AN EVERLASTING CIRCLE

MERCER UNIVERSITY PRESS

Endowed by

TOM WATSON BROWN
and
THE WATSON-BROWN FOUNDATION, INC.

AN EVERLASTING CIRCLE

Letters of the Haskell Family of

Abbeville, South Carolina, 1861–1865

Edited by Karen Stokes

MERCER UNIVERSITY PRESS
Macon, Georgia
1979–2019
40 Years of Publishing Excellence

MUP/ H979

© 2019 by Mercer University Press
Published by Mercer University Press
1501 Mercer University Drive
Macon, Georgia 31207
All rights reserved

9 8 7 6 5 4 3 2 1

Books published by Mercer University Press are printed on acid-free paper
that meets the requirements of the American National Standard for
Information Sciences—Permanence of Paper for Printed Library Materials.

Printed and bound in the United States.

This book is set in Adobe Caslon Pro.

Cover/jacket design by Burt&Burt

ISBN   978-0-88146-719-2
Cataloging-in-Publication Data is available from the Library of Congress

CONTENTS

Dedicated to the memory of the defenders of Charleston, 1861–1865

ACKNOWLEDGMENTS

Many thanks are due, first to Dr. James E. Kibler for his generous assistance. He has been a friend and mentor for many years, and I am indebted to him for reading a draft of the manuscript and offering me much encouragement and many invaluable suggestions which improved the book significantly. I must also mention Sara Fair, a descendant of Langdon C. Haskell. A number of years ago, she was responsible for having many of the Haskell letters at the South Carolina Historical Society transcribed as she explored her family history. Reading some of the transcribed letters of Mrs. Sophia Haskell sparked my curiosity about her and her family, and so I am indebted to Sara for this. She also provided Haskell and Wardlaw family history, as well as a wonderful original photograph of Capt. William T. Haskell that is now at the South Carolina Historical Society. Another Haskell descendant, Charles Thomson (Tom) Haskell III, of Omaha, Nebraska, was very generous with genealogical information, some of which he passed on from other descendants. The staff at Magnolia Cemetery in Charleston assisted me in locating old records I needed, and in Abbeville, Ann Waigand and her mother, May Hutchinson, the church historian, graciously checked nineteenth-century church records for me and provided valuable information. Doug Bostick and Herbert (Bing) Chambers were always helpful when I consulted them for their expertise in South Carolina military history, and Dr. Richard D. Porcher helped to clarify some Porcher family genealogy. Thanks are also due to the staff members at the South Carolina Historical Society, South Caroliniana Library (University of South Carolina), Georgia Historical Society, Wilson Library (UNC Chapel Hill), Rubenstein Rare Book and Manuscript Library (Duke University), the Library of Congress, and the Albert and Shirley Small Special Collections Library at the University of Virginia.

EDITORIAL METHOD

These letters were transcribed largely as written, with little abridgment except for illegible sections, but punctuation and capitalization has been added, especially where sentences began and ended with only a dash and lacked initial capitalization. Questionable words or phrases are indicated by brackets, and missing words or sections are indicated by an italicized explanation in brackets. Brackets are also sometimes used to spell out abbreviated words for clarity. Miss Sophia Louisa Lovell Haskell is referred to in the letter headings as Sophie Haskell to differentiate her from her mother, Mrs. Sophia L. Haskell. The closings of letters have been omitted, but the salutations have been retained for the purpose of further clarifying family relationships among members with very similar names. Datelines have been standardized.

Most of Alexander C. Haskell's letters included in this collection are from his papers in the Southern Historical Collection at the Wilson Library, University of North Carolina at Chapel Hill, but many also came from the Charles T. Haskell Family Papers at the South Carolina Historical Society in Charleston, SC, and from the South Caroliniana Library at the University of South Carolina. Almost all of his wartime correspondence is outgoing. Many years after the war he wrote that his papers, which presumably included letters he may have preserved from family and friends, "were destroyed on the last march (Richmond to Appomattox)." Two much less extensive collections of the letters of John C. Haskell are found at the Wilson Library and within the South Carolina Historical Society's Charles T. Haskell Family Papers, and the latter is the source of all the letters of his brothers Langdon, Charles, and Lewis, and of his parents and his sister, Sophie. Most of the letters of William T. Haskell and Joseph C. Haskell are also in this collection, but a few of William's letters came from the Langdon Cheves Papers at the Georgia Historical Society. A few of Joseph's letters are found in the Rachel Susan Bee Cheves Papers in the Rubenstein Rare Book and Manuscript Library at Duke University.

Most of the wartime correspondence of the seven Haskell brothers and their parents has been included, but a small number of letters were omitted principally because they were incomplete, repetitious, or unreadable in whole or part. About a dozen or so of Alexander C. Haskell's letters were too faded to be legible. Eight of his letters excerpted in Daly's *Alexander Cheves Haskell: The Portrait of a Man* could not be found and may be among this illegible material. They are dated February 15, 1863; March 7 and 27, 1864; April 12, 1864; April 28, 1864; May 2, 1864; August 31, 1864; and January 31, 1865.

ABBREVIATIONS OF MANUSCRIPT REPOSITORIES

DUL: Rubenstein Rare Book and Manuscript Library, Duke University, Durham, NC

GHS: Georgia Historical Society, Savannah, GA

LC: Library of Congress

SCHS: South Carolina Historical Society, Charleston, SC

UNC: Southern Historical Collection, Wilson Library, the University of North Carolina at Chapel Hill

INTRODUCTION

America's deadliest, most brutal war began in 1861. Thousands of families, North and South, were swept up in this vast, horrific struggle—countless husbands, sons, and brothers leaving home to fight and perhaps be maimed or killed by wounds or disease. *An Everlasting Circle* is the story of one Southern family, the Haskells of Abbeville, South Carolina, who sent seven sons into the tragic, ruinous conflict commonly called the "Civil War."

Why did the Haskell brothers, like so many other Southern men, risk their lives in this war? Why was their family willing to suffer and sacrifice so much? The letters of these remarkable individuals, written during the most tumultuous period in our country's history, reveal not only their motives and ideals, but also their sources of strength and perseverance in the midst of unimaginable trials.

The story of the South Carolina Haskells begins with Major Elnathan Haskell of Massachusetts, an officer in the Continental Army whose military service brought him into South Carolina during the American Revolution. After the war, Elnathan settled in St. Matthew's Parish in central South Carolina, where he married a young woman named Charlotte Thomson. She was the daughter of Col. William ("Danger") Thomson, the officer in command of a patriot force that famously repulsed a British attack at Breach Inlet near Charleston in 1776. Elnathan and Charlotte had nine children, the fifth of whom, born in 1802, was Charles Thomson Haskell. As a youth, Charles attended Phillips Academy in Andover, Massachusetts, and later went on to Harvard. In 1827, he joined the South Carolina Society of the Cincinnati on the basis of his father's Revolutionary War record.

Charles married Sophia Lovell Cheves in 1830. Born in 1809 she was the eldest daughter of Langdon Cheves (1776–1857), an attorney and planter from the South Carolina upcountry district of Abbeville who achieved national eminence, serving as Speaker of the United States House of Representatives and later as director of the Second Bank of the United States. The first home of the newlyweds was a plantation located near Fort Motte in the district of Orangeburg, in an area which is now part of Calhoun County, but they would soon leave this place to put down roots in Sophia's ancestral soil. A history of the Cheves family written by a descendant, Susan Smythe Bennett, takes up their story here:

> At first the Haskells lived at the old Haskell home (Zante) at Fort Motte, but some time in the 1830's Mr. Cheves and Mr. Haskell

went to Abbeville District in search of a home, the house at Fort Motte being left to Charles Haskell's mother and sisters. Several fine places near the "Flatwoods" by Davis' Bridge were bought, from which many of the farmers had removed to Mississippi and Alabama: The Home Place, Ellington, Turkey Hill, Charley's Hope, etc. There they settled and lived ever after.

At their plantation called the Home Place, Charles and Sophia prospered and became the parents of a large family. Twelve children were born to them, two of whom died as infants. Nine of their children were sons, and of the eight sons who survived to adulthood, seven would serve in the Confederate Army. In order of their birth, their names were Langdon, Charles, William, Alexander, John, Joseph, and Louis.

Although Charles T. Haskell and Sophia Cheves were third cousins and both of their families owned plantations in St. Matthew's Parish, they did not become acquaintances until around 1825. Sophia was a well-educated young woman who had enjoyed a varied and sophisticated upbringing. The daughter of a Congressman, for several years she lived in Washington, DC, and later, while her father was director of the Second Bank of the United States, the family resided in Philadelphia and then in Lancaster, Pennsylvania, until moving back to South Carolina in 1829. Her sister was Louisa S. Cheves, who would later marry David J. McCord and become a noted author and intellectual.

In Philadelphia, Sophia had attended a seminary (school) for young ladies, and one of her classmates there, Eleuthera Du Pont Smith, became a lifelong friend. In July 1830, Sophia wrote to Eleuthera to announce her engagement to Haskell and relate their plans:

> In the first place, it is to be a pure love match, very little alloyed by any encumbrance of fortune on either side. Now the southern plan, in such cases, is to go into debt immediately by taking property on credit, live on your plantation, on hog and hominy, to use a very expressive country saying, and disappear from the world till you can afford again to reappear. I cannot ask you what you think of such a plan, for you know, I suppose, but little of a country life to the South. I do not know much more but I am sure it will be very pleasant, when I have once learned to make bacon and raise poultry, till then there will be some little danger of suffering from famine. But I will be able to tell you all about it by next Spring I hope. I dare say you will laugh at the idea of my becoming a sober country lady, after having been so long a giddy girl.

Later in her letter, Sophia described her romantic history with Charles, which began around 1823, just after he had left Harvard. At the time of their first meeting (somewhere in the North), she was a schoolgirl, and he, "a young dandy just from college." Her letter continued,

> I was travelling alone with Father, and during the day we were together, [Charles] was good natured enough to take some trouble to amuse me and thought I was quite a nice little girl. Two years and a half after we met again, but then it was on a more equal footing. I was...on a visit to our friends in the South. My Aunt's plantation is but three miles from his Mother's—his sisters two very pleasant girls, the only young ladies in the neighborhood, and he the only beau we had. Had not he a fine chance! And he did not neglect it. We rode a good deal on horseback, and he made his sisters ride that he might show us the prettiest rides.

During this reunion Sophia and Charles became "the very best of friends," and about two years later, they were engaged. Sophia described her future husband's appearance: "If you want to know what kind of looking being he is, all I can tell you is that he is well looking enough for me to think him as handsome as I choose. He is as dark as an Indian, dark hair, dark eyes, and teeth as white as mother of pearl."

Another letter from Sophia to Eleuthera gives some details of her early married life after she and Charles took up residence in Abbeville District. This was during a period when a number of South Carolinians were migrating to other states such as Alabama and Mississippi in search of better land and opportunities. Sophia wrote in December 1833:

> We have moved too as you may see by the Postmarks, and are now living in what is called the upper country. Though not much more north than our former residence, yet from its greater vicinity to the mountains, the character of the country is very different, and the whole style of living and manners, seemed changed along with it. They [sic] people are much more like the farming population of the Northern states, the greatest part of them working their own fields, and Squires, Colonels and Majors ploughing their own corn, and driving their wagons. Indeed they form an industrious, hardy, intelligent set of people with as strict moral and religious habits as you could anywhere meet with but not offering much improved society. They look with a jealous eye on <u>Lowcountry</u> people, and as such we are treated rather shyly. We only came up here last February, and left it again in June, and have but just returned. During the time we were here, my health and other

circumstances did not permit me to go out, so that I know no one. Our beautiful Fort Motte was too poor to grow rich on, and as my good husband thought it was incumbent on him, to increase our little property, that we might have hominy and bacon for our little children, we have removed to this <u>terra incognita</u> instead of taking the more beaten track to Alabama. You would be not a little amused to see how we live up here. Our house has two pretty good rooms, a piazza and three small shed rooms, no upstairs but a dark loft, and not a particle of paint or paper, and no shutters to the windows, only calico curtains instead.

Charles would enlarge this first residence, and in 1845 he built a new, spacious plantation house of eight rooms, four on each floor, with two large attics. In addition to running his plantation, which produced cotton and other crops, he engaged in public service by serving as a state representative and as a trustee of the Abbeville Clear Spring Association (chartered in 1851 "for educational purposes"). For many summers, he took his family to reside at "The Cabins," a pineland settlement located about four and a half miles southeast of Abbeville.

As a planter, Charles was also a slaveholder. The 1860 census for Abbeville District lists him as the owner of 160 slaves. One of his sons, Alexander Haskell, recorded many affectionate memories of these servants (as the Haskells called them) in a memoir and described how his mother served as their head nurse, who "daily visited the sick, for the health standard was high." He recalled that one slave called Old Daddy Simon, born blind, was "water carrier and our devoted friend," adding of him, "Simon's mother was said to be a Moorish princess. She was brought to Charleston on one of the slave ships, which were all from England, or New England, and my grandfather, Major Elnathan Haskell, and his wife, touched by her appearance it was said, bought her and she lived and died head nurse in charge of their children."

As plantation mistress, Mrs. Sophia Haskell devoted herself to the welfare of her home and the nurture and supervision of her children and servants. Susan Smythe Bennett wrote of her, "Sophia Cheves Haskell was a woman of the highest character and judgment, brave, calm, tolerant; kind and generous. The mother of a large family of high-spirited sons, she needed all her qualifications, and found her life full."

The Rev. William Porcher DuBose, a family friend, admired Mrs. Haskell as a person of deep faith and gave her much of the credit for the fine qualities her sons would exhibit. He regarded her as a great woman, describing her as a cultured and accomplished lady who "trained up, in all that adds

nobility to noble natures, eight sons, of whom seven served with distinguished gallantry, and two consecrated with their life-blood the cause which
they believed to be that of justice, patriotism, and honor." In his reminiscences, DuBose compared her to Cornelia, a noblewoman of ancient Rome.
Celebrated as the supreme model of virtuous motherhood, Cornelia educated and raised her two sons, Tiberius and Gaius Gracchus, with a high sense
of duty and character. Such women as Cornelia and Mrs. Haskell, wrote
DuBose, were "the mothers of distinguished sons who owed a great part of
their greatness to the personalities of their mothers."

Two eminent characteristics of the Haskell family emerge from a study
of their lives and letters—an ardent patriotism and a deep Christian faith.
Their devotion to God and country sustained them in their many trials
throughout the war.

The conflict of 1861 to 1865 is often called the Civil War, but most
Southerners regarded it as a war for independence and self-government. The
seven Haskell brothers who fought in it had both a grandfather and a great-
grandfather who served with distinction in the first American war of independence, and they were mindful of their heritage. Like many others in the
South, they were proud of the part their ancestors had played in the American Revolution, and when the seceded states formed a confederacy, they
adopted many of the images and symbols of that time. The banner which
hung over the table where the South Carolina Ordinance of Secession was
signed bore the image of a rattlesnake poised to strike (as appeared on the
Gadsden flag) and a palmetto tree (symbolic of the patriot victory at Fort
Sullivan in 1776). The Confederate States of America put an image of
George Washington on its national seal, and Washington's image, along
with that of another Revolutionary patriot, Francis Marion (the "Swamp
Fox" of South Carolina), also appeared on Confederate currency.

When South Carolinians declared their independence from the United
States and seceded in 1860, the delegates of the Secession Convention compared the position of the South to that of the American colonists in 1776,
stating in one of their published documents: "The government of the United
States is no longer a Government of Confederated Republics...it is no longer
a free Government, but a despotism. It is, in fact, such a Government as
Great Britain attempted to set over our fathers; and which was resisted and
defeated by a seven years' struggle for independence."

In a letter that Sophia Haskell penned to her friend Eleuthera on
March 28, 1861, she described the patriotic fervor of South Carolinians just
prior to the outbreak of the war, also alluding to the first American Revolution: "We have been in a state of singular excitement all this Winter. I have
never seen anything like it. There is a steady spirit of firm resolution I could

not have imagined. The spirit of '76 could not surpass it." While serving in the Confederate Army in Virginia, William Haskell wrote to his mother on June 2, 1862, adding after the dateline of his letter: "In the second year of this war of liberty."

The orthodox Christian faith of the Haskells was characteristic of many if not most Southern families during this period. There were, of course, families and individuals who were more or less religious than others, or not religious at all, but in the nineteenth-century South, traditional, biblical Christianity was a deep and pervading influence in society. Chester F. Dunham observed: "Southern Christianity, or the theological position of Southern Christian Churches, was thoroughly orthodox. Religion in the South, by and large, supported the civilization, culture, and social order south of the Mason Dixon line."

Historian David D. Wallace noted that the morals of South Carolina gentlemen of the Victorian antebellum era were generally superior to those of earlier generations because of religious influences that increased in the nineteenth century. "Standards of private and public conduct were higher in the generation before 1860 than earlier in South Carolina," he wrote. "The frank grossness of the eighteenth century and the cynical degradation of the Regency disappeared before the invigorating of all the churches following the Wesleyan revival and the toning up of religion and morals by the Evangelical and Oxford Movements, etc., in England and America." In the first half of the nineteenth century, a Presbyterian evangelist named Daniel Baker sparked major religious awakenings in South Carolina, most significantly in Beaufort District in the early 1830s, where he converted a number of men who would go on to become influential ministers and hold high office in their respective denominations. One observer, an Episcopalian, gave Dr. Baker credit for the ascendency of the evangelical party in the Episcopal dioceses of South Carolina and Georgia. Later, in the 1850s, Baker's preaching brought revival to other parts of South Carolina, including Abbeville District.

As any mother would, Sophia Haskell prayed for the safety and success of her sons in the army, but it is evident from her letters that the spiritual welfare of her children was her foremost concern. In a letter of October 18, 1863, she expressed the happiness she had in "seeing my young children one by one turning to God in their youth."

Describing Sophia as "that pious Christian woman Mrs. Haskell—who looks into your very soul with those large and lustrous blue eyes of hers," the famous diarist Mary Chesnut recorded a conversation that took place in 1862 just after the death of young Decca Haskell, the wife of Alexander Haskell. After a friend commented, "This is the saddest thing for Alex,"

Mrs. Haskell said to her, "Death is never the saddest thing. If he were not a good man, that would be a far worse thing." The friend was amazed and protested, "But Alex is so good already." Mrs. Haskell replied, "Yes. Seven years ago, the death of one of his sisters, whom he dearly loved, made him a Christian. That death in our family was worth a thousand lives." Mrs. Haskell was speaking of her daughter Mary Elizabeth Haskell, who passed away in March 1855, and whose death affected her brother Alexander deeply and was also likely influential in the spiritual transformation of her brother William Haskell. In his memoir, Alexander recorded that William was desperately ill with pneumonia at the time of Mary's death, and that when he recovered, he was "a changed boy...and he was to the end the most perfect character I have ever known."

Prior to this loss in the family, Dr. Daniel Baker's ministry had worked a profound effect upon the eldest Haskell brother, Langdon, who likely heard the evangelist while he was preaching at Upper Long Cane Presbyterian Church in September 1854. In October of that year, Langdon wrote the following letter from Abbeville to his brother Charles, who had just embarked on a career as a civil engineer:

Dear Charles,

We are all in rather a gloomy state of affairs. There have been so many deaths in the place lately among the families whom we know. The last is the death of William Lyon, a brother of John. He (William) was a late convert under Dr. Baker's preaching here. There has been a great effect produced by the Dr.'s preaching. Lyon we all believe was a true convert and he died professing entire confidence in his salvation in consequence of his repentance and through his belief in Christ as his savior. There has been a great change in this place as to religious matters of late, from being one of the most careless communities, there so hardly a man now who is not thinking more or less of our future salvation and the means to be used to secure our future good. Dr. Baker's preaching brought the matter so directly home to everyone that it was impossible to be indifferent to it.

And my dear brother without making the least pretensions myself to any worthiness or authority to advise, I would recommend [the] subject of religion to your sober and serious consideration. You cannot imagine how much I regret that I was not earlier brought to think seriously on the subject, for now I am convinced that it is by far the better path. It no doubt will appear strange to you that I who have been so utterly careless on the subject should be now speaking of it in this way. But I feel it my duty to warn you of what I have felt, and of how much easier it would have been for me to have yielded to the influence of religion if I had undertaken it earlier. You must not understand from this that I am professing myself as one converted. I only pray that I may be.

You have not been through half that I have and have not evil at all as I have so that I think it will be easier for you to feel the truth and influence of religion. You must not think that I am carried away by a temporary excitement on the subject. But it is my firm and sober conviction that no man not a Christian has at all the happiness, even in this life, that one has who is, and I can't help thinking on the passage of Solomon "come unto the Lord in the days of thy youth."

I feel very differently with regard to becoming a Christian than I did. I am convinced that it is nothing to be ashamed of. For though we would not profess openly that we are ashamed of it, still many of us act it. I am convinced that in Christianity there is nothing deviating from manliness or that there is anything low-spirited in it, and I am sure that we cannot commence it too soon.

My dear Brother, you must not, I repeat, suppose that I have at all come up to what I here write, but I only hope to do so. I hope that I feel deeply on the subject and that I may become better. Often we advise where we cannot do and lay down precepts that we do not follow. Look at our mother. I think of her and I feel that the power of Christianity is great. She may be sometimes disturbed, but I have noticed that we are the cause of that disturbance. I think that we could mutually help each other in amending our ways. Listen to the preacher not to cavil at his imperfections, but hear the truths he speaks.

I feel drawn toward you since I have been thinking of these things and I hope that we may all amend.

Some information later imparted by a family friend, Octavius T. Porcher, may explain why Langdon manifested such concerns about his brother's spiritual welfare. In a letter of 1863, Porcher related a conversation some years before in which Charles had confided in him about recent moral and spiritual struggles. Charles told Porcher that after working as an engineer on a railroad project in South Carolina, he had "entered fashionable society" in Charleston, and, becoming "absorbed in its vanities," he found that his heart had been drawn away from God, and consequently he became tormented and miserable. Porcher, a devout man, assured him of God's love and faithfulness, urging him to "begin afresh," and before they parted, Charles made a promise that he would do so. His fulfillment of this promise is documented in a letter written shortly after his death in 1863 by his brother Alexander Haskell, who recorded his deep emotions at witnessing the confirmation of Charles at St. Philip's Episcopal Church in Charleston in 1855.

During the war, Alexander Haskell wrote to his mother that she need not fear for the eternal fate of any of her sons. In a beautiful letter of April 2, 1863, he assured her that he and his brothers were "Soldiers of Christ" who "have prepared for death knowing the value of life."

In the same letter, he reminded his mother that should he fall in battle, that his death would only mean a brief parting from his loved ones—a temporary separation until the family circle was once again unbroken for eternity. "I lie down to rest until the gates of Heaven are opened," he wrote, "and all we love are once more joined together."

THE HASKELL CHILDREN

Langdon Cheves Haskell

Langdon Cheves Haskell, the first child of Charles and Sophia Haskell, was named for his famous maternal grandfather. He was born in St. Matthew's Parish on October 25, 1831, before the family moved to Abbeville District. In physical appearance, he strongly resembled his father. His brother Alexander Cheves Haskell (who will be referred to as Aleck hereafter), described Langdon in his memoir as "dark and swarthy, his hair a very black brown, his eyes hazel, his features straight and his face rather long. He was sometimes called 'The Indian.'" Aleck summed up Langdon's temperament as "nervous and sensitive, with a tendency to gloom and depression, though often very bright, and socially charming."

Nicknamed "Lally," Langdon was tutored at home until he entered the South Carolina College in Columbia at the age of sixteen. "Through all this College experience," Aleck recalled, "my dear brother went very pure in heart and in life.... He was a gentleman of polite letters, of a retiring and romantic disposition."

In an unpublished portion of his memoir, Aleck Haskell wrote about Dr. Daniel Baker's influence on Langdon and his sister Mary. "[Baker] came to Abbeville in the summer and preached at Long Cane Church, established in early days by the Scotch Presbyterian settlers. Langdon and Mary attended regularly & joined the church. It had a great effect on the subsequent career of their brothers and of all the family."

After graduation Langdon read law for about two years, studying under Samuel McGowan of Abbeville. When of age, he became an attorney, and, in the winter of 1856, after practicing law in Abbeville for a short period, he set up an office in Charleston. He lived at a boarding house on King Street, where he met and fell in love with a governess—"a fascinating French woman," as Aleck described her. Hearing of this unsuitable attachment, family members soon intervened, and Langdon left Charleston for Italy to take care of a consumptive uncle, Robert Hayne Cheves, who died in Florence in August 1856.

After his return home, Langdon became engaged to Ella Coulter Wardlaw, the daughter of Judge David Lewis Wardlaw of Abbeville. They were married on September 21, 1858, and the following year, the couple left South Carolina to begin a new life in Arkansas, where Langdon's father had purchased some farmlands. Settling on a plantation called Boscobel near Pine Bluff, they found planting a difficult endeavor. As war loomed in 1861, Langdon and his family moved back to South Carolina, where he began his military service as a volunteer aide to Col. Maxcy Gregg in Charleston. In January 1862, Langdon became Gen. Maxcy Gregg's aide-de-camp, ranking as a lieutenant. He would later serve on the staffs of Gen. Samuel McGowan and Gen. Richard H. Anderson. During the Seven Days Battles in Virginia in 1862, the divisional commander Gen. A. P. Hill would praise Langdon Haskell for "conspicuous gallantry."

Mary Elizabeth Haskell

A daughter was born next to Charles and Sophia Haskell, on May 16, 1833. They named her Mary Elizabeth. In his memoir, Aleck recalled that Mary was educated at home by a tutor, "and by our Mother, who was highly educated herself and of a very high order of intellect." Aleck continued of his sister, "She was wonderfully beautiful and charming. Her temper had in early life been affected by ill health, but all this passed away and she was one of the sweetest dispositions I ever knew. She was loved by all."

Mary spent the winter of 1854 visiting cousins in Philadelphia, but the summer after her return home, she began to show signs that she had contracted tuberculosis. For the next five or six months, as she grew ever weaker, Aleck, who was living at home during this time, was her constant companion and "devoted attendant."

Mary's older brother, Langdon, was especially close to her. In January 1855, while he was in Florida exploring the possibility of settling there, he wrote her long letters about his observations and experiences on the trip.

After her death on March 24, 1855, Mrs. Haskell told a friend that Langdon was grieving for Mary "as if his heart would break."

Charles Thomson Haskell

The second son in the family, Charles Thomson Haskell, was named after his father. He was born on March 28, 1835. Aleck's memoir records the following about him: "Charles was a 'big boy,' generous, impulsive, and energetic. He was led by the excitement between North and South and the fire of the Mexican War to go to a military school, and it was the regret of his life. He was a splendid soldier but, led by his military schooling, he joined the 'Regulars' of South Carolina, and was held to service in defense of Charleston."

In July 1852, Mrs. Haskell wrote to young Charles while he was in school at the Citadel in Charleston, "You do not know how much I miss you and how great a pleasure it would be to all of us to have you with us. But it gives me so much pleasure to think you are doing well and exerting yourself in the way of your duty that I ought not to wish you to leave it."

A biographical sketch in *The History of the South Carolina Military Academy* by John Peyre Thomas described Charles as "a person of fine and imposing physique, about 6 feet and 2 inches high and well proportioned. He was warm hearted and generous—a man every inch of him—gallant, chivalrous, and of resolute will." After graduating from the Citadel in 1854, Charles began a career as a civil engineer. Aleck recorded that his first project was as "a construction engineer building the North Eastern Railroad, now the Coast Line, from Charleston to Florence." According to a memoir written by his brother John, Charles was working in Mississippi in 1860 and came home soon after he heard that South Carolina had seceded.

Charles was commissioned as a first lieutenant in Company B of the First South Carolina Infantry Regulars and soon became the acting regimental quartermaster. His brother John also mentioned in his memoir that in April 1861, Charles "was on staff duty with Colonel Richard H. Anderson, then in command of Sullivan's Island." In May 1861, Charles was promoted to captain of Company D. Although designated as infantry, this company effectively functioned as an artillery unit during much of its service.

His letters of early 1861 reveal that the governor of South Carolina, Francis W. Pickens, chose Charles for a partly secret mission. The public purpose of this assignment was the carrying of dispatches to Isaac W. Hayne, the attorney general of South Carolina. Hayne was in Washington to convey a demand to President James Buchanan that the Fort Sumter garrison be removed and to offer a pledge from his state that the United States government would be compensated for the monetary value of Fort Sumter and its contents. It was hoped that these actions would prevent a "collision" that might lead to war. Hayne was unsuccessful in his efforts, however, as were the Confederate commissioners who came to Washington soon afterward seeking a peaceful resolution of the crisis. President Buchanan refused to remove the US garrison from Fort Sumter, leaving this fateful situation in the hands of his successor, Abraham Lincoln, who took office in March 1861.

The principal but covert purpose of Charles Haskell's mission in January and February 1861 was the recruiting of men in Baltimore and elsewhere for service in the defense of South Carolina. He had also been given "other mysterious directions" from the governor but seemed to regard them as insignificant, suggesting that Pickens was "making a mountain out of a mole hill." Some newspapers reported his movements as a "Special Messenger from South Carolina," and the *New York Herald* mistakenly identified him as "Col. Haskell, aid-de-camp to Gov. Pickens." In a letter dated February 17, 1861, Charles told his father that a newspaper had reported his "special errand" to Baltimore and that the governor of Maryland "sent a Marshall after me as one of the conspirators to take city of Washington. Finding me a far less important character than he had imagined I was let alone but my errand became suspected and every obstacle thrown in my way." Not long after Abraham Lincoln's election, rumors circulated that there was a secessionist plot to assassinate the president-elect and capture the city of Washington, DC, and later, after President Lincoln called up troops for an invasion of the seceded states, there were real fears in the North that the first move of the Confederacy would be against Washington. These fears were never realized, but Charles found himself caught up in the suspicions and tensions of that period.

Charles returned to Charleston in March 1861, and later that month, he was tapped again for another special assignment. Gen. Pierre G. T. Beauregard, the commander at Charleston, had received a message from LeRoy Pope Walker, the Confederate secretary of war, dated March 18, 1861, directing him to order Lt. Charles Haskell to Baltimore, where he was to inquire for W. T. Walters and L. T. Wigfall. Louis T. Wigfall, a US senator from Texas, had taken it upon himself (with permission from Walker) to open a recruiting station in Baltimore a few days earlier, and William T. Walters, a Baltimore businessman, was advancing the money necessary for the recruiting efforts. This trip was to be something of a reprise of Charles's earlier recruiting mission, however, he had to turn down Beauregard's request, and another officer was sent in his place. Time was of the essence for the mission, and Charles would have been delayed too long by matters necessary for turning over the office of quartermaster to another officer. Beauregard wrote to Secretary Walker on March 21: "Lieutenant Haskell cannot go immediately to Baltimore. Department better send another one from Montgomery."

During the remainder of 1861, his company saw service on Coles Island near Charleston, then on Edisto Island, and in December, Charles was ordered west on another recruiting mission. The following year, he was sent to command the Breach Inlet Battery on Sullivan's Island (later known as Battery Marshall). In 1863 he supervised the enlargement of the battery. Aleck's memoir states that this fortification at the east end of the island was located at the same place where patriot troops under the command of his great-grandfather, Col. William Thomson, "held the British Army at bay while [Gen.] Moultrie, at the West end, fought their fleet approaching Charleston by way of the channel." This great Patriot victory of the Revolution is still celebrated every year on June 28th as Carolina Day.

In the summer of 1863, Charles would die in an attempt to hold another invader at bay on a different island in Charleston Harbor. John Peyre Thomas noted in his biographical sketch that Charles had long been concerned about an enemy attack on Morris Island, where the Confederate batteries named Wagner and Gregg were situated. In January 1863, Charles and his uncle Capt. Langdon Cheves had held a meeting in Battery Wagner in which they deplored the lack of fortifications on the south end of Morris Island, "since they felt satisfied that the decisive assault on that Island would come from that undefended quarter." Charles believed that the attack would come from nearby Folly Island, which was occupied by Union forces, and in July 1863, after four enemy monitors (armored warships) appeared off the bar, he went on a scouting mission to investigate that area, of which Thomas wrote: "In his anxiety on the subject of the Confederate tenure of Morris Island, upon special permission following application, he and Col. W. P. Shooter, S. C. Regiment, went over to Folly Island to make a special reconnaissance." Johnson Hagood, a Confederate general from South Carolina, also recounted this episode in his memoirs. "On the night of the 8th of July," wrote Hagood, "a scouting party under Captain Charles Haskell visited Little Folley [sic] and discovered the enemy's barges collected in the creeks approaching Morris Island." This discovery gave indication that preparations for an attack (some of them well concealed) were underway. In his history of the siege of Battery Wagner (also known as Fort Wagner), Timothy E. Bradshaw stated that the observations made by Captain Haskell "provided enough evidence to spoil the Union's element of surprise for the attack on Morris Island."

On July 9, Charles was stationed at Battery Mitchel (Oyster Point) on the southern end of Morris Island in anticipation of an attack. Johnson Hagood continued: "On the night of the 9th July...the whole of the infantry force on [Morris Island] was kept under arms at the south end. At five o'clock on the morning of the 10th July, the enemy's attack commenced by heavy fire from a great number of light guns, apparently placed during the last forty-eight hours in the works lately thrown up on Little Folley [*sic*] Island." The monitors crossed the bar at about the same time, bringing their formidable fire to bear on Morris Island, which was also under fire from enemy howitzers on barges on Light House Inlet. At about 7 A.M., flotillas of boats brought thousands of enemy troops who eventually effected a landing on Morris Island.

John Johnson, author of *The Defense of Charleston Harbor*, described how the Federal infantry forces, after landing on the island, "took battery after battery, and drove the infantry support out of their main line of rifle-pits in full retreat up the sandy length of the island toward Fort Wagner." This two-day fight, known as the First Battle of Fort Wagner, ended unsuccessfully for the Union forces, but on the first day, they took control of much of Morris Island. Among those killed in this fierce struggle of the first day was Capt. Charles T. Haskell. A fellow officer, Capt. James W. Owens, was near him when he fell and reported his last moments. On July 23, the following account by Captain Owens was published in the *Charleston Daily Courier*:

> The many friends of the brave and lamented Captain Haskell, who fell in the first fight on Morris' Island, on the 10 inst., would perhaps be gratified to know something more of his last moments. I was the last to speak with him. He acted nobly and beyond my powers of description. He fell near myself, standing in the rifle pit encouraging his men, and while speaking was struck with a minnie ball which went through his body. He extended me his hand and said: "Tell my mother that I died for her and for my country." I rendered him every service in my power. Being compelled to leave him, one of my men afterwards passed as he was breathing his last, having been struck afterwards by another minnie ball, which entered his head. That was the last I saw or heard of the gallant and lamented Captain Haskell.

Lt. James Moultrie Horlbeck, who wrote to Charles's father on July 11 to report his death, gave as his last words, "Tell my mother I fell fighting for my country." No matter which wording is the more exact, it is clear who and what was foremost in his mind as he died.

A letter from Captain Haskell's uncle, dated the day after his death, indicates that efforts were made to retrieve his remains from Morris Island. William E. Haskell wrote from Charleston: "I have been to Gen. Beauregard & have made every arrangement to go down, as soon as the enemy will receive a flag of truce & get his body & have it put into my vault until I know your wishes. I will have the service as soon as I can get it. I hope to do so today but can't say positively as they are still firing." There is no further word in the surviving letters, however, about whether William E. Haskell was successful. John Peyre Thomas asserted that Charles was buried by the enemy on Morris Island. "As to Haskell's fate," wrote Thomas, "there were conflicting rumors, but they were dissipated by General Gillmore. He gave the information that his gallant foeman had been killed, and that he had been buried by the Federals on the field." In an article about the siege of Charleston dated October 13, 1863, quoting *The Richmond Dispatch,* the *Empire* (a newspaper of Sydney, Australia) stated the following: "Captain Haskell's and Lieutenant Bee's bodies fell into the hands of the enemy." (Lt. John Stock Bee had been mortally wounded on July 10 and would die in enemy hands eight days later.)

An obituary for Capt. Charles T. Haskell, which was published in the *Abbeville Press* on July 17, 1863, reported: "It is understood that his body fell into the hands of the enemy and has not been recovered." A Wardlaw family history authored by Judge David Lewis Wardlaw in 1865 (but not published until 1891) also states that Charles T. Haskell's body was not recovered.

Although there is a ledger stone bearing his name in Magnolia Cemetery in Charleston, the cemetery's "Register of Burials" does not list the name of Charles T. Haskell. The only interment recorded for July 11, 1863, is that of his uncle Capt. Langdon Cheves, whose body was brought to Charleston from Battery Wagner (which had not been captured). It has been stated in some writings about the Haskell family that Charles's body was transported to Abbeville after the war and reinterred in the same plot at the Trinity Episcopal Church graveyard with his brother William, but the records of Trinity Church do not reflect this. The gravestone in Abbeville bears the names of both brothers, but for Charles, it appears that this marker, like the one in Magnolia Cemetery, is only a memorial—a cenotaph.

On July 10, 1863, while Charles and his men were under fire, his uncle Capt. Langdon Cheves was with the artillery garrison at Battery Wagner, a fortification which Cheves and Capt. F. D. Lee had designed and built. Word quickly reached Cheves that his nephew had been killed. In his *Confederate Defence of Morris Island*, Robert C. Gilchrist recounted what happened to him soon afterward:

Captain Cheves, son of the late Judge Cheves, to whose engineering skill and untiring zeal Fort Wagner was to be henceforth famous in history, was sitting in his quarters overwhelmed with grief at the tidings just brought him of the death of his nephew, Captain Chas. T. Haskell. But as the sound of approaching battle grew louder, he roused himself to action, and stepping across the threshold of his door, towards one of the magazines, he was stricken to death by a fragment of the first shell hurled at Fort Wagner.

The article from the Australian newspaper quoted above adds the following: "Captain Langdon Cheves, an accomplished and very efficient officer of the engineer corps, was killed almost instantly by a shell from a monitor exploding in Battery Wagner, and striking him in the head."

Two batteries on nearby James Island were named in honor of Charles and Captain Cheves shortly after they were killed. Battery Haskell at Legare's Point was a large fortification situated to fire on enemy troops on Morris Island as well as their ships in nearby waters. Battery Cheves, located on the southeastern shore of James Island, was designed to protect the area between Battery Haskell and Fort Johnson from an amphibious attack from Morris Island.

William Gilmore Simms, South Carolina's foremost man of letters of the nineteenth century, paid homage to the Confederate defenders of Morris Island in his poem "Fort Wagner," making particular mention of Charles and his uncle:

> Their memories shall be monuments, to rise
> Next to those of mightiest martyrs of the past;
> Beacons, when angry tempests sweep the skies,
> And feeble souls bend crouching to the blast!
> A shrine for thee, young Cheves, well devoted,
> Most worthy of a great, illustrious sire;
> A niche for thee, young Haskell nobly noted,
> When skies and seas around thee shook with fire!

Charlotte Thomson Haskell

The fourth Haskell child was Charlotte Thomson, who was born in 1836 and lived less than two months. According to Aleck Haskell's memoir, she was buried in the graveyard of the Rocky River Presbyterian Church near Abbeville. Charlotte's maternal grandfather, Langdon Cheves, was born in this area, and his mother, Mary Langdon Cheves (1754–1779) was also buried at Rocky River. There is a gravestone bearing Charlotte's name in the Trinity Episcopal Church graveyard in Abbeville, but this may only be a cenotaph. This headstone gives her date of birth as September 26, 1836, and her date of death as October 29.

William Thomson Haskell

William Thomson Haskell, born December 11, 1837, was named for his great-grandfather of Revolutionary War fame. According to Aleck's memoir, William was in early life a "problem" child with a "will of iron." Aleck continued,

> He was my companion, and my tyrant and oppressor. This first drew Langdon to me and he was my defender. I fought, but William was too strong.... William was finally sent to school, to Mr. Rivers in Charleston, and lived in the family of my Father's sister Claudia.... When Mary died he was lying desperately ill of pneumonia. He recovered, and was a changed boy. All the force of his nature went to overcome evil, and he was to the end the most perfect character I have ever known.

William entered the University of Virginia in 1856, and in spite of an inauspicious beginning as a scholar, he made a name for himself and acquired many friends and admirers. Aleck wrote of his brother's college days, "He was of a slow mind, and when he entered he was dull and awkward in debate, not brilliant in anything. When he left, he was the editor of the Magazine and, men of that day say, the master debater in their Societies." A memoir written by his brother John records the following of William:

> He was a remarkable man. At college he made no great success, barely getting his degree though a faithful student; yet many years after the war several of his old professors of the University of Virginia said to me that they expected more of him than of any student who attended the institution for many years. Fellow students, like Bishop Dudley of Kentucky and others distinguished in their lives, have told me how he was the most admired man in the University.

In 1860, William graduated, and, according to J. F. J. Caldwell, who wrote a history of Gregg's Brigade, he "was just entering upon the profession of the law when the war began." William and Aleck enlisted together in the Abbeville Volunteers, which would become Company A in the First Regiment South Carolina Volunteers under the command of Col. Maxcy Gregg. In the spring of 1861, Mary Chesnut briefly recorded in her diary an encounter with William, recalling an earlier meeting with him in Virginia: "Last summer at the White Sulphur he was a pale, slim student from the university. To-day he is a soldier, stout and robust. A few months in camp, with soldiering in the open air, has worked this wonder. Camping out proves a wholesome life after all."

When the regiment was reorganized after a six-month enlistment, William and Aleck joined another company under Gregg, the Richland Rifles, and were soon on their way to Virginia. William later recruited another company of men and served as its captain through many battles.

As a company commander, William enforced a strict discipline, which at first was not well received by his soldiers. One of them, Corporal Berry G. Benson, who had known and admired William before serving under his captaincy, wrote of him and one of his lieutenants in his well-known memoir, "Capt. Haskell was not, strictly speaking, a martinet, but he was the strictest officer in the regiment (except it might be Lt. Rhett) and the whole Regt. was soon hating him and Rhett cordially. But after a time, they not diminishing their discipline, all the men came to see that this discipline was best for all concerned, and at last they were esteemed as highly as they had been hated deeply." Captain Haskell and his officers made their company the best drilled and most proficient in the regiment, so much so that they were jealously and derisively referred to as "The Models," but Benson noted wryly that "the other officers began to 'model' their companies also."

In early June 1863, William was chosen to command a select group of men as a battalion of sharpshooters in McGowan's (formerly Gregg's) Brigade. The battalion consisted of handpicked soldiers from five regiments in the brigade, among whom were Berry Benson and his brother Blackwood Benson, natives of Hamburg, South Carolina. Soldiers like the Bensons, who occupied a somewhat humbler station in life than many of their officers, looked up to such men and also aspired to their status. In his biography of Sergeant Berry Benson, Edward J. Cashin described Benson's relationship with Captain Haskell and his officers:

> Haskell's officers included lieutenants John G. Barnwell, Grimke Rhett, and Charles Pinckney Seabrook, all from old and distinguished South Carolina families. Berry respected them. The prevailing philosophy in the South of Berry's day was that nature divided persons into categories according to their natural talents. Thus society was provided with its clerks, manual laborers, preachers, and merchants. At the top were the natural rulers.

While leading his men at Gettysburg on July 2, 1863, William was killed in action. During much of the battle, his battalion of sharpshooters had been stationed along the front line of Pender's Division, but late in the afternoon, they were sent to repel enemy skirmishers from the road in front of Cemetery Hill. Col. Abner Perrin, who was in command of McGowan's Brigade at Gettysburg, reported that "the gallant Haskell" made a daring charge on the enemy and drove them back. In his biography of Berry Benson, Edward J. Cashin described what happened next: "To get a better view of the scene, Haskell climbed upon an outcropping of rock. A Union sniper on the roof of the Bliss Farm, five hundred yards away, took aim and fired. The bullet pierced Haskell under the shoulder, and he fell dead."

William's leadership and character had inspired a deep devotion in his men. To give an example, J. F. J. Caldwell recorded that one young private in his regiment, Jim Ouzts, who was "devotedly attached" to the captain, "often said that he would die for Captain Haskell if necessary." After William was killed, Private Ouzts "seemed to be regardless of fear...and fought with desperation as if to avenge the death of his fallen chief. Often during the day his splendid shots were noted by his comrades, and late in the evening, he was killed almost instantly. He died without a struggle, with a smile on his face, as if he had courted death to be again with his Captain, who he knew could not come back to him."

William's surviving letters do not disclose a great deal about the inner man, but Aleck's description of his brother as "the most perfect character I have ever known" is borne out by many other accounts, all of them unanimous in their estimation of him as a man and an officer. J. F. J. Caldwell wrote of William Haskell in his brigade history:

> In camp he was the most thorough, yet the most discriminating, disciplinarian, on the drill-ground, he was infallibly accurate, on the march he was indefatigable, in battle he was the very spirit of gallantry and self-possession. In all places he held his command perfectly, swaying them equally through their affections and their admiration. He was the model line-officer of my acquaintance. He endured the extremes of heat and cold, sunshine and rain, forced marches and listless inactivity, the thousand small annoyances of camp and the terrible dangers of battle, with unbroken equanimity. He was never known to fret or complain, and never to criticize, except in the most impartial spirit.
>
> Yet this Roman fortitude was accompanied by a most Christian conscientiousness and purity. He was amiable, pious, delicate and refined in all his actions. While he dared all and suffered all him-

self, he dealt tenderly with other men's weaknesses. And his social virtues were not inferior. He was companionable, fond of conversation, fond of all the rational enjoyments of the world.... If I should be required to sum up the character of his mind and his heart in one sentence, I should express it as, care, energy, resolution, grounded on conscientiousness. He presented not much upon the surface, but his depth of thought and feeling was wonderful to those who sounded him.

Many years after William's death, his brother Aleck wrote of him, "I feel now as I have always felt, that he was the only man in that army who could have filled Stonewall Jackson's place." In his memoir, his brother John described William as "deeply and simply religious as any man ever was, never obtruding it on anyone out of place, but never failing to assert it in the right place. More than one clergyman has told me how William's life in the army had converted him and made him devote his whole life to the church. Hundreds of his fellow soldiers have delighted to bear witness to his bravery and devotion."

Berry Benson's brother, Blackwood Ketcham Benson, published a novel in 1900 in which Capt. William T. Haskell appears as a major character. In *Who Goes There? The Story of a Spy in the Civil War*, the author depicts Captain Haskell using his real name, as well as the actual names of many other men in the regiment. The novel tells the curious story of Jones Berwick, a Union spy who loses his memory and winds up as a soldier in the Confederate Army. Berwick joins Captain Haskell's battalion of sharpshooters, and several chapters record their interactions, including a few lengthy conversations on weighty subjects such as mortality, military strategy, and slavery. Like his brother Berry, Blackwood K. Benson knew and served under William T. Haskell in Company H, but how much (if any) of these conversations were actual accounts can only be a matter of speculation. In replying to a reader who had asked him how much of his book was factual, Benson explained that the second half of the novel (chapters twenty to forty), in which his main character becomes a Confederate soldier, was "very true," adding that "the names of the Confederates (men and officers) in that part of the book, are all true, and so far as I know and believe the acts were done." (This letter is found in the Albert and Shirley Small Special Collections Library at the University of Virginia.)

Chapter 27 of Benson's novel is entitled "Captain Haskell," and chapter 31 portrays how Captain Haskell's men reacted to his death at Gettysburg.

On the morning of July 2nd, Company A still lay behind the brigade, which was in line a little to the south of the Seminary. The sun shone hot. The skirmishers were busy in front. Artillery roared at our left and far to our right. At times shells came over us. A caisson nearby exploded. In the afternoon a great battle was raging some two miles to our right. Longstreet's corps had gone in.

At four o'clock I saw some litter-bearers moving to the rear. On the litter was a body. The litter-bearers halted. A few men gathered around. Then the men of Company H began to stir. Some of them approached the litter. Who was it? I became anxious. The men came slowly back—one at a time—grim.

I asked who it was that had been killed.

"Captain Haskell," they said.

My tongue failed me as my pen does now. What! Captain Haskell? Our Captain dead? Who had ever thought that he might be killed? I now knew that I had considered him like Washington—invulnerable. He had passed through so many dangers unhurt, had been exposed to so many deaths that had refused to demand him, had so freely offered his life, had been so calm and yet so valiant in battle, had been so worshipped by all the left wing of the regiment and by the battalion, had been so wise in council and so forceful in the field, had, in fine, been one of those we instinctively feel are heroes immortal! And now he was dead? It could not be! There must be some mistake!

But I looked, and I saw Lieutenant Barnwell in tears, and I saw Sergeant Mackay in tears, and I saw Rhodes in tears—and I broke down utterly.

William was buried in a well-marked grave on a farm near Gettysburg. After the war, his body was brought home to Abbeville, and he was reinterred in the graveyard of Trinity Episcopal Church. William Porcher DuBose described William's return to Abbeville: "In November, 1866, the remains of William Thomson Haskell were raised from the field of Gettysburg by the hands of his comrades and brought to his native town. At the depot they were met by the survivors of the old company with which he had originally entered the service, and escorted to the Episcopal Church, where, with solemn services and amid deep emotion, they were interred in the adjacent cemetery."

His remains arrived in Abbeville on Monday, November 5, 1866, as noted in an obituary in *The Abbeville Press* (published on November 9, 1866). The funeral services were conducted by the rector of Trinity Episcopal

Church, the Rev. Benjamin Johnson, who discoursed on a text from Jeremiah 31:10 ("Weep ye not for the dead") "whilst paying a touching tribute to the virtues of the deceased and the great cause to which they were consecrated." During the service, Rev. Johnson doubtless made mention of William's fallen brother, and the ledger stone marking William's grave also memorializes Charles T. Haskell. The stone is adorned with a pair of crossed swords and two linked laurel wreaths, over which there is a banner bearing this inscription in Latin: "Dulce et decorum est pro patria mori." A quote from an ode by the Roman poet Horace, it can be translated, "It is sweet and fitting to die for the homeland." The word "patria," from the Latin word for father, could literally mean one's father's lands—that is, one's home.

Alexander Cheves Haskell

Alexander Cheves Haskell, the fourth son born to Charles and Sophia, came into the world on September 22, 1839. Aleck was fair, with blue eyes, one of which was flecked with spots of brown. He wrote of himself, "My hair was white as cotton and I was called 'Ecky,' which is an old Scotch form for Alec or Alexander. I was also called 'Cotton Head,' sometimes in endearment, sometimes in derision. I was a stutterer and a nervous, timid child." (In addition to "Ecky," he was also called Alex or Alic.) He was tutored at home, and then, after attending a school in Charleston, he entered South Carolina College in 1856. Aleck suffered bouts of ill health during his teenage years, including a serious case of malaria, but survived to take his final college examinations in December 1860, graduating second in his class. It was in that month that South Carolina seceded, and Aleck felt sure that a war was coming. As the year 1861 began he recalled,

> We had our last celebrations in the old home. William, my dearest friend, was with us, having graduated in July. The week wound up with the New Year's celebration at William Henry Parker's. I never forget the innocent merriment and frolic. Judge Wardlaw and old Mr. Armistead Burt were fighting with sofa cushions and the room full of delight and fun, when a telegram came in announcing that a "Company from Abbeville" would be accepted in the formation of the First Regiment under Col Maxcy Gregg. There arose a cheer and rejoicing. I felt the reverse but said nothing.... We went home, and two days later William and I came into town and enlisted in the First S. C. Volunteers.

William and Aleck joined Gregg's First Regiment, South Carolina

Volunteers. This six-month regiment would become reorganized as Maxcy Gregg's First Regiment, South Carolina Infantry. Later, it would be known as First (McCreary's) Infantry Regiment, under the command of Col. C. Wickliffe McCreary.

Ambitious and able as a soldier, Aleck steadily advanced in rank and responsibility as the war progressed. In the first year of the conflict, after serving as a private in the Abbeville Volunteers, he became an officer on the staff of Col. (later Gen.) Maxcy Gregg. That year, Aleck also succeeded in winning the affections of the beautiful Rebecca Singleton, a young lady he had loved for years since meeting her in Columbia, South Carolina. Decca, as she was called, was a petite, vivacious young woman with reddish-gold hair—a popular belle of Columbia and Charlottesville who became deeply religious during the last two years of her life. She was the daughter of John Coles Singleton (1813–1852), a South Carolina planter, and his wife, Mary Lewis Carter, of Virginia. Mary Chesnut knew both the Haskells and the Singletons and wrote about them on a number of occasions. One of those occasions was Aleck's engagement, about which Mrs. Chesnut announced in an entry for August 8, 1861: "Alex Haskell, Gregg's aide-de-camp, who has all human perfections except that he stammers fearfully in speech—though he fights without let or hindrance—is engaged to be married to Rebecca Singleton. We are all glad of it."

Mrs. Chesnut chronicled their wedding in Charlottesville, Virginia, in September 1861, recalling how Decca's mother called her "the worst girl in love I ever saw." The ceremony took place on September 10, and Mrs. Chesnut gave up her room for them in the crowded city for their wedding night.

Aleck and Decca's days together as husband and wife were very happy but brief. On June 20, 1862, she gave birth to a daughter named Rebecca, and less than a week later, on June 26, the young mother passed away. Decca died at her mother's home on Senate Street in Columbia, South Carolina, and Mrs. Chesnut recorded her last days and her funeral in that city:

> Decca is dead. That poor little darling! Immediately after her ba-
> by was born, she took it into her head that Alex was killed. He
> was wounded, but those around had not told her of it. She sur-
> prised them by asking, "Does anyone know how the battle has
> gone since Alex was killed?" She could not read for a day or two
> before she died. Her head was bewildered, but she would not let
> anyone else touch her letters: so she died with several unopened
> ones in her bosom. Mrs. Singleton, Decca's mother, fainted dead
> away, but she shed no tears....

In a pouring rain we went to that poor child's funeral—to Decca's. They buried her in the little white frock she wore when she engaged herself to Alex, and which she again put on for her bridal about a year ago. She lies now in the churchyard, in sight of my window. Is she to be pitied? She said she had had "months of perfect happiness." How many people can say that? So many of us live their long, dreary lives and then happiness never comes to meet them at all. It seems so near, and yet it eludes them forever.

Decca's death was a devastating blow to Aleck, and although he tried to accept it with Christian resignation, he admitted his overwhelming grief in a letter to his parents in August 1862. "A broken constitution, and weakness," he wrote, "have forced me to give way to a sorrow which I vainly thought I could have borne as a follower of Christ."

Aleck loved and admired his "gallant chief" Maxcy Gregg. He was angry and indignant when, at the time some soldiers of Gregg's six-month regiment refused to volunteer for service in Virginia, another officer made accusations against him which Aleck contended were slanderous. In a letter to his father written in early May 1861, he defended Gregg as "a brave, honest, gallant soldier & a man as fierce as a tiger to be sure, but as tender as a woman."

When General Gregg was mortally wounded at Fredericksburg in December 1862, Aleck came to his deathbed, grief stricken, to hear his last messages for his family. Gregg gave his sword to Aleck and further demonstrated the high regard he felt for him as an officer by making a request to Gen. A. P. Hill for his promotion. After Gregg's death, Aleck served on the staff of his successor, Gen. Samuel McGowan, and he rose to the rank of colonel in the summer of 1864, commanding the Seventh South Carolina Cavalry Regiment in the Army of Northern Virginia, a unit formed in March 1864 and reorganized in June 1864.

Aleck was wounded four times during his military service, most seriously in October 1864, when he was shot in the head. His friend Gen. Edward P. Alexander later wrote of this incident in a book published in 1897, *The Story of American Heroism.* The story is dramatically retold in a chapter entitled "The 'Killing' of Colonel Haskell." According to General Alexander, on October 7, 1864, Aleck Haskell was in command of a brigade of cavalry that was engaged on a battle on Darbytown Road near the James River in Virginia. Amid fierce fighting, Aleck was struck down by a ball that entered his left eye and came out behind his left ear. He was left for dead, but one of General Longstreet's scouts eventually found him alive and brought him to a house, and from there an ambulance took him to Richmond. As General

Alexander related,

> He was conscious until put into the ambulance. After that, he had no recollection, though it chanced that the ambulance mules took fright and ran away, throwing the driver from his seat. Haskell was seen to raise up and seize the lines, and then to fall back, as it was supposed, dead. But the mules were safely stopped by an Alabama infantry brigade on the road, and Haskell was taken to the residence of Mr. Dudley, the father of Bishop Dudley. Here he lay for many weeks between life and death, and when, finally, recovery was assured and convalescence began, he was as one born into a new world. Language came back by slow degrees, and names of persons, places and things all had to be learned anew.

Aleck lost the sight in his left eye, but otherwise made a remarkable recovery and returned to his command to serve to the end of the war. In April 1865, Gen. Robert E. Lee chose Colonel Haskell to lead the surrender of the Confederate cavalry which were with him at Appomattox Courthouse.

More is known about Aleck than any of the other Haskells owing to his extensive correspondence and a memoir, all of which formed the basis of a biography compiled by one of his daughters from his second marriage, Louise Haskell Daly. Daly's *Alexander Cheves Haskell: The Portrait of a Man* was privately printed as a small edition in 1934. The book was mainly intended for the family and not for the general public, but several years later a Haskell family member sent a copy to author and historian Douglas Southall Freeman, who is best known for his biographies of Robert E. Lee and George Washington. Impressed with the book, Freeman wrote to Mrs. Daly about it in a letter dated June 13, 1939, stating of her father's letters and memoir, "He exhibited the nobility of his inheritance and the splendor of his own character in a hundred ways." He judged this work one of the most important personal narratives of the war and asked her permission to include excerpts from one of her father's letters in a new book he was working on (*The South to Posterity*, published in 1939). In it, Freeman pronounced a letter Aleck Haskell had written to his mother in 1863 the noblest and "most beautiful born of war" and held him up, along with such outstanding figures as Robert E. Lee and Stonewall Jackson, as one of the highest examples of Southern character.

John Cheves Haskell

John Cheves Haskell was born on October 21, 1841. He entered the South Carolina College in Columbia in 1859. In January 1861, he wanted to join the Abbeville Volunteers along with Aleck and William, but his father forbade it and insisted that he return to school. At least three months would pass before John entered military service.

Late in life, like his brother Aleck, John wrote down his wartime recollections. Douglas Southall Freeman made use of them in manuscript form for his book *Lee's Lieutenants*, and they were finally published in 1960 as *The Haskell Memoirs: The Personal Narrative of a Confederate Officer*. In his memoir, John recorded that just after he arrived in Charleston in April 1861, he became a volunteer aide to Col. Richard H. Anderson, commander of the First Regiment, South Carolina Infantry Regulars. He was then "appointed to a lieutenancy in the battalion of regular artillery and was assigned to Company A." This was the Sumter Battery, also known as the Calhoun Battery (and other names), commanded by Capt. William Ransom Calhoun. It was part of the First Battalion, South Carolina Artillery Regulars.

In a letter written on April 12, 1861, the first day of the bombardment of Fort Sumter, Charles T. Haskell wrote of his younger brother John: "While walking upstairs today at the Moultrie House a forty-two passed through the house throwing splinters over him. John watched the course of the ball, which fell directly, pursued it and carried it home. It was one of the only two which struck the house & those were accidental." It was later revealed that the cannonballs mentioned by Charles were, in fact, not accidental shots. They had been deliberately fired at a group of non-combatant spectators on the beach of Sullivan's Island by one of the gun crews in Fort Sumter, who sent two "42 pounders" at the crowd. The first struck the beach about fifty yards in front of the crowd, bounced over their heads, and crashed into a hotel called the Moultrie House. The second shot followed much the same course.

In April 1861, John's company was at Fort Moultrie and was subsequently stationed at Fort Sumter for three months until it was sent into Charleston and then to Virginia in late July. Company A participated in no engagements in Virginia and was ordered back to South Carolina in December. John resigned at this point, and Gen. Joseph E. Johnston invited him to join his staff as a volunteer aide. He served in this capacity until Gen. Gustavus W. Smith offered him a place with the rank of major, and, as John recalled, "I went on duty as assistant to General Horace Randal, his inspector general." In March 1862, John joined the staff of Gen. D. R. Jones as Commissary of Subsistence. In June of that year, he lost an arm at the Battle of Gaines' Mill, Virginia. During this engagement he was serving as volunteer aide-de-camp to Gen. James Longstreet, who sent him in to carry orders to another general, and, as it happened, within a short while, John was heroically leading soldiers into the thick of the battle. He recounted in his memoir how his right arm was torn off at the shoulder by cannon fire at close range, and how the doctors who first tended to him off the battlefield expected him to die. He was taken by ambulance to Richmond, where Thomas U. Dudley, a prominent merchant, took him into his home. "To this I certainly owe my life," John recalled, "as I was cared for with a devotion equal to what I would have had at home, and had the attention of the most skillful surgeons of the Confederacy." John's parents traveled to Richmond to nurse him as well as his brother Joseph, who was extremely ill with typhoid fever.

After a "long and weary wait," as he described it, John went back into the army in late 1862. Of this he wrote: "I finally returned about the first of December, and spent time at General Headquarters until the Battle of Fredericksburg on the 13th. I was then a volunteer with General Lee, though I had almost nothing to do but sit on Telegraph Hill, where he stood during most of the battle." When fully recovered, John was "ordered to North Carolina to organize the artillery." In North Carolina, he took part in a winter campaign of 1863 commanded by Maj. Gen. D. H. Hill, who assigned Haskell's artillery to Gen. James J. Pettigrew's brigade.

In early June 1863, John was ordered to Culpeper, Virginia, and assigned to share the command of an artillery battalion in Longstreet's Corps with Maj. Matthias Winston Henry. Henry's Battalion fought at Gettysburg in July, suffering the loss of four dead and twenty-three wounded. John wrote of this campaign in his memoir, explaining how the lack of rations and supplies in the Army of Northern Virginia necessitated this move into enemy territory to obtain "arms, clothing, medicine, and even food" for the soldiers and their horses. While in Pennsylvania, Lee's troops were under strict orders concerning the treatment of civilians and their property. "Our army had daily orders to do no damage," John recalled, "and no troops could have passed through the country of their best friends with less harm."

After Gettysburg, when Major Henry was promoted and sent west, John assumed command of the battalion, which would become part of Brig. Gen. Edward P. Alexander's First Corps. John continued in this capacity through many engagements that followed, including the Battle of the Wilderness, Spotsylvania, and Cold Harbor. Around January 1864, he became engaged to marry Sarah (Sally) Hampton, the daughter of Gen. Wade Hampton of South Carolina. Mary Chestnut took note of this event in her diary, commenting, "Another maimed hero is engaged to be married. Sally Hampton has accepted John Haskell." That summer, John's artillery was ordered to Petersburg, Virginia, where a long siege began in June. He wrote of it: "At Petersburg both armies fortified their lines and lay opposite each other until the following spring. We did a great deal of fighting, gradually wearing out our half-fed, half-clothed men. When we got there, we were just in time to keep Grant's troops out." His memoir gives a riveting account of the Battle of the Crater in July, in which his artillery played a principal role. In his "Defence of Petersburg," W. Gordon McCabe described John's leadership of his artillery in that fierce struggle, praising him as "a glorious young battalion-commander, whose name will be forever associated with the artillery corps of the Army of Northern Virginia."

Gen. William T. Sherman was conducting his brutal, destructive marches through Georgia and the Carolinas during the same time of the long siege in Virginia, which *Confederate Military History* described as "dreary, suffering, starving months in the trenches around Petersburg. Soldiers have never been called upon to endure more than the Confederate soldiers were there forced to stand, and to stand with a full knowledge that their distant homes were being ruthlessly devastated, and that the pangs of hunger were pressing cruelly upon their unprotected families."

In a fight on the Darbytown Road in Virginia on October 7, 1864, John suffered a grazing wound to the head, and Aleck was even more seriously wounded in the same engagement, receiving a wound to the head that destroyed his left eye. On October 11, a South Carolina newspaper, *The Lancaster Ledger*, reported a dispatch from Richmond about this battle: "A fight commenced this morning on the Darbytown Road, on the north side of James river, and extended along the line to Fort Harrison, and ceased at 2 o'clock. We carried, it is reported, two lines of breastworks, took 300 prisoners and 9 pieces of artillery, and 100 horses.... Our loss is slight, but that of the enemy heavy." The article also noted the officers killed or wounded, including Colonel Haskell and Major Haskell.

Gen. Edward P. Alexander, who became a good friend of Aleck, John, and Joseph Haskell during the war, wrote about them in his memoir, and in it he described how John narrowly escaped death on the Darbytown Road:

> John was riding a tall & beautiful horse.... When we started our fire, advancing, he sent that horse to the rear, & mounted, instead, a small & ordinary battery horse. During the fight a musket ball struck him at the top of his forehead, exactly in the centre. It split the scalp & scraped the bone of the skull for nearly six inches & passed on. Had his horse been a half inch taller he would have been instantly killed. He did not leave the field, however.

John was back in active service in a matter of three weeks, and Aleck returned to duty by the end of January 1865. In February 1865, John was promoted to the rank of lieutenant colonel, commanding Haskell's Battalion in General Alexander's First Army Corps, Army of Northern Virginia. When General Lee surrendered at Appomattox, he designated John to surrender the artillery of that army.

Joseph Cheves Haskell

Joseph Cheves Haskell was born on December 1, 1843. He was the youngest of the Haskell brothers to serve through all four years of the war, and his letters often betray a lingering boyishness. In a letter that his mother wrote to a friend in 1857, she described Joseph as "a fine boy of thirteen but very tall and stout, and promises to be the finest looking of the family; not near as studious or thoughtful as his elder brother John, but a good boy enough." Mrs. Haskell also mentioned that John and Joseph were attending a boarding school in Abbeville, coming home "every week or two on Saturday."

When the war began, Joseph was a student at the South Carolina College in Columbia. He was in Charleston for the bombardment of Fort Sumter in April 1861, but he returned to the college in May. A letter written by their mother on May 5, 1861, mentioned that both Joseph and John had gone back to college in Columbia, but, as it happened, neither would stay there for long. William came to South Carolina to recruit during the summer, and in August, when he returned to Virginia with some new troops, Joseph was with him. Joseph's service records document that he first enlisted as a private in Company C of the First South Carolina Volunteers under the command of Col. Maxcy Gregg.

In early June 1862, Joseph sent a letter to his father in which he reported that Gen. Joseph E. Johnston wanted to give him a commission, but learning his age, could only offer him a cadetship. This rank was a kind of apprenticeship given to some young men in order for them to gain experience and skills as a staff officer. Joseph's cadetship on Johnston's staff dated from the day of the Battle of Seven Pines on May 31, 1862. In a letter dated June 3, 1862, Aleck wrote of his younger brother and the general, who was wounded in that battle: "Joe is a very gallant looking soldier, very much improved, and must have behaved well. He was at General Johnston's side when the General fell & will probably be out of employment for some time in consequence of the General's illness. Johnston is getting better, of a very severe and painful though not dangerous wound."

At Fredericksburg in December 1862, Joseph was appointed a volunteer aide-de-camp to Edward P. Alexander. A colonel in command of an artillery battalion at that time, Alexander wrote of it in his memoir: "Joe Haskell joined me & offered his services as an aid which I gladly availed myself of, & found him exceedingly useful as well as a delightful companion." In his official report regarding the operations of his artillery battalion at Fredericksburg, Col. Alexander expressed "especial thanks" to Cadet Haskell, "who volunteered me his services and rendered me indispensable assistance in the supervision of so extensive a command."

In early 1863, Joseph was appointed a lieutenant and became adjutant to his brother John in his artillery battalion. Later, in June of that year, Joseph was assigned to duty as adjutant to Maj. David Gregg McIntosh, the commander of an artillery battalion in the Third Corps, but soon afterward, in the latter part of July, he was again on the staff of Col. Edward P. Alexander, who wrote of his appointment as adjutant: "Haskell was with me to the last day of the war, not only admired but loved by everybody on the staff, & in the command. Nature has not got any more admirable or attractive type than that in which the whole family of the six Haskell brothers in the war was stamped."

In late 1863 and early 1864, Joseph was with Alexander's Battalion in Tennessee. In February 1864, when Edward P. Alexander was promoted to the rank of brigadier general, Joseph served as his assistant adjutant general with the rank of captain.

Sophia Louisa Lovell Haskell

After giving birth to six sons, Mrs. Sophia Haskell was finally blessed with another daughter. Sophia Louisa Lovell Haskell, who was usually called Sophie, was born on December 25, 1845. She was named after her mother and her aunt, Mrs. Louisa S. McCord. In a letter that Mrs. Haskell wrote to a friend in March 1861, she described her daughter's appearance and character: "Sophie is but fifteen but she is tall and womanly in appearance, not at all like me, but decidedly well looking, bright, intelligent, and impulsive, sometimes maybe, impetuous would be the right word. She is going through the first years of her schooling which is pretty hard for a spoiled child." At the time this letter was written, Sophie was a pupil at Madame Togno's School for Young Ladies in Charleston, a prestigious, exclusive boarding school where only French was spoken. Some of her fellow pupils there were Bessie and Adele Allston, the daughters of R. F. W. Allston, a former governor of South Carolina. Later, in 1862, Sophie was sent to a boarding school in Flat Rock, North Carolina, which was operated by two French sisters, Beatrix and Eliza de Choiseul. While in Flat Rock, Sophie spent her weekends at Acton Briars, the home of her aunt Isabella Middleton Cheves and other relatives. In October 1862, Isabella's sister Harriott Middleton wrote of "a pleasant visit from Isabella's niece, Sophy Haskell. She is at the school of the Misses de Choiseul, and is to spend her Fridays, Saturdays and Sundays here. She is a very intelligent womanly girl of sixteen, and has so much that is interesting to tell." Harriott added of Sophie's brothers in the army, "They are a noble set of brothers, Carolinians as they should be."

Through their wartime letters, Sophie was sometimes the recipient of gentle brotherly advice and correction from her elder siblings (who sometimes spelled her name Sophy). On April 3, 1863, Aleck counseled her: "You have a strong nature and should seek early not to crush it but to subject it to control & make its every act and energy subordinate to the desire to serve God and do well to your fellow creatures. Then will its strength be a blessing, where uncontrolled it would be a curse."

Sophie returned to South Carolina by 1864 and thereafter divided her time between Abbeville and Columbia. She naturally matured during the war, and like so many South Carolina women, worked diligently to raise money for the war effort. In a letter of January 1865, Aleck commended his sister for her war work in Columbia: "Sophie is useful and I think a model in company for the ladies of this generation. There her talent, good taste and good manners are well and modestly enough exhibited."

Louis, Paul, and Robert Haskell

The two youngest Haskell brothers alive during the war were Louis Wardlaw (whose name is often spelled Lewis in the letters), born February 5, 1848, and Paul Thomson, who was born on March 6, 1850, and named after a favorite uncle of his father. Another Haskell brother, Robert Hayne Cheves, was born in July 1852 but only lived about two weeks. Aleck wrote of him, "I went with Father that long and weary drive and helped to bury him at Rocky River Church, where his little sister had been laid to rest."

Louis and Paul, along with their little sister, Sophie, were tutored at home by their older sister, Mary, and after Mary's death, Mrs. Haskell took over that role. In a letter of 1857, Mrs. Haskell informed a friend that she had "a very small family now at home; only three of my youngest, Sophie, Louis and Paul, for whom I pretend to keep school." In the same letter, she describes Louis and Paul as "stout healthy little fellows." Mrs. Haskell's letters of 1861 give a few more details about her youngest sons as well as an orphaned nephew who was living with the family. Russell Noble, born 1847, was the son of Eugenia Lucy Lovell Haskell Noble, a sister of Charles Thomson Haskell. Mrs. Noble passed away in 1851 as a widow, and sometime thereafter her son, Russell, was taken in by the Haskells.

In a letter of March 28, 1861, Mrs. Haskell mentions that there is also another young nephew living in the Haskell household but does not name him. This was John Bachman Haskell, who is mentioned by name later on. "Johnny B." was the son of William Elnathan Haskell, a brother of Charles Thomson Haskell, who lived in Charleston. William E. Haskell was a merchant, banker, planter, and state militia officer. Johnny's mother was Harriet Bachman Haskell, and his maternal grandfather was the Rev. John Bachman, a Lutheran clergyman of Charleston and an internationally renowned naturalist. A friend of John James Audubon, Rev. Bachman collaborated with him to produce *The Viviparous Quadrupeds of North America* (published in three volumes in the 1840s), providing much of the scientific data which informed Audubon's beautiful paintings. A specimen of one of the animals featured in their book was obtained from Dungannon, William E. Haskell's plantation located in St. Paul's Parish near Charleston. According to Claude H. Neuffer's biography of Rev. Bachman, John Bachman Haskell "though only sixteen years of age, served with the defenders of Charleston until incapacitated for military duty." After the war, William E. Haskell and his family lived with Dr. Bachman at his home in Charleston, and John Bachman Haskell would follow in his grandfather's footsteps to become a Lutheran minister.

In February 1861, Mrs. Haskell wrote to her daughter Sophie about the boyish activities of her cousin and brothers, who were helping at home with the gardening: "We are all quite well. The boys are as busy as they can be. They have divided the goat team and Louis takes the big one, Russell the small one and each drives his own cart. One takes the hind wheels, the other the front wheels. They have commenced gardening in their usual style, which consists principally in hauling manure."

It is likely that the education of the younger boys at home suffered to some extent due to the exigencies of war, and Louis's earliest letters offer some evidence of this, but in the second year of the war Mrs. Haskell made arrangements for their formal schooling. In the spring or summer of 1862, Louis and Paul were sent to a boarding school that had been established by Octavius T. Porcher near Willington, South Carolina. Russell Noble was also a pupil there, although at some point he became a cadet at the Arsenal Academy, a state military school in Columbia. Porcher, who would be ordained as an Episcopal priest after the war, had formerly been a teacher at the prestigious classical school in Willington established by Moses Waddel. In his history of the Episcopal Church in South Carolina, Albert Sidney Thomas described Porcher's establishment as "emphatically a Church school," adding,

> The boys were instructed in the principles of the Christian religion...and the daily services of the Church were maintained with

regularity. The course of instruction was based upon that employed in the great English preparatory schools. Latin and Greek were especially emphasized.... The school was maintained until 1864, when boys from 16 to 18 were called into service. Mr. Porcher then closed the school and himself entered the service until the end of the war.

Paul, who was still too young to enter military service, was sent home to Abbeville in late 1864, while Louis enlisted in Company G of the First Regiment, Junior Reserves, South Carolina State Troops. This regiment was commanded by Col. James Benjamin Griffin, formerly an officer in the Hampton Legion. The Junior Reserves were organized in September 1864 at various places in the state, but these young soldiers were then sent home before reassembling later in the year at Hamburg, South Carolina. According to a memoir written by Samuel W. Ravenel, the members of the "Boy Brigade" were mustered into active service on December 1, 1864, and transported by train to Grahamville, South Carolina, a village in Beaufort District. The Battle of Honey Hill, in which a Union expeditionary force made a failed attempt to cut off the Charleston and Savannah Railroad, had taken place near Grahamville in late November. Louis's regiment of reserves was stationed in the area to help protect this vital railroad line that ran between the two port cities.

While in South Carolina in January 1865, Aleck Haskell arranged for Louis and a young cousin, Langdon Cheves, to be transferred to his cavalry command. Aleck returned to active service in Virginia by the end of the month, and his letters just prior to that time indicate that Louis returned to Abbeville sometime in late January or early February. Louis was supposed to join his cousin Langdon in Columbia or Abbeville so that the two could ride to Virginia together, but this plan was apparently disrupted when General Sherman's army began its assault on Columbia in mid-February. Soon afterward, Louis started out for Virginia with his brother Langdon, and their cousin Langdon Cheves left Columbia with the evacuating Confederate troops and later made his way to Virginia in the company of another cousin from Abbeville. Near the North Carolina line, Langdon C. Haskell's horse was taken sick, and he was forced to make the rest of the journey by rail, while Louis continued on horseback alone, not arriving in Virginia until late March. In his memoir, Gen. Edward P. Alexander noted that Louis showed up a few days before the Confederate forces evacuated Richmond (on April 2), describing him as "a well grown young fellow of about 17, who came on to be a soldier, the 7th of that family of brothers." He had arrived in time to briefly serve as a courier for his brother Lt. Col. John C. Haskell and would be with him to surrender at Appomattox.

Setting the Stage

In the second year of the war, uncertain of what lay ahead, but anticipating fierce battles, Aleck wrote to his mother from Virginia, "I can only tell you of how we feel in our little share of the great drama—a tragedy soon." By this time, the war was indeed becoming one immense tragedy that would only grow worse over the next two years—but the stage for this "great drama" had been set much earlier.

In the 1850s, the influence of the abolitionists had increased in the North, and in that decade, a series of events and publications worsened sectional tensions. In 1852, Harriet Beecher Stowe published her famous book *Uncle Tom's Cabin*, and in 1859, John Brown instigated a raid against the Harper's Ferry arsenal in Virginia. With the weapons he hoped to seize there, he planned to lead an armed slave rebellion. After Brown's capture and arrest, it came to light that his efforts had been funded by a number of prominent Northern abolitionists. Southerners were shocked and outraged that many Northerners looked on John Brown favorably and even praised him as a martyr after his execution.

When Abraham Lincoln ran for the presidency of the United States in 1860, he was viewed by Southerners as the candidate of a political party (the Republicans) which was purely sectional and concerned mainly with promoting the interests of the North. Consequently, his election in November provided the catalyst for South Carolina to secede from the union and reassert her independence. A state convention was convened, and an Ordinance of Secession was enacted in Charleston on December 20, 1860.

In their *Declaration of the Immediate Causes which Induce and Justify the Secession of South Carolina from the Federal Union*, the delegates of the Secession Convention defended states' rights, condemned Northern abolition societies which had "sent emissaries, books and pictures" into the South to incite insurrection and violence by the slaves, and contended that some northern states were violating the Constitution and federal legislation regarding slaves by refusing to enforce the fugitive slave laws. The *Declaration* pointed out that the United States Constitution was a contractual agreement (or compact) among the states and that if any of the parties did not abide by its obligations, it was rendered null and void.

The Secession Convention also published a document entitled *Address of the People of South Carolina,* and one its chief complaints against the government of the United States was the tariff, or taxes on imports. After comparing the position of the South to that of the American colonists in 1776, the *Address* stated:

[The Southern states] are a minority in Congress. Their representation in Congress is useless to protect them against unjust taxa-
tion.... For the last forty years, the taxes laid by the Congress of
the United States, have been laid out with a view of subserving the
interests of the North...to promote, by prohibitions, Northern interests in the production of their mines and manufactures.... The
people of the Southern States are not only taxed for the benefit of
the Northern States, but after the taxes are collected, three-fourths
of them are expended at the North.

The 1860 platform of Lincoln's party called for adjustments, that is, increases, to the tariff on imported goods. The promise of a protectionist tariff
was a notable factor in the election of that year and helped the Republicans
secure crucial electoral votes that would secure the presidency for them in
November. The Morrill Tariff Bill was working its way through the US
Congress in 1860, passing in the House of Representatives in May of that
year and in the Senate early the following year. President James Buchanan
signed the bill into law on March 2, 1861, two days before the inauguration
of Abraham Lincoln, and it raised the average tariff rate from about 15 percent to over 37 percent, with a greatly expanded list of items covered. The
constitution of the Confederate States of America outlawed such protectionist tariffs, effectively creating a free-trade zone within its borders, which
many Northern newspapers decried as a dire threat to the North's economy.

In his inaugural address in March 1861, President Lincoln stated that
the only reasons he would use force against the seceded states would be "to
hold, occupy, and possess the property and places belonging to the [US]
government, and to collect the duties and imposts" (duties and imposts
meaning the tariff revenue). After South Carolina's secession, the state, now
an independent commonwealth, no longer allowed the collection of federal
tariff revenue, and the rest of the states that seceded followed the same
course. They also took possession of most forts and arsenals within their
borders. The federal government in Washington was left with this choice:
allow the South to go in peace or resort to war.

Writing to Eleuthera DuPont Smith in Delaware on May 5, 1861,
Mrs. Haskell laid out the case for South Carolina's secession, emphasizing
the political hostility of the Republican Party:

I cannot tell you in words that would convince you why we know
and feel we are in the right. Why we feel we had to separate or
sink into miserable provincial dependence on a people disposed to
crush us into obedience to their fanatical rule. It is not your North
that hurt us, you are almost Southern, but that party you call

small, has grown, like the cloud not bigger than a man's hand, till it has strength and power to exclude us from the territories, to lay on a new and enormous tariff, to set at defiance the laws for the return of our negroes, for, for one returned five hundred were kept back. Strong enough to <u>Canonize</u> John Brown to spread arson and murder through districts in Texas and to scatter emissaries through the whole of the South.

In a letter penned on August 3, 1861, John C. Haskell commented that after Lincoln took office, his party "looked on it as a fixed fact that the South was now theirs, that their tender consciences were to be salved by the suppression of slavery and that their pockets were to be filled by the suppression of free trade &c." The platform of the Republican Party in 1860 did not call for the abolition of slavery, but it did express opposition to any expansion of slavery into the US territories, which was a prohibition, or "suppression," that the Southern states saw as an unconstitutional assault on their equality in the Union and an effort to reduce their political power. Ironically, another plank in the Republican platform denounced "the lawless invasion by armed force of the soil of any State or Territory, no matter under what pretext, as among the gravest of crimes."

South Carolina's secession in December 1860 was followed in the next two months by Mississippi, Florida, Alabama, Georgia, Louisiana, and Texas. When President Lincoln called for 75,000 volunteer troops in April 1861 to invade the seceded states, Virginia, Tennessee, North Carolina, and Arkansas promptly seceded in outrage and joined the Confederacy. Less than a week after South Carolina proclaimed her independence in December 1860, Maj. Robert Anderson, the commander of United States garrison at Fort Moultrie on Sullivan's Island, made a fateful decision to transfer his men to Fort Sumter, a new fort located in Charleston Harbor. At night, the soldiers of the garrison spiked the cannons at Fort Moultrie, set the gun carriages on fire, and took boats a short distance across the harbor to Fort Sumter. At about the same time, representatives from South Carolina were in Washington, DC, where they had been sent to seek the removal of United States troops in Charleston, to negotiate for a peaceful settlement of questions of Federal property in South Carolina, and to offer to pay the state's share of the public debt. Their negotiations with President James Buchanan and his administration abruptly came to an end when news reached them of the startling and unexpected events in Charleston. In response, South Carolina took possession of the Federal arsenal and the other harbor forts in Charleston. Another incident which South Carolinians viewed as warlike occurred shortly afterward. In early January 1861, in an attempt to put in more troops and provisions at Fort Sumter, the US government sent a civilian merchant ship, *Star of the West*, to Charleston. The South Carolinians were aware that there were armed troops and munitions concealed below its deck, and after sending a warning shot that went unheeded, they fired on the ship, and it reversed its course and steamed away.

The garrison at Fort Sumter was permitted to receive food and other provisions from Charleston, as well as mail, on a daily basis. (This went on from the latter part of January until April 7, when it was learned that warships were on the way to Charleston Harbor.) In February 1861, the Confederate States of America was formed in Montgomery, Alabama, electing Jefferson Davis as president. Davis sent three commissioners to Washington to negotiate the same matters that earlier representatives from South Carolina had been sent to discuss, to seek recognition of the Confederate States, and to establish friendly relations between the two governments. President Lincoln would not meet with these men, however, and his administration refused any direct negotiations or any recognition of their government.

In March 1861, US Secretary of State William H. Seward gave assurances to the Confederate commissioners through an intermediary that his government would remove the Fort Sumter garrison. As the whole country watched and waited to see what the outcome of the Fort Sumter crisis would be, newspapers speculated about President Lincoln's intentions. The *New York Herald* newspaper observed on April 7: "Unless Mr. Lincoln's administration makes the first demonstration and attack, President Davis says there will be no bloodshed. With Mr. Lincoln's administration, therefore, rests the responsibility of precipitating a collision, and the fearful events of protracted war."

On April 8, a message from President Abraham Lincoln was delivered to Francis W. Pickens, the governor of South Carolina. It notified the governor that an armed naval expedition was on its way to Charleston to supply Fort Sumter with provisions, by force if necessary. Despite Seward's assurances that Anderson and his men would be evacuated (given as late as April 7), Federal warships, troops, and supplies began making their way to Charleston harbor. President Davis decided that strengthening a fortress that could be used against Charleston and the harbor batteries could not be tolerated, and he determined that it should be reduced before it could join forces with the approaching warships. Confederate general Beauregard sent messages to Major Anderson on April 10 and April 11 requesting he evacuate the fort, but Anderson refused to leave or remain neutral in the anticipated engagement, and on April 12, the Confederates began a bombardment of Fort Sumter.

In his book *The Rise and Fall of the Confederate Government*, President Jefferson Davis wrote of his decision to bombard the fort: "He who makes the assault is not necessarily he that strikes the first blow or fires the first gun. To have awaited further strengthening of their position by land and naval forces, with hostile purpose now declared, would have been as unwise as it would be to hesitate to strike down the arm of the assailant, who levels a deadly weapon at one's breast, until he has actually fired."

In New Jersey, an editor of the *American Standard* newspaper declared on April 12 that the warships were not sent down by Lincoln to provision Fort Sumter but were actually sent as "a disingenuous feint...a mere decoy to draw the first fire from the people of the South, which act by the predetermination of the [United States] government is to be the pretext for letting loose the horrors of war. It dare not itself fire the first shot or draw the first blood, and is now seeking by a mean artifice to transfer the odium of doing so to the Southern Confederacy."

Throughout the bombardment, the Federal vessels which had just arrived lay off the bar and did not enter the harbor to brave the guns firing from Morris and Sullivan's islands in order to render assistance to the besieged fort. After Major Anderson surrendered on April 13 (with no deaths of combatants resulting from the shelling of Fort Sumter), he and his men were treated respectfully and allowed safe passage home. On April 16, 1861, the *Buffalo Daily Courier* editorialized: "The affair at Fort Sumter, it seems to us, has been planned as a means by which the war feeling at the North should be intensified, and the [Lincoln] administration thus receive popular support for its policy....War is inaugurated, and the design of the administration is accomplished."

Act one of a great tragedy had begun.

me with one lock hair

Silhouette of Mrs. Sophia Cheves Haskell as a young woman.
Courtesy South Carolina Historical Society.

Charles Thomson Haskell, Jr. The background of this
carte de visite, probably taken in the late 1850s, indicates
that the photographer was George S. Cook of Charleston.
Courtesy South Carolina Historical Society.

Captain William T. Haskell. This carte de visite
was produced by Quinby & Company of Charleston.
Courtesy South Carolina Historical Society.

Alexander Cheves Haskell. He was probably twenty-one years old
at the time this photograph was taken in 1861.

Courtesy Tom Haskell.

John Cheves Haskell. This carte de visite was taken prior to June 1862, when he lost his right arm at the Battle of Gaines Mill.

Courtesy South Carolina Historical Society.

Joseph Cheves Haskell. This photograph appeared as an illustration in T. C. De Leon's book *Belles, Beaux and Brains of the 60's*, published in 1909.

Sophie Haskell (later Mrs. Langdon Cheves). This photograph of Sophie was produced by W. B. Austin of Charleston, ca. 1890.

Courtesy South Carolina Historical Society.

Louis Wardlaw Haskell. This cabinet card photograph was taken
by Alman & Company of New York, ca. 1885.

Courtesy South Carolina Historical Society.

Paul Thomson Haskell. This cabinet card photograph
was taken by Alman & Company of New York.
Courtesy South Carolina Historical Society.

Langdon Cheves. This carte de visite was taken between 1861
and July 1863 by Quinby & Company of Charleston.
Courtesy South Carolina Historical Society.

General Maxcy Gregg. A carte de visite produced
by Wearn & Hix of Columbia, South Carolina.

Courtesy South Carolina Historical Society.

Detail from an illustration in *Frank Leslie's Illustrated Newspaper*, February 23, 1861, depicts "General McGowan" addressing the Abbeville Volunteers from the Charleston Hotel. Samuel McGowan held the rank of major general in the South Carolina militia at the time.

Courtesy Library of Congress.

Detail from an illustration in *Frank Leslie's Illustrated Newspaper*,
May 4, 1861, depicts a view of Fort Sumter and Sullivan's Island
from Morris Island during the bombardment in April 1861.
Moultrie House is on the far right in the distance.

Editor's collection.

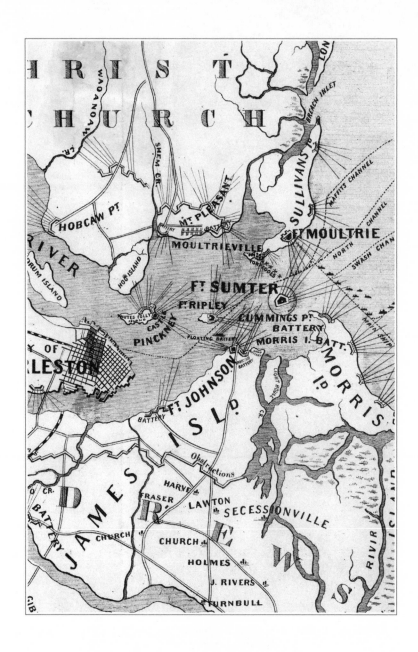

New Map of Charleston Harbor. This 1863 map (detail) by G. W. Tomlinson shows the locations of the Confederate harbor batteries and forts.

Courtesy Library of Congress.

Alexander Cheves Haskell. This portrait appeared in the *Cyclopedia of Eminent and Representative Men of the Carolinas*, published in 1892.

Courtesy College of Charleston Special Collections.

Sophia Cheves Haskell. This photograph of Mrs. Haskell in her later years appeared in T. C. De Leon's book *Belles, Beaux and Brains of the 60's*.

1

WAR OR PEACE?

8 JANUARY 1861 – 17 APRIL 1861

As 1861 begins, three of the Haskell brothers—William, Charles and Aleck—are in Charleston serving in the state troops. Stationed at Sullivan's
Island and Morris Island in Charleston Harbor, they await the outcome of a
crisis precipitated by Major Robert Anderson's stealthy abandonment and
sabotage of Fort Moultrie and subsequent occupation of Fort Sumter. The
South Carolina authorities desire a peaceful separation from the union, but
make defensive preparations after Anderson's actions, which they consider
warlike. War looms as a terrible possibility, although many hope for peace,
especially after reports circulate in March that the Lincoln administration
intends to remove the U.S. garrison from Fort Sumter. Aleck's first letter
home is one of solemn foreboding, while William writes optimistically, anticipating a peaceful resolution. Their sister Sophie is also in Charleston at
this time, at Madame Togno's boarding school. Charles, an officer in the
First Regiment, South Carolina Infantry Regulars, leaves Charleston in late
January on a partly secret mission for the governor of South Carolina, Francis W. Pickens. Newspapers report that Charles has been sent to deliver important messages to Washington, D.C., but his covert, more urgent purpose
is the recruitment of men in Maryland and elsewhere for service in South
Carolina. Aleck joins Colonel Maxcy Gregg's staff as his military secretary in
mid-February. In March, Charles returns to Charleston to take on the duties
of regimental quartermaster, while Langdon begins his military service as a
volunteer aide to Col. Gregg. The younger brothers Joseph and John arrive
on the scene in April, and on the twelfth day of that month, after an armed
United States ship is sighted off the harbor, the bombardment of Fort Sumter begins. The North has chosen war.

Alexander C. Haskell, Charleston, S.C., to Sophia C. Haskell (UNC)
8 January [1861]
My dear Mother,

I enter on duty tonight. Major Anderson from his tremendous fortress, has announced to our Governor that he will sink any boat or vessel seeking to land at any of our four fortified points. This is a blockade which annihilates our power & cuts off those forces at the respective commands from all their supplies. This power is great & his insolence is greater. I trust in God that we may resist the one & punish the other without too awful a sacrifice of life.

Our destination is unknown. Do not be uneasy if you hear nothing from us. We are no longer allowed pen & paper.

God bless & keep our State and all friends & relations & all in our family. Love to family & friends.

William T. Haskell, Charleston, S.C., to Sophia C. Haskell (SCHS)
9 January 1861
Dear Ma,

I write a few lines to say that we are all well and to give the news which is quite exciting this morning. At 7 o'clock this morning the "Star of the West" tried to enter the harbor and was fired into by Major Stevens[1] with the cadets from a battery of five guns on Morris Island. The range was long but two shots are said to have taken effect. Three shots were also fired from Fort Moultrie. Sumter, contrary to her promises made no reply. The steamer turned and went out of sight where by last accounts she still remains.[2]

We are at a loss to account for the silence of Fort Sumter. Some say the object of the Gov't was simply to draw So. Ca. into a decided act of hostility—that effected, for the present things are expected to remain quiet. But this is mere surmise. I still retain my faith in peace in which many join me. We may go to Sister's tomorrow. Love to all.

---

[1] Major Peter Fayssoux Stevens (1830-1910).

[2] Major Robert Anderson took no measures to defend this civilian ship which had entered Charleston harbor with troops and munitions concealed below its decks. Anderson sent a note to South Carolina Governor F. W. Pickens to ask if the ship had been fired on with his sanction, adding that if he did not receive a prompt reply that he would fire on any vessel that came in range of Fort Sumter's guns. The governor answered that the firing had been justified, and that he had instructed his battery commanders to fire a warning shot across the bow of any unauthorized vessel entering the harbor. When Anderson learned that the *Star of the West* had disregarded the warning shot sent across her bow, he decided not to carry out his threat, which would have effectively blockaded the port.

William T. Haskell, Moultrie House, Sullivan's Island, to Sophia C. Haskell
(SCHS)
20 January 1861
My dear Mother,

We are very glad to hear through two or three letters lately received that you are all well at home & as for ourselves here can inform you that we are beyond all question as comfortable soldiers as can be found anywhere on a summer's day. We are now in the Moultrie House[3] again after two day's absence at the upper ward of the island among the myrtles where we were stationed in our turn to guard a small battery whose object is to protect the point as in the former attack of Sir P. Parker.[4] There our quarters were tents & our fare somewhat rough. The duties without being severe give us something to do. They consist of three drills & a parade every day with guard duty & other occasional services such as the economy of the establishment requires.

Our fare is very good being much improved by two boxes which Pa sent over to us & others which others of the mess receive. We received two boxes last evening on our return from ladies who thus kindly remember us, one from Columbia the other from Charleston. No names were sent but I think I recognize the directions. Such supplies, with Titus' cooking & catering, keeps us going very respectably.[5] What adds much to our convenience ... [*missing section*] ... being directed to the channel from points which are not commanded by Fort S[umter] or at least are somewhat protected. Such are that on Morris Island & another about half a mile above the Moultrie House. In spite of all these signs of war & the possible chances for it I still adhere to my belief in peace unless some accident precipitates hostilities. I don't find the fault with the Governor which many think they discover. I think we have been brought on our way thus far prosperously & the omens of the future seem to me good. Alic says he is going to write a long letter in

---

[3] The Moultrie House was a fine hotel on Sullivan's Island. It opened in 1850, and was located just east of Fort Moultrie. John McLaren McBryde, one of the Abbeville Volunteers who was a messmate of Aleck and William, gave the following details about their stay there in his memoir: "The unit was quartered in the Old Moultrie House, an immense summer hotel just above Fort Moultrie. My mess occupied the quarter on the first corner of the second floor and next to us on the inner side and just at the head of the steps was the mess of a group of our special friends. The regiment held a dress parade every afternoon." McBryde, "An Eyewitness to History," 38.

[4] Sir Peter Parker (1721-1811), a British naval commander who led an attack against Fort Moultrie (then called Fort Sullivan) in June 1776.

[5] In his memoir, Aleck Haskell related that while he and his mess were quartered in the Moultrie House, they had "Uncle William's old man servant, Titus, to cook for us." Daly, *Alexander Cheves Haskell*, 44.

which I daresay he will discourse of war as I have of peace. But he is under a high war pressure & can see nothing except in that aspect. We are both quite well. I am sorry London[6] does not get better. Do tell him so & remember me to the servants generally. Give my love to Pa & all the rest, & say I will try & keep up a regular report of our state & actions.

Alexander C. Haskell, Camp Moultrie, Sullivan's Island, to Charles T. Haskell (UNC)
Sunday [January 1861]
Dear Pa,

I got your letter from home yesterday afternoon, just as we tramped in from Camp Oyster,[7] where we have been roughing it for two days, taking our turn in guarding the North point of the Island on which a landing would probably be attempted if the enemy resolve on active hostilities.

Our return was a most joyous affair. A general outburst of feeling indicated the pleasure with which the Red Coats[8] found themselves once more in their comfortable barracks to which we have formed a home-like attachment. We stand close to each other and completely segregated, except in the way of daily civilities, from the other companies in the House. Our quarters are kept so nicely & with so much pride on our part that we feel at home in ours soldiers' lodge in a way that you can hardly conceive. All looks familiar, even Mr. Anderson's (as a simple backwoods soldier styled Fort Sumter) has become almost a necessity as we look from our window in the gray morning, as it looms through the mist in all its magnificent strength, frowning as proud a defiance upon us as if it stood like bold Leonidas against the tremendous odds in number (for so they put it) & feel heroic in proportion to our useless number & their own brick walls & tremendous artillery. But still I am convinced we will & even if we would not, must have the elephant at

---

[6] London was a family slave, of whom Aleck Haskell wrote in his memoir, "Our favorite man servant, brought up by my parents, was 'London,' called 'Lunnun' for short." Daly, *Alexander Cheves Haskell,* 13.

[7] Camp Oyster likely was likely located at or near an oyster plantation at the east end of Sullivan's Island near Breach Inlet. John McLaren McBryde recorded in his memoir that the Abbeville Volunteers were ordered there without camp equipment or rations. "So we had a hungry time of it, and were forced to literally to live by our own wits. Some of us caught crabs and fish in the inlet between our island and the next outer one, and some enterprising members discovered an oyster bank belonging to a man who supplied Charleston with that bivalve. After that we lived almost entirely on oysters, raw and cooked, but unsalted, and before we were done we loathed the very sight of them. And we had to pay for them out of our own pockets." McBryde, "An Eyewitness to History," 38.

[8] Part of the uniform of the Abbeville Volunteers was a red flannel jacket.

all cost, & then keep him for useful purposes at home. Nobody knows what is to be done or what is contemplated. We only know that fortifications & batteries are being multiplied with a view to arresting reinforcements & if needs be bombarding "Mr. Anderson's."

Our noble company is being drilled and disciplined & is improving in these points quite rapidly. They are a splendid set & will do good service if they have a chance. It will only be a pity if they are cut up too much. The Regiment generally is in fine spirits and ready for service.

We are living royally. Titus is a perfect "fidus Achates"[9] and an Ulysses for cunning wisdom in expedients. We are supplied by the commissary with the ruder materials for supporting existence, but more grateful stores pour in from every side. Last night on our return from camp we were summoned to the orderly's room to receive some parcels. One was a huge box weighty & well filled, directed to Messrs. W & A Haskell & Mr. McBryde[10] "The young soldiers who have come so far to defend their State." "From some ladies of Charleston &c." Just think now what a soldier that ought to make. Why it takes me back to the days of Chivalry when Knights fought & died for the gentle lady love. But in all truth and earnest I felt more willing to die in a storming party than I ever had done before. Such remembrances & such attentions are inexpressibly touching and must be addressed to brutes indeed if they did not excite the noblest impulses of our souls.

But when it came to my turn to open a box addressed to A. C. Haskell Abbeville Volunteers & found in it such evidence of woman's delicate care and all that a mother could have done if a sickness or any other misfortune should render such attention necessary, I felt very grateful & very happy. I could not find out who sent it for with true woman's wit (for it was a lady & no doubt) the name had been cut out of every newspaper in the box & all other landmarks erased, but I can make a pretty sharp guess. It came from Columbia.[11]

Well I feel quite foolish today & think that more people remember a poor private soldier than he has any right to hope for or expect. It is a queer life we lead here, quiet & orderly, & happy enough & work enough, but a restless reckless feeling of wanting to be doing one way or the other. I did not know exactly how to answer the other day when somebody asked me if I was homesick. I feel well & cheerful, work as hard as any man in the company until some of the old hard-fists gave up & said they didn't know those

---

[9] An Achates is a faithful friend or follower.

[10] John McLaren McBryde (1841-1923), a member of the Abbeville Volunteers.

[11] The box was probably sent by Aleck Haskell's aunt Mrs. Louisa Susanna Cheves McCord (1810-79), his mother's sister, who lived in Columbia, S.C.

Haskell boys before. But Rothschild answered the question.[12] I went to hear him play in the Capt.'s room, when he began in such strains of feeling as I never heard "Home Sweet Home." It was too much for me. I escaped unobserved, but not till the floodgates had been opened.

Dearest love to Ma & all the boys. Goodbye.

Charles T. Haskell, Jr., Charleston, S.C., to Charles T. Haskell (SCHS)
27 January [1861]
Dear Father,

I leave tonight for Washington with despatches. Then I return to Richmond on business for the Ordnance board & then go to Baltimore on business which I have no right to speak of.[13] My business there is very ticklish particularly as I go accompanied by a sergeant. The worst tho that can happen to me will be a <u>temporary</u> arrest as I am acting under explicit instructions from the Secretaries of war & state & the Executive.[14]

[P.S.] It is absolutely necessary that you should keep to yourself what I now write.

William T. Haskell, Moultrie House, Sullivan's Island, S.C., to Charles T. Haskell (SCHS)
28 January 1861
My dear Father,

I write to keep you informed of our position in the progress of affairs here. You hear by the papers of the prospects of war & peace. I think the expectation is in favor of the latter, but that is of course involved in all the doubt which has hitherto attached to it.

---

[12] Benjamin Rothschild, a member of the Abbeville Volunteers. A native of Baden, Germany, he was a music teacher in Abbeville, and died in 1862 at the Second Battle of Manassas (Bull Run). On December 19, 1856, an Abbeville newspaper, the *Independent Press*, reported on entertainments at the Opera House, noting "some excellent performances on the violin by that accomplished musician, Mr. Rothschild, who evoked the most rapturous applause, and enthusiastic encores."

[13] Charles was on a covert recruiting mission, and was to make contact with Louis T. Wigfall and W. T. Walters in Baltimore. William Thompson Walters (1819-94) was the owner of W. T. Walters & Company of Baltimore. Because of his pro-Confederate activities, he found it necessary to leave Maryland in the summer of 1861 and take his family to Europe, where they remained for the rest of the war. While abroad, Walters studied and collected art, and after his return to America his fine collection eventually formed the basis of the Walters Art Museum in Baltimore.

[14] Governor Francis W. Pickens' secretary of war was David Flavel Jamison (1810-64), and his secretary of state was Andrew Gordon Magrath (1813-93).

I think the question will be definitely decided before the 4th of March. Preparations are going on with considerable vigor, mortar batteries being erected at various points for a future bombardment of Fort Sumter. I have no faith in its impregnability. We have a fair chance at their guns in "barbette" as they have at any of ours, & in fact better for all the guns at Fort Moultrie were protected by our merlons, such as you saw in process of construction. These are being lined outside by palmetto logs which present quite a strange face to the attacking guns. The place is considered now as strong & tenable for some time. We are quite comfortable in our quarters here, which is more than we will be if we change as is somewhat anticipated to Morris Island. Our drills & duties are quite constant & prevent our time from hanging very heavily on our hands. The governor's wife[15] came over here this evening & reviewed the regiment which as being kindly meant I take quite as a compliment, though some dismiss the matter otherwise. The place though not tiresome as yet may become monotonous. We have no regular employment except the aforesaid drills & guard duty. The life we lead is a very healthy one whatever may be its other features.

Charley you will have heard ere this has arrived & received an appointment of first lieutenant at first in the engineer corps but has exchanged it for the infantry—Simkins' company.[16] We have not heard from home for some time but I suppose soon will. I will write & keep you informed as to the news & our welfare.

Charles T. Haskell, Jr., Richmond, Va., to Sophia C. Haskell (SCHS)
29 January [1861]
Dear Mother,

I have stopped here on business for South Carolina until the next train comes on, when I will go on to Washington & deliver despatches that I have charge of & then enter on my duties. I will be for some time almost altogether in Baltimore & Norfolk. Do not think of writing to me at either of these places, but to the care of Major John Dunovant,[17] Charleston. What I do will depend for its success on its being done clandestinely & letters di-

---

[15] The governor's wife was the beautiful Lucy Holcombe Pickens (1822-99).

[16] John Calhoun Simkins (1828-63) was the captain of Company B of the First South Carolina Infantry Regiment. He later held the rank of major and then colonel. A native of Edgefield District, he married Rosalie Maria Wardlaw (1831-91), a daughter of Judge David Lewis Wardlaw of Abbeville. He was killed at Battery Wagner in July 1863, and a battery (Shell Point) on James Island was renamed in his honor.

[17] John Gore Dunovant (1825-64), a native of Chester, S.C., was the major of the First Regiment, South Carolina Infantry Regulars. He was killed in action near Petersburg, Va. in October 1864 with the rank of brigadier general.

rected to me from Carolina might compromise me. Major Dunovant has the means of communicating with me otherwise than by mail.

Charles T. Haskell, Jr., Willard Hotel, Washington, D.C., to Langdon Cheves (SCHS)
30 January 1861
Dear Uncle,

I am stationed part of the time here & part of the time at Baltimore, on a peculiar service as an officer of the So. Ca. Regulars. From the nature of the service in which I am engaged I shall be obliged to remain here some time.

Having been obliged to leave the west in great haste on receiving my appointment & orders from the Governor, I have been compelled to come on here, low in funds. If you can lend me two hundred $200, to be returned whenever I can do it, you will relieve me from considerable embarrassment.

P.S. Please if you send it let it be directly, as I may be ordered off any hour &c to the Gilmore House Baltimore.

Sophie Haskell, Charleston, S.C., to William T. Haskell (SCHS)
[January 1861]
Dear Willy,

Titus came here this morning & told me he had been here yesterday, but the child that opens the door forgot to say anything about it. He tells me you wanted me to write to you. I asked M[ada]me to let me write you a line about Charley as perhaps you have not heard from him. You know he was sent off on Saturday evening very unexpectedly no one knew where for it was secret but Mme showed me a piece in the morning's courier which explains it.[18] She gave me the paper to send to you. She says you might like to see it. She is in a [glorious] humor, or rather she is so frightened that it makes her gentler to the girls. I heard last night that Hayne had demanded the Fort, but [H] was expected home today, but the piece about Charley seemed to contradict that. I heard that it had been refused & then that the President

---

[18] A Washington newspaper, the *Daily National Intelligencer*, reported the following on Saturday, February 2, 1861: "The Charleston Courier of Wednesday says: 'Mr. C. T. Haskell has been dispatched on a special mission to Washington with important despatches and instructions for Colonel L. W. Hayne [*sic*]. Mr. Haskell it is thought will reach the above city to-day. Mr. Hayne will await the receipt of these before taking any final action on the subject with which he is charged.'" Isaac W. Hayne (1809-80) was the attorney general of South Carolina. In January 1861, Governor Pickens sent him to Washington as a special envoy to negotiate a peaceful settlement of the transfer of Fort Sumter.

had referred it to Congress, but of this I know nothing. I suppose Hayne must be home soon & then it will be decided. I try to think they won't fight but I can't see how they can avoid it. I have not heard anyone say anything this morning one way or the other. If they do fight I suppose it must be soon, but from what the Courier says I don't see how Hayne can have already demanded the F[or]t.

I got a letter on Monday from Ma. She says they had had terrible weather, raining, freezing & sleeting. She says the trees were a good deal broken by the sleet but not as much as she expected. She seems rather lonely she says since Joe has gone. The house seems desolate though the little boys make enough noise to remind her that all are not gone.

I have had & still have a dreadful cold, the first really bad one I ever had, & it makes it very hard for me to go on with all my lessons & regular duties & makes me wish that I were at home to be coddled up & made much of. What is most unpleasant I have a dreadful pain in the chest the whole time especially when I cough. I hope it will get better soon, for I never had such a cold before & it is not pleasant. Good Bye. I have stretched the time, allowing to the utmost limit, & besides Titus has come for the note. Best love to Alic.

William T. Haskell, Moultrie House, Sullivan's Island, S.C., to Charles T. Haskell (SCHS)
31 January 1861
My dear Father,

I have no news but merely write to keep up the communication. Alic is now in town on account of some indisposition which I was afraid his imprudence would extend into something worse. He is doing well only with a bad cold which was getting better when I left him at Pinckney's this morning.[19] I saw Sophy this morning. She looks pretty well but complains of a bad cough. The doctor has seen her & given her some medicine & put a mustard plaster on her chest to relieve a pain which she says is now better. Charley as you will see by the paper is on duty in Washington. We had an alarm here the other night by some firing on our own vessels which gave no signals. The regiment was drawn up & heard some balls whistle by. Love to all.
[P.S.] Tell Ma if she sends a box, send eggs. I hope London is better.

Alexander C. Haskell, Charleston, S.C., to Sophia C. Haskell (UNC)
2 February 1861

---

[19] "Pinckney's" refers to the home of Mrs. Martha Caroline Haskell Pinckney (1834-91), a cousin. She was the wife of Bartholomew Gaillard Pinckney (1830-1906).

Dear Ma,

You will be surprised to hear from one of your soldiers in so pleasant a place as Mrs. B. G. Pinckney's comfortable little domicile, but so it is. I have not deserted or run or been expelled the company, but was very foolish in getting sick and remaining so for several days with prospect of more, which so worked upon my kind officers, specially Lythgoe, our good Capt. being absent, that I was ordered up to the city on the sick list.[20] The Colonel sent for me in [state] and in [state] was I borne from the Moultrie House on the bottom of a car big enough to haul thirty men and hired by government for my special accommodation. I arrived in Charleston safe & without much fatigue. One night of good nursing and sound sleep broke up & drove off my fever & I am now well but not quite strong enough for duty, so I shall wait a day or two more to break my cough & cold.

I think the Doctor (James Mabry, who is as kind and attentive as possible & affectionately so) was afraid of pneumonia if I remained on the island exposed to so much noise and alarm as one is subject to in barracks, so ordered me off & my recovery shows his prudence.[21] The third night that I was sick he gave me a great deal of blue pill and sudorific teas and told me not to move from under my blankets until late in the next day. I had a good deal of fever, but went honestly to sleep.[22] In about two hours a man burst thro my room "The war has begun" &c with startling outcry. The next instant a 48 thundered and the ball went with its screaming whistle over the house. There was no sleep then. Drums beat. The Col. ordered the regiment to form on the beach & to remain where they could "see the fight until they were fired into, then retreat "as they did no good." I could not stand all these calls specially as I heard we were to be marched up to meet a landing force, so up I jumped, bundled on my traps and was out at roll call with the company.[23] I was soon captured however & sent in under guard of Surgeon Bull who doctored me into quiet & then put me to bed & in a few minutes the regiment was marched in too.[24] We found out to our infinite mortification that it was nothing but a fleet of our own boats & steamers coming in with palmetto logs. They had put up wrong signals and had been most alarmingly

---

[20] Augustus Jackson Lythgoe (1830-62).

[21] This was Dr. James Fletcher Mabry (1824-78). Aleck Haskell wrote of him in his memoir: "We had a physician for the family and negroes and he came with great regularity whenever needed—Dr. Mabry—most of my early life ... one of the greatest doctors I ever knew." Daly, *Alexander Cheves Haskell*, 11.

[22] Blue pill may have been a medicine also called blue mass, prescribed for many different complaints. A sudorific was a substance used to induce sweating.

[23] Traps was another word for clothing or baggage.

[24] Surgeon Bull was likely Dr. William Izard Bull, Jr. (1838-1917).

responded to by Forts Morris & then Fort Moultrie, whose four balls & shells whistled as they passed over & glanced on the water in front or burst between us and the moon in splendid style. Those on board the boats say that considering the distance and the darkness the shooting was awfully straight. It was delightful to see how the brave fellows handled their guns perfectly careless of Anderson & his fort. The very guns cracked so cheerily & freely in the quiet night it sounded like the ratification indeed of independence.

As for our men they thought it a doubtful alarm, but only hoped it was true & to my surprise we could not keep from being charmed with the sound of the guns & still more so the balls, although we expected nothing but Anderson rattling right thro us the next moment. As one man said, the balls went laughing on their way. It was true & tho we felt solemn we felt like cheering the music if it came to be ours. Willy & all else are well. We are getting on with health & comfort (apart from my failure). The company is in glorious spirits. If you could make up your mind to the undertaking & and send a mammoth box to the company, to the brave Abbeville boys, it would be great and don't think sweets unimportant. [*illegible words*]

Love to Pa & all the boys. Good-bye. God bless and keep you all at home. I will write again before troubles grow worse.

[P.S.] Caroline is as kind as kind can be. She says if you and Pa will come down, you are a thousand times welcome to the room.[25]

Charles T. Haskell, Jr., Baltimore, Md., to Charles T. Haskell (SCHS)
3 February 1861
Dear Father,

I got here yesterday from Washington where I remained for some days by the advice of Wigfall[26] & Col. Hayne. I do not know whether I can accomplish my object or not—recruiting a large body of men—but am perfectly satisfied that I will not be safe here but for a short time & shall therefore in a day or two shift my quarters to Washington City or more probably to Norfolk.

Sophia C. Haskell, Home Place Plantation, Abbeville District, S.C., to William T. Haskell (SCHS)
5 February 1861
Dear Willy,

---

[25] Caroline was Mrs. Bartholomew Gaillard Pinckney, a first cousin to Aleck.

[26] Louis Trezevant Wigfall (1816-74), a Texas senator, and a native of South Carolina.

We received yours of the 31st yesterday evening. I was very glad indeed that you wrote or we should have been in much anxiety, for we had just received a message that Mr. [Fair] had returned from Charleston and had not seen you, that Alec was sick and that you had gone over to Charleston to take care of him. I hope your account is quite exact and that it is nothing serious. I had been uneasy too about Sophie and was glad to hear that she was in the D[octo]r's hands, as from her account I thought it was perhaps necessary. You ask after London. He gets no better, and I fear very much I will have no news to give you but what will give you pain. He is still sitting up and goes out a little when the weather is fine but he looks very thin and badly. You may be sure we are taking all the care of him we know how, and he is so good that every one seems to wish to be kind to him. All the rest are well. Your Father is feeling much better now, tho ever since his return from town until the last two days he has been ailing a good deal. The four boys get on very well together. I teach them a little now and then and try to keep them from forgetting the little they knew before. Johnny Bachman is improving in looks very much, and is a fine little fellow. He and Louis are great friends. I will get you a few eggs when I can send you a small box but they are not very plenty yet. We have had no mails since Saturday night. The Cars ran down as far as Saluda but could not reach the river as the embankment was washed away, some say the bridge. They waited but heard no news of the Car from Columbia, and it is supposed there is serious damage to the Road below Newberry. Richard waited in the village till 5 o'clock this afternoon but the Car had not returned. Your Father goes in tomorrow and I hope he will bring us some news. A day's delay is painful in these anxious times. I am glad you were not in Camp during this very bad weather we have had lately. Thank you very much for taking care of Alec. I knew you would and have felt less anxious.

God bless you my dear boy. I must conclude in haste.

Sophia C. Haskell, Home Place Plantation, Abbeville District, S.C., to Sophie Haskell (SCHS)
5 February 1861
Dear Sophie,

We have received all of your letters up to the 29th and are very much obliged to you for writing so often. We would have answered them sooner but for the great interruptions from the bad weather. The river was very high for two days and now the R. Road is so much injured there have been no mails to the village since Sat. 2nd. When this letter will go or when we will get letters I cannot tell as we have not as yet any information as to the extent of the injury to the Road. I have been quite anxious about your cough, and hope you will take as much care as you can of it. You were very right to speak to M[ada]me and if necessary you must make more complaints at the risk of a scolding. I do not understand what gave you so much pain in your chest. You must put on your under vests if it continues if you have not done so already. I was glad to hear from Willy that the Dr. was prescribing for you. Tell me particularly how you are. I was sorry to hear that Alec was suffering from cold too. Willy does not speak of it as very serious and said he was at Pinckney's and better. His letter was written Thursday afternoon after his return to the Island. We have the Courier of the 1st but no news since, which is a long time to be without hearing. The last accounts however lead [*sic*] us to think that affairs will remain without change for some days as Hayne made his demand for the Fort the day after Charley got to Washington, and the President required several days to consider before giving his answer. We are all well at home. Your Father seems much better again. Poor London gains nothing and I fear is gradually failing. He does not seem to suffer much and is cheerful and patient. We do all we know how for him and the servants, particularly Dick and Lucy, are very attentive to him.[27]

I have Jonas at present to work in the garden and in the last few days have done a good deal towards preparing for the Spring. I have trimmed all your roses and fixed up your little garden. The violets are blooming by thousands. I have sent for 4 new roses and for a Gardenia, a Laurestinas, two Myrtles and two Eunomias plants which I expect home tomorrow with a bundle of fruit trees and grave vines from Summer.[28] I do not know if I can get the boys to write. They are very lazy about it tho they promise very fairly. Do give my love to all friends when you see them particularly Kate.[29] Livie wrote to me a few days ago and says she has been very well this winter but

---

[27] In his memoir, Aleck Haskell wrote: "Our cook was 'Daddy Dick,'" adding that his "family stayed on at the plantation with many of the other negroes, 'after Freedom,' and whose daughter was still with us in 1886.'" Aleck described Lucy as a nurse who "reared our family of ten children from the oldest to the youngest. Her name was Lucy and she was one of the most pious and devoted women I have ever known." Daly, *Alexander Cheves Haskell*, 10-13.

[28] These roses were obtained from one of the finest nurseries in the country, the Pomaria Nursery in Newberry District, S.C., which was owned by William Summer (1815-78). According to Dr. James E. Kibler, an authority on Pomaria, the nursery records list an order placed for "4 roses" by Mrs. Charles T. Haskell on January 28, 1861. The order also included fruit trees and other flowers. Additional orders for trees and other plants were placed by Charles T. Haskell in 1860, 1862, and 1863. James E. Kibler letter to editor, January 6, 2018.

[29] Kate Haskell (1840-1910), a first cousin of the Haskell brothers, was the daughter of William E. Haskell.

says Lucilla is in very poor health.[30] I am very sorry to hear it. I was in hopes she would mend. Good by dear Sophie. Take care of yourself and let me hear soon that you are better, but do not say so unless it is quite true. It would make me very anxious if I thought you would make yourself out better than you really were. Love from all.

Alexander C. Haskell, Headquarters, First Regiment, S.C.V., Sullivan's Island, S.C., to Charles T. Haskell (UNC)
[February 1861]
Dear Pa,

    I wrote you from town telling of my recovery from slight sickness. I am and have been well since. Most of today not spent in drill has been passed by me in company with Col. Blane (I don't know how to spell the name, but Blane is the sound).[31] He introduced himself to us as an old college friend of yours, and had he been a near relative and a dear one he could not have been kinder and even more affectionate. He took leave of me and even with tears in his eyes begged me to call on him as my father's "old friend" for anything in which he could aid us. He is a noble Christian gentleman and has shown it in his interest in our regiment and especially of our company, which he has specially selected & presented with a considerable number of admirable religious works so well chosen for their interesting matter, that they are read by every soldier in the company. He sends affectionate remembrances to you, and tells me to inform you that Major Anderson is a brother of Lars Anderson, who was a classmate of yours in college.[32] This brother was the one who

---

    [30] "Livie" refers to Susan Olivia Haskell Venning (1830-89), daughter of William E. Haskell, and the wife of William Lucas Venning (1825-1919). Her sister was Eliza Lucilla Haskell Lee (1836-1905).

    [31] Aleck is referring to Allard Henry Belin (1803-71) of Charleston and Georgetown District, S.C. His rank of colonel is likely a state militia rank. He was a graduate of Harvard.

    [32] Larz Anderson (1803-78) was the brother of Major Robert Anderson, the commander of the U.S. garrison occupying Fort Sumter. He came to Charleston in early January 1861 and paid two visits to the fort to see his brother. A Massachusetts newspaper, the *Lowell Daily Citizen and News*, reported on January 11, 1861: "Larz Anderson of Cincinnati, brother of the major, has just returned from Charleston. After the first interview with his brother, the surveillance was not continued, and he had free communication with him. The major considers his position entirely secure, and is fairly supplied with provisions and other necessities, except coal and wood, for military purposes, in case that extremity should be reached." At Governor Pickens' request, a prominent citizen of Charleston, Robert N. Gourdin, accompanied Larz Anderson on his first interview with his brother. Gourdin was a friend and correspondent of Major Anderson's during the Fort Sumter crisis, making arrangements for provisions to be sent to the garrison from Charleston merchants. Larz Anderson also corresponded with Gourdin after he left

came on not long ago to see the Major and excited general sympathy by his own worth and the affecting scene with his brother in the fort. This same fort stands still stronger by every means wh[ich] Anderson's skill and energy have been able to bring to bear. A fine battery has been erected on Cumming's Point, 1200 yards from Fort Sumter, well provisioned with guns & mortars. This will be ready in a few days, perhaps tomorrow, & together with the forts, Morris, Johnson & Moultrie, will, it is supposed, open fire on Anderson as soon as completed in every particular of preparation. People here of every grade of position and opinion seem to have come to a sort of inevitable conclusion that the fight is to begin in a few days. Our regiment received orders this evening to report in readiness for anything tomorrow at ten o'clock. This probably means nothing, but it may mean everything. Our destination, if we move, is probably Fort Morris. But I don't know what part we are to play or how we are going about it or when. In fact we know nothing about it and war may be very far off, but everything conduces to a contrary opinion provided the Southern Congress do not take some means to avert it.

Tatoo stops me. My dear Father & Mother I am thinking constantly of you. I trust we shall all meet again. Whatever comes we will try to do our duty to God and our state. Love to all the boys & remembrances to friends.

Sophie Haskell, Charleston, S.C., to William T. Haskell (SCHS)
[February 1861]
My dear Willy,

I am just writing a few lines in bed because it is some time I have written. You must not imagine from my being in bed that I am sick but you know I told you some time ago that I had a bad cold. The D[octo]r saw me for several days & my cold got better as long as he prescribed for me, but as soon as he stopped coming M[ada]me stopped doing anything & it has got a good deal worse again, but with much less pain in the chest but I got a letter from Ma yesterday & she seemed quite anxious about it so I determined to nurse myself up & get well. Cousin Caroline[33] who I saw yesterday told me she thought I ought to stay in bed one day at least & apply a Mustard Plas-

---

South Carolina, informing him on January 8 that he had attempted to prevent the *Star of the West* from being sent to Charleston, and writing on January 10, "God save us from fraternal bloodshed!" Robert N. Gourdin's brother Henry Gourdin (1804-79) corresponded with Langdon Cheves (1814-63) about the Fort Sumter situation during this period. Racine, *Gentlemen Merchants*, 424-429.

[33] Cousin Caroline was likely Caroline M. Mason (1832-1919). She was the sister of Ann Graham Florence Mason Rhett (often called Folly or Follie), who was the wife of Thomas Grimke Rhett, a first cousin of the Haskell brothers.

ter which I determined to do & have done accordingly though it is very unpleasant, for Mme has all the morning been talking about the queer way
some people have of making a fuss about anything & when I begged for the
Plaster she said, "Oh, certainly have what you please, doctor yourself up. I
have no doubt you are very experienced." At any rate she can't say it is to get
off from my lessons for it's Sunday.

I got a letter from Charley dated the 4th. He had only stopped in
Washington for a day to deliver his despatches & then went on to Baltimore
where he wrote from. He was about to start for Norfolk. Of course he did
not say what his business was. He said I had best not write to him & he
seemed doubtful whether I would get his letter but I suppose you have heard
from him probably later than I have. Ma says in her letter that the mail had
been stopped by an accident on the road & that they had heard nothing at
all since the 30th. I suppose it is all right now. She says all are well but poor
London who is no better at all. Oh when you write beg her to come down. I
really thought she would if you & Alic were to write to her. Do give my best
love to Alic. I do hope he has got over that cough. It made me so uneasy.
Please when you have time write me a little note.

[P.S.] I don't know if you can read this for I can't write lying down.

*William T. Haskell, Moultrie House, Sullivan's Island, S.C., to Sophia C.
Haskell (SCHS)*
7 February 1861
My dear Mother,

I got your letter today & am very glad to hear that you are all well. We
are in a like good condition, Alic having returned now already two days
looking quite well. Things here are just as usual, occasional rumors of reinforcements, etc., etc. I believe in none of these until ocular demonstration is
given. In any case the whole affair is in hands above ours & there as far as
uneasiness goes I am content to leave the matter. Our last news is Hayne's
return & the prospects which it opens. Of the details the papers give the best
account & later than I can furnish.

We are quite comfortable & hope to remain but may soon be sent to
Morris Island where our quarters will be less convenient & elegant. Do send
what news of Lally, Ella & family when you write next time.[34] Sophy, Ecky[35]
brings word, is quite well & I suppose over her cough. I got Pa's letter two
or three days ago & will follow his counsel & keep before me your wishes &

---

[34] Lally was a nickname for Langdon Cheves Haskell. His wife was Ella Coulter
Wardlaw Haskell (1835-87), the daughter of Judge David Lewis Wardlaw of Abbeville.

[35] Ecky was a nickname for Alexander C. Haskell.

anxieties. I hope your next account of London can be better. Love to all & thanks for all letters received this morning.

William T. Haskell, Moultrie House, Sullivan's Island, S.C., to Charles T. Haskell (SCHS)
7 February 1861
My dear Father,

Not to allow a long interval I commence again to give no news from the seat of war. Things here I think, although immediate preparations for war are fast [maturing], are growing more & more peaceful in their aspect. The formation of the So[uthern] Confederacy is the most effective course I think of this. They will make a formal demand which if refused will I suppose lead to the immediate bombardment of the Fort. For this we are very nearly ready. I suppose in three days six points will be prepared to throw effective shot & shell into Major A's quarters. The <u>floating battery</u> will be longer in completion. But now as the question seems deferred until some near the fourth of March next, this present delay makes little difference.[36]

Sophy is quite well as are also Alec & myself. I have not heard from Charley since he left the city.

I am very sorry to hear that London is no better. Do send me any accounts of Lally & family. I must end my letter as our very efficient quartermaster Lawson has to go the boat with the mail.

Give my love to Ma & all the boys.

Sophia C. Haskell, Home Place Plantation, Abbeville District, S.C., to Sophie Haskell, Charleston, S.C. (SCHS)
11 February 1861
Dear Sophie,

I mean to write you just a short letter tonight so I have no room for scolding. I am much obliged to you for all your letters, if they do not occupy too much of your time. They always give me pleasure, for I believe, as you say, that it does you good occasionally to have someone to speak freely to and let off a little steam when Madame blazes up.[37] Take things easy; she

---

[36] The idea of a floating battery was proposed to the South Carolina Executive Council by a naval officer, Captain John Hamilton, and it was supposed to be completed within three weeks. "Actually the floating battery was more than a huge barge roofed over with iron which was able to contain two 42-pound guns and two 32-pound guns." It had to be towed into position. Burton, *The Siege of Charleston*, 23.

[37] "Madame" was Rosalie Acelie Guillon Togno (1815-1913), a widow who operated Madame Togno's School for Young Ladies. The scholastic year at her establishment on Meeting Street consisted of two sessions (Oct. 1 to Feb. 15, and Feb. 16 to June 30).

don't mean half what she says, and words are not half as strong in French as in sober English. A *mensonge* is not near so bad as a *falsehood*. I knew you would find school hard though I should have preferred a more gentle ruler, but believe me the worst is over and I think you will be able to improve in your music and studies more than you think. I have not at all given up the idea of paying you a visit. I think I may very likely come down with your father after a while, but he is waiting for some time of more interest. He does not think the Fort will be attacked soon, perhaps never. We hope strongly that Virginia will join us and with her will go all the border states. Every step seems steadily leading to this blessed end. God grant that it may be so, and then we will be safe, perhaps escape all our dreaded troubles. I hope so with all my heart and pray God it may so end.

We are all quite well. The boys are as busy as they can be. They have divided the goat team and Louis takes the big one, Russell[38] the small one and each drives his own cart. One takes the hind wheels, the other the front wheels. They have commenced gardening in their usual style, which consists principally in hauling manure. I have given them all the piece of ground from the French pear trees back to the fence, and am to take back all that is not well cultivated by May. I have set out the plants in your garden: 4 roses, Cloth of Gold, Gloire de Dijon, Granville [Pink], and Woodland Margarette, a new and beautiful white rose. The violets are beautiful, they form a purple wreath all around the center bed and perfume the whole yard. The hyacinths are beginning to peep out but they were not all to be found when I went to plant them. The pretty little crocuses are showing themselves. We have had a great deal of rain and will, I rather fear, have an early Spring which may again endanger the fruit.

Your letter from Charley was some days later than any we had received. I suppose it may be some time, perhaps two or three weeks, before he returns. In the meantime, I do not think you need have any anxiety about him. Your father has a pretty good idea as to what is his business. You never have mentioned going to the dentist. Do if possible, have your teeth attended to at once. Tell Madame I am very anxious on the subject. Who have you in your room instead of Louise? And are you the only two who have the same bed? Lilly is quite well and takes her meals just where she can get them though she was very spiteful today and wanted to fight the cat for looking at her. Joe and Johnny are well but I am afraid the latter is in a very bad humor

---

In 1862 she moved her school from Charleston to Columbia, where she leased the Barhamville Academy.

    [38] Russell Noble (1847-65) was the son of James Noble and Eugenia Lucy Lovell Haskell Noble (1809-51), who was the sister of Charles Thomson Haskell, Sr.

at not being allowed to volunteer in the Company for your father will not consent to it.[39]

Good night my dear little girl, may God bless and protect you and may we all meet next Summer in peace and happiness.

Alexander C. Haskell, Moultrie House, Sullivan's Island, S.C., to Sophia C. Haskell (UNC)
13 February 1861
Dear Ma,

I write this evening after sending message by some of my comrades who returned to Abbeville today to execute the sad duty of conveying to his last home the mortal remains of our poor soldier boy Clarke Allen.[40] He was a beautiful bright hopeful boy, just come among us, he died last night not in battle for his flag and State, not in battle for his God and right, but by the hand of a friend and comrade. He ran against a bayonet held in the hands of poor honest John Wimbish.[41]

It pierced the eye and brain. He neither spoke nor uttered a cry. A few throbs in life's last struggle with death, and he was no more. When we closed his eyes, no wound marred his faint pale face as we sent him in his last sleep to his poor mother and father. He was their hope and pride. A few minutes after his death I got a letter enclosing a beautiful little bunch of fragrant violets & geranium. I placed the withered flowers on his breast, fit emblems of his blighted youth. T'was all I could do for the gallant soldier boy that died so far away from home.

---

[39] In his memoirs, John Haskell wrote that his father, "who was very much accustomed to rule in his own house," would not allow him to enlist with his older brothers in December 1860 "until he came of age," adding, "I submitted for the time being but went back to college very much dissatisfied, and in April, hearing that Fort Sumter was to be attacked, I left on the next train." Haskell, *The Haskell Memoirs*, 3-4.

[40] James Clark Allen (born 1843) was the son of Charles Henry Allen and Catherine Livingston Clark Allen of Abbeville District. John McLaren McBryde, a fellow soldier in the Abbeville Volunteers, wrote in his memoir that Allen was the first casualty of the war. "About a week or so after our arrival, a young friend of mine named Clark Allen left the University of Virginia and came to us, joining the mess next to ours. Shortly after his arrival, returning from dress parade to his room, after putting up his gun and equipment, he hurried out of his door. A messmate, also returning from parade, carrying his gun at trail with bayonet fixed, started to enter the room just as Allen came running out, so that the bayonet entered poor Allen's eye, piercing the brain." McBryde, "An Eyewitness to History," 38.

[41] John Wimbish (or Wimbush) of Abbeville District was the son of Alexander F. Wimbish (or Wimbush). He was born around 1832, and on July 5, 1862, he died of wounds in Richmond, Va., as a member of Company B of Orr's Rifles.

It is a terrible warning sent to show these careless reckless soldiers, taken as we are from Christian churches and pious influences, that there is a God to fear and death other than before the cannon's mouth to show us too, how awful a thing it is to meet that God still unprepared to die. My dear Mother it was a terrible blow to us all. I have prayed & still do pray that it may be sanctified to us and blessed by the redemption of some souls at least, even though few. When I last wrote I thought and our Capt. thought from indications in high quarters that we must fight before two days were over. It passed by and we are in the hands of the Southern Congress.

I still believe we will fight though many say peace, and before the fourth of March. We cannot hope for any reason or wisdom or justice from the insane God-forsaken fanatics who are in power. We are now resting on our oars awaiting the orders of the Congress of our Southern Confederacy.

Willy and I are both quite well. I was stopped last night just above by tattoo & have not time to finish this morning.

Do give my love to all family & friends. I write just what we feel here. I think I am wrong sometimes in giving you our alarms and prospects of war, but I suppose that you would rather have them than a "suppression veri." My dear Father & Mother love & goodbye for the present.

William T. Haskell, Moultrie House, Sullivan's Island, S.C., to Sophia C. Haskell (SCHS)
13 February
My dear Mother,

I take occasion of the return of several comrades on a sad mission to send you this note. We are quite well here but very sad at the sudden accidental death of little Clark Allen. He ran suddenly from a room into the passage & struck upon the bayonet of a musket carried by John Wimbish.

The immediate prospect of war has been at least deferred. I told you in my last that Sophy was well. Since then I have a note from her saying that she wrote in bed on Sunday, having by [Dolly's] advice applied a mustard plaster to her chest, her cold being [renewed]. I don't know that it is much, but I think you had better ask Uncle W[ilia]m to see her [occasionally]. Alic & myself are quite over our colds.

If you send my box to us send by Thomas Robinson who will leave on Monday. Please don't trouble yourself about the eggs but as much butter as you can send will be acceptable. Love to Pa & all. Tell me how London is.

Alexander C. Haskell, Headquarters First Regiment S.C.V., Sullivan's Island,
S.C., to Charles T. Haskell (UNC)
15 February 1861
Dear Pa,

I write to inform you of my promotion into Col. Gregg's Staff.[42] I am Military Secretary not a commissioned officer, though the Col is trying to make it so. I wear uniform of an officer and a sword. I live in the Col's Quarters. I am constantly with him on his walks and expeditions. I hold a very pleasant place, with prospect of advancement.

I thought it right to take a place which may bring me a lieutenancy, although it will involve considerable expense for a time. If however I get my commission, my pay will be sufficient to meet my expenses. I have to draw on Uncle Will for an outfit.[43] We move to Morris Island on Monday next.

War is as near or as remote as ever. Do give my love to Ma and all. Direct letters to Head Quarters First Regt S C Volunteers.

[P.S.] We are all well. I am told the box has arrived and is very fine.

William T. Haskell, Moultrie House, Sullivan's Island, S.C., to Charles T.
Haskell (SCHS)
16 February 1861
My dear Father,

Since my last & the receipt of yours we have been prospering in good health & quite an important item. Have received the box from home. It contains the best of everything we wanted & we are still luxuriating over its contents, from the "side of pork" which we anything else but "despise" to the boys scaly-barks which furnish good amusement for leisure moments.[44] Speaking of the boys, whom I have constantly in mind as indeed everything at or concerning home, do tell them to exercise their [indents] in writing to me just as many letters as possible telling me whatever they can think of. I hope you still entertain your idea of visiting & bringing Ma & Sophy of

---

[42] Colonel Maxcy Gregg (1814-62) was the first commander of the First South Carolina Infantry Regiment. He was later a brigadier general in General A. P. Hill's Light Division.

[43] William Elnathan Haskell (1805-72), a brother of Charles Thomson Haskell, Sr., lived in Charleston and at Dungannon, his plantation in St. Paul's Parish (Colleton District). The 1860 Charleston city directory lists his residence as 8 Ashley (Avenue), and his place of employment as the Planters' & Mechanics' Bank. From 1863 to 1865, he held the position of cashier there. In the early 1850s, he served at least one term in the South Carolina General Assembly representing St. Paul's Parish. He was also an officer in the South Carolina militia. In 1853, he was listed on the General Staff of the militia as Lieutenant Colonel W. E. Haskell.

[44] "Scaly-barks" may refer to hickory nuts.

whom I have made mention frequently. Alic saw day before yesterday & reports as well. I suppose Alic has notified you of his quite pleasant appointment as secretary to the Colonel. Smith is appointed Major of the regiment. His success certainly is wonderful. I hardly think he has the head for it.

I am sorry London is no better. I hope some change will allow better reports. Our regimental surgeon is I am told about to resign, in wh[ich] case it is thought Dr. Jim Mabry will succeed him. I will write soon again. Ecky leaves with the Col. tomorrow for Morris Island. Our comp[any] stays here. Love to Ma & all.

Charles T. Haskell, Jr., Newton's Atlantic Hotel, Norfolk, Va., to Charles T. Haskell (SCHS)
17 February 1861
Dear Father,

I have just returned here from Charleston, where I have been with a force of recruits for the Regular service. I collected them from Baltimore, Philadelphia, Norfolk, and Portsmouth. I feel mortified (that after having had so much confidence placed in me by the authorities, as to send me so far North on a delicate errand) that I have not been able to do more than I have done. The only satisfaction I have is that I have the perfect approval of the Secretary of War and the Major of my regiment. And also that (little as I have done), it has been vastly more than has been done by another officer (an old army officer) who was sent on the same errand as myself.

The trouble has been with me that in spite of every effort that I made to prevent it, my name got publicity at once. I was sent on by Gov. Pickens with dispatches to Washington. I delivered them quickly and having to wait a day or so for any answer, kept myself from being noticed as much as possible and could have done so but that Col. Hayne, who was in Washington at the time, wishing to be polite to me took me out to a soiree where I met a great many very distinguished characters, who were very civil but were far more interesting to each other than they were to me. The consequence of this was that a piece came out in the paper next morning about Col. Haskell [etc.] that he had gone to Baltimore on a special errand [etc.] and the consequence of this was that Gov. Hicks[45] (of Maryland) sent a Marshall after me as one of the conspirators to take city of Washington. Finding me a far less important character than he had imagined I was let alone but my errand became suspected and every obstacle thrown in my way. I leave for Baltimore

---

[45] Thomas Holliday Hicks (1798-1865).

tomorrow where I think I can still get some more men if I am not arrested. We are all <u>ordered</u> to be in Charleston on the 25th.

[P.S.] Do not speak of what I have written out of the family.

Charles T. Haskell, Jr., Newton's Atlantic Hotel, Norfolk, Va., to Langdon Cheves (SCHS)
17 February 1861
Dear Uncle,

I am much obliged to you for your kindness in the matter that I wrote you of & would have acknowledged your letter sooner but that I have been, since the receipt of it, very much harassed by the business—and its consequences—which has been entrusted to me.

After delivering despatches in Washington my main errand was to raise men, wherever I could, for the So. Ca. regulars. I had other mysterious directions given me which the Governor, with his usual policy of making a mountain out of a mole hill & a mole hill out of a mountain, still enjoins on me to keep to myself. What I consider my main errand—raising men—I have been very much baulked in by the publicity given to my name, in the papers, on account of visit [*sic*] to Washington.

Just as soon as I got to Baltimore, I was waited on by an official from Gov. Hicks (who seemed to think that I was conspiring against the city of Washington) & as I refused to answer any question asked me except such as I was compelled to & as they had no shadow of evidence against me, they turned me loose. After doing all I could however, I determined to leave Baltimore as I found that my object being suspected, every obstacle was thrown in my way. I left therefore for Charleston carrying about thirty "Plugs" & have returned to this place where I hope to have better success. I shall make one more trip to Baltimore where my agent telegraphs me that I can get about thirty more. Taking these with such as I can get in this place, Portsmouth, Richmond & Petersburg I shall return to Charleston, where we are all ordered, <u>rather significantly</u>, to report by the 25th. Do give my love to Aunt Charlotte & the girls & little Lang.[46]

---

[46] Aunt Charlotte was Charlotte Lorain McCord Cheves (1819-79). She was the wife of Captain Langdon Cheves (1814-63), who was a brother of Sophia Cheves Haskell. Charlotte was the mother of Langdon Alexander Cheves ("little Lang"), and two daughters, Emma (1844-1910), later Mrs. Gilbert A. Wilkins, and Mary Elizabeth (1846-1921), called Mamie, who was later Mrs. Charles Nephew West. Langdon A. Cheves, a graduate of Virginia Military Academy who became a physician, went to Memphis, Tennessee, to help during a yellow fever epidemic there in 1878, only to succumb to the disease. He was twenty four years old at the time of his death.

P.S. I do not know that it is a matter of consequence, but don't speak to strangers of what I have written.

Charles T. Haskell, Jr., Newton's Atlantic Hotel, Norfolk, Va., to Sophia C. Haskell (SCHS)
17 February 1861
Dear Mother,

I have written for the last two hours letters which I was obliged to write & am rather tired. I have just written Pa a long letter & shall therefore make this very short. I would rather talk when I see you than write now. I was in Charleston day before yesterday but only remained five hours & had not time to see Sophy & the boys. I was in Philadelphia the other day & saw Uncle Dulles & family.[47]

You remember the cross I wrote you about. It was stolen from me by a negro. I recovered it, broken, & it is now at Hayden's in Charleston being repaired.[48]

Alexander C. Haskell, Headquarters First Regiment S.C.V., Morris Island, S.C., to Charles T. Haskell (UNC)
18 February 1861
Dear Pa,

I write from Morris Isl. where I have gone with Col Gregg as a member of his non-commissioned staff. As I wrote a few days ago this promotion will involve expense. I will make application to Uncle William for what I am obliged to have. I merely drop a line to tell you of my change. I will write at length when I have learned something of our position. I have only been here a few hours. Tomorrow I hope to go over the Island and examine the works. This is the point of interest as being the one which must take Fort Sumter or destroy our hopes. Smith[49] has been promoted Major. This place has been filled by an old friend of mine, Ferguson a recent cadet son of the old Colonel.[50] He with Alic McGowan,[51] Capt Kennedy[52] & several others, Lieut

---

[47] This was Charles's great uncle Joseph Heatly Dulles (1795-1876), whose sister Mary Elizabeth Dulles (1789-1836) was the wife of Langdon Cheves (1776-1857), the grandfather of the Haskell brothers.

[48] Hayden & Whilden of Charleston were military outfitters, jewelers, and silversmiths.

[49] Augustus Marshall Smith (1827-62) of Abbeville District. He died from wounds received at the Battle of Gaines' Mill in June 1862.

[50] The "old Colonel" was James Ferguson (1784-1874), a veteran of the War of 1812. His son Samuel Wragg Ferguson (1834-1919) was a captain in the First South Carolina Infantry Regiment. A West Point graduate, he became a brigadier general in 1863.

Col Hamilton[53] &c constitute Col Gregg's household. A very pleasant one for me. Col Gregg is a gentleman and a soldier, as kind as can be and as stern as Brutus. I felt very much grieved this morning at even taking a temporary leave of our noble company. We loved each other too well to part without sorrow.

Willy was quite well this morning in fact in better condition than ever in his life. I will write soon. Love to Ma & all. War is waiting on Jeff Davis.[54]

Joseph E. Brown[55], Executive Department, Milledgeville, Ga., to Langdon Cheves (SCHS)
2 March 1861

SIR: It affords me much pleasure to transmit to you the annexed copy of a Resolution passed by the Convention of the State of Georgia,[56] and to unite with that body in tendering to you the thanks of the people of Georgia, for your patriotic conduct evinced in placing at the disposal of the State, without charge, in January last, a number of your negroes, to be employed in making such repairs upon Fort Pulaski, and the ditch surrounding it, as the safety of the State required should be immediately made.[57]

I am informed by an official statement before me, that you furnished two hundred and twenty one days' labor; and that thirty one of your negroes were employed. I desire, with your consent, to make a gratuity, in money, of fifty cents per day, to each slave engaged in the work. Enclosed you will find a check for $135.50 payable to your order; which sum you will please distribute among them.

Hoping that the blessings of Heaven may attend you in all your efforts to advance the glorious cause of constitutional liberty in the Southern States,

---

[51] Captain Alexander H. McGowan (1832-63).

[52] This may have been Joseph Kennedy (b. 1814), later a major, who was commissary of subsistence on Gregg's staff.

[53] Daniel Heyward Hamilton (1816-68).

[54] Jefferson Davis (1808-89) was the president of the Confederate States of America.

[55] Joseph Emerson Brown (1821-94), a native of South Carolina, was the governor of Georgia from 1857 to 1865.

[56] The Georgia Secession Convention voted to secede from the union in January 1861.

[57] Fort Pulaski was a coastal fortification located in Georgia on Cockspur Island near Savannah. It was surrounded by a moat.

and that you may long live to enjoy prosperity and happiness under the new government formed upon the basis of the old Constitution.[58]

I have the honor to be, very respectfully, your obedient servant, Joseph E. Brown

[Resolution]

Whereas, certain patriotic citizens of Georgia and South Carolina, placed in the service of the State a large number of their slaves, without remuneration, who were actively and laboriously employed at Fort Pulaski, for about two weeks. Be it

Resolved, by the People of Georgia in Convention assembled, That the Governor be requested to convey to each of the gentlemen who contributed this force, the thanks of this Convention for their patriotic action. And be it further

Resolved, That the Governor be also requested to make a suitable gratuity, in money, to the slaves thus engaged.

A true extract from the minutes of the Convention.

A. R. LAMAR, Secretary[59]

Alexander C. Haskell, Headquarters First Regiment S.C.V., Morris Island, S.C., to Charles T. Haskell (UNC)

6 March 1861

Dear Pa,

I just write to ask a simple question, to which you may be able to reply better than I can.

What do you think is the chance of raising twenty five or thirty good men with good horses, in Abbeville, to volunteer with our Regiment & under my command until the fourth of July?

No proposition has been made to me, but I hear the Colonel & General agree that it would be desirable to have such a force on Morris Island. If I could offer to raise a good troop I might be commissioned lieutenant commanding the platoon.

Do not say a word of my suggestion but I will be glad to hear your opinion as soon as possible. Love to Ma & all.

---

[58] Although much of the Confederate Constitution was copied word for word from the original U.S. Constitution, it explicitly and significantly limited centralized (federal) power in favor of states' rights. Its preamble affirmed the sovereignty of the states, and invoked "the favor and guidance of Almighty God."

[59] Albert Reese Lamar (1830—89), a lawyer of Americus, Georgia, served as the secretary of the Georgia State Convention.

*Alexander C. Haskell, Headquarters First Regiment S.C.V., Morris Island, S.C.,
to Sophia C. Haskell* (UNC)
10 March 1861
Dear Ma,

I take a moment this morning to write saying that both Willy and I are quite well. The Regiment is much more comfortable than could have been expected, & soon will be sent to Secessionville.[60] However we must take whatever comes.

I don't know whether you have heard of a very amusing accident which happened here the other day. Major Stevens was drilling recruits at the Iron Battery,[61] firing blank cartridges, by accident a 64 pound shot in one of the Columbiads, it was fired, ricocheted & struck the wall of Fort Sumter near the gate, making quite a neat little impression, but doing no serious damage. The scene was very amusing as related. Major Stevens seated himself on a gun and indulged in a very hearty fit of laughter, but was called to himself by seeing the portholes fly open in Fort Sumter. No further demonstration however was made. After a while Col Gregg sent Maj Stevens to explain the accident. He found Major Anderson just sending over a note expressing his sense of the accidental nature of the whole affair. Anderson was very courteous, expressed his desire for peace & declared he could not see the use of keeping him there. He certainly is very hypocritical & or very stupid in holding to shadows of honor & etiquette, losing the reality.[62]

The prospect of a fight is just where it always has been. Love to Pa & all the rest. Five new batteries are being rapidly erected along the channel defences.

Alexander C. Haskell, Headquarters, Forces on Morris Island, S.C., to Sophia C. Haskell (UNC)
14 March 1861
Dear Ma,

I have written but little since you went away, yielding to one of my fits of aversion to the pen. But I must give you some intimation of our present

---

[60] Secessionville was a settlement on James Island which served as summer retreat for island planters. In June 1862 it was the site of the Battle of Secessionville.

[61] The Iron Battery was an ironclad battery at Cummings Point on Morris Island.

[62] The diarist Mary Boykin Chesnut wrote of Major Robert Anderson just before the bombardment: "Why did that green goose Anderson go into Fort Sumter? Then everything began to go wrong. Now they have intercepted a letter from him urging them [the U.S. authorities] to let him surrender. He paints the horrors likely to ensue if they will not. He ought to have thought of all that before he put his head in the hole." Chesnut, *A Diary from Dixie* (New York: D. Appleton, 1905), 34.

condition. In the first place we are all well & comfortable. In the next, reports worse than ever, rumor after rumor each more uncertain than the last, are brought in as authentic information by credulous news mongers. It is generally believed in Charleston that the Fort is to be evacuated.[63] This has some show of credibility, as it has the aspect of being a military necessity. But even supposing it evacuated, although we gain a strong place, which we will get anyhow, the war I fear is by no means ended.

President Davis apprehends that Pensacola will be the great battlefield, if so we may be ordered to the support of that place.[64] Captain Ingraham is put in command of the Pensacola Navy Yard, & five thousand men ordered there.[65]

It was excessively disgusting to think of Anderson leaving Fort Sumter with all the honours of war as if for mere expediency, and not from fear as would be the case, after all our trouble and preparation. But I was glad to hear Beauregard's[66] decision, as reported to me this evening by Lieutenant Warley. He says that two have a word in the matter, and that Anderson will leave Fort Sumter not by General Scott's,[67] but Beauregard's order, and not as a commander simply transporting his forces, but on the terms wh[ich] General Beauregard sees fit to grant him. I think we have at last the upper hand & that we can both reduce Sumter and drive back reinforcements.

From what I hear, Charley's well and busy in the multifarious distractions of the Quartermaster's Department. Willy is very well, as are all the members of our Company.

Love to Pa and all at home. Kind remembrances to all friends.

I am as ever your affectionate son,

---

[63] In March 1861, William H. Seward, President Lincoln's Secretary of State, gave assurances to Supreme Court Justice John A. Campbell that Fort Sumter would be evacuated, and Campbell so informed the Confederate commissioners in Washington.

[64] In early January 1861, enacting a scenario similar to Major Anderson's actions in Charleston harbor, a small United States garrison at Fort Barrancas on Pensacola Bay spiked the guns in that fort and moved across the bay to Fort Pickens. Fort Pickens dominated Pensacola harbor, and its commander refused demands for its surrender by Florida's governor.

[65] Duncan Nathaniel Ingraham (1808-91), a career navy man, was appointed as a captain in the Confederate States Navy in March 1861 and was assigned to command the Warrington Navy Yard at Pensacola, Florida. In November 1861 he was assigned to command the naval station in Charleston.

[66] Pierre Gustave Toutant Beauregard (1818-93) commanded the defenses of Charleston.

[67] Winfield Scott (1786-1866) was the commanding general of the United States Army at this time.

Alexander C. Haskell, Headquarters, Forces on Morris Island, S.C., to Charles T. Haskell (UNC)
17 March 1861
Dear Pa,

I write again just to keep up the communication. News is of course as contradictory as ever, but thanks to having a head at the helm, we go on simply disregarding all reports except to redouble watch & preparations whenever a very strong assertion of <u>peace</u> comes from Washington, which unhappy place seems to have been converted into a huge patent machine for the evolution of lies and fabrications. General Beauregard is firm and reliant on our strength. He will never allow Anderson to evacuate Fort Sumter with his sword at his side and his colours flying. He will give no such loop hole for the escape of the mortified vanity of the United States. Submission or defeat are the alternatives. His plan seems at present to be a blockade, effectually keep out vessels and then reduce by shell & starvation, more of the latter than the former, if we have time given us.[68] For two days past we have been looking for some war steamers, but I suppose we shall hear in about a week that they have passed on to Texas or Florida. I find now the advantage of my place. Whenever anything is expected I have a share in it. Night before last I was with the Colonel in the saddle until one o'clock. And last night until two, there was an alarm of many rockets flying in a suspicious quarter, and I was up and on horseback by four where I remained until daylight. Then laying aside my armour I resumed the peaceful toga & have been writing or acting as a mediator for petitioners ever since. I thing if the island was blown out of the sea some dark night a sentinel would rush in to "Mr. Haskell" or "Captain or Lieutenant Haskell" to make the announcement to Col. Gregg & find a remedy. I will certainly soon be known to, if I do not know, every man in the regiment. I must stop here all of a sudden to attend to business. Willy is well. All the company are perfectly well & in fine spirits. Only ten men sick out of 1063 in the regiment. We had a visit yesterday from Mrs. Singleton & Miss Deka, like angels' shadows passing by.[69] I was getting very heartsick for some friend and lady friend especially since Ma left & I can't go over to see Sophy.

Love to all boys & friends.

Charles T. Haskell, Jr., Charleston, S.C., to Charles T. Haskell (SCHS)
22 March [1861]

---

[68] General Beauregard's plan was not necessarily that of the provisional authorities. See the letter written on April 2, 1861, by Charles T. Haskell, Jr.

[69] Mrs. Mary Lewis Carter Singleton and her daughter Rebecca (Decca) Singleton, Aleck's future wife.

Dear Father,

I have just arrived from the Island to meet with a very bitter disappointment. I was selected the other day by Genl. Beauregard without application on my part to go off on a special service for the army of the Confederate States. Being regimental Quarter Master it was impossible for me to go off before settling my accounts & getting from successor a receipt for the stores for which I had already receipted. Genl. Beauregard tells me that altho he approves my conduct he is compelled to send some other officer in my place, as the matter will admit of no delay. So I have lost a first rate chance of going directly into the Southern army without even making an application, not to speak of the opportunity lost of acquitting myself in such a way as to gain the approval of the Secretary of War. However it cannot be helped, tho it seems hard that I should lose a good opportunity of advancing myself. I have spoken to every army officer in Charleston whose opinion I care about & they all agree in telling me that I could not have acted otherwise without seriously involving myself personally & pecuniarily.

I have sent out my application to Montgomery[70] endorsed by Genl. Beauregard for a captaincy. I went to see Sophy this morning. There have been five cases of measles in the house. Sophy has been allowed to sleep in the same room with some of them but has not contracted the disease. The doctor thinks she will not & at all events removal now I imagine would do no good.

Alexander C. Haskell, Headquarters, Forces on Morris Island, S.C., to Charles T. Haskell (UNC)
23 March 1861
Dear Pa,

Here we are still, but how much longer, nobody seems to know. Great pow-wows are going on, on all sides, as to our probable destination in the event of an evacuation of Fort Sumter by the enemy. This latter fact seems to receive a very general credence, and to be looked upon already as quite a matter of course. But I don't know about believing it until I either hear it officially or see it, and [again] the modus-operandi is a trouble. Anderson must treat with us before he gets out. Orders are given to sink him going out, as readily we would reinforcements, if he attempts to slip away. Every passage is guarded. A proposition is before the regiment to extend their time of service over six months additional to our term of enlistment so that we might be received by the Confederate States, but it has been almost unanimously rejected by the regiment and I believe rejected because they are con-

---

[70] Montgomery, Alabama, was the first capital of the Confederacy.

vinced that there is to be no fight. If we were engaged actively they would go anywhere & even now will cheerfully take the Florida campaign if ordered within six months.

We look now either to peace, or to a general war, or to [*illegible word*] the southern parts in the civil wars of Virginia, Maryland &c. Many think that the Convention will disband if the fort is given up. All are well. Charley is on Beauregard's staff & gone to Baltimore again. Beauregard has recommended him for a captaincy in the army. Love to Ma & all.

Sophia C. Haskell to Sophie Haskell, Charleston, S.C. (SCHS)
[March 1861]
Dear Sophie,

We have just heard of you from Charley who says you continue well. I do not know whether you can escape the measles but leave you now to your Father. Only if you should be seriously sick I will come down and take care of you. I have just packed up all the articles I promised you, 2 dresses, 1 apron, 2 chemisettes, two pair sleeves and 2 collars, and two under bodies. I am afraid they will not fit well as I had to work so much by guess. I am afraid the dresses are too long, but I was afraid to shorten them. They are a little longer than my longest dresses. The [travelling] dress you wrote for cannot be lengthened in the least so I do not send it. I enclose a little frill of linen cambric to wear with your pink muslin dress. I never saw the ring you were to enclose for [Leah]. If it is lost get another instead and send it up by your Father.

We are all quite well, but I am sorry to say the fruit has suffered very great damage. What will escape we cannot yet tell, and then come the April frosts. Your little garden looks pretty well tho I fear the myrtles will not live, and the cloth of gold does not put out tho it still looks quite green. The frequent frosts killed the hyacinths and spoiled their beauty. The Spirea has all its buds killed too. How is Piciola.[71] Perhaps you could get one or two more geraniums to raise for me or get them and send them up by your Father to raise for you tho they might be too troublesome for him to bring up. You will find in his trunk a cake which is a present from him and a can of peaches which I thought might be good for you if you were sick.

Robert Barnwell Rhett to LeRoy Pope Walker[72] (SCHS)

---

[71] *Picciola* was a novel published in 1836 in which one of the characters was a flower called Picciola.

[72] Robert Barnwell Rhett (1800-76) was a South Carolina politician, newspaper editor, and Confederate Congressman. LeRoy Pope Walker (1817-84) was the Confederate Secretary of War.

28 March 1861

The undersigned respectfully applies for the situation of Second Lieutenant in the army of the Confederate States.

John C. Haskell

Dear Sir,

John C. Haskell is a grand son of Langdon Cheves and of Major Haskell, one of the officers in the revolution of 76 who appears in Trumbul's picture in the Rotunda at Washington.[73] He is in every way worthy of an opportunity in the army of the Confederate States.[74]

Sophia C. Haskell, Abbeville, S.C., to [Eleuthera Dupont Smith][75] (SCHS)
28 March 1861

My dear old friend,

I have received all your letters and answered every one, but except the first. I do not know that you have received any from me. I have been intending to write to you for some time past but have had an unusually large correspondence to keep up and have been twice to Charleston in the last few months. We went there last month with the expectation, almost amounting to certainty, to see the taking of Fort Sumter. Three of our brave boys, our second, third, and fourth, were there. Two privates in our Abbeville Volunteers, the other Charles, an officer in the Regulars of the Provisional Army. I felt if that attack once began, I could hardly hope to see them all come home again, and indeed they are noble boys and hard to part with. Everybody praises them and you must forgive me if I boast a little. I have earned the right by many an anxious hour this winter. When I was busy trimming my trees and pruning my vines, I could not help asking myself, but too often, who will be here when these ripen, and which bright face will be missing at our summer family gathering? And the first one I always thought of was my

---

[73] Major Elnathan Haskell (1755-1825), an officer of artillery in the Continental Army, is one of the figures in John Trumbull's painting "Surrender of General Burgoyne," which was placed in the Rotunda of the U. S. Capitol in 1821. The painting depicts the surrender of General John Burgoyne to the American General Horatio Gates after the Second Battle of Saratoga in 1777. After the war Major Haskell married Charlotte Thomson (1769-1850), the daughter of Col. William Thomson of South Carolina.

[74] In this letter, John C. Haskell's application is also endorsed by James L. Orr (1822-73), a U. S. and Confederate Congressman (and later governor of South Carolina), and by William Porcher Miles (1822-99), also a U. S. and Confederate Congressman from South Carolina.

[75] Eleuthera du Pont Smith (1806-76), the widow of Thomas Mackie Smith (1810-52), was a friend who lived in Delaware. Formerly a classmate of Mrs. Sophia Cheves Haskell at a Philadelphia boarding school, she was the daughter of the founder of E. I. du Pont de Nemours & Company.

merry blue eyed boy Alec. He was in no more danger than the others but he seemed to have gone with all the ardour of the days of chivalry to lay down his life for his God, his Country, and his Lady Love.[76] An uncertain vision the last but not less earnestly worshipped. His letters were almost wild with excitement, and all the world seemed brighter and fairer as he seemed to feel he was taking his last look at it, and ending his letter to me he said "whatever may happen my trust is in God. God save our Country! For such a Country and such a people it is easy to die."

But I meant to write you a sober, quiet letter. But we have been in a state of singular excitement all this Winter. I have never seen anything like it. There is a steady spirit of firm resolution I could not have imagined. The spirit of '76 could not surpass it. What seems so wonderful that it looks almost miraculous, is the wonderful unanimity we feel, as if in the hand of an almost Visible Providence which turns everything to our advantage and has so far lead [sic] us through a bloodless revolution. Our people are one and the idle rumors of the Northern papers are utterly groundless. I wish you could have seen the gathering of the Abbeville Volunteers. One hundred men almost all young, the flower of our district, came forward at the first call. More offered, but those who were most needed at home were left behind. They were to leave in three days. The ladies met to offer their help to sew for them. Mothers, wives, sisters, all ready to do what they could, but no word of doubt or hesitation. These are the men and hundreds more like them (almost) who have been working for three months, with wheelbarrow and shovel, drilling, standing on guard, sleeping in tents on the floors, on the sand, anyway, and no complaints. It is much harder than to fight. The Tribune[77] says we must be deeply in debt for such works cannot be done and troops maintained but at immense expense. We are in debt no doubt, but hundreds of negroes were sent and gentlemen would go with them to superintend, some even furnished their own food, when work was needed. All these forced loans are mere nonsense; many have contributed in money, provisions, every way they could but it was not even asked.

Now I have got off my sober track again and maybe you do not sympathize with us, I hope you do, your state has Southern feelings at least in part. What we have done we had to do. We had no choice. For thirty years has this storm been gathering and the North would take no warning. And with its huge mass was slowly crushing us to death. We can draw breath now for we are free. As to coming back, it is an impossibility, we could not. No one dreams of such a thing, they would rather submit to England than to the

---

[76] Rebecca (Decca) Coles Singleton (1838-62), Aleck's future wife.
[77] A New York newspaper.

Black Republicans. We are all politicians in a small way now, and I and our overseer's wife have just had a talk over the state of the country and how the Fort is to be given up. So you must not wonder if from the abundance of the heart my pen writes nonsense.

All my family are well. Our own eldest son with his wife and two babies [are] out in Arkansas. The three next in Charleston, and Sophie there at boarding school, nos. 5-6 at college in Columbia so that I am left alone with my two youngest boys, who with two young nephews form our present family. I hope now that we may all meet next July. They are all growing up fast, my youngest is just eleven. Sophie is but fifteen but she is tall and womanly in appearance, not at all like me, but decidedly well looking, bright, intelligent, and impulsive, sometimes maybe, impetuous would be the right word. She is going through the first years of her schooling which is pretty hard for a spoiled child.

If this reaches you I will write again, but do send me your direction that our future letters may not be lost. Mine is as I have given it before.

Warrenton

Abbeville District

South Carolina

Or simply direct to Abbeville Court House, South Carolina. There are so many Warrentons in other states that letters from the North often take a long journey before reaching us. Do remember me very affectionately to the Grimshaws and give me news of them.[78]

Charles T. Haskell, Jr., Sullivan's Island, S.C., to Sophia C. Haskell (SCHS)
2 April 1861
Dear Mother,

I write from the upper end of Sullivan's Island where we have been stationed for some months, at least part of my regiment has been, I having only arrived some weeks ago, as you know. We are beginning to find things very monotonous indeed as we have got very much through our preparations for action & have settled down into the regular routine of camp life. An assault on the fort has been so long looked for in vain that I think even the most rabid of the volunteers no longer feel much excitement on the subject. I do not, now, think that there is any probability of an assault being made from the simple fact that the officers of the old federal army have too much knowledge & experience to instruct Anderson to hazard the chances of an

---

[78] This likely refers to Isabella Grimshaw (1810-95) and her sister Charlotte Grimshaw (1807-82), who operated a seminary for Young Ladies in Wilmington, Delaware. Their mother, Harriet Elizabeth Milligan Grimshaw (1788-1826), operated a seminary for young ladies in Philadelphia in the early part of the 19th century.

assault or of a bombardment or to attempt to reinforce the fort. As soon as we open fire on Anderson I believe that he will haul down his colors, as I think he is now only holding out because he is allowed to do it by the provisional authorities.[79] I do not know what the policy is of allowing him still to retain the fort entailing the necessity of paying & supporting several thousand more men than would be otherwise necessary. I suppose however that there is some sufficient reason for it as I do not think that Genl Beauregard is a man to lie inactive without some good reason.

You ask me to write concerning my application to Montgomery. As yet there has been no result & I think it likely that there will be none for some time, as I am told that there are being very few appointments made when Fort Sumter is taken or surrendered. I think that I shall go on to Montgomery myself & urge my own application. Pa who I suppose will have reached home by this time can give you later news of Willy, Alick & Sophy than I can. If you have any hams to spare or anything else to eat I wish you would send me some. If you do, send them to somebody's care in Charleston & notify me by letter.

Alexander C. Haskell, Headquarters, Forces on Morris Island, S.C., to Sophia C. Haskell (UNC)
4 April 1861
Dear Ma,

I am here and so is Willy, to imitate the graphic style of the native orator, but how long I will be able to inform you of the interesting fact I do not know. Though official communication has not been given us, we have every reason to believe that Anderson has been cut off & is consequently under blockade & is closely invested. If he does not surrender at once he may cut off our communications by way of retort & then our mail will be uncertain. Last evening we dared the fight by firing on the U.S. flag coming in on a schooner.[80] It was drawn down, cut down, & trailed in the water & Anderson pretending to hold a fortress of the U.S. from conscientious motives, did not assert or sustain the dignity of his government by a single shot. He de-

---

[79] The "provisional authorities," that is, the Confederate government, through Governor Francis W. Pickens, allowed Major Anderson to receive and send mail and to obtain food and other supplies from Charleston during most of his occupation of Fort Sumter.

[80] The schooner was the *Rhoda H. Shannon* which had blundered into Charleston harbor under the mistaken notion that it was the port of Savannah, Georgia. The Confederates fired warning shots first, after which the schooner lowered its flag. The firing continued, and the ship turned and sailed away a distance. The officers from Fort Sumter went out in a boat to make inquiries, after which the schooner put out to sea.

clared at the time of Star West affair that the next time he would fire, but he failed lamentably. Our batteries were cleared for action, so Anderson [trained] his guns & there it stopped. Two of Anderson's officers came to the point with a flag of truce, asked why we shot and asked leave to go & see if the schooner was hurt. They were allowed to go out & came in reporting to us on their way that it was "some fool who did not know any better" & asked us to let him in. Sad style for officers of the army.

I should not be surprised if the bombardment begins in two or three days. All are well.

Alexander C. Haskell, Headquarters, Forces on Morris Island, S.C., to Charles T. Haskell (UNC)
6 April 1861
Dear Pa,

I have nothing of interest to report except what you will or have seen in the Mercury relative to the formidable preparation of the coercion party who are proving that a strong wealthy people can raise "the sinews of war" even at a sacrifice of interest when they are fairly excited and maddened by a course which they have indeed pushed upon us but which will result in their serious detriment. These reports I know to be confirmed by telegraphic communications to the officers high in command. Work has recommenced on the Island at the rate of 400 to 500 men day and night. It seems they are never ready. The plan seems to be to sweep our Island from the rear & take the batteries. Our infantry will have a word to say before it comes to that. Goodbye.

Alexander C. Haskell, Headquarters, Forces on Morris Island, S.C., to Sophia C. Haskell (UNC)
8 April 1861
Dear Ma,

We are all well & waiting. Anderson is cut off from supplies & here we stand: a fleet is afloat, with a tremendous armament bound either for this place or Pensacola.[81] I have no intelligence to give except that we are making preparation to win a victory or a glorious defeat. Six companies in addition are coming to this Island tomorrow making about 1800 or 2,000 in all, with about 1500 on Sullivan's Island, & others scattered about, making about 4000 in the field. Things look earnest & will I think soon be settled one way

---

[81] On April 8, 1861, General P.G.T. Beauregard informed his superiors that Major Anderson's provisions had been stopped the previous day, April 7th.

or the other. Willy says he will write but has no conveniences for it which makes him irregular.

Love to Pa and all. Goodbye.

Alexander C. Haskell, Headquarters, Forces on Morris Island, S.C., to Charles T. Haskell (SCHS)
11 April 1861
Dear Pa,

I write a few lines today, we are all well. We are watching day and night for an enemy. For three nights past I have been almost constantly in the saddle, last night until daylight, from 8 o'clock, but my Col[onel] is with me in all the work so that it is both pleasant & profitable. Col Gregg is now in command of about 2500 men on this Island, soon to be 3000 or more, perhaps 4000. We are determined if the Yankees do land to give them the most terrible thrashing that ever a parcel of piratical scoundrels were blessed with. Orders are to whip them wherever they land & not to give back an inch under any circumstances. [Ten] men keep them at work till the rest come up. I am overwhelmed by a small avalanche of business as soon as day comes, for I am acting, although not in name, as Col Gregg's chief of Staff as a [Brigadier] & am becoming a popular or hated man as circumstances may be by signing the Col's name or refusing it. My place is now important, responsible & pleasant in proportionate degrees. Love to Ma & all. Goodbye.

Sophia C. Haskell to Sophie Haskell, Charleston, S.C. (SCHS)
[April 1861]
Dear Sophie,

I write a few lines to say we have heard from all and are now waiting most anxiously for news today. We have news up to early yesterday morning. I wish I could be with you but many reasons make it best I should stay at home. Your Father has decided not to go down today but I do not think he can stand this uncertainty much longer. I hope still, tho there is mad fanaticism and ignorance of the real state of affairs and they would like to hurt us, and would not mind the sacrifice of a few hundred soldiers of their own if they could effect our conquest, or humiliation. But my dear child we must put our trust in God. Our cause is just and our dear boys are doing their duty and if sorrow should come it comes from a merciful Father who does not willingly afflict his children, and I still hope we may be spared. Before this reaches you affairs must have taken a more decided turn. Keep up good courage, but if it should be expedient for you to leave town, which tho I have no idea of, apply to your Uncle William at the Bank or his house. I suppose you have seen John. He has given us the slip at last, but I could not scold him if he were here much less now that he is in Charleston. Your Uncle writes that he has been suffering from the effects of a severe fall but was getting better. I am glad you find such pleasant friends in your cousins. Now that you are all growing older I hope you may be with them frequently as it would give me great pleasure that you should have them for friends. I am sorry Madame is in such a worry but hope you may not have any particular trouble. Give my best love to any of the boys if you see them. God bless you and them.

Charles T. Haskell, Jr., Sullivan's Island, S.C., to Charles T. Haskell (SCHS)
12 April 1861
Dear Father,

The bombardment of Fort Sumter commenced this morning at twenty minutes of five A.M. & has been kept up constantly though deliberately throughout the day & still going on now 9 o'clock P.M. The Floating Battery (from the steamboat landing on Sullivan's Island), the Enfilade Battery, Ft Moultrie the Mortar Battery & Butler's Mortar Battery[82] have been throwing shot & shell during the whole time. Stevens Battery & a Mortar Battery on Morris Island & James Mortar Battery on James Island have also been actively employed. No impression has as yet been made on any of the works on this Island nor on the Iron Battery on Morris Island & to the best of my belief, none on any of the others. The Floating battery has been struck at least five times directly, but the balls have in all cases glanced down. The buildings in Ft Moultrie have of course been torn to pieces but that is a matter of no consequence. Fort Sumter has had several Barbette guns disabled & has been compelled to depend on the casemate guns as the men are driven back immediately, by shells, whenever they attempt to man the former. Stevens has played havoc all day. As far as can judge [*sic*] he has silenced the guns bearing on Morris Island. They have not opened fire in that direction for two hours. Stevens has not sent a shot in vain. Sending about one every five minutes he brings a cart load of bricks every time. I am satisfied that he has stopped up their embrasures. Many shells have burst in the fort & must have done damage. The shelling however on the whole is bad.

At half past twelve o'clock today four war steamers & sloops appeared off the bar supposed to be the Pawnee, Harriet Lane & others unknown. An attempt to reinforce & a land attack are both looked for tonight. I think however that the night is too stormy. The land attack will probably be at-

---

[82] Captain William B. Butler (1831-1910), a native of Greenville, S.C., commanded mortar battery no. 2 on Sullivan's Island, located east of Fort Moultrie.

tempted at Thomson's point at the same place and the same way that the British tried it. Strange to say not a man on the Island has been killed <u>or wounded</u>. Anderson made a signal of distress as soon as the enemy's vessels came in sight. John is here, apparently, edified. While walking upstairs today at the Moultrie House a forty-two passed through the house throwing splinters over him. John watched the course of the ball, which fell directly, pursued it and carried it home. It was one of the only two which struck the house & those were accidental. Anderson shows no disposition to fire on anything but the batteries.[83]

April 13th 6 A.M.

At ten o'clock last night all but the Mortar Batteries ceased firing, Sumter having ceased some hours before. Shells were thrown about one every five minutes with considerable effect until about midnight when the Iron Battery thundered out again & continued throwing round shot throughout the night & is still doing so. The Mortar Batteries steadily throwing shells. Throughout the night Anderson did not open fire once, nor has he up to this time. From ten to twelve o'clock repeated discharges of musketry were heard on Morris Island. Either the men were grossly slack in their duties in firing guns throughout the night or there was some land skirmishing. The former I think most probable. The war vessels put to sea last night, but this morning having broken beautifully bright & clear, two are again lying just outside the bar & another the largest just [heaving] in sight. I have no doubt that the fourth will soon make her appearance. Probably they will make an attempt to reinforce before midday. I have a chance to send my letter this morning & can therefore write no more now.

Charles T. Haskell, Jr., Sullivan's Island, S.C., to Charles T. Haskell (SCHS)
16 April 1861
Dear Father,

I suppose that the papers have already told you of the bloodless fall of Ft. Sumter. About eleven o'clock on the second day, the fort was fired by a bombshell apparently from Morris Island producing a most terrific scene. For a short time the fire from all the surrounding batteries doubled their fire, while poor Anderson seemed to have the greatest difficulty in firing a single

---

[83] The cannon balls that crashed into the Moultrie House were not accidental shots. They had been deliberately fired at a group of non-combatant spectators on the beach by one of the gun crews in Fort Sumter. The first cannon ball struck the beach about 50 yards in front of them, bounced over their heads, and went into the Moultrie House. The second shot followed much the same course. James Chester, an officer of the Fort Sumter garrison, described the incident in his article "Inside Sumter in '61."

gun about once in ten minutes. From time to time his own shells and gre-
nades exploded within the fort, throwing up columns of black smoke and
followed by thundering reports. At half past one, Stevens cut down his flagstaff. It was raised again after a long interval however, and one more feeble
shot fired by the fellow to show that he was game to the last. At two o'clock
he raised a flag of truce and hauled down the federal colors, upon which the
firing instantly ceased. In an instant the whole garrison rushed to the ram-
parts to escape the fire and smoke which was almost smothering them.

It is no use however to write more as you must have got everything
from the papers. Joe and John are both well. I have had a chill and fever but
have recovered.

Charles T. Haskell, Abbeville, S.C., to His Excellency F. W. Pickens, Governor &
Commander in Chief (LC)
16 April [1861]
I do not like to trouble you with a personal application as I know your
time is much occupied, and therefore I make this petition, that you should
appoint my son John C. Haskell as a Lieutenant in the Regiment of Regulars which you are now raising. He is twenty years of age, has lately been in
the junior class in the South Carolina College, but has now left college. He
is extremely anxious to go into the regular service, and if he is fortunate
enough to get a commission I think I can venture to promise for him that he
will discharge all the duties of the position firmly and bravely.[84]

Alexander C. Haskell, Headquarters, First Regiment S.C.V., Lighthouse Hill,
Morris Island, S.C., to Charles T. Haskell and Sophia C. Haskell (UNC)

17 April 1861
Dear Father & Mother,
You have long before this been made happy by hearing that Fort Sumter has been taken, not only without the loss of any of your sons, but not
even one of Carolina's. A glorious day it was, and marked so deeply by the
protecting hand of divine providence that it calls to mind the miraculous
victories of the chosen people.

The fire & cannonading was tremendous & conducted by a skill which,
although exhibited by volunteers, has excited the wonder and admiration of
our veteran commander, & of our gallant foes. They did prove themselves

---

[84] This note appears on the second page of this letter: "I know John C. Haskell very
well. He is a young man of fine mind and body. He has been well raised and is spirited. If
you have any vacant third lieutenancy I have no doubt whatever that it would be a good
appointment to fill it with the name of John C. Haskell." It is signed "S. McGowan."

men at the last, & gallant ones. Fort Sumter is a terrible wreck. Amid all the rejoicing, it was rather a bitter day for the 1st Regiment, who after toiling day & night in the trenches under our gallant & skillful Colonel, were pushed aside & neglected in the whole affair. Ten hours before the fight began, Simons, a pompous coward who shielded himself & staff during the whole engagement under the Hospital flag, came over & with an amount of injustice which he could execute, [superceded] Gregg in command & sent him off to the end of the Island.[85] The whole Island was thrown into confusion by a host of upstarts who came over at the same time to snatch away what honour was to be reaped, while the organization of the 1st Regt alone, fed and transported & supported the whole Island. We have done the whole work & had Colonel Gregg chosen he could have made them feel their insolent assumption, but he worked manfully & has helped them out of their troubles even at the expense of his own Regiment. Such however is military style, merit is not always appreciated at the right time & place.

But it will be long before "Hospital Jim" & the holiday officers will be forgotten.

The artillerists who fought the battle are gallant fellows and deserve all the credit that can be given. It is rather a bitter pill to swallow & when we think of having been cut out of the whole affair which we have been waiting three months to share. We were sure once of a fight from the Men of War off the Bar crammed with soldiers, but the dastardly wretches disappointed friend & foe alike by not striking one blow for their flag & burning Fort. The soldiers on our side gave a cheer to Anderson at every shot towards the last, & a groan for the cowards in the fleet. It was as gallant an affair as the world ever witnessed, & when the officers in the Fort were told of it afterwards, it affected them almost to tears.

The prospects all are now, though I won't triumph, on my side of the argument, war and a long & bloody one. I feel as if I was going to be made a soldier whether I would or no. I hope I will get home though one of these

---

[85] South Carolina militia General James Simons (1813-79), a prominent lawyer and politician, was the commanding officer of the forces at Morris Island at this time. John McLaren McBryde wrote of him: "A few days before the attack on Fort Sumter, a brigade of South Carolina troops was sent to Morris Island, and the commanding general established his headquarters in a summer home, the one nearest the end of the island, to be away as far as possible, unfriendly critics declared, from the guns of Fort Sumter." McBryde, "An Eyewitness to History," 39. In her diary entry of April 15, 1861, Mary Boykin Chesnut recorded, "There is frightful Yellow Flag story. A distinguished potentate and militia power looked out upon the bloody field of battle, happening to stand under the waving yellow hospital flag." A rumor circulated that Simons had avoided the risk of enemy fire, earning him the nickname "Hospital Jimmy." Chesnut, *A Diary from Dixie* (Cambridge, Mass.: Harvard University Press, 1980), 39.

days. Though the prospect at present is small. I have but little idea of being able to leave at the end of the six months.

I am here now, in the field in tents & messing with the Colonel &c. I would be very glad if you could send me something to contribute my portion to the mess.

I hear that a Cavalry company is going from Abbeville to Florida. I wish very much I could get a good cavalry company to take up on the 12th of July or before & go on with the war as an officer instead of private. I wish now very much that Willy had the place McGowan[86] offered him, or that it were possible for him to get it.

Do tell me if anything can be done in my old country in the way of organizing a troop to go into the war. Give kindness & love to all.

---

[86] Samuel McGowan (1819-97) of Abbeville was in command of a brigade of South Carolina troops at Fort Sumter in April 1861.

2

TO VIRGINIA

20 APRIL 1861 – 29 AUGUST 1861

On April 15, 1861, President Abraham Lincoln calls up troops for the suppression of the "insurrection." After this, the states of Virginia, Tennessee, North Carolina and Arkansas secede. The Confederacy calls for troops to defend Virginia, and Colonel Maxcy Gregg offers his regiment. Several companies remain in South Carolina, among them Captain James M. Perrin's Abbeville Volunteers, and the regiment is reorganized to some extent. Langdon stays in Charleston, but wishing to remain with Gregg, Aleck and William join the Richland Rifles and arrive in Richmond, Virginia, in late April. After brief assignments at Manassas, Centreville, and Fairfax Courthouse, Colonel Gregg's troops return to Richmond. Their enlistment ends in early July, and consequently they do not participate in the great first battle at Manassas on July 21, but the colonel soon raises another regiment retaining the same name which is enlisted for the duration of the war. A momentous event takes place in Aleck's life in the summer of 1861, revealed in his letter of the 9th of July—an ecstatic announcement of his engagement to Decca Singleton. In Charleston, John is appointed as a lieutenant in an artillery battalion (which is sent to Virginia in August), and Charles, captain of Company D of the 1st Regiment, South Carolina Infantry Regulars, is stationed on Coles Island near Charleston, where he is busy constructing new fortifications. In August, William makes a trip to South Carolina to enlist men for a new company, returning to Richmond in the latter part of the month with some new recruits and his brother Joseph.

Alexander C. Haskell, Headquarters, First Regiment S.C.V., Lighthouse Hill, Morris Island, S.C., to Charles T. Haskell and Sophia C. Haskell (UNC)
20 April 1861
Dear Father & Mother,

We march this morning for Norfolk, Virginia. Willy & myself with perhaps five others of the Abbeville Company.[1] For some hitch with respect to Field Officers & special umbrage taken to some remarks of Colonel Gregg's, the Regiment has refused to go. About 350 will go, the mere skeleton of the noblest Regiment ever formed in the State. We are few & perhaps not the best in the Regiment, but will do our best to sustain the Palmetto Flag with untarnished honour. We have as many as the Palmettos had in great battles of Mexico.[2]

It has been a bitter day of division & disappointment. But Virginia has a claim upon us for the magnanimity with which she came forward in the time of our need. Goodbye & God bless you all. I entered for my Country & have sought earnestly that I might not fear to die for my Country, led as she is by the God of right & justice. My prayer is that God may grant us a happy reunion on earth or one far happier in heaven. Goodbye. I go full of hope.

Alexander C. Haskell, Headquarters, First Regiment S.C.V., Richmond, Va., to Sophia C. Haskell (UNC)
25 April 1861
Dear Ma,

I write from Richmond where we have arrived safe & well with 500 men. Our reception has been warm and enthusiastic to a degree which has given us as much pleasure as surprise. At every stopping place on the road, everybody, men, women & children, young & old, rich & poor, turned out to welcome the "gallant soldiers from Carolina." Smiles welcomed us, tears & blessings sent us on our way. It makes my very soul expand with pride & gratitude to the good old State to find what a name she gives to us abroad. Crowds along the streets are overheard in most extravagant praises, & when

---

[1] John McLaren McBryde wrote in his memoir that the captain of the Abbeville Volunteers, Abner Perrin, urged his company not to volunteer to go to Virginia. "The next day Colonel Gregg had the regiment drawn up and in an eloquent speech urged us all to volunteer for service in Virginia. In closing he asked volunteers to step to the front. Some companies came forward in a body and Perrin's was the only company in which a majority refused to volunteer. Only 11 of us, nearly all from my mess, stepped to the front. Perrin refused to speak to us afterward. We joined the Richland Rifles from Columbia and the next night the regiment, still nearly 1,000 strong, boarded a freight train for Virginia." McBryde, "An Eyewitness to History," 40.

[2] The Palmetto Regiment, an organization of South Carolina volunteer soldiers, was celebrated for its service in the Mexican War of 1846-48.

they hear that we are the Morris Island troops, there is no limit to their enthusiasm. I have had my hand wrung by old men & ladies too on the sole credit of being a "Morris Island Boy," until I am sure the print of the friendly pressure must be left.

Our probable destination is Washington, but I can learn nothing very definite yet. Things are in great confusion in the old government, & I think we can crush them here, beat them down once & forever in their home & stronghold. It is veritably related to us here that the Enemy was driven from Norfolk with their work half done, by an ingenious R. R. conductor who ran so many extra trains that they thought Beauregard & the 1st Regt were upon them, & they fled like good fellows at the bare mention of us.[3]

Goodbye & love to all. Willy is well.

Alexander C. Haskell, Headquarters, First Regiment S.C.V., Camp Pickens, Richmond, Va., to Charles T. Haskell (UNC)
28 April 1861
Dear Pa,

I got your letter last night. I have written to Ma several times, but had no idea that you were still at home. We are as well as you could desire, received as more than brother soldiers by the Virginians. Duty certainly called us here. It is only moving the battle field & its horrors away from our own dear State. I feel great sorrow for those of our forces who determined to remain at home, except those who were compelled to remain. I will write more at length as soon as possible. We do not move immediately against any enemy. Dearest love to all.

Alexander C. Haskell, Headquarters, First Regiment S.C.V., Camp Pickens, Richmond, Va., to Charles T. Haskell (UNC)
30 April 1861
Dear Pa,

Encamped very pleasant at Richmond. We will probably remain here for some time. General Lee[4] in command desires to wait until he can make his advances sure & comparatively safe, at the head of a large & at least tolerably disciplined force. Washington or Maryland will in all probability be the points of attack & concentration on both sides. The force in the field is either exaggerated or underrated in such degree that I can give you no estimate. From five to twenty-five thousand Yankee troops & as many on our

---

[3] The navy yard at Norfolk, Va., was set on fire by the United States garrison, who also scuttled ships there.

[4] Major General Robert E. Lee (1807-70) was at this time the commander in chief of the Provisional Army of Virginia.

side. No move, so far as I can learn, is contemplated, short of two or perhaps three weeks.

This is the place for service at present & I only hope we can give such a repulse as will keep the enemy from our homes. I regret very much that our whole Regiment did not come & hope that those at home will not put us in the wrong who have sacrificed so much to what we deemed our duty.

Prayers & blessings were showered on our way as we came from dear old South Carolina, smiles at meeting & tears at parting, in every town we passed. At some places the enthusiasm was unbounded. Palmetto cockades or leaves are begged on every side & treasured when obtained, to that extent that there is hardly one left in camp though I suppose a thousand left Carolina. Just this morning I was begged out of my last spare palmetto button as I walked along the street.

In my present situation I will be obliged to make immediate & pretty heavy expenditures. I intended to have seen Uncle William to arrange with him, but was ordered off on duty with despatches & it was only by the kindness of friends that I got a shred of baggage to Virginia. I found it all safe however, when I overtook the Regiment at Weldon. Do make arrangements with Uncle to honour draughts on him at the Planters & Mechanics Bank when I am forced to make them. I may be under the necessity now of buying a horse, which however I can sell as soon as I am done with him.

Goodby & dearest love to Ma & all. Willy is well & pleasantly situated.

Alexander C. Haskell, Headquarters, First Regiment S.C.V., Camp Pickens, Richmond, Va., to Sophia C. Haskell (UNC)
1 May 1861
Dear Ma,

Still at Richmond & no knowing when we will leave. We came on for a brilliant dash on Washington & a hard fight when we got there, but policy & wisdom probably have put a stop to such proceedings & Gen. Lee is waiting for his time. Virginia has plenty of men but, as yet, a military organization & supply if munitions much inferior to our own. War will no doubt be the result, but we must again draw upon that patience which we learned so well to exercise on Morris Island.

To say Virginia is kind & hospitable, is to say nothing by way of expressing the flattering reception which our officers & soldiers have met at the hands of the Virginia ladies & soldiers, for into these two classes is the southern population at present resolved. Camp discipline is too strict for us to see much of the city, but Mahomet has gone to the hill & the city has come to us.

I write a line as often as I can. When you don't hear, count all well. Willy is in fine health & spirits, & enjoying himself very much.

Goodbye. Love to Pa & all.

Alexander C. Haskell, Headquarters, First Regiment S.C.V., Camp Pickens, Richmond, Va., to Sophia C. Haskell (UNC)
3 May 1861
Dear Ma,

I write my diurnal to say that we are well & getting fat to an extent that is terribly alarming. War must be upon us but when & how it is coming I can't say. I only hope & trust that we may give a good account of every sacrilegious foot that supports an invader of Southern soil. Richmond is a beautiful & a hospitable place. Ladies & friends come visiting & endowing us with all manner of good things. Have our clothes washed, mended &c.

Scott they say & truly is making tremendous preparation in Washington for the subjugation of Virginia. What Gen. Lee is doing besides collecting & drilling troops I don't know. We are directed as yet upon no special point. The people here are bold & true, but with more fear of Yankees than we ever felt. I suppose they are nearer dangers. Love to Pa & all. Goodbye.

Alexander C. Haskell, Headquarters, First Regiment S.C.V., Camp Pickens, Richmond, Va., to Sophia C. Haskell (UNC)
4 May 1861
Dear Ma,

We are still well though nearly frozen by the most unseasonable weather that ever chilled the merry month of May. My hand shakes too much for me to write! We have now near 1500 Carolina troops in Richmond & could you but hear the reliance these Virginians place upon the honour, chivalry & invincible courage of every man that wears a palmetto button, you would feel proud of having two sons who shared in the public admiration. The plot is thickening & all military movements seem to my mind to be checked by the greater necessity on both sides of vast & serious preparation for a war of subjugation & extermination on one side, of a just & righteous defence of home & families on the other, spurred on by all the rage & hate that can be excited by the approach of an impious, piratical, bloodthirsty invader. I much fear the Yankee horde have forgotten the laws of war & have not natural honour & chivalry enough to [suggest] them or the conduct they enforce. I think they will hang or otherwise murder any prisoners they catch at first & will keep on at it until fire & sword have driven them trembling & suppliant to ask for mercy. Invasion of their states & cities is the only way to keep them in check or in their senses. New York & Boston in flames would do more to

establish peace than a dozen battles won. I do hope soon to see the war carried into Africa & see how they like the sword & torch at once, as these are
the weapons they deal in. They caught a Southern officer the other day, imprisoned & ironed him with other abuse. He narrowly escaped with his life.
They I suppose did not comprehend the meaning or idea of a parole.

I am obliged to draw on Uncle W. for money $100 & will perhaps be
forced to get $150 in a few days to buy a horse which is now requisite. Willy
is having a pleasant time. We go out today to a great dinner at Mr. Free-
land's. Love to all

Sophia C. Haskell, Abbeville, S.C., to [Eleuthera du Pont Smith] (SCHS)
5 May 1861
My dear Friend,

I am very glad indeed that you received my letter, for I did not like you
to think I would neglect you after all the kind and affectionate feeling you
had show [*sic*] towards me. I am very sorry to hear of all your sorrows and
afflictions, yours has been a life of trial, but I can well understand how great
must be the comfort you feel when you think of the blessed death of your
dear good Sister, but oh! how much you much [*sic*] miss her in every moment of the day, one who has been the partaker of almost all your joys and
sorrows through a long life.[5] I pray God may raise you up someone to comfort you in her stead tho none can ever fill her place.

All are well with me as yet; how long it will be so no human knowledge
can form any idea. I am not superstitious but I can hardly say how much I
am cheered and comforted by the wonderful almost miraculous, bloodless
victory of Fort Sumpter [*sic*]. I had been down on Morris Island and had
looked through the embrasures of the Iron Battery at the awful fort which
was to deal death to those near & dear to us all, our own three boys in their
uniforms and many a young friend beside were there. I told all good by but it
did not seem possible that all should meet again. Sunday the 14th we went
into Abbeville village to church; we knew the fight had commenced Friday
morning, an extra train had been sent to Columbia to bring us news. It was a
sad and anxious day, all our young men gone, five of our own on the Islands
in the batteries from behind; and as Alic wrote us word orders issued to our
men to stand their ground if but ten men till help should come, but not to
yield an inch of ground. Just imagine what we felt when the news came,
"The Fort Surrendered not a man killed on either side." It was hard to believe the people seemed wild with joy and the negroes for sympathy in a state

---

[5] Eleuthera Du Pont Smith had a sister, Evelina Elizabeth Du Pont Bauduy, who
died on January 19, 1861.

of ecstatic delight. It was hard to believe it could be true for many where [*sic*] in great danger; our son John who was acting as a sort of volunteer aid had one cannon ball to pass just over his head and another threw splinters over him. Young Rhett had lain down to rest a little and a ball fell in his bed, the Chaplain while dressing had his bed knocked to pieces by a cannon ball, and not one wounded. Alic says "it is like the battles of the chosen people." I cannot tell you in words that would convince you why we know and feel we are in the right. Why we feel we had to separate or sink into miserable provincial dependence on a people disposed to crush us into obedience to their fanatical rule. It is not your North that hurt us, you are almost Southern, but that party you call small, has grown, like the cloud not bigger than a man's hand, till it has strength and power to exclude us from the territories, to lay on a new and enormous tariff, to set at defiance the laws for the return of our negroes, for, for one returned five hundred were kept back. Strong enough to <u>Canonize</u> John Brown to spread arson and murder through districts in Texas and to scatter emissaries through the whole of the South. Then where was our good name; through all Europe vilified and stigmatized, English and Scotch Reviews overflowing with utter falsehoods. Brazil and Spain both slaveholding nations, are not treated so. They had no <u>Brothers</u> to tell they [*sic*] world how infamous they were. Look in this very struggle how the Papers of the North misrepresent everything. Charleston <u>Mobs</u>, starvation, forced loans, immense taxes, &c &c and not one word of truth in all; the taxes were increased, but people thought hardly <u>enough</u>; there never was greater plenty nor peace in the City from the absence of so many gentlemen, ladies went about more by themselves than usual, but without a thought of danger, and not one single act of violence or rudeness committed, and I had many opportunities of hearing by the thousands of volunteers who have been coming & going since Christmas. We have now as far as I can learn 2000 troops gone to Virginia. 1000 regulars to defend the forts in the harbor and about 5000 more volunteers encamped in different parts of the State to be drilled and disciplined in case they are wanted anywhere. Two of my boys are with Gregg's regiment at Richmond. Willy who you know something of from our young friend and Alic who comes next to him. Charley is with his Regiment on Sullivan's Island. John and Joe have gone back to College a few days ago. What is to come God only knows but come what may we can never never never yield. We must be let alone. It is all we ask, but we must have our forts, we must be allowed to go out from the North and it is useless to try to keep us. We breathe free now, the Glorious Union had almost smothered us and we do not want to try it again. Forgive me if I am too warm. I cannot help it. I know you cannot feel with me, I should be sorry if you did, but if Delaware ever joins us then you will be a true Southron in feeling I know, so write as you please it will not give my any offense I am sure. I hope you may not be troubled, I know harm will not come to you, from our side if we can help it. I send you a Charleston paper with the President's Message, do read it. Write to me again and I will be sure to answer, so trust me if you do not hear that it is by some accident. God grant I may still write good news of my boys. It would do you good to hear all the praises I have heard of them this Winter. If I see John Darby I will give your message.[6] His Father & Mother are both cousins of Mr. Haskell. We have lived so far apart that I have never seen him but always heard he was a fine boy. Some of my sons know him. I hope he will not suffer by givin [sic] up his profit for his duty; it is what thousands are doing. Good by my dearest friend with kindest love to Charlotte & Isabell. Tell Isabell I am teaching Caesar to my boys every day, the [school] most having volunteered [sic].

Alexander C. Haskell, Headquarters, First Regiment S.C.V., Camp Pickens, Va., to Charles T. Haskell (UNC)
6 May 1861
Dear Pa,

I was very glad to get your letter yesterday giving me some home news. Since I last wrote, yesterday, we have had no developments except a rumor current that Scott is to retake the navy yard, Harper's Ferry & then by a bold stroke Richmond. This is not incredible & will give us a handful. We are not very many but I can say of the regiment to which I belong now 700 in number, that if in defence of our friends & allies here, we are thrown alone before & even deserted by a retreat of other troops under the steel & fire of an enemy superior in force, the noble fellows will scorn to turn the back or yield an inch before the Yankee foe. The Virginians are brave but they look on the Yankees more as equals & with too much respect as a formidable invading force, to feel as we South Carolinians do the withering shame of a surrender or retreat.

I really believe that if it were not for our presence here, Richmond would be in a panic now, but they look over the heads of their own [gay] troops to praise and trust the ragged, battered old "Fighting First." We feel what a tremendous responsibility is resting on every movement of ours in action. We have the honour of the state in our hands, & our lives will defend it & vindicate our position. It is a bitter thing for us, standing to our arms and what we believe our duty, to hear occasionally from a Carolinian whose

---

⁶ This is likely John Thomson Darby (1836-79). A noted medical instructor in Philadelphia, he returned to the South when the war broke out and first served as a surgeon in Hampton Legion.

every whisper we listen for now, that our gallant Colonel is maligned, and through him his whole regiment, by the most infamous falsehoods & vilest slanders uttered by & even published by a disappointed, ill-tempered and cowardly scoundrel, Capt. Warley, left in command on Morris Island.[7] He has not hesitated at anything which could put us in the wrong & himself in the right. For those gentlemen & brave soldiers who were obliged to remain at home I feel the most cordial sympathy and regard towards them. But Warley & some others held back from bad, wrong motives & finding how they were regarded have endeavoured to throw all the blame on a brave, honest, gallant soldier & a man as fierce as a tiger to be sure, but as tender as a woman. Warley has acted as their exaggerated representative & if we get back alive from the war I fear his life will but ill atone for the mischief which his black heart and lying tongue have done not only in our regiment, wh[ich] despite the talk made volunteered more unanimously than any other, but in all the other volunteer regiments in rendering them disaffected. We of the staff from our personal devotion are particularly reflected upon, but if it be hard to bear now when we hear of backbiting slanders, public voice will re-pay us either in case we return with the laurels of victory or if we fall in a gallant effort to sustain a name which once covered us all, but which now we have to fight for with half our force.

We would not mind the loss of numbers if we had been given their honest reasons & not disgraced the regiment by their snarling malice & falsehoods as to persons. I trust & believe that in my dear old company there is none of this feeling against us, but in case there is any manifestation of it I cast them off now, here, & forever. All the Abbeville men are well & doing well.

Willy is quite well. Goodbye. Dearest love to all.

[P.S.] Yesterday for the first time in four months I spent the morning in church & knelt down once more before the communion table. It was a deep pleasure & happiness to feel once more & has aided me to feel content with whatever may be God's will. I would tear my letter up, but I do want you to know what we feel though I will banish it hereafter.

---

[7] Frederick Fraser Warley (1830-76) was the captain of Company B (the Darling-ton Guards) in Gregg's Regiment. He was resentful of the way that Colonel Gregg re-quested volunteers for Virginia in April 1861, and most of the men in his company de-clined. After the incident, Warley made a number of accusations against Gregg, including a charge that the Colonel had supplied liquor to the soldiers to induce them to change their minds about volunteering. He also said that Gregg had told the soldiers that their refusal to volunteer was disgraceful. Warley's version of the story was published in a newspaper, *The Edgefield Advertiser,* on April 19, 1861.

Don't be anxious. I will try to write in advance of war motions. I have been angry whilst writing this letter, but it is true and blame from home cuts our hearts like red-hot steel. I hope I do now feel more kindly since I have spoken out & will try not to be angry again.

Alexander C. Haskell, Headquarters, First Regiment S.C.V., Richmond, Va., to Sophia C. Haskell (SCHS)
8 May 1861
Dear Ma,

I am strongly disposed to have a printed form stating that Willy & I are well &c, current news of the war &c leaving blanks for the date & place, & enclose one every morning until something occurs to render this form inapplicable. I feel so stupid sitting down to write & rewrite the same old story. We have not marched from Richmond, and I don't know when we will. Other troops are being moved to Norfolk, Harpers Ferry &c wherever Scott makes a demonstration, but some shrewd thinkers apprehend that these moves of Scotts are mere feints to draw the force away from Richmond, to give room for a destructive descent upon the place to glut some of his savages with plunder & strike terror into the hearts of Virginians. The Yankees are like ferocious monkeys which I believe the Spanish proverb makes the most cruel, wicked & capricious of tyrants, emboldened by the effects of their descent on Baltimore in paralysing the unhappy Marylanders, they hope to find as ready cowardice & compliance in Virginia.[8] But I think they are seriously mistaken. Although there are suppressed traitors in Virginia who will spring up like mushrooms at the sound of the tread of invasion, upon which they can rely, yet Virginia as a whole is true & brave & only falls short of Carolina in the lack of the bold confidence to which we are accustomed & the unflinching determination wh[ich] in our State never dreams of retreat or defeat. This is replaced in Va. by a vague dread & horror of the invaders with a dim vision of defeat. But when the Yankees beat them & all their allies they will like Pyrrhus exclaim such another victory & c but the idea is disagreeable & improbable & they are not worthy of the comparison. The accounts of the brutal soldiers in Washington which you see in the papers are not overdrawn.[9] I see many refugees from Washington & they have

---

[8] In April 1861, there had been riots in Baltimore when U.S. troops passed through the city. Soon afterward, the Maryland House of Delegates voted against secession, but several months later, many of the legislators were arrested by the Lincoln administration on suspicion of disloyalty.
[9] An article entitled "The Reign of Terror in Washington" appeared in the Charleston *Mercury* newspaper on May 4, 1861. In it a "Special Correspondent" reported on the plight of residents who refused to take the "odious test oath by which every citizen

inspired me with the conviction that butchery is none too bad for the beasts assembled there.[10]

Goodbye, dearest love to all.

Joseph C. Haskell, Columbia, S.C., to Charles T. Haskell (DUL)
12 May 1861
Dear Pa,

I have not written for some time for as you knew that I was well and there being nothing to write I have nothing to say. The only thing that has made any stir is the news not that the Niagara[11] off the bar, which she really is, but that they have mounted the rifle cannon on the Lady Davis and are going to try the effect that a few shots will have on the blockading ship.[12] This will be a very safe experiment, for it is nothing more, as the Lady Davis is but 42 feet long and at the distance from which they have to fire it would be next to impossible to hit her. This is no rumor but a positive fact. It was told me by a student just from Charleston who said that he had heard it from the officer who commands her and that he saw the cannon mounted on her bow. I hardly think it possible that they will be able to do anything but if they should by any lucky chance, it would be something to be proud of.

We are getting fixed down in College with about 75 students who are doing almost nothing. There is a great deal of sickness here and one student

---

and sojourner is sworn to war upon the South." They were "at the mercy of a ruthless gang of licensed vagabonds, horse-thieves and cut-throats, who, under the lead of the notorious Border Ruffian, Jim Lane, have transferred the scene of their atrocities from the Western frontier to the Federal Capital. These men are the chosen bodyguard of Abraham Lincoln. They desecrate with their quarter the spacious and magnificent reception hall of the Executive mansion so well known as the 'East Room,' and daily go forth in brutal squads from its tapestried precincts to threaten, plunder and slay such of the citizens as are not 'in the wool.'"

[10] In a pamphlet published in 1861, Edwin A. Pollard, a recent resident of Washington, addressed a letter to President Abraham Lincoln, stating: "I congratulate you upon your almost perfect establishment of military terrorism over a parasitical city. You have filled your capital with troops. You have set up a political inquisition in Washington, by the process of military TEST OATHS, wringing from men's consciences all that is precious to men's freedom ...You have surrounded yourself with every element to inspire terror around you. Your minions and your parasites are this day hunting through the streets of Washington, to do violence, by threats, at least, to every man who dares to oppose your Administration." Pollard, *The Southern Spy*, 22-23.

[11] The USS *Niagara* arrived at Charleston on May 10, 1861, for blockade duty.

[12] A Charleston newspaper, the *Courier*, reported on April 25, 1861: "Lieut. Stockton has been assigned to the command of the steamer gunboat Lady Davis, which received the pet rifled cannon 'Prioleau.'"

is desperately ill, and the increasing warmth of the weather lessens his chance of recovery. Mr. Venable[13] leaves for Virginia this week so that I don't know what will become of us. I was delighted to hear last night from Lou[14] that she was expecting Sophy and Miss Jeannie[15] in a few days. Columbia is rather dull but I suppose they can find some amusement down here. The principal one now is riding up to the fairgrounds in the evening to see the dress parade. Do ask Ma to send down the suit of clothes I left at the tailors to cut out and if she can to send me one or two thin linen sacks as I have not a single article of summer clothing of that description. I have not heard anything from the boys in Virginia, but have heard of Aleck who appears to be enjoying himself. Do write to me something of Willy and whether Charley has got his commission or not. John is still I believe on the island. I am very glad of this as it is the healthiest place he could be although it is not as pleasant as it might be.

I must come now to me the most important part of my letter, that is that I would be very much obliged if you would give me a check for 75 dollars. I hope that you will not think that I have put off writing until I was pushed for money, for I did not know until I had commenced this letter that we had to pay into the library this week, that is before Friday. Nothing is deducted for our absence and as I spent a good deal more whilst in Charleston than I do in college, I am out of money. Do give my love to all.

Alexander C. Haskell, Headquarters, First Regiment, S.C.V., Camp Charleston, Richmond, Va., to Charles T. Haskell (UNC)
12 May 1861
Dear Pa,

I have not written for several days for as many reasons. Just as I was worried by having my watch stolen & I did not want to write until I had exhausted all means of recovery & was sure of my loss. Again we have transferred our position to camp on the other side of the city which prevented me yesterday as I was constantly busy. But we have moved & I have been to church once & now got through most of my days work so am quiet & at leisure.

I was lucky enough in my search to hit on the very rascal who had stolen my watch & although it was not at the time on his person, I scared him

---

[13] Charles Scott Venable (1827-1900), a native of Virginia, was a mathematics professor at South Carolina College. After serving in the military in South Carolina, he left to join the staff of General Robert E. Lee.

[14] Louisa Rebecca McCord (1845-1928), a cousin.

[15] Jeannie Wardlaw (1842-1921), was a daughter of Judge David Lewis Wardlaw of Abbeville. She was later Mrs. Francis Turquand Miles.

so by having made a direct shot the very first time & hitting on him, that he sent it up to me the next morning with a contrite message & as his brother is already in the penitentiary I thought it best not to persecute the family & therefore dropped all proceedings.

News as to military movements is impossible. I can hear but little & believe less. There was a little skirmish on the York river the other day between a battery on the bank & the steamer Yankee which resulted in the retreat of the Yankee.[16]

I do hope that people in Carolina & everywhere in the South are waking up at last to the assurance that we are to have a real true & true, bona fide war of terrible magnitude & intensity. Never again do I expect to see the chivalrous bowing & scraping of Fort Sumter repeated. I am more than half inclined to think that if an army or naval officer of the old service chance to be among the first prisoners, they will try the hanging game which will of course put into most active operation the "Lex talionis" & rope will rise in price on both sides.[17] I am becoming somewhat anxious now as to my position at the expiration of the six months. I must go right on & I feel competent now to a commission or even would not fear at all to undertake a company. I am very desirous to get into some organization for the war in which I can obtain a commission. I thought of Hampton's Legion but I can learn very little of its constitution & less of the chance of obtaining a commission in it. Though I don't believe much in the Colonel commanding the Legion it is a service which I would very much like.[18]

Do write me what sparks of military ardour are yet burning in the district & what chance of getting a company.

I would prefer to remain under Gregg, but I much fear that his enemies have made him odious through the state. I see that Warley has at last written some of his atrocities & published. His worst enemy could not have wished for more. He has now sealed his own fate & fixed his position beyond hope of retreat.

We are under general orders to hold ourselves in readiness to march at a moments notice, but I do not think now that we will be moved from her to garrison any other place, but that the moment the enemy makes a decisive move we will be thrown before them with the greatest possible speed. The staff are now under the necessity of purchasing horses. I have to get uniform

---

[16] The exchange of fire between the *Yankee* and Confederate batteries took place at Gloucester Point, Va., on May 9, 1861.

[17] Lex talionis means retaliatory, corresponding punishment.

[18] Colonel Wade Hampton (1818-1902) had no military experience when he organized his legion, but would prove to be an able commander and rise to the rank of lieutenant general.

& horse & live for which I must draw for $300. Horses are not very cheap here & I have been disappointed in getting a cheap government horse. They are all high. I draw on Uncle Will.

Goodbye & love to Ma & all. Willy is quite well. Out today to church & dinner. Quite overwhelmed by the ladies.

William T. Haskell, Camp near Reservoir, Richmond, Va., to Sophia C. Haskell (SCHS)

14 May 1861

My dear Mother,

My long neglect in writing home even though somewhat justified by the great many drawbacks & inconveniences with which I have been impeded [*illegible words*] which I must seek to redeem by its future avoidance. I have had no tent since leaving Charleston, sleeping in the open air, but under a sort of shelter when it rained. I have found no hardship, but have quite missed the comparative privacy which the tent affords. A change of camp within the last few days has made my situation decidedly more civilized & convenient.[19] We left Charleston you know very suddenly & quite broke up our establishment. We have now again settled into an organized state of mess & movables. All the Abbeville men are with me & quite a nice one from Columbia. Our journey on was almost a triumphal procession, the arrival quite in keeping & our kind entertainment all that kind hospitality in war times can devise. All this from the beginning tended to reassure where any misgivings were entertained, and now you could persuade no one to return on any account. For myself I have been of one mind throughout. Alic says he has received an old letter from Pa concerning our [further] service. I have not as yet seen it. I am interrupted by the inevitable drums.

A day has intervened & I now commence anew. Our camp is visited every evening by a crowd of ladies whose repeated coming & patriotic spirit have given many of our men opportunity to make fair acquaintances, so that there is quite a new feature in camp in the matter of beaux & belles. A no less real advantage is found in the aid afforded by the good people in the shape of sundry loaves of bread—better than we get—buttermilk from the country round & then any sewing or work which ladies can do be it much or little. I have the advantage of many in knowing many fine friends in the city & many of it who the times have gathered here. Of the war though I of course cannot deny that hostilities are somewhat imminent. Yet there is evidently a prudent policy of delay & preparation observed which gives time for

---

[19] William's regiment was apparently encamped near the Marshall Reservoir at Richmond.

the development of any peace measure which a little time must I think give rise to the north.

Camp life has become quite a matter of course with me now & I find various ways of diversifying the times viz I drill every day part of a new company here, a very good practice for me. I have too a squad practicing the bayonet exercise, so that learning & teaching together I am improving myself. I spoke of my friends in the city. My chief difficulty is that I can but seldom go out of camp to see them. I promised Lee to write to him of our experiences. I have not been able hitherto but may soon. I am sorry to see & hear of wrong impressions & statements made concerning our regiment & its officers, do not hesitate to say from all the heat & excitement felt by some in the matter in which I have never joined, that such impressions and statements are unjust & unreliable, particularly those of Captain Warley which [add] absurdity to the other qualities. Love to Pa, Sophy & all the rest & say I will write soon.

Charles T. Haskell, Jr., Charleston, S.C., to Charles T. Haskell (SCHS)
17 May [1861]
Dear Father,

I have just received letters from you & Ma. I suppose that you have already received my note stating my return from & lack of success at Montgomery. I shall follow implicitly your advice as to retaining my position. I shall do what I can with John. My impression of him is that he is liberal to an excess but not naturally extravagant. He belongs now to a very expensive mess from necessity. I hope he will be able to get out of it before long. I have no fear of his being deleteriously influenced as he has too much character & nothing but official respect for those who might otherwise mislead him. I have not in myself anything of an example for him but may be able by my experience to preserve him from my own errors.[20]

Alexander C. Haskell, Headquarters, First Regiment S.C.V., Richmond, Va., to Charles T. Haskell (UNC)
18 May 1861
Dear Pa,

You no doubt are more exercised by rumours of war, than those of us who are upon its very borders, as I find that these rumours grow by change

---

[20] John C. Haskell was at this time in the Calhoun Battery, commanded by Captain William Ransom Calhoun (1827-62). The "errors" Charles refers to were likely his own experiences of getting himself in debt while living in Charleston before the war.

of air and rapid motion. It is indeed very difficult, to keep the [run] of the defensive or aggressive movements on either side, as bewildering as the occupation of the man who tends the rise & progress of a mushroom bed, so sudden & irregular are the modes & processes of increasing the force. The strength of the enemy concentrated in Washington is calculated at about 40,000. The number of our forces I cannot tell but although smaller it is steadily increasing. The great trouble is in the fact that they being an aggressive and invading body with choice of many important points at which to strike, are able to concentrate a tremendous power in Washington without developing its destination until they are ready and in motion to have it upon the destined spot, with all their brutal accompaniments of plunder and outrage, while we on the defensive, and as Scott says ten days behind him, are obliged to cut up & distribute our force at each of these various points, holding all in a fluttering & uncertain attitude, ready at earliest notice to fly to the scene of action.

Public opinion seems to have settled upon Harper's Ferry as the probable scene of the first action, on account of its importance to both parties. It is said that the enemy are now marching upon it from three several points with a view to [invest] & finally seize the stronghold. We have there about 10,000 men under the command of Brig. Genl. Johnson[21] of C.S.A., an officer I believe of considerable ability. Major Whiting,[22] of Morris Island memory, called to see us yesterday as he passed through from the Cape Fear works in N.C. on his way to Harper's Ferry. He expressed a great deal of regret that the So. Ca. troops had not yet received orders for his destination, as "at their side he felt sure of brilliant victories in battle & soldierly fortitude in labour & hardship." I should not be surprised if his order was but the forerunner of ours & if we were at Harper's Ferry in a few days. We want to be wherever is the first fight.

We are still well & prosperous notwithstanding what I can't help seeing in the paper occasionally of some small but malignant vapouring at our expense from our old comrades in arms, who unhappily cannot candidly confess a fault or false step or give the right reason for, in many cases, a right step, but will seek self-justification in blame & bitter reproach of those who adopted a different course. But it will all be straight one way or the other when we get home, after the war. I fear that we will be obliged to return

---

[21] Aleck Haskell is referring to Joseph E. Johnston (1807-91), who became one of the most notable and important high-ranking generals of the Confederate Army. His name is misspelled as Johnson in a number of these letters.

[22] William Henry Chase Whiting (1824-65), a West Point graduate, was a major of engineers in the Confederate States Army. He worked on the defenses of Charleston and was later promoted to the rank of brigadier general.

temporarily at a most important crisis, but it will be to raise a new force to reenter the service & there continue until the last pirate of this unholy and unrighteous invasion has met the lot of wickedness & crime.

I don't know what will be the opportunity of rising at the end of the six months service, but I think that Col. Gregg & his field stand some chance of being held in commission, so entirely has the Colonel held & commanded respect amongst the higher officers, and in this case I think whatever he can do for me or for Willy will be exerted in our favour in the event of a reconstruction of a new regiment for the war.

It is needless to tell you more of the kindness of the Virginians. It amounts to an enthusiasm which has no check or abatement. The ladies & old men & young too need but to hear the name of So. Carolina to welcome dearly & warmly. If it was not wartime we could all marry to unspeakable advantage. I can't write more. Goodbye, dearest love to Ma & all at home.

William T. Haskell, Camp at Manassas Junction, Va., to Sophia C. Haskell
(SCHS)
25 May 1861
My dear mother,

We have changed our quarters as you will see by our superscription & now are within about 25 miles of Alexandria which is now held by the enemy. Of course our proximity to the adversary increases the excitement & adds to the imminence of a fight. Yesterday morning Alexandria was occupied with the usual circumstances of deceit & dishonesty which seems to have characterised the action of the U.S. Govt. so far. I learn all the circumstances from old friends who are among the military leaving the place. At half past four in the morning a flag of truce came from the Pawnee to the officer commanding in Alexandria demanding the evacuation & giving him until 9 o'clock A.M. to withdraw his troops amounting in number to between 4 & 500 from the town. Before however the flag of truce returned at 5 ¼ the sentinel on the wharf saw two boats of troops approaching. These he halted. On their commencing again to advance he leveled his piece at one of the boats, the men stooped in their boat while all in the other aimed their rifles at him. Just at the moment the officer (Lieut Lowry)[23] with the flag of truce under which he had entered the town appeared & by interposing himself stopped the fire for a moment. The sentinel then began a retreat as rapidly as possible firing as he went & escaping from amid a storm of bullets. The alarm thus given put all the military on the alert & probably saved them all from a capture which befell through some of bungling or mistake a

---

[23] Lieutenant Reigart Bolivar Lowry (1826–80).

squadron of 25 cavalry. Morril[24] the sentinel who shot & was shot at is an old University acquaintance of mine & gave me as also many others this account. Col. Ellsworth was shot by a man named Jackson from whose house they took down a C.S. flag.[25] Jackson was a very brave man & had for some time promised this fate to anyone who touched his flag. He was of course immediately shot down. I have been interrupted for a long time & must now be short as Alic is also writing. He seemed to think that we are just on the eve of any amount of hostilities—it may be so but there is still room for the contrary, if it does come we make no doubt of the result.

With love to all. I remain in excellent good health & condition your affectionate son

P.S. Having had my hair cropt today I saved you a lock.

Alexander C. Haskell, Headquarters, First Regiment S.C.V., Camp near Manassas Gap, Va., to Charles T. Haskell and Sophia C. Haskell (UNC)
26 May 1861
My dear Father & Mother,

I have not time to write but a few lines before I will be off on duty for two days and nights. My horse & myself have been going at all hours & 6 hours together with half an hour or a little more of quiet. I give this to show why I could not write but more to give you an idea of our position. We are about 18 miles from the nearest large force of the enemy. 30,000 are within 30 miles of Washington & Alexandria & our forces in Alexandria were driven in yesterday about 550 in number. In Alexandria after it was occupied Col. Ellsworth commanding N.Y. 7th Regiment of Zouaves attempted to pull down our flag at the head of his forces. He was met defied & killed by a single unsupported man James Jackson of Virginia. He killed Ellsworth as he laid his hand upon the flagstaff.

This is the spirit & it must succeed if we can only get time & collect a little more force at this point (we have now about 1500 & will have 800 more tonight). I think we will be able to give a good account of ourselves.

---

[24] William Todd Morrill (1838-62), a member of the Alexandria Riflemen. J. Lipscomb Johnson wrote of him: "When the State of Virginia passed the Ordinance of Secession, the 'Riflemen' were called out to do guard and picket duty in and around Alexandria. On the 24th of May, 1861, at daylight, Morrill was on guard at Cazenove's wharf, opposite the point where the United States steamer *Pawnee* was lying at anchor in the Potomac river; he was one of the first to observe the advance of Federal troops, and it is said that he fired the first shot as the boats full of men approached the shore of Virginia." Johnson, *The University Memorial*, 128.

[25] Col. Elmer Ellsworth took down a secession flag flying from the Marshall House in Alexandria. The hotel keeper, James Jackson, shot Ellsworth dead, and was immediately shot and killed by another United States soldier.

Goodbye & remember that there are many chances in war & I hope I am ready for even the extremest. If ever there is a gratification in having sons it must be when they can be given to protect their country & their homes from the brutal ruffians (for such they really are) who are invading with murder & plunder for their war cry & incentive.

Goodbye. Dearest love to all, Sophy, Lewis, Paul & all the rest.

Alexander C. Haskell, Headquarters, Advance Forces, Centreville, Va., to Charles T. Haskell (UNC)
28 May 1861
Dear Pa,

I write from Centreville the advance post of the Alexandria Department, within 19 miles of Alexandria & about the same distance of Washington. We marched to this point 3 days ago to meet an expected, or rumored, advance of the enemy, and to take & hold a very advantageous position which was selected by our Colonel's keen eye & endorsed at once by generals and engineers. [He] was sent on as the advance guard of the Alexandria movement with our 600 to 700 gallant Palmetto boys about 70 horse & a fine field battery of 4 pieces. We are honoured by holding the right wing of the Confederate forces in Virginia, when in line of battle & of course when thrown into column we are at the head. Justice has been done to us at last at least in our position in the Dept. of Alexandria with which we are presently to deal. If our course is short I have hopes of its yet being glorious. Kershaw's 2nd Regt. S.C. Vols is in our rear about 2 ½ miles ready to come up to our support.[26] About 4 miles behind him at the Manassas Junction are the Virginia troops in some force. I don't know exactly what, as it is constantly shifting.

Our men received the order to advance with every evidence of satisfaction and I do think that if we get them once in reach of the enemy they will add a leaf to the laurels of Carolina which will surpass the greenest of them all. Twice have I seen them when they thought but a few hundred yards separated them from the enemy & never have I expected to have seen such noble, dauntless courage pervade so large and promiscuous a body of men. I can well understand Major Whiting of the U.S. old army, the directing officer at the bombardment of Sumter, when he said that it had been worth whole years of his military experience to have spent those few months with

---

[26] Joseph Brevard Kershaw (1822-94) of Camden, S.C., was the colonel of the 2nd South Carolina Infantry Regiment. He was commissioned as a brigadier general in February 1862.

the S. Carolina troops, just to learn how laborious, patient, cool, and un-
dauntedly courageous men could be. Often he has spoken of our Regt. too,
when he was trembling for his batteries on Morris Island with the enemy's
fleet ready to land an invading force, that when he passed the irregular
troops below & came to our lines he was at rest again.

But day before yesterday was a fine sight to be seen. We marched from
Manassas the night before after dark, stopped half way & bivouacked under
the bushes. The men woke up as lively as could be & we marched in to Centreville. We reached the place about 9 o'clock, very hot & dusty with a furious wind blowing. In a few minutes after couriers came hot & furious on
reeking, panting horses to say that they had left the enemy in force varying
from 1500 to 5000, about 3 miles behind them rapidly advancing. The report was soon confirmed from all quarters, so the Colonel rode to the head
of the Regiment, very quickly gave his orders. The men stood without a
word or a cheer, quietly gratified, some looking earnest, some smiling, some
hugging their rifles & muskets quite excited with delight. They went into
position in line of battle in this spirit, sat down to rest & wait, but sent their
servants off for dinner which they cooly discussed, looking over the brow of
the hill for the enemy. We were disappointed however after all. The information was false, started partly by treachery, partly by cowardice. I was going
to write more but must stop. We are in the midst of traitors & have to look
sharp.

Goodbye. Dearest love to Ma, Sophy & boys. Willy is quite well.

*Alexander C. Haskell, Headquarters, Advance Forces, Centreville, Va., to Charles
T. Haskell (UNC)*
1 June 1861
Dear Pa,

I write again from Centreville with much fear that my letter will not
reach you. We had a brush this morning about 3 o'clock at one of our outposts about 6 miles off. Now if I had command of my troop I could have
made a big name. At Fairfax Court House, we had about 90 Virginia cavalry
& one company of Virginia rifles attached to our Regiment, but sent to an
outpost. They were surprised, their sentinels shot or captured & the whole
concern was thrown into confusion by a brilliant dash of about 80 of the 2nd
Regt. U.S. Cavalry. The Virginia horse scattered like partridges & never
halted till they reached Col. Gregg 6 miles away. The rifles stood their
ground & repulsed the enemy without loss to themselves, and with the capture of several prisoners & more horses & arms which we are much in need
of. A squadron of cavalry at the post behaved in the most disorderly & dastardly manner, retreating almost without a blow & flying on the wings of

terror. I was roused out of bed by the announcement in accents tremulous from excitement & terror of one of the flying horse that the enemy were upon us in thousands, & this was confirmed by each & every of about 60 of the fugitives. The Colonel dismissed them however with some contempt & we went quietly to work to turn out our boys on their picked battle field, where they are always anxious to be summoned, & showed their ranks in perfect order in a very few minutes. Troop after troop of the horse kept pouring in.

I just hear that Capt. Marr of the Virginia rifles was killed in the action, a noble fellow.[27] The enemy have lost several.

Goodbye. God bless you all & dearest love.

Charles T. Haskell, Jr., Charleston, S.C., to Sophia C. Haskell (SCHS)
1 June 1861
Dear Mother,

I am just on the eve of departure for "Coles" Island lying southwest of Charleston where I am to take command of two companies, mine & another.[28] The news came on me this evening so suddenly that I can write but a few words. Mrs. Tom Rhett is now in Charleston having been compelled to leave Alexandria.[29] She has been generally asked by different members of the family to visit Abbeville. I know that within a short time such a visit would be very agreeable to her as she has been very anxious about her two little children as to their health. I hope you will write to her if it suits you, asking her definitely. Direct care of Roland Rhett.[30]

---

[27] Captain John Quincy Marr (1825-61) of the Warrenton Rifles. At the court house in Fairfax, Va., there is a monument memorializing him as the first Confederate officer killed in the war.

[28] In his memoir, James R. Hagood described Coles Island as "about a mile in length and from 150 to 350 yards wide" situated on the Stono Inlet about ten miles southwest of Charleston between the islands of Folly and Kiawah. Hagood, "Memoirs of the First South Carolina Regiment," 37.

[29] This was Ann Graham Florence Mason Rhett (1823-85), the daughter of Judge Thomson Francis Mason (1785-1838) of Alexandria, Virginia. She was the wife of Thomas Grimke Rhett, a first cousin of the Haskell brothers. She died in 1883, and only two of her children, Charles Hart Rhett and Florence Rhett, survived to adulthood. She is usually referred to as Cousin Folly (also spelled Follie) in these letters.

[30] Roland Smith Rhett (1830-98) was commissioned as a major in the Confederate Quartermaster Corps in December 1861 and served throughout the war. He was the son of James Smith Rhett and Charlotte Haskell Rhett, and was a first cousin of the Haskell brothers.

Alexander C. Haskell, Headquarters, Advance Forces, Centreville, Va., to Sophia C. Haskell (UNC)

2 June 1861

Dear Ma,

Rumors are flying so thick and fast to So. Carolina that it distresses me to think of how you must be worried & harassed if you give them any credence. We are now within arm's length of the enemy. Two hours sharp ride will put me at any time in the enemy's lines. Night before last the enemy with about 90 splendidly armed and mounted dragoons made a brilliant dash on Fairfax C. H., our advance post about 7 miles from here. Killed a noble captain, but fortunately did no other damage. Our cavalry was not prepared to meet them & consequently broke, but about 70 riflemen stood firm & repulsed them, taking several prisoners & a good many horses. 6 horses have been found dead on the road by which they retreated & a minister who met the troop counted 15 empty saddles. We are in a beautiful country & one in which from its natural features, many of the singlehanded achievements of border warfare will be accomplished.

I am liable now to being on pretty hazardous duty, acting body guard to the Colonel & am almost without arms having but a single pistol.

I wish that if possible Pa would send me by Adams Express or some officer of the regiments coming on a good pair of saddle holsters, one or two pistols if they can be got, & if obtainable a horseman's rifle of [single shot] of course a Maynard's is the best, with a good supply of ammunition for all. These may be of very material importance to me & can't be got in Virginia, for love or money. The greatest expedition is desirable.

Willy & I have made as usual some very kind & pleasant friends near this antiquated village, "Sholte Turberville Stuart" & family in an ancient Virginia mansion of half a century's date "Chantilly" by name.[31] A most beautiful spot, & here we spent a very pleasant day. By the way you may rely for information on the letters in the Mercury which are written regularly by Mr. Spratt,[32] who being my bedfellow & associate on the "Volunteer Staff" can give information for both at once. He is a very pleasant gentleman & of great intelligence, come to view the war and battlefields for which he has so long labored with his pen.

I am doing reasonably well, I hope laying a foundation for future position or promotion, acting again as chief of staff in the office department to Col. Gregg, who is in command of about two regiments, of the whole ad-

---

[31] Sholte Turberville Stuart (1821-84) owned a farm named Chantilly in Fairfax County, Va.

[32] Leonidas W. Spratt was the Virginia correspondent for the *Charleston Mercury* newspaper.

vance force, and as his nearest Aide de Camp in the battlefield, where we have stood now three times and been disappointed. Davis is in Richmond & Beauregard is at Manassas in a few miles of us. Good hands to be in.

I am as ever your loving son. Goodbye. Dearest love to Pa & all.

[P.S.] Smith has been quite sick but is now well, sitting by me writing to his wife. In case my letter comes first do let her know. Remember me most kindly to them all.

Alexander C. Haskell, Headquarters, Centreville Outpost, Va., to Sophia C. Haskell (UNC)
5 June 1861
Dear Ma,

I write again the most interesting news—that we are all well. We have occasional starts from the enemy. Last night two of our cavalry videttes were chased in by some scouts of the enemy. I was refused my application to join the party that went after them, but made up for it by sleeping very soundly with my spurs on my feet & my pistol under my head & my sword at my side, in spite of which armament I had almost to be rolled over by the scouting officer on his return from his reconnaissance, before he could prevail on me to awake.

We have lost no more men & I think have some twenty or thirty of the enemy. We hear constantly of a contemplated advance against Manassas Junction in which case we will have a chance before the Regiment is to be disbanded. If we are obliged to return home to be disbanded, I hope to lead a troop of light horse into Virginia to harass our invaders. Spies are numerous among the population, and those that are on our side are so indifferent that they give us no aid and do the enemy no harm. An invading army in Carolina would fare very differently.

I got a piece of wedding cake from some friend. I don't know who. I am afraid too much of that will be going on whilst we are far away. If I return to Carolina this summer it will be for a short time only, but even this is doubtful. I do not care to recede in the face of the enemy.

Willy is quite well. Goodby & dearest love to Pa and all the rest at home & friends abroad.

Alexander C. Haskell, Headquarters, Centreville Outpost, Va., to Charles T. Haskell (UNC)
8 June 1861
Dear Pa,

I write still from Centreville where we stand, along with the enemy, I think gradually closing up to advance either upon this position or Harpers

Ferry. The federal commanders have landed about 3000 troops at the White House below Mount Vernon on the Potomac, quite a strong position in defence of the rivers passage. I think that their object is to fix themselves at a number of commanding points from which they may readily concentrate on any designated point, though we hear that they do not intend to move until the 4th of July. There are many circumstances which induce me to believe this an absurdity as it contains in some degree the proposition that Scott & Lincoln are waiting for law and order, of wh[ich] they have long since proved themselves independent. I think that a movement will be made shortly, and then we will have to undergo the mortification of seeing our Regiment go ingloriously out of service in the very face of the enemy and from the most <u>advanced position on the line of advance</u>.

I wish very much that you would ascertain as far as possible the means of obtaining arms and equipment for a troop. I am resolved if I am forced to come home to endeavour to train a troop to go on to Virginia & show those fellows that horses are made for something besides getting out of the way of the enemy. The Virginia cavalry behaved most disgracefully in our little brush of the other day, in which as I believe I told you we lost but one man killed, a gallant captain of Virginia rifles, & five prisoners of the race riding cavalry, the enemy losing about 30 in killed, wounded & prisoners, & about a dozen horses. We are on constant and arduous duty expecting an advance daily and nightly. This is very exhausting to our men, but they go it bravely and cheerfully. Willy is quite well and we are cheered occasionally by some little testimonial from the friends we manage to find among the nicest people of the country.

I may be at home about the middle of July but if I can get an appointment here I will deem it my duty to remain.

Don't let Joe come on in that college company, as I hear they have offered. It would be mad, cruel & useless to let those boys come here.[33] Goodbye & love to Ma & all.

Alexander C. Haskell, Headquarters, First Regiment S.C.V., Centreville, Va., to Charles T. Haskell (UNC)
10 June 1861
Dear Pa,

I have nothing of any importance since my last. We have had no action though we came very near shooting a parcel of Tories the other night. They, however, unfortunately discovered our ambuscade of riflemen of whom Wil-

---

[33] The South Carolina College Cadets volunteered for service in Virginia in June 1861, but Governor Pickens would not allow them to go.

ly was one, and retreated on their horses. We were ruined in this expedition by the blunder of some of our Virginia cavalry who are very raw and stupid. A good many of them have been captured (near ten) at outposts by their own carelessness and negligence.

You will probably hear of us soon nearer the enemy, for they don't seem inclined to approach us since they find they can't surprise us.

We are all well. I mean all whom you know. One of our young poor young fellows died yesterday of typhoid pneumonia, a sad case. He was of the Camden company, Gardner.[34] But in the Mexican war about this time, as many as 14 died in one day in July in our regiment, and hundreds in all, while this is but the 2nd death in our body.[35]

Goodbye. Dearest love to Ma & all.

Alexander C. Haskell, Headquarters, Centreville, Va., to Sophia C. Haskell (UNC)
13 June 1861
Dear Ma,

I am quite unwell today and therefore not on active duty, which gives me as much time as I want & more than I feel inclined to use. I merely repeat that we are still awaiting marching orders, rather excited by hearing of the splendid little victory of our forces near Hampton, where on the 10th or 11th about 4000 Yankees attacked about 12 or 1500 of our men & to their astonishment retreated with between 200 & 300 killed & wounded.[36] We are in the main well & doing well enough, except that we fear we won't get a fight before our term of service is out. I will probably return home about the 10th of July to make arrangements for reentering the service.

Goodby & love to Pa & all.

William T. Haskell, Camp Centreville, Va., to Sophia C. Haskell (SCHS)
14 June 1861
My dear Mother,

We are still at Centerville and all well, except that Alic has been a little ailing for the last two or three days. The regiment has just moved on according to previous arrangement, viz, that we should take that position as soon

---

[34] This may have been Corporal John Gardiner, who enlisted in the DeKalb Rifle Guards at Camden, S.C. This company was originally part of the Second South Carolina Volunteer Infantry Regiment, and then volunteered to go to Virginia in Maxcy Gregg's regiment as Company N.

[35] This refers to the famous Palmetto Regiment of South Carolina.

[36] This engagement took place as described at Big Bethel, Va., on June 10, 1861. It was an encouraging victory for the Confederates.

Cash's Regiment[37] arrived. The Col. Leaves me here with Alic in a very kind family of which he has no doubt spoken (Dr. Alexander's)[38] with order's from the Dr. (Powell)[39] who says that nothing is the matter with him, to bring him out to Fairfax tomorrow when he will be "all right." I have got well of a bad cold in the head which has been stupefying me for the last week.

The time has nearly come for the disbanding of the Regiment. There exists in the Regiment a feeling which I think will become general, if recruiting a Regiment under Col. Gregg for further services. He is universally regarded as the best Col in the service and this opinion he has gained among the Virginians.

I have in hand an idea hardly an enterprise as yet of recruiting a comp. for the purpose. I wouldn't have much of a chance at home but here I have, where they know me, a better prospect. My object then is to get as many men as I can in the regiment, when it disbands, and have as many gathered from all sides at home and elsewhere by men who have offered to do so, and who indeed first started the idea. But at most the success is doubtful. I can say more of it hereafter. Its prosecution will not allow my return home where I am not quite certain that you and Pa would care to see me just now. I have spoken to Col. Gregg who tells me to go ahead. In case he succeeds in raising the regiment he will, I am sure, provide for Alic.

For all home news we have the greatest appetite and desire. Say to Pa we got his letter a few days ago.

Charles T. Haskell, Jr., Fort Palmetto, Coles Island, S.C., to Charles T. Haskell
(SCHS)
15 June 1861
Dear Father,

I got letters from both Ma & yourself a day or two ago, the first news I had received from home for some time. Your letter gave me the news of Joe's intention of probably going on to Virginia. I must say that I am very sorry to hear it, he is so young, but I can very well understand his desire to go. You ask me about the health of the Post.[40] I cannot say that I consider it a per-

---

[37] Col. E. B. C. Cash (1823-88) commanded the Eighth South Carolina Infantry Regiment.

[38] Dr. Robert Alexander, a surgeon.

[39] Dr. John Walker Powell (1823-78), a native of Fairfield District, S.C., was the surgeon of Gregg's regiment. He died at Hernando, Mississippi, during a yellow fever epidemic there in 1878.

[40] Fort Palmetto was an artillery battery built on Coles (or Cole) Island to defend the entrance to the Folly and Stono Rivers. It was also known as Battery No. 7.

fectly healthy place, but I think it much better than any of the places at which I have spent the 1st part of the last six summers. There is a perfectly healthy island about 300 yards off from this occupying a far more commanding position than this, but unfortunately the two batteries under my charge have been already built here by ignorant people & we have to stay here. I intend to apply to Col. Anderson[41] for permission to build a battery on this other Island—Folly Island—as it will give me an advantage in range of at least 800 yds, enable me to fire on vessels before their entering either Stono or Folly rivers & if war vessels should approach as near to us as they have done once or twice, I could fire into them with the little guns that I have— 24 pounders. If Col Anderson allows me to do so it will render the Post far more defensible than at present.

Of course we could not move there, as these batteries that we now have occupy nearly the whole command, which consist of only 135 men, one company of Confederate & one of Provisional troops—but I could send an officer there with a detachment & could send over officers & men who may be taken with fever.

I have no very great apprehensions of sickness, however, as we have a wide opening right out to sea which is distant four miles. I do not like the live oak growth on the fresh water holes. The latter I am having filled up as fast as I can & the former I have had cleared out as far as is necessary to give a free circulation of air. I am in short taking every possible precaution as to health.

As to the probable mode of attack, if any, the enemy has but one & that is to make an attempt to enter Stono or Folly rivers, to do which he would have to pass directly under both of our batteries, unless we should be shelled out first. I am rather in haste as the mail boat is waiting.

Alexander C. Haskell, Headquarters, Advance Forces Fairfax Courthouse, Camp Hamilton, Va., to Charles T. Haskell (UNC)
22 June 1861
Dear Pa,

I write from near Fairfax where we have been for several days, a mere handful of 600 in reach, 8 miles of 4000 of the enemy & a heavy battery of 8 guns. It has not caused to pass any sleepless nights except those who were on duty, but some anxious thoughts of a bloody acre and friends at home have made us feel badly when we had nothing to do, but today we are reinforced

---

[41] Richard Heron Anderson (1821-79) was the first colonel of the First Regiment, South Carolina Infantry Regulars. He was promoted to the rank of brigadier general in July 1861.

by Kershaw's, Cash's & Bacon's regiments, with Kemper's 4 [little] guns and I feel convinced that we will have a tremendous fight with the enemy at Falls Church a few miles off before long.[42] I think we are sure of being in at least one short fight before July. If we get through that I hope to see you all again.

If I get home it will be to try to raise a company to go into Gregg's new regiment. I feel competent by my experience to command one, & hope I will get it. Willy is quite well & hopes to raise a company here in Virginia.

Goodbye & dearest love to all.

[P.S.] Kiss to Ma & Ella, Sophy & the little ones. I don't know when I will write again.

Alexander C. Haskell, Headquarters, First Regiment, S.C.V., Fairfax, Va., to Sophia C. Haskell (UNC)
25 June 1861
Dear Ma,

We are all quite well in spite of my last letter, in which I expressed my conviction that we would soon be upon the enemy's lines. We did not advance at the time contemplated, but are concentrating troops at about 6 miles from the enemy's advance lines. One column of advance is about 17 regiments, several batteries & a good force of cavalry, I suppose about 16000 in all, though I am not sure, & still increasing. Beauregard is in command with 3 or 4 brigadiers under him, Bonham, Ewell, Jones & don't know who else, perhaps Johnson, at Harpers Ferry with about 11,000 will join us as he is also under Beauregard.[43] My present plan is not to come home, deep as the happiness would be of seeing you all whom I left & the dear arrivals from the West,[44] but so long as I can be of any service here I feel it my duty to remain. Overtures were made to me this morning by a young Virginian to take command of a company of Virginians which he is confident he can raise & which Col. Gregg will receive with his Regt. I have written to "Bill Robinson of Penny's Creek" to know if he will come on to join me with a part of a company.[45] If Pa can in any way aid in this movement he will do me great

---

[42] Colonel Joseph Brevard Kershaw (1822-94) was in command of the Second South Carolina Infantry Regiment. Colonel Ellerbe Boggan Crawford Cash (1823-88) was commander of the 8th South Carolina Infantry Regiment. Bacon's regiment was likely the Seventh South Carolina Infantry Regiment, of which Thomas Glascock Bacon (1812-76) was elected colonel in March 1861. Kemper's Battery, also known as the Alexandria Light Artillery, was commanded by Delaware Kemper (1833-99).

[43] The generals mentioned as Beauregard's brigadiers were Milledge Luke Bonham (1813-90), Richard Stoddart Ewell (1817-93), David Rumph Jones (1825-63), and Joseph E. Johnston.

[44] Langdon Cheves Haskell and his family.

[45] There was a W. J. Robinson on the roster of the Abbeville Volunteers.

service. They will be armed in Richmond. If he can provide them with uniforms, let them be <u>strong</u>, blue or black grey blouses of Georgia, N.C. or Va. cloth. Don't wait however if it is difficult though it is better to be provided, & with blue or grey flannel shirts summer & coats in winter. Goodbye. Dearest love to Pa & all.

William T. Haskell, Camp Gist, Fairfax, Va., to Langdon C. Haskell (SCHS)
26 June 1861
My dear brother,

    I have this morning heard of your—of our—sad loss.[46] It is inexpressibly sad to us all. I can say nothing to make it less so, only that I share it with you. You know whence all comfort comes, you have already sought it. One of my brightest visions of home is taken away and a shadow is thrown where, on my return, I hoped and prayed to find all sunshine.

    Alic, I think, will soon return for a time. I will probably remain here.

    Give my best love Ella and little Pete[47] and believe me praying that God may bless and comfort you both.

William T. Haskell, Camp Gist, Fairfax, Va., to Charles T. Haskell (SCHS)
30 June 1861
My dear Father,

    I have heard by your last letter of the sad [cause of sorrow] which must fill you all at home as well as Alic & myself here. I am glad that you are all well & am able to report the same of ourselves. You have received my letter sometime since speaking of not returning home. My business now is by all means in my power to raise a company of riflemen to serve under Gregg who has promised to receive me. The sooner I can organize this company the better. I have already advertised in Charleston & written to Uncle William & others to assist me & have friends in Beaufort & Fairfield who will assist me also. I will make efforts in Va. to get as many men as I can so that using all means in all places I may within twenty days if possible assemble 64 men, the necessary number. I do not know what chances there are in Abbeville, but any help in any way which you can devise in getting respectable volunteers at home or elsewhere is most desirable. If Alic retains his idea of raising his comp. about home I do not wish to impair his success. At present

---

    [46] Mary Sophia Haskell, the infant daughter of Langdon C. Haskell and his wife Ella, was born in 1859 and died on June 21, 1861.

    [47] The context of the letters indicates that "Pete" was a nickname for Langdon Cheves Haskell (1860-1929), a son of Langdon C. Haskell and Ella Wardlaw Haskell. Family history sources say that he was called Cheves to distinguish him from his father, and he is called Cheves in at least one letter (May 8, 1863).

he seems doubtful. Do write to Charley so that if it comes in his way to give me a lift he may do so. I do not now know where he is or I would write to him. I have two Citadel men, Dwight & Gaillard[48] aiding me & these I hope to have as lieutenants. Their ability & knowledge will be all that I want to make a first-rate company if I can [only] get it together.

Any number of men from one upwards is desirable. For means of transportation, subsistence & mention of the rendezvous I will communicate them as soon as possible. Meanwhile I just want names taken & engaged. It might be well to advertise. You know best.

We have now a telegraph to Fairfax so that you can get news promptly. The Regt I think will disband in Richmond, leaving here on Wednesday next. No news. Love to Ma & all the rest.

Alexander C. Haskell, Headquarters, First Regiment, S.C.V., Richmond, Va., to Charles T. Haskell (UNC)
[June or July 1861]
Dear Pa,

I have been waiting for some days to endeavour to mature my plans before writing, but have failed to arrive at any definite conclusion. Col. Gregg's new regiment will soon be formed & if possible he will give me a place on his staff, probably as adjutant, which I would I believe rather have than the captaincy of any but a crack company. The Sec. of War however reserves the right of appointing the staff & I must be a lieutenant before I can be an adjutant. Of this there is but small chance. After much delay our regiment will be disbanded in a day or two & go home. Much as I desire to see you all, I do not think it well for me to leave Va. as I am determined to see the war through. We are all quite well & I hope Willy is succeeding with his company. If I could have got home 3 weeks ago I might have stood by him in the line, but I am not offered an appointment. I will probably go into Boykin's Rangers, which is a gallant corps with many gentlemen in it.[49] Do if possible send me on to Richmond one or two copies of those numerous cavalry tactics which I have at home & tho it is a shabby thing to ask for a present back again I would be infinitely obliged if you would mail to me your fountain pen wh[ich] I have wished for a hundred times in the campaign. Goodbye & dearest love to Ma & all.

---

[48] These were likely Richard Yeadon Dwight (1837-1919) and Alfred Septimus Gaillard (1839-70), who were both Citadel graduates.

[49] Boykin's Rangers was a cavalry company designated Company A of the Second South Carolina Cavalry Regiment. Funded and equipped by Alexander Hamilton Boykin (1815-66), who served as the company's captain until October 1862, it was mainly composed of men from Kershaw District.

Alexander C. Haskell, Richmond, Va., to Charles T. Haskell and Sophia C.
Haskell (UNC)
9 July 1861

To be read in private by only Pa and Ma then tell Langdon & Sophy & Ella &c.

My dear Father & Mother & all at home,

I wrote because I have done something which though of deepest interest to me, is yet of great importance to all who love me. Now here you must stop & really keep a secret until I write to reveal it. I am engaged to be married & intend, if I get through the wars, to bring you as noble a daughter as your hearts can desire. Deka Singleton has rewarded my two years, three years, of faithful affection, and has promised to be my wife. Don't it sound strange to you? She says that the war convinced her that I was not alone in my anxieties & doubts during last winter's campaign, & then it was that my fortune came into the ascendant.

Do try to be as happy as I am, for although she has faults which you can see, which she will tell you & which I plainly see, yet there are few women as pure, as honest, truthful & noble. I am indeed happy to have won such a prize. Willy is the only one in reach to share my happiness which he does from his very heart, well knowing who it is I have got. For all know one little thing generally dreaded. She is nearly a year older than I! But for all I care she might be ten years older if she were in all other things as good as now.

It was the only objection she made, & it was made until I avowed myself quite reconciled to the fact. Do Ma & both of you write to Deka to my care (enclosed). Tell her how gladly you will welcome her for I know she fears. She has not always had a congenial though a loved home.

As to my prospects, I must remain in Virginia. Gregg has twice told me that he preferred me to anyone else for Adjutant of his new Regt & will give me as fine a position as a young man could desire if he can oust the young Army officers who want it & get me appointed by the President. Willy will probably succeed with his company. He is warmly seconded by Colonel Gregg who really takes our cause to heart as if it were his own. I hope Langdon will not think of coming on unless he can get a good commission in one of the new Regts called from the State. His duties are far above the ranks. I have seen & know this. John Bacon[50] joins me in urging it.

Goodbye, love to all.

---

[50] This may have been John Edmund Bacon (1829-95), commissary of the Seventh South Carolina Infantry Regiment.

William T. Haskell, Richmond, Va., to Sophia C. Haskell (SCHS)
9 July 1861
My dear Mother,

I slip a sheet into this letter to tell you of my state of somewhat ennui which a tedious & unexpected delay in the city causes. I hope soon to get away & further my design of raising a company. This I have got to regarding as a fixed fact but still there is as ever room for failure & disappointment. Hence the need of every effort to hasten & secure the formation of the comp. This will require 64 men. A small part of these I have already got & others rely on getting by efforts made in Charleston as indicated by advertisement in Mercury, in Beaufort & Colleton & Columbia by friends who are [trying] to aid me. I have taken measures to get a few recruits in Richmond if possible, but this is doubtful.

I wrote to Pa on this subject some days since. Do ask him to find out as he can who will come on immediately to Richmond & I will write giving directions for transportation to Richmond. If any men never how small the number can be secured I want & need them at once. After I have the sixty four I can take my time but speed is on many accounts necessary now. Major Smith will I suppose soon return & when he comes back will bring the men for me. Love to all.

Alexander C. Haskell, Exchange Hall, Richmond, Va., to Sophia C. Haskell (UNC)
12 July 1861
Dear Ma,

I got your letter yesterday, but you had not time as yet to have got my letter of two days since, in which I told you of my happy engagement to Deka Singleton. Since then she has been sick, threatened with typhoid fever, but I am happy to say is much better today, and I hope out of danger of a recurrence of her illness. She has not been well for a long time, but promises to be for the future. I have been allowed to see her every day, a wise old doctor to the contrary notwithstanding, and I don't think it has done her any harm. My only regret is that you all cannot see us to learn our happiness as we feel it. I feel it my duty to my military prospects to remain here as in this way I will probably obtain the Adjutancy of Col Gregg's Regt whenever raised. And this is a position well worth waiting for. Tom Rhett's[51] advice is

---

[51] Thomas Grimke Rhett (1821-78), a career military man, was a first cousin of the Haskell brothers. His mother was Charlotte Haskell Rhett (1793-1871), the sister of Charles T. Haskell, Sr. Rhett was commissioned as a Confederate major in March 1861 and served on the staff of General Beauregard. In July 1861, he became assistant adjutant general and chief of staff to General Joseph E. Johnston. He was later transferred to the

that I should prefer it to a captaincy of the line. In case this should fail I would be much pleased to be elected to the command of a troop but I would not accept of a lieutenancy where I feel more knowledge & experience than perhaps my commander has had the opportunity of acquiring. I have not received Lomax's[52] letter nor Pa's only a hint of it in a note last night.

I perhaps might have neglected my prospects in going home had I not been so fortunate as to meet somebody in Richmond, for I really could not stand it any longer. You remember my confession last winter. It was then & is now day by day & almost hour during the whole long half year & the thought has beset me in one way or other, either to fill me with hope or apprehension as I was elated by hopes of success or heard of the chances of losing my prize. I must have gone to Columbia, if but for three hours to settle the question & then go to my duties again. I am received by the family in a manner that would warm your heart towards them. Mrs. S[ingleton] disapproved very much at first of the circumstances of the affair & its future, but spoke to me in the kindest [*sic*] so that after one day's disputation & argument and persuasion I carried my point all round & feel every inch a conquering hero.[53]

I am in haste. Will keep you advised. Goodbye & dearest love to all. Do write some kind letters to the dearest girl in the world. Tell Langdon I expect his best wishes & want to hear from him. You & Pa I hope have written already.

Goodbye.

Alexander C. Haskell, Richmond, Va., to Sophia C. Haskell (UNC)
16 July 1861
My dear Mother,

I don't know what to write or what to say about myself or my prospects. I was on the eve of starting for home today, but news has come that the Regiment in part may start very soon for Virginia. In this case Willy advises me & I can't but think Col Gregg advises it though he won't say, that I should remain to watch my chance for Adjutant. If I get that I am made for the war. If I do not I am thrown adrift with a hole in my pocket, which is

---

Trans-Mississippi Department and served as chief of ordnance for the District of Arkansas and then chief of artillery for the Trans-Mississippi Department.

[52] This may be Colonel Tennent Lomax (1820-62), commander of the Third Alabama Infantry Regiment. Later a general, he was killed at the Battle of Seven Pines. He was originally from Abbeville District, and there were other Lomax family members living there at this time including John Willis Lomax (1810-96) and Samuel Robertson Lomax (1816-86).

[53] Decca's mother was Mary Lewis Carter Singleton (1817-87), a widow.

being deepened by this waiting. Governor Pickens & Jeff Davis together are somehow in my way. Colonel Gregg however assures me that the matter shall not lack his urgent application as soon as the Regiment begins to be organized. This ought to get it for me.

As to my private personal matters I feel as if nothing could go wrong. I don't expect you to know how happy I am until long months have rolled away to the termination of this horrid war. Then when she is your daughter you will know what "Decca" is.

Nobody else has ever known her and nobody but myself knows now what a treasure I have got. She is the truest, noblest heart that ever lived & will I am sure be all you can desire. It is hard indeed that so many things now should keep apart those who so long to be together, but I feel it due to everybody now to cast everything into the scale to secure me a position of credit for the war for I fear it will be long enough to enter seriously as a long dark page in the chapter of our lives. If I could only be at home now I would be very happy.

I hope you have been getting my other letters for if not all this must sound more than strange.

I have found however to my cost how irregular the mails are, in my never having received three letters relative to the cavalry company. Do tell Mr. Lomax why it is impossible for me to answer what I never received. The command of a troop I am now competent to with a little practice & would give a great deal if it were in any way possible to get the place as a certainty in a company that wanted to come immediately into service. I heard yesterday from Tom Rhett. Mr. Tracy[54] tells me that Tom is quite well & has been made Colonel acting (or about to be) acting Asst Adjt Genl to General Johnson which I know he very much desired.

I have not heard a word from any of you since I have been in Richmond. Do write me & do write a kind letter to Decca, or she will dread that you are more hardhearted than her mother, who has not only relented, but has quite won my heart by her gentle kindness. I believe she really loves me already as if I were her son. She has a good deal to worry her as you know, two sons in the field & another hard to hold.

Goodbye & dearest love to Pa & all.

[P.S.] Decca sends love. Willy is quite delighted.

---

[54] This may have been Carlos Tracy (1825-82), a Walterboro attorney and politician who volunteered his services to the Confederate military. He served as a volunteer aide on the staff of Gen. Thomas F. Drayton and others.

Charles T. Haskell, Jr. to Charles T. Haskell (SCHS)
July 19th 1861
Dear Father,

I have been too sick since I left home to write before. I have suffered dreadfully from what I used to suffer from so awfully five years ago & had to be relieved by very severe treatment. I am pretty well now altho very weak still. In a few days I will write more fully.

Rebecca C. Singleton, Richmond, Va., to Charles T. Haskell and Sophia C. Haskell (SCHS)
22 July [1861]
My dear Mr. and Mrs. Haskell,

I thank you with my whole heart for your kind letters which I received yesterday. It gratifies me very much that you should be willing to take me on faith, and if a desire to please on my part will win you over, I shall feel quite sure of a small place in your hearts. I have made up my mind however not to be disappointed should you not think me quite worthy of your son, but always remember that you have unselfishly yielded the first place in his heart to me, and I shall only feel proud of the love and admiration you lavish upon him. I assure you your impatience to see me is not greater than mine to know you and having not met so many members of your household only increases my desire to become acquainted with the rest.

We have just returned from Ashland having gone up to take leave of my brothers who left this morning for Manassas.[55] The news of this awful battle made it harder than ever for us to bid them goodbye and my poor brother is quite overcome now that excitement is passed. Your sons are most impatient to resume their position in the advance and quite inconsolable that the great battle has been fought and they had no share in it. I fear the time is not far distant when they will be off and that there will be many more dearly bought victories before we can hope for peace.

Tell Sophie I hope she will write to me since it seems I have interested her sufficiently for her to make me the subject of a letter some time ago.

[P.S.] Give my love to Masters Louis and Paul. I have heard so frequently of them, that I am impatient to make their acquaintance. Decca.

Charles T. Haskell, Jr., Coles Island, S.C., to Sophia C. Haskell (SCHS)
26 July 1861
Dear Mother,

---

[55] Decca's brothers were Richard Richardson Singleton (1840-1900), Charles Carter Singleton (1842-99), and John Coles Singleton (1844-1919).

I have written very little for some time on account of having been sick. I am now however quite well again. I have heard as yet but little of the great action[56] that has taken place in Virginia, enough however to know that Bee,[57] Johnson[58] & Bartow[59] have all fallen, all of whom I knew, the two former quite well. I do not feel the uneasiness which I did at first with regard to those in whom we are most interested, but I have heard no particulars as yet.

I am no longer entirely in command of Coles Island, as Major Lucas has been sent down here to take command of all the Stono fortifications & of course of my batteries among the number.[60] There are now being constructed two more batteries on this Island & Major Trapier,[61] the engineer who ordered them, told me that there would be three hundred more men & a good deal more heavy artillery sent down here. Where the men are to come from I have no idea. Give my love to all.

John C. Haskell, Richmond, Va., to Charles T. Haskell (UNC)
3 August [1861]
Dear Pa,

I got your letter last night and I wish I could think with you that the war is virtually at an end, but I believe the grand struggle is yet to come. The whole party now in power have been for many years on an arc now pledged by political tenets to carry out their policy of the restriction and final destruction of all institutions predjudical [*sic*] either to their interest or mock humanity (free trade and slavery for instance).[62] They have been instilling

---

[56] The first battle near Manassas, Virginia, a Confederate victory, took place on July 21, 1861.

[57] Brigadier General Barnard Elliott Bee (1824-61) was mortally wounded at the Battle of First Manassas (or Bull Run).

[58] Lieutenant Colonel Benjamin Jenkins Johnson (1817-61), a field officer in Hampton Legion, was killed by a cannon ball that struck him in the head.

[59] Colonel Francis S. Bartow (1816-61), a brigade commander from Georgia, was shot down and killed at the Battle of First Manassas.

[60] James Jonathan Lucas (1831-1914) was appointed to the rank of major in June 1861 and was in command of the Fifteenth Battalion, South Carolina Artillery, also known as Lucas's Battalion, South Carolina Heavy Artillery, or the Dismounted Dragoons. In his memoir, James R. Hagood wrote that in addition to his regiment, "the First S. C. V.," there were "150 regulars under Major J. J. Lucas, and two companies of Volunteers" stationed on Cole (or Coles) Island during this period. Hagood, "Memoirs," 49.

[61] Major James Heyward Trapier (1815-65), later a general.

[62] John is referring to the Republican Party, a sectional party favoring northern interests. Its 1860 platform did not call for the abolition of slavery, but it did oppose the expansion of slavery into the U.S. territories, which was a prohibition, or "suppression," that the Southern states saw as an unconstitutional attack on their equality in the Union,

their principles into the people until a majority came to look with anxiety for the time when the South should be powerless in the hands of the North, to be despoiled at their pleasure. And when the present President went into office they looked on it as a fixed fact that the South was now theirs, that their tender consciences were to be salved by the suppression of slavery and that their pockets were to be filled by the suppression of free trade &c. All these golden visions must be dissipated by hard experience and hard knocks I believe before the people of the North will be willing to let the South be and mind their own business, and before this war stops I believe that they will have to be made so sick of it by starvation as to [rise] against their rulers and depose them from all power, for their rulers are the very men who have been for the last twenty or thirty years exciting their cupidity by false promises by which they hoped to get into power and afterwards to make good by oppressing what they thought would be the unresisting South. They have succeeded in getting into power. They have utterly failed so far in accomplishing their promises and unless they succeed in doing by force what they expected to do by knavery, they justly fear that they will be treated as impostors and hurled from their already precarious seats, so that with them it is a matter of life to keep up this war and I believe that actuated by no patriotic feelings they would rather engage the European powers in war[63] than give up an object (the subjugation of the South), the failure of which they know will be the death knell of their political influence and character, and I believe they hope that superior as they are in numbers, and taught as to their faults by the last fight to see their errors, to be able in the next encounter to wipe out their defeat by a brilliant victory, and though I feel confident that we will whip them in the end yet I cannot but think the event of the next battle exceedingly doubtful for from all the most authentic accounts on the day of the fight many on our side behaved most shamefully. A captain and fifty of his men belonging to the famous Legion were when Bee was killed four miles from the battle field, and Davis when he got to Manassas met between two and three hundred of the upper South Carolina regiments there and many

---

and an effort to diminish their political power. The Republican Party platform also called for increases in tariffs on imports, while the Southern states favored free trade. The promise of a protectionist tariff was a factor in the 1860 election, and helped the Republicans secure crucial electoral votes that would win them the presidency in November. In late 1860, the Morrill Tariff was working its way through Congress. It would raise the tariff rate to close to 40 per cent (later even higher) and greatly expand the list of taxed items.

[63] In early April 1861, William H. Seward, the U.S. Secretary of State, sent a memo to President Lincoln which suggested that the way to bring avert a war between the North and South would be to unite both sections in a war against foreign powers, namely Spain and France.

slunk off when they ordered back [*sic*]. They are the worst case that I have heard of, and they are trumpeted about in every direction by Virginians and citizens of every other state all of whom [seem] most jealous of So. Carolina. Nicholas' eyes are better.[64] They keep getting better and then worse. He is I am afraid rather too delicate for the very severe exposure that he will have to undergo and I can't get him fat. Sometimes he eats well and then again he scarcely eats his food at all and seems [sick] but I hope he may in time get more used to it. I have written, rather will write, several letters which will arrive with this.

Charles T. Haskell, Jr., Coles Island, S.C., to Sophia C. Haskell (SCHS)
8 August 1861
Dear Mother,

I only write to say that we are getting along much as usual, considerably extending the line of field fortification & improving the batteries & getting ready in every way by enlarging the magazines, hospital & quarters to make a hard fight some time after frost, when I suppose it will come if at all. Do tell Russell that the gunsmith cannot mend his gunlock without having the gun. I will send back the locks to him if he desires it. How is Joe getting? [*sic*] Do you think that a trip down here would do him good. The health of the command is perfect.

William T. Haskell, Camp near Richmond, Va., to Charles T. Haskell (SCHS)
18 August 1861
My dear Father,

I got here on Friday last at mid-day with eleven men besides Joe. The eight whom I expected from Camden failed to meet me at Timmonsville.[65] They did not receive my letter in time. I hope for their arrival here still at any moment, but cannot count on it certainly. I have here now 45 men whom I can depend on. If only now Grimke & Wigg are successful in Charleston I shall I think succeed, but great haste is necessary.[66]

I find the men much without supplies. Blankets & shoes are lacking & no immediate prospect of supply. I can say nothing certain as to results of my Comp. I think I will yet succeed but I may fail. Joe is domiciled with George Smith quite comfortably & although somewhat lonely & forlorn he does very well. I hope to make him quite easy soon.

---

[64] Nicholas was John C. Haskell's horse.

[65] Towns in South Carolina.

[66] These were John Grimke Rhett (1838-62), and (likely) William Hutson Wigg (1838-97), both of whom were second lieutenants in William T. Haskell's company. There was also a Samuel Patterson Wigg (1842-62) in the company, a corporal.

I do not know what to expect about more men from Abbeville. McGowan has telegraphed to W. Wardlaw[67] to come on. Cuthbert if coming has started. As to Boyd I have not been able to see Dr. Powell yet about his appointment as he has not come into camp. If he would come on however I have little doubt of his appointment.

C. T. LeRoy (King) I am told by his brother-in-law Belot intends coming on here in about ten days. If some blankets could be sent by him they would in case of my success be very desirable.[68]

I am in the midst of a dozen arrangements now & all the time. Am getting on however & making the men pretty comfortable which they were not by any means before. Do give my love to all, Ma Cousin Folly,[69] Sophy, Lou & all the boys. I will write again soon & be able to tell you more the next time.

Charles T. Haskell, Jr., Coles Island, S.C., to Charles T. Haskell (SCHS)
20 August 1861
Dear Father,

I have just received several letters from home & elsewhere, which have been delayed for some time in the office of the Quarter Master in Charleston. I wish hereafter that you would have my letters directed to "Coles Island Box 585 Charleston Post office." One of these letters informed me that Alick was at home & that Willy was in Charleston. I am sorry that I did not hear of it sooner that I might have gone up to meet him there. I wish I could do something to help him in raising his company. The same letter tells me that Joe is going to Virginia. I have heard nothing of John since he went on & should be glad if you hear from him to know where he is. The health of the post continues perfect, altho we have had excessive rains, & I think that if we can get safely through September, we will have nothing to fear.

Alexander C. Haskell, Charlottesville, Va., to Charles T. Haskell and Sophia C. Haskell (UNC)
26 August [1861]
My dear Father & Mother,

I write to you both again, to record the second happy event & to call upon you to redeem your promises. Decca has consented to terminate our engagement as soon as I think the necessities of our position demand. You may readily imagine how short a time will elapse before my marriage, it will

---

[67] This may have been William Clarke Wardlaw (1837-93) of Abbeville.
[68] This may have been Charles T. Leroy of the 19ᵗʰ South Carolina Infantry Regiment, who died on August 9, 1864, and is buried in Georgia.
[69] Ann Graham Florence Mason Rhett.

only await your arrival & perhaps some arrangements supposed necessary, which will not occasion much delay.

Mrs. Singleton was alarmed & shocked by the sudden nature of my proposal but like a good kind mother gave up after a few warm hours of persuasion. Decca took conviction from me the more readily, as she can hardly suppose anything unreasonable that I ask, so affected is she by the idea of the coming separation. You will not, cannot see into her or appreciate her until time has discovered her true nature to you, but then you will feel that I have had a happy lot indeed, in winning so noble and devoted a wife (I will soon write it so). I have found her among her relatives in Charlottesville & from them have received the most flattering evidence of affection & good will. I have found a Grandfather & Grandmother[70] who seem really quite & earnestly ready to win those names from me by their kind affection. Her aunt Mrs. Peyton[71] is my strong & devoted ally taking to me first from old attachment to Willy & Decca & now for my own sake. I will return to Richmond in a day or two & from there will write although you may be on the road by that time, for I assure you it may of necessity be a matter of extreme haste, as there is no rule for military movements. You may have to stay a few days in Richmond with me & I am sure you would enjoy it as a mere pleasure trip, independent of the fact that your son is to be married with so little of home about him, & that his wife must needs want some assurance of the same sort as your presence will give me. I won't mind the absence of the usual paraphernalia of a wedding if I can have you with me so you must come. Folly will either come with you or keep house for you until you go back. Bring Sophy if you can. I suppose I can get Willy & maybe the other two in Virginia & then those we love most will be with us. There will be no groomsmen &c but in times like these such things are not necessities.

Write instantly that your letter may be a forerunner.

Tell Folly I have found Tom's bundle of bedding in the hospital store in charge of Mrs. A. C. H. (that is to be) & that it will be forwarded to the proper destination tomorrow by Mr. Barnwell.[72] I am writing in haste. Do write to Charley at once. Tell him I will write too but that I am not at all sure of his direction. Goodbye, love to all. Prepare to come.

---

[70] These are likely Decca's maternal grandparents, Charles Warner Lewis Carter (1792-1867), a physician of Charlottesville, Va., and his wife Mary Chastain Cocke Carter (1796-1888).

[71] Martha Champe Carter Peyton (1830-1902) was a sister of Decca's mother Mrs. Singleton.

[72] This was Rev. Robert Woodward Barnwell (1831-63), who was married to Decca's sister, Mary Carter Singleton Barnwell (1837-63).

Alexander C. Haskell, Charlottesville, Va., to Charles T. Haskell (UNC)
28 August 1861
Dear Pa,

I wrote yesterday to you & Ma both to tell you that I have carried out your counsel to its fullest extent. I am to be married at once, before the Regiment is ordered off, & wait for your arrival, when both must come prepared for a wedding & to make it as hopeful as possible. Mrs. Singleton is so confounded at the mode of conducting the affair that she can't cheer up things much, & it would not be needed so much, but that Decca is very unwell & feels rather weak & dispirited. I hope though by the time you get here she will be much better, & that my departure may not have such bad effects. I am just writing this in haste in case my letter of yesterday miscarried.

Of course Willy & Joe or John will be the only supports on the interesting occasion. Several old ladies & middle aged ladies of this town I find were either confidantes or otherwise friends of your gay days.

Charles T. Haskell, Coles Island, S.C., to Charles T. Haskell (SCHS)
29 August 1861
Dear Father,

I have just received your last letter. I hoped to get by it some news of your crop as the rains down here have been so heavy as to prove very disastrous to the prospects of the planters of the vicinity. I hope however from my having heard nothing from you, or anyone else, on the subject that you have not had the same weather at home.

We are now most actively engaged making preparations for action. Telegraphic dispatches have been received from the War Department ordering all appliances to be brought to bear to put ourselves in the best possible condition for a fight. I have had the signals of various schooner rigged vessels and one steamer, all belonging to John Frazer & Co[73] sent to me by Gen Ripley—Major Lucas being absent—which vessels we expect to run in to Kiawah Bay under the shelter of our guns.[74] I know well enough from the maps & still better from my own soundings that whenever these vessels get within range of our guns they will be beyond all possibility of pursuit by the enemy except in gunboats or very light steamers so that I look for no fight arising from them. I think however that before the end of the year unless the enemy meets with a succession of reverses on the frontiers that we will have

---

[73] John Fraser & Company was a Charleston commission merchant firm engaged in blockade running.

[74] Roswell Sabine Ripley (1823-87), a Confederate brigadier general in command of South Carolina coastal defenses.

an attack in force on this coast, & therefore I must candidly say that I received with satisfaction this evening an order from Gen Ripley stating that near 1,000 troops would arrive at this post tomorrow. Of course this will put down Lucas & myself lower in command, but I do not mind that when I consider that without this reinforcement we would continue to be exposed as we have been throughout the summer to certain annihilation in case of an attack of the enemy in force.

3

LOVE AND LOSS

20 SEPTEMBER 1861 – 31 AUGUST 1862

Aleck, a newlywed, writes that his "long-waiting dream of happiness has been at last realized and accomplished." After his wedding in Charlottesville on September 10, 1861, he is ordered with his regiment to Suffolk, Virginia, taking his bride Decca with him. They set up housekeeping in a "very comfortable little establishment" in the town, and Aleck spends his days at the nearby brigade camp, where his brother William, now captain of Company H in the First Regiment, is stationed with the other newly reorganized troops under Colonel Maxcy Gregg's command. Langdon arrives at the camp in late September. In South Carolina, Charles is with his regiment on Edisto Island, where, in early November, he observes a Federal fleet bound for Port Royal, South Carolina. He soon reports, "the enemy is now in possession of Beaufort." In December 1861, when Maxcy Gregg is promoted to the rank of brigadier general, Aleck becomes his Aide-de-Camp with the rank of lieutenant. That same month, Charles is sent on another recruiting mission, John is appointed Commissary of Subsistence to General G. W. Smith with the rank of major, and Aleck makes a trip to South Carolina with Decca, leaving her in the care of his family in Abbeville for a while. As the year 1862 opens, Aleck is a captain and General Gregg's Assistant Adjutant General, Langdon is a lieutenant and Gregg's Aide-de-Camp, Joseph is in Richmond, and Charles has returned to Sullivan's Island, stationed first at Fort Moultrie and then at Breach Inlet. In March, John joins the staff of General D. R. Jones as Commissary of Subsistence. In early 1862, most of Gregg's Brigade is stationed on the southern coastal area of South Carolina, where they remain until returning to Virginia in April. Aleck is overjoyed when news reaches him of the birth of his daughter on June 20, but barely a week later, he is devastated to learn that his beloved wife has died. On June 27, 1862, Gregg's Brigade fights at Gaines' Mill, Virginia. Aleck misses this battle and others due to illness, but numbered among the severely wounded at Gaines' Mill is his brother John, who lost an arm while serving as Volunteer Aide-de-Camp to General James Longstreet. Mr. and Mrs. Haskell travel to Richmond to nurse John and his brother Joseph, who has typhoid fever.

William T. Haskell, Camp Huger near Suffolk, Va., to Sophia C. Haskell
(SCHS)
20 September [1861]
My dear Mother,

Since seeing you in Richmond we have changed quarters to this place where the prospects are we will remain for some time drilling regularly and steadily until we may call ourselves a well drilled regiment. The post is they say an important one; the RR being subject to attack by the enemy if he makes an incursion up through the Dismal Swamp or thereabouts.[1] Of the probability of this, I know not. We were a good deal disappointed at our direction being changed from Manassas to this place, but I dare say, it's all very well and I never think twice of it but shall wait and see what "turns up." You may have heard of someone's having ridden off Alic's mare the last evening I saw you. I am glad to say it has been recovered and is now safe in hands here. Alic is regularly installed as adjutant and is comfortably lodged in a good house a few hundred yards from the camp where Deka finds the quarters not unpleasant.

Joe is looking quite well and is now hard at work performing all the duties of a soldier which he is well able to stand & which will do him good. The place in which we now are is one quite preferable to our former one and also affords a better and less expensive diet. We are 22 miles from Norfolk and have heard several guns in that direction.

I have been quite well until the last two days when I was taken a little sick. I am happy to say now however that I am again all right. Do give my love to Pa, Sophy & all the rest and believe

Alexander C. Haskell, Suffolk, Va., to Sophia C. Haskell (UNC)
20 September 1861
Dear Ma,

I have been too busy for several days past to write an account of myself, but my good little wife took it upon herself to inform you that we were not only alive but well & to the admiration of the world, formal & conventional, together still. I spend the day in Camp & go in the evening to a pleasant, hospitable house in the town, about 1/3 mile off where Decca has a very

---

[1] Two railways ran through Suffolk, Va., namely the Portsmouth and Roanoke Railroad, and the Norfolk and Petersburg Railroad. The latter ran through the Great Dismal Swamp.

comfortable little establishment, besides this I dine with her every day. In the mornings she walks out shopping or receives a few visitors & in the evenings we generally have calls from the Regiment. Altogether it is a strange experience, but it would astonish an unsophisticated world to see how the "young creatures" manage to take care of themselves. Good luck has attended us from the beginning, in the midst of apparent misfortunes. We left Charlottesville, stayed two days in Richmond where I had the satisfaction of learning that my horse had been stolen, then receiving orders to march, Decca found to her horror a few hours before we started, a telegram informing her that she must leave her maid in Richmond, to take care of her sick master. She was an old family servant lent to Decca for the "Tour!" We left her and nothing daunted set out arrived in Petersburg that night. I went to work, found a very nice free woman trained to the business who was willing to follow us next day. I engaged her at once & she is giving the greatest satisfaction. There is good luck no. 1. Yesterday just as I was trying a broken kneed hack, trying to replace my mare cheaply, a man rode up on my mare, just arrived on the train from Richmond, found & sent down to me. There's luck no. 2. I was so happy to see Decca on her back this evening galloping along the beautiful roads here, that I felt the mare would have been a priceless loss. And what makes me not least happy is that I hope and believe that Decca's health is better. I am convinced that she is much happier and more contented & is willing to bear a great deal. She thinks & talks a great deal of you all, her dear Mamma & Papa, and will I am sure give you interest upon the affection you expend upon her. I am fairly in harness as Adjutant going regularly through my duties and to my own satisfaction and the infinite relief of my good Colonel without the shadow of difficulty from my disappearing impediment. I had no idea what a weight it was upon him, until the agony of the first trial was over.

It is bed-time & I am very tired. Decca I know sends her dearest love. She is not in the room, but wouldn't forgive me if I did not send it. Love to Pa, Ella, Sophy & the boys. I have got the best wife and am one of the happiest men in world [*sic*].

Rebecca S. Haskell, Suffolk, Va., to Charles T. Haskell (SCHS)
23 September [1861]

Whilst I am waiting for an answer from Sophie or Mama, I hope you will not consider, dear Papa, a letter misdirected if it is addressed to you. We have all been hoping most anxiously to hear of your safe arrival in Carolina, but suppose our letters are lying at the post office in Richmond and we must continue to wait for the pleasing intelligence. Letters directed to the obscure town of Suffolk in Nansemond County will find us out not much sooner than those sent to the metropolis where the office is so crowded with business. Indeed our little village has its advantages, and I shall be quite content to remain here for some time to come. I tried to make General Huger[2] tell me what was the probable destination of the regiment, but he affects to be ignorant himself. I had such a kind visit from the old gentleman this morning, and feel so self-reproached and condemned for all the unkind things I have presumed to say against him. A man so overflowing with the milk of human kindness will commit errors only of judgment not of heart. Do not think he won my heart because he spoke kindly of Alec, for I am so accustomed to hearing that from all the world, that I question if there was not something else which pleased me.

Elaine has been found, and I ride her out every evening to see the Adjutant on dress parade. The Colonel says he has a great deal of modest assurance to go through the district as if he had been accustomed to the place all his life and one of the captains would scarcely believe me that Alec had not had a military education.

Joe rode with me out to camp yesterday afternoon in his red flannel shirt which I think very pretty, but the company is getting heartily sick of. One of the Lieutenants went to Richmond yesterday for the uniforms, and I hope Willie's mind will soon be at rest about the comfort of his men. Joe has had one days holiday to go on an excursion to Drummond Lake which he says he enjoyed very much. When will Langdon join us? Alic seems to think he may abandon the idea of since the regiment has not been sent to Manassas. Give Mama, Sophie, Louis & Paul my love. I am sorry I cannot send Alic's, but he is at camp.

Alexander C. Haskell, Headquarters, First Regiment S.C.V., Camp Huger, Va., to Charles T. Haskell (UNC)
26 September 1861
Dear Pa,

I have just received your letter & write in answer what I have been wanting to say for some time but have been prevented by a constant demand upon my business hours. We are at Suffolk and Decca is with me as happy and contented a wife as ever made a husband feel reconciled to having brought his wife from her comfortable home to share the inconveniences & discomforts of his wanderings. I am in camp during the day, but the Colonel is so wondrous kind that I go into dinner every day & then every evening after dress parade I am released from camp until next day. I assure you I can hardly realize so far that I have been married in a time of war & trouble

---

[2] Benjamin Huger (1805-77), a brigadier general from South Carolina.

when marriage was to be but a doubling & aggravation of all discontents & troubles.

It has proved a panacea for me and I can say I am contented to meet my fate very cheerfully. I don't know what to say about your "little daughter" more than I have said already except that she is a most wonderful little wife or else if she is not a wonder, all wives are wonders. She is a noble, good & true woman & makes me feel ten times more of a man to rely & make my way in the world.

She is at a pretty comfortable house but very much alone. Her only amusement is to ride out in the afternoon to dress parade on her "beautiful Elaine" & then I join her if I can borrow a horse, or rather I have to bring her out if I can borrow a horse, & then take a ride. This is so essential to her health & happiness that my great wish now is for another horse that I may never disappoint her in her favourite exercise & amusement. I am very much tempted to run the risk and buy a horse to sell when she leaves me & have found a magnificent young mare at $225 but that sounds very high.

I have as you have learned before recovered my mare, without heavy expense & much to my delight as she surpasses as a lady's horse.

I must stop here for my drum has beat. Dearest love to all. Lang arrived today, is well & at work. Love to Ma & Sophy, Folly & all. Goodbye.

I am a happier son than I ever deserved to be of such a good father. Goodbye.

Charles T. Haskell, Jr., Edisto Island, S.C., to Sophia C. Haskell (SCHS)
26 September 1861
Dear Mother,

I write only a few lines to acknowledge various letters which I received yesterday, some of them quite old. The butter & everything else reached me in excellent condition. I have just arrived, from Stono, to rejoin my regiment. I do not much like the post, but no place can be healthier as we are all encamped on one of the finest beaches in the south.[3]

Alexander C. Haskell, Headquarters, First Regiment S.C.V., Camp Huger, Va., to Sophia C. Haskell (UNC)
30 September 1861
Dear Ma,

I write a line from my office to tell you we are all well and happy as circumstances & these by no means adverse will permit. Langdon is with me in

---

[3] Edisto Island is a sea island south of Charleston. Company D was headquartered at Camp Barnard E. Bee on the island.

my tent, of which I very often leave him sole possessor. He is rather disgusted at the idea of inactivity here, and really so far as I can judge by appearances I think our chances of wintering in this country are by no means small. Under the supposition that no active campaign is to be conducted on the Potomac, it is much best for us, for here in a healthy and mild climate the regiment will pass through all the camp diseases & become somewhat inured to service besides being well drilled before it takes the field.

It may be the policy to make the most of the 12 months volunteers & we being for the war to save us that we may step out in full condition when the others retire, which they certainly will do when their term is out. It was a great disappointment to us but I expect very good consequences to result.

Suffolk is a queer old town with no marked peculiarities save a certain Jewishness in all dealings with soldiers, but that is a propensity of the times which nothing but force of military law will correct. An amiable gentleman with whom I obtained lodging having found the exact amount of my account, charges it in full for my board & then with a show of prodigal hospitality, entertains the regiment.

It is rather a dull life I suppose for Decca, but she seems entirely willing to endure it & certainly to prefer it to going away. Mrs. Smith will soon be here too & make it more pleasant by the companionship.[4] I meant to write another page but am stopped.

Goodbye. Love to all, Pa, Sophy, Cousin Folly & the little ones.

I am your loving son, Alex C. Haskell

William T. Haskell, Camp Huger, Va., to Sophia C. Haskell (SCHS)
1 October 1861
My dear Mother,

I have not written this letter as soon as I had promised myself. I hope it will find you well as also all at home. Lally who arrived here some days ago brings us good accounts. Since our arrival here I have been more at home in the regular routine of the camp by far than in Richmond. Things are now more settled & I am beginning to reap in some degree the fruits of my labors & work & anxiety.

I have plenty to do & employ me, drilling, ditching, draining, sweeping, inspecting & other such constant points of duty & discipline so occupy my time that I wish sometimes for a little leisure.

Alic & Deka are quite well & happy. Alic has just got a new & better, cheaper place than hitherto to which he will move tomorrow. Langdon is

---

4 Mrs. Smith was likely the wife of General G. W. Smith. Her name was Lucretia S. Bassett Smith (1822-81).

quite well. Joe I think has begun his measles for which I have fixed him quite snugly in my tent on a comfortable cot with a floor beneath. All the measles so far have been of a mild type & I expect him to get over his as well as most for he looks otherwise much stouter than usual. If he needs it I will put him in a house in town.

Tell Sophy I have a letter in store for her. Love to Pa & all.

P.S. I will send the measures for the men tomorrow. If the pants, or so many of them as you can finish are sent to Charleston within 20 days my Lieut Wigg will be in Charleston & bring them on.

Alexander C. Haskell, Headquarters, First Regiment S.C.V., Camp Huger, Va., to Sophia C. Haskell (UNC)
11 October 1861
Dear Ma,

It is sometime since we received your letter, but being very busy I asked Decca to let her answer include both for the present, & she gave you I believe the information you asked for about Mr. Pringle from whom I hired George. I can't remember his initials. I think they are J. M. or J. W. but am not sure.[5] At any rate he is the only reverend of the name in Columbia & pastor of Christs Church, so that a letter to him can't go amiss & I would be glad to know that he had been written to & paid & I hired George early in August at $15.00 per month. I would be glad to know too if Mr. Pringle desires me to keep him or return him before I lay in his supplies for the winter, or if Pa would not find it more economical to send me Bacchus or some other who can't now be of any use in making cotton, but who could take care of my horses, learn to be a good servant & save $180.00 a year.

We are trying to live upon our means [as] I know times are hard, & though everything is fearfully expensive we may get along, but this boarding is prodigious everywhere we go considering that is the style of our living which however is very comfortable now, but this takes $50.00 a month & our soldier charities which we have to contribute to the poor sick & almost dying soldiers, some have died, of our regiment. It would certainly be a temporary saving & certainly a great final gain to me, if Pa would but give me now Bacchus to train as my future groom & domestic. In case he should agree with this view of the matter, he could send him on by express for one month's of George's wages, & you must supply him abundantly with neat, coarse, warm clothing, flannel hats & shoes & stockings, for it breaks me to get them at Virginia prices. But here I am rambling through business as if I had nothing else to write about.

---

[5] This was Rev. James Maxwell Pringle (1822-1905).

We are still as happy as your heart could desire, and though the honeymoon has passed we laughed with its last moments as it glided out & felt very sure that if permitted to live to see them, many, many months would be to the full as bright as that had been. It is hard I know to realize & prepare for all that may happen to us, but we try to be ready for the worst & if we escape that, will never quail beneath any of the lesser stings of fortune & pains of life.

I have more & more reason to assure you that I have got a treasure in my dear wife & one that will make me a very happy & a better & more earnest man than I could have been without her.

But the drum has beat & I must mount the guard, but while writing I must ask you about a maid for Decca. I think our hired servant is about to take her leave & Decca's maid is too sick to be serviceable enough to come on. Can you help us? Can you set us up in housekeeping now by giving us the use of [*illegible words*] or find out where I can hire a good servant for her. Decca knows nothing of this & says she is going to do without a maid and I don't think that right, leading the life we do.

Love to Pa & all, in haste.

[P.S.] I have given up my extravagant notions of buying another horse. We must get on as we are.

William T. Haskell, Camp Huger, Va., to Sophia C. Haskell (SCHS)
22 October 1861

I suppose you hear from the other boys in camp sufficiently often not to observe how derelict I have been of late in my duties of letter writing. If anything can take away one's inclination and faculty for writing, camp life in the form in which we now pass it seems most fitted for the purpose. My occupations though small are numerous and engrossing to an extent which I cannot well account for myself, there always exists that peculiar consciousness of something to do and not much done. This, no doubt, time and experience, system and regularity, instilled and attained in to by my men and self will remove. I am already much at ease compared with my condition in Richmond and really quite enjoy many points of camp life and habit as in the few months previous.

Your kind diligence in regard to the clothes will be most highly appreciated by the men whose wardrobes are in such a condition as to make the addition quite a grateful one. You told me to say what else would be wanted. In answer I would mention all kinds of coverings, thick or thin. I wonder the thick cotton blankets which the negroes used to get are not used. They are better than the woolen ones now used. A good cotton shirt would not be amiss for each man, some large and some small.

If you remember I spoke to you of some cap covers of which I have neglected to send you a pattern. The best material is some waterproof stuff, if none of that, thick woolen cloth which indeed may be the best. The form is simply that of a cap with a cape attached, a round piece is the top, two pieces form the circumference and then a full "skirt" falling on the shoulders with a button so as to be fastened in part under the neck. These would be good against rain and cold equally and tend much to preserve the caps. I am writing in the dark, will finish when I get a candle.

The candle has come and with it supper which leads me, as I believe I have finished other matters, to speak somewhat of my domestic economy. We, myself and three lieutenants, have two good servants who cook pretty well and are quite satisfactory in other respects. Supper is before me in the shape of a good loaf of cornbread, a plate of biscuits, a new and ambitious effort, molasses, pretty good coffee, butter has given out. Our dinner is beef frequently added to by fish, oysters, or poultry alternately. The company fares also quite well for camp and is in very good spirits and pretty good health.

Do give my love to Pa, Sophy, and the boys. All are well here. Joe better than before he had the measles. I will try and write soon again. Do send the things you have as soon as possible.

Joseph C. Haskell, Camp Huger, Va., to Sophia C. Haskell (DUL)
29 October 1861
Dear Ma,

I received your letter of the 20th yesterday evening and was very glad to get it. You have no idea what a treat it is for us here to hear anything from home. I am perfectly well again and though I have not commenced going on duty I am perfectly able to do so. It was a great comfort to me during my sickness, having the boys here with me as it saved me from a great deal of discomfort if nothing more.

We were very agreeably surprised today by a visit from uncle William who is on his way from Manassas where he has been to see Willie who he found recovering from a case of jaundice. This is very prevalent in our camp, quite a number being sick with it now. We were delighted to see him on his own account and because he had just left John and Willie. It is no use for me to write what he tells us as I expect he will be at home before this letter reaches you or perhaps with it as I will try and send it by him.

I am very much obliged to you for making those clothes I wrote for and hope you can send them soon. The blanket will be very acceptable as it is getting quite cold here. We had ice here this morning. The men all get up by daylight here to warm themselves by the fire, they find it so cold in the tents. I have no fears for myself as I am well provided for, but I am afraid it will get very hard with some of them here. Our company will get on very well I think from the supplies Willie is collecting. An installment of 40 woolen scarfs came this evening from the ladies there and is expecting [*sic*] some more soon. 3 recruits came in this evening and 4 more are expected here soon. I am afraid you will work yourself too hard, and I am afraid if you saw how much such contributions add to the comforts of the men, that you would only work harder.

The health and spirits of the Regt. are improving very much and I think will continue to do so since the cold weather has come on. The weather is beautiful. Every morning a perfect longing comes over me to take a good hunt. I could not stand it the other day so taking Lally's little gun and my pointer puppy which is very fine one, I sallied out and after having walked about 10 miles without killing anything returned home perfectly satisfied. Fine sport can be had here though, with a good dog and a person who knows the country.

I spent a great part of the day with Deka who appears to be in excellent health and spirits as far as I can see. She expects her horse tomorrow which I expect will make her time her much pleasanter. Do give my love to cousins Caroline and Follie if they are with you, Pa, sister Sophie and the rest.

Alexander C. Haskell, Suffolk, Va., to Charles T. Haskell and Sophia C. Haskell (UNC)
29 October 1861
My dear Father & Mother,

I received both your letters together, and so must answer them if I would have the response surely carried. Uncle William will tell you all about us, how and where we are.

I merely want to write & tell you what I meant to do before.

You offered me an income some time ago, which I am entirely conscious you cannot now give & which I would not think of asking for. And knowing that you had but little money & plenty of negroes I supposed you could easier help me by the services of a servant who could not do much good at home now, & that you could be spared the <u>money</u> expense by this arrangement. This was my reason for making the proposition that I did about Bacchus. The present arrangement is entirely satisfactory if not too expensive.

My other request had not this simple plea of expediency in which I had no selfish feeling, but I must confess it was very unreasonable, & soon as it was made and the letter sent, I repented of it and wished it unasked, but I was very much worried and still am, about Decca's having no servant, for her hired maid left some time ago. She says she does very well & does when quite well, but when sick or feeling badly I don't like the idea of her being so dependent on herself or the good graces of our hostess who, however, is quite kind.

But Decca was shocked at hearing of my demand & says she can do very well without. And I hope she can. So having cleared up this I must stop as Decca has been overexerted today seeing some friends & taking too long a walk, & feels sick and tired. I must stop writing and go to comfort her.

Joe is getting quite stout again. Willy & Langdon are perfectly well.

As to money matters, I have not drawn since you were in Richmond & at the wedding. I will draw on Mssrs. W & W if I find it necessary. It will be quite enough for our present wants as we are entirely alive to the necessity of economy, but there are a great many demands of common humanity to the sick & suffering around us that we cannot refuse, wh[ich] make us [live] up to our own means, but I hope we can keep inside of them.

Love to all. We hope to see Pa soon.

William T. Haskell, Camp Huger, Va., to Charles T. Haskell (SCHS)
31 October 1861
My dear Father,

Since my last letter to Ma I have been going on as usual quite domestic & busy in my mode of life, drilling, drilling all the time, not getting tired but quite occupied. In general we are getting on quite well, health is mending & spirits are good. A general content & cheerfulness with the usual allowance of special grumbling pervade the camp & shows the men enduring very well their probationary period of hardening and toughening. Col. Gregg inspires great confidence & has a thorough control of the command. Winter is very late in its approach, there having been no killing frost here until within the last two or three days.

The cold is of importance to us in regard to its requiring blankets & clothes beyond our capacities to furnish them. In respect to blankets my want I am afraid will be considerable. I hope to get substitutes by any means in all places. Supplies are beginning to come in from friends which will add much to our comfort. The pants Ma has will be a most acceptable present & come in very good time. If a package is sent to Charleston by the 15th or 16th of Nov, I will have a man to bring it on. I don't want to be extravagant or troublesome in my requests but I would suggest that a set of jackets, something of the style of the pants which you are making would be very acceptable.

If the good people of the neighbourhood could consider me within the pale of their charities & unite in a combined, associated jacket movement, a sufficient number for me might soon be made. If such a thing can be done I would mention as guides to manufacture full shoulders.

But I find I am only writing the common sphere of my daily thoughts & must leave it for matters of more interest. Joe received a letter a day or two ago from John who seems quite settled in his position which he owes no doubt to Cousin Tom. He has certainly sped well. I feared at first that he had gotten beyond himself but after diligent notice & examination I think he will & can hold his place with credit.

Joe is as well as the rest of us, in a high state of preservation & looking better every day. Uncle William has I suppose seen & given you full account of all things here. Do give my love to Ma & all the household.

Charles T. Haskell, Jr., Edings Bay, S.C., to Charles T. Haskell (SCHS)
4 November 1861
Dear Mother,

I have just rec[eive]d a can of butter and other things for which I am much obliged to you. I am just in the midst of moving from camp to quarters. Our camp was suddenly flooded last night by an extraordinary tide & we had to move off during a pouring rain & through the dark, about a mile, to the village which is now being fast abandoned by the inhabitants.[6] Eleven of the great fleet have past [*sic*] us last evening & this morning, up to ten o'clock & probably many of them during the night apparently bearing for Port Royal.

Charles T. Haskell, Jr., Edings Island, S.C., to Sophia C. Haskell (SCHS)
8 November 1861
Dear Mother,

I do not know whether you receive my letters or not but I scarcely think that you can have received several lately that I have written as there were several questions which I asked that, and altho unimportant, I am sure you would have answered. Before you get this letter I suppose you will have heard the bad news that we have been worsted at Port Royal, & that the enemy is now in possession of Beaufort with, I suppose, about 15,000 troops.[7] I do not know this officially as yet, but cannot doubt that what I have heard is correct in the main. I have been in full hearing of the whole affair & in sight of the smoke of the guns & towards night of the first day I

---

[6] Edings Bay, better known as Edingsville, was a village on Edisto Island which was a summer retreat for the island planters.

[7] A massive Union fleet descended on Port Royal harbor in November 1861 and succeeded in capturing the town of Beaufort and neighboring areas including Hilton Head Island.

thought that I could see occasionally, just above the horizon, the flash. With such a force as they have, probably landed of course, they will give us a great deal of trouble, & I suppose that South Carolina will be one of the scenes of action throughout the winter. As yet there are not at most more than 7,000 men on our side concentrated near Beaufort. They are enough however if properly commanded. There is I fear our weak point, Ripley, whether he has or has not the requisite ability for a commanding general, and I think he has not. Certainly is not relyed [*sic*] upon by those who serve under him. I am sure that the prestige of having a commanding general in whom we all could feel confidence would be of immense service to us & I sincerely hope that one will be promptly sent. As there is no certainty as to the movement & destiny of our little regiment of 600 men I will tomorrow pack up all my effects that I have with me, except such articles as I need & send them to Uncle William in Charleston.

Do not be alarmed too much if you do not hear from me, as I think that the mail communication will be cut off. I think that there will be bloody work during the rest of this month. You had better cease writing to me at this place & direct instead to care of Hutson Lee,[8] Charleston.

William T. Haskell, Camp Huger, Va., to Sophia C. Haskell (SCHS)
17 November 1861
My dear Mother,

I got y[ou]r letter two or three days ago & have to thank you for it very much, for as I write less I feel I have less right to expect letters, & value them the more when they come.

I cannot thank you enough for your kindness & trouble in working at my interminable pants & other articles of botheration. The hospital boxes which you spoke of before & sent by Wigg came safe to hand & were very gratefully rec[eive]d by Dr. Powell, as also two others which you mentioned as being on the road & which arrived yesterday evening. All that I have heard of Sophy lately is that she is devoted exclusively to the manufacture of stockings. Do tell her to write to me whether she has time or not to devote from her vocation.

We have been much excited & moved about the news from Beaufort, which is certainly not good. But I regard it as one of the accidents, [inevitable] results of the inequality of force, & when the first blush is over it will I think be no more than a naval occupation of the harbour giving employment

---

[8] Major Hutson Lee (1843-99) was the Confederate quartermaster in Charleston. His wife was Eliza Lucilla Haskell Lee (1836-1905), the daughter of William E. Haskell.

for a good many troops on our part but involving not much more loss than what has already taken place.

The weather is getting quite cool here & making us quite active about preparing winter quarters. The cold spurs up the work & the hope of returning to Carolina rather dulls the spirit. About going home I have now scarcely any expectation & perhaps no wish considering the matter with reference to the continuance of the war. For if we go down on the coast it will be simply I think to establish a kind of land blockade of an indefinite duration, while here we are nearer the seat of active operations & may be called on at any time to join in the positive & aggressive warfare which is to succeed the present mode of defensive policy.

The regiment is rapidly becoming a very efficient one, occupied chiefly in drilling, grumbling, etc., etc., etc.

Double quick is now our great institution. The drill will soon be entirely of that kind giving us ample exercise & promoting in this cool weather health & digestion.

Do give my love to all at home. We are all quite well here. I very seldom see Deka, I am so entirely confined to camp.

John C. Haskell, Centreville, Va., to Sophia C. Haskell (UNC)
7 December 1861
Dear Ma,

I got your letter together with Pa's and Sophie's some days since when I was too sick to be able to write at all. Since then I have got well and at last up. I am still so weak that I cannot walk about but very little. I believe I had what they call camp fever, which lasted about seven days and then left me. This is the second day since I have been free from fever and I am beginning to feel like a well man again.

Cousin Tom treated me very kindly while sick, and all the other officers were exceedingly kind but still I never want to be [sick] in camp again.

They have again raised the cry of fight and it was so much credited that Genl Johnston summoned all officers back and they are getting ready. They even had the plan of attack [fixed] but it seems to be growing less likely and I am afraid is a false report.

I don't feel well enough to write much but will write again in a day or two. Do give my love to Pa and all.

Charles T. Haskell, Jr., Atlanta, Ga., to Charles T. Haskell (SCHS)
7 December 1861
Dear Father,

I have been sent off again on recruiting service & have been a week at this place. I have met with no success thus far & shall therefore leave tonight for Nashville. I have success very much at heart for the very existence of our regiment depends on our getting several hundred recruits. If we fail, my predicament will be a most unpleasant one next spring, when the term of enlistment of the men we now have will have expired, as not more than half of them now show any disposition to reenlist. For the next week at least I will be at Nashville, & will notify you of any change of post.

Alexander C. Haskell, Camp Huger, Suffolk, Va., to Charles T. Haskell, Abbeville, S.C. (UNC)
9 December 1861
Dear Pa,

I got your letter day before yesterday and certainly on reading it reciprocated all the apologies for not having written. It certainly is, if not an age, a considerable part of one, since I have either sent a letter, or received one from home.

I am just turning to the point of escape from a very trifling attack of scarlet fever which has kept me in bed and house for some days past. I am up today but not yet out, though I think I might be if they would but let me. The part of the business that annoys me most is that my dear little wife, who has been nursing me as diligently as if I had been really ill, will probably take the fever. I only hope that if she does it will be as light as it has been with me.

I believe Decca has been writing to all of you, but has never heard whether her letters have been received. In them was information conveyed of our intention of endeavouring to pass the winter in a log hut, made as comfortable as can be with our present small notions of comfort, which we are obliged to cut in accordance with the extortion of the Jews who hold in their hands such treasures as frying pans, tin spoons, oak split chairs, and no et ceteras for these about fill the list.

The only trouble however is that it is very difficult to get the hut such as it is, built and daubed.

The men have been very busy with their own quarters & will continue so for some time to come as they are but slow workers. I have wished for

Cuffee a thousand times, as he would show them a new mode of handling pine poles.[9]

Mud huts have decidedly risen in the social scale when a young married pair ask for nothing but that theirs may be allowed them. I am coming fast to Grandpa's conclusion that a cover for our heads is all we want, only provided it is warm & keeps out most of the wind and rain.

I trust in a few weeks to write to you from "Mud Cottage" if I can get out to see to its building. I wish that you would help me in a small matter that is a great trouble here, viz, getting some winter clothing for George, my servant, and a pair or two of very heavy shoes about no. 10 or 9, at least one suit of heavy coarse cloth, coat, vest & pants is necessary, with some coarse warm shirting and under clothing. I can't get them here except at great expense & if you could have them made and sent by express, I would be very glad. Write to Mr. Pringle about it if necessary and perhaps deduct it from the wages. I would be glad to have a serviceable old overcoat sent to him, if such can be had. He is about Richard's height & stouter. His coat had best be a long sort of jacket sack, wh[ich] is sure to fit.

I commissioned Uncle William to get me an overcoat, of which I am much in need. The one he mentioned would ruin me. $20.00 is more than I can stand. I don't want anything finer than good homespun if I could get it, any heavy dark or grey cheap cloth that will turn snow & rain will answer. We have had snow already on the ground for four days but it is all gone & the weather is quite mild again.

I have not answered Uncle William as I have been sick when I meant to do so, but I hope he has had no idea of ruining me by sending the coat he mentioned.

I am truly grieved at the state of things in Carolina, and if I did not feel so weak & badly now might express the desire I feel to be there and share the common lot & give the Yankees a taste of "Gregg [*unitellible words*]" in all modesty I think it would surprise them after Drayton.[10]

I have just received orders from the Colonel to get well as fast as I can as he wants me at post again in obedience to warnings from Head Quarters as matters are coming to "now or never" in Virginia.

Decca sends her dearest love & says she does not consider your apologies for not answering her letter at all necessary as she writes without waiting.

Kiss all for me.

---

[9] Cuffee is described in Aleck's memoir as "a black African and the best carpenter, all around, that I ever knew." Daly, *Alexander Cheves Haskell,* 12.

[10] Brigadier General Thomas Fenwick Drayton (1809-91) was in command at Port Royal, S.C.

John C. Haskell, Centreville, Va., to Sophia C. Haskell (UNC)
18 December 1861
Dear Ma,

I suppose you got my short answer to your letter which I received while I was sick. You ask about the bundle which you sent me. I have never received it or heard of it though I got three persons to look for it when I heard that it was down there. They could not find it and then Cousin Tom wrote to the Chief Q[uarter] M[aster] Clerk at Richmond and he searched every store house but could not get it or find anything about it, and wrote back that it had probably been lost. I have managed to get more blankets from the Quarter Master but I am really in need of some other things. And if it is not too much trouble I would be very much obliged if you would send me more thick drawers and a few white shirts as all my supply of both these things besides other articles of clothing were burnt up in the cars on the way from Richmond by a spark falling in the car where my valise was. I had some colored flannel shirts which I have been wearing ever since but every now and then, aids are called on to dress respectably, and I should like to have them. When with you say you sent me a quilt which would have been very acceptable if it had only come [*sic*]. I am very glad to see that Col. Gregg has been made a Brigadier as I think he will be a decided improvement on any that we have in Carolina unless it is Genl. Pemberton.[11] And I hope that he will make Alex his Adjutant General. They have not commissioned me yet, but General Smith wrote again last night urging my appointment and if they do not give it to me I can still get the position of Adjutant General on Genl. Elzey's staff if he does not get on before it has been offered to me again, but I would much prefer remaining on Genl. Smith's staff if I can get a commission on it.[12] It is getting very tiresome here and I don't think there is the least chance of a fight, though I heard both the Generals say yesterday that they were more certain now of a fight than ever, but I don't know what their grounds are. When we get into winter quarters and get everything settled I intend to apply for a furlough and I have no doubt but that I can get it as all the rest of the staff have had leaves of absence and it will be my turn. If I can get it I will come home for a little while at least sometime this winter but I can't say when.

Do give my love to Pa and all the rest.

P.S. I forgot to say that the way to send anything to me is to send it by Adams Express Co. at Manassas.

---

[11] Brigadier General John Clifford Pemberton (1814-81).
[12] Brigadier General Arnold Elzey (1816-71).

Alexander C. Haskell, Charleston, S.C., to Langdon C. Haskell (UNC)
24 December 1861
Dear Lang,
    You are the General's regular Aid. I am his Asst Adjt Genl, Captain. I start in an hour for Columbia. The General will be in Columbia at convention.[13] Meet him there.
    All is right. We go to Port Royal.
    God bless you all & a happy Christmas for which we should be grateful.
    [P.S.] The General offered your place & then I told him enough to make him sure you were obliged to him for it & would accept.

Langdon C. Haskell, Abbeville, S.C., to Charles T. Haskell (SCHS)
26 December 1861
Dear Father,
    Yesterday I received the letter which I send you, announcing Alick's promotion & my appointment as regular Aide de Camp with the rank of Lieut[enant]. Knowing that I should not be wanted at once, I will remain here today. Tomorrow morning I go down.
    Joe's interests will be looked after by Simkins and the Judge, also by Alick and the General, if he is willing to say anything for him. We are a good deal troubled by Louis Simkins being taken with the measles in the house.[14] I suppose poor little Pete will have to have them. I don't see how it can be avoided, though Ella has sent him off to Parker's[15] to be put out of the way. Give my love to all at home.

---

    [13] Maxcy Gregg was made a brigadier general in December 1861. The convention that he was attending in Columbia began as the Secession Convention in December 1860, of which Gregg was a member and one of the signers of the Ordinance of Secession. The convention reassembled in December 1861, effectively superseding the regular state government by the creation of an Executive Council with legislative and executive powers. The convention dissolved in December 1862, and the Executive Council was abolished by the state legislature.
    [14] Lewis Wardlaw Simkins (1854-1903) was the son of John Calhoun Simkins (1828-63).
    [15] This probably refers to the household of William Henry Parker (1828-1905). His wife was Lucia Garvey Wardlaw Parker, (1833-97), the sister of Ella Wardlaw Haskell (Mrs. Langdon Haskell).

John C. Haskell, Centreville, Va., to Sophia C. Haskell (UNC)
29 December 1861
Dear Ma,

I got your letter a day or two ago in which you say that you have heard of my being sick but have not got any letters from me. I have written five or six times and where they are lost I can't imagine. I don't know whether you have got my last letter to Pa. I have been commissioned and have given up all idea of what I wrote about as I don't on further looking into the matter believe that it will succeed or in fact be attempted. What my rank is I don't know but have received other news from the Adjt Genl that my commission has been made out and I expect to receive it soon. I have just heard that Alex has gone South with Genl Gregg but I have not heard in what capacity and as he never answers my letters I don't suppose I will hear from him. Do when you write next tell me what his position is and when and how Deka is. I wrote to both of them several times but never got any answers but perhaps my letters to them met no better luck than those which I write home. We move in a few days into Winter Q[uarte]rs which are nearly completed. For the last day or two there has been some little excitement and a little skirmishing on the front and a good many think a fight is intended but I have lost all expectation of a fight before next spring and will not look for one till it comes.

You say in your letter that Charley is in Nashville recruiting. I wish he would give up his Regiment where he can not in all probability get above a captaincy and try to get up a Regiment for he would make a much better colonel than nine out of ten who are in this army and he would have more chance of showing himself.

Do give my love to Pa and all.

Alexander C. Haskell, Columbia, S.C., to Charles T. Haskell (UNC)
29 December 1861
Dear Pa,

I am in Columbia with Decca within one day of you & can't run up for a few hours visit. The General is here under orders, attending the Convention, liable to being summoned by telegraph at any moment. And of course as his chief of staff I must be ready to move with him. For this reason he was obliged positively to decline allowing me to go out of the telegraphic region. It is a great disappointment not to have seen you and it would have been very pleasant to have brought Decca to you myself. She will come up to Abbeville with Joe when I go away, which will be I suppose in a few days. I am sure you will find her a pleasant addition to the family and I feel much confidence in her finding a comfortable & cheering retreat in your midst. I sup-

pose I will be in a battle, perhaps several, before the war is over, though I
have been singularly excluded heretofore, and in case of such events becoming common, the company one bears very materially affects the manner in
which such anxieties can be borne.

I am rather uneasy about Decca's health. She was very strong until last
winter when she was very sick, & her health suffered much. Though much
better I think she still needs care, though she don't admit it, and a great deal
of walking & driving in an open buggy. To this [department] special attention must be devoted & I think she will recover entirely. I want Ma to cure a
dreadful cold & cough that have been hanging to her daughter for some
time & she will have fulfilled the requests of her son who is mightily impressed with the greatness of the trust which has come upon him.

You no doubt have heard of my appointment & consequent promotion
to at least the rank of captain. It is great good fortune which has taken possession of the family & wh[ich] I hope will carry it through. I have been so
accustomed to hearing of "old Major Haskell" that I have been ambitious of
achieving it for myself. The prospect of success is fair if the war lasts long
enough.

I shall probably be in Columbia two or three days longer. Langdon
went to Charleston this morning. Joe stands some chance for an appointment. The Governor told him he had reserved a commission for me not
knowing I was provided for, which I shall tomorrow ask him to transfer to
Joe.

Goodbye. Love to all.

Charles T. Haskell, Jr., Nashville, Tenn., to Sophia C. Haskell (SCHS)
31 December 1861
Dear Mother,

I have been now some time in Nashville, since my last letter from Augusta, Georgia. I wish very much that I was through with the business that I
am engaged in as it is worrying enough. It is labourious enough to get the
men & after you have got them it is very hard to keep them as there are
many other recruiting officers here who do not scruple to steal them. Only
yesterday I lost through the tricks of a set of lawyers nineteen out of twenty-
five men. I think that I shall try & get relieved from this post, if not entirely
from the recruiting service as I find it anything but a pleasant place. I suppose that I shall be here tho at best a week or so more and will receive any
letters you may direct here.

Alexander C. Haskell, Headquarters, Second Brigade, to Sophia C. Haskell
(UNC)

7 January 1862

Dear Ma,

I won't attempt [*sic*] disguise the fact that it is very hard for me to write to anybody else than my dear little wife, when I have a leisure moment with my pen; but I am afraid you will begin to think I have forgotten you, unless I write to tell you I have not stopped loving you all, and do more now than ever, for the care you are taking of my treasure. Decca writes to me of her reception & her establishment in my home. I hope she will be as happy as I have been there, and I feel quite confident that nothing will be lacking from her father, mother, brothers or sisters to make her forget that it is a very sad thing to be parted from her husband, whom she has taken such a strange and unaccountable fancy for. I wonder even now how it is that my long-waiting dream of happiness has been at last realized and accomplished. After a while when you have won your daughter really to your heart and found out what is in her, write & tell me if you are not happy in my fortune.

You have heard of my whereabouts & doings by my letters to Decca. Everything is quiet about here and it is the old game of waiting for the Yankees to advance. I assure you we would not wait if there was any feasible mode by which we could get at them, but this is I believe entirely impracticable. We have a fine country here for defence, and one in which as small may successfully cope with a greater force and give us a certain victory if our men but remember their name and blood.

I have strong hopes in the conduct of the men since Gregg has come among them. He has a wonderful way of inspiring daring & confidence, by his air & presence, without a word to his troops. Men who would scamper like rabbits with other leaders, would follow him into the breach as a forlorn hope. This is all that our men need to make victory certain if the enemy land. For beyond dispute the Roundheads of this day will run if the Cavaliers do not.

Langdon is quite well & seems to be enjoying the life as much as I do. Do give my love to Ella & Pete. I have just time to write this line before dinner. I leave Decca's letter for the small hours of the night. After finishing her letter last night at 1 o'clock I went to bed & was just well asleep, when comes a rapping at the door—despatches from Head Quarters—up I had to get & sit shivering & writing till nearly 4 o'clock, to send off answers & orders, when back to bed I went & not even Decca's paper comfort could get me warm until this morning's sun called me up. Tell Decca I was never better in my life in spite of these irregularities. I feel as fresh & well as she could possibly desire. Kiss my darling for me twice & give my love & kisses if you will to Pa & all members of the household.

Alexander C. Haskell, Jericho, S.C.[16], to Charles T. Haskell (UNC)
16 January 1862
Dear Pa,

I am glad to see that you do not regard my attentions to "my dear little wife" as you very properly call her, as by any means rendering me worthy of being cut off from other family favour. The truth is I have been kept very constantly at work and one letter a day after holding my pen in my hand from eight to twelve hours, was as much as I could manage, however I am less occupied now. I am writing five letters tonight.

I am really glad to hear of your fortunate escape from an unfortunate accident & hope that Robin[17] will never do so anymore. I wish he had the feet & legs of the swiftfooted Elaine under his powerful body & then not even falling through a hole would endanger you.

You speak of Joe. As to "little offices" about me I am sorry that such things do not really exist and I cannot with propriety drag one in. Besides were the General to allow any such, which he certainly will not, he is forestalled on every side. I think if Joe is determined on service, the pleasantest place for him would be in the "Marion Artillery" of Charleston, a fine light battery & commanded by Edw[ard] Parker, who married Emma McCord, a man, from all I can learn, combining those amiable & excellent traits of gentlemanly character & ability of such order, as to make him a singularly good captain.[18] The Company is composed of young men of good family & position. Chas. Pinckney, Hen. Frost, Ed. Mazyck, Lowndes & many others of like character, some of them known to Joe, & many friends of mine, who will make the association very pleasant to him.[19] Their term of service will not be more than a year & probably within the State. It allows more chance of change than most others & will probably be disbanded (temporarily) in case hostilities should cease in this quarter. I think it would be better for him than to go back to Virginia.

Langdon got a letter from Uncle Wm. this evening; he speaks of your coming down & bringing Decca with you. I know she would come with the hope of seeing me, in which you must not encourage her, for much as I

---

[16] There was a plantation in St. Helena Parish in Beaufort District called Jericho (or Jerico), but it is unclear from the letters if this was the place being referred to or another place by the same name.

[17] Robin was a Haskell family horse.

[18] Edward Lightwood Parker (1828-92) was the captain of the Marion Light Artillery, at this time an independent artillery organization for coastal defense, also known as Parker's Company. His wife was Emma McCord (1830-50).

[19] These were likely Charles Cotesworth Pinckney, Jr. (1839-1909), William Henry Frost (1841-1926), Henry Deas Lowndes (1829-95) and Edmund Mazyck (1840-93).

would give to see her, I could not do it now at a less cost than my commission. The orders are positive against furloughs for any cause but sickness. It is very hard thus to dash away the hope if it existed, but I fear I am compelled to do it decidedly. I could not go to Charleston unless I could get some serious hurt or sickness to send me there. And though I might wish this Decca would not. I am very glad to hear that she is looking better. She writes constantly of your kindness and affection to her at home and is I believe as happy as she could be, if I, unfortunately, could be left out of the question.

I hope the prospects of next year are cheering. I don't think the war will last to the end of this. However the turn you have given your planting operation is wise whether we have peace or war, for cotton will bring small prices at first I fear. Two crops in hand & many mills stopped in Europe.

Give my love to Ma, Sophie & all. Kiss Decca & let her pass it for me to Ma & Sophie.

[P.S.] There is not a word of war news to give. I forgot that I was in the army except that I was away from home.

Alexander C. Haskell, Headquarters, Jericho, S.C., to Sophia C. Haskell (UNC)
22 January 1862
My Mother,

I received your kind letter of the 19th this evening. It is true that I hear very constantly from you all, and you well know how pleasantly, but I would not willingly forego the pleasure of getting a letter from you every now and then as in old times. You know the only news I care about much in the letters is to hear that you are all well. There is something else in the thoughtful kindness of them that affects me much more.

I assure you I appreciate your few words, though many for you, about Decca, because coming from you I know they are true & sincere. It would have taken much from the happiness of my married life, had I brought discord into my own family, or carried it into that of my wife. But I see how you have adopted her; and you know how I have been warmly & cordially welcomed as ever son and brother was, so that all in these respects, is as happy as we could have wished. I daresay I seem very foolish, but I cannot help my importunity, and now you will fully understand my solicitude, and feel why it was that I so wished my Mother's heart and care and sympathy to be given to my poor little wife. God bless you & all for your love and kindness. It takes a load off my heart. I have said enough, perhaps too much, but I know well to whom I am speaking. If anyone should know my heart, besides my wife, it should be my Mother.

We are all quiet and well here, nothing doing and nothing in immediate prospect. Lee has been represented in satirical pictures, with a double barreled spy glass in one hand, and a spade in the other reconnoitering the position of the enemy, ready to retreat a little & throw up fortifications, the instant he set eyes upon them. This is unjust to a fine officer, but it does somewhat exhibit his very cautious policy, cautious now with a good reason, but I think he might by vigorous measures put himself on an aggressive footing. Defence however is his fixed policy.

The climate here is too warm, it is pleasant for a while, but I preferred the bracing cold of Virginia. We have had steady rainy weather for a week, with almost summer warmth. I hope for clear weather and a more active life.

Langdon has received the funds of which you spoke, and will soon get a horse. Joe need be in no special haste, and if Pa wants him to go to Arkansas I think it an excellent opportunity for him to see something of the western life and country. It is late. Goodbye my dear Mother. Love to Pa & all.

William T. Haskell, Camp [Butler], Franklin Depot, Va., to Charles T. Haskell
(SCHS)
14 February 1862
My dear Father,

I have been so much more than ordinarily busy of late that I have not written before of our movements & excitements neither having been very great as yet however.

I am at present one of three comp[anies] stationed at the Blackwater on the Roanoke & Seaboard R. R., our occupation obstructing the river, constructing light defences at favorable points, thus forming a guard to the R. R. bridge & the navigable stream reaching up to it. These objects we are able without difficulty to effect as the river is very narrow allowing trees to meet when felled on either bank. The change from our comfortable quarters to camp in tents is made very agreeable so far by the fine weather that we have had, but rain I am afraid will put an end to this. All parties seem in good spirits at having something to do. I have not heard from any of you for some time but I suppose will soon.

The enemy have Edenton about 80 miles from here. I suppose they will hardly come up this high 150 miles.

The taking of R. island with its particulars you have seen more than I daresay as I have hardly seen the newspapers since coming here.[20] Direct letters as usual. I don't think there is special ground to expect much further immediate effort on the part of the Y[ankees].

---

[20] Roanoke Island in North Carolina was captured on February 8, 1862.

Alexander C. Haskell, Headquarters, to Sophia C. Haskell (UNC)
16 February 1862
Dear Ma,

I have nothing to tell about but myself & not much at that. Never since the beginning of the war have I had such a dull uninteresting time. It seems to my wistful imagination now, that if I had the Virginia life over again, I could write a romance every day for Decca's amusement. But here as usual all my vacant hours are filled with thoughts of her & home, and if they don't give me something to do pretty soon I am afraid I will get homesick. I have not heard from any of you for a long time except Decca, and I suppose you think she gives me more than my share of news. She does tell me of everything that goes on and how happy and well & contented she is, but I want a little extraneous evidence. Really her health has been so delicate for the last eighteen months, that I feel very anxious to hear of Abbeville having worked wonders for her that it has for some others. But I suppose I must be content to hear that she is as well as when I left her. Nobody except the soldiers are expected to improve much in war times.

Military events are taking a more stirring & exciting turn of late & by the latest intelligence from the west, I hope a turn in our favour. Having been in service now more than a year & not having been in action I suppose our turn must be coming before long & when it does I trust it will be such a turn as will give our dear country a decided lift out of her troubles.

I wish Pa was at home again, not for any danger there is in his journey, but because with the rush of troops & munitions of war, the RR route must be slow & fatiguing. It may interest him however & do him good.

I have not seen Charley but hear that he is looking very well and I am really glad to say, recovering his hair. He is success [*sic*] in his recruiting expedition seems to have been very encouraging. I can't leave my post even for a day or I would try to see him. I live in hope however of getting a short leave after a while to run up to Abbeville, just to see what will be the sensation of finding myself actually a married man on the old place where I was a child, and for the happiness of finding my wife established there as your daughter. Not to speak of the greater considerations of seeing that wife and my mother again. They say I make a pretty good soldier, but I feel very little like one when I think about home. I am nothing but a softhearted boy again, & worse than I ever was. Decca is to blame for this aggravation of any tenderheartedness. Goodbye. Kiss Decca for me, give love to Ella, Sophie, cousins & the boys.

Charles T. Haskell, Jr., Fort Moultrie, Sullivan's Island, S.C., to Sophia C. Haskell (SCHS)

19 February 1862

Dear Mother,

I am again stationed in Ft. Moultrie after over two month's absence. I am glad to get back as I have suffered very much the whole time with a very bad cough which I hope now I may get rid of. Otherwise I am very well. I have not seen either Alick or Langdon since I returned here but have heard from them. Any letters that you may have written me for the past month or six weeks have not been received. Love to all.

Charles T. Haskell, Jr., Fort Moultrie, Sullivan's Island, S.C., to Sophia C. Haskell (SCHS)

28 February 1862

Dear Mother,

I was glad to hear from you the other day by your letter which was the first I had received for some time. I heard about the same time too that Pa had returned from Arkansas. One of my sergeants returning from furlough met him on the R.R. Langdon I also heard from yesterday. He was well. My cough which you ask about is getting better & I have in great measure recovered the use of my voice.

Langdon Cheves, Delta Plantation, S.C., to Charles T. Haskell (SCHS)

5 March 1862

My Dear Sir,

I have just received yours of the 28th. I certainly agree with you that the negroes must have meat. They have been so regularly accustomed to it that a sudden change would produce great discontent, if not disease. Their usual allowance was about 2 ¼ lbs bacon side each fortnight, with a quart of molasses in the interval week. For the last season I have substituted fresh beef and mutton—about 4 lbs—and never have had so healthy a gang. The expense here has been much less than that of bacon. I don't know how it will be with you, whether stock cattle can be bought or whether there are any facilities for pasturing them. But, fresh or salt, I think that a half to two thirds the above quantities will do, the work being light. If molasses are not excessively dear they go far to substitute the meat.

Decidedly it will be better not to purchase land at the present excited prices. If the present troubles last, land will be cheap enough next year; if they don't, I should have my purchase heavy on my hands; and without a costly outfit I could not do much this year at any rate.

I was at first inclined to send up my mules, but I can hardly get on without them here in any contingency. If, by an attack on Savannah, our retreat by the River should be cut off, they would be absolutely indispensable for removal to a place of safety.[21] On the other hand, if as is now generally believed, we are to be left in comparative quiet, and I can plant a crop with my reduced force, the mules are my only means of giving it the necessary cultivation. I have learned to use them successfully both in the planting and cultivation and hope with their aid to put in nearly a half crop with my little remaining gang of hardly 30 hands. Besides, as I am killing off my working cattle for food, I shall want more mules whenever I am reestablished. If possible, therefore, I think it will be better to buy what are absolutely necessary, even at a high price. I will take the first opportunity to see what can be done in Savannah. But I do not expect to find tolerable mules at less than $200. First rate ones are out of the question. The army Quartermasters monopolize them. If that price with transportation & risk is better than you can do in Abbeville please let me know. Will not the superabundance of hoes almost dispense with the animal force?

I am so deficient in the data for balancing the cost of their purchase and feed against their probable result on the crop, that I must rest upon your better judgment, only repeating that I shall want, when my negroes return, as many as you will probably think of buying.

I have said so much in response to your inquiries, but I have entire confidence that whatever you, upon the spot, find best, is very preferable to my speculations with imperfect knowledge of the circumstances. I am quite prepared for heavy expense and no returns. [If] my people can be kept in health & tolerable comfort I am content.

Young Oliver left here at only twenty four hours notice, and is probably destitute of many necessaries. Please provide for him liberally.

I must beg Sophie's pardon for not answering her letter. It came the same day with yours and I postponed it to a more convenient season which has never come. It was very gratifying to me and ought to have been acknowledged.

William T. Haskell, Camp Huger, Va., to Sophia C. Haskell (SCHS)
11 March 1862
My dear Mother,
This place has lately assumed the importance of a prospective point of attack from the enemy, & as reports & expectations expand proportionately with distance I write to give you the true state of the case, viz we are all here

---

[21] In 1852, the elder Langdon Cheves (1776-1857) divided his Savannah River rice plantation, Delta, into two tracts and gave the section called Lower Delta to his son Langdon Cheves, Jr. (1814-63). During the war Langdon Cheves sent many of his slaves to the Abbeville District plantation of his brother-in-law Charles T. Haskell, Sr.

quiet as ever drilling as usual, our force on the spot 7000 & [11] pieces of artillery with other troops easily available. Such a force with the [country] we would have in case of need to fight is considered amply sufficient particularly now as the success of the Merrimac has rendered the use of gunboats in roads & rivers questionable & those protecting Suffolk from an attack by the Nansemond River which comes directly up to the town.[22] For the present there is no imminent attack here. The movements at Manassa [sic] John no doubt keeps you acquainted with. I do not know exactly what they are but I understand they indicate a retrograde movement. If so I think it is a very good idea to get them farther from this "point d'appui."[23]

The box has not come & I am afraid has followed the erratic course of Joe's so long expected but as yet not come to port. Is there any chance of getting some light stuff for a summer fatigue jacket for my company. Brown linen like our old hunting coats would be just the thing if it is possible to get it. I w[ou]ld like very much to know whether such stuff is to be had & at what price, if there be any about Abbeville. The city stores are exhausted. We are enjoying weather here which feels as mild & gentle as the spring at home. The health of the place is excellent. The regt has gone over the catalogue of most camp maladies & is now pretty tough & when it has done enough marching will be pretty hard to hurt. I have no news, I just write to let you know that I am well.

Love to Pa & the whole household. I hope the place has not been called Belmont.[24] I have only heard of it from Lally & think it must be a mistake.

Charles T. Haskell, Jr., Richmond, Va., to Charles T. Haskell (SCHS)
16 March 1862
Dear Father,

I am now here in Richmond where I have been ordered, much against my will, on recruiting service. Until the day I left for Richmond I fully expected to go to Abbeville but now I do not know when I will be there. To go off on leave of absence is out of the question, but I meant to try & get up there about the first of next month. I do not know when the draft goes into effect, but think that if I can be there at the right time I may be able to get men to come with me in preference to being forced into positions which

---

[22] This refers to the CSS *Virginia*, a Confederate ironclad warship that was built from the remains of the scuttled frigate USS *Merrimack*. It was used successfully against regular Federal vessels on March 8, 1862, in a naval battle near Norfolk, Va., and the next day, engaged in its famous battle with the Federal ironclad *Monitor*.

[23] A place of assemblage for troops before a battle.

[24] This may refer to a Haskell plantation in Arkansas.

they would perhaps find less desirable.[25] If I had not been ordered off I intended to have spent the rest of this month canvassing the district with that object & even as it is I hope to do something on [saleday] in April if I can get there & it is not too late. I wish if you have the opportunity that you would mention to any good subjects for enlistment that I will be there at that time unless something very unforeseen should happen & that I will pay them sixty dollars in cash before they leave home & that they will have the privilege of going into any company they please in the Regiment. There are four Abbeville officers, Tatom & myself, captains, & Marshall & Perrin, lieutenants.[26] My company is full, but I will be able to fulfill any promise made to them that they can go into my company by transferring men who I now have & taking them in their places. If you think it worth while do get Joe or Langdon if they are at home to have some notice to the above effect published either in the paper or by placards, or both, giving however only the important points such as the amount, time of payment &c but don't let any printing expenses over $10 or $15 dollars be incurred. I doubt however whether this would do much good.

William T. Haskell, Camp Huger, Va., to Charles T. Haskell (SCHS)
19 March 1862
My dear Father,
    Joe arrived here day before yesterday giving me a very pleasant surprise, as he brings the first intelligence of home in a full & authentic manner. Yesterday he employed very unpleasantly to himself in undergoing a fit of bilious cholic which happily by prompt remedies was prevented from going far. He was pretty well this morning & left at one o'clock for Richmond where he arrives about dark. The Dr. has directed a regimen of bitters for him & thinks that he will have no difficulty in doing well.
    This evening we have orders to make ready to go to Goldsboro.[27] This may bring us in the course of human events into a fight & if we do get into

---

[25] The Confederate Congress passed a conscription bill on April 9, 1862.

[26] The officers mentioned were William T. Tatom, a native of Abbeville who died in 1863; Lewis Wardlaw Perrin (1839-1907); and probably John. Hugh Marshall (1833-73).

[27] In his novel *Who Goes There?* B. K. Benson records a conversation in which a soldier in Gregg's Brigade explains why his regiment (Col. Hamilton's) was sent to Goldsboro, North Carolina. "You remember, when Burnside took Roanoke Island it was thought that he would advance to take the Weldon and Wilmington railroad; we were sent to Goldsborough, and were brigaded with some tar-heel regiments under Anderson. Then Anderson and the lot of us were sent to Fredericksburg. We were not put under Gregg again until we reached Richmond."

one I sincerely hope that our fighting may show that we know & feel what we are fighting for.

I like both the Johnson's movements & think that if we do something creditable here things will soon wear off the ugly mask [now] assumed.[28] The Merrimac will make another excursion in about a week. Both the boxes sent I am afraid will never come. Love to all, Ma, Sophy, Decca, Ella & [boys].

[P.S.] I am making ready as we expect to go tonight else I would write more.

Alexander C. Haskell to Charles T. Haskell (SCHS)
11 April 1862
Dear Pa,

I am too unwell to write much at length & just enclose this note to Decca. I am without a servant & most uncomfortable for that reason. Fair trial has shewn me that a hired servant is far from satisfactory or safe as he may be taken away at any moment. Meaning to take that expense upon myself in future it would cost me $200 a year, the interest on near $3000. I can much better afford to buy a servant paying in installments by the end of the year. From old attachment & knowledge of his efficiency I desire to try to get your old servant Butter. Mr. Perrin has never valued him as he deserved & though he is a useful [hack] I think would give him up. This I beg that you will attend to for me & as promptly as possible for we may be moved at any time in common with all soldiers. I know all of Butter's faults & hope that you will try at once to get him notwithstanding these faults. His age ought to make his price a low one. Such is his devotion to the family & his earnest wish to return that I am confident of his willingness.

Charles T. Haskell, Jr., Sullivan's Island, S.C., to Sophia C. Haskell (SCHS)
28 April 1862
Dear Mother,

I am still at the east end of Sullivan's Island in camp. Altho I have a very lonely time the situation has its advantages. I have no one to interfere with me except the commdg general & therefore have pretty much my own way in everything. I have plenty to occupy me too, as I am now on engineering duty, without giving up the charge of my company. The duties however assigned me are not very onerous as they only relate to a small brick fort which is being built just by my camp.

---

[28] A reference to the operations of Confederate generals Joseph E. Johnston (in Virginia) and Albert Sidney Johnston (in Tennessee).

I got the butter the day before yesterday, perfectly fresh. No news down here except an occasional sloop or schooner that slips in or out by the inland passage. The enemy ran one ashore a few days ago within a hundred yards of my camp throwing shells at her which fell in very uncomfortable proximity to us.

Joseph C. Haskell, Headquarters, to John C. Haskell (SCHS)
29 April 1862
Dear John,

I got your letter yesterday evening and came over to head Qrs this morning to ask Genl. Smith about it.[29] Cousin Tom told me this would be the best way to find out what you wanted. He says that in the present state of affairs, you will be assigned to D. R. Jones command but that if it is possible he will try and get you back as he was very sorry to part with you as were all his staff. He says they often talk about you and miss you very much. When I was going away he said give him my kindest regards and tell him for me that he must not leave home until he is entirely well as it will be an act of the greatest folly to do so. You leave [*sic*] has no limit but the state of your health and you owe it to yourself and to your country to get well. You can not be of any service until you are well and you stayed entirely too long here before. He said a great deal more that I don't remember. I did mean marching when I spoke of Nicholas as he came by land all the way from Rapidann. When we left all the spare horses were sent with the wagons and each officer was allowed one. We thought we would have something to do immediately and I wanted something that could carry me so I took Tartar. Both of them are improving and Daniel takes excellent care of them. I have not seen Genl. Jones but will do so soon as I can. Cousin Tom tells me to say to you that he has sent you the sixty days leave and says make use of it all. If you can get a good saddle for me I wish you would as there is no chance of getting one here of any kind. The whole army is down here except Ewell's division which is near Gordonsville.[30] People seem to think that McClelland [*sic*] is afraid of Genl. Johnston and that there will be no fight down here.[31] I will write to you again as soon as I can. I am just going out now to try and get a saddle I saw. Do give my love to all.

---

[29] This refers to General Gustavus Woodson Smith (1821-96).

[30] At this time, the army of General Joseph E. Johnston was at Yorktown, Virginia.

[31] General George B. McClellan (1826-85) was in command of the United States Army of the Potomac.

William T. Haskell, Army of the Rappahannock, Camp Anderson[32], Guinea Station, Va., to Charles T. Haskell (SCHS)
30 April 1862
My dear Father,

Since my last we changed our position from Goldsboro to within 12 miles of Fredericksburg. The enemy are just beginning to occupy the place but everything goes on so slowly when you come up to it that matters seem scarcely to have progressed since my arrival here. McClellan too seems to be at a standstill. The only explanation which I can see for it is that he expects strong [gunboats]. We are all looking with much anxiety to N. Orleans. If it falls it will be a severe blow but if it must come I believe we will in some measure be compensated by the dissipation of the enemy's forces & the sterner temper given to the war.

My solitude from homefolk will soon be broken by Alec's & Langdon's arrival. [Genl's] brigade is already arriving & about eight miles from us for the present. How is John? I hope doing well. Dr. Powell's certificate I sent some time ago to [Weldon] & after learned from Mr. [Campbell] had been forwarded to Abbeville.

I will if I can send another in this letter if not any surgeon will do. I hope you too are again quite strong. I wish I could write in a less <u>mechanical</u> way, & make my letters more interesting than I do but the indescribable inconveniences & engrossments of camp [plowed] over the reflective moods conducive to correspondence. I am feeling more savage of late than is my wont & hope to tell of some Yankee falling before my "bow & spear" before long. Love to Ma & all the household.

Alexander C. Haskell, Richmond, Va., to Sophia C. Haskell (UNC)
30 April 1862
Dear Ma,

I hope you have sometime since received my letter giving notice of our move to Virginia. Delayed for a few days in Richmond by the tardy progress of the brigade over the worn and overtaxed railroads, we start for Fredericksburg tomorrow. McGowan's the 14th & Barnes' the 12th Regt. have preceded; the 13th has not yet come up.[33]

---

[32] Camp Anderson was named for the brigade commander, General Joseph Reid Anderson (1813-92). Guinea (or Guinea's) Station was on the Richmond, Fredericksburg & Potomac Railroad.

[33] Samuel McGowan was by now colonel of the Fourteenth South Carolina Infantry Regiment. Colonel Dixon Barnes (1816-62) was in command of the 12th South Carolina Infantry Regiment. Barnes died from wounds received at the Battle of Sharpsburg (Antietam) in September 1862. Colonel Oliver Evans (or Evins) Edwards (1819-63) of

I don't know exactly the extent of the enemy's menace or preparation on this line, but they are considerable. It is generally expected that Gregg's bad luck will be broken at last and that he will get a chance at the enemy. It is very difficult however to tell tho points at which they mean seriously to strike. I rather concur in the opinion which assigns as a battlefield the country between the Chickahominy and the Pamunkey, and within twenty miles of Richmond. Every gun will sound in the ears of the poor people here of the anxious administration for glorious triumph or the beginning of a desperate partisan struggle. I suppose the next great battle will decide the conduct of the war. If it is a victory for us I can't believe that we will not seek the enemy in his own home. If it is a defeat for us, our whole country will have to be opened to them and we will have to follow in the footsteps of the partisans of the last years of the Revolution. I have great hopes however of victory and almost an assurance of it if we can meet them in the fair field. But I do not believe that an advance will be made against Richmond until by slow degreees the gunboats have been worked into the upper waters of the James, Pamunkey & Chickahominy Rivers. When the enemy has this reserve to fall back upon to prevent our reaping the fruits of a victory, then his great land army may advance. The country has strangely altered since this time last year. The people have by continued contemplation rendered themselves much more indifferent to the chances of war. And the loss of New Orleans does not cause one hundredth part the excitement which followed the capture of a little sand bank & handful of men at Hatteras.[34]

I hear constantly of Willy & suppose will see him in a day or two. He is reported well and prospering. I hear of Joe's having been here some time ago with Tom Rhett, and that he was quite well. I have nothing more recent. Langdon is quite well, entirely recovered from sore muscles & bones with which he groaned for a day or two after our R.R. accident from the ill consequences of which we so happily escaped.

I have a servant but as my luck is in my unavoidable haste, I pay high wages for a perfectly ignorant youngster whom I will have the pleasure of training. My horses are deplorably pulled down by the journey, the gray I fear seriously injured, but they will get over it if I can give them time before hard work commences. They look like skeletons of themselves at present, except their legs which as much swollen as their bodies are contracted. This

---

Spartanburg District, S.C., was in command of the Thirteenth South Carolina Infantry Regiment. These regiments were in Gregg's Brigade.

[34] This is likely a reference to the Federal capture of Fort Hatteras, N.C. in August 1861. The United States flag was raised over the customs house and city hall in New Orleans, La., on April 29, 1862.

gives you [our] general state & condition & the last item was too important to be left out. The horses are often the most important members of the staff.

I found Decca suffering very much with cough & cold in Columbia but hear that she is better. I expect she will, if she is not afraid of giving too much trouble, send to ask you to have some purveying done during the next month or two, for in sober earnest people can't get anything to eat in Columbia. I must be about my business. Love to Pa & all at home. Goodbye.

William T. Haskell, Camp Anderson, Guinea Station, 12 miles from Fredericksburg, Va., to Sophia C. Haskell (SCHS)
[April or May 1862]
My dear Mother,

Since my last we have been [hurried] into a new position near Fredericksburg which the enemy have entered, but as yet not occupied. Whether this change brings us nearer to a fight cannot be said, but we are coming certainly to closer quarters by degree. We are as yet without tents & having been occupied [during] this morning putting up shanties which serve our purpose, though now as evening is coming on, it looks like clearing up & the rain ceasing.

We passed through Richmond only one day earlier than our arrival there last year & have moved on more in our original direction than I ever of late have expected. They say that McClellan is again making a feint on the Peninsula wishing to draw our force to that point & then having his own up the Rappahannock towards Fredericksburg before our army can be assembled to meet him to advance on Richmond from that point. In consequence of such anticipations it is said that we are sent to this point. Whether it be so or not I cannot say, but I don't think that McClellan can be shuffling in such a persistent way. It would [come about] of the generalship for which we have hitherto given him credit. If he should then change his mode of approach it would give our army with its ordinary modes of intelligence time to meet him in the new direction.

Joe I suppose is getting rapidly better. Do tell him for me, it's no use his getting impatient & thirsting for the conflict as Achilles of old. It will be plenty soon enough when he is strong & well again.

I have nothing more to write about. Do ask Pa to advertise in the papers for volunteers for my company. The period of volunteering is limited now to about three weeks after which time conscription will fill up the comp[anie]s to 125 each. The advertisement may say that I am armed with Enfield rifles & am on the left flank of the Regt.

Love to all.

Charles T. Haskell, Abbeville, S.C., to Langdon Cheves, Savannah, Ga. (SCHS)
4 May 1862
My dear Sir,
    I am sorry to inform you of the death of Sharper, one of your negro men, on yesterday. He died of pneumonia after a tedious illness. He was carefully attended to by Dr. Mabry. The general health of the negroes is good. I have ordered osnaburgs[35] for the summer clothing of your negroes from a company in Greenville. I pay ten cents per yard. I hope that this may meet yr approval as I was forced to act promptly for fear of having to pay a higher price. I shall be able to procure sufficient corn to [furnish] bread for the negroes but when the present small supply of meat is out I am totally at a loss to know what to get for them to eat. I am giving 100 lb. per week and have enough for several weeks at that rate. Meat is normally at 30 cents per lb. but there is none for sale. What small quantity there was has been bought and carried of [*sic*] by speculators.
    I cannot buy cows, except at exorbitant prices. I have furnished the nurse with one good cow for the children, but am unable to spare more. Every thing to eat or wear is almost unattainable. The children are quite healthy and are looking remarkably well. A woman was confined two days ago and is doing well. Love to all yr family.

Alexander C. Haskell, Headquarters, Second Brigade, Army of the Rappahannock, Massaponax Hills, Va., to Sophia C. Haskell (UNC)
22 May 1862
My dear Mother,
    I have received your letter of the 10th and though rather old, the home news is very welcome. I feel farther away now than I ever did before. The actual distance is not so great, but our communications are threatened at several points and I feel no certainty but that each day may not be the last which will bring me any tidings of the dear ones at home. I would gladly though cut the communication with my own hands and place hundreds of miles more between all that is dear to me on earth if I could only form part of an army strong enough to drive the horrors of war into the heart of our enemy's country. All mercy, all pity for their barbarous soldiery, that I have been weak enough to feel when I have seen them fleeing or in prison & suffering, has gone since the turn given to affairs in New Orleans by the barbarity of that cowardly fiend Butler.[36] A few words have changed the whole

---

    [35] Osnaburg is a type of plain, coarse fabric similar to linen.
    [36] General Benjamin Franklin Butler (1818-93) became known as "Beast Butler." He executed a civilian in New Orleans, and on May 15, 1862, issued an order to his occupying army in the city to treat any Confederate woman who showed them disrespect as

complexion of the war, and I have spent this morning in the task of spreading before our soldiers in orders these words that I trust will make their blood like fire and their sinews like steel. Sentimentality is at last killed out, and the eyes of the most foolish are at last opened to what the wiser long since have seen. The enemy, confident of their triumph, are beginning in the insolence of conquest to draw the veil from their true purpose and intentions. One corner has been lifted, and the picture revealed has struck a chord in every Southern heart, and lighted a fire of vengeance and desperate hate, before which the ranks of our foe will melt like chaff before the flames. If we can't fight and defeat them now I can look with little concern upon the fall of those who now amongst us prove recreant to the cause. No determined army ever was or ever will be defeated. They are now applying to us the only element which is absolutely necessary to success under our many disadvantages, and that will insure victory with bayonet & knives before the best appointed army of invaders that the world ever saw. Men are saying now, and they feel it, that they have dreaded death in battle, but that death is easy now if it insures victory. Still though we are kept from our enemy. Within five miles of him we are kept week after week inactive. He is perhaps strengthening in our front, we are not yet sure. He is certainly insinuating his forces between us and Richmond to cut off our R. R. With an army before and one behind we will have a harder task than to have whipped double our number or three times on an open field, & in our front. It may possibly be that we will be called back & allowed to share with the great battle for Richmond, for our Country, our homes, our honour and our Religion. I feel more proud of our cause this day than I ever did before, now that I see from what it is that we have separated ourselves in time to save truth & honour, and more confident of the blessings of God and that his spirit will nerve our arms until victory has crowned us with triumphant success.

We know nothing, hear nothing of the army plans. We are just awaiting orders and I hope every man so waits with an increasing determination to make a desperate fight whenever the opportunity is presented to them. I cannot but expect that Johnston will give battle for Richmond, and in that the present fate of our country is balanced. From the outside of the whirlwind you can see more than can one who is in its midst. I can only tell you of how we feel in our little share of the great drama—a tragedy soon.

I ought not to talk about the war after your kind peaceful home letter that made me forget all but the associations it called up. I hope Pa will not continue to suffer from ill feelings but that he will settle down for a comfort-

---

"a woman of the town plying her avocation." Jefferson Davis, the Confederate president, declared General Butler an outlaw deserving of capital punishment.

able summer. You must remind all the powers concerned that the "last colt" is mine and that I hope to see it a fine charger that I can ride in the sixth year of the war. I think your disposal of Paul and Lewis[37] a wise one and I wish very [*sic*] that Pa could, and I hope that he can, find means of sending Sophie for the summer at least to my friends, I so consider the school, the DeChoiseul's at Flat Rock.[38] I fear however that there is no chance now. But if it were possible it would tend much to [conform] Sophie's health, which is doubtful, and give a steady direction again to her education.

There is no satisfaction hardly in writing in such an office as I have. I wrote down to hear about midday, and now after tattoo is my first opportunity to renew and end my letter, for I have yet to write a little letter to Decca. The dear girl has been as usual working for my comfort, and I have just received a nice little bundle of shirts and other useful things which she has made and sent on by John. You can hardly know how I feel your kind affectionate expressions about my dear Decca. She is indeed a noble and good girl, but I could not expect others to feel with me as you do. I could not resist the temptation of sending her an extract from your letter last night. It will encourage and cheer to know what feelings she left behind her. And poor child she needs all the support I can give her, though her letters are very brave and cheerful, and I thank God that it is in Him that she puts her trust. We can look for no other source for help now, and His mercy will not be withdrawn from us in our troubles. I have not been writing regularly since I left Richmond, but I asked Decca to pass on the news. Don't expect me to enlighten you about the army movements, it is impossible. Dearest love to all. I don't know who you have by this time.

---

[37] Aleck's younger brothers Paul and Louis Haskell were sent to a school operated by Octavius Theodore Porcher (1829-73) at his plantation home (Farm Hill) near Willington, S.C. In the early 1850s, Porcher had been a teacher at the prestigious classical school established by Moses Waddel (1770-1840) called Willington Academy. In his history of higher education in South Carolina, Colyer Meriwether stated that after Willington Academy's last teacher departed around 1858 or 1859, Porcher revived the school and moved it to his home. Albert Sidney Thomas wrote that after teaching at the Willington Academy, Porcher "established a school of his own." Thomas, *An Historical Account*, 779.

[38] Beatrix and Eliza de Choiseul, the daughters of the former French consul in Charleston, began operating a school for girls in Flat Rock, N.C., in the fall of 1862. The school closed down about two years later after the sisters were assaulted by marauders. They fled to Greenville, S.C., where they lived out their days.

William T. Haskell, on the Mechanicsville Turnpike on the Chickahominy River, Va., to Sophia C. Haskell (SCHS)

2 June 1862

In the second year of this war of liberty.

My dear Mother,

We have arrived by pretty hard marching from Fredericksburg starting on the 24th May. We have been in the vicinity of Richmond for three days, resting & moving until we have finally taken up a regular position at the superscribed place about 4 miles from Richmond. The Y[ankees]'s are in full view on the opposing hills wherever the gaps in the woods allow an open sight. When we came here yesterday the enemy commenced & kept up for a little while a pretty sharp fire of shells thus introducing us at last to the fact & feelings of being "under fire." The range was such however as to make it ineffective for that time.

Day before yesterday the right wing of our army, Longstreets & Hugers divisions were engaged in a very severe battle.[39] The result has been, though bloody, favorable. Such will be the character I believe of all the fighting to be done here.

Yesterday, by the firing, we know the battle was continued in the same direction. The results I have not learned. I may hear before closing this letter.

This morning I have heard a few guns & the Y's are amusing themselves by sending up balloons which serve the same purpose for our own side.[40]

I have seen all the boys. Joe is with cousin Tom & the General. John with D.R. forces.[41] They are all well. Joe looks better than I ever saw him.

The crisis is rapidly, I think, approaching. All seem confident of the result, we <u>must</u> conquer. Jackson by a splendid success is moving on it is said across the Potomac, thus making a diversion in our favor. Washington is said to be his destination. The army is pretty healthy, the march has for a short time broken down a good many but they will soon be well & ready. We are still in the same brigade, though anxious to join Gregg, & in Maj Genl A. P. Hill's (a g officer) division.[42] When our time in the fight will

---

[39] The Battle of Seven Pines (or Fair Oaks) in Virginia began on May 31, 1862. General James Longstreet (1821-1904) was in command of several brigades of General Lee's army, and General Benjamin Huger was a divisional commander under General Joseph E. Johnston.

[40] Observation balloons.

[41] Department of Richmond.

[42] Major General Ambrose Powell Hill (1825-65) was the commander of the "Light Division," an infantry division in the Army of Northern Virginia.

come I do not know but we are ready I trust for it & what I most hope is that you all at home will not be troubled with apprehensions. God will dispose things according to his will, & we are in his hand.

Love to Pa & all.

Alexander C. Haskell, Headquarters, Second Brigade Light Division, Sheppard Hill, 9 Miles North of Richmond Va. on the Chickahominy River, to Charles T. Haskell (UNC)

3 June 1862

My dear Father,

I received your very welcome letter today and feel quite reproached that I have not been a better correspondent to have left you so long ignorant of my motions, however I have written three times not once. You must charge two letters to the mail. As a matter of course I am quite well as is Langdon. And as for being contented, I think I am a model. I have never ceased to enjoy the more active life of the army & its hardships (for we have an impracticable General who runs us about without transportation, and we [starve] & sleep on the ground on several occasions) and I am consoled when I get very homesick by the reflection that I am trying to do my duty both for my country & my home, and that in that consists my present value. It is not so hard either to be away from Decca when I hear so regularly from her that she is quite well and see that she is being as brave as a soldier's wife should be. It never ceases to be a pleasure to me to hear you speak of her in such terms of affection as I find in your letter, and I feel my singular good fortune in not only having got the best possible wife, but in having her so warmly received that she feels as if she has just gone into another home and I have a warm welcome from every relative of her family. As a sample tonight I got a letter from a cousin in Richmond, Mrs. Brown, who has just returned to her house at Richmond and upon opening it for the assistance of wounded friends has made her first work to write to tell me that she has kept a room for me, and that I must come to her if I am wounded or sick.[43] Perhaps she feels responsible as it was in her house my fate was decided. But to return to the momentous subject of the war, Joe & John were both in the fight the other day for a time, Joe in the earlier part, John towards the last.[44] I have seen Joe. He tells me John is well & little Willy.[45] Joe is a very gallant looking soldier, very much improved, and must have behaved well. He was

---

[43] This is likely Mary Southall Brown (1834-1920), a cousin of Decca Haskell. She was the wife of Col. John Thompson Brown (1835-64), an artillery officer.

[44] This refers to the Battle of Seven Pines, Va., which began on May 31, 1862.

[45] Little Willy (or Willie) is likely a cousin, William Elnathan Haskell, Jr., 1841-1910, the son of William Elnathan Haskell (1805-72).

at General Johnston's side when the General fell & will probably be out of employment for some time in consequence of the General's illness.[46] Johnston is getting better, of a very severe and painful though not dangerous wound.

We are upon the extreme left of the army in the Light Division commanded by Maj. Genl. A. P. Hill, a good and gallant young officer. We watch the right wing of McClellan's army and guard the best crossing of the Chickahominy River. We are constantly moving and on the alert, with the advance guards of the enemy poking up to about two miles from our Head Quarters. Our army came from Fredericksburg under every disadvantage resulting very much from mismanagement of some subordinate officers of another brigade which so much delayed the march as to make it first perilous & then tedious. We were wanted at Richmond & were already more than partially cut off in our rear but had about a triple force in front of us. Considering these circumstances we made a good start, stopping several times to fight, and spending the last night in a wedge between the enemy's lines. Our scouts for this evening have just come in from across the river, report the enemy not advancing, and say that they (the enemy) have told the country people that their loss in the battle was 4000 killed. Ours is roughly estimated at 1000 killed & wounded. This would make theirs four times as great as ours but I much doubt whether the difference is so great. We are informed tonight too that the enemy is falling back. I can't imagine what for. Lee has assumed command. They say G. W. Smith is threatened with paralysis or would have had the [prize].[47]

We must whip the Yankees now and get into their country. Food & forage are getting very scarce. My horses are worked hard but are true and fine animals, both very much reduced by the journey, have not recovered flesh yet but are now improving & work always with fire and spirit. Dusenberry is invaluable. Langdon could not do without him at all. He can't work him hard enough to keep down his vicious disposition. I won't make requisition for Robin until my poor mares are killed. I think the old fellow might then take the field. I hope the Arkansas place will be saved, but if it goes it will be one among the many.[48] If it be necessary I think all who survive this war will be strong enough to battle with the wants of life. Goodbye. Dearest love to Ma & all at home.

---

[46] General Joseph E. Johnston was wounded during the Battle of Seven Pines.

[47] General Gustavus Woodson Smith took command of the Army of Northern Virginia after General Joseph E. Johnston was wounded, but was replaced the next day by General Robert E. Lee when President Jefferson Davis found Smith to be suffering from a partial, temporary paralysis

[48] The Arkansas plantation of Langdon Cheves Haskell.

William T. Haskell, Camp on Mechanicsville Turnpike, 5 Miles to Richmond, Va., to Charles T. Haskell (SCHS)

5 June 1862

My dear father,

We are in status quo & [*paper torn*] … no very definite prospects of changing our condition. But "things" are so near each other that the critical moment or moments may at any time be imminent.

The battle of Sunday was not of as important result as was hoped for, but still was a decided success.[49] We took 15 pieces of artillery, about 2000 stand of small arms, 500 prisoners, a number of tents & camp equipage, lost from 1500-2000 killed & wounded. This account is correct. On Sunday nothing important was effected. Joe was with Johnson when & before he was wounded, acting as aid continually exposed to fire he escaped entirely unhurt. Little Willie with other couriers of Whiting[50] did the duties of aid on the field & was in the head of the fight. He & Joe were together for a good part of the time. Johnson was shot down while giving an order to Joe. The ball entered the right shoulder ranging across toward the other. The wound though severe is said not to be dangerous. Lee is in command. No one can supply the place of Johnson.

The enemy were in sight & keep up a desultory fire from guns on different points of the opposing hills.

Langdon, Alic, John & Joe are all as well as they can be. The life we are leading now & rather the [roughness] we have had yet, one chief cause of which will I hope soon abate viz the rain. We have it nearly every day & night.

I have not been into Richmond yet, for we are properly kept close in camp, but I hear of many sick & wounded, hospitals full &c &c &c. The health of my company is very good. A few have not yet got over the effect of their march but I think soon will.

We have a rumor this morning that Jackson in the valley, has defeated Shields[51] somewhere I suppose around Strasburg. As to the battle here it is thought that we can scarcely have anything like a general engagement but a series at several points.

---

[49] The Battle of Seven Pines was concluded on Sunday, June 1, 1862.

[50] Brigadier General William H. C. Whiting was in command of several brigades at the Battle of Seven Pines.

[51] Brigadier General James Shields (1810-79), commander of the Second Division of the Fifth Corps of the Union Army of the Potomac.

Rebecca S. Haskell, Columbia, S.C., to Charles T. Haskell (SCHS)
8 June [1862]
My dear Papa,

That letter with which I threatened you on leaving Abbeville I hope you have felt no doubts as to its ever arriving. I do not write as often as I think of you all because I am so lazy and stupid that I am loath to appear before you in so unfavorable a light. But, being unwilling you should forget me, sometimes I venture upon a letter which I hope recalls your new daughter in law to your affectionate remembrance. I am sure you missed me at table, as I engrossed so much of your time and attention, and I hope you will let me come back one of these days to your seat on the right, for Alic himself could not be more watchful of my wants or ready to supply them and I rebel at a fresh daughter in law supporting one.

What would you give now for a glimpse at some of Alic's letters, when he has something to write about, and could tell you the secrets of the grand Army! He does not tell me anything very bright or encouraging, however much he may try to put the best face on affairs. But whipping the Yankees has not proved as easy work as our men anticipated. I won't say anything more about the war for fear you will class me with your fat neighbor (who spends the sociable day that he might have a long talk on the affairs of the nation), and find me equally tiresome. My last letter was as late as the fourth in which he mentions Langdon and Willie as being quite well and speaks of Joe's having ridden over to see them since the fight, and that he was looking splendidly. So tall and slight that he envied him his proportions. Alic regrets the illness of General Smith as it places Lee in command whose policy they seem to think is just the opposite of that of Johnston and Smith. I hope John has not lost his place with Gen. Smith that Mama speaks of his being on someone else's staff. Give my love to Charlie when you write. I suppose his spirits have risen with the prospect of hot work around Charleston. Tell Sophie not to be discouraged at my silence but to write me another long letter. I want to hear of Louis and Paul and whether Mr. Porcher appreciates them as they deserve and if they have grown too big to be home sick. Has poor little [Snip] pined away since Paul has deserted her? I hope some chance will soon occur that she may be sent to me. I have not seen Cousin Isabella but mother has called and went last evening to take her to drive.[52]

My love to Cousin Folly, Kate and Sophie and embrace Mama for me. Don't groan at the thought of answering my letter. I expect no such tax upon

---

[52] This refers to a first cousin of the Haskell brothers, Isabella Sophia Cheves (1833-88), the daughter of Isabella Middleton Cheves (1826-1912), who was the sister of Mrs. Sophia C. Haskell.

your time or patience but make Sophie write sometimes to let me know how you are and if you do not find the constant anxiety upon your mind hopeful as you may be of success is not wearing away to the body. Don't coax Mama into giving you [physic] nor think me saucy.

Joseph C. Haskell, Manassas, Va., to Charles T. Haskell (DUL)
9 June 1862
Dear Pa,

I received your letter of the 24th two days ago and have put off writing simply because I had nothing to write about us. Everything has settled down into a state of quiescence which is perfectly astonishing when you think how close these two armies are. I was down at Mechanicsville the other day on a visit to Willie when he asked me if I wanted to get a sight of the Yankees, and took me about a quarter of a mile from the camp to the top of the hills bordering the Chickahominy, from which you could see them on the other side of the river, about 800 yards off, walking about perfectly unconcerned though our videttes were not more than [1000] yards from them. Our men are instructed not to fire at them as it would only provoke them into shelling the camps around which they can do with perfect impunity, as their guns have a much superior range to ours. I found Willie in fine health and spirits, but living in very primitive style without a tent, its place being supplied by a piece of ticking just large enough to cover Grimke and himself. I was able to add somewhat to his comfort by the gift of a fine oilcloth I got from the Yankee camp on the day of the battle. I am in such spirits today that I have almost forgotten the gloomy state of affairs around us. Cousin Tom went over to the Genls. this morning and as soon as he went into the room the Genl. asked after me and then said that I must have a commission, but on asking my age said that could not be got, he was afraid, but that he would get me a Cadetship and have it dated on the day of the battle[53] and best of all intended to keep me with him.[54] And what gratifies me very much is that Cousin Tom has not asked him to do it, but I have not the vanity to suppose that it was done without his influence. If I got this it will be far more than I ever hoped to be, for I consider a Cadetship from him more than a captaincy from any other and will have more cause than ever to thank Cousin Tom for the kindness he has shown me. The Genl. is still getting better, but is quite weak and it will be a month I expect before he will be able to take command.

---

[53] The Battle of Seven Pines.
[54] Joseph C. Haskell became Acting Cadet on the staff of General Joseph E. Johnston.

Jackson is doing his part like a hero. The news has just come of another victory but no particulars as yet, except the notice of the death of Col. Ashby who is a great loss to our army and whose place it will be hard to fill.[55] I have seen all the boys in the last few days and they were all well. I am sorry to hear that Cousin Follie was sick but hope she has entirely recovered. Do give her my love and tell her that I have not got the box with John's things and my boots but hope to soon. Do give my love to her and all the rest.

John C. Haskell to Charles T. Haskell (SCHS)
23 June [1862]
Dear Pa,

I suppose you have all quieted down after the news of the fight of which I suppose even the details have ceased to be news. Here people have stopped even talking about it and the all absorbing theme now is the arrival of Jackson and the battle which it is supposed will almost immediately ensue. He, Jackson, is expected here by some tomorrow, others say the day after, and others again and I think these are the best informed and most truthful, say that they have no idea of his whereabouts or when he will be here though all agree that he is on his way.

I see all the boys constantly now as they are all near, Langdon, Willy & Alec being not more than a half mile off. Joe is farther but I see him pretty often. Langdon lost Dusenberry (his horse) the other night whilst attending a wedding in Richmond, but found him again after he had begun to give up all idea [sic]. It was certainly very fortunate as the horse was stolen and a courier of General Gregg accidentally met the man a day and a half afterwards, whereupon he drew his sword and charging him made him dismount and give up.

I am at present in quite an awkward predicament as the servant I have had some time and who is just lately good for much is taken away by his master and I can't get another for a while. I can get along on the charity of friends but that will not do long and I want to beg you to send me Caesar if you can spare him who I think I can make a good groom and waiting boy of, and he would suit me well as he is light enough to allow him to ride my horse when I want to send anywhere.

General Johnston is doing well though I don't know when the physicians expect him to be out. It is said that the Davis party will make a strong attempt to keep him out of the command of this army and to retain General

---

[55] Col. Turner Ashby (1828-62), a Virginian, was General Thomas J. "Stonewall" Jackson's cavalry commander.

Lee. General Smith is still too unwell to take command and is I believe going to our Sulphur Springs.

Do give my love to Ma & Sophie and to cousins Follie and Tom and all the rest of them and tell the boys to write how they are getting on at school. I have only got one letter since I have been out here.

Joseph C. Haskell, Mount Erin, Va., to Sophia C. Haskell (SCHS)
24 June 1862
Dear Ma

I received your letter of the fourteenth on Sunday, but as I was going down to see the boys next day I put off answering it until I returned. I went down yesterday and had the pleasure of carrying Aleck the first news of the birth of his little daughter. It was almost too much for him at first but he managed to survive it. Mr. Barnwell happened to meet me at church on Sunday and told me if I met Aleck to let him know the dispatch had reached him I think on Friday night but he was too busy to send it to Aleck. He however came down yesterday to congratulate the young man and entirely appeased him. He and Langdon were both a little unwell, Aleck from confinement in the office and Lally from a bad cold. Willie company [*sic*] was out on picket when I went and found him looking as well and [rusty] as ever and when I left was busily engaged in endeavouring to find some way by which he could kill or capture the Yankee picket in front of him Genl Gregg having given him permission to try it. I do not know what was the result as it got so late I had to leave. Langdon was highly delighted at having recovered his horse which I suppose you heard had been stolen from him. One of their couriers saw a livery stable man riding him and took possession at once and also made him produce Memmingers[56] which was taken at the same time. They were very lucky in recovering them so soon. Coming home I stopped at the Legion camp[57] to see Willie who I found quite well but very much disgusted at not having gone to Jackson's army. I suppose at home you are all very anxious about Charleston. Here everybody is so taken up with the army and the thoughts of the coming fight here that they do not regard the fight down there of sufficient importance to be worth any notice. I heard this morning that they were shelling Morris Island and am very anxious to hear something more definite. I am very much inclined to think that they will meet with a more stubborn resistance at Charleston than the [*sic*] have yet encountered. That fight on James Island is only a specimen of what they

---

[56] "Memmingers" were paper money. Christopher Gustavus Memminger (1803-88) was the Confederate States Secretary of the Treasury.

[57] This is the camp of Hampton Legion.

will meet with whenever the [*sic*] attempt a land attack.[58] I hear so little from home now that I am almost in the dark as to anything going on there. I would like very much to be at home for a little while. I met a young fellow named Mitchell, brother of the bank officer who has been at home much later than I have, and from what he told me I suppose I would not know half the people in Abbeville. I don't believe I ever wrote you that I met Eddie Cheves[59] in Richmond going on with Lawton as Aide. He was rather a queer looking little officer but I liked him very much after I had seen a little of him. He must be very much like what uncle John was at his age. He told me that aunt Anna spoke of paying you a visit. Suppose however she gave up the idea as you have never mentioned it in your letters. What is uncle Pinckney doing. I should think that in times like these he might be very useful with his knowledge of engineering and genl information. Eddie told me of several infernal machines which uncle John have [*sic*] devised and had placed in the river and that he was at time engaged in obstructing the Charleston harbour. I do not pretend to give you any news from here for I could only write the rumors I hear on the street and the [*sic*] are so unreliable that I don't care to send them.

Do give my love to Pa, cousin Follie, Sophie and all the rest at home.

Langdon C. Haskell, Headquarters, Second Brigade, to Joseph C. Haskell (UNC)
31 June 1862
My dear Brother,

I don't know what to say what I felt on receiving your news this morning. I feared the worst for poor John but hope and trust in God's mercy that he will spare him to us though I can hardly hope. Do give him my most earnest love and tell him to keep up his spirits and trust in God's mercy. Willy and myself are safe. We went through a hot fight last evening but came through it without being touched.[60] I have felt very anxious about poor Aleck. I feared that his trouble was almost more than he could bear. [Has] he been told of Decca's death, if he knows it I feel relieved that the ... [*illegible words*] ... and tell him for me though I can't write that, but it is no use trying to say how I feel for him. It would not help him and I only might be more comfort to him if I were with him.

I write this in the greatest haste as we are under orders to go to the support of Longstreet and will probably march in a short time. Perhaps he will not have to move as our Division is terribly cut up and those uninjured

---

[58] The Battle of Secessionville.
[59] Edward Richardson Cheves (1842-62), a first cousin of the Haskell brothers, was the son of John Richardson Cheves (1815-69).
[60] This was the Battle of Frayser's Farm, or White Oak Swamp, on June 30, 1862.

are utterly exhausted. I can hardly say what we are doing. The enemy are apparently retreating towards James River and we are following them but they make a hard fight the whole way. Give my love to Aleck and John and if it is possible send me news tomorrow. Do make every effort to do so. Direct any thing you may write to the care of Brig. Genl Longstreet.

Charles T. Haskell, Richmond, Va., to Sophie Haskell (SCHS)
3 July 1862
Dear Dau[ghter],
    I wrote you all yesterday. Our dear John is still doing well and at present very thin. Looking favourably for him. Langdon and Willie are safe up to yesterday evening. May God in his infinite mercy continue to preserve them thru the awful dangers of the battle. Langdon and Willie have been in the actual battle from Sunday up to Tuesday evening.[61] Alick & Joe are free from fever today. I wish you to send the letter to Edwards so that he can get Elizabeth to Columbia at once. I telegraphed to your Aunt Louisa today & shall continue to do so frequently, every other day if everything goes well and often if necessary.

Mary Cheves,[62] Madison Springs, Ga., to Sophie Haskell (SCHS)
11 July 1862
My dear Sophy,
    Do write me a few lines to us know the last you have heard of Johnny. We have only heard through Papa that he was severely wounded, and are very anxious to hear more of him and of your other brother also. I believe they are all safe. We were very much distressed to hear of Decca's death, tho' we scarcely knew her well enough to appreciate her. Poor Alick! How dreadful for him and for you all. Did Aunt Sophia go down to Columbia? We hoped she might have been with Aunt Rache in her affliction. Poor Aunt Rache & Min. I don't know what they will do, for Eddie was everything to them. He was so good & kind, so gentle & intelligent, we will all miss him most terribly. I cannot realize his death, tho' I can think of nothing else.[63]

---

[61] The Battle of Savage's Station was fought on Sunday, June 28, 1862. It was followed by the Battle of Frayser's Farm (or White Oak Swamp) on Monday, June 30, and then by the Battle of Malvern Hill on Tuesday, July 1, 1862. McGowan's Brigade was engaged in all these battles and lost almost a thousand men in them.

[62] The writer of this letter is Sophie's first cousin Mary (Mamie) Elizabeth Cheves (later Mrs. Charles Nephew West), the daughter of Capt. Langdon Cheves (1814-63) and Charlotte Lorain McCord Cheves. She had a sister named Emma.

[63] Edward Richardson Cheves was killed at the Battle of Gaines' Mill, Va., on June 27, 1862. He was the son of John Richardson Cheves and Rachel Susan Bee Cheves

I know you will have no inclination to write just now, but if you will only send me a few lines to let us hear of Johnny & the other boys, I will be so much obliged. We are so out of the world here that we hear nothing, or very little of what takes place in it.

I will enclose a letter to Johnny, which I wish you would forward to him if he is well enough to read it, as I do not know where he is, or how to address him.

Mamma & Emma join me in a great deal of love to you all.

Alexander C. Haskell, Columbia, S.C., to Sophie Haskell (SCHS)
13 July 1862
My dear Sister,

I have been too sick and exhausted to write to you before, and now have but a moment while the mail courier waits. I left John on the 9th. There is every hope of his recovery. Joe has been quite sick but was better.

My poor little baby is as well as possible and I have reason to hope that God will spare me this comfort in my dreary, desolate life. I need not attempt to tell you. You know what I have lost in my Angel and you know what I suffer, and I am sure I have your sympathy. Love to all. Goodbye, my dear Sister. Though my heart is crushed you are all dear to your loving brother.

Charles T. Haskell, Jr., Breach Inlet Battery[64], Sullivan's Island S.C., to Sophia C. Haskell (SCHS)
13 July 1862
Dear Mother,

I have not written thus far as I have felt too anxious, until I got a telegram yesterday, directed to Col Keitt,[65] stating that John was out of danger.

It would be a great relief to me to be on with you but that is impossible. Poor Pickens Butler my first Lieutenant suddenly got the news the other day that his youngest brother had been killed in action & that his mother had

---

(1821-88). His sister, Mary Elizabeth Cheves (1844-1915), who was called Minna or Minnie, later married Joseph C. Haskell.

[64] The Breach Inlet Battery was a seven gun work located on the far eastern end of Sullivan's Island. In 1863 it was enlarged and renamed Battery Marshall, in honor of Col. Jehu Foster Marshall (1817-62), a native of Abbeville who died at the Battle of Second Manassas.

[65] Colonel Lawrence Massillon Keitt (1824-64) of the Twentieth Regiment, South Carolina Volunteers.

died within the day on getting the news.[66] Even he got leave with difficulty to go home for a few days.

I wrote a long letter to Alec a few days ago but tore it up afterwards. I wrote to him such a letter as I would like to receive under similar circumstances, but feared that it would perhaps tend to keep alive the great grief which I should rather try to dispel but which I feel I cannot do. I can give him sympathy, but not comfort. I can think of no words of consolation which I am sure have not suggested themselves to him already with more force than I could express them.

John ought not to feel sad for himself and I don't suppose he does. If every one of us had lost a limb I would feel it would be far far better to go maimed through life than suffer such a loss as Alec has. Everything has been sad for some time. I met uncle John at the funeral of his only son. He seems very sad ever since but scarcely allows anyone to perceive it. He works very hard all the time & seems systematically to be trying to forget. He now has sole charge of the harbor obstructions at Charleston.[67] I know you cannot have time to write but if Langdon or Willy is in Richmond do ask them to write me. All I know is that John has lost his arm. I have not received a letter & but one telegram since the battle commenced.

Sophia C. Haskell, Richmond, Va., to Sophie Haskell (SCHS)
13 July [1862]
Dear Sophie,

I am getting quite anxious for news from home now that the boys are a little better. I have time to begin to wonder we have no news from you. I have not written much for my time is so much occupied but we have sent several letters and telegrams, and have only received in return a letter from Ella of the 9th and one from Quattlebaum of the 11th which tell us you are all well.[68]

John is recovering but is very weak still.[69] He alarmed us very much yesterday by getting out of his head very suddenly, in part the effect of ano-

---

[66] Andrew Pickens Butler (1839-99) was the son of South Carolina governor Pierce Mason Butler (1798-1847). His brother Edward Julian Butler (1842-62) was killed at the Battle of Malvern Hill, Va., in July 1862. Their mother, Miranda Juliette Duval Butler (1803-62), died on July 9, 1862.

[67] John Richardson Cheves (1815- 69), a brother of Mrs. Sophia C. Haskell, was put in charge of engineering obstructions and torpedo defenses in Charleston harbor.

[68] This may be Paul Quattlebaum (1812-90), an industrialist and planter of Lexington District. He was unable to serve in the military but contributed to the Confederate cause and had sons in the army.

[69] William Porcher DuBose, a friend of the family, wrote from Richmond on July 29, 1862: "Mr. & Mrs. Haskell are at Mr. Dudley's nursing their two sons John & Joe

dyne which he has often been obliged to take to give him rest, and in part from a little fever. He is free of fever today but does not feel well enough to sit up as he had been doing for a little while for some days before. He needs a great deal of attendance particularly incessant fanning tho not now at night. Last night I sat up with him till four o'clock, tho generally we leave them now to old servant who is very attentive.

Joe I hope is a little better. He fed himself today for the first time and tho very feeble seems more willing to talk occasionally. We think he is taking a turn for the better. We cannot yet have any idea when either of them can be moved, possibly in a fortnight. Willy came in today. He is looking very well and handsomer than I ever saw him. Langdon is not so well but Dr. Powell thinks nothing serious. You must not feel too much distressed about John's lost arm. I hope he will bear it cheerfully and we must all help him. It seems almost a miracle he escaped at all. His conduct must have been very brave indeed to judge by all the notice taken of him by the Generals and other officers. They praise him very highly. All who are in Richmond. The Genls have been to see him and more visitors than can be admitted.

Friday morning

I was so often interrupted I could not finish last evening. This morning both John and Joe are better tho Joe is too weak to do more than raise his head in bed. He is very patient and uncomplaining. John will sit up again today.

If you are at home tell the overseer to have some peaches dried for me as soon as they are fit and tell Dick to dry in the oven. Jenny can help him. I hope to hear from you soon. Your Father is quite unwell today but I hope it is only temporary. Do write often to Charles. Love to everybody Ella particularly.

[P.S.] Your Father says please write about the crops and if there has been rain.

---

former recovering from the amputation of his right arm at the shoulder joint and the latter from Typhoid fever." DuBose, *Faith, Valor and Devotion*, 82.

Charles T. Haskell and Sophia C. Haskell, Richmond, Va. to Charles T. Haskell, Jr. (SCHS)
20 July [1862]
Dear Charley,

Your Mother has just received your letter of the 13th. I am sorry that you have remained so long without the particulars of John's wound. I have sent you two telegrams directed to the care of Hutson Lee, Q.M. I think that John is entirely out of danger. His arm is amputated at the shoulder joint, an operation of great danger, but attended in his case with complete success. John is cheerful and hopeful. Joe has [*sic*] severely ill but is now free of fever.

I heard from Alic who writes in a resigned spirit and appears to be much comforted in his little daughter. We hope to leave Richmond early in August but it is not certain, as much will depend on John's strength. He is at present quite weak from loss of blood. I yield my paper to yr mother.

Dear Charley,

This is my third letter besides your Father's and sundry telegrams he has not mentioned. I hope you have received more news before now. I think Alec would be comforted by any letter you would write him. He bears it gently and piously and looks for strength to God. Her death was so resigned and lovely that it seemed to loose [*sic*] much of its agonizing bitterness. I could as you say give no consolation to such a grief, for his loss is irreparable, but God I hope and believe will be with him. He wrote to Sophie to meet him in Columbia. She writes to us from there. She says the baby is as I thought the image of its Mother and perfectly well and healthy. London's sister Elizabeth has been chosen as its nurse and Alec says gives satisfaction. Johnny bears his trouble cheerfully and has at least the comfort of having gained the applause of many officers of distinction. Gen. Whiting has just sent him an extract from his report, very complimentary, and all the generals of his acquaintance have been to see him.[70] He does not suffer a great deal and has had but little fever. Willy is perfectly well, so is little Willy, but Langdon is somewhat ailing. Dr. Powell says he thinks he can keep him from a serious attack. He wrote word yesterday he was better. They are en-

---

[70] In his official report on the Battle of Gaines Mill, Brigadier General William H. C. Whiting stated the following: "Though not on my staff, I should not do right were I not to mention here the chivalrous daring of young Major Haskell, of South Carolina, belonging, as I am told, to the staff of Gen. D. R. Jones. His personal bearing in a most deadly fire, his example and directions, contributed not a little to the enthusiasm of the charge of the Third. I regret to say that the brave young officer received a terrible wound from a shell, but walked from the field as heroically as he had gone into the fire." *Official Records of the Union and Confederate Armies*, ser. 1, vol. 11, pt. 2, 564.

camped at Laurel Hill Church 5 miles from Richmond. They have only been in once to see us. Be sure we write whether you receive letters or not.

Sophia C. Haskell, Richmond, Va., to Sophie Haskell (SCHS)
22 July [1862]
Dear Sophie,

I am glad to say that the boys are still improving though it is pretty slowly. Joe has been free from fever for several days, and yesterday sat up for a half hour to have his bed made and sometimes is propped up to eat. John has suffered most from want of sleep but last night he had the best nights rest he has yet had and feels much better from it this morning. This cool weather too seems very favorable to them both. John's arm is doing very well and the wound is healing very well. You must not grieve too much for our losses nor think the future must be all dark. I hear so much of sorrow and suffering all around that I cannot but feel grateful we have been so much spared. Willy and Lang were dreadfully exposed and both behaved with great bravery and coolness. Lang carrying orders through the thickest of the fire and Willy when separated from his Reg., joined another and went on through everything. Pinckney Seabrook told Joe that he took the Colours of the Reg. that was wavering and carried them several hundred yards. Langdon is with us today, come in for little rest and change. I think he is improving though he looks thin and worn.

When you go home, if not there now, make the best disposition you can of the fruit and vegetables and send, at least on Post Office days, whatever is to spare to Ella and the girls at the Village. I can give no directions as to work for the servants but to tell them to spin what they can nicely as it is for their own clothes and the boys. I have heard nothing of poor little Johnny since I have been here. I hope he is improving. Tell me how all are doing. I heard from Charley who still does not seem to get our letters though he has some news. We wrote again in answer. Letters come very irregularly. Our friends here are as kind as ever and never seem to feel anything a trouble to them. Tell me how Sallie Smith is when you write, and if you know anything of Mrs. Singleton's arrangements for the summer.[71]

I suppose we will see Alic here before we leave. Poor fellow, I feel for him most of all but God does everything in mercy and He will show him by and by that it is all for the best, but it is hard now for him, but you my dear must be hopeful and trustful and try and submit all your will to Him who is

---

[71] Sallie Smith was Sarah Margaret Wardlaw Smith (1839-1911), a daughter of Judge David Lewis Wardlaw. She had recently lost her husband, Augustus Marshall Smith, who died on June 30, 1862.

careful for us and does not willingly afflict us. Do write to Louis and Paul for me and give love from all. Write care of Thos. U. Dudley.[72] Good bye and love to all.

William T. Haskell, Camp at Laurel Hill Church, Va., to Brigadier General Maxcy Gregg, Second Brigade, Light Division (UNC)
23 July [1862]
General,

I have the honor in accord with orders to report the action of my Company on Friday 27 of June.[73]

Having advanced from its bivouac at daylight across the Mechanicsville turnpike beyond Ellerson's Mill Creek, the Regt. rested under an artillery fire in a wood. From this point my Company was deployed & having advanced for about half a mile with its left flank resting on the road came in sight of a body of troops which I found to be Jackson's army.

The Regt. again moving forward left in front for about a mile, I was ordered to deploy to the right of the road in a large field my left flank joining Capt. Cordero's right.[74] I then proceeded for about a mile, much of the way very difficult, to Gaine's Mill where I met & engaged the enemy. My men had but little or no cover while their opponents were well protected by large trees & the mill. Here I lost three men. The Regt. having come up crossed the creek & the men now much exhausted by fatigue & heat rested for a short time, & again advanced with light skirmishing across a large field. Then the regt. coming up we assembled on its right & charged across a field which the enemy rapidly left. I then took my proper place in line on the left.

Soon the Regt. advanced & entering a pine wood was [severely] engaged. After being under fire for some time & having just well begun to reply, I was told that there must be an order to retire as some companies to the right were falling back. This I did not mind expecting a direct order. Very soon however Lt. Rhett who was on the right of my company called at me that the whole Regt. had fallen back.[75] I then gave the order. It was obeyed

---

[72] Thomas Underwood Dudley, Sr.

[73] The Battle of Gaines' Mill, Va., also known as the First Battle of Cold Harbor, was fought on June 27, 1862.

[74] John Cordero of Richland District, S.C., was the captain of Company C of the First South Carolina Infantry Regiment.

[75] This was Second Lt. John Grimke Rhett (1838-62) of Company H, First South Carolina Infantry Regiment, who was killed in action at this battle. The son of Benjamin Smith Rhett (1798-1868) and Mary Pauline Haskell Rhett (1808-51), he was William T. Haskell's first cousin. There was, however, another Lt. Rhett in Company I, Robert Woodward Barnwell (1838-1862), the son of Robert Barnwell Rhett (1800-76), who was wounded at this battle and died several days later.

& the Comp. fell back in as good order as the ground would allow to the stream just at our rear. From the loss of my first & second Lts. which had now taken place the Company was diminished by some men following other companies with which the irregularities of the ground threw them. At the stream I halted not knowing till long after that the right had retired further. Not hearing anything of it I joined a force which came up to our left. With about twenty men not all my own, I placed myself on the left of a regt. about to charge across from the left to the right of the field which the First Regt. had lately [fronted].

We made the charge at the double quick as far as the road to the right of the field, putting the enemy to flight & taking some prisoners. This advance was made directly toward a battery whose practice was very severe on us. In a few minutes joining another regt. we charged in the same direction across the road causing the enemy to leave their battery in our front, while they assailed our left flank with a fire which caused the regt. to retire. Seeing that this regt. would do nothing more I joined one of Garland's brigade[76] of Longstreets Div. to the right & advanced a short way with it but the enemy now gave way & then it being night the battle ended. I then had with me Lt. Seabrook & nine men all very tired & worn out.[77] The rest from wounds or the rapidity & frequency of our movements, &their fatigue were scattered. My loss on that day was four killed & twelve wounded, several stunned or severely bruised by spent balls. Among the number Lt. Rhett & Barnwell whose services were invaluable & their loss proportionately great.[78] My men behaved well, several detached from me joining the other companies & continuing the fight & rejoined the Regt.

Charles T. Haskell, Jr., Sullivan's Island, S.C., to Sophia C. Haskell (SCHS)
7 August 1862
Dear Mother,

I have just returned from the city where I heard that you had arrived in Columbia with Joe & John. I wrote a long letter a few days ago to Alick directing to Richmond Virginia. I thought at the time that he had gone back & do not even now know to the contrary. I should be very sorry to hear that

---

[76] A Confederate brigade commanded by General Samuel Garland (1830-62).

[77] Cotesworth Pinckney Seabrook (1839-63) was the son of Archibald Hamilton Seabrook (1816-94) and Phoebe Caroline Pinckney (1816-92). He first enlisted in the Washington Light Infantry and later became a second lieutenant in Company H of the Fisrt South Carolina Infantry Regiment, and was killed at Chancellorsville on May 3, 1863. He was usually called Pinckney.

[78] John Gibbes Barnwell (1839-1918), a 1st lieutenant in Company H, was wounded at this battle. He was later a staff officer under General Samuel McGowan.

he has not received it. I scarcely think it possible to get off but I will try to do so for a few days & come up to see you.

Charles T. Haskell, Jr., Sullivan's Island, S.C., to Charles T. Haskell (SCHS)
26 August 1862
Dear Father,

John & I arrived here yesterday. John quite well. I tried to execute your commissions in Charleston but found that Edgerton had neither the over-coat cloth nor the black that you wished coat or pants from.[79] He has some blue cloth which I cannot recommend, at $15 pr yard. There are two vessels however now in the harbor that have just run in with assorted cargoes & Edgerton thinks that he will be able to supply you soon. I will get the information from Uncle Langdon as soon as I can see him or get an answer from him to a note I have written him. He is now on Morris Island. Gen. Pemberton is in Savannah.[80] I will ask him about the arrangement of the negroes as soon as he returns.

Alexander C. Haskell, Albemarle Plantation, S.C.,[81] to Charles T. Haskell and Sophia C. Haskell (UNC)
31 August 1862
My dear Father & Mother,

It is with regret that I am now forced to acknowledge to myself how much more time I [could] have spent with you had I not been both impatient and somewhat imprudent. I go tomorrow (Monday) and you may rest assured that I go in good health. I cannot say any more as in old times that I go in good spirits but thank God I do go resigned and contented with His decree. I do not hurry off to drown thought in excitement. I go to do my duty to the best of my ability and continue to try to serve my country. No one wishes more sincerely though some with brighter hopes may wish more ardently, than I, for the end of the war. You need feel no anxiety on my account more than for the others. I will run no more risk and have less to lose and more to gain. The power of God can strike as surely in the quiet of the happy home we have left as upon the fiercest battlefield. Why then should you feel more anxiety for me upon the field of battle than in the quiet of peace? It may be the cannon ball, it may be disease, but if it is the will of God that I shall live to do this work or to save my own soul, harm cannot

---

[79] Edgerton, Richards & Company was a Charleston business listed in the 1860 city directory as "drapers and tailors."

[80] Major General John C. Pemberton was at this time in command of the Confederate Department of South Carolina and Georgia, headquartered in Charleston.

[81] Albemarle was the plantation home of Decca's family near Columbia, S.C.

come near me. I do not pretend to insensibility as to the prospect of death, but so plain is the hand of God in all his dealings, that when I reflect like a reasonable creature, I feel as near death in my quiet chamber as when I thought I could not stretch forth my hand without intercepting a ball on its errand of destruction. A battle only makes us feel what we are, and in whose hand. A broken constitution, and weakness, have forced me to give way to a sorrow which I vainly thought I could have borne as a follower of Christ. And I would not that others should mourn for me as I have mourned my lost one. Death is but an era of life more appealing in appearance than the first birth, and is only terrible when met without preparation. When a Christian is born again and borne to Heaven tis for ourselves we mourn and not for the glorified soul. It is not now with me a desire to call back my beloved Decca, but my soul is bent to join her in Heaven. It is not long, nor always even now can I say this with truth, but with fire I have been purged and I have hope. She is happier than I could have made her on earth and for this I should be and am thankful.

I will write regularly and endeavor to alleviate your anxieties. My dearest love to Sophie, cousin Folly and all the boys. Goodbye. Baby is still doing well, very fat and growing fast.

SOLDIERING ON

4 SEPTEMBER 1862 – 28 JUNE 1863

On September 17, 1862, Gregg's Brigade sees action at Sharpsburg, a battle Aleck calls "bloody but glorious." Of all the brigades participating in this engagement (which ends in a draw), Gregg's suffers the most heavily in killed and wounded. On Sullivan's Island near Charleston, Charles is the commanding officer at the Breach Inlet Battery (later named Battery Marshall). In the latter part of 1862, Sophie travels to Flat Rock, North Carolina, where she becomes a pupil at the boarding school of the Misses de Choiseul. The letters give few details about the Battle of Fredericksburg (December 11-15, 1862), but Aleck suffers a wound to the shoulder in that fight, and General Maxcy Gregg is killed there. During this time Joseph takes the role of Volunteer Aide-de-Camp to Colonel Edward P. Alexander, the commander of a battalion of artillery in Longstreet's Corps. In January 1863, when General Samuel McGowan takes command of Gregg's brigade, Aleck becomes his Assistant Adjutant General. Also in January, Mrs. Haskell attends the funeral of her nephew Captain Langdon Cheves McCord. In March 1863, John and Joseph are in North Carolina with forces under the command of Major General D. H. Hill. As part of his strategy to take New Bern, a Union stronghold, Hill sends General James J. Pettigrew to attack Fort Anderson (also called Fort Barrington), described by Joseph as "an earthwork situated across the Neuse from Newbern and just on the river bank." Now commanding a battalion of artillery, John is assigned to Pettigrew's brigade, and Joseph, who is with him as his adjutant, recounts the Battle of Fort Anderson in his letter of March 21, 1863. General D. H. Hill's next move is against Washington, North Carolina, which is garrisoned by Federal troops under the command of Major General John G. Foster. On April 2, 1863, still grieving over the loss of his wife, Aleck pens a moving letter to his mother which has been called "one of the most beautiful born of war." Later that month, he visits the battlefield at Fredericksburg and reflects on events there. At the end of April, Langdon is appointed Aide-de-Camp to Brigadier General McGowan, whose brigade fights at Chancellorsville in April and May. During this battle, which is considered one of General Robert E. Lee's greatest victories, Aleck is wounded again, taking a shot in the left ankle, and William loses some of his best officers and men. General McGowan is also seriously wounded. While in Richmond the following month, Aleck has the sad duty of telegraphing the mother of Rev. Robert W. Barnwell that her son has died. Rev. Barnwell's wife Mary, who is Decca's sister, dies two days later. In June 1863, Joseph is serving as adjutant in McIntosh's Artillery Battalion. His battalion, along with John's (Henry's Artillery), is with the Army of Northern Virginia as it moves into Pennsylvania. In early June, William is given command of a battalion of sharpshooters in Lee's army, and in his last letter, a cheerful one written on June 28, he reports that General Lee has ordered "strict respect to noncombatants & private property."

Alexander C. Haskell, Richmond, Va., to Charles T. Haskell (UNC)
4 September 1862
My dear Father,

I write from Richmond where I arrived yesterday after a tedious journey. I can learn nothing of Langdon, Willy or the General, only I hear no bad news and trust that God has again spared the noble fellows.[1] Is it not hard that I should again be away from them when danger is to be met, glory won, and our country saved? I much fear that this victory has cost us more dearly than any of its predecessors, but they are all worth their price. Even here I am delayed again but hope to get on tomorrow. I find Evelyn my gray mare entirely unfit to go into the campaign. She is with foal & I am obliged to leave her in a government stable until I can find some trusty man to ride her home, where I know you will take that care of her which I wish to bestow until her death. This has caused me an embarrassing delay. I cannot buy a horse at the exhorbitant prices asked, or just now at any prices and have spent my morning looking for one in the Qr Master's stables. I hope to secure one for the journey to carry my servant and baggage, and then I will try to get on with my bay mare, who I hope is in condition though I have not yet seen her.

I am obliged to go on horseback to join the army & hope to start tomorrow to go about 130 to 150 miles.

---

[1] Gregg's Brigade fought in the Battle of Second Manassas, a Confederate victory, in late August 1862.

Since writing the foregoing I have met Mac Haskell who tells me that Eugenia is in Abbeville.[2] I rode my mare a little way this morning and find that her wound still bleeds and discharges most profusely. She is entirely disabled.

I hope to get off tomorrow. Love to Ma & all at home. Goodbye.

Charles T. Haskell, Jr., Breach Inlet Battery, Sullivan's Island, S.C., to Charles T. Haskell (SCHS)

12 September 1862

Dear Father,

I received a long letter from Ma yesterday evening in which she says that she has not heard of John but once since he left home. John writes with considerable difficulty & has therefore asked me to write home concerning him & I think I have mentioned him in three different letters but I am not sure. John is very well indeed as to general health & I think has improved very slowly. I hardly think that he will be fit for service before the 1st of November & I should be glad to see him stay out of it until the 1st of Jan. '63. I have received a list of 100 negroes assigned to my post who will be here today. Four negroes are not among them. I will take the most prompt measures to have them transferred to me as soon as I can find out where they are. As soon as I can go to town I will attend to your clothes.

Alexander C. Haskell, Headquarters, Gregg's Brigade, Light Division, to Sophia C. Haskell (UNC)

23 September 1862

My dear Mother,

I can write to you but a line before the messenger must go to tell you that we have all been spared through two more fights, one a short but bloody one in which the fighting was desperate but successful and our loss heavy.[3] Langdon & Willy were not touched. The General was bruised by a ball & had his horse killed under him. My pet mare was shot severely but not mortally & carried me bravely on. Our army is small but fights gloriously. No part of it fights better if as well as the Division to which we belong. Great numbers of the men have straggled off until none but heroes are left. They fill me with admiration in the fight. You can tell McGowan that his Regiment had no loss in the Sharpsburgh fight of the 17th but in a stubborn de-

---

[2] Eugenia may have been Eugenia H. Noble (born 1839), who was the daughter of Eugenia Lucy Lovell Haskell Noble (1809-51) and the sister of Russell Noble (1847-65) and James Noble (born 1836). No information could be found on Mac Haskell.

[3] This refers to the Battle of Sharpsburg (Antietam) on September 17, 1862, and probably an engagement near Shepherdstown, Va., on September 20, 1862.

fence we made of the crossing of the Potomac in which we endured an awful cannonade for nine hours without being able to cross to take the guns. He lost about 10 killed & 20 wounded. They won the admiration of the whole Brigade by the manner in which they closed up the line three times when shell struck them fairly making fearful gaps each time. The 14th never staggered nor rushed but kept on a steady march at the common step as ever the Old Guard did with Napoleon himself in its might, just giving a stern shout of defiance. On the [17th] at Sharpsburg in Maryland one regt the 12th 175 strong crossed bayonets with over a thousand of the enemy, routed them & came out with 104 killed & wounded. Such fighting as this will tell against any disparity of numbers.

Our life is rough & exposed, exactly what I wished & needed. My health is perfect and my strength rapidly returning. Don't fear for me nor for your others. We are in God's hands. I rose from my seat for a moment [just where] yesterday an officer took it & was shot. I can feel no [ease] seeing so plainly the hand of God around me. The fire through which we rode the other day & which struck our horses was aimed directly at us as we were the only objects visible & within 200 yards of a Brigade was most terrific, missed us and after we had passed on the & the fire had ceased a stray ball from it killed a general officer, Branch, who had come up to ask after our safety a few moments before.[4] Such are the strange chances of battle.

Give my dearest love to Pa, Sophy & all at home. May God bless and protect you all my dear Mother. Tell Ella that Langdon is quite well & give her my best love.

Alexander C. Haskell, Headquarters, Second Brigade Light Division, Bunkers-ville, Va., to Sophia C. Haskell (UNC)
28 September 1862
Dear Mother,

I have just heard of an opportunity of sending a letter but must be in haste.

The fighting seems to be over for the present. The enemy have not crossed the Potomac in force at any point near us and we have fallen back towards Winchester and are now within ten or twelve miles of that place.

Our whole army forms line on a strong range of hills of which we occupy Bunker's Hill, the left. Here our Generals would be glad to meet an attack from the enemy but do not seem at present disposed to make an ad-

---

[4] Brigadier General Lawrence O'Bryan Branch (1820-62) of A. P. Hill's Division. He was killed by an enemy sharpshooter, and the same shot wounded General Maxcy Gregg.

vance. The Indian summer may possibly pass as quiet as it did last year and we may renew an active warfare in South Carolina next winter. I would like then to be among the number sent to Carolina to keep a watchful eye over my dearest treasures.

Our very successes have complicated the aspect of the war. Some say peace will soon break upon us. The range of vision is singularly contracted and circumscribed in the army. We see but little & foresee nothing. We pitch into fight and those that come out then go quietly on in the hard work of [march] or the routine of camp and really enjoy the army life with all its painful accessories. We certainly are training an army of soldiers who will loth to give up the profession. I was surprised to hear Willy the other day when he seriously asked my advice as to the advisability of his seeking a commission in the army after the war.

I have lost an hour at this point by orders in haste from Headquarters and my messengers are in haste.

I saw Richard yesterday looking well though a little thin.[5] He had been for some days staying quietly with the wagons drinking sulphur water which had improved his health considerably. Carter is quite well though I have not seen him yet.[6] John dined with me a few days ago looking remarkably well. Tell Mrs. Stark that Lamar came to see me a few days ago.[7] He was quite well & supplied with boots though he has not received the pair I left in Richmond.

Genl. Hampton has not been hurt in any of his skirmishes & fights & is the boys tell me well.[8] I have heard nothing of the progress of the application made on behalf of Richard. I do hope it may be successful.

If you or anybody else will trouble yourselves to write to me give my full direction, in full care of Brig. Gen. Gregg, A. P. Hill's Division & send the letter to Richmond with a request on the envelope to have it forwarded. God grant that I may hear of your welfare and that my little darling is as well and happy as when she was with me to assure me by her perfect health that she would be spared to me. Give my dearest love to Mary & Lessie[9] and tell the latter that she must spend some of her idle time in writing me how many of my wise precepts she has followed, and how many miles she walks every day.

---

[5] Decca's brother Richard R. Singleton.

[6] Decca's brother Charles Carter Singleton.

[7] This was likely Thomas Lamar Stark (1844-83). His mother (Mrs. Stark) may have been Eliza Cary Lamar Stark (1814-88).

[8] Brigadier General Wade Hampton (1818-1902) of South Carolina.

[9] Lessie was Decca's sister Lucy Everette Singleton (1848-90), later Mrs. David Hemphill.

God bless you all. Kiss baby for me a thousand times & it will not express to her my love for her. Goodbye my dear Mother.

Alexander C. Haskell, Headquarters, Second Brigade Light Division, to Charles T. Haskell (UNC)
2 October 1862
My dear Father,

My letters are not frequent for though we have been quiet for nearly a week we have no regular mail arrangements and the transmission of letters is so precarious as to discourage the frequent writing of them. And writing is difficult nowadays of excitement unless you have a battle to describe and if you have a battle the theme is too great for the scope & power of any ordinary pen. However I can give you still the welcome intelligence that amid the death and ruin around us your sons are still unharmed. The battle of Sharpsburgh was bloody but glorious where Hill's Division met the enemy and cost us many noble friends and comrades.

Colonel Barnes of the 12th S.C.V. was mortally wounded there, since dead. The State never lost a nobler or more generally esteemed officer. The battle of Shepherds Town too of which you have seen ridiculously exaggerated accounts spared us though it cut off men from our very sides. Our army has increased I think much more than one half in fact in some divisions, as in ours, is nearly double what it was in Maryland. This great increase in our week of repose is occasioned by the arrival of men who have straggled, or who have been toiling up from Richmond and other points to join the army upon recovering from sickness or wounds. We are in far better condition in every respect than when we first invaded the cold treacherous soil of Maryland, and I trust before the Indian summer has passed to be feeding our hungry army in the rich fields of northern Maryland & Pennsylvania. It is a point which we must gain, it seems, to give Maryland & Kentucky a fair vote. I trust however that Kentucky will vote herself into, and Maryland vote herself clear out of, the Confederate States. Pennsylvanians could not have looked more Yankee or received us more coldly than did the Marylanders. Of course Baltimore & the eastern shore are much more Southern in their secession feeling, but given they are so Yankee in their habits and ideas that I should much regret to see the boundaries of nature infringed upon & the Potomac crossed to bring such uncongenial spirits into the Southern League.

Langdon & Willy are looking very well. The General is well & quite recovered from the bruise he got at Sharpsburgh, by a flattened ball at the same time that his horse was killed and my brave mare so dangerously wounded.[10] I am truly glad however that my horse friend as well as the General has recovered and the wound is rapidly healing. I write in haste.

Dearest love to Ma & all at home. I have heard that my little one is well and thank God for this mercy. God bless & protect you all.

Charles T. Haskell, Jr., Breach Inlet Battery, Sullivan's Island, S.C., to Sophia C. Haskell (SCHS)
5 October 1862
Dear Mother,

Since writing my last letter I have quite recovered which is very fortunate as I have a great deal of work to do. The fortifications have been greatly increased in their plan at this point, so much so that I have had one hundred & twenty hands employed here for nearly a month & had to report yesterday that I must have at least one hundred more to finish the work in two weeks. A few evenings ago the Yankees shelled me again, throwing long Parrot & eleven inch Dahlgren shells. Several of the latter failed to burst & I have them here now. One of their gunboats came barely within range of my heaviest gun & I fired several shots at her, striking her [[once]]. I suppose that John is at home now. Do tell him, in case he failed to receive a letter that I wrote him, that he left a silver [cup] here which I will send him when an opportunity presents.

Alexander C. Haskell, Second Brigade, Light Division, to Sophia C. Haskell (UNC)
10 October 1862
My dear Mother,

Of course we never hear from home, or very seldom. I believe Willy has had one letter, & Langdon a few, but I hope by this time you have heard of us. Willy told me you spoke of not having heard from me. I wrote from Richmond, and then as soon as practicable afterwards several times. We are all well and weaning away a tedious time of repose on the Virginia side of the Potomac watching the drilling of the Yankee thousands on the other side. The condition of our army is good and prospect cheering. I have heard indirectly of both Joe & John, that Joe had his appointment, and that John would soon rejoin his General. Their good fortune is merited. Langdon & Willy are about as usual, nothing unusual occurring. Idleness in military life is the unbearable thing we are now forced to bear, and I am I confess heartily sick of it & long for some change, but the room for such changes is very small.

---

[10] General Maxcy Gregg.

I have heard once from—I can't write her name again—my little one, that she was well. Thank God for this much. I trust that you are all well. Goodbye. Dearest love to Pa, Sophy & all at home.

Sophia C. Haskell, Home Place Plantation, Abbeville District, S.C., to Sophie Haskell (SCHS)
13 October 1862
Dear Sophie,

I have missed you a great deal particularly as I have been a good deal alone tho your Father being so unwell I have had more of his company than usual. He had an attack yesterday morning which alarmed me very much, a violent palpitation of the heart which lasted nearly an hour. The Dr however who came in the afternoon said it was nothing of importance but only a new phase of his dyspepsia. With the exception he has been somewhat better since you left. He felt better for his trip with you and the next day drove me over to pay a visit to Mrs. Graves. The next day, Saturday, he went into the village with Follie who after many demurs determined to leave the children and accept Mrs. Burt's invitation and come back Monday, but wrote me a note by the return of the carriage saying that Jeannie had pressed her to pay them her long promised visit and begged me to send in Katy and the children this morning, which I have just done.[11] The boys too have just gone this morning after a very pleasant visit at home, for this time I saw a great deal of them, and we were all much more chatty and confidential. No further news from the boys but a few lines from Charley urging your Father to visit him at once while the weather was so pleasant, and promising to make him comfortable. John had just arrived Wednesday and was "busy eating new oysters." Why he specifies the oysters I do not know. I will have the fragments of hoops hunted up but I fear not much is to be found as heretofore I think they have been considered fair spoil and have gone to help the display at the Baptist Meeting.

Monday evening. I have just received a note from Follie at the village and she received a telegram from Tom Rhett telling her to meet him in Columbia to stay several weeks. She sent Katy back to pack her trunk and leaves by the cars in the morning. I have also a letter from Joe. He is well but as yet has made no progress in his own affairs. An Aid of the President whose business is to receive applications told him that his application &c were in the hands of the President but would not be acted on till after the adjournment of Congress. He says he has no doubt of his ultimate success but is

---

[11] Mrs. Burt was probably Martha Catherine Calhoun Burt (1809-69), the wife of Armistead Burt (1802-83) of Abbeville.

very weary of the whole business and is rather sorry for having gone on so soon, as there is no hope of Gen. Johnston's reporting for duty in less than a month. Good night now my dear little girl. May God bless and protect you and guide you in all your ways. Your Father seems better today. Tomorrow is the Election and he is going to Loundsville.[12]

William T. Haskell, Camp Barnes, Va., to Sophia C. Haskell (SCHS)
15 October 1862
My dear Mother,
 Still resting in our lazy camp. We have nothing to occupy us except two drills a day & a constant watch for news, which comes mainly from the West viz K. Smith, Bragg, Van Dorn.[13] Our latest of home manufacture is the return of Stewart who with a considerable body of cavalry & 6 or 8 pieces of art[iller]y crossed in to Maryland near Williams Point next to Chambersburg Pa. & [then] returned crossing near Leesburg. His exploits were burning stores, workshops & machinery, plundering a bank & bringing back about a 1000 horses without the loss of a man.[14] Little Willy was of the party & probably had a fine time. Do give my love to all my cousins in the village. I can hardly think of those domesticated there & almost at times forget the fact. I think our movements here depend much on those of Bragg, Smith & the weather, on the two former we are wanting & hope the latter will wait on us. The best thing hoped for though hardly expected is that McC[lellan] should cross the Potomac & attack us. As yet there are no symptoms of <u>anything</u> anywhere hereabouts. What we shall have for dinner is the chief question & the inevitable answer is beef & flour which last we make into very passable bread using salt water & flour soured for yeast. The men who in our easiest times & best condition were in anything but Jobs now never grumble at anything. I have a few, over half my camp, present—a good proportion now-a-days. The sick and wounded as far as I can hear of them doing well. Many of my men are reduced to the smallest possible wardrobe. Anything in the shape of under clothing would be specially acceptable. Send thro Rev. Robt. Barnwell. It is likely to be rec[eive]d. Love to Pa, who I hope is by this time well, & all the rest.

---

[12] Lowndesville, formerly called Rocky River, was a town in Abbeville District.

[13] Those mentioned are Major General Edmund Kirby Smith (1824-93); Major General Braxton Bragg (1817-76), commander of the Army of Mississippi (later called the Army of Tennessee); and Major General Earl Van Dorn (1820-63).

[14] In the first part of October 1862, Major General J. E. B. Stuart (1833-64) led a daring raid on Chambersburg, Penn., seizing horses and supplies. An attempt was made to take money from the town's bank, but it had been removed.

Sophia C. Haskell, Home Place Plantation, Abbeville District, S.C., to Sophie Haskell (SCHS)
21 October 1862
Dear Sophie,

I find my letter written Sunday evening left by mistake so I will open it to say I received yours yesterday and also letters from Lang & Alic. All are well in Virginia. Lang writes Ella a long letter quite cheerful and holding out hopes of coming home after a while. Poor Alic is short and very different from his bright old enthusiastic letters, but we cannot hope for anything for him yet but that God may give him strength to submit to his great sorrow, and heal his wounds in his good time. Your Father still continues to improve a great deal of late and is quite cheerful again; he feels badly at times but has much more ease and comfort than a week ago. I was in the village yesterday and saw everybody at the Society.[15] The subscriptions are large and we will have the clothes soon made up. Now for your letter. Kerrison's ship has arrived but unfortunately at the yellow fever port of Wilmington so for at least a time the goods can not come on.[16] What you write for I think all very reasonable and if I can I will try and lay in some small supplies for the family and include yours. Keep the money, the $10 for your weekly allowance. I will get for you what I can. Your shoes are not done yet. I will send for them Friday. When they come I will get the box ready. I will look for the handkerchief but fear it has gone the way of the rest, probably lost. I think you have enough to do if you attend to all the lessons you mention and I think it may be as well to differ [*sic*] the Italian till you are better used to them. Do speak french and for that purpose seek the society of the ladies. It will be at least as improving and if nice people perhaps quite as interesting as the girls.

Charles T. Haskell, Jr., Breach Inlet Battery, Sullivan's Island, S.C., to Sophia C. Haskell (SCHS)
22 October 1862
Dear Mother,

Do let me hear when you write again anything that you can tell me with regard to any of my brothers in Virginia. Joe I heard from a few days since. He was at Richmond & I suppose is still there. Everything is going on much as usual down here. Vast fortifications gradually growing up all around the harbor. Really, when I look back to the condition of the defences this

---

[15] This refers to one of several ladies' societies in Abbeville organized to supply and aid Confederate soldiers.

[16] Edwin Lane Kerrison (1813-93) was one of the directors of the Importing and Exporting Company of South Carolina, a blockade running enterprise. He was also the owner of a Charleston department store, Kerrison's.

time eighteen months ago or even six months ago & compare them what they are now & consider that we felt very confident then it seems ridiculous that we should feel doubt now. But I fear that rapid as our increase of the means of defence has been, theirs has been equal in means of attack. It yet is a question to be solved whether their iron [roofed] boats can be penetrated by our projectiles or not. If they cannot, all our defences are as nothing. If they can be, there will be room for the display of any amount of heroism on both sides & we can hardly doubt the results. The yellow fever continues in Charleston where there have been undoubtedly a few cases for six weeks or two months. Altho the papers stated nothing about it, there is, I believe, no doubt that it was the cause of Col. Lamar's death.[17] I am glad that it has not become epidemic as frost is now so near that not much injury could be done by it should it become so now. I see Uncle John always when I go to town & Aunt Rachel & Minna occasionally. They all seem to be well generally, altho both Aunt Rachel & Minna were sick when I last saw them. If Aunt Charlotte & the girls are in Abbeville do give my love to them, also to Cousin Folly & Ella.

Alexander C. Haskell, Headquarters, Second Brigade, Light Division, Camp Barnes, Va., to Charles T. Haskell (UNC)
24 October 1862
My dear Father,
   I received a letter of the 6th from Ma last evening at the same time that Langdon & Willy got dyspeptic attack, originating I cannot doubt from the frequency of such cases, in your prolonged stay in the pestilent atmosphere of Richmond. I trust that the approach of winter will restore your health and strength, as the last two months of active life have brought back mine. What is left of our army, and it is a pretty large one still, is in fine condition, but dreading the approach of winter. Frequent pittances of clothing, shoes and blankets have however covered the cases of sharpest suffering, though we still have a good number without shoes, and who have to trust to a comrade's charity for the share of a blanket. I feel an abiding confidence though that we will weather it all and triumph before long.
   I would warn you in a quiet way to have vaccination on all who have not yet received it, as we have smallpox in the army, and it may find its way home. It is very slight as yet & I hope will not be serious. We have but two cases in our brigade. Our great trouble is in procuring vaccine matter. About 40 of our men who had never been vaccinated received it this morning, con-

---

[17] Colonel Thomas Gresham Lamar of Edgefield District, S.C., died on October 17, 1862. Fort Lamar on James Island was named for him.

suming all the vaccine matter & leaving hundreds still exposed. In a few days the matter will be abundant & we can all be vaccinated, and as the cases have been isolated, I apprehend no serious spread of the disease.

We are still near Winchester spending our time watching and defying McClellan and tearing up the Baltimore & Ohio, and tributary rail roads. We have just returned to camp from an expedition of three days against the R.R. near Harper's Ferry in which in full view, and almost under the guns of McClellan's Grand Army, we tore up miles of this valuable road, burned the wood & bent the iron.

The enemy submitted quietly to both loss and insult. After this defiance and submission I almost think we will not have another great battle this fall, though it is hard to see the fine weather and good roads wasted. If we don't fight, I suppose our army will be distributed for coast defence and in search of food. The great valley of Virginia, having fed two hostile armies for a year and more, is now a trampled desert.

We may be on the coast of South Carolina again for the campaign of the coming winter, but I would rather see the decisive blow struck here before the great army of many victories has been dispersed.

Langdon and Willy are as well as I ever saw them. My own health is good. I am glad to hear of John's recovery and of the ease with which his one hand subserves most of his wants. I hope that some duty will be found suited to his condition. I am glad to hear that Sophy has gone to school with my other little sister.[18] It will do them both good.

Dearest love to Ma & the boys, to Sophy & Charley when anyone writes. Love to Cousin Folly, and to Aunt Charlotte and her daughters. Goodbye.

Sophia C. Haskell, Home Place Plantation, Abbeville District, S.C., to Sophie Haskell (SCHS)
2 November [1862]
Dear Sophie,

I was glad to hear you were well and happy as well as from your Aunt as from yourself. She is certainly very kind both to you and to your Father who will gladly accept her offer as he thinks a little wine would benefit him and I have written to your Aunt Charlotte who left here last Thursday for Savannah to try and put some of her valuables in some place of safety, either from friends or foes, for either army is sure to do mischief. The girls were with Jeannie when she left, but were to have returned on Thursday, but

---

[18] Along with Sophie Haskell, Lessie Singleton (Decca's sister), was apparently a pupil at the de Choiseul school in Flat Rock, N.C.

there was to be some tableaux party of the children on Friday to which they stayed and they will come out on Tuesday and Ella and Jeannie also I believe. Follie has returned from Columbia and stopped in the Village to try and find a servant. Katy left her for another place in Columbia. I fear she will hardly succeed in getting one to suit her. Tom Rhett is ordered to report to Gen Holmes[19] across the Mississippi, and in spite of Gen Johnston's efforts, he has to go. I am afraid from what he told your Father that he has exasperated the President very much by what he has been doing in Richmond during the sitting of Congress but the less said about it the better.[20] We heard from Joe. He has no answer yet to his application but thinks it must be decided soon now. He stayed a week at a boarding house, but Mrs. Thompson Brown gave him so kind an invitation that he was spending some days with her. He was at the boarding house to share the room of Bob Elliott. I am sorry your shoes are not done. When I sent the thread the main said he could not make them in less than three weeks. Your Father in Columbia found some beautiful English shoes $15 a pair. Unfortunately mine are too narrow. I hope yours may fit. Hannah McCord could not get them on.[21] Her instep was too high. But Lottie put them on easily so you may judge.[22]

The boys are at home. Mr. Porcher gives November instead of January, that he may go down and take care of his wounded brother. Dwight and DuBose are both safe and well.[23] Charley quite well and very busy. Alec writes on the 24th all well. He has quite regained his health. They had been tearing up the R. Rds in the face of the enemy uninterruptedly. Little Willy well too. He had been to Pennsylvania with Stuart.[24] John went to Richmond with Major Rhett. He had hired a good servant and one for Joe also. Good by my dear little girl. I will write again soon.

---

[19] Lt. General Theophilus Hunter Holmes (1804-80) had recently been assigned to the command of the Trans-Mississippi Department.

[20] Major Thomas Grimke Rhett had served as General Joseph E. Johnston's chief of staff, and he was the nephew of Robert Barnwell Rhett (1800-76), a Confederate Congressman and newspaperman who often opposed the Davis administration. "His exile to the Trans-Mississippi can perhaps be explained by his association with General Johnston and Senator Rhett, both vocal administration opponents." Allardice, *More Generals in Gray*, 198.

[21] Hannah Cheves McCord (1843-72), a cousin, was the daughter of Louisa S. McCord. She later married John Taylor Rhett.

[22] Lottie was Charlotte Reynolds McCord (1842-1923), the daughter-in-law of Mrs. Louisa S. McCord.

[23] Richard Yeadon Dwight and William Porcher DuBose.

[24] The famous cavalry commander Major General James Ewell Brown ("Jeb") Stuart (1833-64) led a daring raid into Pennsylvania in October 1862.

[P.S.] Cheves McCord mending fast.[25] Little Decca is a little darling (says Papa) only almost too fat.

John C. Haskell to Charles T. Haskell (UNC)
13 November 1862
Dear Pa,

Since I wrote last I have been with the army trying to get my accounts wound up and have at last succeeded in doing so though I found it very troublesome. I will go down to Richmond day after tomorrow to hand them in and will probably return very soon and will be assigned immediately to the command of a Battalion of artillery in Longstreet's Corps provided I can get transferred which I think will be done very easily as Genl Longstreet has requested that it should be done for this special purpose. I suppose that it is decided by this time whether or no [*sic*] Joe will get his cadetship and I think that he will be able to get a position in the So[outh] Ca[rolina] Regulars if his application for a cadetship has failed.

I have not heard anything of Langdon [and] Willy or Alex since I came on as they are in Jackson's Corps and communication has been very difficult between the two portions of this Army, but yesterday news came that the Yankees are falling back and there are none of them between here and the mountains. There has been a good deal of skirmishing on the front and I saw quite a sharp little fight day before yesterday between about twenty five hundred of our men (principally cavalry) and their advance forces. We beat them back about [six] miles skirmishing all the way and late in the evening they beat us back a mile but continued their retreat next morning. I was riding the sorrel who acted beautifully and did not mind the fire at all though it was at times pretty heavy. Our loss was small and we took a good many prisoners. Do give my love to Ma, Aunt Charlotte, Mary & Emma and all the boys and direct to me at Genl G. W. Smith. The sorrel horse is looking well and stands the work finely and is as pleasant a riding horse as I ever saw. I will write from Richmond.

Charles T. Haskell, Jr., Sullivan's Island, to Charles T. Haskell (SCHS)
14 November 1862
Dear Father,

Judge Wardlaw has probably spoken to you on the subject of salt making down here, or will if he has not.[26] I cannot pretend to offer advice as the

---

[25] Captain Langdon Cheves McCord (1841-63), the son of Mrs. Haskell's sister Louisa S. McCord, was wounded in the head at the Battle of Second Manassas in late August 1862.

only objection that can be urged is the risk of the undertaking. I think in view of the fact that I am posted here with a powerful battery, that the risk will not be appreciable & I will be very glad to give my attention to the enterprise should you enter into it.

Sophia C. Haskell, Home Place Plantation, Abbeville District,
to Sophie Haskell (SCHS)
16 November [1862]
Dear Sophie,

We are all looking for your letter telling us what arrangements you can make for coming home. Mamie says I must give you her love and tell you how glad they will be to see you here. Your Aunt Charlotte has not yet returned. She is working under many difficulties to save her household [goods] but I suspect she will be up this week. Your Cousin Follie is well and the children. She bears the trial of Tom's going away very well but I am afraid she feels it very much. She has heard from him as far on his way as Montgomery. He says he had to shoot his fine mare and John said he would have to shoot Nicholas. I believe they were suffering from some severe and incurable disease. John by the last accounts had left for Culpepper to get his horse and settle his accounts. He was then to take the place of Inspector of Artillery on the Staff of Gen G W Smith until he got a position which he preferred. Gen Smith said he would be glad to keep him there but both he and Gen Whiting advised him to try and get a position in the line, that is in a Reg[iment]. Several Gen[erals] have recommended him for promotion, but he did not expect it. Poor Joe I think is doomed to be disappointed though he still hopes that so many recommendations as he has had will not be neglected. He had been staying for some time with Mrs. Thompson Brown who very kindly insists that she wants his company, but he says he feels very much ashamed of sitting down in Richmond while his brothers are all hard at work. I suppose his suspense must soon end. We have no news from the others since the 27th. All were well then. The papers give us no definite news. Jackson's Brigade have been skirmishing successfully that is all known. A young man from the Army told Dr. Livingston[27] that Greggs Brigade had been engaged but none killed, but three wounded.[28] We cannot tell what is

---

[26] Judge Wardlaw was David Lewis Wardlaw (1799-1873) of Abbeville. He was a signer of the South Carolina Ordinance of Secession.

[27] This was Dr. John Frazier Livingston (1803-67), an Abbeville physician and planter.

[28] J. F. J. Caldwell's history of Gregg's Brigade describes an engagement in 1862, stating: "On Sunday, November 2, a small engagement took place between the Light division and the enemy, near Castleman's Ferry, on the Shenandoah. Our brigade and

the position of our Army but I hope it is good and that we may have good news. In the West things I fear look dark. As yet all is quiet along the Coast. Minna wrote to Emma two or three days ago and spoke of no alarm. You must not be disappointed I have done nothing as to trees or evergreens and I would get the Japonicas with pleasure if you were at home but it would be no use till we have some place to keep them. They would only die. I cannot undertake the care of them without some place to protect them. As to your clothes I do not know what to do but when you come home I will try and get you what you want. I will write to Matilda to know what sort of dress can be got in Columbia.[29] I fear little you would like. Black silk is $7 a yard and very poor at that. Do give my love to Isabella and write as soon as you can. Your Father will send you what money you will want to come home. God bless you my dear little girl.

Sophia C. Haskell, Home Place Plantation, Abbeville District, S.C.,
to Charles T. Haskell, Jr. (SCHS)
16 November [1862]
Dear Charley,

I am afraid nobody has written to you for some time so I will write to tell you I have no news but that all are well at home & abroad by our last news. Your Father's health is quite good now and I hope by prudence in diet he will keep so. Our last news from the Army was Langdon's letter to Ella written from Berryville two days after leaving Martinsburg. The papers tell us they have been skirmishing since but nothing serious as far as we can see. John was well and had gone to Culpepper to get his horse and settle his accounts. He was to go on the staff of Gen. G.W. Smith as Inspector of Artillery for the present, but wished to get a position in some Reg. to serve in the line. Gen. Smith and other friends recommended that course. Several Generals had recommended him for promotion, tho he did not seem to expect it. Joe I fear will be disappointed. He is getting very weary of the uncertainty and I hope something will be settled soon. He wishes he had never left Willie's comp[any], then he would at least have been doing his duty. I feel sorry for him, but he must take patience.

Nov. 18th I left my letter unfinished and have since heard of Langdon as late as the 8th. Ella told your Father she had heard from him by yesterday's

---

Thomas's were placed on picket, to oppose the crossing McClellan was thought to meditate. Two batteries of artillery assisted us. But the enemy did not cross, and the only firing that occurred was between the artillery of the two sides. The brigade had three men wounded, one mortally." Caldwell, *The History of a Brigade of South Carolinians,* 55.

[29] Matilda Eulalie Mason Rhett (died 1871) was the sister of Folly Rhett. She was the wife of Charles Haskell Rhett (1822-95).

mail that he was well but he had no hope of coming home either on furlough or with his Division. As he did not mention his brothers we suppose both are well. We hear from them at long intervals. Willy writes cheerfully as usual but I think he has past [*sic*] through many a painful scene with his company whom he really loves and who have suffered so terribly. Twice he has gone to battle and lost once nearly half and once half of his little band of heroes, "brave to a fault" he says, and men of Orr's old Reg., now Livingston's, have told your Father Willy was a perfect hero himself.[30] John McKeller says the best soldier in the Army, "as brave as anyone, never sick, never." Alec writes in better spirits particularly when in active service. His baby is fat and well as can be. Judge Wardlaw gave us news of you. Mamie sends her love to you. Sophie is well and happy, will be home all Dec. All send love and are glad of any news. Mamie & Emma are very proud that "Papa's battery & yours are the best of all."[31] The boys' direction is still Richmond, Gregg's Regt, Hill's Light Div. Goodbye. God bless and guard you.

Charles T. Haskell, Jr., Sullivan's Island, S.C., to Charles T. Haskell (SCHS)
21 November 1862
Dear Father,

I received the letter with regard to stopping Jonas & June too late. I could very easily have kept them here, as I have now nearly 300 negroes under my charge & could have employed them either in getting wood or have hired them on the public works under my charge. Should you have made no other arrangement as yet I would suggest that if you do not like to send down your own negroes, you should hire what number you may need from Mr. Benj. Rhett.[32] I am now hiring six boys from him, "four of them very likely" at $12 pr month & I could arrange the matter so as to turn them over to you should you desire it.

---

[30] Col. James William Livingston (1832-86) resigned command of the First South Carolina Rifle Regiment (Orr's Rifles) in November 1862 due to health reasons and was replaced by James Monroe Perrin (1822-63).

[31] Mamie (Mary Elizabeth) and Emma were the daughters of Capt. Langdon Cheves (1814-63).

[32] Possibly Benjamin Smith Rhett (1798-1866), or Dr. Benjamin J. Rhett (1828-84), both of whom were relatives.

Alexander C. Haskell, Headquarters, Gregg's Brigade, Camp near Fredericksburg,
Va., to Sophia C. Haskell (UNC)
10 December 1862
Dear Ma,

Your letter to Langdon reminds me that I have trusted too much to his giving you all desired information as to our movements, and that I seldom take up my pen unless for some unusual occurrence. We have completed our retreat from the valley and once more face the enemy on the line of the Rappahannock. Great as is the pressure upon Burnside to become the active assailant, I do not believe that he can attack us with any prospect of success, even in his own view of the matter, without an entire change of position, perhaps to the south side of the James River.[33] In my opinion therefore you can lay aside all anxiety until you hear of another great change of base.

I got your kind letter a few days ago in which you offer so much of comfort for the winter already upon us. For myself I have no wants which have not been already supplied so that I cannot think of anything to trouble you with. Our soldiers have been relieved from their most pinching necessities. Clothes have been supplied in considerable abundance. Shoes and socks are still deficient but we have promise and prospect of supply. I only fear that the people at home will deprive themselves of too much in contributing to the comfort of the soldiers, but even if they should do so they will be repaid by the thoughts of the terrible suffering from which their prompt and generous action has saved their friends in the army.

I still hear of poor Joe as undergoing bitter disappointment, dancing attendance upon the War Office. They really have ill-used him.

I am glad to learn what a pleasant household you have in holding possession of such a treasure as Cousin Follie and making such an acquisition as you have in Aunt Charlotte and her daughters. It really is a comfort to know that you are spared the dreariness which war has brought upon so many deserted homes. Do give my love to Aunt & cousins. Sophie I suppose has come home for her holidays. I meant long since to have written to her at school, but she must believe that it has been neither carelessness nor forgetfulness of her that has prevented my doing so. I am pleased to know that she is contented and doing well at her new school, and hope that she will continue on the most pleasant terms with her kind and accomplished teachers. She must write to me, though, and I will promise to answer. I heard of Pa's sickness, but am relieved by your news of him and hope that the winter will quite restore his health & strength. You ask, I remember here, for some

---

[33] General Ambrose Everett Burnside (1824-81) had succeeded General McClellan in the command of the Army of the Potomac in November 1862.

news of Edmund. I am glad to be reminded of it & to assure his Mother of his continuance in health and good behaviour.

Only a few days since I recovered my lost baggage in which I had his clothes, and a letter from his mother, I read the letter to him, and as the little fellow listened to the kind & good advice contained in it, the tears flowed in a manner which shewed both appreciation & intention to profit by good counsel. He is really a remarkably useful little fellow & Lucy may be proud of him.

Langdon and Willy are both in their usual good health. I am perfectly well. Our winter has been severe but the health of our troops has never been as good in the field or garrison as it is at present. Their power of endurance & resistance deprives hardships of all reality.

My dear Mother you must not wonder that I am sometimes long silent. The routine of camp recalls nothing & it is a relief. But these hours devoted to communication with dear ones at home bring their bitter fruits of memory with them, and here of all other places so crowded with recollections of the associations of six short months ago, I have felt but little able to take upon myself more than was already forced. It gives me pleasure to write though, & I will try to be frequent & regular with my letters.

Goodbye. Love to Pa & all at home. May God bless you all & give you as happy a Christmas & New Year as times of such trouble can admit.

Sophie Haskell, Home Place Plantation, Abbeville District, S.C., to [Charles T. Haskell, Jr.] (SCHS)
December [1862]
My dear Brother,

I cannot write much as I am just out of bed having had a bad cold and fever tho I am quite well now. We have heard nothing from the boys in Virginia except that they were all fine in the Battle before Fredericksburg and we say [sic] in the Columbia paper that Alec had been wounded but not severely from [sic] which we hope that none of the others are. We feel quite sure of Brothers safety at least, for we think he would have been mentioned and indeed we have some hopes of seeing him here quite soon, as if [sic] Alic is well enough to [spare] him. We think he has been sent on with poor Genl Gregg's remains in Columbia.

We heard that Johnny in Longstreet's Division probably in command of an Artillery Battalion tho we don't know, had had one or more horses killed under him in the little fight of the first day but we have heard nothing more of any of them.

I hope brother will be here at Christmas. Could you not come for a little while. It would be so very pleasant. Emmy says don't pretend to appear before her without some oysters for her use.[34]

I cannot write any more as I feel rather weak and amuse myself by efforts to convince myself that Christmas will come in a week & that then I will be seventeen. If you and brothers come home it will be a very pleasant one. Love from all.

Willliam T. Haskell, Camp near Fredericksburg, Va., to David H. Bellot[35]
11 December 1862
My dear Bellot,

I got your letter some days ago & am glad to see by it that your spirits are better kept up than your body. I hope however that the latter will catch up in due time. Take care of yourself & don't practice that singular half-hammond of yours too much at first. With patience I dare say you may equal old Dick Yeadon's celebrated feat in that way.

I was much surprised to hear from you that your brother Louis was not at home.[36] I sent him a descriptive list to Lynchburg whence I thought he would start immediately for home. I hope he has arrived though by this time however & that you make a pair of merry cripples together.

I send you a "Descriptive list" in case you have not got your pay otherwise.[37]

I hope speaking more seriously that your wound will in time allow a full return of your strength and activity. It is a severe trial to be bound by an infirmity at our time of life. I trust that if this is your case you may receive strength to bear it well & in the right spirit.

The loss of the comp[any] so far has been 12 from battle, 8 fr[om] sickness. I am sorry to say that poor old Grant is among the first.[38] He died

---

[34] It appears that "Emmy" is Emma Cheves.

[35] This letter was taken from volume one of A. S. Salley's book *South Carolina Troops in Confederate Service*. The recipient, David H. Bellot (1836-89), enlisted at Abbeville in August 1861 and was wounded at Cold Harbor on June 27, 1862.

[36] Louis Gideon Bellot (1838-1915) enlisted at Abbeville in August 1861. He was wounded at the Second Battle of Manassas on August 29, 1862.

[37] This identifying "Descriptive list" was enclosed with the letter and gave the following description of David H. Bellot: "Private, age 25, blue eyes, dark hair, fair complexion, 5 feet 8 inches high, born in Abbeville, S.C.; a teacher; enlisted for the war at Abbeville, August 17, 1861, by Capt. W. T. Haskell."

[38] This was Neely Grant, who enlisted in Charleston in August 1861 and was wounded at the Second Battle of Manassas on August 29, 1862. He died of his wounds on September 15, 1862.

of his wounds at Warrenton. Of Godley too I have apprehensions.[39] If they are realized it will add one to the above number.

We have been disturbed this morning by a furious cannonade toward Fredericsburg commencing before day. The musketry also has been heavy. I estimate the reports of artillery at full 3500. It is now 12 [n.] & all sounds of battle &c have almost subsided. How soon they may recommence I know not. We are cocked & primed, ready to march at a moments notice. The brigade is encamped just where Genl. Gregg was last spring about a mile from our old camp. I walked over there last evening with Alic & looked at the old place. Looked down Co "Es" [old well] & recognized every tree & spot by some association with some one of the comp[any], too often some one who shall join the ranks of Co. H no more.

Tomorrow is my birthday. I dare say we may celebrate it with a battle. If we do I am sanguine of success. Our army is stronger in efficient numbers than ever before & composed of men who have learned their business by victories. We meet a raw or well drubbed enemy. If my part of the army does as well as hitherto we will do well. The co[mpany] did splendidly at Manassas & also at Sharpsburg & we marched from Winchester here on twelve successive days with a single straggler.

We have a good deal of "snow & that sort of thing" & no tents, but it does take a good deal to hurt this army. Remember me to y[ou]r brother & write again.

Charles T. Haskell, Jr., Battery Marshall, Sullivan's Island, S.C., to Sophia C. Haskell (SCHS)
25 December 1862
Dear Mother,

I have not written for some time but I have been very busy indeed scouting the different Islands. I leave today to make a somewhat more extended reconnaissance & think it likely that tonight I will a party of the enemy on Bulls Island.[40] It will be but a small affair if anything. The main object being to break up the rendezvous of runaway negroes on that island. It is another queer way of spending Christmas but perhaps it will be the best day

---

[39] This refers to Henry D. Godley, who enlisted in Colleton District in August 1861. He was wounded at the Second Battle of Manassas on August 29, 1862, and died of his wounds on December 15, 1862. He and Neely Grant are buried in the town cemetery of Warrenton, Va.

[40] Bull Island (or Bull's Island) is a barrier island on the South Carolina coast between Charleston and Georgetown.

as they will be less on the lookout probably than at other times. Give my love to all at home & do not feel uneasiness on my account.

Joseph C. Haskell, Richmond, Va., to Sophia C. Haskell (SCHS)
1 January 1863
Dear Ma,

You must be somewhat surprised at my not having acknowledged the receipt of either of your letters, but the reason is that I did not receive them until the day Willie left and I begged him to tell you so. I suppose he has arrived at home before this will reach you. I expect you will be as much surprised and delighted by his unexpected appearance, as I was when he came and knocked me up at 1 o'clock the night he came down. It is a most fortunate circumstance that he was ordered home because he never would have got there in any other way.

I told Willy all I knew about my affairs and Langdon's too so I will not write a word about them. I was delighted to get your two long letters, especially the last as I wondered if you could have forgotten me, and felt ashamed of myself for thinking so when I got the letter, and I feel now like entering the new year with better spirits than I did before. I have just come back from spending the day at Mrs. Dudley's.[41] I went with her and Mr. Dudley down to the Monumental Church[42] and was sorry that I had never done it before not only on account of the pleasure it seemed to give her, but because I was so much pleased with the church and the minister.[43] John did give her the pepper but he says don't let that stop you if you feel inclined to send her any more. I gave your love to her and Mr. Dudley, which I never fail to do, as they seem always so glad to hear from you, and he often speaks of Pa and says how much he hopes he may meet him again. You know what I and John used to think of Mrs. Gibson.[44] I have completely changed my opinions and like and admire her very much and Miss [Mary] is without

---

[41] This was Martha Maria Friend Dudley, the wife of Thomas Underwood Dudley, Sr. John Haskell wrote of them in his memoir: "Mr. and Mrs. Dudley did all for me that my parents could have done. He was as noble, big-hearted a man as ever lived." Haskell, *The Haskell Memoirs*, 37.

[42] An Episcopal church in Richmond, Va. It was designed by South Carolina architect Robert Mills.

[43] George Woodbridge (1804-78) was the rector at the Monumental Church from 1843 to 1878.

[44] Ellen Eyre Gibson (1817-89), the wife of Charles Bell Gibson (1816-65), a noted physician and Confederate surgeon from Maryland. T. C. DeLeon wrote of them: "No home in Richmond welcomed its guests with more genuine and genial hospitality than that of the Gibsons." DeLeon, *Belles*, 165.

exception one of the pleasantest young ladies I ever knew.[45] My kind friend Mrs. Browne is still up in the army with her husband. I miss the pleasant household round there very much.

I was glad to hear such a good report from Aleck as I was afraid from what Mrs. Barnwell told me that his wound would be a very troublesome one. I will be very much obliged to you for the shirts you spoke of as I am almost entirely out. I don't care particularly for stockings as long as there is any chance of getting cotton ones, I prefer them so much. I was very glad to hear that Pa is doing so well. Do give my love to him and say that I will write him in a day or two about my plans in case I fail in the application I am making. Willy said he would speak to him about it. Do give my love to Cousin Follie and all the rest at home.

Alexander C. Haskell, Columbia, S.C., to Charles T. Haskell (UNC)
8 January 1863
Dear Pa,

Mrs. Singleton will be glad to see you and Ma and will expect you on Monday or as soon thereafter as the weather will permit. From present appearances travelling will be for some time both difficult and unpleasant. Mamie asked me to write whatever I could learn about the condition of the roads. Do tell her that the damage has been repaired between Branchville and Augusta and by this time between Abbeville & Columbia but that the roads are so disordered that it will be very unpleasant travelling until the weather becomes more mild. Detentions & loss of connection are now almost certain. I take it for granted that they could not have started on the day appointed, and hope that they will wait.

If it is possible or rather not too inconvenient I would be glad if you could bring the wheat for Mrs. Singleton, and tell Ma that we are cut off from Mrs. Singleton's plantation by the stoppage of the Camden trains, and then she must bring down some butter which in answer to her inquiries I told her would be always acceptable.

I find no orders from Richmond. It is clear that Col. Preston[46] has failed to carry the point which was made but the Bureau is alive at last to our necessities and we will get as many conscripts as can be collected in the next few weeks or until we get our number (450). Tell Joe that Fickling's Battery

---

[45] Miss Mary Gibson, her mother's "able assistant in all social matters" was "one of the most popular and most quoted of Richmond's women." She married Dr. Edwin Samuel Gaillard in 1865. DeLeon, *Belles,* 165.

[46] This was Lt. Col. John Smith Preston (1809-81).

will share with us all others being excluded from the [contest] for some time.[47]

I saw Uncle William yesterday. He was quite well. Love to Ma & all at home.

Sophia C. Haskell, Abbeville, S.C., to Sophie Haskell, Flat Rock, N.C. (SCHS)
18 January 1863
My dear little girl,

I have missed you very much since you left us and have regretted very much you were not with us to meet your brothers. Willy very unexpectedly arrived last Wednesday, sent home to collect those absent who ought to be on duty and last night the mail boy brought a note from Charley at the village. He was not quite well and had no means of coming out, and would stay at the Judge's. He is up for only two days. Langdon & Ella are with us and had intended on going in yesterday to have little Charley christened today but it was very cold and Langdon had been sick all Friday with cold and fever and they had given up the intention, but as Charley is to be his Godfather, and Ella having written to him a few days ago on the subject, they thought he might have come on purpose.[48] At any rate they would make an exertion and go, so this morning in spite of the cold they got up to an early breakfast & left at eight o'clock and are to bring home Charley this evening. Hannah has not been very well so I proposed [Cis] to take her place who seemed much pleased and looked very nice in a dark dress of yours, and will no doubt have great tales to tell of the painted windows and the organ &c. I wonder what the weather is with you? It is intensely cold here, one of the sudden changes that we have sometimes. It was so warm on Wednesday evening that we had no fire, and when Louis got home Friday 1 o'clock he was half frozen. This morning, just as the sun rose the thermometer stood at 20 in the piazza. It had risen when the party left and they were so well wrapped up with a foot warmer in the carriage that I do not think they will suffer at all. We heard from Joe & John. Joe is still waiting but in better spirits. John says he is confident he will succeed and his commission will be well worth the trouble. He, John, has joined Gen. G. W. Smith and is now a Major of Artillery and was to go into camp the day he wrote. He is well and likes his position tho he would have preferred being with Gen. Longstreet in Va. He writes to send him on Jim and something to eat if I can. Willy looks quite well, rather thinner I thought but he says not. He leaves us on

---

[47] Fickling's Battery, or Brooks South Carolina Artillery, was commanded by Captain William W. Fickling (1832-94), a native of Beaufort District, S.C.

[48] Charles Thomson Haskell, who was born on March 2, 1862, was the son of Langdon C. Haskell.

Wednesday for Columbia and Charleston for his business does not be near home and I suppose we will not have him much with us. Tomorrow he goes to the village to meet his Sergeant. Langdon and the girls go also on Wednesday and perhaps your Father too tho Charley's visit may prevent him. The girls got to Columbia with Jeannie as proposed. Emma looks thin still but seems quite well again. Your Aunt Charlotte left last Wednesday for Greenville. She received a letter the evening before saying Julia McCord was desperately ill, but on the cars at Hodges met Capt. Murden who told her she was still living and better.[49] From her letter last night I hope she may recover, but if any worse news should come the girls will be stopped by it on Tuesday at the village. I am very sorry Lang & Henry did not come.[50] You need never fear inviting anyone to our house as far as I am concerned, for I am only too glad to do anything that will please you, but with them it would have been a great pleasure to me to see them for their Father's sake. He was a very dear little brother. I scarcely knew him as anything else. I am very much disappointed about the piano. Is there any chance of their getting another. I feel it a serious disadvantage to you and perhaps it may be a reason for not remaining as long as intended. Try and learn as much French as you can, particularly to speak and make the most of the old ladies that you can.

Alexander C. Haskell, Columbia, S.C., to Charles T. Haskell (SCHS)
19 January 1863
Dear Pa,

I am disappointed in my recovery and expectation of immediate return to the army. I had fixed upon today for my departure but a [cold] or some other irritation which has fallen upon my arm will detain me at least a week or ten days longer. I have received the box for Mrs. Dudley, but am much disturbed as to the best disposition to be made of it. If there are any perishable articles among its contents, which I presume there are, they may be seriously injured by this necessary delay, and if this be the case and you approve, I must risk the box by the express, which I hope will carry it with fidelity and despatch.

I regret any delay chiefly from the hope I had that in going on some chance might occur which would enable me to forward Langdon's prospects.

---

[49] Julia McCord (1837-1920) was the step-daughter of Mrs. Louisa S. McCord, the sister of Mrs. Sophia C. Haskell. In October 1864, Julia married Captain Henry Wemyss Feilden, an Englishman who was serving in the Confederate Army in South Carolina. Captain Murden was Edgar O. Murden, a Confederate officer who was probably related to the Murdens who were Julia's friends in Charleston.

[50] This refers to Mrs. Haskell's nephews Langdon and Henry Cheves, sons of her deceased brother Charles M. Cheves.

I had considered his success as certain until I received his own gloomy statement of affairs. I have seen Col. Preston, who with every disposition to oblige yet has it not in his power to give any assistance by having Langdon commissioned with a view to going on duty in the Enrolling Service, for he has just received a list of over sixty disabled officers ordered to report to him for duty, and he has not employment, nor can he make it, for one half of them. I can learn nothing as yet, definite or otherwise, as to who will be our Brigadier General. I am disposed however, though it is not current, to hear of James Chesnut as a prominent candidate for this military preferment.[51] He is at present Aide-de-Camp to Mr. Davis, but is not a man to be satisfied with a staff appointment (for which I respect him). His military aspirations are high. He would have a Regt. into the field long since but for the demand by the Convention for his service in the Council. The explosion of this political enormity has restored to us the valuable services of a true and valuable man with a strong turn for military affairs.[52] The President is aware of all these circumstances, is strongly predisposed in favour of Mr. Chesnut, and will be glad to give an appointment, which I believe was offered months ago, & which is so sure of being a good one. The objection, and it is one very difficult to meet or combat, is that Chesnut has seen no service in the field, and would in his appointment take the command of men who have passed, some with wounds and remarkable merit, through one of the most arduous and certainly most glorious campaigns that the world has ever seen, and the one on which our history depends and on which it will dwell when able pens begin to dramatize the scenes with which the names of these men are linked and on which they build their hopes of honourable fame. For the humblest soldier there is a struggle in submitting to a man who has never seen the fields on which they bled for victory; much harder is it then for men who on these very fields have won a claim to rank as high as his whom fortune has placed, all untried, above them. Notwithstanding this objection Chesnut would succeed as a commander, and if it could be removed would be a choice reflecting honour on the State. If I could be at all sure of his applying for the place I would at once write to him on behalf of Langdon.

---

[51] Col. James Chesnut (1815-85) of South Carolina, the husband of the famous diarist Mary Boykin Chesnut. He was not promoted to the rank of brigadier general until 1864.

[52] The "political enormity" refers to the Executive Council, a body of five men appointed to handle military affairs and to oversee public safety in South Carolina during the early part of the war. The Council came under much criticism for allegedly abusing its delegated powers. Only a few persons were arrested under its authority (some for selling whiskey) but were not held for long.

If McGowan[53] gets the command he ought to reserve a place for Langdon, though I heard some rumour of his having offered it to young Proctor in case of his success.[54]

This necessity for a good officer to be seeking at office doors for a commission which is his right and which he ought to receive with promotion, is a most disagreeable part of our system.

I spent some days with Charley—found him looking remarkably well, better than I have seen him for years, and astonishing the island by his performances in his seven league boots.[55]

Baby and all here are quite well. Mrs. Singleton is much obliged for the barrel of nice flour. Love to Ma & all at home.

Alexander C. Haskell, Columbia, S.C., to Charles T. Haskell, Abbeville, S.C.
(UNC)
20 January 1863
Dear Pa,

I received your letter last night too late to get in an answer, which however was not important as I had just sent three letters home stating that I could not start for Virginia within ten days of the time I had appointed. If you send Jem down I will take pleasure in doing all I can to get him safely to his destination.[56] If there is any haste in the matter I can send him very safely by Express with some additional expense.

My arm is much better this evening. I have not been out of the house for four days, two of which I spent in bed. This prudence is bringing its reward. Do give best love to all at home. I hope Aunt Charlotte has hopeful intelligence of her sister. Our last news, several days old, was that she was a little better.

---

[53] Samuel McGowan was promoted to the rank of brigadier general in January 1863, replacing Gen. Maxcy Gregg, who was killed at the Battle of Fredericksburg, Va., in December 1862.

[54] This was likely James Toutant Proctor, a nephew of Gen. Beauregard. He was promoted to the rank of Second lieutenant in the First South Carolina Infantry Regiment on January 13, 1863.

[55] Seven league boots were magical boots of fairy tale lore that enabled the wearer to take a stride measuring seven leagues (about three miles) with each step.

[56] Jem, a slave, is sometimes referred to as Jim.

Sophia C. Haskell, Home Place Plantation, Abbeville District, S.C.,
to Sophie Haskell (SCHS)
26 January [1863]

Many thanks dear Sophie for your kind cheerful letter. I meant to write you a long letter but have only time for a few hurried lines. Our boys are all well, John at Goldsboro, Joe still without an answer in Richmond. But I have very sad news for you. Our fine young soldier Cheves McCord is gone.[57] We know only that he died suddenly in Richmond of inflammation of the brain occasioned says the paper by the wound in his head. Willy was at your Aunts and says they received the news of his illness Friday and of his death that same evening and begs me to come down.[58] We leave tomorrow morning but will go into the Village this evening so I have no more time to write. Mamie and Emma went down last Wednesday with Willy. God bless you my dear little girl. I will write from Columbia. All at home are well.

Sophia C. Haskell, Home Place Plantation, Abbeville District, S.C.,
to Sophie Haskell (SCHS)
[January or February 1863]
Dear Sophie,

We got home last evening pretty well but both suffering from severe colds which makes us both feel pretty badly today. I received your letter of a week ago but not in answer to either of my two last, one last Sunday the other written from Columbia. Alec arrived from Richmond on Thursday evening not having suffered from his long and painful journey. It was a sad sight to see poor Cheves brought back to his home, his mother and his sisters, in his coffin. They bore it with quiet gentle grief which made us feel all the more for them. The glass covering the face was so large as to give a full view of the head and shoulders and it was a comfort to them that his appearance was but little changed. Poor Lottie could not share this sad pleasure for she was at her Mother's not well enough to leave her room and it was thought best she should make no effort to see him. Willy had remained in Columbia and assisted Alec in all necessary arrangements and with the three girls your Father and myself accompanied your Aunt and Cousins to the Church where the Episcopal service was performed. The Church was very full. Mr. Shand objected to Mr. Palmer preaching the funeral sermon in the

---

[57] Mrs. Louisa S. McCord's only son, Captain Langdon Cheves McCord, died on January 23, 1863. He had been wounded in the head in 1862 at the Battle of Second Manassas and eventually returned to active duty, but died soon afterward. Mary Chesnut wrote about his death and grieved bitterly for him.

[58] William T. Haskell was in Columbia, S.C., at the home of mother's sister, Mrs. Louisa S. McCord.

Church, he being a Presbyterian, so that he delivered a beautiful address at the grave, to which his remains were escorted by the Cadets and all the officers of the Post by order of Col. Preston.[59]

He was buried at the new Cemetery out of the town.[60] Many friends joined the procession and indeed everyone seemed to feel and to show respect and sympathy. The coffin was covered with wreaths and flowers from many ladies and letters of sympathy and condolence came by every mail. Everybody grieves for them I hope it is some little comfort to them. Mamie & Emma went down yesterday to Charleston with Willy to see their Father and will be back in about a week. Jeannie stays with the girls till their [return] and all come home [today]. Alec remains in Columbia till his wound heals. It has been retarded by exposure but is not serious. Gen McGowan is now a Brig[adier]. He has written to request Alec to keep his position under him and offered Langdon the Aidship [sic]. Langdon in the meanwhile has gone to Richmond. Alec passed him on the road last Wednesday [&] may be back any day but cannot I suspect stay long. Louis was quite sick while we were away but has recovered very fast and will probably go to school this week. Your Father has sold all his wheat already and has none left. It is scarce and dear as well as everything else. All send love. I will write again soon.

Sophia C. Haskell, Home Place Plantation, Abbeville District, S.C.,
to Sophie Haskell (SCHS)
8 February 1863
Dear Sophie,

I received last night your letter written to Columbia. I had left before it arrived and the weather has been so bad we missed our mail both Thursday and Friday. It came accompanied by a gentle sad letter from poor Lou to

---

[59] The Rev. Peter J. Shand (1800-86) was the rector of Trinity (Episcopal) Church. Benjamin Morgan Palmer (1818-1902) was a prominent Presbyterian minister and theologian from South Carolina. In December 1862, Palmer had delivered the funeral address for General Maxcy Gregg. The Cadets were from the Arsenal Academy, a state military school in Columbia. They fired a salute over McCord's grave. Col. Preston was Lt. Col. John Smith Preston (1809-81), who was in command of a conscript camp of instruction in Columbia. A notice published at his request in *The Daily South Carolinian* newspaper requested his officers to attend McCord's funeral, and stated of him: "Amongst the thousand young heroes who have fallen in our glorious struggle, not one has earned a nobler fame than the pure, zealous, high-toned and gallant Cheves McCord."

[60] Captain McCord was buried at Elmwood Cemetery. The funeral took place on Friday, January 30, 1863 at Trinity Church, followed by a graveside service at Elmwood.

your Aunt Charlotte announcing the birth of Lottie's baby, a fine little girl.[61] This was of course a disappointment to all especially to Aunt Louisa and Lottie, but Lou says the dear little baby girl will be a great comfort to them all and that she feels as if she could not love it any more than she does already. Poor things! I feel for them all very much but I hope they will be comforted, and that their sorrow will be blessed to them. They have much comfort in his late letters and think that he had with God's help been prepared for his sudden end. If so it was a mercy that he was spared the sorrow of parting and never was conscious that he was in any danger. I hope your Aunt will be helped to bear her trouble by the necessity of supporting and caring for the two girls now entirely dependent upon her. I felt often as you do that tho I grieved for them I could not but often think of ourselves, but it is not good to dwell on possible or even probable misfortunes. God has been wonderfully merciful to us and we must try to be grateful and thankful while it lasts, and perhaps it may be continued to us through this whole dreadful war. I do not think we will be any less well prepared to be resigned to God's will when trouble comes if we are thankful and not fearful. He knows what is best for us and we must try and trust him. I know it is very hard but if we begin and practice it in small things, we may have strength given to us when great trouble comes. I hope and trust our dear boys are trying to serve God, and the wonderful escapes from danger which they have made will help to lead them to him. With the confidence that they were happy I could part from any of them as from our dear Mary, and my constant prayer is for that.

In the paper of yesterday I saw a letter from the correspondent of the London Times. He mentions the bursting of an immense gun and that Captain Phillips, Major Venable and Major Haskell who were near seemed only saved by a miracle. It did indeed seem so for they were in a pit which had been dug to protect the gunners when it burst, crumbling to pieces like clay instead of iron or their death would have been inevitable.[62] Willy and the

---

[61] Lottie (Charlotte Reynolds McCord) was the widow of Captain Langdon Cheves McCord . Her baby, a little girl, was named Langdon Cheves McCord (1863-1940) and was called Chev or Chiv. She was born shortly after the death of her father.

[62] A correspondent for the *London Times* reported of this incident, which took place on "General Lee's hill," December 13, 1862, during the Battle of Fredericksburg: "From this hill ... a thirty-pounder Parrott gun, cast at Tredegar Works in Richmond, poured a destructive fire into the Federals. Suddenly, about three o'clock in the afternoon, on its thirty-seventh discharge, this gun burst with a dreadful explosion, but happily did no injury to any of the bystanders. At the moment of its explosion, Captain Phillips, of the Grenadier Guard ... Major Venables, of General Lee's staff, and Major Haskell, were conversing within a few feet of the gun. Their escape without injury was little less than miraculous." *Rebellion Record,* 110. Captain Lewis Guy Phillips (1831-87), a British military officer, was an observer at the battle.

girls where [sic] in Charleston and did not expect to leave till Monday or Saturday yesterday. Mamie writes that there was a great panic in Charleston and her Father was disposed to send them off with Alice Middleton and the Blakes who with numbers of others were leaving the city but they begged to stay a little longer.[63] I fear they have had a dreary visit. The weather has been very bad and the house where they were with Minna and Rachel as cold and comfortless as it well could be. I begin to hope the alarm at Charleston may again pass off though the grounds for it are very strong at present. We are looking now for Alic, Langdon and Willy. Alic is in the village and we have sent for him. Lang has been expected for the last two days but had not arrived in Col[umbia] on Friday. Willy we expect on Tuesday. He and Alic will no doubt leave in a few days for Fredericksburg. Lang may stay a little longer before he resumes his position of Aid under Gen. McGowan. Alic I believe also resumes his old [sic] as I have heard of no prospect of any other. Joe I hope will have some definite answer now as besides all his recommendations Mr. Simpson the newly elected member of Congress has also promised to recommend him from his District which alone would almost insure him the position.[64] He was well not long ago and we hope to hear from him now very soon. Of John you have as late news as we have or later. Lang may give us some more details. He carried little Jim on to him. Charley has been scouting about Bull's Island again and caught two officers on a shooting expedition as the papers inform us, but had no part in the expeditions which have been so successful.[65] Louis, Paul and Russell all left us Wednesday morning. It was very cold and we proposed they should wait but it was well they did not for it has been much worse since [illegible words] at Mr. Porcher's. Your Father sends his best love to you and wants to know how you are coming on and how you stand the cold. Do be careful and dress warm. A cotton body under your [skirts] would be a great addition in cold weather and could be taken off when it grew too warm, and avoid sitting in wet shoes. Do give my love to Lessie and if you have not written already send word if you have given the check to Mad[moiselle]s De Choiseul. I will finish after Alic comes.

---

[63] Alicia (Alice) Middleton (1840-1915) was the daughter of Henry Augustus Middleton (1793-1887). Her sister Isabella Middleton Cheves was Sophie's aunt.

[64] William Dunlap Simpson (1823-90), a native of Laurens District, S.C., was a member of the Confederate House of Representatives.

[65] Captain Charles T. Haskell's report of this incident is found in the *Official Records of the Union and Confederate Navies, series 1, v. 13*, 575. On one of his reconnaissance missions to Bull Island, he and seven of his men ambushed enemy soldiers from a gunboat, the USS *Flambeau*, anchored just offshore.

Alic has just arrived, his wounds almost well tho he has a cold. Lang has also arrived in the village and is well also. I think your list of studies is very good. Don't be afraid of doing too little. Just keep on steadily. God bless and keep you my dear child. Write to me always. I am glad to hear everything you can write. Baby is quite well and Lottie and baby are doing well.

Charles T. Haskell, Jr., Battery Marshall, Sullivan's Island, S.C., to Sophia C. Haskell, Abbeville, S.C. (SCHS)
9 February 1863
Dear Mother,

I write in a hurry by Jonas who is just starting off to tell you that everything is quiet altho we are looking for stormy times before long.

The Ironsides is no longer off the bar but I expect she will soon be back with a host of others.[66] Willy is, I suppose, still in Charleston, but I have heard nothing from him. I will try to go over & see him if he stays a day or so longer.[67]

Sophia C. Haskell, Home Place Plantation, Abbeville District, S.C., to Sophie Haskell (SCHS)
15 February 1863
Dear Sophie,

I am very sorry that you should have been annoyed by any forgetfulness about your letter. I think I destroyed your letter in which you must have written about the check before I went to Columbia and when we came back and your Father asked about it I told him you had not mentioned it that I could recollect, but it is all right now. I am very glad you seem to enjoy the cold. I was afraid you might find it too severe when the hard cold came. It was uncommonly cold here for several days and the ground covered with a hard frozen sheet two or three inches deep which looked very much like snow, but it all soon disappeared and we had some mild spring days. It is cool and damp now but our winter I think is nearly over. All the boys are well when last heard from but Joe has been sick several times in the last month with bilious fever and bad cold. He was quite sick [Thursday] fort-

---

[66] The USS *New Ironsides* was an experimental ironclad ship created to counter the threat of the CSS *Virginia*. Considered to be the most powerful Union vessel at the time, it joined the blockading squadron at Port Royal in January 1863 and was ordered to patrol off Charleston Harbor soon afterward.

[67] Captain William T. Haskell "had served through all campaigns after First Manassas and according to reports had never been absent from his unit except for a single month in the winter of 1863 when, under orders, he went to South Carolina to round up absentees from the brigade." Haskell, *The Haskell Memoirs*, 114.

night but on Tuesday after writes me word he is well again tho he looks very doleful and thin. He was in better spirits. He seems to think his waiting must come to an end very soon and he hopes successfully if the President reads all his letters of recommendation. He says he will think him a very extraordinary young man. Charley writes me word he is well and told Jonas who brought me the letter from Charleston to tell me he had caught two Yankees and killed three. All is quiet in Charleston again and the panic was soon over but we do not know how long it is to be so, maybe a long time yet. There seems no danger of fighting anywhere in Va. at present. The mud is omnipotent. Mamie, Emma and Willy where [sic] still in Charleston by last reports. They may be in Charleston now. They expect to stay there some time. Cousin Follie has been sick for a week but is doing very well now. She lost an infant born dead last Monday morning. It is a great disappointment to her, but I am very thankful that she is doing so well tho the Dr. says she must keep her bed for at least two weeks. I wrote to beg Matilda to come up and stay a while with her but unfortunately she is just moving into a house near Barhamville[68] and had carpenters &c at work and unless necessary could not leave home at present. I hope in a week or so she may be able to come up and see her. We have not heard very lately from Julia McCord but I think it likely she and her sister Mary will come up and see us for a little while. Alec came up and stayed till Wed. morning. He leaves for Va. probably to-morrow. John was well and has little Jim as his only servant at present, but he was looking out for another. Lang, Ella and the children are all well and with us. Little Charley is delicate and pale, still cutting teeth. He has five out. Good by my darling. Papa and all send love and best wishes to you.

Joseph C. Haskell, Richmond, Va., to Charles T. Haskell (SCHS)
15 February 1863
Dear Pa,

I expect you will be as much surprised and nearly as much pleased as I was when you learn that I have been appointed a first Lieut. of Artillery and been assigned to duty as John's Adjt. How it was done I don't exactly know. I am very well aware however that I have my certificate of appointment and will go down to Goldsborough on Tuesday. John sent up the application to me endorsed by Genl. French, the comdg. officer.[69] He stated that John had lost an arm and therefore needed an Ad[jutan]t, tho law does not allow one, Mr. Miles took the paper up to the Secretary of War and after staying about ten minutes came out with it approved. He said he had hard work to per-

---

[68] A community located about two miles from Columbia, S.C.
[69] Major General Samuel Gibbs French (1818-1910).

suade Mr. Seddon but finally succeeded.[70] I will not get my commission until the appointment is confirmed by the Senate, which will be a long time yet. In the meantime I got a certificate from the Ad[jutan]t Genl. which will enable me to go on duty at once. I had very little idea when I used to joke John about putting me on his staff that I would owe my first appointment to him, and now that I am in no particular hurry about it I expect I will my Cadetship [sic]. I can hardly persuade myself of the fact that I am a first Lieut. of Artillery as I have no uniform yet and have constantly to take of the cover of my new cap, when the fact is brought very vividly before me as it, the cap, is of the brightest regulation red. As usual I can not close the letter without asking for something. In this case it is that you will let Aleck get me a saddle, bridle and holsters, all of which I will have to get and they can be got cheaper at home than here. I leave the selection of them entirely to him. Do let him get them and send them by the first opportunity. I will not be in a hurry about getting a horse as John has two and I expect I can use one for a while. John's application was the principal cause of my getting the place, but I must say that I would never have gotten it but for the great kindness of Mr. Miles who has show [sic] the greatest interest in my affairs and has personally interested himself for me whenever he thought anything could be done. It is really a pleasure to be indebted to such a man, and I do feel much indebted to him. I saw Col. Perrin yesterday who told me he had seen you and Ma just before coming on and that you were all well. My next will probably be from Goldsborough. Do give my love to Ma, Cousin Follie, Aunt Charlotte and all the rest at home.

Sophia C. Haskell, Home Place Plantation, Abbeville District, S.C.,
to Sophie Haskell (SCHS)
22 February [1863]
Dear Sophie,

Your last letter gave me much happiness. I am sure you are sincere in your feelings and I am indeed thankful that you have been brought thus early to turn your heart to God, and I most earnestly pray that he will give you grace to persevere through life, that having once commenced the good work, you may never give up but in His strength go on. Doubts and difficulties and fears will arise, but strive not to be fearful but believing, and not to be too much discouraged if you find old faults and follies returning almost stronger than ever. They will certainly seem so if they are not really so, for I think

---

[70] This was probably William Porcher Miles (1822-99), a Confederate Congressman from South Carolina. James Alexander Seddon (1815-80) was the Confederate Secretary of War.

that much that may have passed unnoticed before will now rise up before you to distress and discourage. But remember that you have now put your trust in One who is all powerfull [sic] and if you can go to him he will give you strength to walk humbly in his way, and by perhaps slow degrees to make His will yours. My dear Child I feel God has been good to me far more than I deserve in bringing you one after one to see the right way. I feel deeply how imperfectly I have fulfilled my duties to you all as a Christian mother and far from feeling jealous I feel most grateful that you sought and found in our darling Decca that help and encouragement you needed. She was indeed a dear Sister to you and all I hear and learn of her makes me feel that she was indeed a treasure greater even than we had learned to think her. She was well fitted to aid you, for in many things she had a character not a little like your own, and with God's help I hope you may make a woman like her.

Do not think you are only a trouble to your Father. He is very fond of you, and every little mark of affection or fondness you show him gives him more pleasure than you imagine. Do not be shy and reserved with him. Do not feel hurt or irritated by impatience or faultfinding on his part, but try and avoid those things which displease him and do not dispute his opinions or wishes, and you will be the darling of his old age for we are both growing old now and you are to be the sunshine of our home and to learn to bear with [crabbed] old people. I was very glad to receive your letter but not surprised for I had seen your mind working and had hoped and prayed you might be led aright. These are times to make all serious, young and old. We feel we are in God's hands and know not how long he may see fit to spare us in the dreadful troubles that surround us. Let us try to be thankful now and ready to submit without murmuring when trouble comes. Your Aunt L. and Cousins are well. Mamie and Emma have just returned. They say the girls are pretty cheerful, that they have returned to their usual little occupations and while they were there seemed to do pretty well. Your Aunt is quite sad, more so rather than at first, but that must be so, and her grief must be long and enduring. She feels so anxious about the girls now feeling herself their only protector that for their sakes she will exert herself.

Lottie has not been doing well having fevers at night. I believe nothing alarming but still enough to cause much anxiety. The little baby is well. Alec sent me a picture of his dear little baby. It is a good deal like her but it was so hard to take her that it is rather indistinct. We are all quite well at home. Willy came back yesterday looking very well, and he does think of you and talk of you very often and Mamie tells me has sent you by Alice Middleton a very pretty present. He says it is impossible for him to go see you, it would take him too long. He has not said when he would leave here but I know it will be very soon now. Joe writes in the finest spirits. John has succeeded in having him appointed First Lieutenant of Artillery and Adjutant of his battalion. He had just commenced his duties and writes from the Camp near Goldsboro. He and John I can see are very happy to be together again. I got a begging letter written the same day. John agreed to beg if Joe would write for some hams, butter, sausages and a gallon of molasses. Mr. Miles was very kind in getting the Commission for Joe very promptly. Perhaps he might not have got it at all without his help. He can now wait patiently the result of his application for the Cadetship. Langdon & Ella are still with us. The little boys are both well and have improved very much in the last two weeks. They had both been quite sick before that. Little Charley has six teeth and begins to walk pretty well. Your Cousin Matilda came at last with Willy yesterday. Follie is delighted to see her. She is doing very well and I hope will be sitting up the first fair day. Louis and Paul we sent for yesterday in spite of roads & weather to see Willy. Louis looks a little thin but does not seem otherwise hurt by his sickness. Paul as full of talk as usual. They like very much being at Mr. Porcher's and seem doing very well indeed. Russell is at [Mrs. Rogers] and well too. Little Willy was well and had made prisoner of a Yankee and taken his horse &c. Goodby my little Girl. Papa and all send love. Best love to Lessie.

Alexander C. Haskell, Richmond, Va., to Sophia C. Haskell, Abbeville, S.C.
(UNC)
25 February 1863
Dear Ma,

I have only reached Richmond on my journey to the army after having been eight days from Columbia, four days spent on the Rail Road and four days waiting for the snows to melt and the floods to subside so that the road to the army may be practicable. It will not be good until June. I am rather glad of this unavoidable delay as it is ridding me of the cough which although not sufficient to keep me at home was troublesome.

I was much pleased to learn on the road that Joe had left Richmond as First Lt. of Artillery and Adjutant of John's Battalion. His appointment is very handsome. I have not learned how he got it and I don't like to say "Scissors," but I will make Pa a bet that Joe did not get his cadetship. He had not been well for days before he rec[eive]d his Com[missio]n, but this with lightwood smoke in N. Ca. have worked like a healing charm.

The army of the Rappahannock has been divided. About two fifths of it under General Longstreet have been joined to the Department of Richmond and the Coast. And are now watching the enemy at Suffolk and elsewhere, extending their possible field of operations even as far as South Carolina. The remainder of the army, Jackson's Corps and one, perhaps two divisions of Longstreet, under General Lee await the development of the spring in Northern Virginia. Jackson of course is reserved for the valley which will be the probable scene of great achievements.

If it compensated for our anxiety to know that that anxiety is shared by the Confederacy, we should be satisfied. The attack on Charleston fills every heart and every mouth indeed, for you hear of little else. Certainly everything for good or evil, for hope or for despair, depends upon the issue of the struggle impending there. I cannot feel as confident as others do that this struggle will ever be. I still think against reason that it will not, but if it does, why I should like to be there is the simple expression of every absent Carolinian. But more than this, I do most devoutly pray that there above all other places we may be victorious, for if Charleston falls our home will be on the line with which the Federal arms will belt the middle of our severed Confederacy.

My hope is that the attack will not be made, for with Jordan to make Beauregard proclaim folly to us and our foe, and with Ripley to protest against a division coming to reinforce the place (for fear the Major General would rank him), and with Col. Rhett in command of the over disciplined & cruelly trained mercenaries of Fort Sumter, it would be false to say I feel confident of the result. If however Beauregard's better sense gets the upper hand of his theatrical nonsense and Ripley is suspended from command or hung to a lamp post—I care not which is his fate—and a better man than Alfred Rhett is chosen for a trust as sacred as he has shown himself unworthy to receive, then I will see the battle come with hope & confidence.[71]

I start for the Rappahannock tomorrow. John was well when I heard from him a few days ago. My pen is so bad that with my cold hands I can't manage it any longer. Love to Pa, Aunt Charlotte, Cousin Folly, the girls, and everybody else that ought to have it. Goodbye.

Charles T. Haskell, Jr., Battery Marshall, Sullivan's Island, S.C., to Sophia C. Haskell, Home Place Plantation, Abbeville District, S.C. (SCHS)
26 February 1863
Dear Mother,

I heard from you today for the first time in a good while. I am glad to hear that Joe is fixed at last & I much prefer that he should be fixed as he is

---

[71] Colonel Alfred Moore Rhett (1829-89) was the commander at Fort Sumter during the siege that began in April 1863. In October 1862, Rhett killed William Ransom Calhoun in a duel.

than more permanently, as he may change his mind as to making the army his choice for life.

You need feel no particular anxiety about me now. I thought some time since that an attack on Charleston was a fixed fact, but now the prospect is getting, in my opinion, remote. I believe that there is certain information that more ironclads are being built at the North & if that is really so, I have no idea that they will risk an attack with two or three when by waiting a month or so they may make a much more powerful effort. I think too that considering the dissensions among the commanding officers at Port Royal it will be a month or so before they can get ready for any powerful demonstration by land. Before such a time shall have elapsed it is certainly possible that reverses on the field & revolutions at home may cause them to give up the attempt entirely. I must say that I hope so, for I cannot feel any certainty that we can make successful resistance. Anything that has heretofore been proved [formidable] in assaults on forts I believe we can resist, but a general engagement with ironclads is still an experiment to be made & our own successes with them make me uneasy as to the results when they are brought against us. One must be occasionally on the wharves when the vessels running the blockade come up to discharge their cargoes to form an idea of the greatness of the calamity, if Charleston should be taken.

I will send over some men with cold chisels tomorrow to the wreck near my post that I spoke of when at home & try to get some pieces of sheet iron that may be of use & will notify Pa of the result within a week. There will be no necessity of fastening them together in the first instances as they are strongly bolted together like boiler iron, but they may come loose after a while after exposure to the fire.

Richard Singleton is with me now having reported for duty with the Regiment. He seems very well pleased & certainly bids fair to make an excellent officer. Give my love to all & if you do not hear from me regularly take it for granted that I am temporarily away.

Sophia C. Haskell, Home Place Plantation, Abbeville District, S.C., to Sophie Haskell, Flat Rock, N.C. (SCHS)
1 March 1863
Dear Sophie,

You asked me to send you some of the boys' letters so I send you the longest letter from Charley for a long time. We are all quite well except your Cousin Follie and she continues to improve so that I hope in a few days more she will be out amongst us again. Your Cousin Matilda has been up with her for a week but she leaves tomorrow. Tomorrow is to [*sic*] a great breaking day with us. Willy and Lang both leave us and now for a long time.

May God guard them both and bring them back to us in his good time. They are both in fine health and return to the same positions they have always held in the Brigade. Willy seems in fine spirits but I think poor Lang feels leaving home very much. He has been here now two months and it is hard to leave Ella and his little boys. Pete is getting very interesting tho I am forced to agree that he is pretty bad sometimes. Little Charley will be a year old tomorrow. He can now walk across the room and say Papa and Mamma and I think is decidedly improving in looks tho he still looks very delicate. Willy remains a few days in Columbia & then goes to Charleston for a few days more. Lang goes to Columbia on Thursday and goes on to Charleston with Willy and then they go on to Va. together.

Joe & John seem very happy to be together. I think I told you they had written me a begging letter particularly for a gallon of molasses. I must fix his box tomorrow. They are not hard to please now, anything is acceptable. We sent off yesterday a large barrel of peas to Charley and another of grits and bacon and a box for Willy with bacon lard, dried peaches etc. Tomorrow I have to fix three more for Lang for Mrs. Dudley and for John and Joe. We have a full house now for Mary & Julia McCord came on Thursday.[72] Julia has been very ill & looks very badly—the ghost of herself. Willy has been intending to write and has not forgotten you at all.

William T. Haskell to Sophie Haskell (SCHS)
[March 1863]
My dear Sophy,

I write on this scrap of paper to send you my love & self in the shape enclosed. I would have done this sooner but my old disease has bound me with a stronger fit than common & letter writing has been suspended. Ma showed me a letter from you some time since in which you speak of your happiness in feeling assurance of God's mercy in your salvation. I thank God that he has given you this happiness & pray that it shall never be wanting to you. I go to Columbia tomorrow & in a few days to Va.

I have found home very pleasant & feel saddened about leaving, but no misgivings, presentiments & that sort of thing. I think you will do very well where you are for a while. I stayed for some time with Aunt Louisa in Columbia. It was a sad time. I hope God will comfort where human consolation is so insufficient. I have often intended to write before & often I don't know whether I shall do it or not. I have failed so badly hitherto but I may.

---

[72] Mary McCord (1825-1903) was Julia McCord's sister. They were the stepdaughters of Mrs. Louisa S. McCord. Mary McCord married Judge Andrew Gordon Magrath after the war.

Alexander C. Haskell, Headquarters, Second Brigade, A. P. Hill's Light Division, Camp Gregg, Va., to Charles T. Haskell (UNC)

7 March 1863

Dear Pa,

Never has a time of less incident than the present promoted the natural indolence of winter quarters. Soldiers in winter qrs are very like bears in the like situation; perfect quiet and tranquil repose broken only the slated periods when the paws must be sucked. And unfortunately at this point the analogy seems too close to be all pleasant to contemplate. The ration has been reduced to the amount which is supposed to be the very smallest upon which the average man of the army could sustain health and strength in their full vigour, for those who are cursed with inordinate appetites hunger too often presents itself like an inevitable fate. The usual ration of flour 11/8 pounds is still given and will make in bread a good baker's loaf, in heavy biscuits a very small compass comprehends the weight. Besides this is given but ¼ pound of bacon (most of which is consumed in making the biscuits) with now & then a spoonful of sugar. I am happy to say that this does so far sustain the general health & strength of the army unimpaired.

What we are to do when the warm sun dries the roads, nobody knows. I obstinately expect to see the relieved from its pressing wants the rich granaries and fields of Pennsylvania & Ohio [*sic*]. But I am sorry to find very few who believe with me.

Upon this belief & the equally absurd belief that Charleston will not be attacked by the monster fleet, stake my hopes of distinction as a prophet & will not grieve if Cassandra like I gain no credence, provided the result shows that I was right & that we will be spared on the one hand hunger, and on the other a terrible death struggle.

I only write to tell you that I am quite well & comfortable. All the soldiers are in comfortable huts & tents with chimneys, which [latter] is the pleasantest house in the world.

The mail is waiting. I conclude with a promise to send the news above given at least once a week in spite of the absence of other matters. Love to Ma and all at home, Aunt C., Cousin Follie and the girls as I suppose Mamie & Em are generally designated & classified.

My horses in wh[ich] you feel so profound an interest are half starved, but my [care] is [bringing] them to life again.

Sophia C. Haskell, Home Place Plantation, Abbeville District, S.C.,
to Sophie Haskell (SCHS)
8 March 1863
Dear Sophie,
    We were as we always are very glad to receive you kind pleasant letters
last week. I will leave your Father to answer his another time. I have no news
for you this week except that Lang and Willy have finally left us. I suppose
they will leave Charleston tomorrow by the N. Eastern R.R. for Va., both
quite well. I gave them each a good box of substantials, bacon, soap, lard
candles &c which seems very acceptable and sent a box to Joe & John and
another to Mrs. Dudley besides two barrels of pease [*sic*], grits and bacon to
Charley. These times make very homely gifts acceptable. Did I tell you Joe's
request to send him a gallon of molasses. He is a good deal troubled about
finding a horse. Your Father has written to him he will try and get him one
if can come on for it. It is impossible to send it to him. He thinks they will
move somewhere soon but does not know where it will be. The attack on
Charleston is still postponed. You have seen I suppose the account of the
attack of Fort McAllister on Genesis Point, an earthwork a few miles from
the Ogeechee plantations which protects them and the R.R. leading to Savannah [[word unintelligible]] has stood the attack nobly and baffled the
force of their great Ironclads and two mortar boats which retreated without
doing any material injury after bombarding it for two days.[73] We are looking
anxiously at Vicksburg and Port Hudson as much depends on keeping them.
May God help us in our troubles. We heard from Alec just about leaving
Richmond for the Rappahannock on the 25th. He had been detained four
days by bad weather and roads which had given his cough time to get well. I
have been able to do nothing about hedges at all. The little laurestinas plants
were all dead when I went to look after them, and I am afraid all the evergreens we set out are dead also. They look very badly. Those you sent look
better and I hope some may live. Your Cousin Follie is pretty well again and
says she will come out tomorrow. Her hair dropped out till she was almost
bald and Matilda cropped it off close to her head so that she has to wear
chase caps and looks better in them than I had expected. No news from Arkansas as yet but she hears occasionally from her Mother and Sisters. Do
give my love to Isabella and Sophie and kind regards to the ladies.

---

[73] Fort McAllister, located near Savannah, Ga., was attacked by a Federal naval
force on March 3, 1863.

William T. Haskell, Columbia, S.C., to Sophia C. Haskell (SCHS)
9 March 1863
My dear Mother,

I leave Columbia today. You are surprised no doubt that I am still here, contrary to my intentions, but I met Patrick[74] here who attended to me in the last part of the week & then it was too late to go to Charleston where my main object was to see the dentist & then go to Va. on Monday. Langdon went on down Thursday evening & I will meet him probably on the road. I think I will stop at Goldsboro to see the boys for a day & give them their box which Langdon left with me, as also Mrs. Dudley's which I will get off by express today nothing preventing.

Aunt Louisa & the girls are quite well & cheerful. Jeanny Wardlaw is still with them & is of great benefit by affording them company. They are very much engrossed with Lottie's baby which is doing quite well. Alic's infant is doing remarkably well & is really one of if not the finest children I ever saw—has the perfection of never crying & never being sick.

I miss you all very much. I cannot say how much for that would set me to thinking which would leave me too forlorn.

Do give my love to each & everyone at home & believe me

P.S. I hear of Alic a week ago today. He was in Richmond still & quite well.

Alexander C. Haskell, Headquarters, Second Brigade, Light Division, Camp Gregg, Va., to Sophia C. Haskell (UNC)
12 March 1863
Dear Ma,

I received your letters, including one from Pa, yesterday and right glad I was to get word from home. It was the first that had reached me since I started on a tedious journey and uninteresting camp existence.

Before I forget I will answer some important questions. I did not see Joe in Richmond as I expected. I have not given him a saddle. I am sorry to say that being separated for some time from my baggage, having just recovered it, I have not been able in any way to convey to him his woolen shirts. This latter I very much regret as he may have been wanting them, and it is so long since I have been useful to anybody or taken care of anybody but myself, that I am sorry indeed to have missed this opportunity of accomplishing the only charitable commission entrusted to me.

We are expecting Langdon & Willy every day, and with them I hope to have the late intelligence that all are well in my old home, and in the new

---

[74] This was likely Dr. John Burckmyer Patrick (1822-1900), a prominent dentist.

one where my little Darling forms the centre of many anxious thoughts. When I am with her I feel in my affection that I am guide and protector, mother and all to her, but I realize in [absences] what life will be to the little one bereft of such a guardian as has gone to Heaven before us to light our upward path. May the good God who has promised to be the Father of all such, bless and preserve her.

The army is quiet as in the dead of winter, in fact the winter has hardly broken here yet. I find my position more agreeable than I could have expected. And though not as before the chosen friend of my chosen General, my intercourse with McGowan is of the most pleasant kind and he is really a good officer. The staff is very pleasant too. My first fancy for Hammond[75] is coming back & Andrew Wardlaw[76] has been added to the staff as Commissary. Our troops are still in high condition though it is a question how long they will remain so if the threatened scarcity of provisions comes upon us, but I believe this will not be, and that we will always have enough if the planters will do their duty & the whole people learn to economise.

You mention quite a full household in your letters. I give you my sincere congratulations for having so many pleasant people congregated under your roof. I regret very much that I have lost so agreeable an opportunity of making the acquaintance of Misses Mary & Julia McCord. I am very glad to hear that Cousin Folly is well. I sent her letters from Richmond by a gentleman going to Leesburg. They no doubt will be delivered. Do give my love to her, to Aunt C & the girls, to Pa and Sophie most particularly when you write. Goodbye. God bless you all my dear Mother.

Charles T. Haskell, Battery Marshall, Sullivan's Island, S.C.,
to Charles T. Haskell (SCHS)
12 March 1863
Dear Father,

I find on investigation that all the sheet iron on the steamer "Nellie" except the boiler iron has rusted to such an extent as to be worthless.[77] The boiler I can not meddle with. I priced some pieces six by five in Charleston yesterday & found them to cost about sixty dollars apiece. A month ago the same pieces were selling at $200 apiece & I think that before long they will be down to half their present price. I do not suppose that you will need this iron before July or August & I think that you may rely on being able to get it

[75] James Henry Hammond , Jr. (1832-1916) of Redcliffe Plantation, S.C.

[76] Andrew Bowie Wardlaw (1831-88) of Abbeville, S.C.

[77] The blockade runner *Nelly* (formerly the *Catawba)* was fired on by an enemy ship and ran aground on the beach of the Isle of Palms in May 1862. Orvin, *In South Carolina Waters,* 41.

by that time at a low rate. There is a plenty of it now at McLeish's in Charleston & the salt business is rather flagging.[78] I have not yet heard of the barrels sent me but suppose they will arrive after a while. Langdon has just left me. Willy has not come down yet but I expect him.

Alexander C. Haskell, Headquarters, Second Brigade, Light Division, Camp Gregg, Va., to Charles T. Haskell (UNC)
19 March 1863
Dear Pa,

Langdon arrived yesterday and Willy this evening, both bringing welcome intelligence of the welfare of all at home. Through Willy I heard for the first time in a long month from my little girl. My letters must have been strangely unfortunate. We are still quiet on this part, the right of the line, though on Monday and Tuesday last, 16th & 17th we anxiously listened to the fierce cannonading between Lee's cavalry and the cavalry & artillery of the enemy. It is believed that Hooker had prepared a large division of cavalry and horse artillery for the express purpose of masking a giant "raid" which like all other Yankee enterprises was to eclipse any [other] thing of the kind that the eyes of men had ever beheld. General Lee had timely notice and of course posted his cavalry and artillery to form if possible a small impediment in the way of this avalanche of living beings that were to pour through Virginia and North Carolina even to [Newbern]. The enemy came on & were not only met but driven back with heavy loss by a comparatively small force. Our loss has been severe including some valuable officers.[79]

I do not believe that the grand battle can take place before May & think it possible that we will be the assailants. Hooker will be much [embarrassed] unless he can [keep for] his army all the men who will go out of service in May. I believe that he cannot keep them in service & I know the temper of soldiers too well to think that they will go into battle with alacrity within a few days of the time of discharge. They will not risk their lives when safety and home are so near. Were it to be declared & believed that our next battle would be our last I believe we would be defeated. Men who now will behave with the utmost gallantry would then hesitate to risk all in the last moment when home & safety called them from the field.

---

[78] Archibald McLeish, in partnership with his brother James McLeish, operated an iron foundry in Charleston.

[79] This describes the Battle of Kelly's Ford, in which federal forces crossed the Rappahannock River and were driven back after a fight which resulted in 133 casualties for the Confederates. One of those killed was John Pelham (1838-63), an artillery officer celebrated for his bravery and military prowess.

My military predictions are shallow prophecies but as it all I have to think & write about, I will say furthermore that I believe we will by the end of May have disposed of Hooker & will away for Ohio by way of Pennsylvania, fall upon the rear of Rosencranz & then take peace one by one or en masse from the N. W. states when we have our feet upon their necks & our bayonets at their throats. Hunger will make our policy for us, & if it makes us bold, I hail famine almost as a deliverer.[80]

Love to Ma, Aunt C. & the girls, Cousin F. & the boys & to Sophie when you write.

Joseph C. Haskell, Camp at [Tranter's] Creek, N.C., to Sophia C. Haskell
(SCHS)
21 March 1863
Dear Ma,

I suppose you have not got my hurried note written on the [day] before this in that I said we were on our way to attack Washington.[81] We marched next morning and arrived at this place day before yesterday and there does not appear too much chance of our advancing much farther towards Washington which is about six miles off, as the slight obstacle of a fort with 8 thirty two pounders mounted on it, and an army of about 7 thousand Yankees present present themselves between us and the town, and I think Genl. Pettigrew[82] has come to the conclusion that prudence is the better part of valor, though for all I know we may be attacking before night. It has been raining and sleeting so hard since we got down here until now that it has been impossible to move at all.

We have decidedly seen the elephant since we set out from Goldsboro. We started from that point with three fine batteries, men and horses in splendid condition. Two of the companies had never heard a shot fired and had as one of the men told me never been wet. At Kinston two of our batteries left us and we were given two others and a section of a third. These were nearly all rifled guns. Ours were left with Genl. Daniels [bringing] smooth bores.[83] From Kinston we commenced a forced march for Newbern.

---

[80] Aleck is referring to Union General William Starke Rosencrans (1819-98).

[81] Washington, North Carolina.

[82] General James Johnston Pettigrew (1828-63) was a brigade commander in D. H. Hill's division.

[83] This refers to a brigade commanded by Brigadier General Junius Daniel (1828-64) of North Carolina.

This was the hardest march I have ever <u>seen men</u> make.[84] There was one battery of 20 [pds] the men of which in the three days did not go into camp for more than ten hours. This was caused by the constant [stalling] and breaking down of the guns. They are so immensely heavy, weighing 2,000 pounds and drawn by ten horses, that they would smash through the bridges as if they were nothing. We fortunately however had no men injured and but few horses. At one bridge over a creek six feet deep and the bridge about 8 above the water, just as the gun got on the centre arch the whole thing came down with a crash, precipitating men, horses and everything into the water. Nobody however was hurt and with the assistance of the infantry we pulled the gun out. At another place we passed through a swamp where the water was so deep that it completely covered the top of the ammunition chests and now and then a horse would have to swim a few feet. I doubt if artillery horses passed over a worse road since the war was commenced. The great trouble however was that the drivers would become so exhausted that they would go to sleep and drive the guns off the causeways into the mud, where they would sink above their wheels and stick there until they were pulled out by hand. It would seem strange where 20 horses could not haul out a gun, fifty men could do it.

On the night of the 4th day after leaving Goldsboro we halted at about twelve o'clock, three miles from Fort Barrington.[85] This is an earthwork situated across the Neuse from Newbern and just on the river bank. It is nearly [square] with a deep ditch around it and with but one entrance, that narrow, and in the rear. We were told also that they had a battery of Parrot guns inside ready to run into the [embrasures]. With the pleasant prospect of [storming] this at daylight we were told to [sleep] if we could as we would have three hours rest. John and I had actually hardly gotten off our horses on the whole trip. Our wagon had never caught us and we had nothing to eat except what the doctor could send us now and then by a courier and then it was only cold biscuits and now and then a few potatoes. Jim was along with us the whole time riding one of John's horses. The poor little wretch was perfectly subdued and would submit passively to anything. Whenever we were stopped, broken down by guns, I would take him to one side and [roll] him up in the horse blankets and leave him there until we started [again],

---

[84] John C. Haskell was devoted to General Pettigrew, but criticized him in his memoir for the hard march he forced his brigade to make, which left his men "too hungry and exhausted." Haskell, *The Haskell Memoirs*, 41.

[85] "Fort Barrington" was Fort Anderson, an earthwork which had been constructed by Union forces on the north bank of the Neuse River opposite New Bern, N.C., at a place called Barrington's Ferry. This engagement was better known as the Battle of Fort Anderson.

and at houses where those miserable unionists would not let us have a thing to eat, they would sell him a little.

We started from this halting place about three o'clock in the morning. I was so used up by this time that I would go to sleep on my horse. At last I could not stand it any longer and would go up to the head of the column, get off my horse and lie down. I would go to sleep instantly and would lie there until the rear of the column would pass by. Just at day dawn we got in sight of the fort. We had a Regt. of infantry in front. John comes in next with two light batteries, and I came next bringing up the rifle guns. The surprise was complete. The first information they received of our presence was our skirmishers opening fire on their pickets who were about 3 hundred yards from the fort. They ran in immediately. John then took his two batteries in at a gallop and placed them in position about 400 yards from the parapets within easy rifle range. They immediately opened on the fort with beautiful accuracy. Every shell went inside after a few minutes. Genl. Pettigrew ordered the firing to cease; the rifle guns were then brought up and the whole 15 guns were placed in a semicircle around the fort, and the whole brigade brought within supporting distance. We then sent in a flag of truce demanding the surrender. They demanded a half hour to consider it.[86] We found out from the officer who carried it that they had no guns and but about 400 men. This was a great relief. Two miserable gunboats however hauled up about a mile off and stood ready to commence. At the expiration of the half hour they said they had no answer to make. Pettigrew immediately gave the order to open fire which was done in beautiful style, all fifteen guns [opening] at the same time, half on the fort and half on the gunboats. There was no answer from the first tho they could have picked us off easily with rifles. I think though they were too badly scared at first and the fire was too hot for a man to show his head.

After we commenced, I was on the left with 20 pd parrots, after the firing had been going on for about 15 minutes. I was nearly knocked off my horse by the stunning report of one of them and turning round, saw the whole gun detachment lying on the ground and the fragments of the gun about fifty feet up in the air. The [result] perfectly sickened me. There is something horrible in men being killed by their own gun. On examination we found one was killed, and two mortally wounded. None of the rest were

---

[86] In his memoir, John C. Haskell wrote that although he and another officer urgently advised General Pettigrew to demand an immediate surrender, the general granted the time the enemy asked for. "It seemed hard to realize that a man of Pettigrew's force and of the coolest, personal bravery could have made so grave a mistake, but he was a very tenderhearted, sensitive man, who shrank from the danger and suffering to others, of which he seemed careless for himself." Haskell, *The Haskell Memoirs*, 42.

hurt much. These were the only men hurt but one who was struck by a piece of shell. The firing of the gunboats was very wild at first, though it sounded tremendous as they fired broadsides. After about one hours firing we found we could make no impression on the boats and it was useless to take the fort as they were right in rear of it could soon shell us out. They were beginning to get our range by this time and the metallic coffins, as the little doctor of our command calls the long bolts they fire from their heavy rifle guns, began to fly very close to our heads and took effect amongst the infantry, about 30 of whom were killed and wounded.

Genl. Pettigrew gave the order to retire our guns. Just as the order was given two more boats came tearing round the bend of the river. I never thought guns could be limbered up so quickly. In about 3 minutes the whole column was off at a gallop. The batteries were driven off about a mile and stood the shelling for about 4 hours, luckily without any accidents. John and I kept our horses and went forward to where we could see what was going on as the Genl. said we must be ready to advance the artillery if any movement was made by the enemy. We were both so worn out that we could not keep awake and were afraid to go to sleep as much exposed to the shells as we were. We found an old log at last and lay down behind it. After sleeping about a half hour I woke up and found the log had been struck twice by pieces of shell. I was perfectly unconscious of it, tho John declares I jumped up and started to run both times. [Here] Genl. Pettigrew's adjutant was very badly hurt by a shell throwing sand in his eyes.[87] He was knocked perfectly senseless and is not yet able to see. There are great fears of his losing his eyes.

We staid here until dark and then fell back to where we had stopped that morning. Thus ended the battle of Fort Barrington. I have entered into these details supposing that they would hardly be made public through the press, and desiring that our battles should have a fair showing. We halted that night until twelve o'clock then traveled until daylight, and rested until 1, then went on, and stopped at dark taking a position to repel an attack of the enemy who were reported to be advancing to cut us off. The men were double quicked 5 miles, in one mile I counted 9 men down, five fainted and three in convulsions. This brigade is without exception the best one at marching I have ever seen. We only stopped until the next day when we halted for the night as we were considered safe from any interruptions. We next marched to Greenville, a pretty little village on the Tar River. Marched from that place 15 miles which brought us to this point 6 miles from Wash-

---

[87] Gen. Pettigrew's adjutant was Capt. Nicholas Collin Hughes (1840-63). He was wounded at Gettysburg and died in Martinsburg, West Virginia, on July 15, 1863.

ington. John has not a single gun of his own battalion now with him, all having been sent off in different directions and I think he will be ordered back to Kinston unless we do something here soon. Three of our batteries are up there.

We are both in fine health and excellent spirits. The expedition has not been without its results as far as I am concerned, for at a picket post from which they ran at Fort Barrington, I captured a fine Yankee canteen and five blankets. I kept but one. John gave the rest to the men to keep for him and only succeeded in getting back one. I got five haversacks filled with provisions which I gave to the men without opening them. They told me they found in them sugar, coffee, butter, dried beef and various nice items which I would have enjoyed if I had known they were there. I am glad I did not though, as [they] needed them more than we did. We are on short rations now of corn bread and fat bacon. No flour can be had. I don't know whether you can or will read all this but I don't know when I will be able to write again. Do give my love to Pa, Cousin Follie, Aunt Charlotte and Mamie and Emma if they are there.

William T. Haskell, Camp Gregg,[88] Va., to Charlotte M. Cheves (GHS)
21 March 1863
My dear Aunt,

I take up my pen & lift up a "silent voice" from the depths of a snow bound tent which two companions assist me in crowding & making cheerful, to keep my promise by assuring you of my safe arrival in camp & prospect of preservation in the same.

I made a slow journey from home to Richmond, missed seeing the boys at Goldsboro & encountered an unusual number of delays & disagreeables by the way the road affords spectacles of wrecks & smashes in various places where the cars still lie with wheels heavenward, which sights are by no means pleasant to an imaginative mind. I came through however quite safely to Richmond. Here I spent four or five days quite well seeing various friends of the town male & female. I found Mrs. Chesnut who seems quite "fixed up" there, keeping house & matronizing two of the Prestons.[89] The town is

---

[88] According to D. A. Tompkins, Camp Gregg was located on the Rappahannock River about "ten or twelve miles below Fredericksburg." It was "named in honor of it late Brigade Commander Maxcy Gregg, who was killed at Fredericksburg." Tompkins, *Company K, Fourteenth South Carolina Volunteers*, 18-19.

[89] Mary Boykin Chesnut became a friend of Sally Buchanan (called Buck) Preston (1842-80) and her sister Mary Cantey Preston (1840-91), daughters of John Smith Preston. Buck Preston was a great beauty among whose many suitors was General John Bell Hood. She married Col. Rawlins Lowndes (1838-1919) of South Carolina in 1868.

gay & looks very cheerfully at the horrors of war & famine which are the chief topics of common talk. Such has been my transition from home & happiness to whatever may "turn up."

I think of course of the household I left at home, much, & feel a constant desire to know what is going on & what everyone is doing. Em' & Mamie I know are roaming over the face of the country in their usual enterprising style. I wish often to join in the same. It's much better than plunging through the mud & snow which has not abated at all yet from the winter standard. You must not understand me as disparaging camp though, for I "take to it" with the easy grace of the fish returning to his element. There is almost as much fact as figure in that simile.

Miss Julia I hope is quite well again & able extend [sic] her walks far beyond the piazza. The Y[ankee]s were in quite a commotion the other day & excited the same on our side. It resulted in Stewarts fight & a good deal of marching & counter marching which has now ended & all is again still.

The men here are in fine condition—keep comfortable in small hovels of every conceivable shape & [diminution]. Unless you saw men come out of them you would never think them capable of such contents.

Give my love to Mamie & Em. Tell them I think of them always.

Sophia C. Haskell, Home Place Plantation, Abbeville District, S.C.,
to Sophie Haskell, Flat Rock, N.C. (SCHS)
22 March [1863]
My dear little Sophie,

I hope you have long since got out of the blues, and are bright and happy as I would wish you. I know it is quite a trial to be so long from home to one so little used to it, and though the regime be ever so mild, still you have been so little accustomed to control as to your occupations and studies for some years past that I give you great credit for being so well satisfied. You wished to study and improve yourself and I saw it was utterly impossible for you to do so at home under present circumstances. And though it is no small privation to miss the pleasant company we have now still you must give up one or the other, and I hope when better times come you may have many opportunities of visiting you cousins and being with them for they are such nice girls that I shall always be glad to let you associate with them as much as possible.

I am glad you are making acquaintances in the neighborhood for they are generally persons you will be apt to meet in society here after, and though all may not be exactly what you might prefer, believe me it is above the average society you will meet. You are old enough to think and choose for yourself and I think will have discrimination to like people without imitating their faults. Still remember I do not wish to keep you at school longer that you really wish. It is very hard for me to know what is really best for you and if you would prefer coming home at any time before the period proposed, have no hesitation in saying so. Your father is willing for you to do as you please so I should prefer your acting according to your own wishes.

I think it likely your Aunt and cousins will remain the best part of the summer with us, though I dare say if anything pleasant offers, they may go away for a time. Minna and your Aunt Rachel are still in Augusta but speak of going soon to Savannah if all remains quiet. I have no very recent news from the boys except Alic and I enclose his letter. He wrote me one a few days ago in which he for the first alluded to our dear Decca, as one who had gone before to lead him on to the higher path, he was speaking of his Darling and of how much she now depended on him. He is well and likes his position under Gen. McGowan, I think, feeling apart, it is more comfortable than under his dear old General. Willy and Lang I have not heard of since the 10th.

I got the Calabash seeds, I suppose you mean the large round ones but I will send some of the water gourd also, when the seeds are dry tomorrow. I saw the merino but must take time to get lining and trimming. It is too late for summer and next fall she will be walking. If I can get a pattern for a little walking dress and long cape or something of that sort it will be very pretty. Follie goes to Columbia soon and I can get her to look out for what I may want, and for what you may need also. I can see no way as yet of sending to Nassau. If your Aunt Charlotte should send by her Cousin Mr. Wagner[90] I will try and send for something for you. Shall I make you some cotton chemises and [coarse] at that? Let me know and send a measure of thread the length in front and round the shoulders.

Don't cross your letter when you write to your Father—nobody can read a crossed letter but me.

Charles T. Haskell, Abbeville, S.C., to Sophie Haskell, Flat Rock, N.C. (SCHS)
29 March 1863
Dear Sophy,

I wish you to be very particular in delivering the following message to Mrs. Charles Cheves.[91] Tell her that I am very much obliged to her for the wine which she so kindly gave me, that it has done me more good than anything else I have tried. Also say that amongst the 3 dozen of wine received

---

[90] Theodore Dehon Wagner (1819-80), a resident of Charleston, was a partner in the firm of John Fraser & Company and a signer of the Ordinance of Secession.

[91] Isabella Middleton Cheves (1826-1912), the widow of Charles M. Cheves.

there are some few bottles of Brandy that I have used some and have some left, and Mrs. L. Cheves says that she sent them by mistake not knowing the marks. If Mrs. C. Cheves desires it I will immediately send her what remains of the Brandy. I only learnt this from Mr. L. Cheves who appears to be annoyed by having sent me the Brandy which I used without scruple, believing that it was intended for me. I am sorry if it put Mr. Cheves to any inconvenience. We got a long letter from Joe & one from John, who have been on a very [word unintelligible] expedition against Newbern but have returned without effecting anything of importance. Please deliver my message to Mrs. Charles Cheves correctly in fact you had best read it to her from the letter and write me her answer particularly so that I may know whether to send the Brandy up to her or not.

Joseph C. Haskell, Greenville, N.C., to Sophia C. Haskell (SCHS)
29 March 1863
Dear Ma,

We received orders this evening about dark to march tomorrow morning at daylight. I don't know where we are going or what we are to do. I don't know even what road we move off on. John left this morning with Genl. Pettigrew, on a reconnaissance I suppose. He could not however tell me a word of his movements. He took both horses and his boy along, and my haversack filled with hard boiled eggs, sausages and potatoes. He told me however that he would join us before everything came off. I won't conjecture where he went, for he told me that he had mentioned the destination of this expedition in a letter to Mamie which he was writing when the orders came.

You must suppose from what I mentioned of the contents of the haversack that we are living very sumptuously. We are just at present. These supplies are the result of a foraging expedition which the doctor made about twenty miles into the country. The grand result of the trip there was 20 bushels of fine sweet potatoes, 5 of which he let us have. The potatoes are the only redeeming feature of this country. The Yankees have nearly got all the state that is worth having. We divided our mess some time back, for the servants quarreled so much that we could not get on pleasantly together. John never would stand any interference with Jim.

I am now at my old avocation of housekeeping. Jim is my only assistant and I find him perfectly invaluable. He cooks, waits on the table, arranges the tent and stores, nearly everything but attend to our horses, which the boy and horse [hand] pretends to do. It is really astonishing what he can do. I generally have to cut wood and make the tent for him as he is too small for that but he does all the rest. The only fault with him is that he makes me half homesick every night, for when we are sitting round the fire after supper he does nothing but talk of home and everybody there. I am afraid I am getting too much like him. He said the other day that summertime was coming now and that he was studying too much about home. I don't know what it is in the time of year that has such an effect on me, but when I ride over to town in the evening and see the people sitting out in the piazzas and the gardens all beginning to bloom I feel just the same longing to go home as when I used to be at school in the village. I was almost glad when our orders came to [march].

I know how you want to hear from us. Do give my love to Pa, Cousin Follie, Aunt Charlotte and Mamie and Emma and anybody else at home. Goodbye.

Alexander C. Haskell, Headquarters, Second Brigade, Camp Gregg, Va.,
to Sophia C. Haskell (UNC)
2 April 1863
Dear Ma,

I thank you for your last letter and all that was in it. It came fraught with counsels of love and wisdom which I can remember in your words from my tenderest years. I do thank God with all my heart for the mercies with which he has mingled his just chastening of my unruly heart. It is His mercy now which gives me hope that in the future it will not depart from us. And it is only by implicit trust that I can hope. As yet, as you well say, my poor little orphan has not known her loss. God alone can supply the terrible want which His power has created, when her human heart and will, and her immortal soul demand the care which comes from a Christian mother endowed as hers with all that could under God guard and guide her through perils. What we both have lost, my heart in its agony, in its sad desolation and lonely future, may feel. My tongue has not yet learned to frame the words to express it. But the God who has brought me resignation and granted me submission to His will, can surely protect the Orphan whose cause is pleaded by an Angel Mother. I have not often the luxury of feeling. I can seldom undisturbed remember the past or gaze into the future. Perhaps 'tis best that the Light should not be too much contrasted with such gloom. This was the month in which I last saw her, who I vainly hoped would be with me unto the end. One year has brought its changes, and what a bitter lesson with them. Is life made up of this; have I just begun the stern schooling which tests the hearts of men for the rewards of Heaven? The sword may fall heavily again but its keenest edge is gone. God grant my prayer that I have not suffered in vain. I begin again to fear. Life and hope are awakening anew and I begin already to hug too closely my idols of earth. I dread almost my love for my poor little Baby, lest this too must go. I do not complain, for surely no eye save that of God could see more clearly the depravity of my nature than I do, and how just are the trials to which I may be subjected and how infinite is God's mercy, if through all this He will only grant me the inestimable boon of His pardoning grace. My only prayer for her is that whether summoned before her lips have uttered the wrong her heart may have conceived, or whether taken at the end of life's pilgrimage, she may go with the blessing of Christ upon her and His pardon and love in her heart. Her Mother's last prayer was to teach her the love of Christ. For this I would live, or trust to God if I suddenly die.

I have used the serious word of death, and it is one which at this time at least we should not shun. That God has spared us through perils gives us cause of thankfulness to him that he has granted so much time to prepare us for the future. It is painful to think of losing a dear one, God knows, but learn, both Father and Mother, as I doubt not you have, to look upon the loss of one or more of your sons as the probable event of the ensuing campaign. God in His mercy & for wise ends may spare us, but why should we be chosen for earthly missions. Expect it not with shuddering or dread, but as the consummation of the sacrifice freely, willingly, advisedly offered, for the sake of God and our Country. If you have cause to feel pride in your gallant, wounded, and yet undaunted son,[92] in the noble patient devotion of your eldest and his brothers, or in the generous courage of the youngest in the field, believe me it is because they have prepared for death knowing the value of life. They are Soldiers of Christ, or somewhere in the ranks of your household you might have had cause to blush for your sons. I who am least among them can feel & tell you what perhaps they are diffident to speak. And I tell you because I know what it is to have a Loved One snatched from me when I was far away, and could get no assuring look from her closing eyes, no whisper of faith and comfort from her dying lips. Long before she had stood face to face with Death, she made me listen when I feared to hear the ghastly word from such living lips. Thank God! She did speak and her words, coming from a heart of truth itself, are now my hope, my comfort, my consolation. What misery of doubt did these oft repeated assurances of hers foresee and guard against, thinking even in death of all that might spare me, surviving an unnecessary pang. Expect death among us then, not to dread it with undefined horror, but to prepare to accept God's will with hope and resignation. Forgive me, dear Mother, if I say too much, but I know, oh so bitterly, the revulsion from too great hopefulness.

I write for your comfort. So far as man can see his own heart and the dealings of God with it, I see cause for hope that I have received pardon in

---

[92] This refers to John Cheves Haskell.

Christ. In him I place my trust. I feel as every grateful creature of God does the value and sweetness of life. As every youth does, the yearning to play his part in the great drama. I feel that animal courage is brutish and unreliable, but that trust in God will never fail, and that duty to God and love of God and our Country will bear the weakest through perils where the heart of the lion himself would turn pale with fear. It costs a pang to give up all we hold dear and all who look to us in this world, but for them we trust in merciful God.

The Battle then has lost its terrors and only opens the field for achievements which will crown a man with glory and upon which Angels might smile approvingly. Do not fear that the blood and turmoil of Battle must fill the heart with evil passions. The Christian soldier enters upon a field of glory and ennobled duty, with his mind unclouded, his heart calm, serene and confident, with every energy of intellect and body strung to its highest tension, to do the work for God and right which He has made sacred and inviolable. He has taught us with the sword to defend truth, honour, his Altars & our Country against those who with the sword would assail them. "Be of good courage; let us play the man for our people and for the cities of our God, and let the Lord do that which seemeth to him good."[93]

I forewarn you to this effect. If I fall upon any distant battlefield, if you never hear another word from my lips, if no friend is near me, if all is violent and painful, if all the horrors of a bloody death are marked upon my body, be assured that I go with a bitter parting pang of human grief to part with those I love, but with my eyes upon the gates of Heaven, my heart uplifted in prayer, my hope & trust concentrated on my Redeemer. I lie down to rest until the gates of Heaven are opened, and all we love are once more joined together. Let grief be mingled with joy, and sorrow be tempered with religious consolation.

I am glad to hear of John & Joe that they are so well. I hope that Joe's experiences of hardship will not be much expanded & if they are he can bear it pretty well. I will write to Sophie tomorrow if nothing prevents it. I would write tonight but it is changing to morning. I am truly glad to hear that the dear child has overcome some of the difficulties of her natural temperament and is contented and cheerful. I reproach myself that I have not written to her often as I certainly ought to have done but I have been unreasonably averse to writing. Do send my love to Charles when you write. Langdon & Willie are quite well, both looking fat & stout to such a degree that they

---

[93] This is a scriptural quote from the Old Testament found in 2 Samuel 10:12 and 1 Chronicles 19:13.

almost fear to commence the march. I suppose your household is constituted as usual as you mention no change.

Give my love to Pa, to the boys, and to Aunt C & the girls, to cousin Folly & Ella. Kind remembrances to other friends. I think you speak of Uncle Langdon in your letter though not by name. I hope he has paid his long expected visit & only regret that it was in my absence.

We are all quiet in the Army, though the wind has dried the roads so much in the past 24 hours that Hooker would probably have given us some picket fighting but that a rain has come up tonight as I write.[94] So all quiet for a little time more, & then I hope we will take the initiative, as the assailants are always at advantage.

Charles T. Haskell, Jr., Battery Marshall, Sullivan's Island, S.C.,
to Charles T. Haskell (SCHS)
2 April 1863
Dear Father,

I have not heard from any of you since your last letter in which you speak of the things which you were kind enough to send me. The [grist] came down perfectly, sound & everything in good order. I went out last night with a picking crew to the wreck of the steamer Georgiana & got some excellent sheet iron.[95] There was a blockader lying close by but the night was cloudy & the waves [reaching] very high & they did not see me. I have got a good many things from her lately. As soon as I have an opportunity I wish to send home the sheet iron—over one hundred square feet— & also some quinine, Castile soap, Brandy &c that I got from her. I have given away most of the Brandy to friends & to the hospitals but have kept a few gallons to send you. I can send you quinine enough to last you for the rest of the war. I have given away a good deal of that too but have over twenty ounces still to send up.

The sergeant I lost was the one you spoke of but I consider him above suspicion as to loyalty. He is a man of very indifferent character but he has had me completely in his power again & again within the past two years & he has had any number of opportunities to desert without running any risk whatever. Since the 1st of January he has been several times with me to Bulls Island & have over & over again slept all night within sight of the enemy, with Burke & the very crew he had with him the other night taking it by

---

[94] Major General Joseph Hooker (1814-79) was appointed to the command of the U.S. Army of the Potomac in January 1863.

[95] The *Georgiana* entered Maffitt's Channel on March 18, 1863, and was attacked and run aground off the Isle of Palms by an enemy warship.

turn to watch.[96] If they had watched to desert they would have done it then & I shall never believe that they have done so until I have it positively proved. I wish I could feel sure that they were captured, but am very much afraid that they went down. They were the very flower of my company— men who would go [blindly] to any reckless expedition that I would lead them.

Do thank Aunt Charlotte for me for her letter which I will answer as soon as I have time to do anything. I have been writing officially nearly all day answering complaints that have been made against me to the Brig. Genl. commanding by some officers who I put under arrest some time since, but I don't feel any uneasiness as to the result. I hope about next new moon to go up to Bulls Island again as I think the attack is further off than ever from Charleston.

Do let me know anything you may hear from my brothers as I never hear from them at all.

Alexander C. Haskell, Headquarters, Second Brigade, Light Division, Camp Gregg, Va., to Sophie Haskell, Flat Rock, N.C. (SCHS)
3 April 1863
My dear Sophie,

I am ashamed to realise what a long time has passed since I have sent a word or line to my two little sisters in the mountains. Very tall and old though I suppose you are growing and don't approve of being called little sister anymore, but I will call you so until I know you after this war and recognise the change which time has effected. I hear of you whenever I get a letter from home, and it not only gives me happiness to perceive that your letters are written home in a style of contentment & cheerfulness which affords much satisfaction there, but I also sincerely commend you that you have overcome the inclination to be unhappy, restless or discontented and are now being the sensible good girl that my counsels would have shaped & which I well know you could be when you would. You are getting old enough now to recognise the moral duties of every member of society to offer a cheerful, happy, contented disposition to the world. And when you look deeper, as I trust and pray to God that my dear sister does, you will find that this spirit is the natural fruit of love of Christ, obedience to his teachings, and perfected religious feeling. May God bless you and keep you in the mental struggle & much suffering you must pass in the dawning of religious

---

[96] First Sergeant M. P. Burke was captured by an enemy gunboat on March 21, 1863, while protecting a wrecked steamer. He returned to Company D in September 1863, and died at Charleston on December 15, 1863. Rigdon, *Historical Sketch,* 150.

truth upon your soul. You have a strong nature and should seek early not to crush it but to subject it to control & make its every act and energy subordinate to the desire to serve God and do well to your fellow creatures. Then will its strength be a blessing, where uncontrolled it would be a curse. Remember that I do not theorise—one such noble blessed nature I have known.

I will talk a little now about my own affairs & tell you how the army is doing nothing & how & where we expect (of course each one has his own theory) its activity to dazzle the world with the consequent triumphs. For myself and Langdon, we have settled into our old place, little enough to interest us at present, but liking McGowan of course as we always have very well. Willy is with the little band of veterans who have survived the many battles through which he has led them.

The army is in splendid condition, flushed with success as if its last victory had been but yesterday. We have been weakened by the departure of Longstreet & half his corps, at various times during the winter, but still have a superb army about 60,000 strong under Lee & Jackson. This army with Lee at its head is competent to cut the line of fire which surrounded the Confederacy and hurl itself upon the enemy in the heart of his rich & unmolested country. This I trust we may be called upon to do. If Hooker comes across the river to fight us, we will destroy him & his hosts. If we can get across to fight him, we will still destroy him. And if neither of these happens, we can march, leaving Richmond protected by the troops it now has, passing and threatening Washington, straight to the border. This once attained our battles & victories will begin. If the enemy pursues us, as his people will compel him to do, we can claim the fight upon our chosen ground and defy the mere advantage of numbers which he brings. We can draw him far away from his means of escape and make his defeat final & crushing. Passing through Pennsylvania to refresh our hungry army, we can penetrate Ohio & the great Northwest, fall upon the rear of the Army of Kentucky with Joe Johnston on its front, & forever put an end to the difficulty about the Mississippi line by annihilating its assailants. Then will come the glorious day for our country and for the few survivors of those who have fought so well for her liberties, the day when peace shall restore to us its sweets. A peace not begged or bought with dishonour but won by the blessing of God upon our patriotic hordes.

Now my young lady you may take your map and study our route thus boldly projected to your imagination. Cross the Potomac in the N. West corner of Maryland, sweep round the North & west through Pennsylvania, cutting every R. R. that carries supplies to the East, & follow us into Ohio, thence to Kentucky, perhaps to Indiana, Illinois, etc., marking all the probable points upon our routes with [those] little flags by which the Geography indicates the battles of history & note them as victories won by the Southern sword & bayonet.

You hear perhaps of the sufferings of our army from lack of food. It is true that they are hungry very often but they get quite enough to sustain health & vigour. Our horses are in wretched condition—hundreds, even thousands, have died—and the living are in many cases wretched objects. My two [*sic*] (fortunately poor Evelyn is in Confederate stables in Richmond where she will be until I can get her home) but my other two, poor things, are pitiable to behold. They complain so touchingly that I find myself melted in compassion.

Have you and Lessie quarreled yet?[97] If you have I shall put all the blame on you for spoiling her sweet temper, but I am sure you have not tested it and that it is as good as ever. Be good friends, & help each other along. Kiss Lessie for me & tell her I would have written a letter to her in yours but I am too stupid tonight. I will write to her very soon.

I hear from home that all are well, that Baby has two more teeth without being made sick by it. God grant she may be always as blessed in life as she has been so far. Poor little thing, she has need of his help & especial care. Do give my love to Mrs. Mat Singleton & Helen if you see them. Dearest love to Lessie. Goodbye. God bless you both.

Alexander C. Haskell, Headquarters, Second Brigade, Light Division, Camp Gregg, Va., to Sophia C. Haskell (UNC)
6 April 1863
Dear Ma,

I read your letter to Langdon received this evening. It has put him in quite a flow of spirits and I confess that it is encouraging. We had learned already from McGregor that things were not quite as desperate in Arkansas as we had feared, but were by no means prepared to hear of such a state of plenty and domestic wealth as Quattlebaum describes in his style, eccentric I confess, but certainly forcible and to the point. I trust that he may be able to ward off the evil of conscription as well as Jack Griffin, whom he justly calls a "smart fellow." I would like to have about 800 such to put in the front rank in the next battle. I would introduce them to a field of learning in which I imagine they might add a few things useful if not agreeable to their stock of knowledge. It is shameful that money is allowed to exempt a man from his share in a war like ours. And still harder is it to believe, or submit when we

---

[97] Along with Sophie Haskell, Lessie Singleton (Decca's sister), was apparently a pupil at the de Choiseul school in Flat Rock, N.C.

believe, that money is to rule the world & that when we come home we will take off our hats to these fellows. I would respectfully warn all who calculate upon such philosophical deductions from past experience of mankind that the Army of the Northern Line has subverted rules & principles even more powerful & stubborn that that which makes Mammon God, and Dives King. More and more I dread the evil spirit and treason which prevails among a miserable class at home. The crimes of society are culminating in [those] most ruinous & shameful riots by which all modern revolutions have been disgraced, if not introduced. Mobs of women, in four or five quarters of the Confederacy, traitorous enemies instigated by the Father of evil, have raised such riots. Fortunately we have succeeded in quelling even the most dangerous of them—the Richmond riot—with nothing more than the death of two or three men murdered by these she demons.[98] There is no controlling them. To punish them as men by opening cannon upon them is monstrous, and the life of the best disposed mediator is not safe from their unaccustomed fury. However I agree with one of my friends whose creed is that Providence allows nothing to happen which is not for the benefit of the Southern Confederacy, either spiritually or morally or politically. And this is the creed of our noble army. They deplore the vices of the country, but resolve in their hearts that it shall no longer be that we are an abomination among righteous men, if they are spared to take the reins which they have been forced to abandon. It would shock and astonish you to hear the humblest private on his return from furlough to his home, speak in terms of unmitigated contempt and disgust of the spirit of selfishness and speculation which he has found among those whom he had fondly hoped to find engaged in the peaceful struggle for our salvation, as he is upon the bloody battle field. But so it is & almost universally.

The army is not free from vice, but it is of a different order. Little things which would entail disgrace at home are here shamelessly done, but none go so far as to sin directly and openly against the cause for which their comrades are fighting. Perhaps with reason some of the very people we blame are, unconscious of their own iniquity, horrified at the vices which disgrace and degrade the soldier. The sooner the war is over the better for all parties.

I hear very irregularly from Columbia, so that it gives me much pleasure whenever you can tell me of the welfare of my dear little baby. I suppose

---

[98] The best known of the "bread riots" which took place in the spring of 1863, in which mobs composed mostly of women attacked and looted stores and warehouses, occurred in Richmond, Va., in early April. There were several other similar incidents in cities in Georgia and North Carolina. Food shortages and inflation were two of the main causes for this unrest. In Richmond, the governor called out the militia to restore order.

I must expect to hear of sickness and childish suffering now, as warm weather comes on with her teething, but I pray she may be spared the pain of sickness and may have at least the infantine happiness of being always well. She will learn care and sorrow enough in riper years. So far she has been wonderfully blessed.

I am glad to hear that Lottie and her little girl are doing well. You speak of the McCords, Han & Lou. I suppose they are in Columbia or have they come to Abbeville?

I have been vainly watching the newspapers for news of John & Joe. Your letter gives the first intelligence. I gather that they have had no fighting, but plenty of hard marching. Independent of this I don't blame John much for going to sleep under Johnston Pettigrew's disquisition upon the mode of attacking fortified places, which I take it for granted he gave as preliminary to detailing the place of attack. Very fortunate appearance of gunboats, too. I doubt whether the results would have paid for a bloody fight. I rather think old Mr. Hill will run them round North Carolina a good many times to no purpose.

Edmund is intensely amused at the picture of Jem in the horse blankets being folded away to repose. So different from what he was when for weeks he marched without rest, the wonder and admiration of the soldiers. It was amusing to hear the greeting bestowed upon "the General" (his camp name it seems) and Dusenberry as they came into camp together, recalling to every soldier who had seen them the hardest marches of Manassas and Maryland. I do admire the state of fatigue to which poor Joe arrived when sleeping behind the log. He did not perceive that his breastwork was being bombarded, a good frame of mind for a fight.

Do give my love to them, John & Joe, when you write. I have written to Sophie. Love to Pa, Aunt C. & the girls, Cousin Folly, Ella & all else entitled. You mention Aunt Anna. Do if she comes to see you don't forget my kindest love to her. I should like so much to meet her again.

John C. Haskell, Near Washington, N.C., to Sophie Haskell (SCHS)
10 April 1863
Dear Sophie,

I got your letter some time ago but have up to this time been so busy that I have had time to do nothing besides throwing up earthworks by night and fighting from behind them by day, and sleeping whenever I get a few minutes spare time. I suppose you have heard of our advance and retreat from Newbern. Since then we have, except a short time when we were resting [from] attempting to take Washington which I was sorry to say won't be taken. Ten days ago we got here and immediately commenced operations by selecting positions for my guns and setting the men to work throwing up works. Next morning at daylight I commenced operations by firing on their gunboats which in a few minutes moved down to visit us and commenced firing with great rapidity and a precision which was truly disgusting as our works were by no means bomb proof. In about two hours one of the gunboats backed up the river leaving the other to fight us. About this time our best gun, a Whitworth, burst, and for a while we stopped firing and did not commence again for some time, when we commenced again and soon disabled the boat which was fighting us by firing a shell by into her machinery as she was turning to give us broadside. After this she lay still and fired for a while from the side [lying next] us until we struck and dismounted it. When she lay still for a little while and her crew abandoned her, and soon after she was towed off by tugs and it is reported that she is now lying a wreck at one of the wharves. Since this the boats have generally kept of range [*sic*] of my mosquito batteries, as my guns are facetiously called. Once or twice they have come in range and after getting a few shots have retired.

But a day or so afterwards Genl. Hill[99] ordered me to go down into the marsh close to their boats and see if a battery could be built. I reported that it could not and went down to my batteries. [Next] night about 10 o'clock I got a note from Genl. Hill saying that a battery had been built and he wished a gun put in it. I immediately ordered up a gun and called for volunteers to man it. After some little hesitation eight stepped forward and we started, I taking command and leaving my battalion with a captain in command. About 3 o'clock in the morning we got there and I found that Genl. Hill had put a staff officer in charge who had about as much idea of building works as he had of flying, and had made a bank of marsh mud 6 feet thick. It was nearly daylight and the workmen soon had to leave, and in about an hour it got light enough for me to see four gunboats about 500 yards off. I immediately cleared the battery of all but the detachment and sent word to Genl. Hill that I would fire till we were knocked to pieces and if he would send down at night he would probably find us scattered about in the ruins. Soon after I opened fire and one of the gunboats very leisurely dropped below, another above, and two stayed where they were and got a cross fire on us. As soon however as it got clear, about 9 o'clock. the four boats opened on us and in about half an hour the work was knocked to pieces, and I would defy you to have recognized your respected brother so covered was I with mud knocked over me by their balls and grapeshot, and four of the detachment were wounded and our gun out of order for firing. I then ordered the four able men to take out the four wounded and beat a retreat which did in a

---

[99] Major General Daniel Harvey Hill (1821-89).

splendid style. Two of the wounded, poor fellows, have since died. During the fight I moved from a place where I had been sitting on a [perch] of mud to put in a cartridge as the men would not stand up to do it on account of the grapeshot which was coming like hail, and I had hardly moved from my seat when a cannon ball came in and knocked it all to pieces. Fancy my feelings.

Genl. Hill afterwards said to me it was the most gallant thing of the war and expressed his intention of putting the names of the [devoted] men in the papers but I have not heard of it further. But he has however recommended my promotion. Since this brilliant humbug we have done nothing but pop away at boats and block houses and have burst 3 more guns.[100] They say that tomorrow we will have a field fight but the Yankees who advanced against us are retreating and I have no idea that there will be. Joe is well and flourishing but as yet has not had a chance to distinguish himself or get his head knocked off, and I shall try to keep him from doing the latter as long as possible. When you write to me, direct to care of Genl. D. H. Hill Goldsboro.

Charles T. Haskell, Jr., Battery Marshall, Sullivan's Island, S.C., to Sophie Haskell (SCHS)
13 April 1863
Dear Sophy,

I have not written to you for a long time tho I have been long intending to do so, but I couldn't write except on business when I have so much to think of as I have had lately. The long looked for attack has been made & has proved a perfect failure, without many of the appliances of resistance being brought to bear.[101] They did not get within the line of forts among the torpedoes even, or I think that their repulse would have been far more disastrous. I wish you could have witnessed the whole affair as it was a grand sight. The bombardment of Sumter, which you saw, was nothing to it. I am just setting off to reconnoitre Bulls Bay & only stop to write to you this little note. When I return I will write you a long letter.

---

[100] General D. H. Hill complained that defective ammunition had been sent to his artillerists by the Ordnance Department, which may have accounted for some of the guns which burst on this campaign. Wilson, *Carolina Cavalier*, 184.

[101] Charles is referring to the First Battle of Charleston Harbor on April 7, 1863, a naval assault by a Federal fleet of ironclad warships which proved unsuccessful.

Sophia C. Haskell, Home Place Plantation, Abbeville District, S.C., to Sophie
Haskell, Flat Rock, N.C. (SCHS)
13 April [1863]
Dear Sophie,

All well at home and away, and news from Joe and John up to the 4th from Washington. There are many reports from the N.C. papers of the taking of Washington, etc., but these are contradicted or want confirmation. They did not sink the steamboat as first reported but silenced a gunboat and drove it off by Joe's account and next day tried to blockade the river. But a large gunboat passed up without regarding them carrying reinforcements into the town, and five more were waiting for night to run pass so that there is no chance of taking the place but by regularly investing it. Joe says John had left him and gone across the river to take charge of Gen. Garnett's artillery and he did not know when he would be back again.[102] The news in the papers is much later but unreliable as yet. Alec says he has written to you so you have as late news from them as we have. He has recommenced writing long and frequent letters to me, which I hope will be a comfort to him as well as a great pleasure to us. He has been unwilling to speak of his feelings before and could hardly write much without alluding to his sorrow. Now he has done it he can write more freely. He wrote me a long letter which I shall always keep in prospect of the dangers of the coming campaign, giving us the assurance that he feels willing for anything that God may send and feeling full trust and reliance in His mercy through his Redeemer. And tells us not to fear for his brothers for they are Christian soldiers and that all will be well with them. God grant that it may be so! Pray for them all my dear daughter, and especially that God in His mercy will prepare them to meet His will whatever it may be.

Direct to Joe and John to [Kinston] care of Gen. D. H. Hill if you write. The papers give us news from Charleston which no doubt you hear, we have little else. Charley has not written since the attack. Emma came home from the village last evening. [Col.] Simkins writes every day. He says one shot went through the walls of Sumter and burst on the parade ground. He thinks Sumter could be taken if the Monitors could stand the fire of all the forts for two or three hours, but he thinks that impossible. He went with a flag of truce to the fleet and saw marks of very serious injuries received. All now have passed the bar and gone out of sight. What this means is hard to tell. Charley's battery has not been approached as yet.

---

[102] Brigadier General Richard B. Garnett (1817-63) commanded a brigade in Longstreet's Corps.

The boys came home last Saturday. Russell did not come as he has an irruption called Camp Itch which has got into the school.[103] It is nothing serious but quite annoying, Paul and Lewis have both escaped so far. Charley Allston[104] and John Porcher[105] came up with them and stayed until this morning, for it seems for some reason, Mr. Porcher has changed his holiday from Saturday to Monday. The boys are coming down to army fare. They have no flour, and now the rice and sweet potatoes have given out, and they are reduced to corn bread and hominy. Your Aunt Charlotte was very much amused by watching their hearty meals while here. They took off considerable spoils in the way of ground nuts and gingerbread this morning. They are looking very well though a little thin and growing very rapidly. They seem quite happy and contented. Emma got a letter from Bessie Alston who tells her sister is to be married in June in Charleston taking for granted the enemy will be driven off by that time.[106] Follie and the children left us yesterday for Columbia. It was a lovely day but this morning we have a northeast wind and it is now raining heavily. I suppose she has left the village and is at Hodges by this time. I am afraid the poor boys had a good [dunk] before they got down, though the hardest has come since nine o'clock. The rain is much needed to bring up the corn, and if it will stop at this it will be very useful. The fruit, the Abbeville Press notwithstanding, is not as yet materially damaged, perhaps the pear tree by the smokehouse was hurt as it has but little fruit on it but even the apricots are as yet quite safe.

We heard from Arkansas as late as the 14th March. Quattlebaum had gone to Little Rock to see Major [Rhett] and wrote a letter in his office which he enclosed to your Father. All is well there though 20 of his men had been taken to build a fort which was rather embarrassing his farming operations. Everything is backward here I never saw so late a Spring. We have never been a day without fire yet and generally all day long. Yesterday was the only day at all warm and now I am ordering fire. Emma says she will write in a few days so I have only to say they are both quite well. Sue Ven-

---

[103] Camp itch was a painful skin condition with symptoms of itching, lesions and inflammation.

[104] Charles Petigru Allston (1848-1922), son of former South Carolina governor Robert Francis Withers Allston (1801-64) and Adele Petigru Allston (1810-96). He was a student at Willington until October 1864, when he left to join the Arsenal Academy Cadets. Pringle, *Chronicles of Chicora Wood*, 31-32.

[105] This was likely John Couturier Porcher (1847-1911).

[106] Bessie was Elizabeth W. Allston (1845-1921), a daughter of R. F. W. Allston. She was later Mrs. John Julius Pringle. Her sister Adele Petigru Allston (1840-1915) married Arnoldus Vanderhorst on June 24, 1863. Mrs. Pringle became a noted author, best known for her books *A Woman Rice Planter* and *Chronicles of Chicora Wood*.

ning is nearly well again.[107] Lucilla and Kate did not leave Charleston, I believe further than to go to the farm. Good bye my dear child. We are all looking for you in June or July as it may be. I gave your commissions to Follie to look out in Columbia.

William T. Haskell, Camp Gregg, Va., to Charles T. Haskell (SCHS)
14 April 1863
My dear Father,

I got a letter from Ma yesterday my only one so far except through Alic or Lally. I cannot hear anything of John & Joe except from home, & the newspapers give no general accounts of their movements. I would like much to have a summary of their accounts. I have written to them but get no answer. I suppose they can't receive the letters.

We are in "status quo" waiting for good weather. This has begun two or three times pretty fairly but ended just when we were looking for the old order of "three days rations & fifty rounds of ammunition." All today it has been raining & we have thus another delay, how long we are impatient to know.

The news from Charleston has been very gratifying to our anxiety. It is in our usual greedy style to wish for more to have been done, but I daresay enough has been done for our chief end, our safety by sea.

Mamie & Em no doubt were specially anxious about Battery Wagner & know how much credit is due to it. Do ask Mamie to send me a copy of Uncle Langdon's account of the fight if he writes one. Charley I suppose was a looker on.

I write apart from general topics on a special one to ask you to send me a servant. I have none & today the sickness of the one with us leaves the mess entirely without. I see no prospect of hiring & if I could, such are entirely unreliable. I want a good able bodied young man or lad such as Bacchus.

Sergt. John Wilson of my company is in the village for some days & can bring him on. Wilson is entirely capable. Langdon & Alic are quite well. The former is to return from Richmond today where he has been for two days.

Do send the enclosed note by Louis or Paul. Love to all.

P.S. Mrs. Bellot the mother of two of my best soldiers has had her <u>three</u> sons disabled in battles.[108] I believe she is very poorly off. If you can do

---

[107] Susan Olivia Haskell Venning (1830-89), a daughter of William E. Haskell.

[108] The 1850 Abbeville District census lists a Belot family headed by John Belot (or Bellot). His wife was Josephine Bellot. Their four sons were John E. Bellot, Joseph E. Belot, David H. Bellot, and Lewis G. Bellot. The last two sons were listed on the South

anything to help the family if they need it would be well bestowed. One of the sons was Alic's friend & classmate.

Charles T. Haskell, Jr., Battery Marshall, Sullivan's Island, S.C.,
to Charles T. Haskell (SCHS)
15 April 1863
Dear Father,

I have neglected writing often lately as we have all been looking out for another fight. There seems however no prospect of it. I am just setting off on another reconnaissance of Bulls Bay. I am fixing up the things which I spoke of sending & will have them sent off by express tomorrow. I am much obliged to you for your offer to send down more Grist & Peas. What you have already sent however will last some time longer. If you can send me a little flour however it will be very acceptable as the price is so high down here as to preclude its being used. Do let the [boys] with the money I enclose to buy me any eggs & butter that they can as butter now costs $2.50 per lb.

P.S. There is a little Demijohn in the box marked for Ella. Please give it to her.

Alexander C. Haskell, Headquarters, Second Light Division, Camp Gregg, Va.,
to Sophia C. Haskell (UNC)
16 April 1863
Dear Ma,

I find myself on the point of writing "General Orders" at the top of the page instead of making a proper filial address and the force of habit is such that I think I affix my official subscription of A.A.G. to nearly half the letters I write. Letter writing is however my relaxation at present from the hard task of doing nothing, and I should take more interest in so pleasant an occupation. It would be much easier to write any number of General Orders of terrible import to the poor soldiers who never suspect my innocence of [devising] their drills and labours, than to write a letter of army news. This meaning of course information as to what the army is doing and about to do. The former I can answer. It is doing nothing. And the second I could answer if I were a Spaniard, the [inevitable] & unanswerable "Quien Sabe," but being a Confederate American I can only confess that I know nothing, with the addition that I can guess nothing.[109] Enough has dawned upon me in a

---

Carolina Confederate roster as David H. Bellot and Louis G. Bellot, both members of the First South Carolina Infantry Regiment, Company H. There was also a John Bellot in the Seventh South Carolina Infantry Regiment.

[109] "Quien sabe" means who knows?

visit to Genl. Lee's HdQrs to shew me that though all my former conjectures may have been correct, there had & have no foundation whatever or
probability. I doubt very much whether we can stir before the 10th or 15th of
May.

I spent a very interesting day this week in riding over the battlefield at
Fredericksburgh. I saw once more the spot where I last saw my gallant
chief.[110] I visited the ground sacred in the death of that true brave man that
Georgia lost, and all along the line I bowed reverentially to the humble
mounds where under the unmarked sod, dead to friends and hidden from
sight, but immortal in fame and printed on every well told page of noble
men and noble deeds, lie the patriot soldiers who fell in the arms of victory.[111] Noble fellows, theirs is the hard lot of war. And saddest sight of all,
was that which met my eyes as I rode through the empty city. One old lady
and two or three little children were all that looked home in the place. Soldiers peopled the houses which once were the homes of refined and cultured
families. Almost every wall bore the marks of cannon that dismantled houses, and every church with its violated sanctuaries and shattered walls shewed
the ruthless work of wicked war. Could we have a picture of human devotion
and sacrifice more striking than presented by the empty homes of desolate,
deserted, desecrated Fredericksburgh? These people have not murmured.[112]

---

[110] General Maxcy Gregg was hurled from his horse by a shot through his side.
Soon after, he was carried to a house several miles south of the battlefield, where he died
two days later. One of his last acts was to dictate a wire to the governor of South Carolina
which stated, as reported in the Charleston *Daily Courier* on December 17, 1862: "If I am
to die at this time, I yield my life cheerfully, fighting for the independence of South
Carolina."

[111] Georgia's loss was Thomas R. R. Cobb (1823-62), the commander of Cobb's
Legion.

[112] The fighting at Fredericksburg, Va., in December 1862, resulted in a Confederate victory, but while the federal army had possession of the town it was thoroughly and
pillaged and vandalized. Even churches were defaced and looted, and valuables were stolen from the Masonic lodge in which George Washington had once been a member.
Confederate officer Decimus Barziza later recalled, "Whilst in Gettysburg, I could not
but remark the difference between the conduct of our army and that of the enemy in
invading our country. Here stood the town, after three day's hard fighting around and in
it, almost entirely untouched. No wanton destruction of property of any description could
be seen; no women and children complained that they were homeless and beggars. Then
I called to mind the scenes around the city of Fredericksburg the winter previous; private
houses sacked and burned, books, furniture, and everything perishable utterly destroyed;
women flying from burning houses with children in their arms, and insult and outrage at
full license. I thought as I made the contrast in my own mind, of the utter incongeniality
of the two peoples, and thanked God we were forever divided." Barziza, *The Adventures of
a Prisoner of War*, 30-31.

We had a little fight up the river the [day I] was in Fredericksbug. An attempt by Yankee cavalry to cross. They were driven back without serious hurt to either side. General Lee has been sick with a sort of camp fever but is much better. We watch his health with great solicitude.

Tell Aunt Charlotte I dined with Henry Young on Monday and that he gave me a cup of coffee and a lump of sugar, which proved that as long as a Gourdin survived, there is a votary at the shrine of life who will see that it is properly sustained.[113] Young was very well, is Judge Advocate of the army.

Love to Aunt C. & the girls, Cousin Follie, Ella and all the rest, the boys & Sophie. Love to Pa.

Charles T. Haskell, Jr., Battery Marshall, Sullivan's Island, S.C., to Charles T. Haskell (SCHS)
[17] April 1863
Dear Father,

Since I wrote you this morning it has occurred to me that I did not enclose the money which I spoke of & which I now send. I find too that the box which I have sent off directed to you did not contain the Demijohn directed to Ella that I also mentioned. Please to have two gallons (or ten bottles) sent to her from what is in the box as soon as you receive it as I have written to her about it. The Demijohn directed to her was left out by accident. The main contents of the box are two Demijohns of Brandy, two cases of sweet oil, one square can of castor oil, twenty bottles of quinine, some [much] damaged castile & windsor soap, two or three bottles of chloroform & some axes which may require to be tempered over. I am just off for Bulls Bay.

Louis W. Haskell, Willington, S.C., to Sophie Haskell, Flat Rock, N.C. (SCHS)
19 April 1863
Dear Sophy,

Paul says that he has writen [*sic*] to you three times and you have not answered one yet so I thought that I would try and see what luck I will have with you. When I was coming down from Flat Rock you told me a plenty of things to get at home and I don't think I forgot any, but I don't think you got any of the things that you sent for. When you write you must you are getting on [*sic*] and what you get to eat up there for I can't see. It must be pretty poor consider what [*sic*] we get here. Tell Punch that if he had come

---

[113] Major Henry Edward Young (1831-1918), a native of Grahamville, S.C., was the son of Rev. Thomas John Young (103-52) and his wife Anna Rebecca Gourdin (1805-81). Among other positions, he served as General Robert E. Lee's Assistant Adjutant General.

to school with me this year he would have found a class exactly to suit him, and one for Lang too.[114] I suppose that Paul has given you all the news so I will come to a close. I wish that you would write to us as often as you have time and the inclination to write.

Alexander C. Haskell, Headquarters, Second Brigade Light Division, Camp Gregg, Va., to Sophie Haskell (SCHS)
19 April 1863
Dear Sophie,
      Your luck is bad or I am unjust, I don't know which, but your turn for a letter has come about midnight and on the heel of three other long and somewhat important ones, so that you find me with news exhausted and energies collapsed. Just as well however that it is so, for there was no news before the exhaustive process commenced and my energies are amongst the things that have passed away, or have a future existence to bear date from the moment in which the order to pack and march presents itself to my eye.
      Of Langdon & Willy I might draw the same flattering picture but as they are my seniors I will add by way of Ethiopian compliment that they are quite well and grown "most as big as old Maussa." I heard from John & Joe yesterday. They were still maneuvering in North Carolina under the direction of General D. H. Hill—supposed by some to be an escaped lunatic, by others to be a General of the first stamp—and in a certain benighted portion of North Carolina he is said to be considered as a Demi-God & Demi So. Carolinian, a combination which accounts for anything & everything. We must plead guilty to the fact of his being a South Carolinian. I hope for the sake of our youthful fraternity as well as for the Confederacy at large that he is a pretty good officer & will succeed at his present design of capturing Washington N. Ca. I suppose in your part of the world much doubt exists as to which Washington it is that he attacks. It is Washington on the coast of N. Ca.
      John has had the pleasure of having had two or three guns knocked, it is said, into cocked hats. I don't know as to this, but certain it is that however excellent they may be in future as headpieces, they won't be much service as guns. Joe had come up as official messenger to Richmond for incendiary shells to burn the town. If this is done the garrison will probably be smoked

---

[114] Punch was a nickname for Henry Charles Cheves (1851-1951). Lang was his brother Langdon Cheves (1848-1939). They were sons of Isabella Middleton Cheves and Charles Manly Cheves, a brother of Mrs. Sophia Cheves Haskell.

out, and it is hoped that Foster of Ft. Sumter memory is at their head.[115] It was so stated in the Yankee papers.

Our army is still doing nothing. We might have commenced operations last week but we heard there had been another tremendous battle at Fort Sumter in which like that of April 1861, no lives were lost, and that it was thought in So. Carolina, especially in Charleston, that this awful cannonade—three big guns and brick wall proceedings—must of course put an end to the war.[116] They began it—why should they not end it. In all deference to their opinions we have waited a week, but seeing no indications of immediate messages of peace I think it likely we shall soon hunt up some Yankees to enquire the reason and hasten the [bulletin]. The only drawback to the beauty of our little affairs is that some lives are lost and much ugly blood is spilt to mar the beauty of the action. However, blood has one advantage—it may give us pretty facings to our uniforms as the tailors give to the red artillerists of Sumter.

I am disposed to depreciate the gallant gentlemen who have been unsuccessful so far in Charleston but I would like to see them (just for the expression of their ideas) introduced to one real battle. Tell Lessie I have written to you both once & that she may have half this letter. Love to her. Tell Helen I will fulfill my promise to write her a big letter (in the style of the war correspondents) when we have a battle. Nothing to say now.

Alexander C. Haskell, Headquarters, Second Brigade, Light Division, Camp Gregg, Va., to Sophia C. Haskell (UNC)
19 April 1863
Dear Ma,

I must make you the second apology for giving you the fifth letter tonight. I thought it bad enough to require explanation when I wrote Sophie the fourth but although my little red rooster that I received from the cook has long since sounded his midnight note, I for a wonder am not yet sleepy, and as I have not much to say I had better say it now & let you get it a day earlier than had I put it off until tomorrow night. I dined with Willy today. Langdon's always with me. I am therefore authorized upon personal observation to state that they are both perfectly well, but a little too fat still for the campaign that must be coming though it takes a long time about it. And it may take much longer before anybody in this ancient army would christen it.

---

[115] The town of Washington, N.C. was in possession of Union forces under the command of General John Gray Foster (1823-74), who had served as second in command to Major Robert Anderson at Fort Sumter in 1861.

[116] Aleck is referring to an unsuccessful naval attack on the harbor defenses of Charleston Harbor on April 7, 1863.

The worthy members are as wise as Falstaff to avoid a fight, but I do declare that Hotspur was never braver than they when the fight comes. It is a marvelous sight to look on men who have exhausted the subject of battle with its concomitants, courage, fear, excitement, coolness & a host of other feelings, and who, knowing all, and from the bottom of their hearts [respecting] quarreling in its mildest form, yet move calmly, cheerfully & with determination upon fields which they know as well as if it was already done will be red with blood of near of a third of them before the day has passed. It is a dreadful thought to me, that these men are to be swept away, and the control of the country to go into the hands of men who have either abused this time of war to [their] own advantage, or have known nothing of its realities, speculators who now can scarce count their wealth will long for war again as an instrument of gain. And the gentlemen who have been restrained from the active field, amusing themselves in garrisons with high hats & fine uniforms, will think "Secession" such a remarkably nice thing, such a comfortable way of providing for the [army] of gentlemen like Colonel Alfred Rhett, that they will be inclined to think again and again ad infinitum, as long as the country can pay an officer & maintain the forts. We are all gratified to hear of the success, partial though it was, against the gunboats, but see very painfully in the uproar made in & after the achievement that those men have not learned the lessons of the war. We feel that we will have to deal with a class who do not appreciate what the country has gone through. A paragraph from the Mercury struck my eye, and at the same time, my sense of the unjust and ridiculous, very forcibly. You must take my standpoint of view to appreciate any feelings, in our army where for the last three months, 90 out of every 150 men have gone to bed hungry every night & risen with hunger unappeased, from every [meal]. I see an appeal made in strong terms to the good citizens of South Carolina to empty their stores, hoarded for the sick & suffering, of coffee, to refresh the [wearied] fat gunners of Ft. Sumter after a desperate battle in which not one man was killed & only two or three hurt by an accident & the stupidity of engineers, in which action 90 shot were fired at the Fort & some thirty odd struck what? The outside wall of the fort, while all the men were safe inside. The men may have felt a little fatigue from moving heavy guns but this is not much. They no doubt were somewhat exhausted by their unusual excitement. Now this may seem a little thing but little things mean a great deal, & to one who has seen men on open hillsides exposed to the direct fire of at least 25,000 cannon shot besides millions of rifle balls, & this with but little food perhaps [from] a day before & none for a day after, & not a word about it by any of the actors, the contrast is marked & painful & gives us twinges of apprehension about the future, for there are as many, twice as many, men who are safe from all this as there are engaged in it. But good luck to the gallant defenders. I hope they have said foolish things from the lips & not from the hearts & that they will respect us veterans as we deserve, and if they will wait a little while they will see another act of the scarlet dyes upon [their] coats which make them for a time as [gory] as the redbreasted artillerists. They are all good men & it will all come right after a while. It is hard sometimes to see that Providence [must be] right & whenever we forget it, it does us harm. God keep us & grant we may meet again. I am afraid to think [too] much about home.

Sophia C. Haskell, Home Place Plantation, Abbeville District, S.C., to Sophie Haskell (SCHS)
[20] April [1863]
Dear Sophie,

We heard of you from your Aunt Isabella who reports you well and bright and cheerful. This gives me great pleasure, for a cheerful disposition is not only a great blessing, but I think in many persons to whom it is not quite natural, a great virtue, for it must cost many a hard struggle to put down all the crowd of small discontents and fretfulness which often darken one's mind, and seem so great and so real at the time, but depend upon it much can be done, and if not entirely conquered, still the effort is very salutary. Don't think I mean to lecture you, for I do not think you at all given to despondency, but it is the common malady of most young people who have little but themselves to think of.

We are all quite well and all the boys when last heard of. Joe's last letter of the 8th I mentioned to you in my last. The newspaper accounts speak of little fighting going on at Washington, but hope the town will be obliged to surrender for want of provisions. If I hear anything of interest I will write to you immediately. Charleston seems quite safe and people are returning with the belief that her time of trial is over. Reports say that the whole fleet of Monitors was badly damaged, and will not soon be fit for service. I went into the Village yesterday to see Charlotte Simmons who leaves today for Grahamville near which place her husband is stationed.[117] Livie goes down to Mt. Pleasant in a short time and Caroline speaks of going to Charleston and keeping house with Lucilla. Mr. Pinckney is stationed on Sulli[van's] Is[land].[118] Lucilla and Kate went up to the farm but came back the day of the attack but came back next morning. Ella and the children with Jeannie

---

[117] "Charlotte Simmons" was Charlotte Haskell Simons (1832-92), a daughter of William Elnathan Haskell. Her husband was Benjamin Bonneau Simons (1832-1928).

[118] This was likely Lt. Bartholomew Gaillard Pinckney (1830-1906), whose wife was Martha Caroline Haskell Pinckney, a daughter of William Elnathan Haskell of Charleston.

paid us a three days visit and left here yesterday. They are all well tho I fear dear little Charley will have a hard time with his teeth this Summer. He has six out but the hardest ones are I fear coming now. What chance is there of getting boarding at or about Flat Rock if he gets sick and it is too difficult to go to Mrs. Hills. I only ask to be prepared at all points. Pete is a nice little fellow and tho somewhat wayward a good little fellow. Charley admires him very much & imitates him in everything he can, trys to shout and to climb &c. He is not pretty yet but still improving and is a smart little monkey. Poor Hannah is desperately ill, past all hope of recovery, in a rapid decline. She is at Judge Wardlaw's and Jeannie lets [Maum] Kate give her whole time to her. Ella has hired a woman who nursed all Mrs. Alfred Wardlaw's children, and who had nothing to do now that poor little Alfred has been freed from his long agony of suffering.[119] I do not know if I mentioned he died some weeks ago whilst Susie Venning was so ill. She is much better now tho still suffering badly from whooping cough. Jeannie heard from Hannah yesterday. She gave her no news and writes sadly. She says they feel their loss more and more, and that she cannot feel yet like leaving home. I received a letter from Matilda Rhett who writes for Follie who had gone on to Richmond unexpectedly on business two days after she went down, leaving the children with Matilda. She writes me the price of dresses in Col[umbia]. A very coarse muslin $3.50, a very coarse [Mell] muslin $5 per yard so I must try elsewhere. I may get something better in Charleston tho Carrie told me of calico at $2.60 which is something better. Charlotte and the girls send love to you. The boys are quite well and we will send for them on Saturday. Give my love to Isabella and all with her, and best respects to the Ladies. God bless you my own darling.

Sophia C. Haskell, Abbeville, S.C., to Sophie Haskell, Flat Rock, N.C. (SCHS)
27 April [1863]
Dear Sophie,

I am writing from Sallie Smith's were [*sic*] I am spending the day. All are well but little Charley and he is much better. He was taken sick last Monday the day he came in from our house with bowel complaint and fever. He is looking a good deal worsted by the attack and is very fretful but seems pretty well again today and I am going to take him home with me. Ella is going tomorrow to Columbia with Jeannie and takes Cheves in hopes of getting his picture taken this time and she wants to go to the dentist. They will stay at your Aunts and come home Saturday. Your Aunt Charlotte has

---

[119] William Alfred Wardlaw (1851-63), the son of William Alfred Wardlaw (1816-76) and Iwanowna (Ivy) Tillman Wardlaw (1820-63), died on March 30, 1863.

just determined to go down to Charleston Friday with Mamie and Lang, so that Emmy will be left alone with us, tho I hope Ella and Jeannie will come out and stay with us next week. Charlotte Simmons and family have gone to the Low Country and Livie leaves on Tuesday and goes back to her old home at Mount Pleasant where they think they may now live in safety so that establishment is broken up. Carrie still remains tho she hopes to be able to go down too before long.[120] Poor Mary Pinckney is suffering dreadfully from inflammatory rheumatism. Her Mother says she has not been able to bear having her hair smoothed even for more than a week.[121] She can use one hand a little now and can bend her knees, so you may judge how she has suffered when these things are spoken of to show her improvement.

Louis and Paul are at home both quite well and have holyday till Thursday as Mr. Porcher has gone to William DuBose's wedding at Anderson where he is to be married Tuesday to Miss Nannie Peronneau.[122] I have had letters from Charley, Willy, Alec and Lang. All are well but send no news of any interest except that Charley was going again to Bull's Is. but I suppose he has returned long ago. John wrote to Emmy that they were about to leave Washington after a fruitless effort. Joe had been sent to Richmond for ammunition. All were quite well. I have heard nothing from Follie since I wrote last but suppose she will soon be back in Col[umbia]. If I hear anything of interest I will write again soon. Ella sends love.

Sophie Haskell, Flat Rock, N.C., to Charles T. Haskell, Jr. (SCHS)
28 April 1863
My dear Brother,

Your letter which I received some days ago was the first news I had had of you for some time except that you were safe and well after the attack of Charleston. It [reminded] me too of how long I had neglected writing to you. Up here in this little out of the way corner of the Confederacy we were doubly anxious during the attack as we have only a tri-weekly mail, but at last even we heard that the attack had been successfully sustained and the enemy repulsed. Now that it is over I can hardly help [*sic*] that the fight had

---

[120] This may be Caroline Pinckney (1837-1901), a daughter of the Rev. Charles Cotesworth Pinckney (1812-98). She was later Mrs. Julian A. Mitchell.

[121] Mary Elliott Pinckney (1833-1912) was the daughter of Charles Cotesworth Pinckney (1789-1865) and Phoebe Caroline Elliott Pinckney (1792-1864).

[122] William Porcher DuBose (1836-1918), an officer in Holcombe Legion and later a Confederate chaplain, married Anne (Nannie) Barnwell Peronneau (1836-73) on April 30, 1863. The Reverend John H. Elliott conducted the wedding in a small ceremony in Anderson, S.C. After the war, DuBose was ordained as an Episcopal priest and ministered at Trinity Episcopal Church in Abbeville.

lasted longer and that they should have come to closer quarters so that the injury done them being greater this fight might have had a greater influence on the duration of the war. I am very glad that it is all safely over and no damage done to you or anyone I know.

I have no news to give for my school life tho' pleasant is perfectly monotonous indeed! Living as I do it is very hard to realize how differently all of you are living and often in the evening I try to picture to myself how you are all occupied and often I have to wonder where some of you are for lately Johnny and Joe especially seem to have been pretty actively employed in No. Carolina.

Charleston seems to have been quite gay in a quiet way, for war times this winter, and I hope you go over there sometimes for you know any sort of gaiety seems to me so pleasant that I cannot but think it must be so to you too, and besides I want you to keep up the habit of going out for I expect you to carry your small sister about when she is grown up, which will be I suppose as soon as the war is over and not before if it lasts thirty years. Now I have not much time to think of being grown up for without studying very tremendously my time is pretty well filled up and I hope I am making some progress. I read a good deal of history and a great deal of French (for me) out of school so that I have just time for a little walk in the afternoon and never have time for writing except when I am at Aunt Isabella's where I go every Saturday and come back to school on Monday.[123]

This evening it is raining so I take the time which I generally walk to write this little letter. I have such a cold that it stupefies me but on next Saturday I will write again, and try to make some news for the occasion.

Sophia C. Haskell, Home Place Plantation, Abbeville District, S.C.,
to Charles T. Haskell, Jr. (SCHS)
3 May 1863
Dear Charley,

Your box arrived yesterday everything safe, two demijohns of brandy, quinine, two cases of sweet oil and one castor oil, one box of Castile soap and one of Windsor and a box of axes. Everything but the chloroform and that to us is of very little consequence. Your Father says I must thank you for all and say that the axes are peculiarly acceptable. He has given one to Cuffee to grind and try if it needs tempering. The Windsor soap is only a little hurt on the outside but otherwise very nice indeed and such a supply we can furnish all the family for a long time. I gave Emmy and Ella each a

---

[123] Isabella Middleton Cheves, along with her mother, sisters and children, lived at Acton Briars in Flat Rock, N.C., during much of the war.

little package of it and also for your Aunt Charlotte and Mamie. The boys Louis, Paul & Russell each got a cake and Johnny B. who had arrived the day before from Columbia.[124] Paul said that would do for their hands but he could not use it for his feet so each got a slice of the Castile. I gave Ella and Emmy some of that too and when an opportunity occurs I will send some to all the boys, who have been very thankful for the homemade soap.

We have no recent news from them. I enclose a letter from Alec received yesterday. Ella received one from Lang two days later. Up to that time all seemed quiet. The alarming accounts of the last two days make me anxious but I cannot yet believe that a great battle is to be fought.[125] Longstreet has three divisions of Lee's army with him at Suffolk, two of them very strong, said Langdon in a previous letter, and that he thought Lee would not move till he should rejoin him. Their army from what all write is in fine health and condition, only suffering from lack of sufficient food. Alec's wrath was roused by the subscriptions made in Charleston to send sugar and coffee to the soldiers in Fort Sumpter [sic] to sustain their strength, and even to Lang, from their standpoint it was rather galling when as he said 90 out of every hundred of their men went to bed hungry every night and never had enough to eat. Still so far their health does not suffer except that some were taking scurvy. Their brigade is more numerous and in better condition that [sic] at any time since the battles before Richmond, about 2800, of these 250 were usually in the hospital but generally slight cases. Their old reg. tho was not doing well which he much regretted for Willy's sake who has no chance of filling his company. He says the field officers of the reg. are a very mediocre set. I feel very anxious for tomorrows news.

I hope you will see your Aunt Charlotte and Mamie & they will tell you all the home news. Ella has just returned from a very short visit to Columbia at your Aunt Louisa's with Jeannie by particular invitation. They were all very kind but your Aunt seemed very sad tho she would often make an effort to converse cheerfully. I had little Charley while she was away. He has been quite sick from his teeth but is pretty well again. He was cross and rather melancholy but today that [sic] he has his Mother and Pete are with him he is in better spirits. He is a very knowing little character and though very different often puts me in mind of dear little Mary.[126] I hope he will not suffer very much with his teeth. If he does we must help Ella to take him to

---

[124] "Johnny B." was John Bachman Haskell (1846-84), a teenage cousin. He was the son of William Elnathan Haskell of Charleston.

[125] The Battle of Chancellorsville, Va., which was fought from April 30 to May 6, 1863.

[126] This refers to Mary Sophia Haskell, the infant daughter of Langdon C. Haskell who died in 1861.

the mountains. I believe your Father will be as fond of him as of Cheves. Have you received your butter and eggs. Tell me how to direct the next if the last was not right.

Sophia C. Haskell, Home Place Plantation, Abbeville District, S.C., to Sophie Haskell (SCHS)
3 May 1863
Dear Sophia,

All your brothers I hope are well tho I have no recent news from Joe. John was sick when he wrote on the 23rd but if it were anything serious he would have let us know before now, so I take no news for good news. Charley was detained on Bull's Is. by sickness and did not get back for ten days but he was at home again on the 25th pretty well but weak. Ella left Charley with me and went to Col[umbia] last Tuesday. She came back yesterday with Pete, both well, but Pete's picture very unlucky. He is pouting very much.

Now my dear child I will tell you of what is grieving us very much. Our good faithful Lucy is gone. She was struck dead almost in an instant. She had just gone to bed and was speaking to Beck who slept with her, very cheerfully but complained of a little cough, that it made her feel like having a headache. Back recommended lye tea and told Nancy to get her some.[127] Two or three minutes after she heard her breathe badly, spoke to her and getting no answer called for a light and found her already insensible and in five minutes she was dead. I was awake and only stayed to put on my slippers and dressing gown but was too late. Old Nancy only got from her house in time to see her draw her last breath. This was on Wednesday night at 12 o'clock. She had been indisposed the previous week but was quite well all Wednesday and to use Rose's words "She had not seen her Mother so spry for a long time." The Dr. calls it probably apoplexy of the heart. I can scarcely realize her death. Ten times a day I am on the point of calling for her or sending to her. I hope and believe she was a good Christian and that the loss is ours and not hers. She was busy all Wednesday fixing Jonas' clothes to go to Va. to Willy. He wrote word that he could no longer get on, the sickness of a servant belonging to his mess leaving him without attendance. Your Father thought Jonas would be safer and more faithful than a young man and sent him off as Willy directed under the care his Sergeant John Wilson who was in the village and left yesterday morning. I do not know what to think of the news from the Rappahannock. Hooker is in motion and skirmishing was going on but I hope they will not try a battle again.

---

[127] Nancy was Lucy's mother-in-law.

Alec writes to me very often; his great grief is seeking for relief from Heaven and he seems to feel much comforted. He says the religious feeling in the army is very strong and increasing, that the chaplains are making great exertions and with much apparent success. Last Sunday was their Communion under the pines and as the three brothers knelt together he felt how much we all have to be thankful for. It was our Communion too and as I prayed for you all I hoped some day we might have you and our brave boys to thank God with us. If all should not meet again I trust and hope we may hope to meet hereafter. If we should have any news of interest I will be sure to write to you. The Charleston people seem to feel quite safe now. Many are hastening back. Livie, Charlotte and Lucilla have gone, the Ben Rhetts and Bachmans from Col[umbia] and very many others. Lincoln says the attack must be renewed but no one seems to fear it now. It is said in some of the papers that the Yankees mean to avoid great battles and only to ravage and skirmish. I suppose a few weeks now will produce many developments. God help the Right!

I think I wrote you word that Charlotte, Mamie and Lang were going to Charleston. They left on Thursday. Follie we have not yet heard from. I hope she is back again. Goodby my dear child. I hope this week will bring us good news.

Louis W. Haskell, Willington, S.C., to Sophie Haskell, Flat Rock, N.C. (SCHS)
8 May 1863
Dear Sophy,

I got your letter the other day. You said in your letter, I think the one to Paul that for the first time you had seen a strawberry blossom the other day. What [made] me think of it is my having some strawberries by me now to refresh me while I am writing though I have no sugar with them, but I find that they are better than I thought that they would be. Mr. Porcher turns about six of us in the garden everyday two or three at a time and we pick as many as we want.

When I was at home last Ma got a letter from Joe and he said he was going to try and get a furlough to come home for a while but I would not be surprised if this battle in Virginia stopped him. I suppose you have heard of Brother Alick's being wounded in his foot but I hope it will be nothing very bad though those wounds in the feet are always hard to get well. Johnny Bachman has come up to stay with us and I think he is a good deal stronger than he was last year.

Your pony when I rode him last was doing very well and he is not so bad. The last time we went home we had a week holyday and I rode Kitty almost altogether. She was quite bad at first but she soon got to be a delightful riding horse.

Pa is trying to get Mr. Porcher to break my Slouch and I hope he will for he is a fine rider and I think breaks colts well & sometimes I will get a ride.

Sister J[128] returned from Columbia where she had been on a short visit, and from the description that she said Miss Alice gave her of the fare at Madame Togno's, it must be worse than ours.[129] Sister says it is corn bread & [bread] without any butter for breakfast. The same with homony for dinner, and no supper but some corn bread brought in the school room and the young ladies grab, and Madame Togno & her family do not eat with them. I hope you get something better than that. I hope that you can get Lang & Punch to come to school but I don't think they can come this year but if an application is made for them now I think they can come next year or perhaps in the last part of this year. Tell Lang he will have to study Latin & arithmetic a good deal so he can go in Caesar and be a [good] way in arithmetic and Punch must learn to read and write well.

Last night Mr. Porcher got a letter from the ladies of the wayside hospital asking him to take a boy who had come there very badly wounded. They said he is a boy fourteen years old. He belonged to a Mississippy company and has been in six battles.

I don't expect that you can read this or not very easily at enerate [sic] but I have a very bad pen.

Sophia C. Haskell, Home Place Plantation, Abbeville District, S.C.,
to Sophie Haskell (SCHS)
8 May [1863]
Dear Sophie,

All saved again through a bloody battle.[130] Lang, Willy and others were all engaged. Alec is wounded painfully but not dangerously. Lang says he is going to Richmond with him and Gen McGowan. Lang's telegram says Alec's wound is near the ancle [sic]. Mr. Barnwell says in the foot. In either case I suppose the cure will be tedious and we may see him home after a while on crutches. I will let you know as soon as we hear anything more. Your poor Aunt Louisa sends up Mr. Barnwell's despatch with her kindest

---

    [128] "Sister J" was Jeannie Wardlaw, a sister-in-law. She was the sister of Ella Coulter Wardlaw Haskell (1835-1887), the wife of Langdon Cheves Haskell.

    [129] Alice Patterson Wardlaw (1845-1929) was apparently a pupil at Madame Togno's school for girls in Charleston. Rosalie Acelie Guillou Togno was the widow of Dr. Joseph Togno.

    [130] The Battle of Chancellorsville, Va.

congratulations. Poor soul, I feel so much for her. We have indeed cause for gratitude and thankfullness [*sic*] but I feel that we can hardly rejoice amidst so much sorrow. Pinckney Seabrook is sayed [*sic*] to be killed. James Perrin the Col. is killed and poor little Tom Perrin, just about your age in his first battle.[131] This is nearly all we have heard as yet. Is it not strange four Colonels from our poor little Village killed, Smith, Marshall, Lythgoe and Perrin.[132] Ella returned from Columbia Sat[urday] and is with us. Charley is much better only looks quite delicate. Cheves is very well and pretty but his picture is a complete failure. He got scared & worried by repeated trials and pouted exceedingly making rather a ridiculous little picture. He is not much spoiled and Ella manages him very well, but when much noticed he will be bad sometimes. I am glad you have got a dress, if it suits you no matter about the price. Let me know and I will send it. Everything is so monstrous now. I have sent to Charleston by your Aunt Charlotte for the muslin dress if to be had within reason, also for a chintz or brilliant but do not count on them.

William T. Haskell, Camp Gregg, Va., to Charles T. Haskell (SCHS)
9 May 1863
My dear Father,

Sergt. Wilson arrived yesterday with Jonas bringing your letters. I am very glad that I have one so faithful & reliable about me & only fear that he will not be able to stand the fatigues of marching & the exposure of camp. We shall see. I will have to curtail his baggage as he has as much as a brigadier. His axe is the best in camp.

Langdon & Alic will soon be at home & give you an account of the fight from which we have just returned. It was a very severe one ending in the entire defeat of the enemy. I went over the battlefield in various places & have never seen greater slaughter. To add to the usual horror of such scenes the fort in which much of the battle was fought having been set on fire by shell, burned the killed & many wounded, leaving spectacles most dreadful to look upon. Strange to say though nothing seen now on the battlefield of this kind affects me more than so many stocks or stones. The afterthought is worse.

---

[131] James Monroe Perrin (1822-63) of Abbeville District was fatally wounded at the Battle of Chancellorsville, Va., in May 1863. His nephew Thomas Samuel Perrin (1845-63) was killed in the same battle.

[132] Augustus Marshall Smith (1827-62) was a lieutenant colonel. Colonel Jehu Foster Marshall (1817-62) was mortally wounded at Second Manassas. Augustus Jackson Lythgoe (1830-62), commander of the 19th South Carolina Infantry Regiment, was killed in battle at Murfreesboro, Tennessee, in December 1862.

I am saddened by the loss of C. Pinckney Seabrook my lieutenant, my nearest & dearest companion—one of the noblest best men I have ever seen. He was my chief associate & resource in camp, remarkable as a man & an officer. Miller[133] the other lieut. is severely wounded, so I am now alone. Several of my brave men were lost to the service & perhaps will lose their lives—others less severely wounded. <u>Do send me the Mercury or Courier</u> in which my list of killed & wounded appears.

I can't write more now. Love to Ma & all the household.

Sophia C. Haskell, Home Place Plantation, Abbeville District, S.C., to Sophie Haskell, Flat Rock, N.C. (SCHS)

[May 1863]

Dear Sophie,

We received last night a telegram from Langdon saying all were doing well and would leave for home in a few days. All meant no doubt Alec & Gen. McGowan. I received also a letter from your Aunt Louisa containing a despatch from Mrs. Barnwell which says "Alec's wound is slight, he will be home soon." All which is a great comfort and relief to us for I have felt very anxious about Alec's wound so near the ancle [*sic*]. I hope we may receive a letter with fuller intelligence tonight. But there is more bad news for poor Abbeville. Alfred Wardlaw wounded seriously in the temple.[134] I fear that it may be mortally & Arthur Wardlaw severely in the thigh.[135] All our news so far is from the Telegraph. I suppose you have heard of the death of Stonewall Jackson.[136] It is a terrible loss to us. He has been the <u>Hero</u> of the war so far. His name was a tower of strength. We have no news from John & Joe and I fear Joe cannot get a furlough to come home as we had hoped. I am afraid they are in motion again as we have not heard very lately. Charley is trying to get a furlough as Ella writes me word. She went in yesterday to see Allen who is up for two weeks. Under these circumstances would you like to come home at once. If you do, see if you can any escort or company [sic] for the whole or part of the way. If not write word that we may send for Louis

---

[133] This was likely Alexander Fraser Miller (1842-64), a first lieutenant.

[134] Lewis Alfred Wardlaw (1844-63), a sergeant in Orr's Rifled, was the son of Dr. Joseph James Wardlaw (1814-73). His obituary in an Abbeville newspaper described his ultimately mortal wound at the Battle of Chancellorsville: "In the fiercest of that battle when the color bearer was shot down, Sergeant Wardlaw rushed forward, seized the flag, unfurled the colors again, and while cheering the men onward, received a mortal wound through both temples." The obituary also stated that he survived for more than a week and died in his father's home near Abbeville on June 7, 1863. His gravestone gives a death date of June 6, 1863.

[135] Arthur Wardlaw (1845-63) was the son of William Alfred Wardlaw (1816-76).

[136] Thomas J. "Stonewall" Jackson died on May 10, 1863.

to fetch you home. I hope there is so much travelling now you can find some one coming down to Greenville. Your Father sends a check for $40 which he says you can get easily cashed by any merchant. Your Aunt I dare say can assist you. Do not be in too great a hurry but fetch all your things. Get your bills from Madame De Choiseul and if your money does not hold out for your small debts and to pay for your dress I dare say you can borrow from your Aunt. If you can get any thing else you want as you got the dress get it and welcome for there is precious little to be got here and Charleston is little better. Your Aunt Charlotte says the goods there are coarse, ugly and the prices enormous and I do not think she will get any thing. Little Charley has got quite well again and I hope will have a little time to gain strength and good looks before Lang comes home. Alec I suppose will stop for some time in Col[umbia]. Your Cousin Follie is in Col. and will be back in about two weeks. We are quite alone now except Johnny and I am taking advantage of the opportunity to cut out the negro clothes as far as our home made cloth will go so that I may know how much more will be wanted. Gregg has been so obliging to let us have a bale of cloth at about 40 cts which will be very useful for the boys and house servants so we can get on better than I thought. Your roses are looking beautiful and my garden promises well.

Charles T. Haskell, Jr., Battery Marshall, Sullivan's Island, S.C.,
to Sophia C. Haskell (SCHS)
12 May 1863
Dear Mother,

I rec'd by your letter of the 8th the only news that I have been able to get of Aleck except what I have heard through the newspapers. I have telegraphed twice to Richmond but can get no answer. Do write me from time to time anything that you may hear. I am glad to hear that the things reached you safely. The butter etc. was duly rec'd but the barrel of flour has not yet come. Do let anything sent hereafter come by express as I much prefer paying their higher rates to losing the boxes. Pa proposed in his last letter sending me more grist & peas when desired. I will be much obliged to him if he will do so as we are getting towards the bottom of the barrels already sent. The iron is all safe altho I have not been able as yet to send it off. The trouble is to have the large sheets brought across from Long Island.[137] I have got over more than half however & will get the rest.

Joe is I suppose now with you as he left Charleston on Sunday morning. I have seen Aunt Charlotte & Mamie once or twice & expect them over here to see me. I hope to be able to get off towards the latter part of this

---

[137] Long Island is now known as the Isle of Palms.

month. Will Sophie be at home then. If not when will she as I will wait until she comes home if the time is not too long. Tell Paul I have found Bruno again looking rather like a ragamuffin.

P.S. Do tell Paul also that he had best write "used to" instead of "youster."

John C. Haskell, Kinston, N.C., to Joseph C. Haskell (UNC)
21 May 1863
Dear Joe,
    I have returned from Richmond several days and find that there has been a good deal of scheming among the Captains Graham and Starr particularly to get up North Carolina organizations in the artillery, and Genl Hill has winked at it and actually recommended Graham's promotion and that he should have one of my batteries, and told me nothing of it.[138] He has also recommended Moore's promotion (both of these under the governor's recommendation) and that he should have two more of my batteries.[139] This I heard from Archer Anderson and Capt. Bondurant (both of whom had protested against my command being changed and disorganized without my being consulted) and I immediately demanded to be relieved from duty in this department.[140] When Genl H[ill] found out that I was not going to stand it he said he could not spare me and would give me any command I chose or take me on his staff. To this I answered that after his conduct towards me no command that he had would make [amends] for the unofficerlike manner in which I had been treated and that I would not accept any position in his gift, and as for going on his staff that I did not desire the honor as I did not doubt but that I could get a position more satisfactory to me. After this he had nothing further to say but immediately relieved me and I am in a few days going to Richmond to report for duty and will go to Fredericksburg or out West. As I do not suppose you desire to remain here, I send you an order relieving you & you need not be in a hurry to come on. You had better go home and wait until you hear from me or else go to Charleston and go on duty and if you like [then] I can get you ordered there without your going to Richmond.

---

    [138] These officers were likely Captain Joseph Graham (1837-1907) of the Charlotte Artillery, and Captain Joseph B. Starr (1830-1913), a North Carolina officer.
    [139] This may be Alexander Duncan Moore (1836-64), captain of the Wilmington Light Artillery. He was promoted to the colonelcy of the Sixty-sixth North Carolina Infantry Regiment in August 1863.
    [140] Archer Anderson (1838-1918) was an officer in the Twenty-first Virginia Infantry Regiment (D. H. Hill's Division). James William Bondurant (1835-67) served in the Jefferson Davis Artillery of Alabama.

I have sold the colt and bought Edmonston's gray [race] horse. [Derrill] and his Brigade have gone to Virginia. Dr. [Grayson] has applied to be relieved and ordered to report to me wherever I am sent, and the Blues say they will go with me or nobody.[141] I pity the man that gets them in his command. They are getting up a petition to be relieved also but I think I can prevail on them to keep quiet for a while at least. You had better [send] this letter home as I will not be able to write them for some days. You need not write to me till you hear again [sic] as I do not know where I will be.

P.S. You need not report till you hear from me again. I merely send the order to prevent accidents. Keep away from here or you will be [fixed here without the Battn]. I have your commission which I will send you soon. J. C. H.

Headquarters Battalion Reserve Artillery
Kinston, NC
May 21 '63
Special Order
No. 9   }
1st Lieut. Jos. C. Haskell Provisional Arty CSA is relieved from duty with this command and will report to the Adjutant & Inspector General.
John C. Haskell
Major Comdg Battn

William T. Haskell, Camp Gregg, Va., to Langdon C. Haskell (SCHS)
2 June 1863
My dear Lally,

I got your letter a few days ago & now answer without anything satisfactory on any point. We may move but as yet they give no sign. I don't know what we can do but to divide & send sufficient force on F. J. H.'s right flank to make him fall back & then perhaps combine & follow him.[142] There is an idea that he has commenced already to fall back on Washington [mustering] and having [so much] weakened his force. This may be. I think the point is too obvious that we should fight them before very long but how the meeting is to come on is again the question. I have sent to Mamie Cheves our new organization, three corps, Longstreet, Hill, Ewell. Hill has R. H.

---

[141] This likely refers to the Norfolk Light Artillery Blues of Virginia, also known as Grandy's Company.

[142] F. J. H. likely refers to Major General Joseph Hooker, who was known as "Fighting Joe Hooker."

Anderson, Heth[143] & Pender,[144] the latter his former brigade Thomas,[145] McGowan, Lane.[146]

I hope the Genl. (McG) will get well & come back soon.[147] The feeling with which I look upon Col. H's rule is indescribable.[148] He cannot command the confidence of any private in the brigade, but his sensibilities on some subjects are tough beyond accounting for. I don't know what will become of us unless something is done. I feel as if it was criminal almost to refrain from efforts to get rid of him, but the effort might with his plausibilities fail & leave things worse than before. If some inspector could snap him up & make him drill or try to & then stand an examination it might scare him off. His seeking the rear in the fight on Sunday I think cannot bear the mildest scrutiny. Shooter[149] & Butler[150] disclaim it, etc. etc., but I find I am running off on a topic that sickens me. But before leaving it he (H) told Shooter that it was "so unfortunate that I became separated from the regiment." He has never asked me a question or hinted at the subject just as on the Chickahomminy.

I am glad to hear of Ella & the young ones being well. I hope they continue so. It is sad to think of the Perrins, the last blows have been heavy. Alic I have not heard from since you wrote.

If you come on I would just volunteer on some staff for the time. I have no doubt that you would be gladly employed by some of the new Genls, Pender perhaps. I know it would be disagreeable with Col. H. He is full, has Alston, Barnwell, Adams.[151] Inspectors are abolished by order for the present.

Give my love to Ella & all at home.

---

[143] General Henry Heth (1825-99) commanded a brigade in A. P. Hill's Light Division.

[144] William Dorsey Pender (1834-63) commanded a brigade of North Carolinians in A. P. Hill's Light Division.

[145] Brigadier General Edward Lloyd Thomas (1825-98).

[146] Brigadier General James Henry Lane (1833-1907) commanded the Second Brigade in Pender's Division.

[147] Gen. Samuel McGowan was seriously wounded in the leg at the Battle of Chancellorsville, Va., on May 3, 1863. Abner Monroe Perrin (1827-64) took command of his brigade until McGowan returned to the field in February 1864.

[148] "Col. H" was Daniel Heyward Hamilton (1816-68).

[149] Captain Washington Pinckney Shooter (1837-64), a native of Marion District, S.C. He was later a lieutenant colonel.

[150] This probably refers to Andrew Pickens Butler (1826-1902).

[151] Thomas Pinckney Alston (1832-64), Captain John Gibbes Barnwell (1816-1905), and Captain James Pickett Adams (1828-1904). Adams was a volunteer aide-decamp.

P.S. Do ask Ma to send me on two shirts & some candles the first opportunity.

Charles T. Haskell, Jr., Battery Marshall, Sullivan's Island, S.C.,
to Langdon C. Haskell (SCHS)
10 June 1863
Dear Langdon,

On my arrival here I found orders which will probably prevent me from going on to Richmond with you, as I will have to take a force upon the coast somewhere between this place & Georgetown. It will be but a temporary delay however.

I have attended to what you asked me to. Allen Wardlaw[152] says that you can have the cloth. I will send it to Edgerton today. Edgerton says that he cannot possibly have your things ready until some time next week. If I find that I will be absent when you are to come down I will leave a letter for you with Uncle William. Tell Aunt Charlotte that I have seen Uncle Langdon, who is well.

Charles T. Haskell, Jr., Battery Marshall, Sullivan's Island, S.C.,
to Charles T. Haskell (SCHS)
12 June 1863
Dear Father,

I shipped to you yesterday by express a Tranter pistol[153] complete & two bottles of chloroform. You had best study the mechanism of the pistol pretty well before you fire it. When you wish to fire it pull the lower trigger hard, which will cock the pistol but not fire it. Keep the finger tightly pressed on the lower trigger while you aim & when you wish to fire touch the upper one. The balls should be thoroughly lubricated with the ointment in the case.

I enclose an express receipt. The iron has not been sent. I had it conveyed to town yesterday & as I am not able to attend to it myself have written to Mr. Wardlaw requesting him to ship it to you.

---

[152] Allen Wardlaw was George Allen Wardlaw (1837-65). At this time he was an assistant quartermaster in the First South Carolina Infantry Regiment. He was the son of Judge David Lewis Wardlaw of Abbeville, and his sister Ella Wardlaw was the wife of Langdon Cheves Haskell.

[153] The Tranter was a revolver popular in the Confederate Army.

John C. Haskell, Culpepper, Va., to Sophia C. Haskell (SCHS)
13 June 1863
Dear Ma,

I got your letter yesterday which was the first news I had got from home for a good while as I have been moving about so much that it is almost impossible to send letters to you with any certainty. If you direct care of Genl. Longstreet I will probably get any letter you may send me sooner or later. Joe got here yesterday from Richmond but what he will do I cannot [see] yet as there is but little chance of my getting any position where I can have him with me. He has gone over this morning to see Col. Alexander in hopes that he can give him something to do but I am afraid that there is but little chance of that as he has his full complement of officers.[154]

Tell Sophy that I got her letter and am much obliged to her for it and will answer her soon. I did not know before that she was at home. Has she finished school or not. I am sorry to hear that Emma is looking badly. I hope she will soon be well again. Do give my love to all at home. I wrote to Pa a few days ago and suppose he has got it before this time. I am sorry you did not get my letter giving my reasons for leaving North Carolina as the letter was long and I have not time to write it again so but I told Genls. Smith and Longstreet why I had left and they both say that they think my course was right and that I could not well have done otherwise. I have no prospect of getting as fine a command, but I have got a better place than I had any right to expect, but when I asked to be relieved I did so [unconditionally] and with no prospect of any place in view, and if I knew that I would get no position I would do again as I have done.

We are [here] constantly having rumors of an approaching fight and we are certainly maneuvering in a suspicious way. This morning orders have been sent to all troops to be ready at any moment to march or fight. What the [reason] is which brought out this order I do not know but I suspect it is another [stampede]. Do give my love to Pa and all the rest.

Joseph C. Haskell, Richmond, Va., to Sophie Haskell (SCHS)
16 June [1863]
Three cheers for Genl Lee and the army of the Potomac.[155]
Dear Sophie,

I suppose you have pretty well gotten over the effects of my advice and admonitions as to your behavior. I think it is about time to administer a little more with advantage, but I am afraid I must disappoint you as I have not

---

[154] This was Col. Edward Porter Alexander (1835-1910).
[155] This was the original name of the Army of Northern Virginia.

time to do justice to the subject and would therefore leave it to a more fitting period.

Here I am again. I expect as much to your own surprise as my own, and can only explain it by commencing at the time I left Richmond which I did on last Wednesday evening and reached Culpepper on Friday evening by [5] o'clock, distance over a hundred miles. I am quite vain of my merits as a horse jockey since I bought my pony. Every body tells me he is worth from 8 hundred to a thousand dollars. I found John in camp not having left as he expected to. He has written all his affairs I suppose. He is in good spirits and in better spirits than I expected to find him. The mess is quite a pleasant one and they all seem to like him very much. Being second in command he has no chance of working himself to death as he used to in No. Ca. and having a splendid groom he is at ease concerning his horses. The sorrel was appraised the other day at [900] dollars. Jim is already head of the whole establishment. I reported for duty the day after I got there, and was very kindly received by Major Tabor, Genl Lee's Adjt Genl who told me to look and find out where I would like to go and that he would assign me.[156] There were one or two places and amongst them Col Cabell wanted an Adjt. I thought he would the very man [sic]. I had such pleasant recollections of his nice establishment in Richmond that I thought he must live well in camp. He was very much pleased apparently with the idea, but when I went to ask about him, I heard such stories of his inefficiency and genl worthlessness that I gave up the idea at once. Tho I could not help thinking how pleasant it would be to be a member of his family especially if we ever got near Richmond. When I went back to Genl Lee's next morning I found Major McIntosh had written up and applied for me.[157] I did not fancy the idea particularly but I had to do something as Longstreet's Corps marched yesterday and I had no place to stay, so I am assigned to duty as Adjt of the Batt[allion] consisting of four fine batteries. McIntosh is the man who used to be a captain in the 1st S.C.V., and was transferred without his company to Art[illery]. He will soon be Lieut Col. The Batt[allion] is attached to Pender's Division, the one the boys are in so I will be with some of the family again. I was sorry to learn that I missed Langdon who went on today to Fredericksburg. I left my horse at Culpepper as I knew the Division would go up there, and came down today to get my saddle and baggage which I found safe. Do tell Aleck I have left his saddle and blanket at Mr. Dudley's as I had not time to take them back to the stable. If he is not at home write

---

[156] Joseph probably means Major Walter Herron Taylor (1838-1916).

[157] In March 1863, David Gregg McIntosh (1836-1916) of South Carolina was promoted to the rank of major and given command of an artillery battalion that saw service in the Battle of Chancellorsville, the Battle of Gettysburg, and other engagements.

him word where it is. Be [sure] about this as it [may] give him trouble if he does not know where it is. I got my commission and the letter enclosed this evening and was glad to be able to lay my hand on it as they have a loose way of dropping officers here I don't like.

I will go up to Rapidan Station tomorrow about ten miles from Culpepper. My horse is there at Mr. Massie,[158] who kindly took charge of him for me. I stayed there last night on my way down and had a very pleasant time and more [cherries] than you ever saw at home. The recollection of my breakfast and supper there will always form a bright spot in the memory of the vagrant life I have been leading for the last week or two. Carrie Massie[159] my cousin who last year when we were up there was all [eyes] is now one of the prettiest girls I ever saw. She has a beautifully fair complexion, very bright brown hair, and eyes as dark and pretty as Emma. Genl. Hill's corps is moving from Fredericksburg and I expect to meet them at Culpepper tomorrow night.

I stayed the last day I was with the army at Col Coles Chief Commissary.[160] He thinks and every body else does also that the army is starting for Pennsylvania. They are carrying ten days rations for men and horses and when they are done will live off the country. I am going to carry our box up to Culpepper in hopes of getting it along as the question of getting something to eat will be a pretty serious one before long. The men get plenty now but the officers are cut down pretty low.

I am again in want of a servant as my boy has left me. What for I don't know as he did not go through the form of saying good by, intending I suppose to spare my feelings. I have some hopes of getting one in the army tho. That is the only thing I lack now of being completely fitted out for the campaign. I had a very pleasant time in Richmond while I was awaiting orders. The only thing which disturbed my mind was an accident to those blue pants of mine. I was beguiled into going down to Drewreys Bluff [sic] and whilst down there Constance Carey I believe from pure spite begged me to climb an almost perpendicular bank to get her some laurel growing on top.[161] [My] politeness got the better of my discretion and I got the laurel at the

---

[158] This was likely Henry Massie, Jr. (1816-78). His wife, Susan Elizabeth Smith Massie, was a direct descendant of William Thomson, the paternal great-grandfather of the Haskell brothers.

[159] Caroline (Carrie) Thomson Massie (1845-1921) was the daughter of Henry Massie, Jr. She married Captain James Pleasants (1831-98) in November 1865.

[160] Lt. Colonel Robert Granderson Cole (1830-87) was the chief commissary of the Army of Northern Virginia.

[161] This was Constance Cary (1843-1920), who married Burton Harrison in 1867. She was later a noted author.

expense of pants which were I regret to say very much torn, but what was near being much worse the young ladies insisted on mending them. I expressed my high sense of the honor they wished to confer upon me but respectfully declined it. I will put my foot on Constance Carey's dress the next time I meet her at a party. When that would be I would like to know. I had my head shaved tonight and now consider myself in for it. You must consider this letter as belonging to the household for I don't know when I can write you again. Direct to me as Adjt McIntosh Art[illery] Batt[allion], 3rd Army Corps. Do give my love and goodbye to Ma, Pa, Aunt C, love to Mamie and Emma and any body else at home. I hear cousin Follie is still in Columbia. Do write to me often.

William T. Haskell, Bivouac at Stephensburg near Culpepper Court House, Va., to Sophie Haskell (SCHS)
17 June 1863
My dear Sophy,

I write to give an account of myself. You see where I am—left Hamilton's [Crossing] day before yesterday. I felt the march much yesterday but today have done very well though the weather is waning, and you hear every now and then that some poor fellow has fallen down dead—Coup de Soleil.[162] These things will happen. My little company always does well though I say it, I have no struggles though some look as if they may break down in a few days. They are but a little squad left now. I have been marching today with a battalion of s[harp] shooters which I command when it is used, a temporary arrangement.[163] We have just heard of Ewell's success; I expect we will join and follow up F. J. H. in Maryland and Penn. I would not miss my chance at this campaign for anything. I think we make a good start and will go a long way. Our army is strong and confident, Y[ankee]s weaker than usual, morally and physically. I expect to see the Dulles family.[164] To the females I will show some mercy, to the males I will slaughter without mercy except the father of the family who I will admit to a moderate ransom.

I heard you were at home. I thought I should have heard of you from yourself by this time, but I have learned to class you among the uncertainties which depend on strict attention to render such results sure. I hear that Langdon has nearly caught up with us and Alic will soon be. I will be very glad to see them as I am very lonely, but I don't like so many in one party.

---

[162] Sunstroke.

[163] This battalion was dissolved in the autumn of 1863 and reorganized in the spring of 1864 under the name of Dunlop's Battalion of Sharpshooters.

[164] The Dulles family was related to the Haskell and lived in the north.

Joe and John I believe are in Hood's Division, Longstreet corps.[165] Hill's Corps is the rearmost and our Division (Pender's) is its rear. The whole army is stretching out toward the north. Some of us may cross the Potomac east of the B[lue] Ridge, others west. But enough, the newspapers will give you more just as good as any, though not true.

I would like to see all of you at home but cannot like the bird be in two places at the same time. Give my love to Mamie and [Emma] and tell them I have made up my mind never to walk fast again after this war and its marching is over. Such is the present state of my mind. The present is not the most convenient time for writing as I have another man's pen ink and paper, Joel Smith's, who has stopped writing to give me chance so I must conclude.[166] I have been resting on my right elbow and so have not written in the usually good hand for which I am so justly celebrated, but it is good enough and properly spelled you therefore will not criticise nor show your lack of capacity by finding difficulty in reading this. Love to all. I will write again before long.

[P.S.] John is doing well and very good except too old to stand the marching I am afraid. I am trying to beg him a steed worthy of him. I have not heard for some time from [home]. Tell Louis I will answer him soon and to write again. I am keeping a diary to stand in place of letters. I will send it home when I get something beyond the dates.

Alexander C. Haskell, Columbia, S.C., to Charles T. Haskell, Abbeville, S.C.
(UNC)
19 June 1863
Dear Pa,

My movements are rendered uncertain by the very painful rumours amounting now to reports almost certain of Robert Barnwell's illness (keep this quiet for the present) resulting in complete derangement.[167] I have heard not one word by telegraph and this only confirms my worst fears. Before my arrival a despatch had come from Mrs. Singleton which spoke of her daugh-

---

[165] John Bell Hood (1831-79) was a division commander in Longstreet's Corps.

[166] This was likely William Joel Smith (1833-1908).

[167] Robert Woodward Barnwell (1831-63) was an Episcopal minister from South Carolina who served as an army chaplain and headed the executive committee of the South Carolina Hospital Association in Virginia. Emma Holmes of South Carolina recorded of him in her diary on June 6, 1863: "Rev. Robt. Barnwell has been very ill with typhoid fever and is in such a highly excited state, almost crazy from the many distressing deaths and other scenes he has so long been a witness of, that his friends have had to remove him from the position from where he has been such a fountain of blessing to our sick and wounded soldiers." Holmes, *The Diary of Miss Emma Holmes*, 267.

ter as too ill to travel yet, said not a word of Robert, and begged me to await their arrival in Columbia. I have telegraphed but can get no answer. There is just a chance that I may go tomorrow, or I may wait nearly a week. In the midst of such woeful calamity it is distracting to have all the calls of affection and humanity set aside for the cold fulfillment of a soldier's duty, but having given so much already it is no time now to draw back from the work. Death would have been the highest happiness compared with the misery with which the family and friends of this truly noble man will see him suffer under this most terrible of the afflictions of Providence. It is death with none of the relief from the misery of the world, but with every circumstance of pain and sorrow heaped upon it.

I cannot even yet believe it in all its horrible extent, but there is enough to excite & almost confirm the worst we could conceive. The last report is that he has been sent to the asylum at Staunton, Virginia.

With a mind and temperament well balanced and adjusted for the fullest enjoyment of innocent happiness, if he has fallen, it is as the victim to disease of body, which for months past has been making terrible ravages upon his frame.

I will write you again, whatever my movements may be.

The whole fabric of society seems to be subjected to the terrible trial of these times when the manifestations of the workings of Providence are being made palpable and plain to the eyes of men. Among my friends here the death of Frank Hampton[168] has fallen with terrible weight, and before their bowed heads have been raised from his fresh grave, comes the announcement of the worse than death of this beloved and nobly endowed man of God, and as I write, the sad tidings are going from house to house of the same friends, that old Mrs. Hampton, the pattern of Christian charity, the friend of all who needed help, and the beloved head of a numerous house, has breathed her last after long months of agony.[169]

---

[168] Lt. Colonel Frank Hampton (1829-63), the brother of General Wade Hampton (1818-1902), was killed at the Battle of Brandy Station, Virginia, on June 9, 1863. Mary Chesnut wrote of his funeral in Columbia, "Preston Hampton and Peter Trezevant, with myself and Mrs. Singleton, formed the sad procession which followed the coffin. There was a company of soldiers drawn up in front of the State House porch. Mrs. Singleton said we had better go in and look at him before the coffin was finally closed. How I wish we had not looked. I remember him so well in all the pride of his magnificent manhood. He died of a saber cut across the face and head, and was utterly disfigured. Mrs. Singleton seemed convulsed with grief. In all my life I had never seen such bitter weeping." Chesnut, *A Diary from Dixie* (New York: D. Appleton, 1905) 237.

[169] Mary Cantey Hampton (1779-1863), the widow of Wade Hampton (1751-1835), died on June 19, 1863.

Man must be strangely devised to learn so little when God speaks so plainly.

Tell Emmie, though I shrink from adding more sad news, that her poor little friend Ellen Togno died last week after a brief illness.[170] She will feel now the rare pleasure of remembering the kind charitable words she spoke in her defence when she needed kind words, but a few days ago.

I find all well at Aunt Louisa's, the girls looking better. Aunt Anna still here, quite well today though feeling badly yesterday.

I have tried to find the oil you wanted, but the only oil to be had is linseed at twenty four dollars a gallon. You had better make a little cow's foot oil for the delicate machinery, and use tallow or lard, and soft soap for the coarser parts. I have no horse here and am unable as yet to learn anything about the cattle.

Love to Ma, Aunt Charlotte, Sophie, Mamie and Emmie. Don't forget Lang.

Alexander C. Haskell, Columbia, S.C., to Sophia C. Haskell, Abbeville, S.C.
(SCHS)
20 June 1863
Dear Ma,

I have received despatches which require my immediate departure for Richmond. Robert Barnwell is in the asylum at Staunton. Mary is in Richmond too sick to travel, in all probability will not be able to come home for two months, if the poor soul ever sees home again. Of course Mrs. Singleton remains in Richmond. I wish Baby to remain with you and as the time bids fair to be considerably prolonged, I beg that you will adopt such diet and general management as may seem proper to you, without strict reference to any rules or injunctions which may have been laid down by me or others. I am willing to believe with old Mrs. Green that your nine strong children are the best evidence of your judgment and skill in the management of their early lives. If Baby wants clothes, change of air or anything else, do give her anything at any cost but be sure this is entirely a business arrangement and as such to be regarded. Keep an account of her expenditures. My means are more than sufficient for her wants.

I believe I can say no more for Baby but to commit her to the tender care of those who will love her well, and to hope that God will continue to bless her little life with all the happiness of which she is capable.

All my friends here that I have seen send their love to you. Tell Sophie to write to Lessie as kindly as she can break to her all this dreadful news, and

---

[170] Ellen A. Togno was a daughter of Madame Rosalie A. Togno.

tell her that I will ask her mother to let her come down to Abbeville for a while, where the poor child will have the companionship to win her from her grief. She is a sensitive, delicate girl, capable of intense suffering, and I don't think ought to be left alone this summer at school. I know if she comes to you all she will be happier than anywhere else, and you must see that she is not idle. Tell her I will write to her the moment I reach Richmond. I have no time for even a few lines this evening.

Tell Pa I have failed again to get the oil he wanted. I leave the jug. He may get it at some future time when he sees another advertisement. If he uses tallow or any solid form of grease tell him to beware of fire, which is the danger.

All well at Aunt L's and send love. Love to all the house. Kiss Baby.

Alexander C. Haskell, Richmond, Va., to Catherine Osborn Barnwell[171] (SCHS)
24 June 1863
My dear Mrs. Barnwell,

It was yesterday my sad duty to announce to you by telegraph the death of your noble son.[172]

The holy man of God has been called from earth, and amid all our grief we cannot but feel a solemn joy and full of awe when we contemplate from afar the glories of the Heaven he has entered.

Of this, my dear Madam, it little becomes me to speak before you who knew his heart so well. Still less can I speak in the common language of condolence. He has gone at the time when his name was linked, in the hearts of all our soldiers and our countrymen, with everything that is bright and pure in a Christian character, with all that is high and noble in the patient, devoted patriot. He has gone when his peace with God was made perfect. Fast in faith, bright in hope, pure and holy in spirit, at peace with the world, and stretching out his longing arms to meet his Saviour, he has gone. Of all this I can say nothing to you which your heart does not tell. I can only treasure it

---

[171] Catherine Osborn Barnwell (1809-86), the widow of Rev. William H. W. Barnwell (1806-63).

[172] A few days before Robert W. Barnwell's death, arrangements were made ("at his own desire" as noted by Aleck Haskell) for him to be taken to the Western State Hospital, an asylum in Staunton, Va. After suffering some delirium from typhoid fever, he died there on June 23. An entry in Emma Holmes' diary indicates that Barnwell had tried to take his own life. Holmes, *The Diary of Miss Emma Holmes*, 267.

in my own heart and make his example, what his precept has so often been, the light to guide my steps to truth & happiness.[173]

I have waited until this evening that I might put you in possession of such facts as I can as yet obtain.

On reaching Richmond on the 23rd I determined at once from what I heard, to telegraph that he was better and could soon see you. Before I could do this the sad news came. A sudden turn had proved fatal.

As you know, he went to Staunton willingly, indeed at his own desire. He was quiet and composed on the journey, somewhat fatigued but apparently doing well. He was received by Dr. Hamilton, a kind and accomplished physician in charge at Staunton, and from this moment to the last, all that skill & care could do was not wanting to him.[174] Here Dr. Michel left him.[175]

Dr. Hamilton could see no indications of insanity and so told Robert & offered to remove him to a private house. This Robert & his friends declined, he, preferring to have all fairly tested. Soon the symptoms became unmistakeably [sic] Typhoid in their character and from this time he was treated for Typhoid Fever. Dr. Carter, Mary's grandfather, who knew Robert well, was sent for & went twice to see him.[176] Mr. Charles Sharp a cousin of Mary's & of whom Robert was very fond, went with Dr. Carter. Dr. Cabell, a skillful physician of Charlottesville & a friend of Robert's, was also called in.[177] All these gentlemen concur in stating that he was suffering from Typhoid Fever, and that his mind was clear, his reason sound. Our last account, received day before yesterday, the day before I reached Richmond, represented the worst symptoms as having been checked. You know the result. I learn that he was delirious for several hours before his death. Full accounts will be obtained, first from Dr. Hamilton whose statement will be professional, & then from others who can throw light upon his last days.

Dr. Lafar, an associate with Robert in his work here, will accompany his remains to Columbia.[178] It was Robert's and Mary's desire that he should rest in the church yard in the burial place of Mary's family.[179]

---

[173] An obituary for Rev. Barnwell that appeared in a Charleston newspaper expressed high praise for him: "He took rank with our Petigrus, Thornwells, Palmers, Girardeaus, and others, who were distinguished by every accomplishment."

[174] Dr. William Hamilton (1818-89), assistant physician at the asylum in Staunton.

[175] Dr. William Middleton Michel (1822-94), a surgeon to Confederate hospitals in Richmond.

[176] Dr. Charles Warner Lewis Carter (1792-1867), a physician.

[177] Dr. James Lawrence Cabell (1813-89) was in charge of the Confederate hospitals in Charlottesville and Danville, Va.

[178] Dr. Theodore A. LaFar (1831-1912).

I have told you of nothing that passed before Robert's removal. All this you can learn from Dr. Lafar who was by his bedside.

Of poor Mary I have only to say that she is very ill.[180] I fear she will soon rest by her husband's side, apart from this world's troubles. Only for her children's sake I pray that she may live. Her little daughter is alive, I cannot say doing well, though there is much hope that she can be saved to comfort her poor Mother. It may be that Mary is a shade better this evening. She knows nothing of Robert. Life is barely fluttering in her pulses and the least shock would drive it away. May merciful God bless & comfort you and all who mourn.

I am with high respect and deep regard truly your friend, the friend of two of your noble sons.

Alexander C. Haskell, Richmond, Va., to Sophia C. Haskell (UNC)
24 June 1863
Dear Ma,

I am in a house full of sorrow, & feelings of such complicated misery as but rarely falls to the lot of mortals.

Robert Barnwell died yesterday morning in the asylum at Staunton, Va., a sane man, of Typhoid Fever. Two days of delirium before the fever had fully declared its character and at an interval of a week, have affixed to his name the cruel verdict of insanity. He went to the asylum at his own request, a sane and composed patient. He continued so for many days and died. His physician there said that he was not insane & offered to remove him to a private house. He declined, desiring to have his sanity fully tested. His greatest suffering arose from his own apprehension of insanity, which apprehensions I attribute the depressing effect of the disease of the liver from which he had been suffering for months [*sic*]. It was better too that he should be taken away from his poor wife, and he knew it. Never in his whole life has he evinced so high a faith, so pure a holiness as have marked his manner and conversation from the beginning of this illness. He was sure that his death was near at hand, spoke of it as certain, and all his arrangements and conversation referred to it. He died as a Christian, pure in faith and earnest in hope, one of the dearest yet noblest sacrifices that we have made to our sacred cause. His fame as a man could not have been higher. The soldiers of his country will never forget him. His hope as a Christian

---

[179] Robert Woodward Barnwell and his wife were buried in the Trinity Episcopal Cathedral Cemetery in Columbia, S.C.

[180] Mary Carter Singleton Barnwell (Mrs. Robert W. Barnwell) was Decca's sister.

could never have been brighter. Surely God has some choice reward for such as these.

But his poor unconscious, almost dying wife—for so it is—has been more than human. Such faith, fortitude and resignation can only belong to one into whom the whole spirit of God is breathed. Without a murmur she has borne the agony of seeing him taken from her, never again to meet him on earth. And now to tell her that he is in Heaven is the only thing that would bring a last smile to those pale lips. She lingers now only because she believes him still on earth and suffering, and would be near him. She may live, I can hardly hope. For her children's sake I pray for her life. For her own I could fold my hands and thank God that he had taken her. Her little child, a daughter, is alive and seems to be doing well. It is five days old. I don't know how long it can last. If both live this daughter will be a great comfort. She did so wish for it. I am in an atmosphere of death.

My news must be sad I know. Death is always a sad subject for those whom it leaves behind. Do write to Mrs. Singleton to tell her about Baby. May God bless and keep our little darling. I hear nothing from the boys. They are all I suppose on the Potomac. The Dudleys are all well though. I have not yet seen them. I called to ask after them; all were out. Love to Pa & Sophie, Aunt C. & the girls. Give Baby a kiss for me. God bless you all. Goodbye.

[P.S.] I leave Richmond the moment Mary changes for better or for worse, probably day after tomorrow.

Alexander C. Haskell, Richmond, Va., to Sophia C. Haskell (UNC)
25 June 1863
Dear Ma,

Our poor dear Mary was released from her suffering this morning.[181] Four helpless orphans need all our help and sympathy. God have mercy on them. They know not yet what they have lost. The infant, the poor little girl, is barely living from hour to hour. Such a scene of devastation is beyond the power of description. You saw Mrs. Singleton last year but one day later (tomorrow is the anniversary of my sad day). You saw then how fierce and

---

[181] Mary Barnwell passed away two days after her husband died, soon after giving birth to her fourth child, a daughter who would not live for long. Mary's mother, Mrs. Singleton, was with her in Richmond at the time. Mary Boykin Chesnut reported that shortly after Mrs. Singleton received a telegram informing her of Robert W. Barnwell's death, she rushed to Mary's bedside and was told by the doctor that she was dead. Chesnut wrote of Mary, "Not in anger, not in wrath, came the Angel of Death that day; he came to set her free from a world grown too hard to bear." (Chesnut, *A Diary from Dixie* (Cambridge, Mass.: Harvard University Press, 1980), 306.

unbending was her grief. You can imagine then how hard it is to bear comfort to her heart. I am glad to say though that she has softened a great deal & seems much more resigned than at first, more so than I had dared to hope for. She will go home as soon as possible. The children here still have a little whooping cough. Don't send Baby down until she writes for her. It is as well that she should be a little longer away until the new children are fairly established. Poor little creatures! May God spare one & help me that I may do that for them which their Father would have done for mine.

Love to Pa and all at home. I have too much to do to write more though it is a relief to me. Goodbye. God bless & keep you all. Kiss Baby.

Charles T. Haskell, Jr., Battery Marshall, Sullivan's Island, S.C., to Lt. W. D. Gaillard,[182] Acting Adjutant, Forces on Sullivan's Island (SCHS)
25 June 1863
Sir:

I have the honor to request permission to visit the city of Charleston tomorrow, returning the same day. I have been sent for by one of the commissioners appointed to determine what salvage is due my company in the case of the Stonewall Jackson.[183]

Alexander C. Haskell, Richmond, Va., to Charles T. Haskell (UNC)
26 June 1863
Dear Pa,

I am still in Richmond and will be here until Monday the 30th. On that morning I will get Mrs. Singleton and the children off to Charlottesville which is on my way to the army. My horses will meet me there. I think it is better that Mrs. Singleton should go to Charlottesville for a while to her Father & Mother who are old & infirm. To one or both this may be her last visit, though death spares neither the young nor the vigorous. For the children the climate of Va is much better, in their present condition, than the sultry summer of Carolina. The youngest boy is quite sick in teething, but change will cure him. The infant is too young & weak to move. If it lives it will remain with Mrs. Minor in Richmond.[184] It could not have a more devoted or attentive guardian.

---

[182] This may have been William Dawson Gaillard (1837-83).

[183] The *Stonewall Jackson* (formerly the *Leopard*) was a blockade runner from Nassau which arrived in Charleston waters on April 11, 1863. The ship was fired on by blockading warships and ran ashore on the Isle of Palms. The captain burned the ship, and all that was left of it was its iron hull.

[184] This was Mrs. Singleton's sister, Lucy Carter Minor.

Baby of course will remain with you until her grandmother comes home for her. I have no fear of your getting tired of her however much trouble she may give. I cannot urge any more writing to me, that is always done, and the army moves are now too uncertain to make one hope for regular intelligence from home, but I beg that Ma & Sophie will write at once, and after to Mrs. Singleton in Charlottesville care of Dr. Charles Carter. She is so awake now to the apprehension of some new sorrow, that where she loves most she is in constant dread, and her anxiety about Baby is unceasing. She is sacrificing a good deal in staying away from home, but I believe it best at present for the little ones here, and have urged, but am desirous that her anxiety should be brightened as much as possible.

Let Sophie tell Maria the nurse of all that has occurred here, and tell her to take good care of Baby as long as she is away from her mistress. As well as I can learn the army is within striking distance of Winchester, but what they are doing there or whither their steps are tending no one seems at all able to say. I shall soon know for myself something and will then impart. I have a long journey and horses in very bad condition but by taking them through Albemarle where they can recruit, I will do very well. Of the boys I hear nothing. Can learn of no fights in which there is any probability of their having been engaged.

Richmond is full of reports this evening about Yankees cutting the Central R.R. at Hanover C.H. I can't say as to the truth of it. An enterprising cavalry could do much damage by circling around Richmond & harassing all the R.R. lines. I have seen Mrs. Dudley several times, Mr. Dudley & Thomas & Miss Anne, today. All send love & kind regards and express themselves as being in a constant attitude of watchfulness concerning John & Joe & the rest of us. Joe is probably with John, though I can learn nothing positive concerning him except that he got his saddle & his blankets before he left Richmond.

I gave Mr. Dudley the check for $200.00.

The last of the sad scenes of this poor suffering house was finished this morning. John Singleton has gone home with all that remains of husband and wife, to rest, as they hoped in death, together.[185] Their souls, let us hope are ere this, happy in their reunion in Heaven.

I told John if he went up for Lessie to bring her back to Abbeville where they could both be with Baby to whom they are so sincerely attached, and could at the same time, without visiting among strangers, be drawn away from the remembrance of recent sad events. They will be alone some

---

[185] Mr. and Mrs. Barnwell were buried at the graveyard of Trinity Episcopal Church in Columbia, S.C.

time before their Mother can get home. Do write or cause to be written such further expression of this suggestion, as times & circumstances make proper.

Love to Ma & Sophie, to Aunt C & Mamie & Emmie, to the boys too when they come home.

William T. Haskell, Bivouac 7 miles from Chambersburg, Pa., to Charlotte M. Cheves, Abbeville, S.C. (GHS)
28 June 1863
My dear Aunt,

It was certainly my intention to thank you by a more recent letter than this for yours of some time ago, but not to delay longer, I send this, dirty paper & all!

You see from my superscription that we are spending the day— Sunday—in profound rest & peace after marching through scenes which up to the last two or three days spoke of war & its violence in a manner truly sad. That was in Va. This side of the Potomac the appearance is different, particularly in Pa. The country & crops rich & abundant. All the crops please the eye beyond anything I have ever seen. The population I think without prejudice I say it mean & poor spirited in [proportion].

Our progress hitherto has been entirely peaceful & regular, the days rainy, but cool & on the whole favourable for the march so the army is in fine condition, few sick & none struggling. We march tomorrow morning I believe to Harrisburg about 50 miles distant, no knowing though till we see. We hear of no force yet to oppose us. Hooker is left in the lurch, may come after a while. Gen. Lee's orders were for strict respect to non-combatants & private property.[186] Horses & provisions are impressed for army use & money or certificates of purchase payable 6 months after peace.

The horses are fine & everything abundant. I have had no opportunity of buying anything yet but some are purchasing much to their satisfaction allowing no discredit to attach in the way of discount to Confederate notes. But I can write but two minutes more so will change the subject. It is so long since you wrote that I do not remember if there are any points requiring special reply. I think you compared me to a lizard, an animal I detest. By the by do tell Em' apropos of an argument held on the subject between Pa & myself that our army butchers can butcher a beef in 4 minutes, I allowed 8. A bet was made on the subject. She took my side wherefore I beg her to claim the wager. I think gloves. I wear four or fives or [threes] so she can [sew] as

---

[186] In Pennsylvania, General Robert E. Lee ordered his men to pay for any supplies that they obtained from civilians, and strictly forbade the "wanton destruction" of private property.

though for me. I would buy some spare gloves & things of that sort but I suppose Sophy, Mamie and Em' have given up all desire for such vanities.

I must stop here. Everything feels so peaceful here today—no signs of war on the face of the country—that I have enjoyed the cabin just for a day intensely. Langdon, Joe & John are well—seen today. This may reach you or not.

5

THE TRIPLE BLOW

6 JULY 1863 – 19 AUGUST 1863

The Haskell family suffers three heavy blows in July 1863. On the second day of that month, during the Battle of Gettysburg in Pennsylvania, William is killed in action while leading his battalion of sharpshooters. His friend and fellow officer Arthur Parker laments his death as "too dear a sacrifice even at the shrine of liberty & independence." In Charleston, a little more than a week later on July 10, Charles is mortally wounded during the first enemy assault on Morris Island. A fellow officer reports his last utterance: "Tell my mother I fell fighting for my country." Word of his death quickly reaches his uncle Captain Langdon Cheves at Battery Wagner on Morris Island, and not long afterward, Cheves is killed by one of the first shells thrown in by the enemy fleet. In Abbeville, messages bearing the heart-breaking news of the death of a brother and two sons are delivered all at the same time to Sophia Haskell and her husband. Over the following days and weeks, Mr. and Mrs. Haskell receive numerous letters of sympathy from friends and family members, among them Louisa S. McCord, Edward McCrady, Jr., and the Rev. John Bachman. The grieving widow of Langdon Cheves writes to her cousin, "I know not how I shall live without him!" On July 25, Aleck writes to his father: "Of Willy I hear daily praise and affec-tionate comment as though he were still among us. I have never seen such a case. The brigade mourns his loss more than of any man who has ever fallen in it, more even it seems than of Genl. Gregg. This for one so humble in rank has rarely been seen. His own battalion of sharp shooters almost wor-ship his memory and will never forget him on the field of battle." In August 1863, the family suffers another loss in the death of Langdon's infant son Charles.

George T. Williams,[1] Winchester, Va., to Charles T. Haskell (SCHS)
6 July 1863
Dear Sir,

I have only time to write, as I do with profound regret & real sympathy, that your excellent son Wm. T. was killed in the fight of the 2 inst. near Gettysburg, & his body was carefully buried the next day on the farm of J. A. Heintzelman 4 miles west of town, with a head-board distinctly marked.[2] Langdon was safe at 10 o'clk on evening of 3 inst. May God comfort & sustain you! He was a noble son, & I loved him well. Truly we sorrow not as those without hope.

Joseph C. Haskell, Headquarters, McIntosh's Battalion, to Sophia C. Haskell (DUL)
8 July 1863
Dear Ma,

For the first time since we have crossed the river I have a chance of writing, and can hardly make up my mind to do it now for I know anything I can write will only make you feel at home more than ever our terrible loss. John told me this morning he had written you informing you of the death of poor dear dear Willie. Oh Ma I know what a shock it has been to you all and how hard it will be to bear but the moment I heard Willie had fallen I thought of what you had said to me just before I left home, that whatever happened to Willie and Aleck you could always think of them without a doubt as to what their fate had been. What a consolation it must be to you, and to us all. It was what everybody thought of first. When John Barnwell told me of it he said we can't grieve for him, all the good and noble are going from us and he was too perfect to stay, falling at such a time and in such a cause, we can mourn for him but cannot think his lot is hard. It is all for the best I know but it seems very hard to part, I loved him so.

We are now on the eve of another battle. It may be delayed a few days or weeks but must come soon, and when it does some of us may meet with the same fate. If it should be so Ma don't grieve for us, for tho we may not be like him I trust we are all ready to meet whatever fate befalls us.

I am glad poor Sophie is at home where you and Pa can comfort and support her in this terrible affliction. It was so sudden to me, so unexpected, I could not believe he was to fall after having escaped so often. We are still

---

[1] George T. Williams, an Episcopal minister from Virginia, was the chaplain of a brigade commanded by General Alfred Moore Scales (1827-92) of North Carolina. Williams had formerly been chaplain of the First South Carolina Infantry Regiment.

[2] "The hospital sites and wagon park of Pender's Division were located at the Andrew Heintzelman Tavern and farm at Seven Stars." Brown, *Retreat from Gettysburg*, 57.

in suspense as to what has become of Aleck. We can hear of him as far as Richmond but no farther. We trust that the distress about poor Mr. Barnwell has delayed him in Richmond and that we will hear of him before long. I have seen both Langdon and John today, both quite well.

I have old Jonas and will be able to take good care of him until he can go home. He is too old to stand the hardships and exposure of the rough life we lead.

The army is now at Hagarstown about ten [miles] from the river, which is perfectly impassable so that we cannot get back if we wanted to.[3] If the Enemy does not attack us before I expect we will move forward as soon as we can get a supply of ammunition, the lack of which compelled us to fall back.

Goodbye dear Ma & Pa, best love to all at home. You will hear from me whenever it is possible.

Arthur Parker,[4] Staunton, Va., to Sophia C. Haskell (SCHS)
9 July 1863
My dear Mrs. Haskell,

I have just learned of the death of your generous, noble & magnanimous son Willie. I have but just learned it thro Mr. Williams formerly the chaplain to our Regiment. I grieve & lament most sincerely the death of so noble a man, a Christian whose purity of character & consistency of conduct marked him as one of the highest ornaments of society. I would lay my heart to those who weep & mourn his untimely fall!

He was to me Mrs. Haskell a most loved & respected friend, indeed I know no man for whom I had a higher regard. He possessed the highest qualities of a man, was gifted with remarkable talents and to my eye had not a <u>single fault</u>. I give way to you & yours, <u>only</u>, in grief for a man whose noblest attributes render him but too dear a sacrifice even at the shrine of liberty & independence.

Mr. Williams wrote you from Winchester. I pray God to comfort & console you in this most heavy bereavement. Mr. Williams has doubtless told you all the sad story.

---

[33] Retreating from Gettysburg, Lee's army moved toward Hagarstown, Maryland, where some fighting occurred on July 6.

[4] Arthur Parker (1834-1913) of Abbeville District served in the First South Carolina Infantry Regiment and was later a major and commissary for Gen. A. P. Hill's corps.

Theodore D. Wagner, Charleston, S.C., to Charlotte M. Cheves, Abbeville, S.C.
(GHS)
10 July 1863
Dear Charlotte,

War in all its horrors is upon us and we have to mourn the loss of many many dear friends, and I have to do the sad, very sad duty of letting you know in this the death of your much respected and gallant husband Mr. Cheves.[5] It was hard for me to write you this letter as I intended to write to Mr. Haskell but to him also is the very sad intelligence taken to him by this mail of the loss of his noble son Capt. Haskell, both men killed at the early part of the fight this morning when [moving] from Macbeth's Battery to Battery Wagner. I write this in the General office where I have been to see if the bodies can be got but I have no hopes of it. They are in the hands of the enemy. The loss is about 60 killed & wounded. A son of W. C. Bee is also killed.[6] Capts. Macbeth, Heyward missing.[7]

God grant you will be supported in this your hour of trial.

You must bear in mind he sacrificed his life in a glorious cause. I write this hurriedly as I want to [send] this mail. I have but a moment to write.[8]

I feel deeply for you dear Charlotte.

Lt. J. Moultrie Horlbeck[9], Battery Wagner, Morris Island, S.C.,
to Charles T. Haskell, Abbeville, S.C. (SCHS)
11 July 1863
Dear Sir,

I take the liberty of addressing you in relation to your brave & gallant son the late Capt. Charles Haskell. He received orders to report on Monday morning with myself & company to Col. Yates on Morris Island, the duty to storm the battery on Folly Island. After making two unsuccessful attempts he was ordered on Friday morning to repel with his company the advances of the Yankees to Morris Island. After fighting as bravely as man ever fought

---

[5] Charlotte Lorain McCord Cheves was the wife of Captain Langdon Cheves.

[6] This was Lt. John Stock Bee (1841-63) of Co. I, First Regiment, South Carolina Artillery Regulars. He was mortally wounded on July 10, 1863, and was taken to Union-held Hilton Head Island, where he died on July 18.

[7] James Ravenel Macbeth (1839-93), a captain in the First Regiment, South Carolina Artillery Regulars, was captured on Morris Island. Jacob Guerard Heyward (1844-88), a lieutenant (not a captain) in the same unit was also captured.

[8] The envelope of this letter, addressed to Mrs. L. Cheves, Abbeville, S.C., bears the dateline: "Head Quarters, 1st Military District, Department of South Carolina, Georgia and Florida, OFFICIAL BUSINESS."

[9] This was James Moultrie Horlbeck (1841-67).

in the advance the whole time he fell pierced by nine bullets. His last words were "Tell my mother I fell fighting for my country."

I shall endeavour if possible to recover the body and have already spoken to Col. Graham[10] commanding about a flag of truce but have been unable to start on account of the terrific fire from the monitors.

William E. Haskell, Charleston, S.C., to Charles T. Haskell and Sophia C. Haskell (SCHS)

11 July 1863

My dear Brother & Sister,

You have had some heavy trials already in this war and God has mercifully sustained you under them. He now again calls upon you to look unto him and say "Thy will be done" for He is able to support you under even the heaviest affliction.

Upon arriving in Town this morning from Columbia I was met by the report that Charles was among the mortally wounded and immediately afterwards rec'd such reliable information that I could not deny any longer, that he was killed by the enemy yesterday morning in the defence of the 1st Battery on Morris Island, gallantly directing his men, & in the most glorious position; that of defending his Country in the performance of his whole duty. He was shot thro the head & course knew not what hurt him.

He was so highly thought of that you both have the sympathy of the whole command. His body is still with the enemy as they have the extreme end of Morris Island. I have been to the Telegraph Office to let you know early this morning, but as it does not open until after 8 o'clock it was too late to go by the cars from Columbia today. I therefore write. I have been to Gen. Beauregard & have made every arrangement to go down, as soon as the enemy will receive a flag of truce & get his body & have it put into my vault until I know your wishes. I will have the service as soon as I can get it. I hope to do so today but can't say positively as they are still firing. They attacked Battery Wagner this morning by assault but were repulsed with 98 killed in field 130 prisoners to us & 1 field officer shot from his horse. We don't know what to expect. The enemy are still firing. I shall attend the funeral services of Capt. Langdon Cheves this morning at 11 o'clock. He was killed in Battery Wagner, is the reason his body was obtained. All of this I have heard in the few hours since my arrival. I am making arrangements to send all my family & child out of town as soon as possible. God comfort & support you and give you strength according your necessities.

---

[10] This was Robert Fladger Graham (1833-74), colonel of the Twenty-first South Carolina Infantry Regiment.

Alexander C. Haskell, Winchester, Va., to Mr. and Mrs. Charles T. Haskell, Abbeville, S.C. (UNC)
13 July 1863
My dear Father and Mother,

May God in his mercy visit you with comfort in your [great trials]. Arrived at Winchester a few hours since. I was met upon the [street] with the news so full of sadness for us and for his Country, that our noble Willy had fallen, where he prayed that his fall might be, if so soon he was taken from his Country and his friends. He fell in the front of battle at the head of his chosen command. His body must rest for a time beneath the field where he won immortality. His soul has ere this reaped its reward in Heaven. Oh God have mercy upon those he has left and answer the last prayer of his heart, that we might all meet him in Heaven. I feel and I know that you must feel he is happy, that God has taken him in the ripeness of his holiness, that he has gathered him among the chosen ones for whom this earth is not a worthy dwelling, but with this comes a feeling of overwhelming grief that we are deprived of one so dear, so full of promise, so full of excellence in all the relations of life. For this grief I can bring no comfort. I do not feel it yet. Little did I think that death could again so crush my heart. I ought not to write now but I know not when I can at another time and indeed I must seek some sympathy from those to whom there is such need of support. Since we have been away from home and so often meeting death together, and only one another to lean upon, the bonds of love between us brothers have become so close knit with feelings so tender, that now when broken from my nearest & most intimate, my heart is sadly torn. But this grief is but little for me to bear in comparison with what I feel when I remember that he was as dear to all my brothers and sister as he was to me, to many friends too he was dear, and how your hearts were wrapt up in him. Tis your sorrow & the sorrow of all these that fill me with anguish. I do pray to God to comfort you & be with you and support you through this and all your other trials. May God have mercy! But we know that he is merciful. His mercy, his bounty and all his glorious gifts are heaped upon our loved one. He was my little one's godfather and guardian. I looked to him to be a father to her if I was taken. Teach her, if I cannot, to love his name. Tell Sophie for me, to remember her faith and the source of all comfort. Poor child, she [needs] it all. And those poor boys at home, and Mamie & Emma for they feel like sisters, I can only say the same to them.

I can't hear positively of the other boys, but they are reported as well & safe. I hope to be with them tomorrow night. This journey of mine marked by death and sorrow seems interminable. I shall try to leave this place in the morning if I can buy a horse tonight. My mare is broken down and can't move. I shall leave her. The army is said to be near Williamsport.

Love to all and kiss my Baby for me. She may yet be a comfort to you. God bless and comfort you all. Goodbye.

Alexander C. Haskell, Winchester, Va., to Mr. and Mrs. Charles T. Haskell, Abbeville, S.C. (UNC)
15 July 1863
My dear Father and Mother,

Again this evening sad tidings have reached me, too terrible to believe, that Uncle Langdon & Charley have been killed in the attack on Morris Island. If this be true may God have mercy on those who mourn. Poor Aunt Charlotte and those dear girls & poor little Lang, how my heart bleeds for them! Amid our own bitter griefs I cannot but forget all in looking upon their utter desolation, but an earnest longing to bring them that consolation which we must seek from God. Lang, John & Joe are still spared to you. I have been quite sick here for two days but am up and much better this evening. I will try to reach my command tomorrow. Once more do I pray for you all and beseech the mercy of God.

Louisa S. McCord, Columbia, S.C., to Sophia C. Haskell (SCHS)
16 July 1863
My Dear Sister,

Until your letter (received last evening) I had heard nothing of our latest sorrow. <u>Our</u> sorrow I say for I claim to halve it with you. Willy & Aleck, since my great agony, have seemed half to belong to me. They could not fill the place of my own lost darling,[11] but they were so kind & so linked with him in my thoughts, that I took them into my heart as something left of him. Do not think me selfish that I thus put my sorrows side by side with yours for the loss of one of these. I rather think to give you such sad comfort as we find in the recollection of what was loveable in our lost ones; & Willy was not only brave, but very kind, & gentle, & good. It is a great comfort to think (as I said of Charley) that nothing can be more painless, than a prompt death on the battle field. Not death, indeed, should it be called; for death is the struggle, the doubt, the anguish of parting, while the weakened mind dreads the transit which in its strength it could face calmly. Here, in its full strength, it finds an easy passage from <u>life to life</u>. Death has no time to star-

---

[11] Mrs. McCord's son, Captain Langdon Cheves McCord.

tle even with the shadow of its terrors. To us alone (lingerers by the wayside) is left the sorrow & the loss.

Falling as he has done, so far away from us, there will perhaps no relic of dear Willy come home to you, & you will, I think, like to know that I have in my possession the sword which he carried through 12 battles. It was brought to me by one Col. McCrady (sent by Willy) only a few weeks since, for me to take care of.[12] I wrote him word that nobody should touch it till he came for it himself. But to you & his Father it now of right, belongs. Should it chance that a watch be sent to you, do not think it a mistake. I lent him the last one used by Cheves, begging him to wear it in the fight and bring it home to me. I would come & see you but would do you harm. I need to be alone a great deal, and cannot always command myself as I should. With any change I would likely be ill & a burden to you. My girls seem to feel as if their brother was lost a second time. Poor children, these shocks are very trying to them. This fearful war brings to our daughters a sadder fate than to their slaughtered brothers.

Once more dear Sister you know my sympathies are with you all. Would to God, I had anything else to give.

Charlotte M. Cheves to Theodore D. Wagner (SCHS)
16 July 1863

Oh, my dear Cousin, you who know & valued my dear husband can in some measure imagine my anguish at his loss! We are powerless to express how great & how <u>dreadful</u> it is to me & my children! To them he was <u>everything</u>—a tender father & loving friend & companion taking the place of brother, parent & friend! And as for me, I know not how I shall live without him! I experienced nothing but the most devoted & indulgent affection & kindness. Oh, my dear Theodore, I felt drawn towards you when I saw that you seemed by instinct almost, to know how good & pure he was! So much intelligence & knowledge, united with so much modesty & humility—so much patience & gentleness, combined with so tender & kind a heart, & such devotion to truth & virtue, I never knew united in any other man! He made no profession of religion, but he felt always in every act of his life, that he would be accountable hereafter to his God & maker, & he was only fearful of not acting with perfect justice & disinterestedness to others. He had no fear for himself in anything, but labored always for the happiness & benefit of others. He counted himself as nothing. Oh, my dear Cousin, he

---

[12] Lt. Colonel Edward McCrady (1833-1903) was an officer in the First South Carolina Infantry Regiment.

was too good & too pure for this world! Men could not know or value him enough! His whole life was a sacrifice.

For the last two years, he had no other earthly thought, but how he could labor for his country & state! He would let no private wish or tie draw his mind from the work before him. Poor fellow, I believe he would gladly have died could he have believed himself the instrument by which Charleston should be saved! Oh I cannot weep for him, he must have had his reward, but I mourn, & I cannot mourn too much for my children's loss & for their anguish! This is a grief will grow & increase with years & God only can soothe & comfort me!

My dear Cousin in the midst of your affliction, we are not insensible to your kindness. It is a great gratification to know all we can of the last days & hours of our dear one. I hope I may have the privilege yet of seeing someone who was with him during these last days, but I hope & beg that you will not again so unnecessarily expose yourself as by going to that Island for which I fear he has died in vain!

I have only to ask you to request Mr. Ravenel[13] to send up his servant at once, & any little personal effect that he had about him he would value. I hear that the surgeon of Fort Wagner has his watch & spectacles. These my children would love to keep. His horse & other personal effects I suppose must be lost, & poor fellow, he had but little. All his letters & papers I would feel relieved to have, fearing they might fall into the hands of the enemy, or idle people about the Fort. Lieut. Gillam was very kind to think of saving the lock of hair.

Oh my dear Cousin, I would give, [sic] oh I would grieve less if I had remained longer with my dearest Langdon when I was in Charleston, but alas, so shortsighted and blind are we that I never felt less anxiety about him, & for the first time in my life, I parted with him without any misgiving or pain, feeling that we would meet again soon! My poor Emma is filled with anguish & regret at not having been with him! Poor child, when we heard he was no more, we were preparing, that is, she was preparing to go to Charleston on a visit to him, & talked & thought of nothing else for weeks past! I lived only in the thought that we were to see him again soon! For the first time since the war began I was free from uneasiness about him! Oh blind, blind that we are.

My last letter to him was written on a distressing subject & I fear worried & depressed him. This is another pang to me, but I did only what I

---

[13] This may have been Daniel Ravenel (1789-1873), an attorney, banker and author of Charleston. He was the president of the Planters' and Mechanics' Bank of Charleston, where William E. Haskell was a cashier.

thought it was my duty to do. But I had always been in the habit of putting all my cares on him & with my usual selfishness, I continued to do so & I hoped too it might bring him up to us! When he was with us we had no troubles or cares. He was ever ready to lighten them for me, & his whole object in life was to support & assist me, & to relieve me of all trouble.

I have many consolations which I trust I shall feel in time, but for the present I try to [drown] all selfish repining in the belief that my dear husband has gone to his Father in heaven, who lent him to us for a while, as an example of what a good & pure man should be! And in the midst of our overwhelming grief, we cannot be indifferent to the sufferings of others, & to the peril & danger in which Charleston stands! I pray for her safety & for you all, my dear Cousin! Do take care of yourself for the sake of who belong to you & who live through you! And for all who love & care for you! In this dreadful war too many good men have already been needlessly sacrificed!

My poor sister, Mrs. Haskell, has lost another son in Virginia, another at Gettysburg, & bears it with the calmness & fortitude of a pure Christian.[14] The family are sorely afflicted & Mrs. Haskell, who is very much like Langdon, tries to do good to all & to give others the comfort she feels herself in believing a merciful God wills all for our good! My children are a great comfort & help to me & do all they can for me, & Mamie says I am sure Mamma Cousin Theodore will help us at this time with his advice & assistance! So for our sakes do keep out of danger when it is unnecessary & believe me to be always most grateful for your kind thought of us at this dark hour of our anguish!

Our remembrance & regard to Ella.[15]

Mary Elliott Seabrook[16], Flat Rock, N.C., to Sophie Haskell (SCHS)
17 July [1863]
My dearest Sophie,

I have been wishing ever since I saw the death of your brother Charlie in the paper to write to you, & the fearful news we heard today makes me do so without further delay. We were excessively shocked & distressed this morning to hear from a friend that Capt. Haskell had been killed at Gettysburg. Though not personally acquainted with him, Mama & I felt as if we had lost a friend. Indeed we all felt so, for from his intimacy with Pinckney

---

[14] Mrs. Cheves may have been referring to the death of Charles T. Haskell, Jr., mistakenly putting him in Virginia, or she may have been misinformed that Aleck Haskell had been killed, not just wounded.

[15] Theodore D. Wagner's wife was Sarah Ella Warley Wagner (1833-73).

[16] Mary Elliott Seabrook (1843-1918) was the daughter of Archibald Hamilton Seabrook (1816-94) and Phoebe Caroline Pinckney Seabrook.

we had heard so much of him that we felt as if we knew him well.[17] The tears that were shed here today were not only of sympathy, but of real grief. It brings our sorrow back so strongly to our minds, & we can well sympathize with you in your trouble. But how much we have to comfort us, in the thought that our soldiers were prepared to meet their God. That they are now happy, & reaping the reward of all their trials on earth. I know how hard it is at first, to think it is all for the best— God has done it, not only for their but our good—but afterwards it becomes easier, & the time will come, I hope, when we can thank God for afflicting us. How well I can enter into your feelings. Wishing that I could have seen him once more, if only for a few minutes, before death came—& oh! the bitter, bitter grief at the arrival of letters, telling us all, & yet not all, for to us who wish to know every little thing, it seems hard that the writers would not mention more facts. But we were so thankful to get the letters, & amidst our grief is the happy thought, how much he was loved, how much he was appreciated.

Oh! Sophie, I wish you had a friend to write you as beautiful a letter as Capt. Haskell wrote us.[18] But that is impossible. We thanked him so much for that letter, & for the notice he put in the paper. They were such comforts to us. We have heard through our friends what an excellent Christian soldier he was. At one time Pinckney & Charlie[19] seldom passed a day without

---

[17] A Haskell relative in Flat Rock, Harriott Middleton, wrote in a letter of May 1863: "Pinckney was twice offered promotion for gallantry on the field of battle, but declined it preferring to remain with Willie Haskell." A subsequent letter of hers described Seabrook's funeral in Flat Rock, and in another, she wrote of how his body was removed from its grave on the battlefield in Virginia to be transported to North Carolina. "The body had been wrapped in a piece of india rubber cloth and they found it nine days after burial, as if he had just fallen asleep. No change had taken place. He lay in an attitude of perfect repose, dressed in his uniform with his sash around his waist. It was life like." Cuthbert, *Flat Rock of the Old Time*, 36-39.

[18] Part of a letter of condolence that William T. Haskell wrote to the Pinckneys was included in a biographical sketch of Cotesworth Pinckney Seabrook published in *The University Memorial*: "Of his nobleness and piety I need not tell you. Though so long absent, his heart, I know, was ever open to his parents in all things; and I have never known anything of him, but his praises and merits, that he might not tell you. Always mindful of his religious duties, he was of late especially devout, constantly reading his Bible, and often singing hymns with the men, whose affectionate regard for him caused them to take every occasion to be with him and about him. His cheerful, bright humor never flagged, even on the battle-field, where his smile seemed more radiant than ever, while his voice and command gave life and courage to those about him." Johnson, *The University Memorial*, 350-60.

[19] "Pinckney" was Mary Elliott Seabrook's brother Cotesworth Pinckney Seabrook, an officer in William T. Haskell's company. Charlie was likely her first cousin Charles Cotesworth Pinckney (1839-1909), who served in the Marion Artillery.

mentioning "Alick" and "Willie Haskell" & hearing so much of them, & from their friendship with our boys, we always felt an interest in them. It seems today as if almost our last tie with Hamilton's Regiment was broken.[20]

Johnny Bee, lately killed in the battle at Charleston, was one of Pinckney's friends. Every new death I hear of makes me think fearfully "who next?" Papa has now only one near relation in Virginia, a boy of eighteen, & I [dread] to look at the papers when I hear his regiment has been engaged. His sister is a dear friend of mine. She has lost her lover in this war. She loved Pinckney as a brother, & his death was a dreadful blow. In writing to me she says "One by one we are passing away. Seabrook is the only one left now. May we all meet in Heaven." And surely it is a comfort when we think of this, that the day will come when we will all be together. No more parting, no more trials, anxious watchings, tears, all gone! & we will be happy forever! How I long for that day! & I trust my dear Sophie, you do too. Yours has been no common trial. I have never heard of any one losing an uncle & two brothers in so short a time. But if you look above to Him who ruleth all things, He will comfort & give you strength to bear even this.

Carrie Pinckney sends her love to you & says I must tell you how much she admired Capt. Haskell. She knew him well. Grandmamma, Mamie & Mama send love & sympathy to you & your mother, & say how much they are feeling with her.[21] Mama will write to Mrs. Haskell. Annie sends her love to you. We all feel deeply for you & can do little to comfort you but to commend you to the God of mercies who will give you strength in your trial. Please write me when you can say what you have heard.

Joseph C. Haskell, Headquarters, McIntosh's Battalion,
to Charles T. Haskell (DUL)
18 July 1863
Dear Pa,

We have at last learnt the worst about poor dear Charlie & Uncle Langdon. It has been harder to bear from being so unexpected, so little anticipated. We had no right to do so but we had got to looking on Charleston as a place of comparative safety. This teaches us there is safety nowhere and how necessary it is to be prepared to die at any moment.

We have escaped for a long time but it comes very heavy now and there is no prospect of any end now. It seems that we will all have to go sooner or

---

[20] This likely refers to Daniel Heyward Hamilton, who assumed the colonelcy of the First Regiment in Gregg's Brigade after Gregg was promoted to the rank of general.

[21] Mary's grandmother was Phoebe Caroline Elliott Pinckney (1792-1864). "Mamie" was likely her sister Margaret Hamilton Seabrook (1849-1925), who was later Mrs. Henry Middleton Rutledge.

later and it don't make much difference when. I don't care now how soon we meet them again.

We have so much to occupy us here that we don't have time to think of our own grief, but I know how hard it is at home, how hard it is for poor Aunt Charlotte & the girls. We can all feel for one another now.

Aleck was at Winchester yesterday and I expect is here now. Langdon and John both quite well. The Enemy in force on this side of the river but no indication of a fight yet. Goodbye and dearest love to Ma, Aunt Charlotte, Cousin Follie, Sophie, Mamie and Emma.

Alexander C. Haskell, Winchester, Va., to Sophia C. Haskell (UNC)
18 July 1863
My dearest Mother,

I write again from Winchester, not having been able to ride to camp yet, but will go tomorrow if I continue well. Langdon and John came in to see me today, both poor fellows much grieved but finding the greatest consolation in the thought that our dear lost ones are joined in Heaven. Langdon's grief for Willy—the other had come too recently for thought or realization—could only be equaled by his happiness in contemplating the nobleness and beauty of his character, his perfect state of preparation for death, and the perfect harmony in which for so much time we all had lived with him. Their deepest grief, and it must cost us all the bitterest anguish, is in thinking of the suffering of our dear ones at home. You and Pa and the children and poor Aunt Charlotte and the girls are constantly in our hearts, and we do pray for you all that the help and comfort which we are not present to give may be given you from God. I could not help thinking today as I looked on my own dear one's picture how much happier are they who die in the Lord and how wrong it is for us to wish them back again. I would not now if I could recall her angel spirit to undergo these long years of pain and suffering that some of us must pass through before we are fit to appear before our Saviour & our Judge. But I feel how sad it is to be amongst those who mourn and I feel that it is hard to feel satisfied with the mere assurances of the perfect bliss of our loved ones. It is for ourselves we mourn, not for them. Do not think of your sons as cut down prematurely in the bloom of youth. They have been gathered to their Heavenly Father in the fullness of their season, in the ripeness of their powers, and full maturity of their holiness. Can we think of that life as but begun or imperfect which has under God worked out its salvation and won eternal happiness in Heaven? And besides you know not how many souls these dear ones have drawn to God and in this done greater deeds than had they grown gray among the princes of the earth. How many more may be won too by the glorious departure of these from earth, these whom Jesus calls with open arms and who rise before the eyes of all men professing His name and their glorious faith. I shall never forget the impression which more than any other brought me to seek the comfort and protection of the Church. Touched I often had been and deeply by the views of religion, but I had never felt all that is offered and from how much I excluded myself by declining to confess God before men until one Sunday of Confirmation I went with dear Charley to St. Phillips [*sic*] Church.[22] When the solemn services commenced, Charley rose and knelt before the altar. The Bishop placed his hands upon his head with the blessing and absolution of our Lord and Saviour and I felt in my heart that the Spirit of God had descended & yet it had not rested on my soul. Never again did I feel safe until the same solemn service had received me into the sanctuary. Much of my hope and happiness I owe to his pious example and the subsequent conversations of my dear brother. I can write no more tonight, but will pray for you and all my dear ones at home. I will see John & Joe soon and talk to them both.

Do give my dearest deepest love to Pa and Sophie, Aunt Charlotte and the girls. Love to poor little Baby. She does not know that these short weeks have robbed her of five of her dearest relations. Thank God she is happy. Goodbye. Once more God help & bless you all.

Sally H. Rutledge[23]*, Flat Rock, N.C., to Sophie Haskell* (SCHS)
18 July 1863
My dear Sophy,

I hope you will not think me intrusive when I tell you that I have thought so much of your saddened household that I cannot help expressing to you some of the sympathy I feel, for I mourn with heartfelt tears for the dear ones for whom you grieve. Your brother Charles I knew but slightly but heard much of him from others. Everyone recognized the manly qualities, the sterling worth of his character, and his friends all spoke in such high praise of his goodness and kindness of heart that I feel how much you have lost in him. Your brother William I was proud to call my friend. Young as he was when I first knew him, I saw at once in him one of those rare natures, uniting a clear commanding intellect, high toned character & every manly virtue sanctified by Christian grace, & felt that wherever lay his path in life, distinction and success must be his. His influence was even then so

---

[22] A St. Philip's Episcopal Church register records the confirmation of "Charles Haskell" on October 28, 1855, by BishopThomas Frederick Davis (1804-71) in Charleston.

[23] Sarah Henrietta Rutledge (1832-1906) was the daughter of Frederick Rutledge and Henrietta Middleton Rutledge. She was later Mrs. Charles Cotesworth Pinckney.

great that I remember hearing a friend say "it was not only the highest pleasure, it was a blessing to know him." And many will echo the feeling. I rejoiced when we met last winter to see how all the energies of his noble nature were brought out in his devotion to the Cause. To see that the high purpose of his soul was to him an inward light that brightened the path of hardship and danger that he took, & that he was happy with the best kind of happiness.

Words fail to express the sadness that fills our hearts when such men whose lives are so valuable, so useful in the present, so brilliant with hope & promise for the future, to whom we looked as lights and guides for our Country in the years to come, are thus early cut off, leaving in place of their influence and example, the sense of irreparable loss. But while they willingly laid down their lives for their Country, God has called them to "that better country even an heavenly," the prize for which all pure hearts are struggling in this darkened world.[24] But the unutterable grief that their loss must be to your Mother, to you all, is what I dare not dwell on. Still my dear Sophy God has granted to you all the consolation that springs from the remembrance of such noble unselfish lives crowned by heroic death, & what this this world has to give of glory or happiness that can compare with what they have won? May God comfort you all as He only can.

Pray give my love to your Aunt and cousins and assure them of the warm sympathy I feel for their sorrow. I have written more at length than I intended my dear Sophy, and yet feel that all that I have said is miserably inadequate. Do not think of answering my letter. I assure you I do not expect it for I know it is a painful effort, but pray accept this assurance of my sympathy.

Lt. Col. Edward McCrady, Jr.[25], Sand Hills, Clarendon District, S.C.,
to Charles T. Haskell (SCHS)
20 July 1863
My dear Sir,

It has been with the greatest pain that I have learned the deaths of your two sons, Captain Charles T. and William Haskell and of your relative,

---

[24] Hebrews 11:16.

[25] Severely wounded at the Second Battle of Manassas, Edward McCrady was disabled for active duty several times during the war. He was a prominent Charleston attorney, historian, and state legislator, and was one of the most distinguished men of his generation in South Carolina. He served as president of the South Carolina Historical Society, where his extensive papers are located. McCrady wrote William T. Haskell's obituary for the Charleston *Mercury,* which stated in part, "Whatever ties there were to life he was ready to sacrifice them to his country."

Capt. Cheves. In the depth of your grief you must no doubt shrink from anything like intrusion upon the sacredness of your sorrow. But as your son William was my Brother officer and most intimate friend I cannot but hope however that the expression of a sympathy so deep as mine, the testimony to his worth from one who had such opportunities to learn and occasion to value his character may be allowed even at this time, and possibly afford some consolation even in the bitterness of your trouble.

Where so many fathers have cause to be proud of their sons they have given to their country, none have more and few such cause as yourself. Six such sons, any one of whom would be enough for the gratification of an honest pride in any father, it has been the lot of but few, if any, to offer to the maintenance of our cause. Were I otherwise inclined, the occasion forbids anything but the language of truth and soberness, but in such language I can truly say that one might well envy the individual reputation of any of your sons. Each one has made his name an honor to his brothers; how much more so to the father who reared such sons.

With your son Charles who fell so gallantly on Morris Island I was not so well acquainted, but this I have learned of him in common with the public that he has nobly maintained with his life a reputation that it is no little credit to him to say that he earned while leading a life which would have been to most one of inactivity.

But with William I esteem it one of the greatest privileges of life to have been for the last two years upon the most intimate terms. We met upon the organization of our Regiment in Richmond in the summer of '61. Similar tastes and feelings soon drew us together and in a short time I learned to appreciate his remarkable character, a character the foundation of which was a sincere piety. An esteem for him which soon sprung up strengthened and ripened into a regard such as few men could possibly inspire. Duty was truly the rule of his life and however irksome in itself he carried into its performance a cheerfulness which took away from it whatever was hard or unpleasant. He governed others with ease because he governed himself by the same rules. As an officer he had no requirement for his men he did not apply to himself. Their hardships he shared, he allowed himself no indulgence that they too could not enjoy. He could encourage others to endure and repress murmuring because whatever discomforts were to be borne he too shared them. So on the march whatever troops straggled his men kept their ranks because if a stream was to be crossed he sought for no good place himself but plunged into the depth of it; if the road was hot and dusty he sought not the shade for himself while he required others to keep their places. So too I have seen him night after night lay down in the snow with but a single blanket which he carried himself for his covering. In battle he only asked his men to follow him. As duty was the rule of his life so unselfishness was its chief characteristic. Seldom have I ever met one who so completely buried the idea of self. But conspicuous as this was at any time, it was pre-eminently so upon the battlefield. There all thoughts of himself seemed to vanish and the one idea, how to obtain the victory to absorb all thought and energy. His peace made with his God he gave himself to the work of his country, and in doing so none brought to her service a clearer head, or quicker perception or a sounder judgment. Comfort and safety seemed in his opinion to have been for others, hardships and dangers for himself. It was one of his most striking traits that hard as was his rule for himself, he had no such measure for others. His character combined all the elements of greatness, and I often thought how illustrious a man he might have been had circumstances placed him in more conspicuous positions. He was my junior officer but I believe I speak truly when I say I would willingly have changed our relative positions and have served under him. I am sure I looked for approval from none of my superior officers with more anxiety than for his. But the Lord no doubt saw where best for him to do his work and sure am I that his labor has not been in vain. We used to call him the "old Roman" but his character was far more sublime for it was that of a Christian. The Lord has seen fit to take away your son, my most beloved friend. This loss seems to us unbearable but God no doubt in his death works his own purposes. We can only bow submissively to his will. Knowing your son as I have done and feeling his loss as a friend I can truly appreciate yours, for to me he was a friend but to you a son.

In May last thinking I had sufficiently recovered from injuries which I had received in the winter, I went on to the Army intending to resume my duties, but found myself so unfit for the service that I was compelled to return. On leaving camp your son gave me his sword asking me to bring it on to Columbia and to leave it with Mrs. McCord from whom he said you would get it, saying at the time he might fall in the next battle and that if he did so it would be improbable that anything about him would be saved for his friends and it would therefore be a great comfort he thought to you in such an event to have the sword which had been through so much with him. I could not help feeling at the time that there was something almost prophetic in this and since the news of the battle have constantly felt the greatest anxiety to hear of him. I left the sword at Mrs. McCord's and no doubt you have received it before this time. I feel a great gratification in having furnished him an opportunity of sending it to you. He expressed at the time a wish to have the name of the battles through which he had worn it engraved on its hilt.

Thinking it may afford you some gratification I give you an extract from my official report of the Battle of Manassas, the 29th August last, on which occasion I commanded the Regiment, in which I allude to his conspicuous conduct on that day.

"It was now about four o'clock and though wearied we knew the struggle was yet to be renewed. They (the enemy) soon came, now in still greater force, but our little band though greatly reduced yet met them with as much determination as ever. Our men fell fast around us. The 13th after exhibiting the greatest endurance and courage during the day at last gave way and retired from the front and upon the 1st was hurled the full force of the enemy. They pressed on crossed the (R.R.) cut and slowly compelled us step by step to yield the long coveted position. Here again our men fought the enemy at a few yards. Genl Branch coming up at this time with a Regiment took part in the contest. But unused to so terrible a fire his men gave way for a while. This was a most critical moment and I claim for Captain Haskell Lieut Munro[26] and Seabrook much of the credit of having saved the day. Seeing the N.C. Regiment brake [sic] they with Genl Branch rallied and led it or a portion of it back ... The enemy had by this time driven us back some three hundred yards from the R.R. cut and were possessors of the long coveted field. But still a portion of our Regiment with its colors and the N.C. Reg't rallied by Genl Branch and Capt Haskell contended with them inch by inch for it. At this time when all seemed lost Genl Field[27] with a portion of his Brigade came up and charging the enemy they again broke and fled into the field."

This was the only opportunity of I had of placing upon record officially my appreciation of his conduct but in no other battle did he deserve a less tribute to his gallantry and efficiency. Many officers have gained reputations and rapid promotions for conduct not more meritorious and conspicuous than his at Cold Harbor and Chancellorsville. Indeed no opportunities offered that he did not greatly distinguish himself for the most consummate bravery, and efficient services.

I have thus my dear Sir endeavoured to pay a fitting tribute to the memory of my loved friend, your gallant son. I trust you will consider it no intrusion into the sacredness of your grief and hope that it may be some solace to you to know the high regard and esteem in which he was held by all his brothers officers and soldiers, a weak expression of which this only is.

---

[26] This was John Munro, a second lieutenant in Company L of the First South Carolina Infantry Regiment. He was killed at the Second Battle of Manassas (Bull Run).

[27] General Charles William Field (1828-92).

My father begs me to add to mine his deepest sympathy for you in your great trouble.[28] The Lord who only can assuage such grief as yours may & will I trust give his mother and yourself strength to bear it.

Allard H. Belin[29], *Darlington, S.C., to Charles T. Haskell* (SCHS)
20 July 1863
My dear Haskell,

Even at the risk of being considered an intrusion upon your griefs, I cannot resist the impulse to assure of the warm sympathy of Christian friends in the severe bereavement with which our Master has seen fit to visit you.

Hitherto he has drawn you to him by the blessings of prosperity and an unusual exemption from all temporal ills, and now when he has seen fit to recall some of the blessings lent, not given, I have prayed and do pray, that, in accordance with his own gracious promise "As thy day, so shall thy strength be," he would give you power to say "The Lord gave and the Lord hath taken away, blessed be the name of the Lord."[30]

If I could be with you now I know that it would be a relief to your sorrow to descant upon the merits of those who are gone. Write as you would speak, it will be a relief to your own full heart and will meet with sympathy from one who can understand what your trial is, although Providence has hitherto spared me all of my own children who have passed infancy. Yet, it is but a few years since I lost a Nephew who was to me like my own son.[31] His moral and intellectual endowments were both of a high order, and improved by diligence, application and Foreign travel. Just as he seemed about attaining distinction in the profession of Medicine to which he had devoted himself his career was cut short by Pulmonary Disease. I have passed through the deep waters and know that there is but <u>one</u> who has power to aid in such trials and most heartily do I rejoice that you know upon whom to call while being purified by the fire, and that God in his abundant mercy may sanctify these sore trials by the spiritual improvement of yourself and those who are left to you is the sincere and earnest prayer of your friend and Brother in Christ.

[P.S.] I hope that my friend Alex has entirely recovered from his wound.

---

[28] McCrady's father was Edward McCrady, Sr. (1802-92), a Charleston attorney, theologian, and state legislator.

[29] Allard Henry Belin (1803-71) of Charleston and Georgetown District, S.C.

[30] Deuteronomy 33:25, and Job 1:21.

[31] The nephew was Dr. Eben Belin Flagg (1822-56), the son of Allard H. Belin's sister Margaret Elizabeth Belin Flagg (1801-85).

Thomas Dudley, Jr.[32], Richmond, Va., to Sophia C. Haskell (SCHS)
20 July 1863
My dear Mrs. Haskell,

You will not I am sure have attributed my silence to lack of sympathy with you in your great affliction, for you must have remembered that in this case your affliction was mine also. You have lost your sons, and I my more than brother. I had delighted myself with the hope that he would be spared to us, and every battle through which he had passed had strengthened it. But God's ways are not as our ways and we must patiently submit to his decrees. I know, or rather I think I can form an idea of the intensity of your distress, and I would God that I could say aught that might alleviate it. God alone can do that. I pray most earnestly that he may.

The little band who lived so closely and intimately at the University and who loved each other so very dearly, are dropping off one by one. Oh may we who still survive have grace given us to follow the bright example of him who has gone before.

The Daguerreotype shall be sent to you care of Maj. Rhett at Columbia by the first opportunity which I consider perfectly safe. I would not willingly trust it to the uncertain chances of the express or mail.

My wife who loved Willy before she saw him for my sake, and ever since for his own, joins me in love to you and all his friends. I cannot tell you what I feel, my dear friend. You know how we loved each other.

Octavius T. Porcher,[33] Willington, S.C., to Sophie Haskell (SCHS)
20 July 1863
Dear Miss Haskell,

I know you will be surprised at receiving a letter from one whom you scarcely know and only knows you almost entirely through others and I know full well the delicacy of the task I am undertaking, and would be [*paper torn*] did I not [know] that the human heart ever appreciates sympathy, if only if it be genuine and [kind], and I have [felt] so much for your household under its heavy afflictions, that I would do myself injustice did I not attempt to express it to one of you. It is strange how the smallest circumstances connect us with others, and we feel drawn towards people whom we never see, and almost every day for weeks past I have thought of you, as I

---

[32] Thomas Underwood Dudley (1837-1904) was a student at the University of Virginia with William T. Haskell. After the war he was ordained as an Episcopal priest, and in 1884 became the Episcopal Bishop of Kentucky.

[33] Octavius Theodore Porcher was ordained as an Episcopal priest after the war. His nephew the Rev. William Porcher DuBose preached the sermon at his ordination in Abbeville on May 15, 1870.

mounted "Miss Slouch" and started upon my afternoon ride! Your Father sent me word that he wanted her broken for you to ride and this has been as it were, a link between us and I found myself constantly musing and wondering to myself if you would ever appreciate her as I did, if her beauty, her spirit, her pure and [unmixed] ancestry, would ever give you pleasure as it did me.[34] Whether they would ever suggest [*paper torn*] young heart the great and good Being who had filled this world with so many things to contribute to our pleasure, and I felt [then] like writing to you, but it seemed almost foolish to think of it then, but now that affliction has fallen upon you and my heart has been so full of your Father's and Mother's loss, I have thought that perhaps God (who is a God of infinite condescension and love) knowing the future as well as the past, and having this trouble in store for you, may have ordered these seemingly triflingly and disconnected thoughts, that I might be induced to write to you, and might become the instrument in His mighty hands of comfort and consolation to you and yours. Men keep God at a distance and imagine that He is far off in Heaven and cares not for their trifling sorrows—it is monstrous!!! Oh! that I could convince you and every sorrowing heart of the length and depth and breadth and height of His love!! What right have I [to know] your sorrow—why should I attempt to understand it? you may ask, and I will tell you. I had three dear friends dearer to me than my own life itself, a Brother and two nephews. One of them was taken from me after three days illness and another washed away and drowned off Sullivan's Island, and the third was shot and instantly killed by a miscreant in Sumter!!![35] I know full well the awful feeling of sudden and unexpected bereavement! It almost crushes the heart!!! But is any case too hard for God? Can any sorrow be too great for the Holy Comforter? Did you ever think how good it was in God to call this Spirit "the Comforter"? He knew full well how much the world would need comfort, and so He called Himself by a name that will at once draw the heart-broken ones to Him, and oh! if you will only throw yourself in His arms and pray earnestly to Him, I know that He will indeed come to you and give you peace and

---

[34] Porcher indicates that Miss Slouch is a thoroughbred horse, and it is possible her pedigree can be traced back to the Godolphin Arabian, one of the three horses which were the progenitors of modern thoroughbred race horses. William Alston (1756-1839), one of the founders of the South Carolina Jockey Club, owned a mare named Slouch, and her lineage from the Godolphin is documented in his stud book. Miss Slouch may have been from the same bloodline.

[35] The brother who was lost after a brief illness was likely Henry Francis Porcher (1819-1860), who died of pneumonia on January 18, 1860. A nephew, Thomas Francis Porcher (1827-1861) was drowned off Sullivan's Island while trying to rescue a relative. He was the son of Thomas Porcher, Jr. (1796-1843) of White Hall Plantation, who was a half-brother of Octavius T. Porcher.

comfort and joy at last!!! I was very much interested in hearing from Mr. Johnson an account of his visit to your Father on Friday, and very glad to know that you were [then] confirmed.[36] It is the first step and when ever we are reconciled to God, everything is open to us. Remember, Miss Haskell, that Religion is a <u>warfare</u>. <u>It is not ended in a day</u> and <u>our enemies are many and powerful, but God is ever with us</u>, if we only pray to Him, and will not leave us or give us over to them!! He desires our Salvation and loves us and He has begun the good work in you [*paper torn*]...

I cannot close without saying something of your dear, lost Brothers. I knew them well and can understand the void their absence will cause in your circle. I had known them as boys when first I came up here, and while Charles was on the North Eastern R Road I saw him very often at my Mother's and was very much impressed with his noble, manly traits, and all my friends were delighted with him.[37] A little circumstance drew me to him more than you can well understand. He had just imported a fine English gun, and, having to leave the neighbourhood, left it with me to shoot. It was indeed a fine gun and gave me infinite pleasure and I constantly thought of him while I had it. I never saw him again until the fall we had the Fair at Abbeville CH. We dined together at [Smiths], and on our way from the grounds he unbosomed himself to me in a way that deeply touched my heart. He told me that after he left St. Johns he went to Charleston and entered fashionable society there, that he never dreamed it could draw his heart from God and, before he knew himself, he was absorbed in its vanities, and one thing after another drew him on, until he found himself almost wrecked.[38] He told me that he had turned his back upon the communion table on one occasion and came out of the Church, that it tormented him, that he went out west and labored hard all day and tried to drown his reflections, but, when alone at night, they would return to him with redoubled force, and that he was miserable!! My heart yearned towards him. I had never seen a strong man so humbled. He said to me "Porcher I see it now. I relied too much upon myself. I did not appreciate the power of temptation. It shall be my earnest endeavour to warn my Brothers of it, that they may not fall into the same snare." I urged him to begin afresh. I told him of the Sav-

---

[36] Mr. Johnson was probably Benjamin Johnson, the rector of Trinity Episcopal Church in Abbeville.

[37] Octavius T. Porcher's mother was Elizabeth Sinkler DuBose Porcher (1788-1866). She lived in St. John's Berkeley Parish.

[38] Some of the "vanities" of Charleston had led to financial problems for Charles. A letter that he wrote to his father around this time revealed that he had considerable debts. This undated letter was written just prior to his departure for Mississippi to work on a railroad project there.

iour's amazing love, that I knew that God had not forsaken him, or he would not feel so [worried], that it was God's Spirit still striving with him. He promised me with great emotion that he would [*sic*] and we parted. My heart went after him as I left him, and my humble prayer ascended to our good God "that He would indeed bring back this suffering one to His fold." I trust in God that he found that peace that he so much yearned for and that he is now at rest with God. He died most nobly! He was indeed a splendid specimen of manhood!!

I knew William [well], both from my intercourse with him (which was indeed short) and from my nephews William DuBose and Moultrie Dwight[39] both of whom knew and loved him dearly, I can sincerely say that of all the young men who have come under my observation since the war began, none challenged my admiration more than William Haskell, and that his heart was unpolluted by camp and the horrors of war, I want no better proof than the lines penned by his hand upon the death of his Lieutenant (Seabrook I think). When I read them, I said to myself, "they do Haskell as much credit as the subject himself of the obituary." They must be a comfort to you I know. They have lived long enough for themselves!! Life is not so sweet that we should desire to recall them to its cares and trials and temptations. No! No! To those who are left it is indeed terrible. The heart sinks when it feels its want and knows it cannot be returned, but God is near and to Him I would draw you, as to a friend and Brother!!! Who knows but that God is drawing your Father and yourself and all your household nearer to Him!!! I forgot to mention that Willy DuBose said to me very [seriously] "Tavy if you are thinking of enlarging your school you had better try and get William Haskell. I really think him one of the first men I know."

John C. Haskell to Sophie Haskell (SCHS)
20 July [1863]
Dear Sophy,

I have been intending to write to you since I first heard of poor Charley's death but have been unable to until this morning. I know his loss and Willy's will grieve you very much but you must try to bear it well for Father and Mother's sake and I believe you will. I was very much troubled about you all at home until I got a letter from Pa and Ma which showed how well and Christianlike all were trying to bear the terrible affliction. I do not often see any of the boys as our division is continually moving and I have no one

---

[39] William Moultrie Dwight (1839-77) was the son of Isaac Marion Dwight (1799-1873) and Martha Maria Porcher Dwight (1807-42), who was the sister of Octavius T. Porcher.

with whom I can talk about Charley and Willy, but I think of them a great deal and am trying to be like them.

All the boys are well. Alick looks frail and has a cough which he says he is getting over. Langdon and Joe look remarkably well. Joe is now with Col. Alexander which I am very glad of as I consider his the most desirable position of the kind in the army. What I will do finally I do not know. I am as you know temporarily attached to Hood's artillery which is commanded by a very gallant but [incompetent] officer.[40] Whenever Capt. Riely[41] is promoted I will leave and Gen. [Longstreet] says that he hopes he will be able by that time to give me a separate command. I don't know though what will be done. Give my love to Pa and Ma, the boys and all at home.

Alexander C. Haskell, Headquarters McGowan's Brigade, Bivouac near Culpepper Court House, Va., to Charles T. Haskell (UNC)
25 July 1863
My dear Father,

Langdon shewed me a letter from you a few days ago in which, I thank you for it, you remembered to tell me that my little girl was well. In the midst of your great troubles, I don't feel that you can think of anything else. When I feel & know my own anxiety for a babe that I have hardly seen enough to make it feel it has a father, I can imagine your suffering in the loss of my noble brothers who had grown to manhood under your eye. I can hardly face yet the realisation of their loss, so far away from Charley, and of Willy I hear daily praise and affectionate comment as though he were still among us. I have never seen such a case. The brigade mourns his loss more than of any man who has ever fallen in it, more even it seems than of Genl. Gregg. This for one so humble in rank has rarely been seen. His own battalion of sharp shooters almost worship his memory and will never forget him on the field of battle. By our lamented general of division, the noble Pender, who fell in the same battle, Willy was placed amongst his very first officers, and as a man he held a special place in his regard. From all sides, generals & others of the division have taken occasion to speak to me in terms of the highest admiration of his noble character as a man. All that a soldier could win in a glorious death has been heaped upon him. All that a Christian hero could receive at the hands of his Saviour, we are sure that he has won in Heaven.

---

[40] This likely refers to Major Mathias Winston Henry (1838-77), General Hood's chief of artillery. John C. Haskell had only kind words for Henry in his memoirs, calling him "as brave a man as ever lived." Haskell, *The Haskell Memoirs*, 47.

[41] This was probably Captain James Reilly (1823-94) of Reilly's Battery.

Of our noble Charley you know in his last moments more than I do. But of this I am well assured, that a more skillful, and a nobler soldier has never given his life in a holy cause, and that in laying down this earthly life, he has taken upon him life eternal in the presence of his maker. But I do but pain you in recurring so much to your sorrows. I like to speak of them though. When we meet here we talk of them amongst ourselves and it is pleasant to think of them as still living, far happier, and still purer and nobler than they were when with us.

I had formed so high an estimate of Uncle Langdon, and had, even without knowing him well, so deep an affection for him, that this alone would have made me grieve much over his death, but when I remember the devotion of his family, and their present desolation in contrast with their former happiness, I feel that my own sorrow for even my own losses must yield to earnest sympathy for them. May God help them.

I am much fatigued this evening & feeling wretchedly in consequence of exposure while suffering from a severe cold, and write only to let you know that Langdon is well and I suppose John & Joe. They just preceded us on the march and I would know if they were sick. I know they have had no fight. We had a skirmish yesterday in which a few poor fellows were killed and wounded. It was a mere dash of cavalry & artillery upon our line of march. They were scattered as soon as we could come at them.

My own indisposition, though it worried me on the march, is slight, and will be removed by a rest we will have here for a day or two. The march has been made unpleasant by the loss of my best horse—died—but the other one has got well enough to give a comfortable mount again. In the meanwhile I bestrode an old blind buggy horse & had to be vigilant to preserve the pair of necks under my charge. I will write tomorrow more about our movements. I have sent you a great many letters but fear they have missed you, as I have received but one of all that have been written since I left home. Give my dearest love to my very dear Mother, to Sophie, Aunt Charlotte and the girls, and the boys.

J. G. Barnwell, Jr.[42], *In Bivouac near Culpepper, Va.,*
to Charles T. Haskell (SCHS)
26 July 1863
My dear Sir,
I endeavoured to write to you a few days after the death of your son Captain William Haskell. With the exception of Dr. Frost[43] I was more in-

---

[42] John Gibbes Barnwell (1839-1918).

timately associated with him than any one else who I thought might write to you, and knowing how anxious his family would be to hear from the Army I determined to take advantage of the earliest opportunity. But from lack of time & means at first, and afterwards from an unwillingness to address you on so painful a subject, I have delayed writing until now.

Previous to leaving Fredericksburg Captain Haskell was placed in command of a body of picked men chosen from the Brigade to act as light troops. The admirable manner in which this Battalion marched was noticed by everyone.

On arriving near Chambersburg he was detailed by Maj. Genl. Pender to command the rear ground of the Division, but as that service, as he told me, did not suit him at all, he was at his own request relieved and again assumed command of the Battalion.

In the Wednesday's fight, in which our Brigade suffered its severest loss, his Sharpshooters were deployed on the right of the Division and were not engaged.[44] On Thursday he was ordered forward into the field in front of our line to engage and hold in check the enemy's skirmishers. Throughout the entire day a brisk fire was kept up by his command. At about 6 P.M. I was sent to order him to advance his entire line immediately and to drive the enemy from the road some 200 yards in front. On walking out into the field I saw him standing up, his arm resting on a fence. On receiving the order he at once put his men in motion, and, driving the enemy from his position, occupied the road.

A few minutes later while standing in this road fearlessly exposing himself he was shot and his noble spirit passed without a struggle from earth to Heaven. I sent for his body, secured his watch, rings sword &c. That night his remains were sent to the rear in an ambulance & buried by Mr. Williams who has I believe written to you.

Since the battle of Chancellorsville it had been his habit to read prayers to his company every night after letters. As a Christian and as a soldier he had few if any equals in the army—on his other noble qualities it is useless for me to dwell in writing to his Father.

---

[43] This was Dr. Francis LeJau Frost (1837-1912), a surgeon in the First South Carolina Infantry Regiment.

[44] William Haskell was the commander of a battalion of sharpshooters in McGowan's Brigade which would later be reorganized and known as Dunlop's Battalion of Sharpshooters.

Alexander C. Haskell, Headquarters, McGowan's Brigade, to Sophia C. Haskell
(SCHS)
29 July 1863
Dear Ma,

Last night I received your letter of the 19th. It contained the first words from home since the great sorrow had fallen there. You can scarce imagine the comfort it gave me to see that the piety for whose teachings your children in Heaven look down and bless you, and to which your children on earth look up with such admiration and hope, has sustained you and all about you, in the hour of trial so severe. It is like your goodness and self-forgetfulness to try to seem cheerful to comfort one who has so much less to suffer than you who are in the empty home see and feel it. I appreciate such love and thank you for it, but I know too that it is only the assurance of the unspeakable happiness to which our loved ones have been borne that keeps your heart from breaking. Thank God for this assurance. In the little time I could see Joe I spoke to him, and I hope, though it was but for a moment we talked, that his heart is deeply enlisted, and that even now his soul is fixed in faith and seeking higher things. I have had no opportunity to speak to John though I have sought it, but I feel sure of what was once his feeling and I can hardly help agreeing with my friend and religious counselor Robert Barnwell that the soul once chosen may err and wander but will never be lost by the Shepherd, who will seek it in the desert and wild places and reclaim it. I remember well how he read and talked to John and then knelt by his bedside and prayed when the Doctors forbade it. But he answered "better that his body perish than his immortal soul." I thought it almost cruel then that he probed John's feelings so deeply and so kindly but unflinchingly rebuked him that he had ever hesitated, but I feel thankful now and did then when I learned the result, that John had given him full reason to believe that his repentance was sincere, and his faith firm. And I know that John is not one who could be induced rashly to express feeling & hopes of so grave a nature unless they were deep in his heart.

I am glad that you can see how happy were the deaths of Charley & Willy. There is no horror there. It is the most glorious passage from time to eternity that God vouchsafes to man. No pain, no weakness, no grief. They passed from "life to life" in the fullest glory of redeemed and sanctified humanity.

I feel how Pa must suffer. I have written to him and to all of you several times. I fear you do not get my letters, but I can always pray for you, and this I do. I know that they go to the Throne of Mercy and will be answered. I was deeply touched by your mention of Mamie and Emmie. They are indeed noble girls and I trust will find all the comfort their fortitude and resignation deserves. I am glad Mary McCord is with Aunt Charlotte. She will be a comfort to her. If she is still with you please don't forget my kindest remembrances to her. When I saw her she gave me leave to remember her as a cousin. I do and as a very near and dear one if she will let me, for I have seldom seen anyone to whom I have been as much attracted by regard and esteem.

I have written to Sophie. Poor child, she has not known much grief before this. I trust it may be sanctified to her soul's good. She will do well to grasp the comforts of an open profession of religion. Let her once claim Christ as her friend & Saviour and she will turn to Him naturally for aid and comfort. Where chastening so mercifully dealt as ours has been, I can almost see the hand of God directing it to our salvation.

If I could get a few more letters or see you all I could stop talking perhaps about Charley and Willy and our dear Uncle but now I can write of nothing else. It can only excite feeling which though it never does and never should, may long lie peacefully asleep in our hearts. I hope to see the boys this evening if the storm of wind and rain now raging passes by. Thank you for dear Baby's letter. It sounds almost as if it came from her own sweet little lips, only I hope she would not be quite as well satisfied with her little perfections. I suppose she would though. Dearest love to Pa , Sophy, the boys, Aunt Charlotte, Mamie & Emmie.

John Bachman[45], *Charleston, S.C., to Charles T. Haskell* (SCHS)
31 July 1863
My dear Sir,

With the deepest sympathy for the heavy bereavements which have shrouded your house in sorrow & mourning I wish it were in my power to assuage your griefs or to do anything to alleviate those sorrows which these repeated blows of affliction have brought to your home & your hearts. Let us however reason a little on these subjects as men and as Christians.

We are all the creatures of God—created by his hand & redeemed by the blood of his dear son. Thus he revealed to us life and immortality. He never promised us unmixed pleasures here, or an exemption from death, but he has given us the assurance of a reunion & immortality beyond the grave. Moreover I have often witnessed the fact that those whom God intended to remove early are very frequently blessed with traits of character & with

---

[45] John Bachman (1790-1874) was a Lutheran minister of Charleston and a noted naturalist who collaborated with John J. Audubon. His daughter Harriet Eva Bachman (1829-1858) was the wife of William E. Haskell of Charleston. After her death, Haskell married her sister Jane Lee Bachman (1819-1903).

Christian advantages which enables them to be prepared to exchange worlds even in the morning of their days.

Few men in our Confederacy have contributed so largely to their country's defense as you have done. You offered up on that altar your own beloved sons. That country is our Mother. Your brave boys voluntarily flew to her rescue & in defense of her honour & her rights they shed their blood & surrendered their lives on the battle field. How noble was the cause in which they were engaged & how honourable their deaths. How different would now be your feelings if they had lost their lives in a broil, or in a duel. My good wife & myself often spoke of your large family of sons & could not fail to remark, that we had never met a family of sons of which the parents had such just reasons to be proud. They were well educated, intelligent, devoted to their parents, honourable, respectful, virtuous, a reverential regard to religion [sic] & an undying patriotism. The duties of long life are often discharged in a few years. God enabled them to fulfill their mission in a much shorter period of time than others are able to accomplish in a life protracted to many years. They fulfilled their destiny & when this had been accomplished God took them. They exhibited intelligence, courage & patriotism which was an example & should prove a stimulant to all who are interested in the liberties of their beloved & now bleeding & downtrodden country. Such were their characters that we are permitted to rest on the hope, that through the mercy of an atoning savior, they have been permitted to exchange a world of war & sorrow for a land of peace where the wicked cease from troubling & the weary are at rest.

Let me remind you of another fact which I am sure neither of you have overlooked. You have not been deprived of all, you have still a large family of noble sons remaining. I pray to God that they may be spared to you to be your pride, your support & comfort. We cannot recall the dead but we can impart instruction by our precepts & example to the living. Most fortunate was it for these young men that they were blest by the unwearied labours & example of a mother such as is not very often found among the wealthy & fashionable.

As it is my good friends, I need not say to you that your highest solace will be found in the practice of those high & holy duties which religion teaches to men. This will fortify your minds for the trials that are yet before you & comfort you in the sorrows you have already been called to endure.

Remember me affectionately to your good wife & children, & believe me to be, in deep sympathy for your loss, & earnest pray [sic] for your support & comfort.

Louisa R. McCord to Sophie Haskell (SCHS)
July or August 1863

It was <u>very</u> kind of you dear Sophie to write to us for I know it must have been an effort to do it. Oh Sophie it does seem as if we had so much trouble to bear! That we should have to give up so many of those that are dearest to us. It seems as if everything we had to live for is being taken away. It is selfish of me to write so to you but I cannot help it today and I don't want to put off writing to you. After we lost our own darling I felt that all our relations were so much more to us than they had been, that we had to love them now more than we ever had done. It was such a fearful shock to us to hear of the death of our dear uncle and cousin & then Sophie when your letter came last night! When I think of it all I feel that I can do nothing but feel sorry for you and for us all. In our first trouble Alec and dear Willy were so kind, so gentle that we all felt that they were more to us, could take his place more than any we had left. Oh Sophie if you only knew how kind they were. As you say we girls ought to love each other very much the trouble and distress of one is much that of the other. Goodbye dear Sophie. I will write you again.

[P.S.] Dear Sophie I hardly like to send this it seems so cold & short— but you know how much I feel for you & with you.

Alexander C. Haskell, Bivouac near Orange Court House, Va.,
to Sophie Haskell (SCHS)
4 August 1863
Dear Sophie,

For four days I have been unable to write. We have been kept constantly on the alert and moving partly disturbed by the actual danger of an attack, but much more disturbed by the carelessness of Heth (Hamilton's pet General) our temporary Division commander. This man bears a most extraordinary and unfortunate likeness to Col. Hamilton which stamps its impression upon all his acts. All this commotion was at and near Culpepper C.H. where several times we marched up the hill and down again. One evening the enemy's Cavalry in heavy force dashed upon Hampton's little Brigade which although it charged repeatedly and gallantly, was soon sent reeling in upon Culpepper, battered bruised and wearied. One regiment of our brigade with a N. Carolina regiment was on picket near the scene of action extended its battle line of about 170 men over three hundred yards of ground, the men standing singly as skirmishers and in this way, instead of the massive square prescribed for receiving cavalry charges, they met and repulsed repeated charges in front & flank assisted by artillery. Anderson's Division of five brigades was towards dark advanced to the position and swept the enemy before it, relieving our regiment from its arduous duty, and saving the remnant of the N. Carolinians from being taken prisoners. The greater part of them had fled at the first charge. Our regiment then came quietly into the bivouac, mentioned incidentally that they had had a fight with cavalry, reported their loss, and were delighted to be allowed to lie down by the road for a few hours asleep before going out again.[46] We thought no more about it except that our men had saved the cavalry & prevented the Yankees from riding into Genl. Hill's & Lee's Hd.Qrs. in Culpepper, until to our amazement a note came down through the official channels written by Genl. Stuart to Genl. Lee complaining that our infantry had fled in confusion and given him no support. This has flown all over the cavalry and the army. So villainous are reports. One Regt. did run, but it was not a South Ca. regiment. Our brethren over the border. After this we were harassed with marching to & fro under a terrible sun and at last turned our heads in this direction & have taken up a splendid line south of the Rappahannock where as one of my young couriers enthusiastically remarked this morning "if the Yanks want these hills let them come and take them." A soldier is not entirely born one—much is made in him. This boy had a feeling of positive pleasure—as much as Napoleon ever had in choosing his greatest battle fields—at the bare idea of an enemy making a bloody attack upon us in a position which his eye taught him was fatal to a foe. Such are the pleasures of war. Soldiers cannot always feel its horrors. They lie down & sleep as calmly as two hours before a fight which may be their last as peacefully as ever in their quiet homes, and look upon the red field with the same inquiring eye that they would cast upon lands to see that they were well formed by nature for any of the pursuits of agriculture.

We have had no mails and I no letters. I fear you miss my letters as I learned on leaving Culpepper that bushels of letters remained unmailed. I suppose they sometimes send off ten to fifteen thousand a day. I am very stupid this evening, a little tired, and write to say that nothing worse than a little fatigue, which an hour's rest will cure, is the matter with me. I have been living on green apples and stray biscuits for three days and have wished very often that I could enjoy the luxury of a comb, brush and towel, but

---

[46] J. F. J. Caldwell wrote of this period: "On Saturday evening, August 1, we received intelligence of an advance by the Federal cavalry to our picket station. They, it seemed, had attacked our cavalry picket, in advance of the infantry, driven them in, and followed them up to where the Fourteenth regiment lay. This regiment at once formed and met them. The enemy made quite a dash, but they were quickly routed ... McGowan's brigade, with the rest of the division, was marched, immediately, beyond Culpepper, in the direction of the picket-post. But nothing further being done by the enemy we bivouacked in the fields until Sunday morning." Caldwell, *The History of a Brigade*, 110-111.

wished in vain as our wagon was mysteriously wandering to the rear. However we caught it today. I have had a dinner and washed my face and hands. Write to ask your congratulations. The boys are well. I saw Langdon yesterday. Little Willy I learn from one of his officers was not hurt in the cavalry fight.

We will be here some days. I will write again. Write to me your life and our home. God bless and keep you my dear child. Give my dearest love to Ma & Pa, Aunt C., Mamie & Emmie. Ask the boys to write to me.

Joseph C. Haskell, Headquarters, Alexander's Battalion, Va.,
to Sophie Haskell (SCHS)
4 August 1863
My dear Sophie,

I have wanted to write to you for some time but have really had very little opportunity as we have been constantly on the move. I have seen a good many letters from Ma and Pa to me and the other boys for when a letter comes to one we all see it. They have been a great comfort and help to me and I have been hoping we would get one from you. Ma has written of you but I want to hear from you yourself. She says you bear it better than she expected and trusts that you have gone for comfort where it alone can be sought in troubles like ours. Write to me freely if you can, and don't hesitate to say anything you think of. Write of dear Willy and Charley. Tell me all you know of Charley's death—how he fell and all about him. It may be hard but it will do you good to talk and write about him. I think of them both how very differently than I would if I were at home. Here we were all so much separated that we had got to looking on it as a matter of course, and I now often find myself thinking of the six of us that are in the army. And then when I recollect that there are two less now I can do so almost without pain, for I trust that the separation is but for a time. I feel this loss most when we four meet together which we do whenever we can. There is a change in us all. We feel nearer to one another now that we feel how soon we may be parted.

I wish very much I could get home for a little while, but there is no chance of that. We are so busy here. There is so much change. So many things to keep your mind actively employed that you have not much time to think of quiet matters, and when you have the time, perhaps not the disposition. You meet persons every hour of the day who have no feeling or sympathies in common with you and are ignorant of your sorrow or grief. Unconsciously your thoughts and manner take their tone from them and I am almost shocked to find how entirely forgetful I become of everything but what is immediately around me.

Do write to me of home. Tell me all about Aunt Charlotte, Maimie and Emmie and about Cousin Follie and the boys and about everybody I want to try and feel as if I was at home. I have not seen Lally or Alick for some days, for now that I am transferred to the corps I am much more separated from them than before. I hope tho' I will find them out soon now that the army is becoming stationary as it appears to be doing. We are camped about a mile from Orange C. H. in the vicinity of which most of the army is now collected. I am about three miles from Mrs. Massie where I go very often as they are very kind and I find it very pleasant. John, I hear from them, is also a visitor there. They are all very affectionate and always send their love to you and Ma. Mrs. Lewis and her daughter are with them now. I hope Alick and Lally will meet them before we leave here, tho' I don't know when that will be. We may be here for months, as far as we can judge from anything that we can see of the movements of the enemy. So far I wish if we have to remain quiet for any length of time, it may be here. Do tell me what you know of Cousin Tom. I wanted to write to Cousin Follie but I could not make up my mind to write even to her, tho' I want to hear from her so much. Give her my best love and tell her why I have not written but will do so soon. Give my dearest love to all at home. If Aunt Charlotte and the girls have left home, tell me where they are particularly as I want to write.

Good bye my dear Sophie. If I had ever teased you and vexed you it was not because I did not love you.

Alexander C. Haskell, Headquarters, McGowan's Brigade,
to Sophia C. Haskell (SCHS)
5 August 1863
Dear Ma,

Yesterday I received your letter 26 July. It finds us in a new position near Orange C. H. on the south side of the Rapidan holding the high hills which overhang the stream. In all respects the situation is desirable and the army is in good condition to avail itself of all its advantages. Some few feel a doubt as to the spirit of our soldiers & fear to see it tested in battle. These are only weak people who were unduly elated by success and are now proportionately despondent at the first indication of the reverses necessary to the history of armies, but which they had never had the courage to look boldly in the face. Our men will fight as well as they ever did and if God permit will win a great victory if attacked by the enemy in this country.

Many think and perhaps correctly that Genl. Meade will not advance upon us.[47] I rather hope that he will be ordered to do it & will have no option in the matter. He is holding steadily to the R.R. advancing as he repairs it, will probably soon rebuild the bridge over the Northern Rappahannock & come down on us with a very extensive line of communication in his rear. This line he will be obliged to guard, thus weakening his army. And however well he guard it, it is probable that we can cut it at some point, thus harassing him much. The weather is hot & oppressive, the country dry and bare. An army marching to the attack must suffer much from heat, disease and straggling in spite of all efforts to prevent it will diminish its ranks. Marching in retreat as we do, the men lived out to the extremity of endurance knowing that rest is in front and an enemy in rear. If we had marched for the last week with an enemy in front and rest in rear we would have lost nearly a third of our army.

I have not seen John & Joe for several days. Langdon I see often. All are well. Jonas is with me. Joe asked me to keep him until I could send him home, which I will do as soon as Langdon or I can find an escort for him. The old man is very devoted, expresses an earnest desire to stay with anyone of us that needs him, but at the same time it is evident that he suffers from worry & fatigues of our restless life and yearns for home. He has served faithfully & lovingly the master to whom he was sent and has thus discharged his full duty and enlisted all our feelings for him.

It is a great happiness to me to hear such good accounts of my little darling. I was fearful of the effect of those jaw teeth coming out in this hot weather. I dream of her, and indeed in my waking hours have rather fanciful images of her bright little self which make pleasant pictures for the present, whether or not they ever to be realized.

I will shew your letter to Langdon and arrange with him the list you ask for. Please send me a copy of the paper containing Judge Wardlaw's true-friend's tribute to our noble soldiers. I don't like to call them dead. I think of them as living in so far higher & nobler degree than our loftiest ideas can bear our imaginations. God has indeed blessed those whom he has taken to himself. From my heart I return your prayer. May his blessings rest upon those whom he has left.

Dearest love to Pa and Sophie, Aunt Charlotte, Mamie & Emmie. Please don't trouble about writing too much to me. You know how much happiness your letters give me but you have others to write to & I don't like

---

[47] General George Gordon Meade (1815-72) was the commander of the Union Army of the Potomac.

to tax you. I have got two from you in the last six days. Make Sophie write, a great deal. I write to her pretty often but she must do more than return my letters. Goodbye.

Alexander C. Haskell, Headquarters, McGowan's Brigade,
to Sophia C. Haskell, Abbeville Courthouse, S.C. (UNC)
10 August 1863
Dear Ma,

I am about to start for a ride down to Gordonsville to meet Mrs. Singleton who will pass that place today on her way to South Carolina. I saw her sisters Mrs. Peyton yesterday. She tells me that little Edward is much better and will be able to stand the journey.[48]

I can't help regretting very much the idea of your giving up Baby just now but it must be so for the present. She shall not forget you though, nor will this be her last long visit to you. I know how much benefit she has derived from the change of air and mode of life and am thankful that she had the opportunity when it was most needed. I went to church yesterday with Joe, spent the day with him and met Langdon at my quarters when I came back. Both quite well. I find Joe very happily domesticated with Col. Alexander and Frank Huger, and in good spirits. Frank Huger seems to be a fine young man, & Col. A. is a singular & rare combination of gentleman, soldier and scientific man, all of a very high order. I don't think I know of a more valuable example & companion for a young man, especially for whom he has taken to his confidence. John as I wrote you yesterday I believe to be near Fredericksburg. Joe tells me that Uncle John and Aunt Rachel were thinking of paying you a visit. I hope this is true & that Minna will come with them. It will do all the girls good to be together. Give my love to them & regrets that I am not at home to meet them. It is wrong to think of forbidden things, but I cannot help thinking constantly what a happiness it would be could we who are left meet once more at home and let you feel what a strength of love and hope still surrounded you to comfort your age, when age does come, but you are so young in heart & faith & hope that I fear we will always call upon you for the strength and support which you so long have given us and which it is now our turn to render to you. Goodbye. May God bless my dear old home and all who assembled beneath its roof. Dearest love to Pa, Sophie, Aunt C., Mamie & Emmie & the boys.

---

[48] Robert W. Barnwell's son (whose name is spelled Eduard on his gravestone) was born on April 12, 1862, and died on May 30, 1864.

Francis L. Frost, Camp near Orange Court House, Va.,
to Sophia C. Haskell (SCHS)
13 August 1863
My dear Mrs. Haskell,

I have delayed writing to you for so long a time that I feel ashamed, and reproach myself severely for not having written to you before. I have not however thought of you the less, for whom from my childhood I have always felt a warm regard, which has of late years been fostered & increased by a growing intimacy with your sons, & since your recent afflictions, these ties have been still more closely drawn by sympathy & a common participation in your sorrows.

For Willie I had a warm & earnest affection. Aleck stands next in my esteem. These two were more of my age & there was more congeniality between us by reason of their Christian character, their zealous devotion of those talents to their God & Saviour.

In the death of Willie, I have lost a very dear & beloved friend & counselor, one who was always affectionate, kind & considerate; a friend of my childhood, to whom I had become attached in those innocent & susceptible days; for whom my affections had grown warmer day by day, as his powers developed into manhood & for whom these feelings were much intensified by a life of the closest intimacy with him for the last two years, & by the common pleasures, hardships, trials & dangers of war.

Considering these things I feel that I have lost such a friend as I can never again replace; one whom I felt it an honor & a privilege to love & esteem, & to have as a friend; of whose esteem & regard I felt proud. In whose company I derived pleasure & profit; to whom I could apply for advice & council with confidence, for on his judgment I felt that I could rely implicitly, & that I would meet with his sympathy I felt assured.

But it is on his Christian graces that I delight chiefly to dwell, for, altho in common with all others who came in contact with him, I felt the highest admiration for his strict integrity, his stern government of self, his generous, unselfish spirit, his pure & self sacrificing patriotism, his exalted sense of honor, & his unflinching courage & vigorous sense of duty, yet, since his soul has now left this earth, it is to his zealous, unwearied devotion of these high qualities of head & heart to the God & the Saviour whom he loved & trusted, that I look for comfort & consolation. I pray & trust that God may visit you with the rich blessings of his Grace, and that He may comfort you with the assurance that Willie now rests from the cares & toils of this life in the full promise of a blissful immortality at the last great day. I see Aleck daily. He is well & happy. Langdon, John & Jos. are also well.

Alexander C. Haskell, Headquarters, McGowan's Brigade,
to Sophia C. Haskell (UNC)
13 August 1863
Dear Ma,

An absolute dearth of employment beyond duties of daily routine, and lack of incident of any kind, make my brain stagnant. I have no books to keep it alive, and no companions to provoke it to exertion. A captious argumentative friend, provided he had sense enough to be suggestive & stimulating, would be invaluable.

I have never seen the army so settle itself down to repose. Ready at any moment to move if necessary, nothing is farther from their present thoughts. Generals & officers of lower degree & who yet share the high councils set the example of sending for their families to visit them in the pleasant places of Orange. All the rest take this as assurance of present quiet. Vigour is however, being displayed in filling our shattered ranks and in fulling [*sic*] equipping the army for the approaching campaign. Our Brigade was inspected yesterday by the Inspector of the Army, and presented an appearance of strong health & efficiency in arms and accoutrements, such as I have never seen surpassed.

Langdon having entered upon his new duties as acting Inspector was assisting. He will find his new office a pleasant one and he is being well broken into it at the commencement. His diffidence of his tactical knowledge almost made him refuse to act, but this was overcome by persuasion, & will disappear before practice, as indeed it has done in me. Good days work. I envy him his employment.

Joe came to see me one night before last. Was quite well. Has made pleasant acquaintances all over this country, besides finding our cousins the Lewis' & Masseys, whom I have not yet seen, & seems to be enjoying a few visits among them all very much.[49]

Of John as I have written before I hear but little.

I don't answer any letters from home because I am so unfortunate as not to get them. The mail is defective & loses many letters. My last are 26 July & 2nd August, both from you. If you don't get my letters please attribute to mail for I write more than would please you if you got them all.

---

[49] Dr. John Benjamin Lewis (1810-53) of Sweet Springs, Va., married Caroline Sophia Rebecca Thomson (born 1802), the grand-daughter of William Thomson (1729-96) in 1831. Her first husband was Thomas Bolton Smith (1800-25) of Savannah, Ga. Her daughter by her first marriage, Susan Elizabeth Smith, married Henry Massie, Jr. (1816-78) in 1841. His father, Henry Massie, Sr., married Susan Preston Lewis, the daughter of John Lewis of Sweet Springs.

Love to Pa, Sophie, Aunt C. and all the girls. Goodbye. God bless you my dear Mother and all those at home.

Alexander C. Haskell, Headquarters, McGowan's Brigade, to Charles T. Haskell, Abbeville, S.C. (UNC)

14 August 1863
Dear Pa,

I am just up after the sun from a sleep made more profound than usual by a long and late ride last night to see some of your cousins. I went with Joe who is most intimately installed at the house. Mrs. Lewis and one of her unmarried daughters were there. These I had seen before, but to Mrs. Massie and her very pleasant family I had to be presented. I suppose it is chiefly from their memory of you, who seem to have been such a favourite in the family, & partly from their natural kind & warmhearted disposition, but wherever I find a new relation of the Thomson blood, I am welcomed at once with all the cordiality of affectionate & well known kindred, & while I am [ashamed] to feel that I hardly remember how to trace the relationship, they know every member of our house by name & inquire after them with the most kindly solicitude.

I was at once hailed & installed as "Cousin Alec" by all parties in Mr. Massie's house & am glad to know my connection with such good people. One youngster particularly won my heart. Willy is his name. He is so much like Paul in appearance, and even more close is the resemblance in manner & disposition. He is a splendid little fellow. Coming into the room late & while conversation was very busy, he took me for a stranger, & walking up so like Paul, put his hand in mine & sat down by me, that I felt as if it was my own boy as I left him two years ago, for Willy is younger. At the first pause his question of why "Cousin Alexander" had not come was quite enough to put me at my ease by assuring me that my kinfolk had been hospitably expectant. I suppose we owe it all to what their Grandmother & Mother have told them of you & Ma.

Having given you enough gossip I will not proceed to take up the department of "Army Correspondence." I heard from John last night. He is certainly at Fredericksburg, very well & very much disgusted at being sent back to that exhausted country and cut off from all the army. This army is still in profound quiet. As seems to be that of the enemy across the river. Meade is extended from Warrenton to Stafford Heights, we from Orange C. H. to Fredericksburg. A splendid opportunity it appears to me, for either General to [concentrate] his army rapidly & fall suddenly upon the extended lines of his opponent. We however are quite compact about Orange C. H. &

would be delighted by being attacked at that point. I see however no present prospect of a move on either side, though this delightfully cool morning almost makes us hope that the intense heats of summer have passed.

Love to Ma & Sophie, to Aunt Charlotte and the girls. Langdon is quite well.

Alexander C. Haskell, Headquarters, McGowan's Brigade,
to Sophia C. Haskell, Abbeville Courthouse, S.C. (UNC)
15 August 1863
Dear Ma,

I have just directed to you a letter from Frank Frost. You cannot listen to the words of a truer, nobler friend than he is, and in every instinct of his soul a Christian & a gentlemen of rare purity. He appreciated all the high qualities which shown in Willie's character. If not for his sake, for you cannot know him as he is, you ought to love him for the sake of the love he bore to Willie, & still cherishes for all your sons. It is a great happiness to me to talk with him & hear how cheerfully and joyously he talks of Willie, as if one whose words, and almost his presence, were still with us to advise, cheer or help as they so often were when we three were together. And this is from no callousness or indifference, but from the full realization of the hope we must all feel, that Willie is far happier now than all the love of friends could ever have made him on earth.

I see Langdon & Joe daily. They are always well and cheerful. Langdon is busily employed in a position much better suited to him than his old one of Aide-de-Camp. I hope sincerely that he will never return to it. John as I have written but I keep repeating for fear you don't get my letters is near Fredericksburg & just heard from, is well.

Goodbye. Love to Pa and all at home. May God's blessing be with them all.

Alexander C. Haskell, Headquarters, McGowan's Brigade,
to Charles T. Haskell (UNC)
17 August 1863
Dear Pa,

Your letter of the 10th reached me night before last. I need not say how much happiness it gave me. I can only pray that God will continue to temper his chastenings with such abundant mercies as he has poured upon us in all of our afflictions. Rarely is the mercy of God so bountifully bestowed that one of his creatures is permitted in short a time to look upon the death unto life of six those who were nearest and dearest on earth, and grieve only for himself, feeling only that they have passed into Heavenly kingdoms far above the reach of his words to affect save as they rise in humble, earnest supplication to be permitted to enter in and share their joys. I do pray for you constantly. I know how proud you were of them & how you loved them, and how hard it is to give them up even for a little while. Our prayers are heard and are very mercifully answered.

I am happy that my little Darling has so her way into your hearts. I know that for the sake of her dear Mother she can never lack friends, but if she can attract love in herself it will be happier for herself & for her friends. I am sorry she is so soon taken away from you, but the anxiety of her other Grandmother, who has been taken away for a time, I know is uncontrollable. But whether or not I can come to shew her the way again she will never be absent so long as to forget your faces or your kindness.

I spent most of yesterday with Joe. Met him at church and brought him to camp to dine with me. In the afternoon he went with me to see Mrs. Peyton, Mrs. Singleton's sister, and I think enjoyed his evening very much, for while I was being agreeably entertained by my good Aunt and her intelligent husband, Joe was rapidly ingratiating himself with two of the pleasantest looking young ladies I have seen for a good while, Miss Willis & Miss Lee, and I think has added another to the list of good houses at which he can spend his spare time. Joe is quite cheerful and happy. He is surrounded by men with whom I am glad to see him associated and is such a favourite that he is down to a good deal of visiting, which does him good, as he has here an opportunity of meeting some of the best society of Virginia. In these times when all people are drawn near together and the varnish rubbed off, shows all that is really honest and good in people's nature.

Of John I only hear I fear that he is becoming a little discontented with his position & is working for a change. When I last saw him he was much incensed against Major Henery [sic], over whose inertness and bad management, he being the junior, has no positive control. This chafes him a little but perhaps, certainly indeed, is for the best. This old truism becomes more startlingly evident every day and I could not help acknowledging the force of Joe's case, when he spoke last night of his disappointment in not going to the West with General Johnston, and how much better it has resulted for him. [His] present position is enviable to anyone who desires improvement in his profession. You speak of the loss of my horse. I have been unfortunate, for the horse I bought to replace one who died has gone blind. However I am getting on pretty well as my mare who was lame is nearly well. I don't like to buy a horse here. They are very scarce and the prices are enormous. Eight hundred or a thousand dollars for a saddle horse. I will take care that Joe does not lack money and will make him write to you if he needs remittances which is not unlikely, for simple mess bills are now from sixty to a hundred & fifty dollars a month. I made up some deficiencies last month & will look after him in future. Money is such trash nowadays that its only value after food & clothing are procured is to make one friends comfortable, & indeed I suppose this is the true philosophy of enjoying money at anytime.

Dearest love to Ma, Sophie, Aunt C., Mamie & Emmie. Tell the girls I will write the longest letters they ever read if they will only incite my pen to emulation by awaking theirs to activity. Goodbye. God bless & help you all my dear Father.

Alexander C. Haskell, Headquarters, McGowan's Brigade,
to Sophia C. Haskell (UNC)
19 August 1863
Dear Ma,

I saw poor Langdon yesterday evening just after he had learned little Charley's death.[50] He was very sad, but controlled himself better than I had ever before seen him in circumstances of grief. His heart is so sensitive and his affections so strong that he has always had a terrible struggle with sorrow, but like others in this time when death walks openly among us, he has learned I hope, for his sake, to think that it is a blessed thing that an infant should be permitted to enter into rest before the touch of sin and care had polluted its pure soul. Of such are the whitest lambs in the fold of the Good Shepherd.

I pity poor Ella who amid all the grief and anxiety that surrounds her has had this heavy blow brought again to strike upon her heart, but I know how bravely she bears her sorrows and bows in patient & happy resignation to all that her Heavenly Father sees fit to bring upon her. Do give her my tenderest love and sympathy. Fear for my own little darling, I suppose, makes me selfishly appreciate her sufferings. May God spare her further pain.

I saw John last evening. I called to see Joe on my way to General Lee's Hdqrs. Found him quite bright with the prospect of a pleasant evening at a nice house to which a good many people had been invited. I could not spoil his pleasure by telling him of Langdon's sorrow. He will learn it soon enough. At Genl. Lee's I met John who had just ridden up from Fredericksburg. He is looking reasonably well, but as I feared has had a disagreement with his commanding officer whom he represents as being a brave but idle and dissipated officer and is anxious to leave him. He is not pushing the matter at present but feels confident that he will get a pleasant place some-

---

[50] Charles Thomson Haskell, the son of Langdon C. Haskell, died on August 14, 1863, at the age of seventeen months.

where, it is not yet very definite, in a few days or weeks. I don't blame him at all for desiring this change, though I regret it as indulging a little his own restlessness of disposition and giving an appearance of fickleness where the circumstances of the case might not be well known. I shall be glad however to see him succeed in this effort as I think he can hardly fail to improve his position. He expected to go back to Fredericksburg this morning but I think I received a visit from him by promising to give him my hat, a felt one which he coveted, if he would come to see me. He has at last given up Pa's old hat, which he has been wearing so long for fear his head shall pop through some of the holes in it. Otherwise he looked in his brilliant uniform better than I had ever seen him.

We are all quiet and doing well in the Brigade though we regret Genl. McGowan's prolonged absence. We have lost a first rate (in the real sense of those much abused words) commander in Perrin[51] who so distinguished himself and the Brigade at Gettysburg. The only fear is that Col. Hamilton will return before Genl. McGowan and assume command. I hope to scare him off without hurting him [or] make him resign. I have declared intentions of hostile proceedings so plainly that I expect him to hear them. This may frighten him. It is a painful duty to me but as a duty I regard it & shall unflinchingly act upon it. I conferred upon the subject in high quarters last night and think that if he comes back and dares the contest I can defeat him. I trust so at any rate for the sake of the brave fellows he would disgrace and butcher both in battle, for he never retreats until it is death & dishonour to do so, and honour and safety could be found in a bold charge. Goodbye my dear Mother. God bless you all. I suppose Baby has already left you. Thank you again for the love & care bestowed upon her by all in her second home. Love to Pa, Ella & Sophie, Aunt C. and Mamie & Emmie.

---

[51] Almer Monroe Perrin (1827–64) was promoted to brigadier general in September 1863.

6

BATTLES IN TENNESSEE AND VIRGINIA

23 AUGUST 1863 – 24 APRIL 1864

Having recovered from his Chancellorsville wound, Aleck has rejoined his brigade in Virginia after their defeat at Gettysburg. The Army of Northern Virginia maneuvers to keep between Richmond and the opposing army of General Meade, which reaches the Rapidan River by September 1863. On September 22, Colonel Abner M. Perrin receives his commission as brigadier general, remaining in command of McGowan's Brigade until General McGowan returns. In early October, John and his battalion of artillery are at Gordonsville, Virginia, near the camp of McGowan's Brigade. In early November 1863, Langdon holds the rank of captain and becomes General McGowan's Assistant Adjutant General. Aleck's letter of December 3rd gives details of the Mine Run Campaign, which ends in General Meade's retreat. Although Lee's army sees no further major engagements until spring, the winter of 1863-1864 in Virginia is a severe one. Joseph, who is with Alexander's Artillery Battalion in Tennessee during the late part of 1863, writes about the Confederate assault on Fort Sanders at the end of November, and the Battle of Bean's Station in mid-December. Soon afterward, he gets leave to go home to Abbeville, and in January 1864, he travels back to Tennessee by way of North Carolina, where he pays a visit to relatives in Flat Rock. The following month, Joseph is appointed Assistant Adjutant General to Edward P. Alexander (who is now a brigadier general) with the rank of captain. On February 26, 1864, Mary Chesnut records in her diary: "Another maimed hero is engaged to be married. Sally Hampton has accepted John Haskell." In late April 1864, Joseph is back in Virginia with Longstreet's Corps, and Aleck is appointed lieutenant colonel of the newly formed Seventh South Carolina Cavalry Regiment of Holcombe Legion.

Alexander C. Haskell, Headquarters, McGowan's Brigade,
to Sophia C. Haskell (UNC)
23 August 1863
Dear Ma,

The mails are stopped in Richmond by the resignation of the clerks in the Post Office. This makes the transmission of letters and news very precarious and I write this morning to provide against accidents with former letters, to which I can add nothing. Joe and Langdon are as usual well, Langdon happier and more cheerful than I expected. We have many friends around us & I only regret that the confinement [incidental] upon my office prevents my seeing as much of them as I desire. Last evening I had the good fortune to spend with Mrs. Minor, Mrs. Peyton and Mrs. Thomson [*sic*] Brown, as kind Aunts & Cousins as you could wish to have near me in case I was really in want of friends. I have from them that Mrs. Singleton has got home safely with the children and has robbed you of Baby. I fear that she will be obliged to give up the other children to Mrs. Barnwell for such it appears was the wish expressed by Robert to friends in the early stages of his illness. Mrs. Barnwell is a most excellent woman but I think that the children would probably be better reared and more advantageously with Mrs. Singleton. At Mrs. Barnwell's they will receive a share of attention in a house already very large and a full complement of spoiling from all their aunts, and of teasing from their young uncles. They will be cut off from a most devoted and valuable connection in Columbia and will lose many other advantages which I can see in prospect for them if allowed to remain with Mrs. Singleton. However if they go to Mrs. Barnwell I hope her pious care will shield them from harm and bring them up to honourable usefulness. Poor little fellows. I had hoped that they would remain under my eye and within reach if any assistance that my love and care could afford them. For certainly if there were no other claims upon me I should owe this much to them for the warm friendship which was given to me years ago by both their Father and Mother, before and after their marriage.

Our lines in the army continue unchanged. General Meade appears to be in no condition to provoke a fight, in fact he shews an inclination to avoid it as long as possible. I think it probable that as soon as General Lee has raised his army to its maximum state of efficiency, and before Meade's conscripts have become steady in action, he will advance upon the enemy and make one more effort to remove him from the soil of Virginia, or put him beneath it. This is conjecture and may be as far from the truth as words could carry me.

Every announcement from Charleston adds to the certainty of our sad expectation since Beauregard in madness or blind stupidity allowed the south end of Morris Island to fall into the hands of the enemy, notwithstanding the sacrifice of the few brave men who did see its importance and endeavour to hold it [sic]. I have seen nothing but the loss of the whole island and the destruction of that wretched Fort on which all the efforts of blind leaders seem to have been concentrated when it was plain to all eyes that nothing but the cowardice or indecision of the enemy prevented the breaching of it long since. What will be the fate of Charleston now depends upon the nerve of her soldiers and the sagacity of the commander in whom my confidence is but small. If Charleston is taken and [inroads] are made next winter I shall endeavour to obtain a transfer to Carolina & some command in the Militia.

Goodbye. God help the old State and save and bless you all. Love to Pa & Sophie & Ella, to Aunt C., Mamie and Emmie.

The man who is to carry my letter is waiting.

Alexander C. Haskell, Headquarters, McGowan's Brigade, Camp near Orange Courthouse, Va., to Charles T. Haskell (UNC)
24 August 1863
Dear Pa,

In the midst of our perfect repose on our war worn battle fields, we listen with intense interest to every breath that brings us tidings of the death struggle going on in our dear Old State. Every man forgets that he has said 'I have seen enough of battle and of blood' and wishes in his heart that he might be permitted to join his countrymen in defense of his home and honour, and in the breach of every fort be the last to dishonour his name and State by the cowardly surrender which has marked the close of all our sieges. God grant that though every fort and every gun may be shattered by the terrible engines of our enemy, in the hearts of our soldiers these may still be for the State a defence which nothing but death can break down or destroy. When this is done, and all the good and brave fallen, God will himself defend the weak & unprotected for whom so many lives have been offered up. Last night we heard that Fort Sumter had been blown up after the removal of all the valuable guns.[1] If the latter be true I can hardly regret that the Fort is destroyed. Too long the object of misplaced solicitude and interest to our mistaken commanders its possession has led to the manifest neglect of positions infinitely more valuable and which timely labour would have rendered

---

[1] In August and September 1863, Fort Sumter was subjected to heavy bombardments by Federal batteries on Morris Island and by ironclad warships. By September 2, Fort Sumter was demolished, its guns silenced, but Confederate forces remained in the fort.

almost impregnable. One more such work as Fort Wagner placed on the south end of Morris Island, and so far as human vision can go, Charleston would still have been proudly secure. But so it was not willed. The man to whom its defence was intrusted by citizens and commander, presented the shameful spectacle of a man forgetful of duty and honour seeking only to enrich himself in the moment of his country's misfortunes, not his country's either, for I will never recognize citizenship with Ripley or any of his kind.[2]

This is one of the plain and positive acts of retribution which ought to make people think that we cannot hope soon to see peace without a moral reformation.

Supposing Morris Island given up, Fort Sumter destroyed and our soldiers and guns removed to Sullivan's & James Island & Charleston—we have still positions outside of the line which was the chosen one of the ablest man we have in command, Pemberton. When we are reduced to Charleston & the mainland we can still make a long and perhaps successful defence.

Langdon passed a few minutes ago. Joe I see every day nearly. Both quite well. My letter was written before breakfast and now late in the day. I am obliged to hurry in the last words as the carrier waits. I notify you—I believe this is businesslike—that I may have to accept your offer soon of a horse. I lent my half blind purchase to Joe while I was fattening & restoring to health the broken down horse, and much to the poor fellow's concern my horse was stolen from him. I am glad to say that I am succeeding in rapidly restoring Joe's horse to good condition, & when I send him back a new and better horse to his hard riding master I may have to buy one for myself. John is still at Fredericksburgh.

Love to Ma, Ella & Sophie, Aunt Charlotte and Mamie & Emmie. I heard from Lottie McCord yesterday & from Aunt Louisa that all were well in Columbia & that Baby was expected that day, the 14th. I am really grieved that you have to give her up. Love to the boys. Goodbye. God bless you all and help our State.

Alexander C. Haskell, Headquarters, McGowan's Brigade,
to Sophie Haskell (SCHS)
25 August 1863
My dear Sophie,

I have long since written you down as a lazy girl or a self indulgent one who will not make the effort to write to me when it is disagreeable to do so.

---

[2] General Roswell Sabine Ripley was a native of Ohio who married into a prominent South Carolina family. He was put in command of the First Military District of South Carolina in early 1863. Ripley had a reputation for (among other shortcomings) heavy drinking and moral looseness.

I will however in consideration of the mails give you the benefit of the doubt and lay aside my just indignation sufficiently to give you a temperate scolding. I know writing is good for young people and specially good for you. It is a safety valve. You can pour out confidences, indulge in reflections, wander in dreamland in a manner which the restraints of presence and the fear of ridicule prohibit in conversation. Now although these restraints are very salutary it is pleasant sometimes to escape from beneath them, and the pleasantest medicine for the party who evades the law is this ancient stilus whether it make its mark upon the bark of the papyrus, tablets of Roman [war], sheets of rosy tinted note paper, or the plain Confederate sheet, upon which latter I suspect more of doubt & hope, and love & sorrow, war and trouble, trust in God and noble vows to Liberty have been inscribed than upon all the others put together in any like portion of the life of this world in which for a time we move. This door gives liberty to many a tender, beautiful or noble thought which shrinking from vulgar observation would never have stalked through the broad customhouse gate of social intercourse, where every idea of the brain & every emotion of the heart must pay its tax to the exacting conventions and prejudices of the world. But pen and paper must not be abused as I am now guilty of doing, except I find excuse in the virtuous pleasure of communicating with home. There is an excess of the mania for writing which the Latin satirist has horribly called "Cacoethes scribiendi."[3] This must be avoided (you see, on principle I give you two Latin words in each letter to stimulate your studies but must translate for yourself with the last two I sent you & let me see if your version is correct.)

I went yesterday evening to see a review of General Richard Anderson's Division. It passed very handsomely before our Lieut. General A. P. Hill. Its thin but steady ranks and tattered banners both illustrated the past and gave high promise for the future. Each time that a precious ration of our army is consumed in the fire of battle, the value of the remaining columns, like the volumes of the Sibyl, undergoes a two fold increase. The work that one year ago was assigned to a hundred thousand men is now given with confidence to thirty thousand. This saves us from despondency when we look upon our constantly diminishing battalions. Tis true the same applies but not in near so high a degree to our enemy, and now that he is reduced to conscripts if we can strike him while these raw troops are cumbering his ranks we will pass like the scythe through the grain. I would be glad if you could see the army once at least but I am thankful that our country is spared its presence. It is a terrible visitant upon any community, as any army must be. I fear too

---

[3] This Latin phrase means a mania for writing and comes from a satirical poem by Juvenal, a Roman author.

that we will see enough of armed men in South Carolina before the next year is over. If so I hope to be among its defenders. We are in great doubt about Charleston—can't make out what is being done. We only hope and pray that our soldiers will not disgrace their country or be unworthy of their noble comrades who have shewn them the path to glory and honour, and this in war is the only path to safety.

Joe and Langdon were with me yesterday, both well. Tell Mamie that I got her kind and very welcome letter. I have answered it some time ago but fear she may have missed my letter. I am determined to provoke you & Emmie into writing a defence of yourselves by the number and length of my epistles. Get a patent letter writer & copy a few pages. I can at least see by this the style of your chirography. Write one whenever you have anything to say about yourself or anything else. I shall always be glad to hear from my dear sister. Love to Pa & Ma, Aunt C., Mamie & Emmie. Don't spare the ponies in this cool pleasant autumn weather that has surprised us so soon after the dog days.

Alexander C. Haskell, Headquarters, McGowan's Brigade, Camp near Orange Court House, Va., to Charles T. Haskell (SCHS)
3 September 1863
Dear Pa,

Four days ago I was overwhelmed by receiving six letters in one evening, one from yourself, one from Ma & one from Sophie, one from Hannah McCord, another from Aunt Louisa and the sixth, from a one armed classmate who is resting from his battlefields where he left his other arm, asking my advice about going into service in his maimed condition, & giving me at the same time most interesting accounts of events & sentiment in South Carolina. I had been suffering for a day or two with so violent an inflammation of the eyes that I could barely get at the contents of my letters, and for three days since have been too blind to write. My eyes have however recovered as suddenly as they failed me & I write today without trouble. I must beg you to present my thanks to Ma & Sophie and my promise to avail myself of restored eyesight, to answer them very soon. I find so much pleasure in the letters I get from home that the correspondence will never flag on my part. Of course all the letters have been full of Charleston & I am rejoiced to see marks of a proper spirit prevailing. I was ashamed at first not by the successes of the enemy, so much as by the dullness & inertness of our commanders which made such success possible. This has changed and with this change my fears have resolved themselves into the settled conviction that if Charleston is taken it will be either by the fault of the troops or by the folly of the commanders, or both combined. It can and should be held. And if our

Brigade could obtain the privilege of joining in the fight I would stake my reputation that part of the line would never fail. But so far I have no complaint to make of the conduct of the troops, except that I believe fine infantry well commanded could have swept every invader from Morris Island before they made themselves so strong. I am not sure but that this could be done even yet. Our line of battle would about reach across the Island, and let these old soldiers go home upon condition of retaking Morris Island I believe they would clear it & still save three or four hundred alive out of the fifteen hundred we have left.[4]

The removal of Ripley & the highly complimentary promotion of so fine an Engineer as Gilmer to take command, is the best possible presage of brilliant success. Gilmer drew out a plan of defence, presented it to the President as Colonel of Engineers, the President hands him a commission as Major General & tells him to execute that which he has so ably planned. This is the way Napoleon made soldiers, and this is all that is lacking to make our Army complete. Once establish a Legion of Honour whose badge is a brilliant promotion & we will have leaders who can carry our noble soldiers through anything. Genl Lee has been in Richmond for a week past. The President & himself are no doubt taking into consideration the state of this continent & the civilised world, & upon this will build the plan of the coming campaign. I have been trying to follow them with my feeble brain, & see only two plans, the first of which is immensely perilous, but brilliant, the second, safe & uncompromising. Either to adopt a line south of Washington, cross Rappahannock & Potomac with a pontoon train too monstrous for description, take Baltimore & then Washington after a battle fought between the two places. Or secondly, to hold a strong line between Richmond & the Rappahannock, defying the enemy to battle & thus hold him in check until the agitations of the Presidential canvass next spring. If the armies in the west & on the coast can hold their own, I believe the latter plan would be the safest. We will see how far we come from the truth. I have had a presage of battle on my birthday, if we miss that I shall begin to look upon the latter policy as the one adopted, and by November we shall begin to try to get to the scene of war in So. Carolina, but this is too far ahead to be counting. For the present we are all well & safe. I saw all the boys yesterday, & the day before. All well. John was with me yesterday up from Fredericksburgh to see Genl Lee on some artillery business, looking fatter & better than when I saw him last. Love to Ma & Sophie, Aunt C. & Mamie & Emmie.Love to the boys & Ella when you see her.

---

[4] Confederate forces withdrew from Morris Island on September 6, 1863.

Alexander C. Haskell, Headquarters, McGowan's Brigade,
to Sophia C. Haskell (UNC)
5 September 1863
Dear Ma,

It is long past midnight but as I am enjoying the rare luxury of two candles which have been inspiring me in the composition of a lengthy petition to be presented by the commanders of [Regiments] to the critical severity of General Lee. I will write a few lines in answer to your long pleasant letter of the 30th Aug., received late this evening. My three of four days of semi-blindness broke up my system of letter writing and everything else in my office, so that I have since been pretty busy and am afraid have neglected you. Our unfortunate commander Col. Hamilton returns tomorrow and tonight has been spent in charging the first mine which it is hoped will waft him gently & easily out of his command, with a subdued explosion, but if this fails there is a much more violent process in store for him from which he will hardly escape. It is really very hard to be obliged to do such unpleasant things & to see how one's efforts to do a plain but painful duty complicate you in other people's petty, selfish schemes. Col. Hamilton has had fair warning. I got a friend to write to him beforehand to tell him that a struggle was in store for him before he should settle into his coveted command. We expect him tomorrow as we were agreeably disappointed by his non arrival today.

My fears on the subject of Charleston are much relieved. All that I hear of Gilmer is highly in his favour.[5] He is not as supposed a young man, but age has not injured him. If the people will only reform their morals and give a ready obedience to the dictates of charity, humanity and patriotism, all will be well, & the siege of Charleston will be among the triumphs of the war.

I see that General Johnston is relieved of his command, it is said at his own request, to attend Genl. Pemberton's Court of Inquiry.[6] If this be so he never ought to be put back at the head of his army, which he is willing to leave at so critical a time. I fear that Hardee his successor is not a man of much ability but we must bide his trial.[7] He may be a genius. I believe I am heretical in saying but with all my admiration for Genl. Johnston's manly, soldierly character, I never have been able to look upon him as a great General. He is without exception the worst manager of an army among our chief generals, & where he has fought (Seven Pines) he made one of the most

---

[5] Major General Jeremy Francis Gilmer (1818-83) was the chief of the Confederate Engineer Bureau.

[6] After he surrendered Vicksburg, Mississippi, John Clifford Pemberton was made the subject of a Court of Inquiry, but it never assembled due to the exigencies of war.

[7] This was General William Joseph Hardee (1815-73).

complete botches of the war. I feel very cheerful about the situation in general. If Bragg can hold his own, Charleston & Mobile will stand & we can hold this line for a century. If we can only keep the enemy at arm's length until the dead of winter, we have him. He will have his own battles at the ballot box & in the army, to fight next spring, when the greedy claimants so long kept out of office muster their bands for the next contest for Presidential spoils. We will have peace in a year & that looks now like a very little while. It is said that our English fleet will positively be over in six weeks.[8] I wonder if it can be true. It looks probable. What a good [answer] it will be for Mr. Davis & Mr. Mallory to give to the people.[9]

Love to Pa & Sophie, Aunt Charlotte, Mamie & Emmie. John is up her for a visit. I will give him your letter in the morning.

Alexander C. Haskell, Headquarters, McGowan's Brigade,
to Charles T. Haskell (SCHS)
8 September 1863
Dear Pa,

I got a short letter from you last night. I will remember your suggestions in case any business transactions are necessary. For the present there is no such necessity. You can tell any of those roaming horse thieves for such are the dismounted cavalry who talk about impressment to which they have no earthly right or authority, that if any of them lay a finger upon any of our horses I will hunt them out in the remotest corner of this army with such authority as will make them disgorge their plunder. In case impressments ever do become necessary you can save any favourite horse by substituting a sound serviceable horse in its place. Such you can always get for money only giving mules. I am in favour of giving up all luxuries which will be really useful to government and it would be right to offer the black horses and all such. I don't think it could ever be necessary to give up delicate thoroughbreds or your own old horse or the girls' ponies. If impressments do commence you may consider Miss Slouch as impressed by me and send her to report at these headquarters.

I have written in the last few days all I could guess of army movements. [Straws] floating about indicate a coming commotion in the military ele-

---

[8] The "English fleet" refers to ships built in Great Britain and expected to be brought into Confederate service. In early September 1863, the foreign minister of the United States warned the British authorities of dire consequences if two ironclads known as the Laird Rams were completed and allowed to be released to the Confederates. The rams were detained by the British government and never turned over to the Confederate States.

[9] Stephen Russell Mallory (1812-73) was the Confederate Secretary of the Navy.

ment. Whether the tide will roll towards Washington or Tennessee is still doubtful. I am beginning to incline to Tennessee. It is said that Ewell's Corps will go. I think it more probable that it will be A. P. Hill's. Either of them will be a great help to Bragg, and though both quit Virginia for any place but South Carolina we will have the satisfaction of knowing that we are defeating the enemy upon his chosen route into the heart of Georgia and the Carolinas. We will buckle up again right cheerfully. I have always been afraid of the enemy making a desperate effort to cut us in two parts making the shears meet us in our own up country, Charleston & Chattanooga being the starting points. They may try the game but I think will not succeed, and I am quite willing to be thrown as one of the obstacles across the path of ruin to our home. Our rations are all strong now & we will have to make judicious [combinations].

Love to Ma & Sophie, Aunt C., Mamie & Emmie, to Ella & the boys. Joe & Langdon are quite well. John [too] is looking better.

Alexander C. Haskell, Headquarters, McGowan's Brigade,
to Sophia C. Haskell (UNC)
13 September 1863
Dear Ma,

John is sitting by me. He has just come up to have it decided whether he is to take command of a Battalion of Artillery in this army, or whether he will go to the West with General Longstreet. General Lee has just sent an answer saying that it is impossible to assign him to the command here until he hears from the present commander, Major Henry. It seems that Major Henry is on his way to Chattanooga of which fact Genl. Lee is not aware. He therefore grants John the alternative desired, permitting him to go to the West with Genl. Longstreet. It may be that it will result in his remaining in this army when the General learns that the only difficulty has been removed by Henry's departure. John goes to Richmond in the morning. If he goes to Chattanooga he will spend a few days at home.

The enemy cavalry has been driving Genl. Stuart from Culpepper towards our lines all day.[10] The cannonade was severe for a little while this afternoon. We cannot learn that the infantry has approached but it is rumoured that the whole army has crossed the Rappahannock is coming against us. If so we are ready waiting and willing to do all that we can to help our country. A good victory would cheer the people. I think we can win one.

---

[10] General Meade's army occupied Culpeper Court House, Va., on September 13, 1863.

I am just going to bed and hope to have a quiet night. It is very aggravating to be roused and set to work before the first round. Sleep is thoroughly enjoyed. We may relapse into perfect quiet in a day or two or we may fight. Of course the paper will supply you with such information by telegraph long in advance of my letters. These affairs came on us very quietly and with gentle warnings that I hope are profitable. I went to church this morning with Langdon and had the happiness of kneeling, at least two of us together, at the Communion table. This solemn service, always stirring to the very depths of our hearts, eliciting all the love and adoration in our natures, is peculiarly impressive in this life of danger and separation from those upon whom our love and hopes of earthly happiness are fixed. A soldier of this long standing cannot feel homesick. There is none of that weak, languishing sentiment left, but I am astonished to observe in others what I feel in myself, the steady increase of the feeling which carries all our thoughts to our homes, & prompts and regulates our actions by this memory.

For tonight I say again "all quiet." For the future may God guide and preserve us, and give us that success which will bring with it peace and happiness to the country. Orders have just come to cook one day's rations "& be ready to move"—a further indication of activity in some direction. Goodbye. Love to Pa & Sophie, Aunt C & the girls. God bless you all.

Alexander C. Haskell, Headquarters, McGowan's Brigade,
to Charles T. Haskell (UNC)
14 September 1863
Dear Pa,

I wrote last night to say that John was with me and in a state of entire uncertainty as to his movements. He received communications in the evening from Genl. Pendleton & from General Lee equivalent to orders to proceed to Chattanooga.[11] This morning however when he went to Genl. Lee to get his orders, he was assigned to the command of Henry's Battalion with which he has been for some time associated, Henry having gone to the west. This arrangement will probably be made permanent.

We were under orders all last night. I was roused several times to receive general orders of increasing significance until it came to one to march at dawn this morning. We are still however in camp at one o'clock and have just received an order to have two day's rations cooked and put in the haversacks. This portends a march tonight or tomorrow morning. It is probable that Genl. Meade has crossed the Rappahannock, emboldened by his

---

[11] This was Brigadier General William Nelson Pendleton (1809-83), who served as General Lee's chief of artillery for much of the war.

knowledge of Longstreet's departure. In our wing of the army we learnt first the particulars of Longstreet's movement from the New York Herald, so perfect is their system of espionage.

A few days may find us again measuring our strength in the jungles of the Wilderness, for I think Meade will incline to that point if he wishes to attack. We will have an army very nearly as large as that with which we defeated Hooker's full force on the same spot, and though without the martial inspiration of Jackson to guide us, I think we still have the highest hope and brightest prospects of success. Col. Hamilton is in command. This fills me with fears for the brigade, but I believe that it will be difficult to conceive a complication of affairs in which our brave regiments will not now take care of their own success and reputation. His case progressed very rapidly and satisfactorily until it reached the War Department, but there seems delay.

Langdon is well, saw him this morning. Love to Ma, Sophie, Aunt C. and Mamie & Emmie. I can't telegraph my messages so that letters of this sort are all forestalled by the newspapers, but they may serve to shew you how near we can come to a fight without having one, and teach you how to value such reports.

Goodbye. God bless you all.

Alexander C. Haskell, Headquarters, McGowan's Brigade,
to Sophia C. Haskell (UNC)
14 September 1863
Dear Ma,

I received your letter of the 6th late this evening. It brings my last news from home and a good deal from yourself to furnish me with reflection. I am happy to hear that John & Joe have written to you something concerning their state of mind and preparation. A young soldier who has embraced his cross and fights under the banner of Christ in the service of his country, although he may be the subject of the tenderest solicitude, can never have the worst fears and anxieties hanging about him, and in the time when man meets man and his faith and courage exalt him above petty fears and cares, he becomes sublime in the eyes that watch and love him. I do believe that John & Joe are sustained in their moral battles as well as in those of their country, by a faith and spirit higher and purer than could possibly be derived from mere education & association however perfect these might have been.

I do think it would be well for you to write to them plainly and affectionately as you have in this letter to me. Your words I think would work with them more for good than anything that could come from anybody else. I do not blame where I cannot judge, but it does appear to me that more zeal exhibited by our Bishop and clergy by their exertions in person holding open the gates of the Church would have been blessed in this army in the most wonderful manner. In my brigade the soldiers have never since the war began been so happy and so joyous. They have never been so free from punishment and restraint of any sort, and yet there has never been so little commission of fault of any kind. With this healthy more tone is exhibited a corresponding warmth and earnestness upon matters of religion. Scarce a day passes without religious exercise in some part of the brigade, and as I write the hymns from the mighty prayer meeting resound from several directions in our beautiful little camp. Where chaplains are not present (& we have but one with the brigade), earnest, zealous soldiers conduct the services, or obtain the assistance of a neighbouring chaplain or a missionary of whom a good many have been with us this summer.[12]

There is no fictitious enthusiasm. I have not heard the word revival since I have been here in connection with these services. No catchwords or devices are resorted to for the purpose of attracting numbers. It is the serious, solemn awakening of hope among men who for years have been walking face to face with all the darkness and horror of a sudden and hopeless death. May God grant that thousands of these our brave comrades may have this weight of doubt and fear taken from their souls and that they will enter with a still higher and more joyful courage upon the battlefields which still lie stretched before us.

I wrote a few lines this morning to tell you that John will remain in this army for the present. I told you too of our state of expectation and readiness to meet the enemy. All is doubtful still but the tide has been rolling nearer and nearer all day. Towards sunset the cannonade became loud and near and occasional rattles of musketry could be heard. I don't know what troops had been thrown to the outposts or to what extent they were engaged. It looks very much as if we would have a battle today or tomorrow or next day. I am glad Joe is away for this time, and if it comes soon John will not be able to get up to us. I would not wish either of them to avoid danger or duty, but if their orders and their duty remove them from one battlefield I feel a right to be glad. I hope Genl. Wilcox will be very strict and confine Langdon to in-

---

[12] In his history of McGowan's Brigade, J. F. J. Caldwell noted that a remarkable "general interest" in religion was manifested in the brigade around this time. "The most ordinary preachers drew large congregations; scarcely a day passed without a sermon; there was not a night, but the sound of prayer and hymn-singing was heard. Often, two or three sermons were preached at once in the brigade, and if there was none among us, we went to the other brigades to hear." Caldwell, *The History of a Brigade of South Carolinians*, 113.

spection duties which sometimes are not quite so dangerous as those of an aide-de-camp in a brigade.[13]

This letter cannot alarm you, for you will hear either of the quieting or bursting of this storm long before this reaches you.

I hear pretty often of Baby. She does not seem to be very well. I hope you will see her & kiss her for me if you should go to Columbia. She must not forget you and twice every year must pay you a long visit. Give my love to Pa and Sophie, to Aunt Charlotte and Mamie & Emmie. Remember Ella and the boys when they come home, and Cousin Follie if she is with you. Goodbye. God bless you all.

P.S. Col. Hamilton is in command. I try to remember your advice. I try to be both "prudent & just." I tried specially to be just and it seems I was prudent, for another commander I feel sure will be given to the brigade, and yet to my surprise he is very friendly with me. If we go into battle soon I shall help him as much as I can, and will do my best for the brigade as it will amount pretty much to commanding it. Above all I will try to do my best in all battles now or hereafter, for my country and my God, and trust to Him for protection here and mercy hereafter. Goodbye.

Alexander C. Haskell, Headquarters, McGowan's Brigade,
to Sophie Haskell (UNC)
16 September 1863
Dear Sophie,

I have a moment before the mail goes to write that all seems quiet this morning. The enemy appeared & established a line pretty near us, but has not pushed on with an offer of battle. He is probably masking a movement down the Rappahannock towards Fredericksburgh.

Perhaps General Meade has discovered that we have an army in his front notwithstanding that we have sent reinforcements to Chattagnooga and to Charleston.

We have now very nearly the force with which we fought the fight at Chancellorsville against a much larger army than Meade can bring into the field.

Love to all. Goodbye for the present.

---

[13] Cadmus Marcellus Wilcox (1824-90) was promoted to the rank of major general in early August 1863 and assigned command of Pender's Division, which included McGowan's Brigade.

Alexander C. Haskell, Headquarters McGowan's Brigade,
to Sophia C. Haskell (UNC)
19 September 1863
Dear Ma,

I don't like to let the day pass by without writing to let you know that all is well and quiet in a time of constant alertness & expectation like the present. We received marching orders last night but after cooking and getting ready we hear nothing more. We infer therefore that the occasion may have passed by.

I write though amid rain and gloom. The day is stormy and lowering and as I write, the solemn march of death from the ringing instruments of brass which speak it trumpet tongued and the roll & sad beat of the muffled drum—which even in death marks the time for the guilty soldiers last steps as he is led to the stake at which he must expiate his crimes—come with fearful distinctness and fall upon my ear with a power of eloquence which is impossible to realise without having undergone this suffering. Two of the victims of [evil] cowardice, treason and the instigation of that North Carolina traitor Holden[14] are to be shot in five minutes in sight if I would look up, and in full hearing of my tent from which I write and in which I have sought refuge in a letter. It is wrong perhaps to be [word unintelligible].

How long will the people of North Carolina permit this pestilence to walk among them? How long to lead their deluded soldiers to the stake of execution & how long incite the ignorant and seditious population to treason & rebellion? If I were a citizen or especially a soldier of North Carolina, I would in my heart believe that I did my God's and my Country's work, in killing that cunning devilish traitor. He revels in every execution of a North Carolinian. He gloats over their dead bodies. The Vampire drains from these the food which sustains the unnatural, despicable party which he has created and delights to foster. It would be well for all to remember these [facts] and as they will against the government, they can effect nothing but their ruin & destruction. The government is trusted by the army, the army is represented by the government, and we the army claim that we truly represent the truth, the worth and the strength of the people. Our name is not "the Army." Our name is "the People." The great, the true people risen in arms to defend our freedom, our country, our homes, our women and old men and little children. And whoever presuming to forge our name and calling itself "the people" raises a voice or commits an act against "the true people"

---

[14] William Woods Holden (1818-92), a prominent North Carolina newspaperman and politician, became the leader of a "peace movement" in the state, promoting a new political party called the Conservative Party.

by striking at their chosen heads & representative will find a ready punishment at the hands of the army which they seem to forget whenever they
speak of the political power of the people.

The army is strong and whenever it chooses will rule. It does not now
choose to discover, claim and punish the traitors, cowards and deserters.
And let no portion of the people at home deceive themselves with the vain
hope that their resistance can avail. For the future let them seek to protect
their friends or at least expose them only to an honourable death by keeping
them in the ranks of the army.

There is a class at home, the virtuous and patriotic supporters of the
army, the producers of all that is necessary for our existence, and who in
friends and children & money have staked their all in the army. With these
we feel a sympathy & would that they should have a stronger voice at home.
But there is another class who reverse this order. Instead of supporting the
war, the war is made to support them, and not content with support, they
claim riches. They obtain riches & with riches [claim] power [*word unintelligible*] importance to call themselves "the people." I suppose this is the class
the Mercury submits to serve and play the mouthpiece when it dares to
speak for "the people & the Army" of South Carolina & declare that they
"have lost all confidence in the President & administration."[15] The Mercury
in its presumption has spoken falsely for the Army of South Carolina, as
represented by the soldiers in Virginia who for two bloody years have fought
under this despised President and are willing to fight under him to the end
of the war. If the Mercury would visit the army he would find his mistake
unpleasantly [obtruded] upon him. For the people he does not speak one
whit more truthfully unless it be for the bogus people I mentioned above.
and as I was going [on to say] this is the people that gives us trouble and that
we mean to punish. I have no [doubt] they [prefer] the army maybe engaged
on the frontier far away from their spoils for thirty years at least.

Pardon me, it does me good occasionally to [review] the crying [*word
unintelligible*] of the day. I generally look at the bright side which is to be
found in the endurance & hopes of [our people] & in the high condition &
spirits of the army.

Langdon is quite well. I feel better [having] occupied a half hour which
I dreaded & turned my mind into different channels.

Love to Pa & Sophie, Aunt Charlotte & the girls and all at home.

---

[15] The *Charleston Mercury* newspaper was well known for its opposition to the poli-
cies of Confederate President Jefferson Davis.

Alexander C. Haskell, Headquarters, McGowan's Brigade, in the field, to Sophia C. Haskell (UNC)
23 September 1863
Dear Ma,

We are still in our lines at the alarm posts on the upper Rapidan but the force which threatened us last evening finding a strong front opposed to this advance where he expected nothing has withdrawn. They all slipped off under cover of night. The day has passed quietly & tediously without anything to excite or interest us except the confirmation of good news from Bragg's army.[16]

I wrote last night, being really doubtful as to the chances of writing after that moment, for I know that the chiefs of the army had been expecting a battle and everything gave promise of one last evening. I hasten to correct what was for the time an error. If the enemy has really been well defeated in the west I hardly think we will have any more great battles this fall. Of course there is always a chance here if the enemy chooses to make an offer of battle, but they may not be hasty to do this if Rosencrans is badly damaged.[17] If we can recover Tennessee & hold Virginia & South Carolina we may trust with much hope I think to the strengthening of army [*sic*] during the winter, the weakening of that of the enemy, and internal dissension as soon as the Presidential campaign comes on the stage. If Providence then smiles upon us we may see afar off the beginning of peace, and if Bragg has been defeated even we may still be full of hope. I can't despair, for I must believe if I would live that what happens to us when we are striving conscientiously to do our best, must be well for us.

As I wrote last night, Col. Hamilton has been transferred to Charleston, where I pray he may do no harm. Perrin has been promoted Brigadier General & assigned to command the brigade until McGowan is fit for active duty. I trust you may soon hear good news of Joe. It is so dark I can't see my lines. Love to all. Goodbye.

---

[16] This refers to the Chickamauga Campaign. The battle of Chickamauga in Georgia, which took place on September 19-20, 1863, turned out to be a Confederate victory.

[17] Major General William Starke Rosencrans was the principal opponent of General Braxton Bragg, and was in command of the Federal forces at the Battle of Chickamauga.

John C. Haskell, Gordonsville, Va., to Charles T. Haskell (SCHS)
5 October 1863
Dear Father,

We are still in camp at this place, and all in expectation of an attack from Meade seems to have died out, but from events of the last few days I think that there will soon be an important move on our part. Provisions and corn are being brought up to the entire exclusion of everything else, and all [spare] baggage etc. sent to the rear and the only explanation is that Genl. Lee is about to move forward and needs surplus rations for this purpose or else the roads are to be soon occupied by troops going from or coming to this army, in either of which cases the surplus rations will be needed to feed the men and horses of this army while the troops occupy the rail road. The general and popular opinion is of course that Genl. Lee intends to advance and drive Meade back to Washington and I think this most probable. On the other hand some think and with a good show of reason that it is intended to further reinforce Bragg at Chattanooga and if it was not for General Lee's well known aversion to weakening his own army I would think this the most likely as well as the first plan, but I do not believe that anything short of a positive order from the War Department will soon remove another brigade of this army.

I suppose Joe is long before this out at Chattanooga. Do when you write tell me if he stopped at home and if he left Jem at home or took him with him. I have not seen Langdon or Alic for several weeks for though they are not far from me they have I suppose not had time to come to see me, while I have scarcely been out of camp from the battalion. When I took command of it was [*sic*] in such wretched condition that it has kept me busy all the time and now it is in tolerable condition both as to horses and equipment and drill and discipline, but I am on a court martial now which keeps me more closely confined than ever.[18]

I have heard [not] from home since I have been here but once when I got a letter from Ma of the fifth of last month though I am expecting letters every day and I know they take a long time to get here. Direct to me, to Haskell's Arty Battn. Army N. V. Gordonsville [or Orange] and they will be sent into wherever I am. Do give my love to Ma, Sophie, Louis and Paul and all the rest at home.

---

[18] John C. Haskell was appointed to the rank of major and given the command of a battalion of artillery in April 1863.

Alexander C. Haskell, Headquarters, McGowan's Brigade,
to Charles T. Haskell, Abbeville Court House, S.C. (UNC)
6 October 1863
Dear Pa,

I just hear of Genl. McGowan's return, probably this week. I change chiefs again, and I confess I give up Perrin with much regret. He is a soldier every inch of him. And a man who having won his own way by merit recognized and generously acted upon, has warm feeling towards the natural rights of others, apart from those rights of mere convention which govern such men as Genl. McGowan. This is no treason against my commander, but the simple truth touching men who have passed through the mill which he has been pounded in since he was thrown into it a rough fragment many years ago. He has learnt that the smoother his own rides become the less he is hurt by affriction with the other particles which are being jumbled against him in the mill. He will nor can do anything for anybody else which brings him into this harsh contact with anybody. I remain with him in spite of any services, the same boy as ever, to be glad to hold my present position on his staff. Perrin on the other hand feels what now that he is about to leave us he has taken pains to express, a high esteem and regard. As long as he remained no occasion would have been omitted for my advancement. With him my career would have been one of advancement to the point where my own abilities failed. I write these things not to be talked about. It is in confidence to you and to explain what may seem to you a strange move. If I have the opportunity I shall quit the staff to take what may appear a second rate position in the line. A splendid regiment made an effort a few days since to make me its colonel. The thing was out of order. I had to discourage it. And besides it could not be accomplished. If such another chance occurs, or even a lieut. colonelcy or majority in the brigade, I think I shall accept it. A majority does not look like much but it gives an opening. Enough of this. I have prepared your mind for revolution, and as you know that this is not my natural temper you will accede to me the probability of being in the right.

Langdon is back in the brigade, and means to delay his application for leave of absence for some time yet. All looks quiet on our lines. Axes are at work from daylight until dark, about one axe to every hundred men, cutting firewood & building little huts to protect themselves from the cold which is becoming pretty sharp. They have so few shoes & blankets that even a little cold is felt. I am in haste & forget if I had anything to write about.

I was very sorry to hear a day or two ago that Jeannie Wardlaw was very ill. I do hope that her strong constitution will carry her safely through the terrible ordeal of typhoid fever. Her illness must come heavily upon the family of which she is so much the life and happiness under their complication of troubles.

Love to Ma and all at home.

Louis W. Haskell, Willington, S.C., to Sophie Haskell (SCHS)
7 October 1863
Dear Sophie,

I thought this evening as I had nothing that I would break through my general rule and write you a letter to console you after going to the dentist. When I was at home, I saw your letter to Ma and in it saw that you had committed the extravagance of paying $50.00 for a $1.50 calico. for that is what is Cousin Follie said it would cost in good times. But one is the thing [sic] that will give you most consolation is my having five sweet little hound puppies that about the time you come home will be old enough to give you pleasant music at night. And I have four more that a Mr. McClinton is raising up this winter. I will have a first rate pack, and if your pony does not run away with you, you can hunt sometimes too.

Pa got me a very good McClellan saddle the other [*sic*] but it is a second hand one and is a little damaged. I like it a great deal better than I thought I could like that kind of a saddle. I was sorry to hear when I was at home that Cousin Em was so sick but I hope she will soon be well, and I think that a few good rides on Fenella will make her perfectly well again. But I don't know what to make of Fenella. The other day I was riding her with the McClellan saddle and I had not quite got used to the seat, and she seemed to know it, for she tried her very best to throw me.

When you come home you must ride about the country raising the subscriptions that you spoke of, but whether you do that or not you must carry out your good resolution of riding every day.

Miss Slouch sends her best love to you, and asked me to tell you her state of health, which she does not think very good and so does not eat all of her food. But she will get fat when she gets at home for I don't think any horse can prevent it.

I saw Cousin Mame when I was at home who was looking very well and went in to the village on Monday morning to see Miss Jenny.

[P.S.] Written when I ought to have been in bed.

Langdon C. Haskell, Headquarters, McGowan's Brigade,
to Sophia C. Haskell (SCHS)
7 October 1863
My dear mother,

I write now specially to beg you to get me something to clothe Edmund with, as usual I find that he has lost, worn out, and thrown away nearly everything which he had and is likely to suffer soon from the cold. I find him very hard to manage and impossible to keep him in clothes. I want a sack and pair of pants of the strictest and warmest material that can be got and a couple of osnaburgs shirts. Do get these for him if possible and have them made as substantially as possible. The pants he has had made are always too big and baggy in the waist. I would not trouble you with this, but it is impossible for me to get anything for him here and he really is in great need. I only lately discover his great destitution as he had constantly assured me that he had clothes put away which it turns out are lost. I wrote you or Ella, I forget which, some time back but I do not know whether the letter reached you. I had hoped that you would send on something for him when Gen. McGowan came on. We hear that he is coming on certainly now in a few days. I hope he is not doing so before he is in condition to assume command for it will just lead to confusion and trouble without doing the smallest particle of good. The Brigade is under an excellent commander[19] and there is no reason why he (McG.) should return if he is not entirely recovered. We got a letter from you addressed to John which has been forwarded. I have heard nothing of him except that he is at Gordonsville with his Battalion of Artillery. We are all of course waiting with the greatest anxiety to hear something more from Bragg as we cannot believe that matters will rest where they are now. As for ourselves here though it may seem hard to believe it still I think the campaign will close without any more fighting of consequence. Fighting however may commence at any day as the two armies are in sight of each other and it will only take a day or two to bring on a general engagement.

I have been glad to get good news from Ella and Chiv for some time back and I hope and trust it may continue. I hope to come home the last of this month or the beginning of next. I wrote to ask Pa to try and get me something for an overcoat. I hope he will get me something as I am obliged to have it, cost what it may. I have written to Roland Rhett to try and get some government cloth from him but I fear there is no chance there. If Pa would write to Uncle William he might be able to get something from Lee who is chief Qr Master of the Dept. Give my love to Pa and all with you.

---

[19] Brigadier General Abner Monroe Perrin.

Alexander C. Haskell, Headquarters, McGowan's Brigade,
to Charles T. Haskell (UNC)
7 October 1863
Dear Pa,

Of all the nights we have had for weeks past, this one of the most unpleasant for anything but keeping up a fire, or for sound sleeping in a snug tent. On this night of all others it is my fortune to hear the splashing tramp of couriers' horses, and sent [sic] out my own messengers bearing the most revolutionary orders. We were settling quietly into our new camp. Many of the men had built nice log houses, and now we are ordered to cook three days' rations, to draw guns, and put ammunition in order, and in short to do everything which is considered necessary in the premises to give General Meade a stubborn fight. Whether offensive or defensive, or whether it will be at all is more than I can say. But I trust and pray that if offensive, and I think it will and should be offensive, that our victory will be a crushing one. This is one of the crises of the war, and it is in these moments that we pray most fervently to God to add his crowning blessing to our efforts. Our army is barefoot and ragged, but strong & brave. If we have ever won victory by our own prowess, I think we may expect it now.

Everything indicates important events. Their shadows have fallen before them. We imagine that we see them, and feel the awe and hope & exultation which precedes our bloody efforts for the independence and peace of our country. I daresay that all our presentiments are wrong. Newspapers will tell you that. My letter will serve to shew how little we know, how blind we are who are made to lead the hundreds who look to our skill and sagacity.

I write tonight despite the general dampness of tent, paper & ideas, because it is possible I may not write again for several days. I must now go to sleep & when I awake I will be ready for what next is to be done.

Love to Ma & all at home.

I heard from Joe, 25th Sept., quite well and at Ringgold. I pray for his safety and for God's blessing upon him and upon you all in these times of trial. Good night.

Sophia C. Haskell, Home Place Plantation, Abbeville District, S.C.,
to Sophie Haskell (SCHS)
10 October [1863]
Dear Sophie,

We are all feeling very anxious about dear little Emmie. Lou's letter to Mamie last evening was somewhat a relief to us and I hope the next will be still better, but I fear the poor child is very sick and that her convalescence will be slow. If there is anything up here of food or physic, beg your Aunt to let us know and we will send it down immediately. We have a few bottles of [oil] still left. Jeannie tried one the other day and found it good. She is mending slowly but continued to have a little fever up to Thursday when [Mina] came home. She had not yet tried to sit up and was averse to making any exertion, but I think she only needs time to be quite well again. We are all well at home. Mamie seems very well and is anxious to go to Emmie as soon as her Mother thinks it expedient. Lang is flourishing. He had a great deal of company while Livie was here with her children tho the school was not interrupted for every morning Lulu had to learn her lessons and Susan to read while Follie and he went through there [*sic*] school.[20] They all left the day Mamie returned. Tell your Aunt if Mamie should leave him, I will adopt him and make him my particular companion, when none better is to be had.

I have had letters from Alec, Joe and John since I wrote last and Ella has heard from Langdon. All were well. Joe was only eight miles from Chattanooga on the R.R. He was a good deal out of humour. Their horses had not arrived and they could do nothing but advance step by step as the R.R. was completed. They had not been met by the Western Army as the heroes of the Potomac felt to be their due, and they were not very well treated in regard to their supplies of provision. These added to a pouring rain dripping on his paper as he wrote all put him in a rather cynical state of mind for our light hearted young soldier. John's letter, I think I mentioned before, it was only a request for some clothes which we sent by Gen McGowan on Wednesday last. Alec wrote a very long and merry letter to Paul inviting him and Louis to come and visit them in Camp next Winter each provided with a barrel of molasses and a bag of dried peaches and promises him a setter dog to sleep with him to keep him warm, said dog being wounded had taken shelter in his tent. His letter to me was one of the 3rd. He speaks of some movements among Ewell's forces which might be a preparation to go to Brag [*sic*] or to go against Meade, he, Alec knew nothing. I suppose you will write to the boys. Joe's address is Hd Qrs Gen Longstreet, care of Col E. P. Alexander, Chattanooga. John's is Major John C. Haskell, Commanding Battalion Artillery Richmond Va. Alec as usual. I have been trying to do as you requested to get provisions for the soldiers and will send some to the Village on Tuesday to be forwarded as soon as possible directed to your Aunt. I was at Church this morning and carried two little circulars begging for everything I could think of and gave them to Mrs. Yarborough and Mrs.

---

[20] Lulu may have been a nickname for one of Susan Olivia (Livie) Haskell Venning's children. She had five daughters, one of whom was named Eliza Lucilla Venning (1855-1932), and another, Susan Bell Venning.

Hunter who both promised to send me something on Monday and to send the papers to their neighbours.[21] Anne Thomas was here on Thursday and promised to exert herself among the members of her defunct society and make up a box also.[22] Alec says Langdon has returned to the Brigade, but says nothing of the probability of his getting the Appointment he desired but he still speaks of coming home early in November or thereabouts.

I did not get my letter written in time to send to Mrs. Thomas this evening so I will say goodbye with love to all particularly dear little Em.

Sunday Morning

We have just heard from Lang 4th Oct. He has returned to his Brigade with no prospect of any change for the present. I think it probable it all should continue quiet that he may be home in a fortnight. God bless you my darling and have you in his Holy keeping.

Joseph C. Haskell, Headquarters, Alexander's Battalion,
to Louis W. Haskell (SCHS)
12 October 1863
Dear Lewis,

I was surprised and pleased to get your pleasant letter this morning. You never have written before but I suppose that is my fault as I ought to have written to you some time, but I forget how old you are getting and still think of you as a small boy. I was completely mystified when I first looked at the letter and could not make out whether it was from Pa or Sophie but came to the conclusion that the hand was more like Pa than any one else at home.

I am very sorry that I missed Sophie in Columbia. When we left we expected to go through that way and I was determined to get left or delayed in some way but when we got to We[st] Col[umbia] they changed the route and we went through by Kingsville. I thought of getting off and going the other way but I found that I could be of a good deal of use by remaining and determined to do so with the best grace I could. I could not have trusted my horses with any one else who would have attended to them as that little scamp Jim is worse than no one at all. I wish very much I could have come

---

[21] According to a U.D.C. history, there were numerous women's associations in South Carolina organized for the relief of soldiers. In Abbeville and environs, there were four, including a knitting society and a hospital (formed in 1865), and "Mrs. Chas. Haskell" is listed as a member of the latter. Mrs. Armistead Burt was the president of the Abbeville Soldiers' Aid Society, which sent supplies to soldiers in the army. *South Carolina Women in the Confederacy*, 21-25, 69.

[22] This may have been E. Annie Thomas (1841-99), the daughter of Thomas Walker Thomas and Elizabeth H. K. Thomas.

home or by Columbia as I have a splendid mare that I brought from Maryland with me which I wanted to leave with Pa and breed more. She is over 16 hands, dark brown, long arched neck. Her limbs are a little delicate. Aleck thinks for the body which is tremendous, her fault is the length of her back. This does not hurt her though she is as active as a cat and I have jumped her over a creek 13 feet broad. She is too large to ride and I can't get enough to feed her on, two great objections, so I am going to swap her off as soon as our battery horses arrive, which will be today or tomorrow. When we left Va. I swapped my brown horse which I bought in Richmond for a mare which the bugler of the Battalion had ridden since Va. seceded. She was a public horse and had to be turned in with the other. The old Dutchman was in despair and was delighted when I proposed to turn in my horse and bring his out in his place. He comes over every day now to look at Fanny and play with her. She is a perfect little lady, the prettiest thing you ever saw. About 10 hands and an inch, bright sorrel with white hind feet and a star in her forehead. She has a beautiful head, neck, and limbs, very compactly built, short back and very large round the girth, with the prettiest action you ever saw. If we both get through out here, I am taking care of her in hopes that I may be able to send her home to Sophie.

Take care of those hounds. If I get a chance to come home, I want to take a run with them after foxes, rabbits, or something else. There is no chance of my getting off now. The President is out here and everyone thinks we will have stirring time soon. Col. Alexander has just come in from a reconnaissance and I expect his report will lead an expedition which will make a move somewhere.[23] If it succeeds you will read of it soon enough. If it fails it won't make much difference in the law of affairs out here.

Tell Ma I will answer her letter in a day or two. These are the first I have received. I don't know what have become of all I have written. I want some socks and drawers very much, and Jim wants everything. He is in the most destitute condition imaginable. A suit of homespun, strongly made and large enough with buttons that could not come off would be invaluable. Give my love to Duff and tell him I want to hear from him. Love to Ma and Pa and all at home.

---

[23] Col. Edward P. Alexander's diary for October 1863 had only three entries: "Oct. 5th, Monday. Shelled Chattanooga. Oct. 10-12. Reconnaissance of Bridgeport. Oct. 30, Friday. Occupied Lookout Mountain & shelled everything daily until Nov. 4th." Alexander, *Fighting for the Confederacy*, 301.

Sophia C. Haskell, Home Place Plantation, Abbeville District, S.C.,
to Sophie Haskell (SCHS)
18 October 1863
Dear Sophie,

I received your little letter last night and we were a little put out on finding no news from Emmy. Your Aunt's letter of Wednesday previous, though it said she was better, had made us feel more anxious about her; but on consideration we decided that your not mentioning her was the best proof that she was on the mend. We shall all be glad to see you back again and will do our endeavor to make home as pleasant to you as we can, though I feel more and more that it is hard for me now to be a pleasant companion for the young. I feel like the old dresses and bonnets of twenty years back— too old fashioned for use and not old enough to be interesting as an antiquity. You come home my dear little girl to be comforted and I pray God to be with you and give you grace to worthily take upon yourself the vow of serving Him in spirit and in truth. Look to your heart and strive to cultivate a spiritual feeling to make God first as much as you can, do this and all things will be added unto you. If the heart is right it is wonderful how everything else soon becomes right too. Don't think my dear I expect you to be able to do this but try for it. I know how hard it is and I feel how poor are all ones performances, how little comfort doing right in the eyes of the world can give, we feel we have not the approbation of God that we have not worked to please him. I wish I could guide and teach you better. I feel how little worthy to have the happiness of seeing my young children one by one turning to God in their youth. But I can pray for you and pray God to give you the guidance of His own spirit to lead you in the way you should go.

I have heard nothing from any of the boys since the letters I sent you. We are feeling much anxiety now that Lee's army is again in motion. Its operations have been carried on with so much secrecy that we hardly can conjecture what Lee is after. We must wait with all the patience we can the development of this crisis of the war. Do try and see your Uncle and arrange with him about coming up. If you could ride out some morning and stop at the Bank and send for him to come out and see you it might be the easiest way of arranging it with him. Be sure to let us know in time so that we could send Louis to meet you at Cokesbury if you should have no one to come all the way with you. Slouch came home in a very sad condition. She had been very sick and was extremely reduced, refusing to eat anything when she came home. No one could account for her sickness. She is much better now and has recovered her appetite and spirit. Do give my love to all with you and tell us how Emmy is doing now.

Alexander C. Haskell, Camp near Rappahannock River,
to Sophia C. Haskell (UNC)
20 October 1863
Dear Ma,

You have seen many mentions of rumours of fights in which Hill's Corps has been engaged. We had really but one, and that an accident, in the last hundred yards of the pursuit of Meade's army.[24] Pressing hard upon him, we struck a corps of his army strongly entrenched at Bristow Station in full sight of and very near Manassas. The two leading brigades were dashed against them and defeated with very heavy loss. Night prevented further fighting and some mistake in Ewell's Corps permitted the enemy to escape, which he did under cover of the night. Our brigade for the first time missed a share in all the fighting that could be had. We were ten minutes & half a mile out of place. Had it happened the day before we would have had it all, or would have got in the day after, but in the rotation of march we happened to be near that evening. The sufferers, for they were nothing else, were Pettigrew's old brigade and Cook's Brigade, both N.C. troops.[25]

Our cavalry behaved splendidly in the campaign and has retrieved not only its position in our own army but its lost supremacy over the Yankee cavalry. John is now in Hill's Corps (reserve) and I often see him. He bears the campaign well and is in high spirits. His health seems good.

We are quietly camped today between the Rappahannock & Culpepper. The campaign though brief has been from lack of shoes and from bad weather a very trying one, but the men stand it well. We are now in high condition and if we can only get shoes & some clothing we will be ready for anything. I hope we will be sent to conclude affairs at Chattanooga. That would be a death blow to the enemy.

The mail carrier demands my letter for the third time. I am glad to hear that Emma & Jeannie Wardlaw are better. I was very uneasy about them both. Love to Pa and all at home.

---

[24] This probably refers to a fight near Bristoe Station, Virginia, which took place on October 14, 1863, in which A. P. Hill's Corps attacked retreating rear troops of Meade's army.

[25] General John Rogers Cooke (1833-91) commanded a brigade of North Carolinians which became part of Heth's Division in October 1863. Over Cooke's protest, his brigade was ordered to attack the enemy at Bristoe Station. He was severely wounded and lost half of his 1,400 men in the engagement.

Alexander C. Haskell, Camp near Brandy Station, Va.,
to Sophia C. Haskell (UNC)
21 October 1863
Dear Ma,

Your long and welcome letter of the 11th October reached me last night. I was a little out of sorts and it did me good. I, and I suppose all, except the very best, of our soldiers, need a reminder occasionally of our duty to serve contentedly and earnestly in the positions which have been allotted to us. There is no reminder so good as a letter from home which recalls in all their force the pure and high principles which should actuate every one of us in the war and draw us back from the danger of enlisting too much professional ambition in our thoughts and exertions. It is in such moments as these that I remember that the suffering and enduring private soldier who conscientiously discharges the humble duties of his station exalts himself above all those officers who in the glitter and glory of the achievements of their commands find pleasure, and more than compensation, for their efforts and sacrifices. I believe I would not run so much risk, if I were a private soldier, of losing my temper and contentment as I do now as a staff officer with all responsibility & a very circumscribed credit, a captain for anybody who by the chances of war is thrown into a command which by me alone is unattainable. My present commander is a good one, was a captain when I was, rose to a colonelcy by a fortunate combination of circumstances. I wrote his recommendation with my own hand, made others sign it & watched its success until it passed beyond Gen. Lee approved by all. This is all well, but the Colonel who stands next as commander was long my subordinate, was promoted by the loss of a better man.[26] Any day I am liable to be following this magnate as his man Friday. I acknowledge that this ought not to fret me, but I can't help it sometimes. I have been specially aggravated of late by this prospect, since the idea of relief was held out by one of the regiments which tried to get me for its colonel, to succeed Perrin, but law & order must have their way and it is my business to enforce them.[27] So I had to quell my friends' efforts & see the aspirant rise regularly by promotion, putting the regiment under the command of a man perhaps as good as myself, but in himself certainly unfit. Thus it goes & thus it will, unless I break off from the brigade to which I am so much attached, & from the brave soldiers of which I receive such evidence of regard.

----

[26] Aleck does not name the officer who "stands next as commander" of the brigade. It may have been one of several officers who had once been captains. These included C. W. McCreary, W. P. Shooter, and A. P. Butler.

[27] Before his promotion to the rank of brigadier general, Abner M. Perrin was the colonel of the Fourteenth South Carolina Infantry Regiment.

You may observe that though I philosophize my heart is not light & has not quite become reasonable. I believe however that pure selfishness is not the only cause of low spirits. I have been much concerned to hear of poor Emma's continued illness, and from the character which is given to it (Typhoid pneumonia) I fear the worst results to one of her delicate constitution. Your letter tells me that she is a little better which is encouraging, but may mean nothing more than a fluctuation of a disease so treacherous & subtle as all Typhoid maladies. I trust she may recover without severer illness, and that this anxiety may be spared to you all who have been so acquainted with grief, for I know that anxiety for one so gentle and winning cannot be confined to her own Mother & Sister but must extend to all with whom she has been associated. I had heard of her sickness in several letters from Mrs. Singleton & others in Columbia before hearing from you, and all seemed to look seriously upon the attack.

I hope from your letter that Jeannie Wardlaw is really convalescent & past the danger which seemed to threaten that she too might be taken from the family which has suffered so much. Such illness affects me much when I see it added to all else which our friends at home are called upon to bear. Especially when it strikes as these cases, among the young & buoyant to whom we look for cheerfulness & happiness. The trial includes all and the test is being everywhere applied. I pray that we may profit by the lessons and fit ourselves for the mercy which is in store. Peace is not upon us, nor can we see it, but I cannot help thinking that I discern the glimmering dawn of the sun which is to spread such joy over the land. There is every prospect that the winter will settle upon us with the advantage resting with our arms. Next spring the armies of the enemy cannot be raised to sufficient force to seriously endanger us unless by other & more stringent laws than they yet have in force. The question will soon be decided in the elections of the enemy & we will know what to expect from their legislation. Besides this hope, there is that which looks to the distraction of the Presidential campaign which opens in May. This may assist us, and we may win independence & peace before the next year has passed away.

We all expected after driving the enemy to the Potomac that one corps of this army would go to Tennessee. There is no present indication of this. We have camped upon the Rappahannock and all is conjecture as to what will be our future movements. John is camped within a hundred yards of me. I see a great deal of him and find him doing well. I think he manages his command well and will get along pleasantly & successfully. If I were leading a line of infantry into battle I would desire no better artillerist to support me. He is bold but prudent & judicious. Langdon is quite well, will come home before very long, but I can't say exactly when. We do not know what has become of Genl. McGowan. How is he? I suppose from what I hear that he is still disabled.

You mention a keg of molasses. I assure you that nothing could be more acceptable. I have as yet heard nothing of it. Send small packages by mail & larger things, boxes, &c, by the Central Association. Private hand is the worst possible conveyance except in a few rare cases.

Love to Pa & all.

Alexander C. Haskell, Headquarters, McGowan's Brigade,
to Charles T. Haskell (UNC)
22 October 1863
Dear Pa,

We are absolutely stagnating. Everybody at fault as to the intentions of the General commanding, and nearly all a little disappointed at our inactivity. It was hoped when we dashed so boldly into the cold waters of the Rapidan on the 9th October that this flank movement would either catch Meade in his camps, cut him off & defeat him, or as it resulted, that it would rid Virginia of his army without a fight, and that as soon as this was accomplished one corps (A. P. Hill's) would take up a rapid line either for Georgia or East Tennessee, and cooperating with Bragg, drive Rosencrans from his stronghold and force him either to disadvantageous battle or the abandonment of our soil. We have neither crushed Meade nor have we flown to the assistance of Bragg, consequently we feel a little flat, though at the same time I must confess that the army is somewhat grateful that Genl. Lee could accomplish his object without spilling the blood of a third of its members. For one, and it expresses a general feeling, I am convinced that General Lee and the President act from higher intelligence than I can, and I am cheerful to submit my judgment to their decisions and take it for a thing assured that the course adopted is in all probability the wisest under the existing circumstances, whatever these may be. I see by a letter of Langdon's of the 15th that Emma is probably better. I trust this may be so, and that the amendment will continue. The duration of her fever makes it alarming.

Genl. McGowan has been for some time expected, but we see or hear nothing of him. I suppose he has been stopped somewhere on the road.

In a letter of Paul's to John I see accounts of several purchases in horses & large collection of dogs promises well for sporting for the youngsters next year, unless the impressment gobbles up your horses. I suspect that you will be obliged to turn over your fine bay horse to me. If so notify me and I will guard him against the impressing officer. I don't need him now but if I can get into the cavalry or some more extensive service than my present in the course of the winter I shall stand in great need of just such a charger, if as I conjectured, you have bought McElroy's bay. John & Langdon are quite well.

Love to Ma & all at home.

Alexander C. Haskell, Headquarters, McGowan's Brigade,
to Charles T. Haskell (UNC)
27 October 1863
Dear Pa,

The long expected barrel of molasses has just driven up to our tent door in an army wagon, quite conscious of its importance. It brings with it two jugs which to friends are very acceptable. If I can get a little Peruvian or cherry bark, I will consume I hope as much as one small bottle in this disguise to drive away the ghost of the Rappahannock ague which racked my bones a few nights ago.[28] Ever since this visitation until today I have been feeling so miserable that I could not write anything which would not have made you gape, and turned your fingernails blue in the reading. Today I feel much better and hope that the malaria is being dislodged. I have taken the regulation amount of quinine and scared off the return of fever.

John is camped within a hundred yards of me. Having nothing on my own table (or rather on the table that I have not got) that I could prevail upon myself to swallow, I went over to test John's housekeeping & found such a breakfast as I believe restored me more than the quinine. I have been a tolerably hardy soldier & thought I could eat anything & can when I am well, but we are blessed now with such an ill-regulated mess & such a beastly cook that my powers fail me. The molasses rescues me. Grumbling fills in the courses, and laughing at misfortune and tough beef & biscuit generally makes up the dessert.

The army is growing slowly, is in fine condition and will soon be well shod. Another campaign this autumn will not present the piteous spectacle of hundreds of brave men dragging their bloody bare feet & sore in the ranks where they <u>must</u> march. This is the cruel task of officers. These men may suffer, do suffer, but they must go, and the officer must see that they do go, and gives the harsh command when his heart is melting behind his pitiless face. This seems extravagant, even to men who have seen these sights, but have not thought upon them, but this is the truth. Shoes are being supplied. The generous and provident South Carolina Central Association has fur-

---

[28] Peruvian bark, also known as cinchona, was a source of quinine, a remedy for malaria. Wild cherry bark was used as a treatment for coughs and respiratory complaints.

nished 800 pair for our brigade, in which there was many a son of a well to do father crouching & trembling along on feet bare of the shoes which are being tossed from hand to hand of speculators at home.

The Yanks say we shall fight before winter and I don't think that Genl. Lee will say them nay, provided they give him battle on such terms as he can in this case exact. Meade is threatened with decapitation if he does not pursue & destroy the Rebel. And the Rebel is sitting in plain view on the bare banks of the Rappahannock. There was a good deal of fighting yesterday across the river a few miles from us. Cavalry & two divisions of infantry. We (our division) were not taken out at all. The enemy was driven back with the loss of between 200 & 300 prisoners. I don't know the loss in killed & wounded. I hear cannon and there seems to be some fighting this morning. All this disturbance is created by the Yankees absurdly trying to prevent our hauling off a few miles of R. R. iron from the north bank of the Rappahannock. They will lose more men & horses by their nonsense than all the iron on the whole road could pay for, valuing a Yankee as Lincoln does at $300 and his horse at $200.[29]

Langdon I think will start for home in a day or two. If he gets there he can stay pretty much at will, as there are no military operations in the winter and I regret to learn that Genl. McGowan certainly cannot be with us until spring. It does seem hard to suffer so great inconvenience from a wound at first considered slight.

Please tell Ma that I have received a package from Emmie with the nice pair of socks she so kindly knit for me, but that the others she mentions seem to have been lost. I am still very uneasy about poor Emmie. She must be very sick, and no letter has said yet that she is really better. I do hope that the weary fever has gone before this and that she is recovering health and strength.

I hear of Joe through home only. He seems to be in trouble, natural enough. Such a change could hardly be otherwise than unpleasant at first, but it will all come right after a while.

Idleness & winter quarters loom up before us though much may be in the interval. This cold weather existence in the mud is trying to me, happiness to others more phlegmatic. I have begun grumbling & quarrelling already. I don't know what it would come to in five months. Tell Paul I will soon answer his letter at length. I do so at present only with my thanks.

Love to Ma & all at home.

---

[29] Northern men who could afford to do so were permitted to pay a $300 fee to hire a substitute for army service.

Brigadier General Abner M. Perrin, Headquarters, McGowan's Brigade, Camp near Brandy, to General Samuel Cooper, Adjutant and Inspector General, C.S.A., Richmond, Va.[30] (UNC)
31 October 1863
General,
I would beg leave most respectfully to submit the name of Captain Alexander C. Haskell, Assistant Adjutant General of this Brigade, as a young officer in every way worthy of an appointment to some office in the Provisional Army more fitting his talents and more in keeping with his long and distinguished service, than the position he now holds.

Captain Haskell entered the Army of South Carolina about the 1st of January 1861 in the Regiment commanded first by the late Brigadier General Gregg, and was soon commissioned Adjutant of that Regiment. He has been continuously in the service ever since, and upon the appointment of Colonel Gregg Brigadier General he was appointed his Adjutant General, which office he has held most ably and satisfactorily up to the present time.

I would recommend that Captain Haskell be appointed Colonel in the Provisional Army and ordered to report to some Brigade where vacancies may exist in some of the Regiments from South Carolina.

I make this recommendation on the grounds of gallantry and skill, and would particularly refer to his conduct in the battle of Fredericksburg on the 13th of December last, and Chancellorsville, for the circumstances, as coming within my immediate observation, of his exhibiting these qualities. In the battle of Fredericksburg, when the right of the Brigade was surprised and swept away by the enemy, and General Gregg mortally wounded, his coolness and daring courage were mainly instrumental in keeping the two right Regiments of the Brigade from being routed from the field, and in having other Regiments so disposed as to repel the enemies [*sic*] attack. In this he was severely wounded.

At Chancellorsville he was again preeminent for the same high soldierly qualities. He went forward in every instance at the head of the Brigade and his courage and skill was of incalculable service in the attack upon the enemies entrenched position. He was again severely wounded at the enemies breastwork and consequently disabled from taking part in the Pennsylvania Campaign. He was equally distinguished at Sharpsburg and other battles he has been in.

---

[30] This is Aleck's copy (in his hand) of General Abner M. Perrin's letter to General Samuel Cooper (1798-1876), the Adjutant General and Inspector General of the Confederate Army.

Captain Haskell is a young officer of fine education. He is remarkable for coolness & good judgment and has all the dash and true pride of the profession of arms that can be claimed for any officer.

It was General Maxcy Gregg's dying request that Captain Haskell should be recommended for promotion.

I would state furthermore that no family in South Carolina has contributed more or made greater sacrifices than the immediate family of Captain Haskell. Six brothers have been in the war from the first, all of whom have earned the most honourable distinction. His brother Captain William T. Haskell of the First Regt. S.C.V. was killed at Gettysburg while in command of a Battalion of picked sharp shooters. Another brother, Captain Charles Haskell of the 1st S.C. Regulars fell at Battery Wagner. And still another brother, Major John Haskell, lost an arm at Gaines Mill but is still on duty commanding a battalion of Artillery in this Army.

Under these circumstances I would beg leave to ask for him the appointment of Colonel in the Provisional Army, and I would suggest that I consider him fitted in a high degree for the cavalry service. As the commander of a Regiment of Cavalry he would have no superior.

Alexander C. Haskell, Headquarters, McGowan's Brigade,
to Louis W. Haskell (UNC)
3 November 1863
Dear Lewis,

Your letter awaked me to a sense of my remissness of late in writing home, and I am much obliged to you for reminding me so pleasantly of the correspondence. I have been sick and thus fell out of the way of writing, and when I got well I was careless. I had a good, old fashioned chill & felt unspeakably miserable for about a week, but I am now quite well again and enjoying the fine bracing weather. I ride a great deal & whenever I take as stone wall or a fence in a flying leap as my mare does famously, I wish that I was with that merry pack of hounds that you and Paul will be meandering after this winter. Don't break your necks, for you will never catch a fox with young dogs. Be content with good rabbit hunting—that is the best fun with such a pack you will hunt this winter.

I am sorry to say that there is but small prospect of it being possible for you to pay me a visit this winter, & there is certainly no probability of my coming home. We will not go into winter quarters until the mud is too deep both in Virginia and Tennessee for any further military movements. So late in the season the army would all be buried in hovels & you would see no more of them than of a parcel of prairie dogs in their dens, and as for the pleasure of riding my little man you would find that slow work at that time of year, deep in the mud & a hungry horse. Very different from their present condition, when both my horses are fat & ready for any fun or frolic. I jumped a whole cavalry camp into submission this morning on my bay, & all had to give up to her powers. The little roan is not a thoroughbred, is of good enough blood though to make her respectable for anybody that is light enough. She is next thing to useless to me, too small.

I saw little Willy today in trouble. He has lost his horse, strayed off a week ago. I hope however that he will get him back. Tell Pa to write at once to the Secretary of War to ask for a safe guard for his horses, unless they have been impressed already. He must give me one saddle horse. It will be better to send them to us than to let Genl. Beauregard's officers be parading on the best of them. Winter is over, perhaps very soon, for I think I will change my service in some way.

Tell Pa to take steps promptly or he will lose all his horses, and then others will have to be looked up for us in the army. So far we have had great good luck with our horses & need very few. If any have to go into service at once, the new bay horse & [Fritzy] would be the best. Miss Slouch ought to be protected to the last, but send her to me if she is in danger, whether she is fit for service or not. I can take care of her.

Love to all.

Alexander C. Haskell, Headquarters, McGowan's Brigade,
to Charles T. Haskell (UNC)
4 November 1863
Dear Pa,

I have just received your letter of the 29th. Am glad to hear that Ella and the new baby are doing well.[31] Give my love to both. I heard from Langdon in Richmond on his way home. I suppose he has reached Abbeville safely and I am glad to hope that he will find Ella and his new boy doing so well.

John is in my tent as I write, quite well. I went with him yesterday to see little Willy who is looking well, rather troubled by the loss of his horse, strayed off but I hope he will be found. Willy had some vague hope of promotion to lieutenancy in his company. He merits this reward for his good services, and I hope he will get it, as he has become so much attached to the cavalry service that he would not leave it to be promoted elsewhere.

I am much gratified by your information that you bought [McKelvy] for me, and unless has fallen into the claws of the harpies before this letter

---

[31] Langdon C. Haskell's son Allen Wardlaw Haskell was born at the home of his grandfather David Lewis Wardlaw in Abbeville on October 28, 1863.

reaches you I think I can secure him. I think there is every prospect of my changing service this winter in some way & it will be more active. I was anxious to get a good horse & for cavalry or staff duty, I don't think I know a horse in Virginia or South Carolina superior to the one you have selected, if my impression from a mere glimpse of him is correct. Before rec[eivin]g your letter I had written to the Adjutant General to get a safe guard for your horses on the grounds of the supply being necessary for your mounted sons in service, but I destroyed the letter & wrote advising you to apply. I have now written to Roland Rhett urging him to obtain a safe guard upon the same ground & send it to you.

I don't know who is in charge of the business but whoever is write to him. The representation that you have sons who of necessity (which is now the case) will look to you for horses can hardly fail to secure the exemption of all the saddle horses & brood mares, and at least two of the carriage horses. Roland Rhett or Hutson Lee can have it done I suppose. I enclose a protest on my own behalf. I have quite recovered from my illness.

Love to Ma & all at home.

Joseph C. Haskell, Headquarters, Alexander's Battalion,
to Charles T. Haskell (DUL)
5 November 1863
Dear Pa,

When I wrote my last letter two or three days ago I thought we were fixed for the winter but a very sudden change has come over the prospects of things out here. On Tuesday we were up on Lookout shelling the Enemy camps until about five o'clock. An order then came for us to move our camps about two miles to the rear and to withdraw our guns as quickly and silently as possible. At daylight next morning we moved and got to this place yesterday evening, Tyner's station on the Chattanooga and Knoxville road. Here we will put our guns on the train and start for Knoxville via Cleveland. All the horses public and private will travel by the dirt road. I don't much like leaving my home for 3 or four days as we will have to do.

The object of this move is to attempt to surprise Burnside who is in Knoxville.[32] McLaws division about a thousand strong is leaving now.[33] I believe our two other divisions Hoods under Jenkins and Walker's numbering in all about 16,000 all told. Burnside has 15,000 but as we will have to attack him where he has choice of position and no doubt is fortified. I am

---

[32] General Ambrose Everett Burnside (1824-81), commander of the 9th Corps of the United States Army.

[33] A division commanded by Major General Lafayette McLaws (1821-97).

afraid our force is not large enough. Everything is done out here by halves. If we accomplish anything it will be by hard fighting. It is a pity they won't send troops enough to make the affairs certain. It is about a hundred miles from this place to Knoxville and the transportation on the R. R. is so limited that I expect it will be a week or ten days before we all reach our destination. We will probably remain here a day or two longer.

Do tell Ma that the box came to hand yesterday after some wanderings in search of its destination but such activity was displayed by the field and staff in hunting it up that it was finally secured and met with the unqualified approval of everybody. All the things were sound but the rusks which to my sorrow and Jim's special grief were spoiled.[34] The potatoes were the very thing I would have asked for and the molasses is invaluable to us especially at a time like this when we are on the march. The Col. would never eat molasses before this came but I induced him to taste it this morning and he says it is the nicest he ever tasted. The flavor is different from the ordinary syrup. He begs to be particularly remembered to you and Ma both. Frank Huger sends his love to Ma and says he must send his thanks too for the box which has been the salvation of us all.[35] The little clay pitcher and its contents were most particularly appreciated. Winthrop[36] was so curious to find out what they were that he eat [sic] nearly half of them the first evening. The S. Ca. Aid Association is a great institution. Not less than 20,000 pounds of eatables have been brought out to Kershaw's Brigade in the last three weeks. You may imagine what an assistance this has been in eking out their rations. I am happy to say that tho it is pouring down rain as it always is doing out in this country, we are free from all [vicisitude] with regard to the rising or falling of the Chickamauga or Chattanooga creek as we are on the safe side of them next the R. R. I am not sorry at leaving this country for I am afraid it will all be swallowed up in a deluge of mud this winter. We gave the last kick yesterday as we came along to every unfortunate bridge that was struggling against its fate and I don't see how it will be possible for any loaded wagon to pass over them now. This Battalion had something of a reputation in Va. but it can't compare with what it has made out here not only in the army but in the country, not having any [horses] when we came out here and our guns being constantly [wanted]. The teams of all the other Art[illery] of the corps

---

[34] Rusks are dry, hard bread, wafers, or biscuits.

[35] This refers to Francis Kinloch Huger (1837-97), the son of General Benjamin Huger. He was a major in Colonel Edward P. Alexander's artillery battalion in 1863, and was later promoted to the rank of lieutenant colonel, then colonel.

[36] This likely refers to Captain Stephen Winthrop (1839-79), an Englishman on Colonel Edward Porter Alexander's staff.

were at different times hauled over to us much to the disgust of the owner, who all belonged to Bragg's army. The Q. M. also were not at all pleased to see their fine teams promoted and placed on Art[illery] duty, and when it came to furnishing us with horses and the fine pairs of carriage horses and fancy buggy horses were ruthlessly torn from their disconsolate owners. The wrath of the community was almost boundless, but the hardest blow of all was when the horses of the fancy Artillery around Petersburg were taken and sent out to us. One battery proposed to match its eff[iciency] against any one of ours and decide the right to proprietorship by the result. I recognised some of the horses which were with us down in No. Ca. So you see in one way or another Alexander's Battn. has got its name up. I hope we will stay in this army until we make another sort. Do give my love to Ma, cousin Follie and all at home.

Alexander C. Haskell, Headquarters, McGowan's Brigade,
to Sophia C. Haskell (UNC)
11 November 1863
Dear Ma,

I have no great feats of arms to sing in heroic strains. I can only say with the Yanks, we retreated successfully (after losing about 1200 men) and are now masters of the situation.[37] Our little army, although it has had misfortunes recently, is not the least bit discouraged or daunted. It still feels gloriously confident of its ability to defeat anything sent against it, whenever Genl. Lee shall make up his mind that it is right to fight. By the way, I dined with Gen. Lee this evening & he wished for some red pepper. Send me a package for him & let it be strong. The pepper you gave me, & that you lately sent John, was most unaccountably mild. Make up a package and send it by <u>mail</u>. I assure you it is the best & only sure way of sending small parcels. Bundles of clothing are frequently sent to the army in this way.

The General looks well in health & seems to be in his usual serene good spirits. He becomes a little sarcastic & savage upon men sometimes, but he never quarrels with fate, or, to be less heathenish, providence. I can remember days of pride when I scorned woolen gloves. I have lately sat upon my horse without overcoat or gloves from the sunset to the sun rising of the coldest night & north wind I almost ever felt. I acknowledge my past errors, and now humbly sue pardon and a pair of dark-coloured woolen gauntlets knit by some skillful hand. Send them likewise by mail, and as soon as they

---

[37] In early November 1863, there were two major engagements as General Meade's army pushed across the Rappahannock River and General Lee began a withdrawal to the Rapidan River.

can be begged, bought or knit. I had to borrow a pair from a courier today, and will borrow them tomorrow as I will be out all day. Meanwhile the good natured youngster who lends them has to keep his hands in his pockets. The cold is severe & is made doubly worse by a sharp north wind which howls incessantly.

John came back from the other side of the river with the rest of us, quite well, & without having had a fight.

The barrel of sorghum (the molasses, not the whiskey which I am delighted to say has vanished like other evil spirits, but by the exorcism of more powerful agents than myself) has cured my chills. It would be very hard to give me another shake now that we have got out of the swamps of the Rappahannnock.

Arthur Wardlaw arrived today bringing me a nice pair of socks for which I return thanks. I am glad to hear from Langdon that all are well and especially that Emmie has quite recovered.

Love to Pa & all at home.

Major General Wade Hampton, Headquarters, Hampton's Division, to James A. Seddon[38](UNC)
12 November 1863
Sir,

Capt. A. C. Haskell, A. A. Genl. of Gregg's old Brigade, who has greatly distinguished himself on various occasions, has been strongly recommended for promotion to a colonelcy, and the only difficulty in the way of this appears to be that there is no command now vacant. There are several unattached companies of Cavalry in So. Ca. & a Batt[alio]n of five companies—the Holcombe Legion—in this state. The Colonel of the latter is, I am told about to take command of the infantry portion of his Legion. If this is the case I recommend that this Batt[alio]n be filled up to a Regiment by ordering five more companies from South Carolina & that Capt. Haskell be assigned to the command of the Regiment so made up.

If this can be done I request that the new Regiment be ordered to report to me. My knowledge of Captain Haskell assures me that he is eminently qualified to fill the position for which he is recommended & I am very anxious to have him in my command.

---

[38] This is Aleck's copy (in his hand) of General Wade Hampton's letter to James A. Seddon, the Secretary of War. The letter was forwarded and endorsed by Major General J. E. B. Stuart, who added, "I hope the Dept. will not fail to reward a gallant officer & add to the efficiency of the army as proposed."

Alexander C. Haskell, Headquarters, McGowan's Brigade,
to Sophia C. Haskell (UNC)
16 November 1863
Dear Ma,

I got a letter from you night before last, half of which fell out of the envelope as I tore it open and was not found until yesterday morning. Just as I was about to answer it, we received orders to break up camp (Winter quarters? Huts & chimneys!) & move instantly to a point down the river to meet the enemy. To give you an idea of the celerity with which our little villages break up when spurs are put to us, we had marched the brigade out upon the road & nearly issued two days "hard bread" (fighting rations) in a few minutes less than half an hour. After this exhausting piece of activity we were repaid with orders announcing the move unnecessary. It appears the enemy were not crossing the river & that it was a mistake of the reconnoitering party. We went into camp, waited until dark for further orders, then unpacked wagons, re-roofed the houses, started fires in the cheery little chimneys and were as comfortable in half an hour, as if nothing had happened.

The weather is changeable & promises rain & perhaps snow. If the latter comes I think that the ordinary chances & calculations are clearly against a battle this season, unless some great emergency should arise for either party, from occurrences in other quarters. And even under a continuance of good weather it is a pretty evenly balanced question, whether or not Meade will cross the Rapidan or the lower Rappahannock. In the event that he declares for battle, I think there is every reasonable probability of his getting a severe defeat. His army to be sure is much larger than ours, but when have we ever met it on any other terms? The late disasters of Bristow & Rappahannock bridge, though very depressing to newspaper warriors, I don't think have hurt the army. In each case, there probably was mismanagement, which there is every reason to conclude, will not occur again. In the first case fifteen thousand of the enemy well posted defeated 2,500 of our people hastily dashed against them. In the second, 1,500 were defeated & about half of them captured by 20,000 Yankees and a river in their rear. Those things mean nothing to the army except the accidents which may be expected, & have not the "demoralizing" effect which popular critics attribute to them.

You mention the recovery of my little blue silk needle bag, which I thought had dropped out of a hole in my trunk after I left home. I suppose it fell out before the trunk was moved from the room. I much regretted the loss of what I valued so much, and am truly glad to hear that I will recover it. Do keep it safely for me. I hope I will claim it some of these days.

I will say in general, in answer to your inquiries, that I will want gloves, socks & drawers, if you have material. Also I would like very much to get some nice homespun gray, enough for pants & jacket.

Do urge upon Lewis & all parties concerned the importance of curing "Reveille's" foot. Tell Paul I do not accept his name, although the owner of the last horse I knew of that name was my good friend and commander. The horse was unworthy of him. I think I will certainly stand much in need of this or some other horse before half the winter is over. We cure such lameness in our army horses very easily if we can rest them, but I know that maladies are more obstinate with the stabled horses of civil life. Bathing in hot water is my great remedy for such a lameness, and I did apply with good results to my mare. Tar & salt (in absence of turpentine), plastered into the bottom of the hoof, with tow.

Goodbye. Love to Pa & all at home, Cousin Follie, Ella & Lang. I am glad to hear that Sophie & the boys are spending their time as pleasantly.

Alexander C. Haskell, Headquarters, McGowan's Brigade, Camp near Orange Court House, Va., to Charles T. Haskell (UNC)
20 November 1863
Dear Pa,

The autumn has almost passed away and the last month of it is made up of a succession of beautiful days which would grace the opening of the most propitious spring. Meade has not yet molested us, and I am beginning to be convinced that he acts now as we do as a force whose movements are contingent upon those of the huge young monster that has grown up of veteran limbs in the west.

Meade will hardly fight unless compelled by Lincoln, & Abraham will hardly imperil the Army of the Potomac in an open field, swelled as it is by the garrisons of Washington, if Longstreet is really in east Tennessee & at Knoxville. A defeat of his army would really endanger Washington in such a case as this for he would not dare to reinforce from the west & his clouds of volunteer locusts are harder to raise now than in the olden time. I think he has filled up Meade's army to prevent Lee's attacking others imperiling Washington. Lee will not attack I feel sure. His policy is peace. The winter will swell his army at least one fourth. It will not increase much, & may deplete, the army of the enemy. Of one thing I feel as confident as I dare feel concerning a battle, which seems more than any other act of life to be taken out of the hands of men, that we can defeat Meade the day after he sets foot upon the south bank of the Rapidan or lower Rappahannock. Our army is in splendid fighting condition & does not fear. I would feel more than confident, hopeful in the highest degree of brilliant and speedy results, if I could only hear of Joe Johnston or anybody else with a decent force moving on Nashville, while Longstreet holds Knoxville, of which I trust he will get possession. Thomas & Grant will have to combine their genius in retreat, or break over Lookout Mt. and make their way for the Atlantic coast, trusting to living, fighting & dying as they go.[39] Such a progress might have a good many in the start but few in the end.

If we can regain Tennessee this winter and hold our line in Virginia, if Congress will throw every substitute keeper into the ranks, and drag away every skulker from his corner, to fill our ranks, we will present a stronger and more threatening front at any previous moment of the war, when the approach of the season for active operations will find the enemy embarrassed in the refilling & reorganizing of the disbanded ranks of his army. Invasion may be effective then and upon its heels we may be granted peace. I believe that this will only come however when all are in the army who can march or fight, and the country is drained of the wicked people who now exhaust us by their villainies. The army is school for repentance for such, and into the army I believe they must be brought.

My aspirations to a colonelcy of cavalry have probably found honourable sepulture in the chiefest pigeon hole in the desk of the Sect. of War, the one in which are filed in numbers untold the letters of young officers who think they might be more useful in a more elevated & extended field of exertion. Mine however is not in the first person nor an autograph. It is all from my commanders. They have given me copies, but I do not appear on my own behalf, which is some consolation in my neglected condition. Time sufficient has passed & I hear nothing of the matter. I will still however have use for "Jeb" to get him in good hardy order with round feet & I will make him as famous as my mare.

Love to Ma & all at home.

John C. Haskell, Orange Court House, Va., to Sophie Haskell (SCHS)
21 November 1863
Dear Sophy,

I have just got your letter written conjointly with Paul. I am much obliged to you for it as I believe I already owe you one in return for the letter you wrote me some time ago. We are still in the same position that we have occupied since we first fell back from Brandy Station, on the south bank of

---

[39] This refers to Major General Ulysses S. Grant (1822-85), who was assigned command of the Division of the Mississippi in October 1863, and Major General George Henry Thomas (1816-70)

the Rapidan where I am afraid we will wait for a long time, for our position is so strong that they will scarcely give us battle, but it is such that they are constantly threatening us without risking anything.

The weather including last night has been very fine but today is gloomy and wet, a day which looks as if it is the commencement of a long spell of wet bad weather. If it is, operations will [mercifully] be suspended for a good while to come. My battalion has been attached to Heth's Division at which I feel considerably disgusted as it [delays] my expected winter quarters indefinitely and with them my furlough which I had hoped to be able to ask for early next month, but something may turn up yet that will relieve the suspense under which we all are now and decide what is to be done this winter. Whatever does turn up however I hope to be able to pay you a visit this winter anyhow though it may be late in the winter. I have not seen Alick for some days but have heard from him yesterday. He is quite well. Tell Paul that I sent him (Alick) the letter which was enclosed in Louis' to me and tell Louis I will answer his letter as soon as I can, but I have not adjutant and have to attend to all office work myself which with the great aversion I have to such work give me as much writing as I feel equal to daily. I had heard before I got your letter that you are riding Miss Slouch, whose old name I believe I like better than her new. I do not admire poetical names for horses but I think let's all call her Slouch still. Tell Lewis I have never named either of my horses yet, but if I ever do I think I shall call them Dick & Bob or some other such names. I wish very much I could get them home for the winter for though they look very [finely] now I am afraid this winter will be a dreadful one for horses, for starvation is staring them in the face already. All the corn that my horses get is hauled fifty or sixty miles and it is getting scarce there and the roads are getting bad very fast. Tell Louis not to spoil the [brown colt] by trying to ride it. She is too young. Give my love to Ma & Pa.

Alexander C. Haskell, Headquarters, McGowan's Brigade,
to Louis W. Haskell, Abbeville, S.C. (SCHS)
25 November 1863
Dear Louis,

I believe I wrote you a letter the night before last and burnt it up. I am not sure of its fate. If you have received it this is a duplicate.

I dined with John today and assisted at the writing of a lengthy document which is intended to smash the claims of a very troublesome Major Henry who in very bad faith has returned to the battalion and is trying to get the command away from John.[40] I think it is pretty clear that Genl. Lee, the final arbitrator, is decidedly on John's side of the controversy. It will be all right soon. I suppose that you and Paul will be obliged to give up all idea of a visit to us this winter. I believe it would be far from pleasant. We don't know when we will be permitted to become quiet and imagine ourselves at rest. Tonight is cold and sleety enough to make me wish I had my chimney and winter quarters, but at the same time comes an order for men to dig rifle pits. Nothing but a snow about two feet deep will settle us down. It will be February before we are permitted to feel at all sure that we are in winter quarters.

Besides this I think I would have no horses for you. An order has just been published reducing me to one. Of this one I will have to take much care. Be diligent and cure Jeb's foot. I am impatient to hear that he is fit for service. My old mare needs rest. I would like to send her home & bring this conscript into camp. I think he is larger and stronger and better able to do all the work by himself. My pony has disappointed me in looks but she has splendid action for a saddle horse, & I would rather get her home for some of you than throw her away here, as will be necessary I fear. She would surpass even your pony as a walker, and has a fine canter. She would make a third nice horse for the girls (or young ladies as I hope your reverence bids you call them) to take out in their rides next spring.

I am glad that Sophie is so well pleased with Slouch, and that she has made really a pleasant saddle horse. She would give Ethel to me for a charger, if I sued the favour as a mighty general. It is very well that a few of the noble animals can be kept out of the war, though they will feel rather badly some of these days when the veterans recite their tales of battle after the good cheer and much corn which their grateful masters will spread before them. By the time I am a major general don't you think that "Whiskey" will be old enough to take the field? Give him a generous supply of oats all this winter and next spring. Urge his growth so that he will move lightly under the accumulated honours which he will find heaped upon his back.

Rumours tell this evening of the Yankees moving down the river towards Ely's Ford as if to cross below near Chancellorsville or Fredericksburgh, but I think this is probably in the imagination of some signal officer, who not being able to see through the clouds, has imagined what is going on beyond them.

---

[40] John C. Haskell wrote of Major Mathias W. Henry in his memoir: "Henry was my junior in date of commission, but by Longstreet's advice I never formally assumed command until after he left, which was not until after Gettysburg." Haskell, *The Haskell Memoirs*, 46.

The President paid us a visit a few days ago but was prevented by bad weather from reviewing the army. The old gentleman is becoming so fond of military affairs that I would not be surprised to see him take command of a grand army next spring with Lee and Bragg for his lieutenants.[41] Then you will see Yankees over the border in short order.

Tell Paul that if I owe him a letter he must write and tell me so. I have forgotten and will await his answer in much suspense. Write to me often while you are at home and have strength from nutritious diet. I cannot expect cheerful letters from your emaciated existence while your brain is undergoing the forcing process.

Love to Ma & Pa & all at home.

Joseph C. Haskell to Charles T. Haskell (DUL)
[November 1863]
[*This letter, the first part of which is missing, describes the Confederate assault on Fort Sanders near Knoxville, Tennessee, on November 29, 1863.*]

… Parts of three Brigades attacked and 4 Colonels were killed and several others wounded. The entire loss was between 5 and 6 hundred killed, wounded and prisoners. The loss amongst the officers was so heavy because the storming column was led by the officers who all went at the head. Our men went most gallantly up to the ditch and most of them jumped into it where they stayed imagining themselves safe. The Yankees brought a gun up and raked the ditch with canister for a moment or two and were then run off not before they had killed about 40 of our men. Some of our men went to the top of the parapet and some went over. The gunners in the fort left their guns and the Infantry also ran when a panic [seized] our men who ran back in the utmost confusion leaving all the killed and wounded and some prisoners in the hands of the enemy.

As soon as the assault was over the Yankees sent out a flag of truce offering to let us have our killed and wounded who were brought about a hundred yards from the fort by their men and handed over to ours. I was very much pleased by the handsome behavior of their officers and men whilst this was going on, all of them showing us every courtesy in their power. Several of the officers came out and asked for Col. Alexander and Major Huger who went in to see them and talked for a long time over old affairs. They had been classmates at West Point. Amongst others the Col. met his old danc-

---

[41] President Jefferson Davis was a graduate of West Point, and an officer in the United States Army during the Mexican-American War of 1846-1848. He also served as the United States Secretary of War.

ing master Ferrero who is now a Brig. Genl. and com[mandin]g the fort.[42] They all spoke in the highest terms of our men and told us that one officer and Adjutant of a Ga. Regt. had jumped over the parapet followed by 5 men and attacked the cannoneers at one of the pieces with his sword and ran them off. He was not followed however and was obliged to surrender. On parting they wanted to give away everything they had, hats, overcoats and all, and at last made Major Huger take a handsome Colt's revolver and a pipe. I was glad to see in all this bitter struggle that there was some pleasant feeling left yet. It will be hard to extinguish the feeling that exists between the old army officers. We killed Genl. Sanders on their side the evening of the 18th when Winthrop was wounded.[43] They all asked after Winthrop. We were immediately ordered to fall back after the repulse and rejoin Bragg but by evening a dispatch came from him directing us to join him at Dalton[44] if practicable, if not to retreat to Va. Genl. Longstreet determined that he could not get to Dalton and has determined to try this place again and if he fails he will retreat to Va. by way of Bristol. Our communications will be cut off after today and in fact I have not much hope of this getting through but will risk it as there is no knowing when you will hear from me again. We are at a desperate game, but put reliance on being able if the worst comes to [cut] our way to Va. Do give my love to Ma and all at home. Goodbye.

Joseph C. Haskell, Headquarters, Alexander's Battalion, to Sophia C. Haskell (DUL)

2 December 1863

Dear Ma,

I wrote a letter to Pa two days ago and have kept it until now hoping that I would have a chance to send it off. An officer will start tomorrow for Richmond and has kindly offered to take these letters on for me so I thought I would give you the news of two days later. The amount of it is that we have had no fight yet, but it is only two days nearer as it must come very soon. The Gens. have been holding a council of war for two days past and it only adjourned this evening. I have not seen the Col. yet to find out what was the result of it but know pretty much what it was as Col. Alexander is the authority on all questions of roads &c and in fact almost everything else,

---

[42] Edward Ferrero (1831-99), a noted dance instructor and choreographer, and author of *The Art of Dancing*, taught dancing at West Point. He raised his own regiment at the beginning of the war and later rose to the rank of brigadier general.

[43] Brigadier General William Price Sanders (1833-63) was mortally wounded at Knoxville on November 18, 1863.

[44] Dalton, Georgia.

as he has to decide on the plans of attack and the [footing] of the batteries &c.

His idea is that we must take Knoxville at all risks and that quickly too, before Thomas can send a large force from Chattanooga after us.[45] Just as I have got so far it is suggested that there is a pretty good chance of this being [captured] no I will not touch further on military matters.

The unfortunate car with our things from home never got any farther than Dalton and has now been sent back to Va., so I have resigned myself to its loss. Jim and myself both made several captives on that trip tho that relieved our immediate necessities and will be able to get on for a while. This is a very fine country out here and as long as it lasts we will live finely, how long that will be tho I don't know.

There is nothing else to write as we get nothing from the outside world. Our Corps is in fine condition and spirits and I think you will hear from us before long. If the Yankees should get us they will pay dearly for their bargain.

Do give my best love to Pa and all at home.

[P.S.] If you write inclose the letter to the Adjt. & Inspector Genl. Richmond. Do write at once as I have not got a letter for 3 weeks. J. C. H.

Alexander C. Haskell, Headquarters, McGowan's Brigade, Camp near Orange Court House, Va., to Charles T. Haskell (SCHS)
3 December 1863
Dear Pa,

I am stupid tonight from the continued fatigue and excitement of seven days and nights maneuvering in closer proximity to the enemy than we have ever been for the same length of time, and though perfectly well as long as it was necessary, I took a sort of a chill last night after seeing the last Yankee across the Rapidan, & still feel a little clouded from its effects. I write however, as soon as possible, to let you know that John & myself are safe and quite well.

The campaign has been short but of excessive severity.[46] The troops have been without a moment's respite, until last night, under arms & on the alert, for six days, since the 26th November, at this hour of the night. We had rain storms on the first two days and afterwards most piercing cold, against which our protection was very inadequate. But I have never seen the

---

[45] Major General George Henry Thomas (1816-70), commander of the U.S. Army of the Cumberland.

[46] This letter describes the Mine Run Campaign in Orange County, Va., November 26-December 2, 1863.

division to which I belong, & I hope the whole army, in such magnificent condition for action. I heard not one complaint though I saw barefoot, ragged & blanketless men, and the division from its commander down would have cheerfully fought & whipped any one or two corps in the Yankee army. On Friday last we marched with three days rations on the Plank Road from Orange to Fredericksburgh, passing through Chancellorsville. We marched 18 miles, within 10 miles of Chancellorsville, where we struck the Yankee advance. Some skirmishing here occurred in which John with his artillery bore the principal part, but without material loss, and inflicting some upon the enemy. We moved back during that night to a position about 3 miles back, where the whole army went to work to fortify itself against Meade's attack. Genl. Ewell's Corps was on the left, resting on the Rapidan River, the line running nearly due north & south. Ewell's Corps crossed at r[ight] angles the turnpike next the river. Hill's left joined Ewell's right between the turnpike & the plank, crossed the plank (which runs parallel to the river & the turnpike) & extended to the R. R. (projected & only graded, running from Orange to Fredericksburgh). First movement in force was up the turnpike against Ewell on Friday & Saturday. On Friday Edw. Johnson's Division[47] whipped two corps of the enemy army, who pursued him as he was changing his position. Finding the line too strong (and here I will say that the performance of our men & officers in field fortification, when they were called upon to resort to this defence, was splendid—it beat the Yankees to death & this almost without tools to do the work with) the line being too strong, Meade on Saturday evening threw two corps across the plank & out to R. R. to take us in flank. The movement was soon discovered. Genl. Hill[48] extended his line & by daylight on Sunday a splendid position & formidable line of work checked the Yankees on our right. Genl. Hampton had gone to the rear of Meade's army & sent word to us that he would come up the plank road Saturday night. He came but at the same time the Yankee corps (two) under Genl. Warren[49] had crossed this road, hemming him in. He lost his way a little, went to a house to enquire, there caught a Yankee of Genl. Warren's household who told him of the proximity of his chief, supposing Genl. H. to be one of their own number. A pistol was applied to Yank's head & his quiet secured, & he astonished to find himself a prisoner. Hampton thus ascertaining his position charged a camp of the enemy, broke it up in confusion, took some prisoners, destroyed some property & with-

---

[47] Major General Edward Johnson (1816-73) was the commander of General Stonewall Jackson's former division.

[48] General A. P. Hill, commander of the Third Corps.

[49] Major General Gouverneur Kemble Warren (1830-82), commander of the Second Corps of the United States Army.

drew, coming round to us on the right or south side of the railroad, where he dismounted his division & formed with it a line of infantry along a marsh & mill pond, at the angles of our line, thus securing us against a flank movement unawares. This was the posture all Sunday. The Yankees threatened all along the line, but kept edging towards our left, while we constantly extended—checkmating them with a new line of works with the same old Confederate faces behind them. The position was magnificent. It made the prospect of battle almost positively enjoyable to everybody. And it could be fully enjoyed as there was very little sharp shooting. We could inspect all our ground to the front & almost go among the enemy's skirmishers without being shot at. Our men were forbidden to waste ammunition in this unprofitable manner, & the Yankees were only too thankful not to begin the game at which they would have been worsted. And in truth both parties were so nearly frozen that they could not shoot. It was ludicrous to see the skirmish lines in an open old field, not more than two hundred yards apart, with the men along them running up and down, their hands in their pockets & their rifles hung over their backs. The tame Yankees were the subjects of many jokes. The artillery fired a little. John had one or two good opportunities & availed himself of them very handsomely. He was a little more to the left than my station, but I saw him very often, and heard one or two cheers elicited by the style in which he scattered some Yankee columns.

This game continued until Tuesday night when Genl. Lee made up his mind that if they would neither fight nor leave his front, he would make them do both. The dispositions were made, and Anderson's[50] & our divisions were to slip to the right (Anderson's did go) and fall upon Meade's left flank, while the rest of the line managed his front. But on Wednesday morning when the movement commenced, the bird had flown. Meade had retreated rapidly on Tuesday night & was across the river before we could catch him.

Their loss in the whole affair was I suppose 600 to 800 prisoners, about the same killed & wounded, more than 100 wagons captured & destroyed, and fully 150 mules (splendid ones) & 100 horses taken. Besides this Mosby damaged them on the railroad.[51]

[*The rest of this letter is missing.*]

---

[50] Major General Richard H. Anderson.

[51] Colonel John Singleton Mosby (1833-1916), a celebrated Confederate cavalry battalion commander.

Alexander C. Haskell, Camp near Orange Court House, Va.,
to Sophia C. Haskell (UNC)
11 December 1863
Dear Ma,

In spite of many ominous [deadly] refusals of all leaves of absences, bringing up pontoons, and issuing of "fighting rations" &c we are still quiet near Orange C. H. & the men trying to make themselves somewhat comfortable before Christmas. We have had some very cold weather but very dry and favourable for military operations. This has made General Lee very restless and I think he still entertains the idea of driving the enemy across the North Rappahannock & back towards Washington again if the weather holds its favourable aspect much longer. Every preparation has been made and the army is ready either for winter quarters or for a freezing winter march and perhaps campaign. This however is hardly to be expected. A great number of applications for leave of absence have come back today "suspended for the present" and this from Genl. Lee is announcement that we are not yet safe from further disturbance. Tonight it has at last clouded up & there is some promise of the snow which the soldiers wish for as the herald, not of peace, but respite from war. If you see snow don't say "poor soldiers" unless we are in the field, for in camp you would hear shouting and laughing and as boisterous glee and merry snow balling as ever delighted a parcel of school boys on the first snow of the season.

I see John as usual frequently. He is quite well and just now relieved from a very annoying contest as to the command of his battalion, it being claimed by Henry the former commander, who, having gone to the west has returned and wishes to assume his old command. The justice of the case was clearly with John but some technical points were against him. Genl. Lee has just decided the matter in his favour and established him in the command. After the matter was thus settled I believe Henry behaved very well in giving up the pretensions. I had apprehended some difficulty at this point of the proceedings but all has been agreeably disposed of.

Your allusions to my plans and hopes are very just. I was for a little while more sanguine than I should have been had I calmly considered the improbability and difficulty of the attainment of such an object as I desired, but I was surprised and flattered into this expectation by the readiness and cordiality with which all my commanding and the cavalry generals urged my promotion & seconded my efforts. If too hopeful at one time I will not be disappointed so soon after by failure. There is a pleasure in having such a decided mark of approval bestowed, even if it brings no [material] fruits. There was neither rank nor profit, but much honour attached to the cross of the Legion of Honour, so I will treasure the good opinions which have been expressed and console myself, for not yet having gotten that fine cavalry regiment, at the head of which I rode in imagination to the grief and destruction of all those bestriding Yankees. There is too a pleasing excitement in an occasional wrestle with [fortune]. I might have succeeded, or may at some future day when I better deserve it. Indeed my [merits] I fear are rather fictitious. There are hundreds of brave fellow who have fought twice as many battles as I have and have better done all their duty, & nobody says a word for them or about them. They find a surer reward in their noble consciousness of duty performed & true glory won. With me it has not been so much the desire for promotion and has been a wish to change my sphere of action to command instead of always acting in another's name & bringing my thoughts and actions to fit themselves to whoever happens to be the commander of my brigade. I am with a general now who makes my [position] as pleasant as its nature admits. On that battlefield as we were a few days ago I could have nothing to complain of. He taxed me to the best of my judgment & powers of command and gave me in everything a full share, but when all this is over & we come down to the petty office drudgery & clerkship I get out of temper and patience. He agrees with me perfectly though sometimes it is at his expense, and will do anything to help me get a command.

Langdon has just been put in the same harness. He is commissioned captain & A. A. Genl. Inspector of the brigade. I will have to send him his commission tomorrow & if he accepts it he will be obliged to come on very soon after Christmas. He takes rank 2nd November '63.

I hope from what I see in papers that Longstreet is safe and trust that Joe is well and unhurt. Do let me have any news you get.

I am truly sorry to hear that Aunt Charlotte & the girls are going away. Emma wrote me from Savannah just before I got your letter. Mamie & Emmie are friends that Sophy cannot replace & we will all miss them very much.

I had no idea of coming home this winter but it dawned upon me this morning. Genl. Perrin surprised me by telling me he desired me to go to South Carolina on business connected with the brigade and the conscript bureau. If such weather sets in as precludes army movements his application may succeed & I may see you for a few days sometime in the course of the winter. That of course is a mere chance.

Love to Pa & Sophie & all at home.

Joseph C. Haskell, Headquarters, Alexander's Battalion, Bean's Station, Tenn.,
to Sophie Haskell (SCHS)
17 December 1863
Dear Sophie,

I am almost discouraged from writing any more. I can't get any letters from home. I suppose then that I am partly responsible for this as I directed that my letters should be sent to the Adjutant Genl's office. There is no necessity for this now, and if the letters are directed simply to Longstreet's Corps via Bristol they will come all right. I don't know whether my letters ever get home, but write [whenever] I get a chance.

You will see by the date of my letter that we have been on the wing again, and have had a pretty sharp fight, I don't [suppose] tho of sufficient importance to get it into the papers.[52] Last Sunday evening when we were near Rogersville we were ordered to be in readiness to move at daylight next morning, as we all supposed on our way to Bristol, but the head of the column was turned towards Knoxville when we started in the morning. It was a horrible day snowing and raining alternately and the road so muddy that men and horses were sliding and slipping at every other step. Over these roads our barefooted men marched sixteen miles and a good deal to our surprise and much more to that of the enemy ran into them about 4 o'clock in the evening, and their line of dismounted cavalry commenced a sharp fight with our skirmishers.

Their tents were standing in full sight and the wagons all in park, which made us hope that we would get a considerable amount of plunder. We were however very much disappointed. Our column had been so much broken on the march that it took a long time to get the troops up, and when Genl Gracie[53] got up at last with his brigade and one of his batteries, he was unfortunate enough to get shot at the first fire from the enemy lines, and his men could not be made to advance rapidly and did not go forward at all until Col. Alexander charged with one of our light batteries three hundred yards in front of the line. The enemy [retired] and some of our old brigades coming up we ran them a mile or more when it became too dark and the men were so perfectly broken down that we had to halt without having done anything but kill a few and [scare] the rest very badly. They had two divisions of infantry and one of cavalry, not all of them were engaged tho. Our loss was about two hundred and fifty and I expect that of the enemy must have been larger. We certainly killed a great many horses. We lost but one man killed

---

[52] This was the Battle of Bean's Station, Tennessee, which took place on December 14, 1863.

[53] Brigadier General Archibald Gracie (1832-64) was shot in the arm at the Battle of Bean's Station.

and one wounded in the battery which was engaged, but as is always the case they were the two best men in the battery. Our cavalry while we were doing this crossed over the mountain on their flanks and captured 55 wagons, many of them loaded with sugar and coffee.

We followed them next morning and drove them with occasional halts within 25 miles of Knoxville, and the cavalry took them in hand there.

We have now established a camp at this place which is about 40 miles from Knoxville and I think very likely will remain here through the winter if we can hold our present position, for by so doing we threaten their communications by way of Cumberland Gap and keep them out of one of the richest valleys I ever saw. I thought our men had behaved as badly as the Yankees could, but the change that has come over this country since we came through it is lamentable in the extreme. It has been literally desolated. The Yankees declared their intention of making the people desolate in order that they might become entirely dependent on them for support. It may [prove] a lesson to these Union people in the country as they have fared just as badly as the Rebels. I was infected with the Genl desire to get back to Va. and civilization once more, but now that I take an unselfish view of the matter, I am very glad to think that we will probably stay where we will be able to subsist without helping to curtail the [scanty] rations of the Va. army. I did hope to spend Christmas somewhere where it would feel something like it, but now I try not to remember the dates in hopes that we will pass it without knowing anything about it. It makes me very sad to think about Christmas now and tho I have not the heart to wish all at home a merry Christmas, I hope [indeed] it may be a happy one for all that are there. Best love to Ma, Pa, Sister, Lally, Cousin Follie, Mamie, the boys and all at home. Give my love to Miss [Joanne] when you see her.

Joseph C. Haskell, Headquarters, Alexander's Battalion, Russellville, Tennessee, to Sophie Haskell (SCHS)
29 January 1864
Dear Sophie,

I had time to write but a few lines to Pa the other day informing him of my safe arrival and wrote merely for that purpose for I knew if the household heard all the stories which I have you would be in a state of considerable alarm. When I got to Asheville I heard that a party of Morgan's men had been fired on between that place and the Warm Springs. Two men and three horses had been killed. I then determined to wait for a party but before I had stayed 15 minutes I concluded to run the risk of Bushwhackers rather than ride with the drunken crowd I saw there, so I started right on and made the ride through entirely alone without any interruption or accident. The first day I left home instead of going by Williamston, I took another road which is more direct, but which was impassable when I came down. Towards evening I began to inquire where I could stay all night. Everyone directed me to [Warren's] store. When I arrived there I found quite a large good looking house and rode up and knocked. Quite to my surprise a [jocund] and very nice looking lady came out and gave a very ready response to my request for a nights lodging and asked me into the drawing room, and after about a half hour conversation requested me to walk into quite a handsome parlor. I was a little surprised at this, but [supposed] the old people were away and that their daughter was determined to the honors of the house. After a while we had a nice supper and then she entertained me until about half past ten o'clock. I was so tired I could barely keep my eyes open and tho I clenched my teeth, the jaw bones yawned in spite of me. About this time she happened to say something about my husband, and I was so surprised that I yawned right out. She took the hint and asked me if I would not like to retire, and I made very little objection. My room was a very nice one with a fine spring bed and I enjoyed it. I found out next morning that the house was now owned and occupied by a young married couple from Greenville, and the husband off at the wars and his wife living here with her mother and some little brothers. The old Mama was off on a visit. I also found what I had suspected that I was considered a guest and treated according [sic]. When I was overcome with surprise next morning and made many apologies for my intrusion she was polite enough to say that the pleasure of my company more than repaid any obligation I had incurred. I am perfectly willing to stay there any length of time on the same terms. The next day I went to [word unintelligble]. I was very much disappointed in my little Rustic beauty. She was dressed for the occasion and did not look half as pretty as before but what was worse she had got over her shyness and began to talk a good deal, which entirely spoilt her appearance. The next day I got to Aunt Isabella's by 1 o'clock and had a very pleasant time. I got a very pressing invitation from Mrs. Seabrook to come over and see her, and as Aunt Isabella was kind enough to lend me her carriage I went. I saw only Mrs. S. and Miss Mary.[54] The visit was pleasant but very sad to me. I found a scarf and pair of socks awaiting my return, a present from Miss Seabrook. I think if I was to stay at Flat Rock long I would get terribly vain. I felt actually ashamed to find how I was monopolizing the conversation sometimes. They have such an artfull [sic] way of drawing one out and making you talk

---

[54] This likely refers to Caroline Phoebe Pinckney Seabrook (1816-92) and her daughter Mary Elliott Seabrook (1843-1918).

in spite of yourself, that it is hard to avoid it. You must not be surprised at anything Aunt I. writes about your industry for I told her some extensive stories about what you were doing. Do give my love to them when you write. I forgot to say that I stopped a few minutes in Greenville to see cousin Lucilla and Kate. They astonished me with the intelligence that Uncle William was to be married again very soon.[55] They made a great deal of fun over it but seemed to feel it nevertheless. I expressed some surprise that Ma and Pa had heard nothing of it from him when they were in Columbia. Cousin L. said Oh the old man was ashamed to tell them he will write about it.

I took Major Huger completely by surprise as I got back a day before my leave expired. Just as I rode up to the tent a coon or some varmint ran by and I fired at it in the dark with my pistol, and roused the whole camp. Hq did not recognize me for a little while. Frank Huger was delighted with his gloves and they have occupied a conspicuous place in the tent ever since, and excite great admiration. We have been very busy since I came back, fixing up the tent. There was nothing but a chimney when I came, and now we have a nice board floor, shelves and racks. The back of the tent is festooned with our old flag, and our swords were crossed over it with pistols gracefully [interspersed] and our [sashes] draped amongst it all. You have no idea how pretty and comfortable it is. Everything is moving down towards the front but two of our batteries, and I should not be surprised to find myself in the vicinity of [Knoxville] soon. The small pox is certainly there I believe and one case appeared in our army caught from Yankee clothing. Do give my love to Ma & Pa.

John C. Haskell, Lindsay's Station, Va., to Paul T. Haskell (UNC)
2 February 1864
Dear Paul,

I believe I have owed you a letter for some time and indeed I am not certain but that I owe you two which I would have answered long ago but I have been so [unsettled] in my idea as to what I would do that I have kept putting off writing expecting to go home but I have just got back disapproved so I have to give up all hopes for the present. I hope I will be at home about the twentieth however and I certainly will if Major Reilly who is absent does not get his leave extended or play me some trick which I suspect he is trying to do but in which I am very sure he will fail. I have been visiting a good deal lately as there are a great many lady acquaintances from Richmond up in the neighborhood on a visit to their relatives in the Artillery. I

---

[55] William E. Haskell married his third wife, Jane Lee Bachman (1819-1903) in June 1864. She was the sister of his second wife Harriet Eva Bachman, who died in 1858.

have just come back from a dinner party given by Major Pegram who is camped quite near to me which was decidedly the grandest affair of the season.[56] There were about twenty ladies old and young and officers ad libitum and he had a really handsome dinner which was I suppose gotten up for him by some of his relatives and relatives of his surgeon who live in the neighborhood.

I suppose you and Louis are at school again by this time and studying hard. Write me word and tell Louis to do the same what books are you studying and whose editions of your latin books, as I suppose you have commenced Latin by this time. Write me word also how to direct your letters whether to the village or to Willington & when. Things are beginning to look badly for our artillery in the way of horses, a great many of which are dying. Major Pegram near me has lost sixty odd in the last six weeks and our other [battalions] of the Corps have lost more. I have lost fewer than any other as the glanders of which they are dying have not broken out in my [stables] yet though I am constantly fearing it.[57] We have at last started to get hay and if the glanders will [allow] my horses to live I think I can keep them up.

Write to me soon and give my love to all at home. Send my respects to Mr. Porcher.

Sarah Hampton[58], Richmond, Va., to Sophia C. Haskell (SCHS)
7 February [1864]
My dear Mrs. Haskell,

Your kind letter to me arrived while I was in Abingdon therefore I only received it a day or two ago. I cannot tell you how earnestly I thank you for your remembrance of me & how truly I appreciate your good wishes. In some happier time I hope to meet you all & feel assured that I shall love you trusting that you also will care something for me.

---

[56] William Ransom Johnson Pegram (1841-65) was a celebrated young artillery officer in the Army of Northern Virginia. He was promoted to the rank of colonel in late February 1864, and was killed in action at the Battle of Five Forks, Va. In his memoir, John C. Haskell wrote of Pegram: "He was probably, at the time of his death, the most distinguished artillerist in our army." Haskell, *The Haskell Memoirs*, 81.

[57] Glanders is an infectious disease primarily occurring in equines and is usually fatal.

[58] By January 1864, Sarah (Sally) Buchanan Hampton (1845-86) had become engaged to John C. Haskell. She was born in Abingdon, Virginia, at the home of her mother Margaret Preston Hampton.

The kindness of all my Haskell family has deeply touched me & already I feel a sincere regard for his two brothers here whose unvarying goodness has made me anxious to know those still at home.

I deeply sympathise with you on sending another son into the army & pray God to watch over all those near & dear to you.[59]

With affectionate regard to Mr. Haskell & Sophie, believe me...

Alexander C. Haskell, Orange Court House, Va.,
to Charles T. Haskell (USC)
9 February 1864
Dear Pa,

I am safe in camp after a very successful journey and find the brigade in the very best condition. Rations somewhat scant, but with the home supplies there is a sufficiency of food. And in the matter of health, high spirits and hopeful courage, it would do your heart good to see them. Two regiments the 1st and 14th being off duty this evening held meetings, and without a dissenting voice but with proud acclamations assured the country of their faith and courage renewing their obligations to serve for the war, to whatever length it may be drawn. This fine example will doubtless be followed tomorrow by the others. These resolutions will convince the country of the spirit of the soldiers. As mere acts of reenlistment it was hardly necessary to go through the form. The brigade sees no period to its services other than the successful termination of the war.

I reached Richmond on Sunday morning in the midst of great confusion and pealing of alarm bells summoning the troops for "Local Defence" to keep Gen. Butler at bay. He was then reported at Bottom's Bridge, 15 miles from Richmond on his way to see Mr. Davis on the question of "Recognition."[60] He was however stopped at this point and about midday my uneasinesss was removed by the arrival of a veteran brigade from our own old army whose march through the city, though it gave an air of gravity to the affair,

---

[59] This letter does not include the year in the dateline, but the content suggests that it was written in 1864 shortly after Sally Hampton's engagement to John Haskell. She was in Virginia at this time in 1864, but would have been in Columbia, S.C., in February of 1865. Her mention of "another son going into the army" must refer to the prospect of Louis Haskell going into military service, though this did not actually occur until September 1864.

[60] General Benjamin Franklin Butler ordered a raid on Richmond for the purpose of releasing prisoners. The expedition included a skirmish at Bottom's Bridge on February 6, 1864. The next day, the Richmond home guard was called out in response to a report that the enemy was "in force" at Bottom's Bridge on the Chickahominy River.

yet brought such an assurance of success, that I was rather anxious to see [an] effort made to take the city by surprise.

Soon after I heard telegrams from Orange announcing a general advance of the enemy across the Rapidann and a pretty sharp fight below Orange in which the Yankees were badly worsted by Gen. Edw. Johnson. I was sure then that my brigade was moving , and hurried from Richmond in the first train, but only got up in time to receive the brigade on its return from a severe but fruitless march in pursuit of the Yankee cavalry, in which there was no fighting.

Both movements have resulted in nothing, and all things are quiet on the lines & will probably remain so until April at least. Genl. McGowan took command of the brigade, mounted his horse, stood a severe march and returned much better than he has been for a long time. His improvement is astonishingly [rapid] now that it has set in & will I hope be permanent. Perrin[61] has been assigned to Genl. Wilcox's[62] old brigade (Alabamians), is well contented and everything is going on pleasantly. Langdon is quite well. I saw John at Gordonsville as he returned from the march up to the front. He is well and expects his leave of absence about the 18th inst. We have heard of Joe's safe arrival in Tennessee. My opinion of "Boxes" has risen amazingly after my two first dinners in camp (both of which dinners came from Abbeville and were very nice). Remember my barrel of molasses. I find my mare rough and warm as a long haired horned beast, but in splendid health and condition, with plenty of forage for the present.

Love to Ma & Sophie & all the boys.

Alexander C. Haskell, Orange Court House, Va.,
to Sophia C. Haskell (USC)
14 February 1864
Dear Ma,

I have been in camp six days and feel settled again in the routine of its duties. I find but little to do but I brought on with me Herschel's Astronomy and whenever I convict myself of having clearly nothing to do I betake myself to the study of a little mixed mathematics. This always effects a cure. It either interests me, or suggests something else to do as a means of escape.

Genl. McGowan continues to improve and seems quite competent to the performance of all that is likely to be required of him. I have been to see Perrin & find him well established in command of very fine brigade, Wil-

---

[61] Brigadier General Abner Monroe Perrin (1827-64).

[62] Cadmus Marcellus Wilcox was formerly the commander (colonel) of the Ninth Alabama Infantry Regiment, and later, with the rank of brigadier general, commanded a brigade that included the Third Alabama Infantry Regiment.

cox's Alabamians. Though not so large as this brigade, it is large enough and of approved good qualities for fighting and campaigning.

I saw John for a few minutes at Gordonsville the day I came up, but my trunk was in the car and I could not get at his bundle. I have but one courier and have for this reason been unable to send it to him, as he is distant some fifteen miles of bad road. I hope however to get it conveyed to him before he starts for home. The weather has been beautiful since my arrival & continues so with a little threat of rain this morning. Rain or snow would not be amiss now as either one would prevent the small agitations and movements which are so harassing to our army in winter quarters. Everything in the army wears a cheerful aspect, except perhaps the artillery, and some of the cavalry horses. The men are in the very best condition and in the snuggest of winter quarters. The rations though not abundant are good in quality & sufficient. In fact with the admirable arrangements for South Carolina troops which are in operation through the Central Association,[63] the supplies from home constitute a very important portion of the subsistence of the brigade. I only wish all others were as well off, which indeed the N. Carolinians, Virginians and Georgians are. The remote western troops are the only sufferers, and these buy and pick up some addition to their fare. Better than all they have contentment with their fare whatever it is and never grumble at the authorities. An Alabama soldier was seen the other day by a friend of mine sitting on a log in front of his hut, barefooted & ragged, munching a piece of dry corn bread & drinking a cup of water. This was his dinner. The same had constituted his fare for two days past and he excused himself for hurrying through his dinner, saying he must hurry up to the meeting and "reenlist for the war." Such is the spirit which will sustain our arms through all the difficulties which lie before us.

Reenlistments are almost unanimous. A few N.C. regiments are slow, but I think will come in. I am ashamed to say that a few of "Orr's Regt. of Rifles" likewise decline the honour, but to conceal their shame the action of the regiment is reported as being unanimous.

I find myself as well contented as ever, not spoiled by, but retaining very pleasant memories of my visit home. Baby's sweet little voice is forever ringing in my ear as I last heard it, calling "Papa" as I left the house.

Love to Pa & Sophie and the boys. Goodbye for the present.

---

[63] The Central Association for the Relief of South Carolina Soldiers established a wayside home in Richmond in August 1863 for South Carolina soldiers in Virginia.

Alexander C. Haskell, Brigade Headquarters,
to Charles T. Haskell (USC)
17 February 1864
Dear Pa,

I have received your kind letter of the 10th. I thank you very much for your solicitude about my getting the servant I wrote to you about. I still have July and would be well content to keep him, for I feel pretty sure that he will not desert to the Yankees, but I am afraid that Carter Singleton may want him, and refrain from expressing his wishes because I have no other servant. Carter's own servant was very sick last year and sent home by the Doctors. I am glad to hear your good accounts of Jeb. I feel pretty confident of his entire recovery. His foot I think will expand with use. I have seen much worse <u>looking</u> cases recover, though I don't remember any that lasted quite so long. I have seen the foot contract more than his and practically separate from the flesh, and yet recover perfectly.

I think it very well that [Frity] is sold as I believe he goes into the Service. There was no need of two pair of carriage horses.

John expects to start home very soon. I wrote to him and got an answer by mail. It is very mortifying that I have been unable to get John's bundle down to him, and don't think that I can before he goes. As well as I could make out the word which was blotted he expected to start today. I hope you will have him at home for 30 days, though it is rather hard to get, these furloughs over 21 days. He ought to have at least double the usual allowance. The approach of that fine box is watched in all stages of its progress. A warm welcome will be in store for it on its arrival. The General has sent home for a box too, and there is every prospect that will we will become a self-sustaining body of the most flourishing character. It is astonishing to see the amount of food contributed to our soldiers through the Central Association. With many of the men it more than compensates for any deficiencies that may occur in the rations.

The Army is in fine spirits. I saw Genl Lee at church last Sunday looking strong and well. [I] trust he is prepared for great events in the next campaign.

Love to Ma, Sophie & the boys. Goodbye.

Alexander C. Haskell, Orange Court House, Va., to Sophie Haskell (SCHS)
18 February 1864
Dear Sophie,

Everything is freezing and my often melted ink will hardly make a mark. I know it will be a solid lump of ice as soon as the fire goes down a little so I take it now while it is still a little dark in colour.

It is really cold. The thermometer this morning in the body of a small well warmed house was only four degrees above zero. What it was in our tents I would not venture to guess. My tent was burnt over my head at 3 o'clock this morning while I was in profoundest slumber and as I had to turn out as I was burning the blankets I know exactly how cold it was [*sic*]. Luckily for me July[64] was sleeping in my front tent which was the one consumed. He was awaked and by his operations & presence of mind I escaped a good scorching and any goods and chattel were saved. Tents burn almost like gunpowder. Mine was an old fellow captured at Harper's Ferry in '62.

I have not much to do & amuse myself with reading, walking and wood cutting. Walking is my standby and drives away idleness whenever it comes upon me. I never ride because the roads are so hard frozen that it would be no pleasure to break up my horse's feet in galloping over them. I had a present the other day of a marvelously little giant of a pony. He is small but pretty & wicked & very strong, and carried a heavier man all last summer. I rode him a few nights ago over rough fields and high hills with Andrew Wardlaw's little boy[65] on the saddle before me and no complaint was made by Genl. Morgan, but I had not hitched him two minutes before he had jumped through his bridle and scampered away to camp leaving me to get home as best I might. He is about half as big as the cream pony and defeats in single combat our largest horse. He can live by his wits and astonishes the natives by his daring and successful raids upon the forage yard. He is almost as good as a big dog except that he can't sleep in my tent.

I was sorry to hear from Hannah McC. of the departure of Primus. They must be at a loss to know who to trust when this young model of fidelity has played them so false.

Remember I expect you to pay your visit to Columbia when John has got through his visit home, and I hope you will be able to get Lessie up to Abbeville in the spring or summer especially too as I want Baby then to make a visit to "Granny & Daddy." Love to Pa & Ma & the boys. Write to me. I am always glad to get your letters.

---

[64] In his memoir, Aleck Haskell described July as "my attendant" and "my man, July." Daly, *Alexander Cheves Haskell*, 104,126.

[65] Andrew Bowie Wardlaw (1831-88), an officer in McGowan's Brigade, had a son named Patterson who was born in 1859.

Joseph C. Haskell, Headquarters, Alexander's Battalion,
Strawberry Plains, Tenn., to Charles T. Haskell (SCHS)
20 February 1864
Dear Pa,

I have not before had an opportunity of writing, since my hurried note just before leaving Russellville the other day. We are as you see by the date of this at Strawberry Plains 15 miles above Knoxville on the north side of the river. Two Brigades and one of our batteries are on the south side somewhat nearer to the town. When we started the other day Genl. Longstreet told Major Huger that he wanted to take advantage of the good weather and commence operations by attacking Knoxville. The day after we started it snowed and since then we have had desperate weather, rain or snow almost every day. This coupled with our crippled condition from the dying of our horses from actual starvation has I think put a stop to the expedition for the present. Tho today the weather is warm again, and I expect if we get some forage which is expected on the cars, that we will be on the move again in a day or two.

It is enough to break one's heart almost to see the condition of our horses. I saw four of these splendid horses which we got from Ga. stop still in the road with an empty wagon and not able to move it [four] times since I came back. The horses have been for 48 hours without anything to eat, not even straw. I stood it as long as I could bear to see my horses starve and the Q. M. get fat on corn that was hidden away, and then I took our Hd. Qr. Wagon and got a load of corn and fodder off which I have been feeding all the private horses in the [Battery]. I sold Robin when I thought they were all going to starve for the small price of 55 d. He was very much pulled down by the trip out and was getting stiffer every day. His stumbling also got very bad. One of our officers who was thrown out of commission by a decision from the War Dept. stating his appointment to have been illegal left his horse to which he was very much attached in my charge, hoping that he might be able to reclaim him someday. It is a pony about 15 hands high with a body about as big as Robins and very powerful and strong. He will be of great service to me this summer. Fannie is looking very well indeed considering. I have got two letters from Ma and one from Sophie since I came out and hope that by this time some of mine have arrived. I got a long pleasant letter from John a few days ago but have not answered it as I expected that he would leave for home soon. I am going to try and get on without horse for a while until I can get a really fine one. I am tired of horses that have to be nursed all the time. Do give my love to Ma, Sophie and anybody at home.

Joseph C. Haskell, Headquarters, Alexander's Battalion,
to Charles T. Haskell (DUL)
7 March 1864
Dear Pa,

I have not written home for some days expecting that when I did so I might give some news of myself and Col. Alexander. He has returned a Brigadier Genl. and Chief of Artillery of this army, and has nominated me as his Adjt. Genl. with the rank of Captain. It is very doubtful tho whether I will get the position as the President [declined] appointing any more Adjt. Genls. until those now unassigned are put on duty. The Genl. hopes that he talked the Dept. into the belief that I was the only man fit for the position, and hopes that I may get the appointment yet. He has been very kind about it and says that whatever happens he will keep me on his staff in some capacity or other, and offers me the position of Ordnance officer or [Aide] in case this appointment fails. It makes me feel ashamed to think how little worth all this [trouble] my services are. But it is very pleasant to be with a man who when he shows you a kindness does it in such a handsome manner. I leave the Battalion tomorrow morning to with him as Adjt. It is quite a break up to leave the old Battalion. It is almost like home to me now and I have made so many pleasant acquaintances and friends amongst its officers and men. I am writing in a hurry so as to send this by Frank Huger who goes off on furlough in the morning. He will be promoted to Lieut. Col. now. I enclose 250 dollars which I wish you would forward to its proper destination, 165 to Edgerton & Richards, and 95 to Mr. [Henri]. This is not exactly the amount but nearly it. I am sorry to say I have owed this for some time having bought the things when I was first appointed and would have asked you to give me the money before, but was anxious to pay this debt myself and have not been able to [send] the money before. I also give Frank Huger 200 dollars to invest for me in something or other and send it to you as I will not be able to sell bonds or anything of the sort and would like to have a little fund at home to [pay] my expenses a little when I draw from you which I expect to do when I get another horse which I will do if I am promoted.

We are all very much put out about this currency bill and trying to dodge it.[66] I have to keep a hundred dollars to pay current expenses and will lose some of that but am determined not to draw any pay for this year until

---

[66] The Confederate Currency Reform Act of 1864, which reduced the money supply in the Confederate States by one-third, was passed in response to the highly inflated currency. It mandated that all large denomination bills be converted into interest-bearing Treasury bonds before April 1, 1864.

the new issue is made, or unless I can get it in five dollar notes. Please tell Ma that the box got here this evening just in time, as I and the Genl. start housekeeping tomorrow. Everything was in good condition, sausages, butter, ginger cakes and all. The peas were very acceptable as beans or anything of that kind always is. The Genl. and Frank Huger say that home and the Association are the institutions of the times. Please ask Ella whenever she sends a box to put in any old knives, forks, spoons or crockery of any kind she has to spare. It is always in demand. The silver we have used very sparingly but I sent out [Jim] foraging this morning so as to commence housekeeping in style. We move our quarters in the morning from Bulls Gap back to Greeneville where Genl. Longstreet is staying now. Capt. Parker too has been nominated as Major and Inspector but I am very much afraid he will refuse to take the place considering himself personally responsible for all the boys in his company.[67] I hope he will take it as he would be a great accession to the staff.

I am so much hurried that I hardly know what I am writing and will stop for the present, with love to Ma, Sophie and all at home. Direct to me hereafter at Genl. Longstreet's Hd Qrtrs, but don't put Captain on my letter till I write that I am appointed. If Ma could send a little box with [two] or three plates, knives &c to Major Huger [care of] Col. Preston Conscription Bureau Richmond I would get them.

Alexander C. Haskell, Orange Court House, Va., to Sophia C. Haskell USC)
14 March 1864
Dear Ma,

Just before going to church this lovely morning, I send a few lines to tell you that we are well. Yesterday, the good Bishop Johns preached in our church, and today offers the rite of confirmation & the sacrament.[68] Solemn always, it is more so than usual, to see the gathering of strong men around this sacred table, humble & earnest. I trust they will be as becomes their twofold character as soldiers.

I hope to see John soon after his return and learn from him all about his visit. I wish he could have made it longer. I have heard nothing from Joe since your last news. I hope that there will be something done to keep him with Col. Alexander, or if this is impossible, with Major Huger.

Tranquility prevails in this army, undisturbed except by the intelligence that Genl. Longstreet has [words unintelligible] and on his return to

---

[67] William Watts Parker (1824-99), a physician, was the captain of the Parker Virginia Battery, and was later promoted to the rank of major.

[68] John Johns (1796-1876) was the Episcopal bishop of Virginia. The church where he preached was St. Thomas's Episcopal Church.

Richmond is accompanied by Genl. Lee, who has not yet returned. I cannot keep half wishing that Longstreet should come back here. I think that with his assistance we might become so dangerous and active as to withdraw the great peril from Johnston, perhaps more effectually than if Longstreet goes directly to his assistance. We hear strange accounts of McLaws' old division being mounted. Nobody knows what to make of it, yet can scarcely discredit what we hear from such good & numerous authorities.

The "Box" is not exhausted yet, by many days & twice at least in each 24 hours recalls your kindness. Love to Pa & all at home. Goodbye for the present.

Alexander C. Haskell to Sophia C. Haskell (USC)
19 March 1864
Dear Ma,

Last night my box arrived with contents all safe. At the same time one came for Langdon, from Ella, which was robbed of most of its contents. Such abundant supplies make us oblivious to the fears of starvation, which hovers around the pillow of the Commissary General. The government appears at last to be taking the sensible step which will enable it to arrive at the actual resources of a much larger extent of country than it has hitherto done.

The R. R. in N. Ca. is impressed for the transportation of supplies. One only bad effect is the stoppage of furloughs to soldiers, which however was expedient other grounds. Its good effects are greatly increased facilities for supplying the army, and a check upon the restless gadding about which has kept people away from steady business & thrown them into the giddy speculations of the times. If R. Roads can be made now merely military trains I believe it would be for the good of the country's morals & develop its powers of supply amazingly.

I have not yet heard of John's arrival in the army, but hope he will not overstay his leave as it is made quite unpleasant now to do so. I propose going to see him in two or three days, when I will be pretty sure of finding him.

I heard from Joe a few days ago. There was nothing to report from the army, but personal news was interesting, as it assured me that he would in some capacity remain with Colonel, now General, Alexander, perhaps as his Asst. Adjt. Genl. If that cannot be, as his Aide-de-Camp or Ordnance Officer.

I am getting on very pleasantly, but still trust to chance to throw me into some command in the line before the summer comes. If not I have a place among men good enough to reconcile one to many smaller disadvantages. The brigade grows in strength and spirit every day & will gloriously sustain itself in the approaching [contests]. There seems to be a general confidence that this summer will end the war in our favour. The general voice of a thinking and suffering people is not often wrong. If this opinion prevails everywhere I would feel almost that a prophecy had been spoken.

Love to Pa, Sophie & all at home.

Joseph C. Haskell, Headquarters, Artillery, Army of East Tennessee, to Sophie Haskell (SCHS)
22 March 1864
My dear Sophie,

Just as I had mailed a letter to Lewis yesterday in which I reproached you for not having answered my letter, I received one from you and also a most thrilling and interesting description from Lewis of the triumphant termination of one of their fox hunts in which Renard surrendered to superior numbers after a most gallant and protracted resistance. It would really have done credit to the Turf Register.[69] I will send this to Columbia where I suppose you will be by the time it gets there, Lou being now engaged and, I therefore suppose, being somewhat subdued.[70] I shall ask to send me an account of your goings on and if you misbehave yourself as you threaten to do, shall write at once to Ma giving her a little advice on the subject.

It is snowing now and the ground is covered at least six inches deep already and you just ought to see me sitting before a big fire in a rocking chair with my feet on the mantle piece in a nicely carpeted room & enjoying the prospect out of doors. What the use of being A.A.G. if you can't be comfortable? The gent submits with a very good grace and enjoys it. The beauty of it now is that we are spoiling the Egyptians staying with a lady who is a thorough Yankee from Minnesota. Her husband is on Burnside's staff. We were looking all over town for a room the other day when we came back from our wild goose chase after the Yankees our old room having been occupied, and applied at this house amongst others but were refused. Went off disconsolate but must have made an impression during the interview, as were

---

[69] There were several 19th century publications which might be referred to here. One of the most popular was the *American Turf Register and Sporting Magazine,* which featured stories about hunting and other sports, and chronicled the pedigrees of race horses.

[70] The Haskells' cousin Louisa R. McCord (1845-1928) became engaged to Augustine Thomas Smythe (1842-1914) in February 1864. (She mistakenly wrote a date of 1863 on this letter.) "Gus" Smythe was in the Confederate Signal Corps. They were married shortly after the war ended.

pursued and caught by a note stating that on second thought had concluded to take us. Went back and immediately, established ourselves in very comfortable quarters and I hope in the good graces of the natives who have been paying us various little attentions in the way of milk cakes and such like, which are very acceptable.

There is one character about the house tho who so far has been impervious to all attacks—a real thoroughbred pretty little Yankee girl who when we first made our appearance always left the room. She has become a little mollified tho and yesterday invited us into the parlor and entertained us for some time. Winthrop and I are endeavoring to show her the error of her ways and if we stay long enough, think we will succeed. Some narrow minded people I suppose would be outraged by this course, but it is decidedly more Christian and civilized than not to have anything to say to her. I think that women have a full right to their presentiments if they don't express them in too disagreeable a manner. Spent an evening delightfully [genteelly] yesterday in the company of Mrs. Blackford, from Va., formerly from near Charlottesville, now the wife of an officer in the military court out here.[71] It is really a treat to meet a polished, refined and intelligent lady out here in the midst of the Barbarians. Never knew her before but made the best use of my evening. Before I left got on offer to work my coat collar and mend my gloves and anything else which needed a lady's attention. I have got horribly selfish lately. By the way how are the gloves getting on. The old fur fellows are good yet and have been invaluable to me this winter. Frank Huger's wore out at the fingers but he has taken them on to Richmond to get them repaired. Mrs. Blackford also promised me a cousin of hers for a sweetheart, the prettiest girl in Va. I hope she will stand up to the promise. John has a great deal of business on hand all the time. What in the world had his Battalion to do in Charlottesville? You had better raise a subscription for your indigent brother since I have lost my little [ten] I am a ruined man, and am afraid I will never get even again. Answer this letter soon and give me all the news from Columbia. Letters are all that keep me alive now. Love to Aunt Louisa, Han, Lou and Lottie. Ask if [they] have got my letter.

---

[71] Susan Leigh Blackford (1835-1916) was the wife of Charles Minor Blackford (1833-1903), a Virginia lawyer and author, and a judge advocate on General Longstreet's military court. Their memoirs were published in 1894, and an abridged version was later published as *Letters from Lee's Army.*

Joseph C. Haskell, Headquarters, First Corps, Army of Northern Virginia,
Gordonsville, Va., to Charles T. Haskell, Abbeville, S.C. (SCHS)
24 April 1864
Dear Pa,

I met John yesterday, who told me that you had written word of a mare
at home which you would buy if any of us wanted her, and he wrote that I
would need her as it impossible for me to buy a good one here. Such is the
case, but I am compelled to buy one of some sort at once, as there is a prospect of active operations commencing any day, and though I would be delighted to get the mare if you are kind enough to buy her, I can't wait for the
chance of getting her on to Va. The horse I get will probably be a government animal and there is no chance of finding a stylish mount yet. I hope to
get an efficient one. 150 horses will be issued tomorrow and I will try and
get one if possible. You can't imagine how disagreeable it is to be without a
horse. Borrowing is out of the question entirely, and here I am in the midst
of old friends and acquaintances and can't see them once a week.

We are going to have a Review of the Corps on Wednesday tho and I
need to be mounted by that time. Aleck was down here the other day and
rode John's old sorrel horse in a race in which he displayed such skill as a
jockey as to inspire the admiration of all beholders. He was victorious of
course. I think my last letter was from Charlottesville, which place we left on
last Thursday to the regret of all parties, as we had enjoyed ourselves up
there very much indeed and look forward to a return there with the greatest
anxiety. If I was to get sick or wounded now I don't know where I would go,
to Richmond, Lynchburg or Charlottesville. I am rather inclined to the latter tho. We stopped one night in Lynchburg and I happened to make the
acquaintance of a Mrs. Speed, a most delightful person and in charge of the
Ladies hospital at that place, of which she gave me such an account that I
was almost tempted to get sick on the spot and would have done so but that
we were on the way to Charlottesville.[72] We are now located in what is generally known as the Green Springs neighborhood and [said] to be a very delightful place. I find we are camped quite near some Orange C H friends we
knew last summer, and spent a very pleasant evening over there yesterday
with John. He is camped about a mile off and we see a good deal of each
other. I go over there whenever we don't have any dinner and manage to
pick up a precarious subsistence in that way. Our supplies which we got in
Tennessee and rations for the whole month of April gave out yesterday and
we had no meat for breakfast, which consisted of biscuits, and did not know

---

[72] Mrs. Catherine Page Waller Speed (born 1819) was the wife of John M. Speed
(1815-66), a lawyer of Lynchburg, Va.

where we would get any dinner when a most unexpected surprise came on in the shape of a ham sent over by John, one which he had got from home. There is no chance of buying anything here as the people have been on rations. Grown ones 1/4 pound of bacon and children get 1/8. All the rest has been impressed. Everyone submits to it cheerfully or without complaint, apparently buoyed up by the hope that this is to be the last year of the war. It is singular how general that opinion has become. I almost begin to believe it myself. It is astonishing to hear the perfect confidence with which everyone in the army speaks of the coming campaign. No one seems to doubt it in the least. It seems to be the confidence of strength and determination. I have not met either Lally or Aleck yet but hope to soon. The box has not come yet. Please give my love to Ma and the boys.

THE FINAL MONTHS

7 MAY 1864 – 26 MARCH 1865

John's first letter in May is written from the Wilderness battlefield, where General James Longstreet has been seriously wounded by friendly fire. After suffering a serious abdominal wound at the Battle of Cold Harbor in late May 1864, Aleck is sent by train to a hospital in Richmond. The following month he is promoted from the rank of lieutenant colonel to colonel, and by the first of July he returns to active service. During the Siege of Petersburg, which begins on June 18, John writes from the defensive lines there that "balls are continually hitting the trench and covering me with dirt." In August, Langdon is at Chaffin's Bluff on the James River with Brigadier General James Conner, who is in temporary command of McGowan's Brigade. As October begins, John is ordered to take his artillery battalion across the James River in an effort to retake Fort Harrison, which had been captured by the enemy on September 29. His battalion is involved in a fight on the Darbytown Road on October 7, during which John suffers a grazing wound to the head, and Aleck receives his most serious injury of the war. Joseph visits Aleck in Richmond the next day, writing: "His wound is in the left eye fracturing the skull and completely blinding the eye." The first letter Louis writes as a soldier is dated November 29, 1864. In December, his regiment of Junior Reserves is stationed at Grahamville in Beaufort District, South Carolina. On December 5, Langdon becomes Assistant Adjutant General to General Richard H. Anderson. Aleck, still recovering from his head wound, visits South Carolina, writing from Columbia in December. In January 1865, he arranges for his brother Louis and a young cousin, Langdon Cheves, to be transferred to his cavalry command, and he returns to active service in Virginia by the end of the month. In a letter written the following month, Aleck is distressed to hear of Sherman's destructive campaign in South Carolina, declaring that he "would be happy even in the misery of a bloody fight if it were against this hateful Sherman." In mid-February, about the time of the burning of Columbia by Sherman's army, John is promoted to the rank of lieutenant colonel, commanding Haskell's Battalion in General Alexander's First Army Corps, Army of Northern Virginia. Louis writes from North Carolina on March 19 while he is on his way to Virginia, mentioning that Langdon is also en route to that destination, returning from a furlough. Aleck's last wartime letter, written during the last days of the Siege of Petersburg, is dated March 26, 1865. Less than two weeks later at Appomattox, he will be designated by General Robert E. Lee to lead the surrender the cavalry of the Army of Northern Virginia. John will lead the artillery.

John C. Haskell, Wilderness Battlefield, Va., to Sophia C. Haskell (UNC)
7 May 1864
Dear Mother,

I have neglected so long to answer your letter that I feel quite ashamed but for some time I have been so very busy that it has been almost impossible for me to write. Day before yesterday we had a fearful fight in which we were victorious, but at a terrible cost. South Carolina (Kershaw's Brigade especially) suffered particularly losing some of her best field officers early in the day when Longstreet went in forming under a furious fire with [Heth's] worthless men breaking through his [lines]. No men in [the world] but Longstreet and his men could have done what he did and he is acknowledged to have saved the day. Later in the day he made a magnificent attack and was driving the enemy in great confusion when poor Jenkins' Brigade which he had been leading began to [cheer him] and Mahone's Virginia Brigade mistaking them for the enemy opened a severe fire at about seventy five yards wounding Longstreet very severely and killing Jenkins and young Dobey of Kershaw's staff who was a classmate and friend of Alick's at college.[1] Longstreet was struck in the throat, the ball glancing off to the right side and passing through his shoulder. I have been with him a good deal since he was hurt. The first day he suffered terribly but yesterday morning he was much better and in good spirits. He went up yesterday to Orange C[ourt] H[ouse] to the house of his Quartermaster Major Taylor.[2] He says he will be back in five weeks but I am afraid it will take him much longer than that. Up to this time the Artillery has had nothing to do worth speaking of. The battle ground is a dense thicket of chinquapin bushes and scrub

---

[1] Mahone's Brigade was commanded by General William Mahone (1826-95) of Virginia. Brigadier General Micah Jenkins (1835-64) of South Carolina was wounded by friendly fire during the Battle of the Wilderness in Virginia and died a few hours later. General James Longstreet, who was riding with Jenkins, was also wounded by friendly fire but survived. Lieutenant Alfred English Doby (1840-64) of Camden, S.C., an aide to General James B. Kershaw was killed in the same battle on May 6, 1864.

[2] Major Erasmus Taylor (1830-1907) was quartermaster of the First Corps, Army of Northern Virginia.

oaks where you can't see a man more than twenty steps in front. You will of course have heard of Langdon and the misfortune he met in having his horse killed before this. I saw him yesterday. He is looking well as are also Genl (McGowan) and Allen Wardlaw. I have just got orders to march in about an hour (it is now about [ten] o'clock at night) to get on the left of the enemy so I suppose at last the Artillery will have its chance. I telegraphed yesterday to Alick at Richmond that we are all well. Joe is camped within fifty yards of me. I saw him a few minutes ago. You spoke in your letter of giving Willy's money which is in Tom Dudley's hands to little Decca. I am sure all of us would like that disposition of it. It was Willy's intention to have [directed] it to a trip to Europe after the war. Please give my love to Pa and all at home.

Alexander C. Haskell, near Drewry's Bluff, Va., to Sophia C. Haskell (USC)
20 May 1864
Dear Ma,

I have been too sick at heart and anxious to write. I have been unable to hear from the dear boys in the great army except reports that all are well and safe. God grant that it may be so. I wrote to Tom Dudley who promised to watch and telegraph to you whatever occurred. There is a lull in the battles for the present. I can form no idea as to when they will be renewed. So far we have much to be thankful for. The enemy is checked and baffled at all points with terrible loss. Our own noble armies have lost many of the best and bravest. For myself I have but little to say. My duties are different from those of former times and the command is as yet merely nominal. With what we had however an immense deal of work has been performed in pick-eting, watching and scouting, but little fighting. A great portion of the work has devolved upon me and sleepless anxious night after night distracted my thoughts from the dear old brigade and army to which I had just bidden adieu. The regt. is assembling today. I hope I can strike some good blows now in the great struggle. May God keep my brothers and friends and help our country in its greatest need.

Love to Pa and the boys and Sophie too I suppose is at home.

John C. Haskell, Petersburg, Va., to Sophie Haskell (SCHS)
21 June 1864
Dear Sophie,

I have been patiently waiting, expecting, expecting a letter from you to start our correspondence but I suppose you have been living such a gay life that you have not had much spare time for writing so at last I have [deter-mined] to take the initiative and write to you. I suppose you have had a very pleasant time in Columbia. I have heard of you there several times.

We are doing nothing of consequence here nor do I think we will at all [in this line] as the Yankees only gained partial success before this army got here, and since it arrived they have made no attempts and our works here have been improved and strengthened, and our men rested, and last but by no means least nearly all Beauregard's men—new issue they are called by our men—have been relieved and their places taken by Lee's army or a part of it. Longstreet's Corps occupies most of the line. Beauregard pronounced his men exhausted after [eleven] days in the trenches so our [fresh] men who had been fighting for only forty seven days almost daily were sent in to relieve the veterans, and for the last five days we have been in this first line which is now almost impregnable, but is excessively hot as it is on a high bare hill where there is not a bush and where if a man shews his head he is certain to be shot at immediately. I am a little more comfortable as some of my men have built me a small [fort] and covered it with the bushes so that I have a place to myself where I can read, whenever I caught a book and where I am writing now, but balls are continually hitting the trench and covering me with dirt which is anything but pleasant. Sharpshooting is continually going on along the lines and several men have been shot close about me today who exposed themselves, but except this [picking] off of stray men nothing is being done nor will be I think. I saw Joe several days ago. He is quite well but I see little of him as this is not a pleasant place to visit by any means. I send enclosed a letter for [Alick] which came with my mail today.

John C. Haskell, near Petersburg, Va., to Sophia C. Haskell (SCHS)
1 July 1864
Dear Mother,

Yesterday the first mails came through that have been received for nearly a month, and as I hear that the mails start South today for the first time I write so as to take advantage of the opportunity before the railroad is cut again. I have heretofore invariably forgotten when writing to thank you for the horses which I have received generally when sorely in need of them. One horse took a little over two months to come but arrived safe at last. It came just as the campaign began and then it was running all over the country to keep out of the hands of the raiders.

Yesterday I got a horse and Joe got one at the same time, there were also two, one for Alick and the other for Langdon, both of which I told the agent to carry on to Richmond. Alick's he carried on, but he left Langdon's here and I am afraid it will be some time before he gets it as his brigade is at Drewry's Bluff. I will try to send it to him if I get a chance for I have no doubt but that he is [indigent] as the [rough] ration which they allow officers to buy now, a third of a pound of bacon and other things in proportion costs within five cents of four dollars a day, and will cost a subaltern nearly a fourth more than his pay.

When Alick comes on I will be very much obliged, if you have plenty of it, if you will send me a bottle of red pepper which I promised to try to get for Genl. Anderson who is [commanding] our Corps. Joe is camped about half a mile from me but I have not seen him for a day or two as I have been quite busy. He sent me word yesterday that he had heard from Pa that all are well at home. I will see him today. Everything is very much the same as it was [the weather also] except that it is not quite as hot and a good deal more dusty. A great many reports are flying about, the last is that Grant was killed yesterday [or in captivity], that Genl. Lee will either attack Grant or send off some more of his army to Maryland but these are only conjectures.[3]

Please give my love to Pa, Sophie and the boys.

Alexander C. Haskell, Columbia, S.C., to Charles T. Haskell,
Abbeville, S.C. (USC)
26 [July] 1864
Dear Pa,

I have succeeded in getting off my horse with prospects of a safe journey. They go by the Danville route. I sent the seeds, turnip & onion.

I got from Dr. Chisolm[4] 4 instead of 2 pounds of mustard. He had the four pounds put up in such nice looking tin cases that I disliked to break your present.

He paid me $276, deducting the mustard given to me & that which you had taken. This money I do not send you. I have devoted $175 to the payment of the sword, a beautiful one, which you ordered for me. The remainder went to keep paying my bill to Dr. Patrick for nine plugs which he put in my mouth. I went to him just in time to save myself great pain & much injury.

I write in haste to say goodbye to all. I am much stronger and I think in good condition for the journey.

Baby is flourishing and will soon pay you a visit. Write and tell Mrs. Singleton of any opportunities in the next two weeks for baby & Lessie to go up. It may be that Mrs. S. will be obliged to start for Virginia, so soon as to prevent her making the visit she contemplated. Jeb is much improved, moves better and looks well. I have as good a horse as is to be found in the service.

Roland Rhett has given me in friendly exchange for my own, the finest saddle I ever saw. It is priceless and a wonder of comfort & security.

---

[3] General Ulysses S. Grant was in command of the Union armies.
[4] This was likely Dr. Julian John Chisolm (1830-1903), a Confederate surgeon.

Goodbye. Love to Ma and all at home.

Alexander C. Haskell, Camp Seventh S. C. Cavalry,
to Charles T. Haskell, Abbeville, S.C. (USC)
2 August 1864
Dear Pa,

I find my strength, health and I regret to add, my appetite improving daily. I am very busy. I find my command in fine heart with a good reputation & confident of their ability to whip cavalry, infantry or gun boats if they have a fair chance, but much reduced in numbers by death, wounds & sickness, horses very thin and suffering. I hope however very soon to improve the appearance of things. [My own] mare I find so weak, [her] wound in bad condition [that] she is worse than useless. I can hear nothing from Jeb & July but hope they will be on soon. I am now riding a horse borrowed from one of my men.

I got a note from Langdon of the 31 July. He was well and had lately heard the same from Joe & John. He says that there is [every] reason to believe that Allen fell into the hands of the Yankee cavalry.[5]

I hear but little from Grant's army, or our own. Things seem as usual.

Our friends in Richmond are well & send love. I suppose baby & Lessie will soon be with you. I think you will find the little one improved & hope that Lessie will be made strong & well by the change. Love to Ma, Sophie & all at home.

Langdon C. Haskell, Headquarters, Aiken's House near Chaffin's Bluff, Va.,
to Sophie Haskell (SCHS)
5 August 1864
My dear Sophie,

I was waked up this morning by the arrival of three letters and one of them from you, which was welcome for itself and then again for the surprise. Our camp life becomes very monotonous and letters form one of the most agreeable relaxations which we enjoy. I am particularly solitary now as poor

---

[5] George Allen Wardlaw, a captain on General McGowan's staff, was captured on July 28, 1864, near Richmond, Va. He was imprisoned at Fort Delaware until he was exchanged in early 1865. According to a Wardlaw family history, he came home to South Carolina for a short rest and then attempted to return to Virginia to rejoin his regiment, but did not arrive until after the surrender. He died on July 9, 1865. His obituary in the *Abbeville Press* stated that "his constitution had been much impaired by long confinement as a Prisoner of War." His gravestone states the following: "Long a prisoner in Fort Delaware. Broken by exposure and hardships, he returned home to die." His father's history of the Wardlaw family states that he died in Savannah, Ga.

Allen has fallen into the hands of the enemy as you will have learned by former letters, and Genl. Conner is not at all an agreeable companion.[6] I fear he must be unhesitatingly classified as an egregious snob and though not wanting in ability, and possibly a pretty fair officer, his snobbery and small restless ambition is too much for this hot weather and I retire to some shady tree and sleep or consume some miserably stupid Confederate publication. I would like to have Sir Charles Grandison in 6 vols.[7] Or some other of those ancient novels now that would last me some time on. I even think I might read that celebrated book of Jordan's the "Evil One Revealed." I have been in low spirits about Allen for though I believe he is safe and only a prisoner in the hands of the enemy, still there is an uncertainty about it which is very distressing, especially when I think of the grief it will cause his father and sisters. But there are times when we must try and put away all gloomy forebodings and take comfort from every day that passes without a disaster to our camp, our friends, and our hopes.

The struggle here before Petersburg & Richmond waxes hot and cold by turn & we have this to encourage us, that almost every time the opposing forces have met, we have wasted them badly. Even in this affair of the mine opening before Petersburg the enemy sustained a loss of near 5 to our 1.[8] It has been a terrible campaign. Today is exactly three months since the first shot was fired and there has not a day passed that we have not (some part of the army) been face to face with the enemy, and some, one or many of our officers and men have fought their last fight. For the last month we here have been at rest except the fight which we had on the 28th July.[9] This was quite a bloody affair for us and would have been a very successful one, but for the failure of other troops to do their duty. Our brigades and divisions are like machines, if any one part of it gets out of order, the machine stops or if forced, breaks. We brought off however one gun out of a battery of four which our brigade captured.[10]

---

[6] Brigadier James Conner (1829-83), a South Carolinian who was in temporary command of McGowan's Brigade.

[7] *The History of Sir Charles Grandison* was an epistolary novel by Samuel Richardson published in 1753.

[8] This refers to an enemy mine explosion under part of the Confederate defense line at Petersburg, the ensuing battle known as the Battle of the Crater.

[9] Langdon is referring to the Battle of Deep Bottom, Va. A regimental history records that McGowan's Brigade suffered 21 killed and 153 wounded in this fight.

[10] In his memoir, John C. Haskell noted that the Federal forces were also throwing shells into the city, and that several non-combatants were killed as a result. "There was no justification for it, and it was done in sheer, brutal wantonness. The firing could hurt no one but women, children, and old men." Haskell, *The Haskell Memoirs*, 80.

We are staying now in tents in a tolerably cool place, but I have always found the heat in Virginia very great, & utterly exasperating when one has nothing to do. The nights however are very pleasant and before morning a blanket is generally quite an addition to your comfort. We are getting very tired of bacon. Nothing but bacon to eat now for 6 months and we sigh for the days when good beef and flour was abundant in Virginia and are inclined to envy our more fortunate brethren under Early their trip to Maryland and Pennsylvania. I understand it was reported at home that we were going to reinforce Early, but there is no such good luck for us. Genl. Lee has cut down his army here as much as is prudent and no more will go from it in my opinion. It was a very bold measure from the first and such a move as no General of ours but Genl. Lee would attempt. We used to think Genl. Lee slow, but he has more dash in him than any of our younger leaders. Hood, however, has a chance now to make himself illustrious & better than this to do more for peace than any man in the Confederacy by whipping Sherman out of Georgia.[11] Matters have come to a standstill here unless their mining operations are continued and I would not be surprised if we remained here for the rest of the summer and perhaps until both armies are rained and snowed out of the trenches. If Grant will cut loose from his fastnesses and come out for a fight I believe we will whip him easily. The slaughter in his army has been terrible beyond precedent. He had the other day what would amount to two large Regts in these days annihilated in the breach made in our lines.[12]

Alick I have not yet seen, but received a note from him announcing his wellbeing and arrival at his command which is some 10 miles from us. If he does not come first I will go to see him in a day or two. John and Joe are both well by very late accounts and John illustrating himself by bombarding the enemy's lines in which they say he is quite successful. He is in general charge of that department of the artillery. I would like very much to be with you all a while, but there is no chance for it until the leaves fall & the wind comes. There is one thing or two which you may do for me. You can make me a jar of sorghum preserves and if you could undertake a pair of gloves it would be of great service to me. I am still wearing, and expect to wear for some time longer those you made me last year. And they have been admired by Genl. Lee who inspected and commended them. A piece of sheep skin

---

[11] General William T. Sherman (1820-91) had invaded Georgia and was making his way to Atlanta with an army of sixty thousand men. His opponent, Confederate General Joseph E. Johnston, was replaced by General John Bell Hood in July 1864.

[12] General Grant was called a "butcher" by some in the North and the South because of the high numbers of casualties he incurred in his operations against the Confederates.

would be the most available or some stout cloth. I left a piece of gray cloth at home out of which a pair might be cut without serious disturbance to it and it will I think do very well.

Love to Ma, Pa and all with you.

Joseph C. Haskell, Headquarters First Army Corps, Petersburg, Va.,
to Sophie Haskell (SCHS)
8 August 1864
Dear Sophie,

I got your letter a few days ago and intended answering it immediately but the weather is so dreadfully hot that I have hardly recovered from the shock of the one I wrote Pa. It is just sunrise now but the heat is offensive. I said nothing in my letter which calls for such recrimination on your part and I believe it's nothing but an attack to cover some of your movements. You need not try any such game as that on me. The fact is tho some of these Va. girls are enough to make anybody to think matrimony or any other foolish thing. There is no knowing what might have been the result of our stay here but for the fact that Grant's shells drove all the girls out of town, with a few exceptions. There was one delightful little exception in the person of Miss Marion Meade of this place, sister of Lieut. Meade who was in Fort Sumter.[13] He was a classmate and very dear friend of General Alexander's, and through the Genl. I got to knowing this most charming family. There are two or three other sisters besides this one, all as pleasant, but none as young or pretty. They are real old Va. people, poor and proud, but have a fine old house handsomely furnished and everything about them in same style. The old lady their mother is a widow, one of the old school people, and I flatter myself I quite won her regard by my respectful attentions. It is my painful duty to say that they have all left town leaving a terrible blank behind them as Col. Huger and myself were in the habit of passing a great deal of our time around there. We are comforted by the reflection tho that it may not be wasted, for the chances of war may bring us back here once more and then...but I will let you know in time.

I was never more mistaken in my life than when I formed my estimate of Virginia ladies by what I saw of them in Richmond. It has only been this year that I've had the opportunities of seeing and judging of Virginians as they were before the war, and I tell you they ain't to be beat anywhere. Make the most of that.

---

[13] Richard Kidder Meade (1835-62), a Virginian, had been an officer in Major Robert Anderson's garrison at Fort Moultrie and Fort Sumter before joining the Confederate Army.

What do you mean by talking about being fastidious and wanting a phoenix or some other outlandish thing. You better be glad to have some human with the usual proportion of limbs for they will be scarce after the war. Lou had displayed her wisdom in taking advantage of her opportunities. You had better do likewise. But my letter will be about as foolish as yours if I don't stop this nonsense and proceed to business. The gauntlets are the very thing. I would send them as soon as possible. I am afraid they won't get here before we start for Maryland. Rumor speaking through the mouth of Robert Gibbes says the infantry of our corps has started already. This is true I know so far as Kershaw's Div. is concerned. Whether the other two, Field's[14] and Pickett's,[15] will follow I don't know but trust they will. None of the art[illery] has been ordered to move yet nor will probably until a large force of the infantry is withdrawn from the line. Everyone seems to have come to the conclusion that this is the only way of getting Grant from Petersburg, that is by threatening Washington and it will probably be done. He caught up the other morning with only Beauregard's troops and one div. of the 3rd Corps, but [we] swept him [away]. The only excitement since then has been our springing a mine under their picket line and blowing some of them to kingdom come.[16]

Major Gibbes who [is] mentioned as being wounded has recovered wonderfully and is now out of danger.[17] [*The rest of this letter is faded and illegible.*]

Joseph C. Haskell, Headquarters, Artillery, First Army Corps,
to Sophia C. Haskell (SCHS)
18 August 1864
Dear Ma,

I received you letter some days ago but have been so busy ever since the Genl. came back that I've not had time to time to answer it before.[18] We've just been run in off the lines by a pouring rain and have a few hours quiet in consequence. The Genl. came back on Sunday and has been hard at work

---

[14] Major General Charles William Fields (1828-92) commanded the division formerly led by General John Bell Hood.

[15] Major General George Edward Pickett (1825-75) commanded a division in Longstreet's Corps.

[16] This likely refers to an incident that took place on August 5 in which the Confederates exploded a mine in front of the Federal 18th Corps at Petersburg.

[17] Wade Hampton Gibbes (1837-1903) of Longstreet's Corps was seriously wounded during the Siege of Petersburg, Virginia.

[18] General E. P. Alexander returned to Virginia from a furlough home on August 15, 1864. Alexander, *Fighting for the Confederacy*, 471.

ever since. Genl. Huger & I thought there was no room for improvement but he has managed to find a good deal. All interest has been centered for the last few days in the operations on the north side of the James but we have gotten up quite an excitement on our right this evening and a brisk fight is going on there now. The Yankees are endeavouring to cut the Weldon road I suppose. We will hear all about it I suppose in the paper.

We are getting very tired of this place and hope very much that we will move soon now that all our infantry has been withdrawn from the trenches here, 1st Corps infantry, I mean. Genl. Alexander speaks of moving in person tomorrow. I think it's more than doubtful tho. There is too much engineering to be done on this line for him to leave [for] a while. All my acquaintances have left town now and I would like to leave too. All of Genl. Lee's army has gone but part of one corps. Major Gibbes is staying with his wife at a very nice place close by our camp and I manage to spend most of my spare time there. His wife, formerly Miss Mason and sister of Mrs. Alexander, is a most charming person and it's very pleasant now that Gibbes is getting so much better.[19] He will probably leave for Columbia on Monday. Do tell Sophie if she is in Columbia at any time when Mrs. Gibbes is there to call on her as a favor to me. She is one of the finest women I've met in Va. and we owe all we can possibly pay in the way of attention and kindness to Virginians. Tell her I want her particularly to see Mrs. Gibbes and know her as being a particular and dear friend of mine, and she's not to mind where or who she is living with, and do Ma remember it too if you get a chance. John is flourishing. Don't know anything of Lally and Alick. Will write soon to make up for this short stupid letter. Do give my love to Pa, Sophie and the boys.

Joseph C. Haskell, Headquarters, Artillery, First Army Corps, to Sophia C. Haskell (SCHS)
6 September 1864
Dear Ma,

Our life here is so uninterrupted and so uninteresting that it is hard to keep in mind the fact that people at home are not aware of the do nothing condition of affairs here and consequently I don't write as often as when we are more actively engaged. The excitement of the past few days has been the unexpected arrival of a box from home. They generally are so slow in coming that their arrival is anxiously looked for and expected long before that happy

---

[19] Major Gibbes' wife was Jane Allen Mason Gibbes (1840-87), the daughter of Dr. Alexander Hamilton Mason (1807-58) of Virginia. Her sister Betty Jacqueline Mason (1836-99) was the wife of General Edward Porter Alexander.

event occurs. This one tho preceded Paul's letter of announcement by a day, and its coming was hardly more unexpected than gratifying. I am very much afraid tho that these boxes will be felt as a real tax at home, that is as far as the bacon goes. Everything else I know is abundant and we accept them with clear consciences, but I am afraid that the above named article will be found wanting at home if you don't stop sending so much to the army. The hominy is a great treat and holds out so long. I had given out the last cup full of what came in the box last month on the very morning this box arrived. Then Genl. brought on a good deal of rice, and Hopin John (I never tried to spell it before) will be an institution in our establishment all this winter.[20] The can of jam got opened and was considerably adulterated with peas but that with the cake made a lunch last Sunday after church when Lally and several other friends called of which I felt quite proud. The tomato catsup is a real treat. The Genl. and John Bull say it's the best they ever saw. You told me to ask for anything I wanted in the eating line. If you could save us some of the white butter beans we have at home every spring I think they would be very nice. What do you think of sweet potatoes at 2.50 a quart. That's what I paid for some in the market this morning. Quite an extravagance, but some friends are expected to dinner and we have to keep up the reputation of Hd. Qrs.

We were all very much disheartened by Hood's disaster at Atalanta [sic], just when things looked so hopeful and bright but the spirit which has sustained our gallant army and people so long lives still, and the struggle is but protracted.[21]

We are very pleasantly camped in a pretty yard in the midst of town. The house was deserted when we pitched our tent in the yard, but the family has returned now and they are as kind as possible in insisting on our remaining. The Genl. wants to leave and is now looking for a camp. The gentleman of the place is a son of old Johnson of Va. of horse racing memory and a very pleasant man indeed. The Genl. and myself were this morning at our kind friends Mrs. Cameron's.[22] I believe I told you about her before. Her husband is Agt. for one of the blockade co.s and is now immensely wealthy. Mrs. Cameron is about 39 without children and with a heart as big as her

---

[20] Hoppin' John was originally a South Carolina Lowcountry dish made with rice, cowpeas, bacon and onions.

[21] General John Bell Hood failed to break General William T. Sherman's siege of Atlanta and evacuated the city on September 2, 1864.

[22] Martha Louisa Russell Cameron (1833-1903) was the wife of William Cameron (1829-1902), who is described in John C. Haskell's memoir as "president of a very successful blockade company and a most hospitable entertainer of Confederate officers." The Camerons lived in Petersburg, Virginia. Haskell, *The Haskell Memoirs*, 89.

body which is not a small one. Gibbes stayed there when he was wounded and we went there to see him at first and now if John or I are not there at least once a day she thinks something has certainly gone wrong. I cannot tell you how much she has added to the actual comforts of our [duty] here. The weather is raw and bleak. I hope will clear off cool. Love to Pa, Sophie and the boys.

Joseph C. Haskell, Richmond, Va., to Sophie Haskell (SCHS)
8 October 1864
My dear Sophie,

I write to you as I think it likely that Ma and Pa will have started for Va. before this reaches you. I came up from Camp this morning and saw dear Aleck for the first time since his wound.[23] The doctor thinks him a little better this morning but all he can say is that there is hope and that is all. So many wounds in the head, apparently mortal, have recovered that doctor Gibson says he has hope, but that the chances are rather against him. His wound is in the left eye fracturing the skull and completely blinding the eye. He is conscious this morning and recognized me when I spoke to him.

All we can do now is to pray for him and trust in God. John is slightly wounded on the left of the head and is going about too much I am afraid for his own good.[24] Fortunately it has turned cool and there is no danger from exposure to the sun. Lally was not over here but I believe he is quite well having escaped so far as I can hear from all dangers. I am as well as ever. It seems all must go before me. Yesterday when that ball struck John and he fell over on me, we were sitting by each other on horseback. I felt almost angry that he should be hit and I by his side should escape.

Love to all at home. I will remain until tomorrow and will write you then.

Louisa S. McCord, Columbia, S.C., to Sophia C. Haskell (SCHS)
9 October 1864
My dear Sister,

Mrs. Singleton will doubtless forward by this same mail the distressing dispatches which she has received. God help us! we must bear, but it is hard! I still trust that the very remarkable recuperation powers which Aleck has hitherto shown when wounded, may aid him through this, so much worse

---

[23] Aleck Haskell was seriously wounded in an engagement on the Darbytown Road near Richmond on October 7, 1864. This engagement was also known as the Battle of Johnson's Farm.

[24] John C. Haskell was wounded at the Darbytown Road fight when a minie ball grazed his head.

than his preceding wounds. (John as Mrs. Singleton will no doubt inform you is well again from a very slight injury.) So long as Dr. Gibson says that there is some hope & the last dispatch does say so, I cannot but have faith in the strength of Aleck's constitution which has so wonderfully stood preceding shocks. I hope that you may have seen through the paper that your boys are wounded & that you may come down by tomorrow's car. If so, you will not receive this. Should you however be still at home I shall hope very soon to see you down. If in my crippled condition I can do anything, let me know, & believe me with earnest sympathy

[P.S.] Should you leave home & Sophie not ready to leave with you let her come down with Hannah & stay till your return.

Alexander C. Haskell, Columbia, S.C., to Sophie C. Haskell (USC)
24 November 1864
Dear Ma,

I am still doing well though my wound is getting slow [*sic*]. Baby is quite well and all our friends here. I expect to come up on Saturday, day after tomorrow. I think it doubtful whether I can ride or drive home the same evening as I am unable still to go any distance without great fatigue. I may spend the evening with Ella at the Judge's and go out next morning. I have no news or ideas about Georgia affairs. I hope I will see Lewis. I will come alone for the present as I must run back here on business before very long. Love to Pa & all.

Louis W. Haskell, Camp near Hamburg, S.C.[25],
to Sophie Haskell (SCHS)
29 November 1864
Dear Sophy,

We have fixed up in camp and I am pretty comfortable as our orderly has a very large wall tent and for the present at any rate all the officers have honored him by making use of his tent. All the rest of the company are making brush tents. We have the finest set of boys as far as I have seen in camp but Capt. Goodwin's Bonham Guards is the best company.[26] It has the advantages of being formed of gentlemen and perhaps what is more ad-

---

[25] Hamburg was a market town in Edgefield District, S.C., located across the Savannah River from Augusta, Georgia.

[26] Artemas Darby Goodwyn (1827-98) served as the lieutenant colonel of the Second South Carolina Volunteer Infantry Regiment. After being wounded in Virginia, he resigned that command in June 1863. While still a convalescent, he raised a company of boys, the Bonham Guards, which became Company K of the Third Regiment, Junior Reserves, South Carolina State Troops.

vantage to still [*sic*] is that they have a good captain, who I found out and immediately claimed kin with him. He invited me to camp, where I met some very nice fellows indeed.

When I got to this part of my letter we had to go down to draw guns. We got splendid guns, Enfield rifles with a cartridge box & everything of that sort complete. Some of the boys are so small that I don't think that they can carry their guns, and when Hopkinson comes he will be among that crowd.[27]

I have got Mr. Porcher[28] the place of 2nd sergeant and if Moses [Tagart] is elected colonel I have made him promise to make him his adjutant.

Last night we had quite an excitement. I was spending the afternoon at Capt. Goodwin's camp and we heard cannon open over in Augusta. The Capt. got on his horse expecting certainly that it was a fight, as it was too late for practicing, but after some time he came back and said they were firing blank cartridges for fun but as soon as it commenced every one of the company packed up everything they had. The slander on the Militia is that as soon as the firing commenced every Militiaman who was in Augusta struck out for the Carolina side, for the defence of their native soil, but I think that this can't be so. At any rate none of my company were there.

A soldier is on a visit to our camp who tells me that J. G. Barnwell is in [Augusta] in the hospital and I am going over to see him. There are a good many reports flying about but no reliable news.

Give my love to Ma, Pa and all at home.

Louis W. Haskell, Grahamville[29], *S.C., to Charles T. Haskell* (SCHS)
7 December 1864
Dear Pa,

This morning we were in our first rain and did not like it so much that I would like to be in another one. We were down in the trenches and the

---

[27] This was likely Francis Hopkinson (1847-98), the son of James Hopkinson (1810-75) of Edisto Island, S.C. Francis was the namesake of his great-grandfather Francis Hopkinson (1737-1791), who was one of the signers of the Declaration of Independence.

[28] Octavius T. Porcher and the older boys from his school in Willington enlisted in the reserves in 1864. They became Company G of the First Regiment, Junior Reserves, South Carolina State Troops. According to a memoir written by Samuel W. Ravenel, these members of the "Boy Brigade" were mustered into active service on December 1, 1864, and transported by train to Grahamville, S.C., where the Battle of Honey Hill had recently taken place nearby.

[29] Grahamville was a village in Beaufort District, S.C. It was burned by Federal troops in January 1865.

rain started about an hour before we were relieved, and the relief came too late to late to save us from the rain, but they are moving about all the time. This evening they intended to move camp for good and carry us down to the trenches, but we had given our guns to the company that relieved us this morning, and we had to stay to draw guns, so that we are not going till tomorrow morning.

Being in the rain this morning determined me still more that I would like very much to indeed to have the tent, and as I think that we will stay here for some time, I think it would be a first rate thing to do with the tent, and we are very much in need of an axe and the mess would buy one but nothing of the sort is to be had here, and while all these things are being sent something to eat would not do me any harm. I expect by this time that you think that I have learnt to beg pretty well for being in camp so short a time, but it seems to me that I have been in camp for at least a month, and when I think how near we are to Christmas, it scares me, for I don't think I will see home.

The election in our regiment was held yesterday but it has not been decided yet whether Griffin will be Col or not.[30] If he is not elected a man who is named Hall, who is not even here, and has never been in the army will be elected. Griffin hate [*sic*] the idea of being beaten by him tremendously, and I think myself that it would be a pretty hard case for they say that he was a first rate officer and kept his regiment in good order. If the other man is elected, he graduated at West Point and has been keeping a military school, so that he will not be a very bad officer I expect after all. A man from Anderson is elected Lt. Colonel, and for Major we have a Yankeefied [edition] of Steven Debruhl,[31] if you remember him, named Dyke. A thoroughbred [Massachusetts] Yankee who has been keeping school in Abbeville for the last five years and has been going round bribing the sixteen year old men with whisky, or so they tell me, and I believe it is certainly so.

I don't know much more news here than you do at home. It seems to be pretty positive that the enemy cut the telegraph between Coosawhatchie & the Tulifinny Rivers. It is not known whether they cut the railroad or not and they burnt the bridge on the public road.

Mr. Porcher sends his respects. Do give my love to Ma, Sophy, Alick & all at home.

---

[30] This was James Benjamin Griffin (1825-81) of Edgefield District, S.C. He was elected colonel of the First Regiment, Junior Reserves, South Carolina State Troops, on December 27, 1864.

[31] The 1850 Abbeville District census lists a Stephen DeBruhl as a resident.

Joseph C. Haskell, Headquarters, First Army Corps, to Sophie Haskell (SCHS)
7 December 1864
Dear Sophia,

I received a letter some days ago and certainly have not shown my appreciation of it by putting off answering so long. My reasons are many and good, and you must imagine them sufficient without demanding a more complete statement. I am anxious to hear from home to know what Louis is doing with the Reserves. I suppose all anxiety with regard to Sherman's movements as far as regards So. Ca. have now been allayed, for tho we can get no distinct account, the tone of all papers correspondents & [presses] cheerful. I have heard nothing since your letter from home but hope to soon. As usual on the approach of winter and the remote prospects of a fight, the Army is becoming very gay, and reviews, lunches & riding parties are becoming the order of the day. I have kept out of these up to this time but would have parties [posted] today in a grand affair, no less than the review of our entire Corps by the Ad. J. Genl. Cooper, to be followed by a lunch and dance at Genl Longstreet's Hd Qurs, to which old Pete[32] had the good taste to invite me, but for an unfortunate rain which is still pouring. If the weather is fair it will come off tomorrow. I was very glad that it had to be postponed today as I was so tired. I could hardly stand, having gotten back to camp this morning about 2 o'clock after attending Capt Shannon's wedding.[33] This event to the surprise of all acquaintances of both parties has at last come off. You know Shannon's reputation and the bride's was worse.[34] This was the first wedding I ever saw in church and it was certainly the rowdiest I ever have or ever expect to see. Everybody went regardless of invitations, and when the ceremony commenced, people, men & women, stood up on the back of the pews to look on. The large church was [crowded], gallery and all. When I get married it shant be in St. Pauls. After the wedding a select few adjourned to the bride's residence, a married sister of Miss Nannie Giles, where they partook of a very elegant collation and after [yawning] around until about 12 o'clock all went home. The bridal party left for So. Ca. this morning at 8 o'clock. Miss Nannie Giles accompanied them. She was exceedingly affable and always meets me as an old friend. She seems to look upon you quite as a friend. I was principally struck last night by the stunning dressing of the ladies. I don't think I ever saw handsomer. There was one beautiful girl there with moire antique dress with an illusion skirt over it embroidered with roses leaves and [grass]. Looked exactly like the

---

[32] A nickname for General James Longstreet.
[33] Samuel Davis Shannon (1833-1900) of South Carolina.
[34] Captain Shannon married Elizabeth Peyton Giles (born 1835). Soon afterward, she divorced him for non-support. They are both mentioned in Mary Chesnut's diary.

pictures in Godey's Ladies book but was very beautiful. Don't you think I must be getting a fashionable man. I certainly shall if we stay here, for tho I don't accept half the invitations I get, I am generally out at least twice a week. I have two more wedding invitations already. John is worse than I am a great deal. The arrival of the Prestons is much the [pleasantest] feature in Richmond society now. They seem to consider John as entirely and myself a little as members of the family and treat us accordingly, which is quite pleasant. Richmond is a very rowdy place and there are a good many people to suit it, but I have got to know who's who now and can always spend a few hours in Richmond to the best advantage.

We are looking rather bluely on to our Christmas prospects, which tho as far as we can see are much pleasanter, their arrival are yet rather slow. I have an invitation to Mrs. Camerons where I know I will at any rate get a dinner worthy of the occasion and that is doing pretty well for war times. I suppose you have heard of Lally's change in position, which I hope he will like. It certainly ought to be pleasanter, as Genl Anderson is one of the finest men I know. Love to Ma, Pa, Aleck and all the boys. Write me word what they are going to do in Columbia this winter about the bazaar I hear everyone talking about as possible and fun. Leaves may be granted after January and I would like to take it on the way home.

Joseph C. Haskell, Headquarters, Artillery, First Army Corps,
to Sophie Haskell (SCHS)
11 December 1864
Dear Sophie,

I have been looking for letters from home for some days, for I knew you would not forget it, and am glad to say that I was not disappointed as your and Ma's kind letters both reached me night before last and made me realize for the 1st time that my birthday had nearly past.[35] No one in camp knew or remembered it but my tent mate a young fellow from Savannah Ridgley Godwin, aide to Genl Gilmer but now on duty with us, a head over heels sort of a chap but a fine kind hearted fellow and makes a very pleasant friend in camp.[36] I am very sorry that he is going to leave us soon, but can't wish him to be disappointed as he looks for a great deal of pleasure from his Christmas at home. We hear all sorts of rumors from Savannah none of which I hope are true, as if they are it must be in some danger. One other little friend in Richmond remembered it, very kindly the Miss Nanny

---

[35] Sophie Haskell's family record lists her brother Joseph C. Haskell's birthday as December 1, 1843.

[36] This was Charles Ridgley Goodwin (1842-94) of Georgia.

Brooke. Ma can tell you all about her. Rather the sweetest little specimen of a Virginian I ever met. I don't know what I might not have done if the Prestons had not come on. Her four years advantage over me had dwindled down to nothing, and it was no longer a question of what were the objections to her, but what were mine. I confess they were harder to get over, but I am of a sanguine disposition and might have tried. Miss Tudie arrived however and one ride on horseback with her settled me for 6 weeks longer at [least].[37] I never saw anyone so improved as she is both in manners and appearance, and on horseback she is most aggravating. She and one other of the ladies will probably come to Columbia to the bazaar, and if a furlough can be begged or stolen, you may meet your affect. brother Joseph in that burg about that time. I wrote to you a few days ago and asked you all about it. Tell me all you know the next time you write. I am afraid seriously speaking that there is but little chance of getting a leave for there is no one here to look after my business in my absence, and now that the campaign is coming to a close, the paper business is increasing very much. Our command is also increased by (3) three new battalions and a large number of new batteries along the river on both sides, and everybody seems to want furloughs or passes or something else.

The tent has filled since I've been writing the last few lines and I don't know what they are, and am principled against inflicting myself with reading my own writing. Your letter and Ma's were read about 12 o'clock night before last, just as I got through writing and sending out the last orders for an attack which we attempted yesterday. It snowed all the day before and when the troops moved out yesterday moving at 4 o'clock it was bitter cold and snow 4 inches deep on the ground. We had a horrid day of it and [accomplished] nothing and I am happy to say did not lose more than a dozen men and killed and wounded more of the enemy than that. They were fortified so that we did not attack. Give my love to Aleck and tell him I hope we will see him in January. Love to Pa and Ma.

Russell Noble, Pocotaligo, S.C., to Sophie Haskell (SCHS)
12 December 1864
Dear Sophie,
    I arrived here safely. We are [seeing] now on pretty hard times. The Yankees are about a mile of us. They shell us continually but do no damage except scaring a [few]. They sometimes come up in an hundred and once in twenty of our breast works but we have driven them back every time and as

---

[37] Tudie was Susan Frances Hampton Preston (1845-1905), the daughter of General John Smith Preston (1809-81). She later married Henry William Frost (1841-1926).

they have shown no disposition for a little time of advancing we think that it is probable that they wish to go to Savannah where we have heard very heavy cannonading. The other night I was on Pickett and could hear the enemy in about two hundred yards ahead of us although we could not see ten feet ahead of us. We were in a [thick] swamp in water up to our ankles.

Louis is here and I see him every day. I am now writing in his camp. Do tell Paul to take care of my cape and if he gets a chance send it to me as I have no more time I must close. Give my love to Uncle C. & Aunt S., Duke and Cousin Carrie. Whenever you can, write to me and direct to Cadet Ru. Noble, Batt. State Cadets, care Maj. White, Pocotaligo.[38]

Dear Sophy,

Russell is over here writing and I take the opportunity of adding a P.S. You spoke of sending me a pair of gloves. If you send them I don't care about having the big gauntlets but only cuffs of the same stuff as the gloves. They ought to be directed to Coosawhatchie. I have no time to write any more, as I am about to go on drill.

Give my love to Pa, Ma and all the rest.

P.S. Do send some me some paper & envelopes by mail. Direct to Charleston. We have a mail carrier going there twice every week. L.W.H.

Louis W. Haskell, Tulifinny Works, S.C., to Sophia C. Haskell (SCHS)
14 December 1864
Dear Ma,

I received my first letter from you today, it was the first time that I have heard from home. I didn't know before how good a thing it was to get a letter and especially such a one as you wrote me, and I got Joe's letter that you enclosed to me. I wish you would make Paul write to me, and tell Sophie if she knew how much I wanted letters she would write to me too, that is if they have not written as often as I have. Up to this time I have not known where to tell you to direct to me but the Capt tells me that arrangements have been made for sending a man twice every week to Charleston to carry and bring the mail, so that hereafter I suppose you had better direct there, wherever we, as this man will continue to go. As I told you in my last letter we are stationed about 3 miles from Coosawhatchie. The militia, officers and all are being drilled four hours every day by the Citadel & Arsenal Cadets who are stationed right by us and a dress parade every evening besides.

---

[38] Major James Benjamin White (1828-1906) commanded the Battalion of South Carolina State Cadets, which included cadets from the Arsenal and the Citadel. The Cadets participated in a battle at the Tullifinny River in early December 1864, but suffered no losses.

Our colonel is coming down on us pretty hard. I see Russell[39] & Haskell Rhett[40] every day as they help to drill.

I wish someone would give Dr. Thomas a hint that he is expected down here.[41] The names of those absent were sent to headquarters today and I hear that all their names are to be published in the papers. The enemy shell the cars as they run by here every day but up to this time they have done no damage farther than making a small hole in the boiler of one of the engines. Mr. Mitchell arrived here today. He say [*sic*] that they are opening new batteries, some say just at his gate, that will make it almost impossible for the cars to run. I don't know however whether this is the case. Frank Hopkinson asked me to ask Pa if he saw his father to tell him where he is and his direction.

I am sorry to hear that Alick is not improving faster. When I saw him on the cars he looked so much better than I expected that I thought he was improving very fast. Do give my love to [him] and all at home.

Alexander C. Haskell, Columbia, S.C., to Charles T. Haskell (USC)
20 December 1864
Dear Pa,

I write today to tell you that [I] will be at home on Friday next and will bring Lessie Singleton with me. I would like to drive home on the evening of the arrival if that is practicable. I expect you will have to send in a cart as there will be two trunks counting my valise as one. I cannot hear definitely of Lewis except that he is about Grahamville. I have brought you 10 pounds of poor brown sugar at 8 ½ dollars per pound. It was the best bargain the town would afford.

There is no news in Columbia. The people are preparing in mind and body to suffer under the invasion of Sherman. I can hear nothing from our Savannah friends except that they will remain, and that probably the Savannah as well as the Ogeechee plantations have been destroyed.[42]

Love to Ma and all at home.

[P.S.] Lessie will only have a hat box, carriage will do.

---

[39] Louis's cousin, Russell Noble, an Arsenal cadet, died of disease brought on by the hardships and exposure of military service in January 1865.

[40] This was likely William Haskell Rhett (1844-1909), the son of Benjamin Smith Rhett (1798-1868) and Mary Pauline Haskell Rhett (1808-51).

[41] This may refer to John Peyre Thomas (1833-1912), formerly a professor at the Citadel in Charleston. He was elected colonel of a regiment of reserves in August 1864.

[42] John Richardson Cheves and Langdon Cheves, uncles of the Haskell brothers, owned plantations on the Ogeechee River in Georgia.

Alexander C. Haskell, Columbia, S.C., to Charles T. Haskell (USC)
16 January 1865
Dear Pa,

I am still in Columbia, kept here by the destruction of bridges & trestle works which renders transportation impossible between Charleston & Greensboro and between Greensboro and Danville. While waiting I have taken a very severe cold and Ben is sick, so that I may wait with philosophy though not satisfaction until near the end of this week.

Sophie is well, getting over her cold and enjoying her time among friends with whom she is a great favourite. She has been disappointed in not meeting Dr. Patrick and considering the condition of the Greenville R.R. I suppose he will be absent some weeks.

I have seen the Governor, and by two visits and some writing, procured his order for the transfer of Lewis. I have some hope of getting the papers down today or tomorrow, if boats have been set to work where the bridge beyond Kingsville has been washed away. I have some hope that Lewis may reach Columbia before my departure. Lang Cheves is here and will go to my regiment in which he is already enlisted as soon as Lewis can get ready.[43] Lang is keeping his horse in Columbia. I hope you can at once supply Lewis as I am exceedingly anxious for them to go together and it is much the best plan to take the journey on horseback. I will endeavour to find some party that they may journey with, but if I cannot they will be very well able to go alone.

I suppose they will start in two or three weeks. Langdon Cheves is entrusted to me by his mother. He is in many points which I have observed a promising boy, but for the moment will require all the assistance and care which I trust my presence and advice may give him.

There is absolutely no news in Columbia except that the attack at Wilmington is being renewed.[44] Nothing is known or heard of Sherman & except by telegraph Columbia has no communication with the rest of the world.

Sophie will write if we can find means of transporting our letters. Dearest love to Ma, Paul and all at home. Tell Pinckney that I received a letter from Tom Dudley some days ago saying that he—Pinckney—will probably be appointed commissary of my regiment. Baby is well, happy and good as any child can be.

---

[43] This was Langdon Cheves (1848-1939), a first cousin of the Haskell brothers.

[44] On January 12, 1865, a Federal war fleet arrived off Fort Fisher, North Carolina, and began an attack the next day. Fort Fisher protected the important Confederate port of Wilmington.

P.S. I will write again and will add as much as I can learn about Lewis' & Lang's affairs.

Alexander C. Haskell, Columbia, S.C., to Sophia C. Haskell (USC)
18 January 1865
Dear Ma,

I write on my last day in Columbia. The R. Roads are not yet repaired but I understand that the journey although slow and difficult can be made. Our being cut off from Charleston has prevented my getting Lewis up before my departure. Yesterday a telegraphic order was sent for him by the Adj. General and on the same day a written one. He will, I hope, be up before many days. I have left with Sophie to give to him his certificate of enlistment and a few written instructions for him. He will go up to Abbeville at once to get supplies and a good horse, saddle, bridle and halter. Let him then return on horseback to Columbia in order to join Lang and take him with him on the journey. I have promised this for Lang. It is important for both boys to go together, and I hope that in this matter there will be nothing to disappoint me. I shall do my best for both the boys. Lewis like his brothers before him is a soldier the moment he enters the field. I feel sure of his success & usefulness. Lang is a fine boy, but requires for a little while my personal care, and this I have promised.

The Bazaar is at work today with some success. Sophie is useful and I think a model in company for the ladies of this generation. There her talent, good taste and good manners are well and modestly enough exhibited. My baby is well and happy.

Public news bears still its full character of punishment and instruction for our selfish and indecisive people. Love and goodbye to Pa, Paul and all at home. May God bless and protect our home for many friends.

Joseph C. Haskell, Headquarters, Artillery, First Army Corps,
to Sophie Haskell (SCHS)
26 January 1865
My dear Sophie,

It's so long since I've gotten a letter from home that I hardly know how to write to you. Your last letter was so blue that I was almost glad of the break of the R.R. which cut off communication. I have heard nothing since and the details in the papers are so meager as to afford very little satisfactory information of what is going on down in So. Ca.

I am almost ashamed to write of our carryings on here, but I have always acted on the maxim that I might as well enjoy myself if I could do so without detriment to the [service] or myself. If people will give parties I will go to them. I have just finished a heavy round of duties as groomsman at the wedding of my old friend Miss Skinner.[45] Don't be shocked by the name. Ma can tell you who she is. I knew the happy man but slightly but was invited as her friend and acted as 2nd groomsman. The rest were rather a green set and I was in my in my element. You would have thought I had never done anything but play groomsman at church weddings all my life. The groom and his 6 assistants were all officers and went in all the uniform that the law allows, and indulgent friends pronounced it the [handsomest] wedding of the season & was followed by three parties all more or less pleasant, the last of which came of [8 last night]. On the same night came off that long looked for news, rumors of which may possibly have reached So. Ca., viz, the marriage of Miss Hetty [Cary] and Genl Pegram.[46] It was a very [proud] [Zoave] affair and passed off well. My bridesmaid has been a Miss Carrie Stewart from N. King George, cousin of the ones gorgeous in a new uniform, and tho I tell all the girls he is engaged [interviews] with me very much. My performance was so successful this time that I am invited next week as groomsman to our [corps] commissary Major Edwards who is to be married to a Miss [Magill] from [Rochester], and I am to have the [pleasure] of standing with my friend Miss Nannie Brooke.[47] Middleton is also to be one of the groomsmen. I do rather hard work these cold winter nights as the Genl is absent on sick furlough, one of his ribs broken by a kick from a horse. I can't leave camp in the daytime and always have to come back the same night so that it's pretty rough. I think it's doing a good deal for my friend. I have become very select in my ...

[*The rest of this letter is missing.*]

Joseph C. Haskell, Headquarters, Artillery, First Army Corps,
to Sophie Haskell (SCHS)
5 February 1865
My Dear Sophie,

I was very glad to get your pleasant letter the day before yesterday and show my appreciation in the only way I can by writing an answer in my first spare moment. Not to say that I am overburdened with labor, but I went up

---

[45] This was Elise Glenn Davies Skinner, who married Thomas Tileston Greene of Alabama on January 17, 1865, in Richmond, Virginia. She was the daughter of Frederick Gustavus Skinner (1814-80).

[46] Brigadier General John Pegram (1832-65) of Virginia married the beautiful Miss Hetty Carr Cary (1836-92) of Baltimore on January 19, 1865. Less than three weeks later he was killed in action at the Battle of Hatcher's Run.

[47] Major John Franklin Edwards (1832-1904) married Virginia Louise McGill (1837-1901) on January 31, 1865.

to town yesterday to see Mrs. Gibbes and to attend to my duties as groomsman at the cutting of the bride's [cake] incidental on the wedding at which I
was groomsman this week. I have had a very pleasant time and my little
bridesmaid Miss Minnie Brooke looks so sweet and pretty that I would not
have minded being principal instead of taking a second part. My time has
not come tho I [suppose] as I cut neither ring of [*sic*] five cent piece.[48] Capt
Middleton, who was first groomsman cut the 5 cents, much to his disgust.
Mrs. Gibbes was apparently much pleased to see me and declared I was not
half as glad as she was. She certainly is a very warm hearted affectionate person. She certainly has found the way into my heart by giving me a very
handsome pair of boot legs which I must get [footed] if I can ever get the
leather. Do beg Pa to send me some. I wrote to him but doubt if he will get
the letter as mail communications with Abbeville is so uncertain. I wrote a
regular begging letter home the other day which I hope has arrived. Pa was
requested to supply me some leather, Ma socks and a handkerchief, and you,
if you are determined not to send me those gloves, to send me a pair of
coonskin gauntlets for a friend, Major [Jordan] of our old Batt[ery]. The
winter is so far gone its almost too late. If you have not left Columbia please
try and get me a pair or two of white thread gloves, and send them on to me
by the mail as soon as you can. Mrs. Gibbes says she did not see much of
you, but loved you very [fondly].

John is happy Miss Sallie[49] is staying with the Prestons, and John
spends most of his time in Richmond. He used to be a little ashamed of it
but goes now with a perfectly composed air and says if he has not got reason
enough he would like to know who has. He talks about applying for leave to
go South, wants to volunteer with the troops down there. I think he wants
to act as military escort to a train which will pass over the road south in a
few days. I wish he could be married. I would like to have Miss Tudie Preston for a bridesmaid. Aleck I have seen a few times since he came back. I
went over and stayed all night with him the other day and had a very nice
time. I want to see that boy Lewis on here, and poor little Lang, who one
year ago could not ride one mile with me because it was too cold. The idea
of his riding on to Va.

I saw cousin Follie yesterday evening who now has rooms in Richmond
and will remain here until affairs become more settled down South. Charlie
was with her a very handsome boy but very much spoilt. I have not seen

---

[48] There was a custom of placing objects in the bride's cake (or wedding cake). A
coin was a promise of future prosperity, and a ring meant marriage within a year.

[49] Miss Sallie was John's fiancée Sarah Buchanan Hampton (1845-86), who was also called Sally Buck. She was the daughter of General Wade Hampton (1818-1902) and
Margaret Buchanan Frances Preston Hampton (1818-52).

[Flo]. Cousin Follie was [larger] than ever. She is a stunner. Middleton,[50] the last one of our staff leaves this week on furlough and I will be left disconsolate with old Cabell.[51] He will run me crazy if the Genl don't come back soon.[52] Didn't you like him. I know he didn't show to advantage on first sight as he always has a sort of spasmodic grin on when he is introduced to ladies, but he is true gold, and twould be a great thing for the army if we had a few more like him. I will make an effort to get back home when he comes back as I am getting to feel very much like seeing you all in spite of the attractions of Richmond society. I was glad to hear where Aunt Rachel and Minnie where [sic] as I had heard nothing but that they were in the Confederate lines. I wish Aunt Charlotte had sent the girls out. She might have stayed. How are Lou and Hannah. You don't mention either of them in your last. I am curious to know if she and her beloved are thinking of joining hands soon. I hope Lou will have the grace to wait until I can get there. You had better pick me out a pretty sweetheart in So Ca and send me on her picture, to shield me from the attacks to which my susceptible nature is daily exposed, or it will be impossible for me to account for what may happen. I have been waiting to have my picture taken all the winter but could never raise money enough to do it. I will send you on one if I am in condition to have it taken and find anyone who can do justice to your good-looking elder brother.

I hated to write such nonsense but it's all I know. The Yankees may be at Columbia before this letter or at Branchville and I suppose you will hardly appreciate it then but I hope for the best and wish it. I wrote you a few days ago directing to Abbeville. Please write to me oftener. You don't know how seldom I hear from you or anyone else. Give my best love to Pa, Ma, Sister, [Duff], Lally, Miss Jane and all at home if you are there, if not to Aunt Louisa, the girls, Mrs. Singleton, Lessie and anybody else that would appreciate it.

Alexander C. Haskell, Headquarters, Seventh S.C. Cavalry,
to Charles T. Haskell (USC)
11 February 1865
My dear Father,
    I write I fear in vain on account of our broken mail, but I hope you will get a few lines to tell you and Ma that I am well and still hopeful though

---

[50] John Izard Middleton (1834-1907) was on the staff of General Edward Porter Alexander.

[51] This was likely Colonel Henry Coalter Cabell (1820-89).

[52] General Edward Porter Alexander had been wounded in June 1864 and was away on medical leave until February 1865.

before this reaches you I fear our State will have suffered great things. I am sincerely anxious to share the pain of the struggle on our soil but I must give up the desire and be happy that even as it is far away from our homes, I am allowed to fight for the sacred cause on the soil of this our noble allied state.

Our congress and government seem to be weakest at the moment we need them most. Our country is suffering deeply indeed before sufficient comes to make us a good and pure people. Each panic brings with it a hope we will be purified and blessed. We have been disappointed on thousands of occasions, but we have not yet by a great deal reached the excess of human suffering, and we have therefore before us a reasonable prospect of delay, but at the same time a hope that accompanies every moment. We are now approaching the deeper state of affairs which must precede the national war and which generally result in the success of the weak, persecuted and suffering rebels who are moved by pure and sacred principles.

Congress is half [mad] upon the subject of African assistance most absurdly declaring against the introduction of freed negro assistance in our ranks. Congress may be right in a logical or in a political point of view. The negro assistance and emancipation may give us a prospect of ruin, but this is not my opinion, and while three fourths of Congress [declared] against putting negros into the field as free soldiers or as soldiers at all, notwithstanding their decision I feel sure of seeing it yet done, and in this think that I recognize the principal element of our success.[53]

I see John and Joe frequently. They are remarkably well and bright. I am expecting Langdon soon and shall endeavour to learn from him something from home. I have not received a single line from Abbeville nor one from Columbia since my departure from each of the two places.

I hear rumours this evening of our defeat in So. Ca. and that Sherman is rushing upon Columbia. I will delay my grief until I receive certain information. I would be happy even in the misery of a bloody fight if it were against this hateful Sherman.

I suppose our home is filling up with suffering relatives and friends. I trust that your home escaping the enemy, you may long have the happiness to be driven from it if affords some refuge for our friends.

Dearest love to Ma, Sophie, Paul and all at home.

---

[53] The Confederate Congress approved the enlistment of black soldiers in March 1865.

Louis W. Haskell, Abbeville, S.C., to his cousin Langdon Cheves,
Columbia, S.C. (SCHS)
12 February 1865
Dear Lang,

Ma is writing to Aunt Isabella to ask you to come up here and start from here to Va. If you come up we have two excellent McClellan saddles, besides the one that I am going to use, one of which you will be very welcome to, as I think that the one that you have will not do for you to ride to Va. with.

Our Col. wrote the other day that we could take our time about coming on. So I have determined or rather been advised by Langdon & Pa not to go on before the first of March at least tho if you should come, I would be very glad to see you up as soon as you feel inclined and you can get used to riding before you start, and I advise you to ride as much as you can anyhow. If you come up here you had better send on your things—all that you don't carry on your horse—by the Central Association. And write to Alick about it.

I hope that you like to come up, if you don't, I wish you would write to me. Give my love to Aunt Isabella, Harry & the rest.

Joseph C. Haskell, Headquarters, First Army Corps,
to Sophia C. Haskell (DUL)
15 February 1865
My Dear Ma,

I have not written for some time as I was entirely uncertain as to whether a letter could get through in the present uncertain condition of things. I suppose they have not been able to, as I have received no letters from home save one came from Pa dated before Aleck left home.

We are all very anxious and uneasy about So. Ca., more so than ever, because things are so quiet on our own lines as to give us nothing to think about. I would not be surprised to hear anything from there now, for if things are not exaggerated Sherman has it in his power to walk up to Columbia or any other front he chooses. It seems that the Yankees are to have a full opportunity of wreaking their pent up wrath on our unfortunate old state and what distresses us all more here than anything else is what we daily hear of the conduct of the people who are represented as proving false to those principles which we all hoped, and many so loudly proclaimed, they would sustain at all hazards. I can't believe it, for I think the army influence would keep people at home right, for I know our soldiers are what they should be. It's a bitter mortification to hear tho what we do every day, especially as many seem to regard it almost as a testament that South Carolinians, when put to the test are no better than anybody else. I didn't know until now how strong the old feeling of state pride was in me. I am almost inclined to sport my old palmetto cockade in their defiance, for I can't help but think the old state will show itself all right under any circumstances.

I had hoped to hear from Sophie before now as she was in Columbia but no letter has come and I suppose that she has returned to Abbeville. All Richmond gaiety has passed off and we are very dull and quiet in camp now. I am specially lonely as the Genl. is still away, and Col. Cabell is a great deal worse than no one at all. I don't think I ever met quite his equal. I am only sustained by the hope that the Genl. will return this week. If he does not I am afraid I can hardly survive old Coalter. Fortunately he spends the greater part of his time in town. John and Aleck were both up there yesterday tho I did not see them. I am looking for Lally's return anxiously as I have a vague hope he will bring me something. What I can't say, but anything would now be acceptable. If he did not get an extension I suppose his furlough must be nearly if not entirely out. I hope Louis and Lang have not started on for the weather has been dreadful for horseback travelling. John has put in an application for leave or rather detail to be allowed to go down South and volunteer, but I don't think he can get it. His real object is I believe to get a place in the army down there as he is disgusted with this one.

Do write me word what you can about our friends & who have been made refugees. I see Cousin Follie often. I think she is fast making up her mind to go to the Trans-Mississippi, where she ought to have been for the last year. I give my love to Pa, Sophie, Sister, Duff and all the rest.

Alexander C. Haskell, Headquarters, Seventh S. C. Cavalry,
to Charles T. Haskell and Sophia C. Haskell (USC)
18 February 1865
My dear Father and Mother,

I heard today of the abandonment of Columbia and that we have no mail to you. I have an opportunity of sending you a note by Captain Gary to tell you that I am quite well.[54] John & Joe are the same. All prospering although sad over the trouble in our homes. I trust that you will be spared from the pain of receiving the enemy in our old home, and that you will have the comfort of keeping our dear refugee friends and relations. I hope that my dear little child is with you, but have not heard one word of her since my departure from home. I have great hopes of Sherman's speedy ruin and perhaps destruction. Until then be of good cheer. May God bless, sustain and comfort our people. Goodbye for this time.

---

[54] This was likely Captain J. Wistar Gary (1837-1915) of the Second South Carolina Cavalry Regiment.

Joseph C. Haskell, Headquarters, Artillery, First Army Corps, to Sophia C.
Haskell (DUL)
25 February 1865
Dear Ma,

I have now hopes of being able to get a letter through by private hand, and write a few lines to let you know we are all well, but very anxious to hear from you all. It is reported by telegraph that Abbeville has been burnt.[55] I can hardly credit such a report, but it is positively stated. Try and send your letters through Capt. Venable if he is still in the Village, and get him to forward them to the Q. M. Genl. at Richmond care of Genl. Alexander.

Neither Lally or Lewis have returned. I met Allan Wardlaw yesterday looking very well, but with a bad cold.[56] He says that his only suffering was from short rations and he was able to supply himself after money was sent him. I suppose you got Uncle Dulles letter by flag of truce, saying that he had sent him money. John has gotten his promotion at last I believe, Lt. Col.

Do take every opportunity of getting letters through as we are very anxious to hear from you at home. When you write tell us all you can about our refugee friends & relatives. Don't worry about not hearing from us, but go on the conviction that all's well until you hear to the contrary. No signs of immediate operations anywhere in this army. We can't help but feel that the Confederacy is all right, while this army is intact. I hope if the Yankees have been at home they didn't get the horses. Love to Pa, Sister, Paul, and all at home.

Alexander C. Haskell, Headquarters, Seventh S.C. Cavalry,
to Charles T. Haskell, Abbeville, S.C. (USC)
27 February 1865
Dear Pa,

Some of my men start tomorrow morning for South Carolina to endeavour to procure horses to remount my regiment. I send a few lines by one of them to tell you that John, Joe and myself are quite well. Of Langdon, Lewis, our little Lang I have not yet heard.[57] Do tell Mrs. Singleton that John is better. He has gone to Charlottesville on [60] days leave. It was too difficult for him to attempt the journey to Abbeville. John writes to me this evening to beg you to send to him his filly the young "Brownie." She can be [led] on the journey. Lieutenant O. G. Rogers near Unionville is in charge

---

[55] The report was mistaken. Sherman's army did not pass through Abbeville District.

[56] George Allen Wardlaw had been a prisoner of war at Fort Delaware, Delaware.

[57] This refers to Aleck's brothers Langdon and Louis, and cousin Langdon Cheves.

of all the parties from the upper section of our State.[58] If you can have the horse taken to him with a letter explaining her destination he will be glad to have her safely brought on. If you wish to send Punch or Toby to Joe, and if you can raise any contributions to the cavalry under my command, you can send them in the same way to Lieut. Rogers, who will have them brought on, it will be some expense to him which it will be well to advance. He will take good care of the horses.

I am making a desperate effort to remount to remount my regt. and could I be heard would make a speech to my whole State which might induce our friends and patriots to help us, and in helping a good regiment contribute largely to the success of our good cause. I suppose too I have personal ambition. I always desired to command the best regiment in service, but am now very desirous to win on the field what I did not win in the Cabinet. My rivals Logan and Bonham have so conducted their affairs as to secure (the first one a proper case, the second one questionable) the only two cavalry brigades to one of which I had some reason to suppose I would be given.[59] I have to make my regiment so good that it will be as serviceable as other peoples' brigades. If this can be done my triumph will be sincere and honourable.

Of public affairs I can tell you but little. We expect to long hold Richmond, to obtain food and fight our enemy with prospect of success. Genl. Lee is well, hopeful and strong. From this our country will gain much assistance. My conviction of two years standing is now satisfied by the relief of Beauregard. Johnston I trust will be successful, not because he is as great a man as is claimed by his friends, but from the fact that his must be a very base human nature if the noble generous mind of Genl. Lee cannot master in it that sad fault of character which has caused personal trouble between Genl. Johnston and his legitimate commander, to do so much to lose our victory and threaten destruction to our country.[60] All our Richmond friends are well, Prestons, Hugers, Dudleys, Gibsons and all others. Tell Mrs. S. that Aunt Lucy & [Champe] are quite well and report others to be so.[61]

---

[58] This was Oliver G. Rogers of the Seventh South Carolina Cavalry Regiment.

[59] The "rivals" were likely brigadier generals Thomas Muldrup Logan (1840-1914) and Milledge Luke Bonham (1813-90).

[60] Robert Garlick Hill Kean (1828-98), chief of the Confederate Bureau of War in Richmond, recorded in his diary in April 1863 that General Joseph E. Johnston was "eaten up with jealousy of Lee and of all his superiors in position, rank, or glory." Kean, *Inside the Confederate Government*, 50.

[61] Mrs. Singleton, Aleck's mother-in-law, had a sister named Lucy Carter Minor. Mrs. Minor had a son named Charles Carter Minor.

I do trust that Mother, Baby, Sophie and Lessie are all safely with you, and that you have with you other friends whom you may help. Kiss my little darling for me. Extend the kiss with dearest love to Ma, Mother, Sophie, Lessie and all at home. Let me have letters by my men as they return.

John looks well. Joe is splendid.

Joseph C. Haskell, Headquarters, Artillery, First Army Corps,
to Sophia C. Haskell (DUL)
5 March 1865
Dear Ma,

I hope some of the letters we have been sending home by private opportunity have reached you and relieved any anxiety which you may have felt with regard to us. None of us have heard anything either directly or indirectly from home since the fall of Columbia, and are very anxious to do so, for tho we have never believed the reports of Abbeville being burnt.[62] Yet we would like to hear from our refugee friends. Neither Lewis or Lally have made their appearance yet and we are looking anxiously for their return. The weather has been so dreadful that traveling across the country would necessarily be slow. This is the first time for 8 days that we have not had rain. If this March wind and spring sun lasts much longer we must have active operations soon. Our Corps will necessarily be the last affected by then I suppose, as we [farthest] to Richmond and not in a position to be flanked. I hope our fortunes will turn before long, as any change must be for the better. Early's last disaster in the valley is the latest. I have not yet learned the extent of it but believe Early himself was captured.[63] What a pity they did not get him six (6) months ago. It would have been a lucky thing for the country. There has been a dreadful panic among the people here on the subject of evacuating Richmond. It seems rather to have died out tho now. While everyone recognizes the chances of our having to do so, few think that the time has come yet. I dread it more than anything which has happened during the war. We have all gotten to feel personally responsible for it, and I feel as if I could never look my friends in the face again if we were to abandon them now to the enemy. It will be a terrible time when it does come.

Cousin Follie after much hesitation I think has given up the plan of attempting to reach the Trans-Mississippi and will go back to Leesburgh [*sic*] as soon as the weather and roads will permit. I believe that is her present

---

[62] Columbia was surrendered to General William T. Sherman on February 17, 1865. His army entered the town that morning and quickly began pillaging. That night, they burnt the city.

[63] On March 2, 1865, General Jubal Early suffered a decisive defeat at Waynesborough, Va. He was not captured, but many of his troops were taken prisoner.

intention. Do write me word if anything was ever done about [Mrs. H.] silver. She is very anxious to know if it was ever sent off from Columbia.

John was over to spend the day with me yesterday looking well and in good spirits. Aleck I see occasionally looking better every time. We only meet in Richmond, generally at church. I am disappointed at missing him today, as I have to stay at home and keep house, the Genl. having gone to church. I will try and get this letter off by his brother who leaves for Ga. in a day or two. Give my love to Pa, Sophie, Paul and all the rest, and ask Sophie why she don't write to me. I am getting very hard up for some of the [necessities] of life and any assistance will be thankfully [received].

Alexander C. Haskell, Camp near Richmond, Va., to Sophia C. Haskell, Abbeville, S.C. (USC)
10 March 1865
Dear Ma,

We hear nothing from home but always hope. We know that our old State has suffered, how much we tremble to ask, but believe that she is bearing it nobly and that all will yet be well. Our armies are being well managed. The spirit of the soldiers is rising and the desertion which had disgraced our army (but not my regiment) is diminishing. Concentration under the great old General Lee begins already to assume character as a form of salvation. This will repay us for the bloody passage across our states. A decided victory on the 8th of March, won at Kinston N. Ca. 30 miles from Goldsboro, by Bragg over Foster, was announced to our troops on the night of the 9th and while they were preparing for humiliation and prayer on this appointed day, poured into their hearts a spirit of sincere thanksgiving which rose today from the lips of earnest thousands.[64]

Congress is about to adjourn. The government will be relieved and more effective power will at once be excercised for our benefit. My old idea of concentration of our Western and Southern with the Army of Northern Va. and the combined movement of this mighty force to the Western interior where we could obtain food and give out defiance, still remains as a good and sound one, but I begin to have hopes of a victory before the Capitol which will hold [us] upon our bloody old field of battle and triumph.

Just as I reached this point I dashed out of my tent upon hearing a rattling fire and cheer in this cold moonlight night, but as it has subsided I take it for granted that it means nothing. But we are on the flank and there is a

---

[64] In March 1865 Confederate forces under the command of General Braxton Bragg moved against a corps commanded by Major General Jacob Dolson Cox (1828-1900), and Bragg was able to check the enemy advance temporarily. This engagement was known as the Battle of Wyse Fort (aka Battle of Kinston).

huge body of cavalry from the valley under Sheridan which is hovering around Lynchburg, Richmond and the Danville road.[65] A part is reported to be moving towards us this evening and I have but a squadron out to meet them. I hope however that we will escape the first fight as my horses are weak and very few in number.

I as yet hear nothing from Langdon, Lewis and Lang Cheves, but hope they are making a safe journey.[66] John and Joe I see. They are quite well and bright. John I believe is Lieut. Col. and Joe is a contented Captain. By the way, I am sorry that you will all be disappointed as to my promotion. I wish you would tell Pa that I may be forced by the absolute impossibility of getting pay, to borrow a thousand—it may be fifteen hundred dollars. If I do borrow it will only from Mr. [Marklay] the Agent of State and will give him a note on Pa. [*Several lines crossed out.*]

Kiss Baby for me. Love to Pa, Mother, Sophie, Lessie, Paul and all at home. Kiss for yourself and each of them. Goodbye.

Louis W. Haskell, Guilford County, N.C., to Charles T. Haskell (SCHS)
19 March 1865
Dear Pa,

I write in hope that there is some sort of mail communication from Chester to Abbeville. Lally wrote a few days ago tho you may not have got the letter saying that he was going to take the cars, on account of Tramps taking sick (he however has got perfectly well again). He was taken sick when we were in Iredell County about fifty miles this side of the N.C. line and delayed us about [five] days and then was unfit to be rode so that Lally had to take the cars. I am getting on astonishingly well by myself, & I have generally been more lucky in getting good stopping places than when Lally was with [*sic*].

This evening I had much more difficulty in getting a lodging place. The first house I tried was a very stylish one belonging to an old Quaker, & from the fine barns & stables I thought that I had come to the very place but old gent was out & the old lady said no so fast that I just left without making another attempt. [Only] next, I had a better commencement, for when I

---

[65] General Philip Sheridan (1831-88).

[66] According to some notes he made in his transcriptions of family correspondence, Langdon Cheves left Columbia on February 17, 1865, evacuating with the last remaining Confederate forces. Eventually he made his way to Abbeville and from there left for Virginia on horseback, accompanied by his cousin Allen Wardlaw. While they were on their way to join the Seventh South Carolina Cavalry in Virginia, they learned that General Robert E. Lee was preparing to surrender. Louis W. Haskell traveled to Virginia separately.

went in the old lady (the old gentleman) was absent again only said she would rather not [*sic*]. I thought then that she only wanted a little begging so I commenced & stated my case as a most pitiable one but still she would rather not, so I had to give it up as a bad job and came on about a mile farther where I am staying.

I am now in the convenient distance of 50 miles from Danville[67] as that it is just two days journey and I have not determined as yet how to avoid it. The black mare I think is getting fatter if anything on the road, and [Edmund's] little mare is standing the trip very well indeed.

I can't hear much news of Sherman's doings, but people seem to think that he will soon have to fight [if] we have about 50,000 men to oppose him. I have no more to write so I have to stop before I have filled four pages. Give my love to Ma, Sophie & the rest.

Alexander C. Haskell, Headquarters, Seventh S. C. Cavalry, to Charles T. Haskell, Abbeville, S.C. (USC)
26 March 1865
Dear Pa,

I have for the present a dull Sunday morning. [I] have failed to get a visit from the Chaplain to whom I sent yesterday and have not yet found it necessary to march out against the Yankee force that was harassing my pickets yesterday and last night. I shall recompense myself for the first loss by a letter to you, and write it at once that it may be completed before anybody calls me out in the cold March wind that is wailing around our quarters. So far we have had not much active fighting but yesterday it commenced at Petersburgh and there are indications that great movements may soon begin. Grant appears to be concentrating his troops on our right flank below Petersburgh and while doing this his line at Petersburgh was attacked by Genl. Lee, two entrenchments and a heavy battery carried, a Major General and 500 prisoners taken.[68] Our loss was considerable and, it being impossible to carry the attack farther the line was withdrawn. We have rumours of Johnston's constant success in small affairs, but lack official reports of facts. His army however, and the North Carolina people seem to be in much better and higher spirits than they were in a short time ago. With the approach of the activity, the peril and struggles of the Spring, the spirit of our old army has vastly improved. Desertion which for a time so vexed our ranks has almost ceased. The men seem brave and hopeful, and evince that species of

---

[67] Danville was a town in Virginia near the North Carolina state line.

[68] This was the Battle of Fort Stedman on March 25, 1865. The general who was captured was Brigadier General Napoleon B. McLaughlen (1823-87).

resolution which enables men to fight even after defeat, sustain their cause and [end] with victory over an enemy who has been spoiled in his triumph. The public panic upon the subject of Richmond's evacuation has somewhat diminished, in fact you now hear very little of it, but it appears to me to hang upon accidents of war, and since accidents of war that I would not be surprised at its occurrence.[69] At the same time, strong efforts will be made to hold the place.

The Yankee chief of cavalry, Sheridan, by his destruction of the canal to Lynchburg and a large amount of provisions from Staunton to Charlottesville to Richmond, has worried us a great deal in the simple matter of food.[70] This is our danger. Our men have so far received a sufficiency, though the four quarts of meal per week which is our most abundant supply appears too small to those who near us still give the allowance of twelve quarts the week [sic] to servants besides the extra rations of home. The smaller which can be seen in this country is eight quarts the peck and is regarded as an approach to starvation when the son of the family or perhaps its father is on the line a few miles away living and laboring on his four quarts. This is no grumbling. I give it simply to encourage home folks who may think we will starve. At present to give this amount to our men it is taken away from our horses and as grass has not yet grown we are suffering heavy loss of horse flesh. I work at the poor brutes until I suppose my men think I neglect humanity for horses, but upon horses human existence, to a large degree, and our possession of Richmond will depend.

I have before written letters telling of Langdon's arrival. I have not heard from him since he joined his General, who is now I believe on the extreme right several miles below Petersburgh. He looked [remarkably] well, I hope continues so. I see John and Joe pretty often, both doing well. I see that John has on two stars nowadays instead of one.[71] Having started he may get a third. If he doesn't get it he will deserve it which is the best thing that can be said about a man, and far the most valuable consciousness [for it in our mind] if he can be made to believe it. It shows that he has done his duty. Joe is bright and brave, making many friends and fully appreciating the pleasure that this is in the world. I expect Lewis in about a week perhaps less time. [I] will give him a few days rest then let him look about for his comrades. There are a good many nice young men, mere boys, of Lewis' age who

---

[69] The Confederate government and military forces would evacuate Richmond on April 2, 1865.

[70] General Philip Sheridan received orders to destroy the James River Canal and a railroad supplying Petersburg, Virginia.

[71] Two stars on the collar of a Confederate officer's uniform indicated the rank of lieutenant colonel. A major wore one star.

have recently come in and I think he will be pleased with his association with such in the duties of the field. I hope that his horse will well bear temporary starvation. Grass will afterwards bring him up.

My command will be strong if I can get three weeks or one month worth more of quiet. This however I cannot expect and must make it strong even without the quiet. Our friends the Dudleys look pretty well, as kind to me as ever. Tom is annoyed and unpleasantly [situated] by the exchange of his former chief Col. Northrop for St. Johns the present Commissary General.[72] The Gibsons are well and hospitable. Mrs. Huger gives a regular home to John & Joe and I would find myself falling into it could I be more in Richmond. I have never seen greater kindness and more sincere or pleasant hospitality. Cousin Folly is in Richmond looking well, but troubled as all are by doubts of the future as well as by present difficulties. The Prestons have just gone to Yorkville So. Ca. leaving their second home in Richmond. When I am writing about such friends it is wrong to begin by using the adjectives. You must repeat them or find stronger which soon becomes in such cases impossible. I hope that the time will come when in a few hours of peace together we can have the happiness of meeting in the happy scene the friends who in time of trouble and trial we have learned to know and to value. Genl. Preston is going on a short leave to see Columbia and to try to do something there for the poor starving people. I begged him to write to you and if he has time to go to see you, as I knew it would give you pleasure to unite with him and you could bring much valuable assistance from Abbeville Dist. and might with him direct energetic representatives of other districts. The Prestons will stay at same place as Hamptons in Yorkville. They will there have a dull time and may find some pleasure in so quiet a visit as one to Abbeville. I assured Mrs. Preston and the girls of the pleasure it would give you to welcome them in a crowded house, and especially invited the young ladies to take Sally Hampton and go there when grapes and peaches ripened, promising that you would let one lead the party on Robin and the other ride whatever she could get. A crowded house in the country adds to the merits of the place. Enough people thrown together can amuse themselves anywhere. I am especially anxious for Sally Hampton to have the visit as I think it will do her a great deal of good in health and spirits and she will be will be brought more easily by making her cousins come with her, though [you] will soon discover that this will not be the only value of such visitors.

---

[72] Colonel Lucius Bellinger Northrop (1811-94), the Confederate Commissary General, was forced out of office in February 1865. Brigadier General Isaac St. John (1827-80) replaced him on February 16, 1865.

Susan Preston will be your favourite. You will find her the general agent, guardian and superintendent of John & his affairs.

I have not yet heard whether Paul's plan of the extra barns or gin house has yet been carried out, but would like much to see home with its present acquisitions. I know it will do Baby and Lessie a great deal of good to be there away from the suffering and depressed conditions of Columbia. The poor old place must indeed be a sad one. [I] as yet have heard but little of my friends and have hopes that many of them have escaped the greatest terrors of that time of possession by brutal enemies.[73] I have heard that Aunt Louisa's household was in possession of the enemy—can learn no more. I do pray and trust that they are safe though the home must be nearly destroyed.[74] Give my dearest love to Ma & Baby and Mother, Sophie, Lessie, Carrie, [Julie] and all others. Goodbye.

---

[73] General Edward P. Alexander wrote of the burning of Columbia: "[Sherman] officially stated that it was burned by fires set by Hampton's men. When the willful falsity of this statement was fully established, some years afterward, Sherman admitted it, but said that he made it as a war measure—to destroy Hampton's popularity in So. Ca!" Alexander, *Fighting for the Confederacy*, 505.

[74] After General Sherman's army occupied Columbia, the home of Mrs. Louisa S. McCord was temporarily used as the headquarters of his second in command, General Oliver O. Howard, who caught his own men attempting to set fire to the house on several occasions. Howard's presence there preserved the house but it was pillaged by his soldiers before his arrival and after his departure.

EPILOGUE

APPOMATTOX

Unfortunately, it appears that none of the letters which may have written by the Haskell brothers in April 1865 have survived. In those last desperate days of the war in Virginia, there was probably little opportunity of writing a letter or getting it home. During the siege that went on from June 1864 to late March 1865, the Army of Northern Virginia took part in the defense of Petersburg, a place crucial to the railroad supply line for General Robert E. Lee's army and the nearby city of Richmond. When Lee's supplies were finally cut off by General Grant's army at the beginning of April 1865, he abandoned the area, retreating westward toward a town called Amelia Courthouse. This retreat would ultimately end in the surrender of his army at Appomattox Courthouse, which was located about fifty miles west of Amelia Courthouse.

In trying to describe the retreat from Richmond in his memoir, Aleck Haskell could only say: "The next eight days are like a dream—moving, fighting, starving. One can only recall the most stirring hours, here and there, and the encounters in which those noble soldiers seemed in their devoted struggle almost more than human. We were advance guard or rear guard every day, and picketed every night. Many of our best were killed, and I lost several very dear to me personally in a bloody fight the afternoon and night before the surrender."

In the last chapters of his memoir, John Haskell described his experiences of the last days of the war in considerable detail. Upon hearing of General Lee's intention to meet with General Grant for the terms of surrender at Appomattox Courthouse, he was disbelieving, but when it was confirmed to him by General Longstreet, his first impulse was to leave and make his way to General Johnston's army. Longstreet persuaded John not to go, however, and soon afterward he was instructed to arrange for the surrender of the artillery at Appomattox.

Another South Carolinian, Colonel James R. Hagood, commander of the First South Carolina Infantry Regiment in Longstreet's Corps, wrote a history of the unit which contains one of the most vivid and moving descriptions of the last days and hours of the war ever penned, revealing the anguish in the hearts and minds of an army of men who had battled, struggled and suffered for four long years—only to learn that this vast sacrifice was ending in defeat.

In the final chapter of his memoir, Hagood described conditions during his regiment's retreat from Petersburg in early April 1865. The colonel and his men evacuated and went to Amelia Courthouse, expecting to find some supplies of rations which were supposed to have been left there for the retreating army, but by some mistake, these supplies had been forwarded to Richmond. "Now the Army found itself in a most distressing condition," he wrote. "The troops, having but one day's ration in their haversacks when Petersburg was evacuated, had already gone nearly a day without anything to eat and the close proximity of the pursuing enemy precluded the hope of foraging to an extent sufficient to supply our wants."

Hagood's descriptions of the army's ensuing struggles closely the accounts found in the memoirs of Aleck and John Haskell concerning those final days, during which the retreating Confederate forces were harassed by cavalry troops under the command of General Philip Sheridan. John recalled, "Day and night we were attacked by Sheridan's men. Whenever we halted to drive off our assailants, they were quickly and heavily reinforced, so we would have a hard fighting, often getting the worst of it, losing men as prisoners besides the killed and wounded." Colonel Hagood concluded his narrative:

> We remained at Amelia Court House until the night of April 5th, during which time some skirmishing occurred with Sheridan's cavalry ... then continued our retreat in the direction of Farmville, thirty-five miles due west ... What now remained of the Army, except Field's Division, crossed the Appomattox on the same night and hurried towards Lynchburg. Our Division, which brought up the rear, was, owing to the sudden eruption of the enemy on our flank, staved off from the High Bridge where the main body, under Lee, had crossed. We did not until the next morning, after a running fight of two hours, reach Farmville ... where we effected a passage and rejoined our comrades. It was in hurrying through Farmville, with Sheridan's cavalry right on our heels, that our men got their first mouthful to eat since the consumption of the ration they brought from Petersburg, except perhaps a few handfuls of parched corn gathered on the route. Their condition had been the most pitiable that the privations of war could reduce them to— brave strong men falling on the roadside from the sheer exhaustion of starvation, or so weak that they had to throw away their guns and accoutrements and, thus relieved, endeavor to save themselves

from falling into the enemy's hands. When we got across the river we destroyed its bridges and also over a hundred of our wagons, which had to be abandoned because the teams were starved to death ... The same evening we had an action of some magnitude some five or six miles farther on ... No mere description would be adequate to express all of the horrible sufferings which our men endured in that desperate struggle to escape the bloodhound pursuit of a remorseless enemy—how, when nearly exhausted by hunger and the fatigues of successive night marches, it was often necessary to suddenly halt and, face one rank one way and the other in another direction, defend ourselves from simultaneous attacks in front and rear ... The smoke and flames of burning wagons which had to be abandoned—artillery carriages overturned in the road—dead and dying horses at every step—added the scenic effects to this horrid drama in which our famished soldiers were the actors ...

Throughout the day and night of April 8th we dragged on our flight with all the speed we could and, for the first time since the retreat began, we were not harassed by the enemy. A faint gleam of hope shot through our hearts as we thought that we were at last outstripping our pursuers, but when daylight arrived we found the enemy drawn up across the road ahead of us while, simultaneously, another closed up on our rear. The game was now decided. A brief effort, like the unconscious jerking of a dying animal, was made to clear a passageway, then we subsided into rest—the Army had surrendered!

This intelligence was first conveyed to our men whilst they were lying on the roadside, pallid and panting from their last exertion, by a courier who galloped up ... The emotion which the news produced can only be imagined—I cannot describe it. We looked in each other's faces, where blank and fathomless despair was written, nor said one word—our hearts were too full for language. We vainly strove to comprehend the reality of our situation but our intellects were stunned by the heaviness of the blow and we could only murmur stupidly and meaninglessly the word "surrendered." It sounded like a knell of damnation.

AFTERWORD

by Dr. James E. Kibler, Jr.

The sum total of this remarkable assemblage of letters is both proof and definition of the high culture which produced them. They tell variously the story of war, grief, endurance, deprivation, devotion to home, family solidarity, faith, virtue, fidelity, sacrifice, bravery, and a strength of character that makes it possible to survive terrible loss and trauma. The stalwart nature of the authors, both women and men, young and old, encourages appreciation of the society that could shape and stimulate such greatness of heart and soul.

Eminent historian Douglas Southall Freeman singled out one of the letters collected here as among the very finest examples of "the war-time correspondence of high souls" and "one of the most beautiful born of war." (*The South to Posterity*, 6). There are at least a dozen additional examples in this collection that equal the high level of writing Freeman singles out—some by the same author he quotes, but others by his family and friends. Freeman accurately gauges Alexander Cheves Haskell's letters following the death of his young wife as testaments to the "deepened seriousness of his nature" and a mind "turned toward the things of the spirit" (6). In the progress of his correspondence, one is able to chart the growth of this "high soul" in its passage through what the poet John Keats called "the vale of soul-making." Few have experienced the vale of the shadow of death as deeply and closely as he. The writing is superb. The words are well-chosen and rise from a depth of character forged by both the events they describe and the culture that sustains him.

The collection includes letters from father, mother, brothers, sister, uncles and aunts, as well as other of their closest connections. Mrs. Haskell's letters to her daughter and sons are particularly interesting in showing life on the home front. All seven Haskell brothers who are fighting for the Confederacy have letters in the collection. Each has his own style, and his letters reveal his personality. All but the youngest are college educated—four at South Carolina College, one at the University of Virginia, and one at the Citadel. The youngest is at a classical academy preparing for college when he enlists. Their studies in the Greek and Latin classics have helped form their writing style, which on occasion elevates the letters to the level of permanent literary value. The well-written letter is recognized as an art form and a legitimate literary genre. A goodly number of letters collected here qualify for this distinction and should take their place in the celebrated body of Southern literature. As previously noted, at least a dozen approach the highest literary rank, and not just of Freeman's category of letters "born of war."

The brothers' college education entailed a depth and breadth of classical studies difficult for the modern reader to comprehend. When Langdon, Alexander, John, and Joseph were admitted to South Carolina College, they were required already to have a sound knowledge of Greek and Latin grammar, to already have read in the original the whole of Virgil's *Aeneid, Bubolics,* and *Georgics,* Cicero's *Orations,* Xenophon's *Cyropaedia* and *Anabasis,* Sallust, the Gospel of St. John in Greek, and at least one book of Homer. As sophomores, they would read Horace and *The Iliad.* A sophomore at South Carolina College described the weekly routine: "Monday and Tuesday, recitations [in Latin and Greek] before breakfast. Every Wednesday and Thursday, we recite in Cicero and the other days in Homer" (Carolyn Matalene, *Carolina Voices: Two Hundred Years of Student Experience* [2001], 6-7). Historian Francis Butler Simkins wrote that from the earliest days, Southern colleges all stressed the classics and that the "devotion of Southern students to the classics and their participation in recitations and debates of the literary societies accounts to a large degree for the grace of manner … and flowing melody" of their prose (*A History of the South* [1963], 168-169). All four brothers at South Carolina College were in one of the two literary societies where Ciceronian prose was the norm. Graduation addresses were in Latin, and a well-educated audience could understand them.

Alexander's serious grounding in Greek and Latin had begun in 1854 with study at the school of Searle, Miles, and Sachtleben in Charleston. Alexander writes that when he first comes there at the age of fifteen, he "has never seen a Greek dialect, having read only a part of Xenophon," so he has difficulty with Homer. Having read Caesar, however, he is able to "work out" his Latin. He then studies Greek "with a love inspired by" Augustus Sachtleben, whom he calls "a superb scholar and an enthusiastic teacher." With Sachtleben, Alexander masters Homer and "dialect Greek" and traces every Greek word "to its root." (Louise H. Daly, *Alexander Cheves Haskell: The Portrait of a Man,* [1934], 27-28). It is no wonder that as a senior at South Carolina College in 1860, he wins a gold medal for a sophisticated Greek composition and graduates with first honors. He writes that his school boy days in Charleston had also included a study of English under James Warley Miles, and that Thackeray's books were "my delight." He saw the English author and heard him read in Charleston (Daly, 30).

The Haskells received an education that was designed to produce a well-rounded gentleman who would be equally at home in his agricultural fields, his library, and his drawing room (Kibler, *The Classical Origins of Southern Literature* [2017], 8-22). John Gould Fletcher's essay in the Agrarian treatise *I'll Take My Stand* published in 1930 concludes that education in the antebellum South was designed to "achieve character, personality, and gentlemanliness in order to make our lives an art and to bring souls into relation with the whole scheme of things, which is the divine nature." Fletcher contrasts the Northern way of education as "producing a being without roots, except in the factory" (111, 120). The "high-souled" quality of some of the Haskell letters along with the proof of the brothers' character, personality, and gentlemanliness—with souls brought "into relation with ... the divine nature"—were no doubt shaped by an antebellum classical education that solidly reinforced their society's Christian underpinning.

The classics, however, contributed more than a felicitous, effective style to the letters in this collection. The cultural, philosophical, religious, and political beliefs that the letters exhibit owe much to the content of the Latin and Greek works that the brothers studied in the college curriculum. For graduation at South Carolina College, the Haskells had to be proficient in the first nine sections of Cicero's *De Senectute* and the last seven sections of *De Amicitia*. Cicero concludes, "There is no life happier than the farmer's ... Of the verdure of the meadows, the even rows of trees and the beauty of the vineyards and olive groves, why should I speak at length! Nothing can be more abounding in usefulness or more attractive than a well-tilled farm" (*De Senectute*, XVI). Cicero makes it clear that the honest and virtuous statesman springs from these local rural men who till their fathers' lands. He writes, "*In agris errant tum senators*"—"senators live on farms." Xenophon in *Oeconomicus* similarly praises rural life.

Writers like Virgil in his *Ecologues* and *Georgics*, which celebrate an independent local life on the land not ruled by a distant authority, or Juvenal and Horace, who satirize Roman vice and depict the city as a source of avarice and crime while extolling the virtues of farm life, or of Homer, who describes Laertes' consolations in cultivating the soil, all point to the desirability of living a life on the land rather than in a Puritan-conceived city on a hill. It is no wonder that Hobbes in his great leviathan of big and bigger centralized government would bar classical authors from his republic. Understandably, Hobbes, Thomas Paine, and Noah Webster all particularly despised Cicero at the same time he was a favorite in the South.

The Haskell letters often declare—sometimes eloquently—what the brothers are willing to sacrifice their lives for, and what their parents are consoled by in the deprivations and loss of their sons in the struggle. The sacrifice is for home, the *patria*, the local, intensely specific family fields, as in Virgil's own specification of his *patria* as his father's fields running down to the Mincio River beneath the beech trees with the broken tops. The Haskells see the war as a struggle against the distant *palatial Romana.*

It is fitting that the inscription chosen for the gravestone memorial to the two Haskell brothers killed in the war comes from an ode by Horace: *Dulce et decorum est, pro patria mori* (Book III, ode ii). It is the *patria,* the specific father's fields of home, that are sweet and fitting to die for. For the Haskells, one does not die for Rome, the *palatial Romana* of empire, or for the "National Idea," especially when they parasitize and make war on the *patria.* It is also fitting that their Haskell plantation in Abbeville District, South Carolina, is simply named "Home Place Plantation." When the Haskell brothers declare in their letters that they are fighting a defensive war for *home,* they most literally mean the "Home Place." With home come the associations of the particular seeds that are being planted, of desiring the little early butterbeans grown there for a meal, or of the roses and fruit trees that their mother and sister are nurturing.

Alexander Haskell, particularly, reveals himself to be more than a gifted and eloquent prose writer. His conception of the war as a modern day version of the old world struggle of Puritan Roundhead against the landed Cavalier shows a broad and informed view of history (letter of 7 January 1862). He was not alone in this comparison. Others said the same on both sides of the cultural divide. For instance, George Ward Nichols, aide-de-camp to Sherman, wrote in his *The History of the Great March* (New York: Harpers, 1865) that he feels the incendiary general to be a more effective Cromwell because he does not go into battle "singing psalms, and uttering prayers, but with a cool and quiet determination which is inspired by a lofty sense of sacred duty" to the National Idea. He feels that the position of Cromwell is more accurately assigned to Gen. O. O. Howard who rebukes soldiers for profanity and will not allow liquor about his headquarters (142). He is the Cromwellian Puritan crusader *par excellence.* Southern author William Gilmore Simms on several occasions made the same comparisons of North and South.

Religious differences did sometimes fuel the conflict. The invader seems to have had a particular hatred for anything "high church." The Haskells were Episcopalians. In 1868, Frederick A. Porcher's insightful treatment of the differences between a secularized Puritan Unitarian-Transcendental philosophy based on a belief that "the voice of humanity is the voice of God" comes into direct conflict with the South's traditional Christian and classical conception of man's limitations (*South Carolina Historical Magazine,* 117 [Spring 2016], 242.) Nichols lends credence to this explanation by declaring that the Southern people "do not know what it is to be an American" because they "have never had any conception of the National Idea," a phrase he uses as a thematic motif throughout *The History of the Great March.* (See for example, pp. 67, 125, 171, 214.) Of Sherman, Nichols writes, he is "a pure outgrowth of American civilization ... There is nothing European about him. He is a striking type of our institutions, and he comprehends justly the National Idea" (125). When Nichols says Sherman has nothing European about him, he no doubt means that the incendiary general has none of those troubling classical ideals that Southerners have. Honour, chivalry, and the love of the local have instead been replaced by the Hobbesian National Idea. It becomes clear that for Nichols, America is an abstract "Idea" based on unlimited material progress and a constant march of man to utopian perfection.

The Haskell letters reveal quite a different conception of "American." Their writings show they believe man to be a flawed creature in need of redemption. Mary Seabrook's letter of 17 July 1863 to Sophie Haskell declares that she feels God sends afflictions such as theirs to make them better. The constant refrain in these letters is submission to the will of God and a quiet acceptance of what befalls one. Those conversant with the Greek authors have learned that to put oneself above God is the greatest sin—the sin of *hubris*—and leads directly and unequivocally to tragedy. The Delphic admonition to "know thyself"—that is, to know your small place before God— is the root of Greek wisdom. The Haskell letters reflect this wisdom at every turn. There is no questioning of divine wisdom. Theirs is a quiet personal faith that has not morphed into secularized Puritan zealotry or the aberration of fanaticism. Mrs. Sophia Haskell on 5 May 1861 identifies the Northern manner as "fanatical."

The Haskell letters reveal that America to them is not an Idea, but home and family. It is most literally *patria*, as we have seen, and not the Hobbesian Nation State. The feelings of the conquering army expressed by Nichols are the diametric opposite. Standing in the desolate, still smoking ruins of Columbia, he asks what South Carolinians would feel at that moment about "state sovereignty," now that the National Idea has rolled over them like a great Cromwellian wave of fire and fury destroying everything they hold sacred. Nichols clarifies for me just why the Haskells feel they must give their all to fight what traditional, classical man would consider a malignancy and an enormous evil. The Haskells show they would never consider they are at war with old European ideals as expressed in a classical and Christian view.

In fact, what one gathers from the sum total of their letters is that the Haskells' Southern world is modeled upon the society of the English rural gentry who value land and family above material things. English Augustan poetry and drama, expressing the beau ideals of that landed squirarchy, are both influences in the Haskells' South that are still honoured in their day, even when romanticism has become the popular new fashion. Their letters often reveal that the family has the sensibility of the landed gentry. The men talk constantly of horses, during war and peace. Joseph Haskell refers to the *American Turf Register* and a fox hunting story in the midst of war. Alexander relates that "I had read the *Turf Register* since I was a boy" (Daly, 28). Throughout his letters, Alexander shows great compassion for his suffering horses, ill-fed and nearly ridden to death. They are "pitiable to behold ... They complain so pitiably, I find myself melted in compassion" (3 April 1863). The letters express rural concerns, from seeds and fruit trees to new ploughed fields and the growing of vegetables.

Stark Young defines aristocracy in his chapter in *I'll Take My Stand* as "an innate code of obligations" and "self-control," and most definitely "not the expression of you and your precious personality." Young continues, "You controlled yourself to make the society you lived in more decent, affable, and civilized" (350). The Haskell letters frequently exhibit this innate aristocratic manner and character, reflective of the manner of the best of the English gentry. The words "code of obligations," "self-control," and a humble disregard of self are descriptions of the brothers' character traits shown throughout the body of their letters. In Young's definition, then, the brothers qualify as aristocratic in the way of the landed gentry.

The Haskells understand home to be the seat of family, much in the way the English Great House or manor house becomes more than a repository of treasured art and *objets virtu*. It houses the sacred *lares et penates* spoken of in the classical writers the family knew well. Their sensibility is again a part of the landed gentry's understanding of a civilized world. The Haskell letters express this understanding fully by word as well as deed.

It is worth repeating in this context that another aspect of a gentry-patterned world is the Haskells' training in the Greek and Latin classics that reinforce a life on the land by defining rural life as the ideal and the source of freedom and independence. From Virgil and Horace to Homer and Xenophon, from Cicero and Juvenal to Ovid and Sallust, the good life is embodied in the rural and not embroiled in the fever of buying and selling. All the classical writers advanced this understanding and condemned a society dominated by a merchant class with a cash-register evaluation of life. The Haskells' classical educations were not window dressing, but instead allowed comprehension of the Western world's definition of the civilized man. Southerners of their class understood that they were the upholders of that tradition, so that a Southern Agrarian writer like Allen Tate could declare of Southern traditionalists, "We must be the last Europeans—there being no Europeans in Europe at present." The Haskells lived their own particular version of the agrarian ideal with the historical and religious scheme of Europe as their example, source, and prototype. Their letters provide a valuable window into that world.

Their landed society also valued the old virtuous concepts of honour and chivalry also revered by the English gentry. Alexander Haskell notes on 4 May 1861 that the enemy "has forgotten the laws of war" along with "natural honour and chivalry." He predicts a war of subjugation and "extermination." The actions of the following four years prove his prediction correct. *Extermination* may at first seem an extreme word, but, as we have seen, Sherman and his aide-de-camp often used the word. This was also the assessment of F. A. Porcher in 1868. The Haskell letters provide ample proof of honour and chivalry in action. Those who demeaned these ideals in the North were pilloried by Simms in his last essay of 1869 (*William Gilmore Simms's Selected Reviews on Literature and Civilization* [2014], 191-193.) Here he also noted that Europeans saw these concepts "as especially belonging to the South"—a fact that angered Northerners (192).

The Haskell letters make it possible to put a face on these abstractions. They display chivalry in action to the extent that the term may be defined thereby. Honour and chivalry are brought down to the personal level. Here the concepts entail far more than duty and a sense of obligation understood in the gentlemanly code as *noblesse oblige.*

The letters are now brought together for the first time from the manuscript collections of the University of North Carolina, the University of South Carolina, Duke University, the South Carolina Historical Society, and the Georgia Historical Society. They are valuable primary documents that go a long way in helping to define a place, a culture, and a time.

APPENDIX 1

THE HASKELLS AFTER THE WAR

General Sherman's path of destruction through South Carolina left much of it in ruins. Some of the destruction in South Carolina and other Southern states had been carried out as part of a strategy to reduce the Confederacy's capacity to wage war, but, as historian Ludwell H. Johnson observed, "most of the destruction was born of a quite different philosophy, one that sprang from a generation of anti-Southern polemics with a strong religious tincture. There was a widespread although by no means universal conviction among Union troops that Southerners were a wicked people who had deliberately started the war and therefore had no rights that the righteous were bound to respect." General William T. Sherman's campaigns were a prime example of this phenomenon. "Sherman and the kind of warfare that he exemplified," Johnson contended, "were not so much harbingers of modern total war as they were a throwback to the religious wars of the seventeenth century, or perhaps even to the wars of the Old Testament."

South Carolina was singled out for particularly savage treatment. Major George W. Nichols, one of Sherman's staff officers, proudly declared, "History ... will be searched in vain for a parallel to the scattering and destructive effects of this invasion of the Carolinas." The invaders left the state by March 1865, but the end of the war a month later was only the beginning of another tragic era in South Carolina. As bad as it was, the widespread physical destruction of towns, plantations, livestock and railways was not the worst aspect of the devastation the state would suffer. Most of the wealth of South Carolina planters was wiped out with emancipation, and by 1867, land values had plunged 60 percent. Worse than all this, the state had lost over a third of the 60,000 men she had sent to war. Countless veterans were maimed or debilitated, and there had also been many civilian deaths in South Carolina and elsewhere in the South attributable to the war's hardships and barbarity.

Ludwell H. Johnson noted that both whites and the freedmen suffered greatly in the years immediately after the war. "Among blacks who had left the plantations and crowded into towns and cities," he wrote, "the mortality rate was said to be enormous. Deaths from disease among black children were especially numerous; it was, said one observer, like Herod's slaughter of the innocents. By 1868 the danger of starvation was past, although widespread poverty became endemic." During most of the period called Reconstruction, the South was at the mercy of the Radical Republicans in Washington, and in South Carolina, corruption was widespread in the state government dominated by Republicans.

In his study of Reconstruction, Hodding Carter observed that "South Carolina and Louisiana suffered most at the hands of the Radicals; and they, together with Florida, would not throw off the Republican yoke until after the presidential election of 1876." In June of that year, Mrs. Haskell wrote to a friend complaining of "dreadful Yankee Radicals who govern the negroes and tax us to death and put all sorts of villainous characters into office." When General Wade Hampton was finally installed as South Carolina's governor after the election of 1876, Aleck Haskell played a significant role in his campaign.

Like other formerly prosperous Southern families, the Haskells had to adapt to the harsh realities and difficulties of the post-war period. In 1865, Charles T. Haskell still owned extensive lands in South Carolina and Arkansas, and although not destitute, he and Sophia were burdened with a large amount of debt. In the spring of 1867 she wrote to a relative, "we are going on credit for almost everything ... we cannot expect ever to be well off again but I hope we will have enough to be comfortable. Our boys must struggle for themselves."

Charles Thomson Haskell died on December 27, 1874, and the vestry records of Trinity Episcopal Church record that he was buried two days later in the church graveyard. Writing to a friend in June 1876, his widow Sophia described her family's life in the aftermath of the war:

> [W]e have been going through hard times and have suffered much. In 61 when our struggle began, we were wealthy, as we look on wealth in this country, after thirty years of work, with a noble family, eight sons and one daughter. Our six eldest all went into the war from the beginning, the oldest 28, the youngest 17 and such noble boys they were! Handsome, brave, honorable and good. I never had cause, thank God to be ashamed of them. I pleaded God to take to Himself our Charles and Willy, the second and third. Charles was killed commanding the forlorn hope at Morris Island and Willy shot through the heart at Gettysburg in command of a battalion. Sometimes we think they were the flower of the flock, but they were splendid men and best of all true Christians from early youth. We almost lost two more but they

seemed spared to us almost by a miracle, one with the loss of his eye and fearful wound in the temple and the other with the loss of his right arm. The other two though in every danger escaped un-injured and also our soldier boy of seventeen who served in the last campaign and had the honor of surrendering with Lee.

We have lost nearly all our property and I have now been a widow a year and a half. My dear husband bore up bravely against our troubles til struck by a partial paralysis which ruined his health. He suffered with little intermission for two years but died without a struggle one Sunday morning as I sat beside him reading to him, and I thank God he was ready and willing to go. I have lived alone since in our plantation home with our only daughter Sophie. She is everything to me now and a very fine girl. She grew up in the War and has learned both to suffer and to act. All our six remain-ing sons have married and I have 22 little grandchildren and six good daughters. And no Mother could wish for more loving chil-dren. So amidst all our losses I feel that the best is left me. Our sons are all working hard and have many difficulties to encounter but I trust God will prosper them in His good time ...

Langdon Cheves Haskell

Langdon and his family returned to Arkansas after the war, and his letters to family members in South Carolina chronicle the difficulties he encountered in trying to re-establish himself as a planter. In 1870 he wrote to his father: "My cotton crop is on two thirds of the place very good and on the other third only tolerable. But everywhere it is too large by far for my force to pick in reasonable time and I have to remain here and try and get it out by hiring all additional labor procurable. This is very scarce and the rates are very high... The great trouble here is to get enough labor. There has never since the war been more than two thirds of crop made on the land as we have to scatter the hands over too much land for their present energies to keep up with it. My corn crop is miserable, in part, due to drought, but more to bad work."

Things did not improve much over the following decade, and in a letter of 1881 Langdon reported: "We have had a terrible season here this year and with the high price of labor, the low price of cotton and the heavy loss in the field will make nothing. There is still a large quantity of cotton unpicked and it is time to be putting in another crop. Ella and the two younger children are doing only pretty well."

The following year, on November 14, 1882, Langdon died of congestion of the lungs and was buried in Bellwood Cemetery in Pine Bluff, Arkansas. After his death, his wife Ella and the children returned to Abbeville, where she passed away in 1887.

Alexander Cheves Haskell

After the war Aleck studied law and eventually achieved notable success in that field and others. He was active in politics in South Carolina, and in 1890, he ran for governor, but lost the election to his opponent Ben Tillman. The *Cyclopedia of Eminent and Representative Men of the Carolinas* (published in 1892), described Aleck's life and career after the war:

Returning from the army at the close of the war, Col. Haskell commenced teaching school at Abbeville, S.C. At the same time he was engaged in the study of law, which profession he had decided to follow. In December, 1865, he was admitted to the bar, and in the same year was elected to the legislature from his native county, where he served a period of two years. He continued teaching school and practicing law until 1867, when he was elected judge of the district court at Abbeville. But he resigned this position in September of the same year to accept a professorship of law in the South Carolina university to which he had been elected the preceding July. The duties which devolved upon him in this new capacity were met with much ability and he continued to discharge them until July 1868. At that time the state convention requested him to be an elector in the presidential contest between Grant and Seymour, the acceptance of which seemed to call for his resignation of the law professorship. He at once began an active and stirring canvass of the state for the democratic ticket, which resulted in much good for his party. At the close of the campaign, Col. Haskell opened a law office in Columbia, and the following year formed a partnership with Joseph D. Pope, which lasted until the last month of 1877, at which time he was chosen associate justice of the supreme bench of South Carolina, a position he held for two years. His career upon the bench was marked by eminent fairness and profound knowledge of the law, and won for him much distinction as a jurist. He was elected for the term of four years, but resigned to accept the presidency of the Charlotte, Columbia & Augusta R. R., an office he continued to hold until December, 1889. In addition to this, he was in 1883, selected for president of the Columbia & Greenville R. R., the duties of which place he discharged for a period of six years. Judge Haskell's qualifications as a business man and financier were duly recognized, when at the organization of the Loan & Exchange bank, of South Carolina, in 1886, he was chosen president, which position he satisfactorily filled to the present time. From 1887 to 1889, Judge Haskell was one of the government directors of the Union Pacific R. R., and was chairman of the committee which reported to the government the best method of dealing with that road. This report was afterward re-iterated by a special commission appointed to investigate the relations of this road with the government. During the memorable campaign of 1876, Judge Haskell acted as chairman of the democratic state executive committee, and his management of the affairs at that time were universally commended as wise and efficient. At its close he was chosen to represent the state at Washington to secure the recognition of Gen. Hampton as governor of South Carolina. The success which attended the efforts and the government established by the vote of the people of the state, are well known and were largely brought about by the skillful manner in which Judge Haskell presented the cause of his state.

The married life of Judge Haskell began in 1861, when Rebecca C., daughter of John Singleton, of Richland county, became his wife. She bore him one daughter and died in 1862, much lamented. His second marriage occurred in November, 1870, Alice V. Alexander being his bride. She is a daughter of A. L. Alexander, of Washington, Ga., and sister of Gen. E. P. Alexander, of Savannah. By this wife Judge Haskell is the father of ten children.

Aleck never forgot his first love, and his daughter and biographer, Louise Haskell Daly, recalled that that there was "a complete openness and confidence" between him and his second wife about Decca, adding, "As long as our Mother lived she never failed on Easter Sunday to place a wreath on Decca's grave in Old Trinity Church yard. I think she felt, and without any bitterness, that Father never recovered from the wound of Decca's death. It was Mother who told me what I know of the sad story. Father never spoke of it."

After a brief illness, Aleck died in the early morning hours of April 13, 1910. The next day, he was laid to rest in Elmwood Cemetery in Columbia, where Confederate veterans sounded Taps at his grave.

John Cheves Haskell

A biographical sketch of John C. Haskell published in *Men of Mark in South Carolina* in 1907, offers the following summary of his later life:

> After the close of the war he located in Mississippi, and for ten years was engaged in planting, but during the last two years of the time he read law, and at the expiration of that period he was admitted to the Mississippi bar. In 1877, Mr. Haskell removed to South Carolina and was elected a member of the state legislature and by successive reelections continued in that capacity until 1896. During the last four years of his legislative service he was chairman of the Ways and Means committee. When the Tillman forces gained control of the state, Mr. Haskell resigned from the legislature and since that time he has not held public office. For two years after returning to his native state he gave much time to planting. He then removed to Columbia, where, when not engaged in legislative duties, he practiced law with great success, until 1890, when he became receiver of a railroad and also of a company which was engaged in mining coal and iron ore and operating furnaces at Bristol, Virginia. He was engaged in this work until 1896, when he received an injury which disabled him, temporarily, from active service. He is a member of the D. K. E. fraternity and of the Clariosophic society of the South Carolina college ... In 1865, Mr. Haskell was married to Sallie Hampton, daughter of General Wade Hampton, of South Carolina, who died in 1886. In 1896 he married Lucy Hampton, daughter of Colonel Frank Hampton. Of his four children, by his first wife, all are living in 1907.

John C. Haskell died on June 26, 1906, and was buried at the Trinity Episcopal Cathedral churchyard in Columbia, South Carolina.

Joseph Cheves Haskell

After the war, Joseph married his cousin Mary Elizabeth Cheves (1844-1915), the daughter of John Richardson Cheves and Rachel Susan Bee Cheves. They were the parents of four children, all of whom were born in Savannah, Georgia, between 1868 and 1877.

An obituary published in the *News & Courier* of Charleston on July 2, 1922, stated the following:

After the war, Capt. Haskell planted rice on the Ogeechee in Georgia and subsequently went to Louisiana where he was head of the large salt mines of that State. Upon his return to the Southeastern States, he was first employed by the Central Railroad as purchasing agent and later became head of the department of all the railroads in the South in looking after cars on the different lines and attending to delays caused by the detention of cars. Subsequently he became head of all the cotton compresses of these railroads and continued to serve with them even after they had disposed of their presses and until his death.

There were few men in South Carolina more favorably known than Capt. Haskell. He was over six feet tall, a graceful rider and a wonderful sportsman. He made no enemies but through his disposition, a combination of amiability and strength, he endeared himself to all who were fortunate enough to be associated with him. He was in harness, as he desired to be, until the last.

He leaves surviving him a son, Mr. William E. Haskell, and a daughter, Mrs. Alexander Marshall. He was the last survivor of the family of his father and mother.

In a letter published in *The Louisiana Planter and Sugar Manufacturer* on July 7, 1888, a trade journal published in New Orleans, a visitor to Avery's Island, Louisiana, mentioned meeting "Capt. Haskell, the courteous and accomplished manager for the American Salt Mining Company (now in active operation)."

In 1899, John C. Haskell was selected to be a member of a delegation representing the state of South Carolina at the funeral of President Jefferson Davis, which took place in New Orleans, but illness prevented his attendance, and his brother Joseph took his place. Records of the funeral list John C. Haskell as a pallbearer, but it is likely that Joseph took his place as such.

Joseph died in Atlanta, Georgia, on June 30, 1922, and was buried in Magnolia Cemetery in Charleston. One of his obituaries described him as "a business man widely known throughout the South."

Sophia Louisa Lovell Haskell Cheves

Sophie lived with her parents after the war, and after her father's death, she was the principal companion and support of her mother. A number of years after her mother's death, in the spring of 1889, she married her cousin Langdon Cheves, who had become a well-to-do attorney in Charleston. As a teenager, he had joined Aleck Haskell's Seventh Cavalry Regiment in

1865, arriving in Virginia only to find that General Lee had just surrendered at Appomattox. Brilliant, but eccentric and parsimonious in his later years, Langdon did not give Sophie the happiness she had likely hoped for in their union. For several years before her death she suffered with heart problems, passing away in Charleston on May 7, 1922.

Langdon Cheves died on the last day of December 1939. In his will he bequeathed a massive collection of papers to the South Carolina Historical Society, where he had been an officer for many years. This collection consisted of his extensive legal, financial, and personal papers and his historical and genealogical research and writings, as well as the correspondence and other papers of families and individuals to whom he was related, including the Haskell, Middleton, Cheves, and McCord families. Thanks to Langdon and Sophie, these valuable manuscripts were preserved, and from them came many of the letters of the Haskell family in this book.

In 1941, as directed by Langdon's will, a handsome stained glass window was installed at Trinity Episcopal Church in Abbeville in memory of his mother-in-law Mrs. Sophia Haskell, and "and her daughter Sophia Lovell Haskell, wife of Langdon Cheves."

Louis Wardlaw Haskell

After the war, Louis worked as a civil engineer and, along with his cousin Langdon Cheves,became a rice planter at Delta Plantation on the Savannah River. Louis married Sarah Gordon Owens (1851-1920) of Savannah in 1872, and in the 1880s, he embarked on a new venture that would bring him notable success as a businessman. He died on June 4, 1920, and most of the available information pertaining to his later life is found in obituaries. A death notice that appeared in a Savannah newspaper on June 5, 1920 (and reprinted a day later in *The Augusta Chronicle*) described him as "vice-president of the Southern Cotton Oil Company and one of Savannah's most prominent businessmen and citizens," further noting, "Business interests called Mr. Haskell to New York some years ago and he and his wife made their home there for about ten years, returning here about five years ago. ... Mr. Haskell is survived by ... two sons and two daughters ..."

At the time of his death he was vice-president of the Southern Cotton Oil Company. A more extensive obituary published in a trade journal, *The Oil Miller*, gave the following details:

> Soon after his graduation at college he was engaged as an engineer in railroad construction, and after this became a rice planter on the Savannah River. When the Southern Cotton Oil Company was organized, by Oliver and others, in 1886, Mr. Haskell noticed in

the news items of the paper that these gentlemen were considering the erection of several plants in the South, and entirely in the interest of Savannah, he wrote them and suggested Savannah as a suitable place for the erection of one of their oil mills ... They were in need of some local man to take charge of the construction and running of this mill, and, without solicitation on his part, the position was offered to Mr. Haskell. He accepted, and became the first manager of the Savannah plant.

Paul Thomson Haskell

According to a letter that Paul wrote to his cousin Langdon Cheves in December 1870, he was leaving South Carolina to move to the vicinity of Savannah, Georgia, where he had obtained a position "keeping all the accounts & buying all the supplies" for some plantation owners. About six years after this, he would find a livelihood on his own plantation as a rice planter. According to the book *North by South: The Two Lives of Richard James Arnold*, Paul purchased a Georgia rice plantation on the Ogeechee River called Cherry Hill in 1877.

In 1873, he married Mary Wallace Footman Owens (1854-99) in Savannah, Georgia, and they were the parents of three sons. The 1880 federal census lists Paul as a resident of Ways Station, in Bryan County, Georgia (in the vicinity of Cherry Hill), and the 1880 city directory for Savannah, Georgia, shows that he also had a residence there, listing him as a planter living at 92 State Street. The 1900 Savannah city directory again lists him as a planter, and gives his residence as 122 State Street. His brother Louis is listed as a resident of 128 State Street in the same directory.

In reminiscences written in 1948 by his niece Elise Haskell Marshall (the daughter of Joseph C. Haskell), she stated that Paul "lived in Savannah Ga. and at his plantation 'Cherry Hill' in Bryan Co. Ga. He was a rice planter and lived at Cherry Hill all his life. Like most of the Haskells, he was very social and spent a great deal of his time at the Old Oglethorpe Club in Savannah and his summers at the White Sulphur Springs in Virginia ... In my long life, I do not think that I have ever known anyone with a keener sense of humor or more ready wit than my 'Uncle Paul.' He was noted as a raconteur."

Paul died on October 19, 1918, and was buried in the Laurel Grove Cemetery in Savannah.

Sophia Cheves Haskell

Survived by six sons and a daughter, Mrs. Sophia Haskell died on July 30, 1881, and was buried in the graveyard of Trinity Episcopal Church in Abbeville. A week afterward, when Langdon Haskell received news of her death at his home in Arkansas, he wrote to his sister Sophie about her.

My dear Sophie,

Last night your letter with John's reached us telling of our dear mother's sudden death. I could hardly believe it and can't yet realize it. I had so persuaded myself that I would once again, even if were but for a little while, live near her, to love, admire & reverence her as I had never done before. I had hoped that the critical state of her health had passed & persuaded myself that so fine & noble a life would be spared to us a few years longer. I know I can't feel her loss as you do, & grieve for your affliction as well as her loss. There was none like her that ever I knew & my heart is filled with bitter and unavailing regret that I did not know or appreciate better what she was in my younger days and show and give her a higher love and devotion. But she knew how to wait—to accept humbly and in faith the present ill in full confidence & hope that all things were for the best. I think she was the noblest exemplar of Christian faith & charity & peace of mind that I ever knew. How often you will recollect she used the expression, "I trust." How slight and often without significance it fell on our ears, but how infinite and full of meaning to her.

Let us pray that her example and remembrance may never pass from our hearts. She was the bond which united us & though John says she loved you and myself the best, I can't think of her as making any difference, her love was so large and so unselfish.

I feel as if one great object of my life were gone beyond reach, to see her and be with her again. Take comfort yourself that you have been so much to her, and been the stay of her old age. She would wish you to be comforted and to be happy.

Your affectionate brother,

L. C. Haskell

APPENDIX 2

The following biographical sketch was written by Langdon Cheves (1848-1939), the nephew of Captain Langdon Cheves. The original manuscript is found in the papers of the younger Langdon Cheves at the South Carolina Historical Society. The original spelling and punctuation have been retained, but a few changes and corrections have been made for clarity. The author erred in his belief that Captain Cheves was born in Charleston; he was in fact born in Philadelphia. The author also suggested that Battery Wagner was named for Theodore D. Wagner at Captain Cheves' suggestion, but it is generally accepted that the fortification was named for Lieutenant Colonel Thomas M. Wagner, the Inspector of Artillery in Charleston, who died from an explosion of a gun at Fort Moultrie in July 1862.

Langdon Cheves (a signer of the Ordinance of Secession)

Langdon Cheves was a son of the Honorable Langdon Cheves (sometime a Judge and a Member of Congress from South Carolina, chairman of the Naval Committee in the War of 1812, and Speaker in 1814). He was born at Charleston (I believe) on the 2nd September 1814. His father, Judge Cheves, having been made the President of the United States Bank and subsequently Commissioner under the Treaty of Ghent went to Philadelphia in 1819 and remained there and at his seat "Abbeville," near Lancaster, Penn., for ten years, and his son Langdon, the subject of this sketch, went to school at Lancaster and in Philadelphia, completing his education at the South Carolina College where he graduated in December 1833. His next birthday after graduating came near to being his last. At Pendleton while practicing pistol shooting with the gentlemen of the neighbourhood he accidentally shot himself in the neck—it was supposed mortally by his companions. His mother writes: "He is a great favourite … a very amiable fine young man … the day before the accident was his Birthday, when his health and good wishes were drank in Champaign. He was twenty. His father drank his health and said, My son … I am happy to tell you you have never given me one unhappy moment."

Mr. Cheves' first military experience was in the Seminole War, where he served as a volunteer, in what rank or capacity I do not know, and was actively engaged. He then read law and was called to the Bar at Columbia in 1836 and practiced there for several years. He was State Reporter for the

Courts of Appeal and Cheves' Law and Equity Reports (published in Columbia 1840, 41) are part of his work for this period. He then married Charlotte, daughter of the Hon. David J. McCord, of Columbia.

After his marriage Mr. Cheves became a rice planter. His father put him in charge of his extensive rice plantations on Savannah River in Beaufort District and later removed to his Ogeechee estate and turned over the Savannah places to himself and his younger brother Charles. He planted these places with most conspicuous skill, ability and success until the war. He greatly assisted in the erection of the "Vernezobre" freshet bank, to protect the Savannah River plantations from its floods, and other plantation engineering works, and reclaimed and planted successfully the neglected peat or "prairie" lands, thus greatly increasing his acreage. His plantations were among the best managed and his people the best cared for in the state. In the cholera epidemic of 1850-51 he and his brother Charles remained with their people, removed them to camps in the pine lands, and greatly mitigated the disease and the sufferings it occasioned.

Mr. Cheves possessed a most endearing personality, winning the confidence and affection of his associates and even of his negroes, who were most loyal and devoted to him. He was a man of unusual ability and information and was constantly called upon to assist his friends in matters of engineering and machinery so often needed on rice plantations. Mr. Cheves was by this time known not only as a skillful and successful planter but a man of great judgment, originality, and uprightness. He was a warm Southerner in sympathy and principle and devoted his time and resources to the cause of the Confederacy from the time of its incipiency. Mr. Cheves was chosen a delegate from St. Peter's Parish to the Secession Convention and voted for the Ordinance.

On the breaking out of the war Mr. Cheves volunteered his services and devoted his time and resources to the defence of the State, and never ceased to labour with constant and unselfish zeal for the good of the cause. He served as an Engineer (for which his studies and his experience in plantation works, canals, banks, etc. well prepared him), and the confidence of his fellow planters of the coast in his eminent powers, justice, and integrity, their knowledge that he took personal charge of the works, and his example in sending his own negroes were of great benefit to the public defences in procuring negro labourers for them.

In the spring of 1861 he volunteered to raise the labour for and superintended the works on Hilton Head. After the completion of these, he became volunteer aid to General Drayton, who assigned him to engineer duty. He was present there with Capt. F. D. Lee at the engagement with the Federal Fleet when Port Royal was taken. He constructed the works at Red

Bluff and was employed on other minor works. In the spring of 1862 Mr. Cheves designed and superintended the construction at the Chatham Armory in Savannah, chiefly at his own expense (I believe), of the only Southern war balloon, made of ladies dress silk bought in Savannah and Charleston, in lengths of about 40 feet and of various colours. He laughingly told his daughters, "I am buying up all the handsome silk dresses in Savannah, but not for you girls." A letter of 7 June, 1862 from his brother Dr. John Cheves (then constructing, under innumerable difficulties, the system of obstructions and torpedo defences at Charleston): "Tell Lang I am using car springs dissolved in boiled oil to coat the wire (for torpedos); it is the best balloon varnish." Mr. Cheves took the balloon on to Richmond just before the Seven Days Battles and remained there to assist in using it. Several ascents were made (amongst others by the late Genl. E. P. Alexander and Capt. Jos. C. Haskell, his adjutant, now chief of the Car Service Association). But the inferior coal gas and the long distance it had to be run out on the railroad (attached to a flat car) from Richmond to the front and back made ascents difficult. It was finally lost at the James River, being cut off by the enemy's gun boats. Capt. Glassford, U. S. A., in his "Sketch of Ballooning in the Civil War" says: "While the use of the balloon by the Confederates is known to have been very scanty, an interesting account of the construction, use and ultimate fate of one balloon—believed to be the only one in the Confederate Army—is given by General Longstreet. He says: "The Federals had been using balloons in examining our positions and we watched with anxious eyes their beautiful observations as they floated high up in the air, well out of range of our guns. While we were longing for the balloons that poverty denied us, a genius arose for the occasion and suggested that we send out and gather all the silk dresses in the Confederacy and make a balloon. It was done; and soon we had a great patch work ship of many and varied hues which was ready for use in the Seven Days campaign. We had no gas except in Richmond, and it was the custom to inflate the balloon there, tie it securely to an engine, and move it down the York River Railroad to any point at which we desired to send it up. One day it was on a steamer down the James when the tide went out and left the vessel and the balloon high and dry on a bar. The Federals gathered it in and with it the last silk dress in the Confederacy."

Mr. Cheves brought home from Richmond the body of his nephew Lieut. Edward Cheves who had been killed in the battle. In July, 1862, he was ordered in charge of the works on Morris Island. He chose the site and built Battery Wagner, and probably suggested its name (after Mr. Theodore D. Wagner, a relative of his wife's who had contributed largely with labourers and otherwise towards its construction) and subsequently considerably improved and strengthened the work. Gen. Ripley writes (see Charleston Year Book 1885, p. 354) "... the works which had been commenced were well and solidly finished during the summer of 1862, notably Battery Bee on Sullivan's Island and Battery Wagner on Morris Island, the former under the charge of Capt. George E. Walker and the latter of Capt. Langdon Cheves." Battery Wagner and Cummings Point with some minor works on the Island were the results of his energy and skill. For more than two years he thus served his country without asking or receiving either rank or pay until about two months before his death when the War Department at Richmond conferred upon him the commission of Captain of Engineers in recognition of his services. Capt. Cheves remained in charge of the Fort until the grand attack of the Federal Fleet and land forces on the 10 July, 1863, when he was killed at the threshold of his quarters by the first shell fired from the attacking fleet.

The Charleston Mercury of July 13, 1863 states: "Even in the midst of our dangers and our preparations for coming trials we must pause in grief at the loss of some of our best and bravest, who fell early in the action of Friday last. Conspicuous amongst these were Captains Langdon Cheves and Charles T. Haskell. Langdon Cheves was killed by the first shell fire by the enemy at Battery Wagner ... In the full vigor of manhood he has fallen at the Battery which he had been at so much pains to erect, leaving a record which will not unbeseem the memory of the sire whose name he bore."

BIBLIOGRAPHY

SECONDARY AND PUBLISHED PRIMARY SOURCES

The 1850 Census of Abbeville District South Carolina. Edited and indexed by Harold Lawrence. Tignall, Ga.: Boyd Publishing Co., 1981.

Allardice, Bruce S. *Confederate Colonels: A Biographical Register.* Columbia: University of Missouri Press, 1991.

Allardice, Bruce S. *More Generals in Gray.* Baton Rouge: Louisiana State University Press, 1995.

"Attapkapas Letter." *The Louisiana Planter and Sugar Manufacturer,* 1 (1888): 126.

Alexander, Edward Porter. *Fighting for the Confederacy: The Personal Recollections of General Edward Porter Alexander.* Edited by Gary W. Gallagher. Chapel Hill: University of North Carolina Press, 1989.

Bachman, C. L. *John Bachman: The Pastor of St. John's Lutheran Church, Charleston.* Charleston, S.C.: Walker, Evans & Cogswell, 1888.

Baker, Gary R. *Cadets in Gray.* Lexington, S.C.: Palmetto Bookworks, 1989.

Baker, William M. *The Life and Labours of the Rev. Daniel Baker, D.D., Pastor and Evangelist.* Philadelphia: William S. and Alfred Martien, 1858.

Bancroft, A. C., ed. *The Life and Death of Jefferson Davis, Ex-President of the Southern Confederacy.* New York: J. S. Ogilvie, Publisher, 1889.

Barnwell, Stephen B. *The Story of an American Family.* Marquette, Mich.: Privately printed, 1969.

Barziza, Decimus et Ultimus. *The Adventures of a Prisoner of War, and Life and Scenes in Federal Prisons: Johnson's Island, Fort Delaware, and Point Lookout.* Houston, Texas: Richardson & Owen, 1865.

Bennett, Susan Smythe. "The Cheves Family of South Carolina." *South Carolina Historical Magazine* 35 (1934):79-95.

Benson, B. K. *Who Goes There? The Story of a Spy in the Civil War.* New York: The Macmillan Company, 1900.

Benson, Berry. *Berry Benson's Civil War Book: Memoirs of a Confederate Scout and Sharpshooter.* Edited by Susan Williams Benson. Athens: The University of Georgia Press, 1992.

Bradshaw, Timothy Eugene. *Battery Wagner: The Siege, The Men Who Fought, and the Casualties.* Columbia, S.C.: Palmetto Historical Works, 1993.

Brock, Robert Alonzo. *Virginia and Virginians: Eminent Virginians ... History of Virginia from Settlement of Jamestown to Close of Civil War.* Richmond, Va.: H. H. Hardesty, 1897.

Brown, Kent Masterson. *Retreat from Gettysburg: Lee, Logistics, and the Pennsylvania Campaign.* Chapel Hill: University of North Carolina Press, 2005.

Burton, E. Milby. *The Siege of Charleston, 1861-1865.* Columbia: University of South Carolina Press, 1970.

Caldwell, J. F. J. *The History of a Brigade of South Carolinians, Known First as "Gregg's," and Subsequently as "McGowan's Brigade."* Philadelphia: King & Baird, Printers, 1866.

Carter, Hodding. *The Angry Scar: The Story of Reconstruction.* New York: Doubleday & Company, 1959.

Cashin, Edward J. *A Confederate Legend: Sergeant Berry Benson in War and Peace.* Macon, Ga.: Mercer University Press, 2008.

Cauthen, Charles E. *South Carolina Goes to War, 1860-1865.* Chapel Hill: University of North Carolina Press, 1950.

Chambers, Herbert O. *And Were the Glory of Their Times. Cavalry: The Men Who Died for South Carolina in the War for Southern Independence.* Wilmington, N.C.: Broadfoot Publishing Company, 2015.

Chesnut, Mary Boykin. *A Diary from Dixie.* New York: D. Appleton & Co., 1905.

Chesnut, Mary Boykin. *A Diary from Dixie.* Edited by Ben Ames Williams. Cambridge, Mass.: Harvard University Press, 1980.

Chester, James. "Inside Sumter in '61." In *Battles and Leaders of the Civil War,* Vol. 1, 50-74. New York: The Century Company, 1884.

Clark, W. A. *The History of the Banking Institutions Organized in South Carolina Prior to 1860.* Columbia, S.C.: The State Company, 1922.

Cohen, Hennig. *A Barhamville Miscellany.* Columbia: University of South Carolina Press, 1956.

Confederate Military History Extended Edition: A Library of Confederate States History. Wilmington, N.C.: Broadfoot, 1987.

Conrad, James Lee. *The Young Lions: Confederate Cadets at War.* Columbia: University of South Carolina Press, 2004.

Cuthbert, Robert B. *Flat Rock of the Old Time: Letters from the Mountains to the Lowcountry, 1837-1939.* Columbia: University of South Carolina Press, 2016.

Cyclopedia of Eminent and Representative Men of the Carolinas of the Nineteenth Century. Madison, Wis.: Brant & Fuller, 1892.

Daly, Louise Haskell. *Alexander Cheves Haskell: The Portrait of a Man.* Wilmington, N.C.: Broadfoot Publishing Company, 1989.

Davidson, Chalmers Gaston. *The Last Foray: The South Carolina Planters of 1860, A Sociological Study.* Columbia, S.C.: University of South Carolina Press, 1971.

Davis, Jefferson. *The Rise and Fall of the Confederate Government.* New York: D. Appleton and Company, 1881.

Davis, R. Means. "Octavius Theodore Porcher." *The Educational* 2 (1903): 86-89; 105-08: 116-19.

De Leon, Thomas Cooper. *Belles, Beaux and Brains of the '60s.* New York: G.W. Dillingham Co., 1909.

DuBose, William Porcher. *Faith, Valor and Devotion: The Civil War Letters of William Porcher DuBose.* Edited by W. Eric Emerson and Karen Stokes. Columbia: University of South Carolina Press, 2010.

Dunham, Chester F. *The Attitude of the Northern Clergy Toward the South, 1860-1865.* Philadelphia, Pa.: Porcupine Press, 1974.

Easterby, J. H. "Captain Langdon Cheves, Jr., and the Confederate Silk Dress Balloon." *South Carolina Historical Magazine* 45 (1944): 1-11.

Fair, Sara Cheves. "Finding my Haskell Ancestors: A Family History Journey." *Carologue*, Summer 2015: 20-27.

Ferguson, Lester W. *Abbeville County: Southern Life-Styles Lost in Time.* Spartanburg, S.C.: The Reprint Company, 1993.

Flynn, Jean Martin. *The Militia in Antebellum South Carolina Society.* Spartanburg, S.C.: The Reprint Company, 1991.

Freeman, Douglas Southall. *Lee's Lieutenants: A Study in Command.* New York: Scribner, 1998.

Freeman, Douglas Southall. *The South to Posterity: An Introduction to the Writings of Confederate History.* New York: Charles Scribner's Sons, 1939.

Gilchrist, Robert C. "Confederate Defence of Morris Island." Appendix in Year Book (Charleston, S.C.), 1884, 350-403.

Hagood, Johnson. *Memoirs of the War of Secession.* Columbia, S.C.: The State Company, 1910.

Hagy, James W. *To Take Charleston: The Civil War on Folly Island.* Charleston, West Virginia: Pictorial Histories Publishing Company, 1993.

Happoldt, Christopher. *The Christopher Happoldt Journal: His European Tour With the Rev. John Bachman.* Edited by Claude Henry Neuffer. Charleston, S.C.: The Charleston Museum. 1960.

Haskell, John C. *The Haskell Memoirs.* New York: G. P. Putnam's Sons, 1960.

Hemphill, J. C. *Men of Mark in South Carolina.* Washington, D.C.: Men of Mark Publishing Co., 1907-09.

Hewett, Janet B. *South Carolina Confederate Soldiers, 1861-1865, Name Roster,* Vol. 1. Wilmington, N.C.: Broadfoot, 1998.

Hoffman, Charles, and Tess Hoffman. *North by South: The Two Lives of Richard James Arnold.* Athens: University of Georgia Press, 1988.

Holmes, Emma. *The Diary of Miss Emma Holmes, 1861-1866.* Edited by John F. Marszalek. Baton Rouge: Louisiana State University Press, 1979.

Johnson, John. *The Defense of Charleston Harbor: Including Fort Sumter and the Adjacent Islands, 1863-1865.* Charleston, S.C.: Walker, Evans & Cogswell Co., 1890.

Johnson, John Lipscomb. *The University Memorial Biographical Sketches of Alumni of the University of Virginia Who Fell in the Confederate War.* Baltimore, Md.: Turnbull Brothers, 1871.

Johnson, Ludwell H. *North Against South: The American Iliad, 1848-1877.* Columbia, S.C.: The Foundation for American Education, 1995.

Johnson, Thomas Cary. *The Life and Letters of Benjamin Morgan Palmer.* Richmond, Va.: Presbyterian Committee of Publication, 1906.

Jones, Samuel. *The Siege of Charleston: And the Operations on the South Atlantic Coast in the War Among the States.* New York: The Neale Publishing Company, 1911.

Kean, Robert Garlick Hill. *Inside the Confederate Government: The Diary of Robert Garlick Hill Kean.* Edited by Edward Younger. New York: Oxford University Press, 1957.

Krick, Robert E. L. *Staff Officers in Gray: A Biographical Register of the Staff Officers in the Army of Northern Virginia.* Chapel Hill: University of North Carolina Press, 2003.

Krick, Robert K. "Maxcy Gregg: Political Extremist and Confederate General." *Civil War History,* 19:4 (1973), 293-313.

"Langdon Cheves." *South Carolina Historical Magazine,* 39 (1940): 96-97.

Long, E. B. *The Civil War Day by Day: An Almanac, 1861-1865.* New York: Doubleday & Company, 1971.

"Louis Wardlaw Haskell." *The Oil Miller,* 11:4 (1920): 31.

MacDowell, Dorothy Kelly. *DuBose Genealogy.* Columbia, S.C.: R. L. Bryan Co., 1972.

May, John Amasa. *South Carolina Secedes.* Columbia: University of South Carolina Press, 1960.

McBryde, John McLaren. "An Eyewitness to History." *Civil War Times Illustrated,* 2:9 (Jan. 1964): 37- 41.

McCabe, W. Gordon. "Defence of Petersburg." *Southern Historical Society Papers,* 2 (1876): 257-306.

Meriwether, Colyer. *History of Higher Education in South Carolina, With a Sketch of the Free School System.* Spartanburg, S.C.: Reprint Company, 1972.

Meynard, Virginia G. *The Venturers: The Hampton, Harrison, and Earle Families of Virginia, South Carolina, and Texas.* Easley, S.C.: Southern Historical Press, 1981.

Moore, Frank, ed. *The Rebellion Record: A Diary of American Events. Sixth Volume.* New York: D. Van Nostrand, 1866.

Nichols, George Ward. *The Story of the Great March, From the Diary of a Staff Officer.* New York: Harper & Brothers, 1865.

Orvin, Maxwell Clayton. *In South Carolina Waters, 1861-1865.* Charleston, S.C.: Nelson's Southern Printing & Publishing, 1961.

Ouzts, Clay. "Maxcy Gregg and His Brigade of South Carolinians at the Battle of Fredericksburg." *South Carolina Historical Magazine* 95 (1994): 6-26.

Pollard, Edward A. *The Southern Spy: Letters on the Policy and Inauguration of the Lincoln War Written Anonymously in Washington and Elsewhere.* Richmond, Va.: West & Johnson, 1861.

Pringle, Elizabeth W. Allston. *Chronicles of Chicora Wood.* Boston: The Christopher Publishing House, 1940.

Racine, Philip N., ed. *Gentlemen Merchants: A Charleston Family's Odyssey, 1828-1870.* Knoxville: University of Tennessee Press, 2008.

Ravenel, Samuel W. "The Boy Brigade of South Carolina." *Confederate Veteran Magazine* 29 (1921): 417-18.

Rigdon, John C. *Historical Sketch and Roster of the South Carolina 1st Infantry Regiment, Butler's.* Clearwater, S.C.: Eastern Digital Resources, 2004.

Salley, A. S. *South Carolina Troops in Confederate Service, Volume 1.* Columbia, S.C.: R. L. Bryan Company, 1913.

Scarborough, William Kauffman. *The Allstons of Chicora Wood: Wealth, Honor and Gentility in the South Carolina Lowcountry.* Baton Rouge: Louisiana State University Press, 2011.

Seigler, Robert S. *South Carolina's Military Organizations During the War Between the States.* Charleston, S.C.: The History Press, 2008.

Sholes' Directory of the City of Savannah. Savannah, Ga.: A. E. Sholes, Publisher, 1880.

Sholes' Directory of the City of Savannah. Savannah, Ga.: The Morning News Print, 1900.

"The Siege of Charleston." *Empire* [Sydney], 15 Oct. 1863: 2. National Library of Australia. Web. Accessed 27 Dec. 2017.

Simms, William Gilmore. *War Poetry of the South.* New York: Richardson & Company, 1867.

Singleton, Virginia Eliza Green. *The Singletons of South Carolina.* Columbia, S.C.: Singleton Family, 1914.

Some Cemetery Records of Abbeville County, South Carolina. Baltimore, Md.: Genealogical Publishing Company, 1993.

The Story of American Heroism: Thrilling Narratives of Personal Adventures During the Great Civil War. Springfield, Ohio: J. W. Jones, 1897.

Thomas, Albert Sidney. *A Historical Account of the Protestant Episcopal Church in South Carolina, 1820-1957.* Columbia, S.C.: R. L. Bryan Co., 1957.

Thomas, John Peyre. *The History of the South Carolina Military Academy.* Charleston, S.C.: Walker, Evans & Cogswell, 1893.

Tompkins, D. A., and A. S. Tompkins. *Company K Fourteenth South Carolina Volunteers.* Charlotte, N.C.: Observer Printing and Publishing House, 1897.

Trimpi, Helen P. *Crimson Confederates: Harvard Men Who Fought for the South.* Knoxville: University of Tennessee Press, 2010.

United Daughters of the Confederacy. South Carolina Division. *South Carolina Women in the Confederacy.* Columbia, S.C.: The State Company, 1903.

Valentine, Ida Massie. "A Memoir of the Thomson Family." *South Carolina Historical Magazine,* 62 (1961): 215-220.

Wallace, David Duncan. *The History of South Carolina.* New York: The American Historical Society, 1935. Volume 3.

The War of the Rebellion: The Official Records of the Union and Confederate Armies. Washington, D.C.: Government Printing Office, 1880-1902.

The War of the Rebellion: The Official Records of the Union and Confederate Navies. Washington, D.C.: Government Printing Office, 1894-1922.

Wardlaw, David Lewis. *An Account Genealogical, and Occasionally Somewhat Biographical, of the Family of D. L. Wardlaw and Other Families with Which It is Connected.* Abbeville, S.C.: Press and Banner Printing, 1891.

Wilson, Clyde N. *Carolina Cavalier: The Life and Mind of James Johnston Pettigrew.* Athens: University of Georgia Press, 1990.

Wise, Jennings Cropper. *The Long Arm of Lee: The History of the Artillery of the Army of Northern Virginia.* New York: Oxford University Press, 1959.

MANUSCRIPTS

Alexander Cheves Haskell Papers. South Caroliniana Library, University of South Carolina.

Alexander Cheves Haskell Papers. Southern Historical Collection, Wilson Library, The University of North Carolina at Chapel Hill (UNC).

Barnwell Family Papers, South Carolina Historical Society (SCHS), Charleston.

Charles Thomson Haskell Family Papers. SCHS.

DuBose, William Porcher. "Reminiscences." UNC.

F. W. Pickens and Milledge L. Bonham Papers. Library of Congress.

Hagood, James R. "Memoirs of the First South Carolina Regiment of Volunteer Infantry." SCHS.

Haskell Family Files. SCHS.

John Cheves Haskell Papers. UNC.

Langdon Cheves Papers. Georgia Historical Society.

Langdon Cheves Papers. SCHS.

Letter of Blackwood Ketchum Benson. Albert and Shirley Small Special Collections Library, University of Virginia.

Rachel Susan Bee Cheves Papers. Rubenstein Rare Book and Manuscript Library, Duke University.

INDEX

Hamilton, William, 236
Hammond, James Henry, 183
Hampton, Frank, 233
Hampton, Mary Cantey, 233
Hampton, Sarah Buchanan (Sallie),
  285; letter of, 340-41; 378, 390
Hampton, Wade, 55, 145; letter of,
  323; 332-33, 404
Hardee, William Joseph, 292
Harriet Lane (USS), 38
Haskell, Alexander Cheves, biographical sketch of, xxxii-xxxv; engagement of, 73; wedding of, 85;
  wounded at Chancellorsville, 220,
  317; recommended for promotion
  by Gen. Perrin, 317-18; requested
  by Wade Hampton, 323; wounded
  at Darbytown Road, 354, 366-67;
  post-war life of, 406-407
Haskell, Allen Wardlaw, 319
Haskell, Charles Thomson, early life
  and marriage, xi-xiv; letters of, 40,
  119, 131, 135, 193-94; 148-49,
  150, 156, 175; death of, 404-405
Haskell, Charles Thomson, Jr., religious life of, xviii-xix; biographical
  sketch of, xxi-xxvi; xxxii; death of,
  243-47, 246, 416; confirmation of,
  256; character of, 256, 258, 264-65,
  267; 318
Haskell, Charles Thomson (Charley),
  164, 173, 176, 179, 214, 217-18,
  221, 223; death of, 283
Haskell, Charlotte Thomson (Mrs.), xi
Haskell, Charlotte Thomson, biographical sketch of, xxvi-xxvii
Haskell, Ella Coulter Wardlaw, 136,
  164, 173, 176, 179, 213-14, 217-
  18, 221-22, 283, 319
Haskell, Elnathan, xi, xiv, 32
Haskell, Harriet Bachman, xlii
Haskell, John Bachman, xli-xlii, 12,
  136, 217, 219
Haskell, John Cheves, biographical
  sketch of, xxxv-xxxix; loss of arm at
  Gaines' Mill, 131, 133; religious
  faith of, 269, 296; wounded at

Darbytown Road, 366; post-war
  life of, 408
Haskell, Joseph Cheves, biographical
  sketch of, xxxix-xl; 123-124; at
  Battle of Seven Pines, 135; religious faith of, 269, 296; post-war
  life of, 409-409
Haskell, Kate, 13, 148, 153, 213, 339
Haskell, Langdon Cheves, religious
  conversion of, xvii-xviii, xix; biographical sketch of, xix-xx; xliii, 70,
  88-90, 102, 105, 108, 111, 124,
  129; letters of, xvii-xviii,130-31,
  305, 359-62, 412; 135-36, 141,
  147, 156-57, 164-65, 167, 173,
  176, 179, 195, 198-99, 211, 217,
  220, 255, 279, 281, 283, 285, 295,
  297-98, 208, 335, 354, 356, 371,
  383, 385, 387, 389; post-war life
  of, 405-406
Haskell, Langdon Cheves, Jr. (Pete),
  71, 102, 179, 214, 217-18, 221
Haskell, Louis Wardlaw, xli-xliii, 121,
  164, 171, 176, 205, 215, 217; letters of, 209-10, 219-20, 304, 367-
  69, 373-74, 381, 387-88; 222, 307-
  308, 310, 318-19, 325, 327, 350,
  354, 370, 373, 375-76, 378, 382-
  83, 385, 387, 389-90; post-war life
  of, 410-11
Haskell, Mary Elizabeth, xvii, xli; biographical sketch of, xx-xxi
Haskell, Mary Sophia, death of, 71;
  217
Haskell, Paul Thomson, xli-xliii, 121,
  171, 176, 205, 215, 217, 224, 280,
  307, 314, 316, 318, 325, 326-27,
  339-40, 391; post-war life of, 411
Haskell, Rebecca Singleton (Decca),
  xxxiii-xxxiv, 29, 33, 43, 73-74, 76;
  letters of, 77, 87-88, 126-27; 81-
  83, 86-90, 92, 94-95, 98-100, 103-
  107, 109, 118, 121, 123; death of,
  130-32, 135; 140, 175, 183, 191,
  193-94, 282
Haskell, Rebecca Singleton, xxxiii;
  birth of, 129; 132, 135, 140, 146,